# The Scenic Route

# The Scenic Route

## Building Minnesota's North Shore

Arnold R. Alanen

University of Minnesota Press
Minneapolis
London

The publication of this book was assisted by a bequest from Josiah H. Chase to honor his parents, Ellen Rankin Chase and Josiah Hook Chase.

Unless otherwise credited, photographs are taken by the author and illustrations are from his personal collection.



Published by the University of Minnesota Press
111 Third Avenue South, Suite 290
Minneapolis, MN 55401-2520
http://www.upress.umn.edu

ISBN 978-0-8166-4138-3 (hc)
ISBN 978-0-8166-4139-0 (pb)

A Cataloging-in-Publication record for this book is available from the Library of Congress.

Printed in Canada on acid-free paper



33 32 31 30 29 28 27 26 25 10 9 8 7 6 5 4 3 2 1

# Contents

The author, at age seven, in Duluth for the first time. This visit established a lifelong fascination with Lake Superior, the North Shore, and Duluth. Also in the photograph are his mother and Matti's wife.

# Preface

I first saw Duluth, Lake Superior, and the entrance to North Shore Drive at the age of seven. This fortuitous event occurred when my mother and I were visiting her parents on their dairy farm, situated sixty-five miles from Duluth along the boundary between Aitkin and Carlton Counties. Fortunately, they also decided that, finally, it was time for my first trip to Duluth, where I could experience some of the city's attractions. While in the city, we stayed with my grandfather's best friend, Matti, his jovial lifetime acquaintance from eastern Finland who had immigrated to Minnesota, married in Duluth, and found employment with the city's street department. (I soon realized that at least some of Matti's cheerfulness was fueled by the contents of a flask he accessed on numerous trips to the car's trunk.) Because Matti's knowledge of Duluth was considerable, we were treated, on a sunny July day, to a lengthy drive that included many stops—some of them to quench his ever-present thirst.

One of our pauses was on Superior Street, the heart of Duluth's business district, where I gazed at my first skyscraper, the Alworth Building, fifteen stories high and even today the tallest structure in the city. This experience was no less awesome than my first impression, more than a decade later, of New York City's Empire State Building. Equally absorbing were the trolley buses that had flexible rooftop poles connected to overhead electric lines, as well as the London Road entrance to North Shore Drive, where the numerous mansions, to my mind's eye, might have housed the city's royalty. We also boarded a Duluth Harbor tour boat that brought us by huge vessels as they were filled with iron ore and grain and passed under one of the city's engineering marvels, the Aerial Lift Bridge. Although the wind occasionally slapped cold water into the boat, this only added greater excitement and delight to my experience.

Nothing, however, proved more impressive and stunning than Skyline Drive. From overlooks along the roadway, panoramic views of the city encompassed silhouettes of downtown buildings; piers, quays, docks, and anchored ships punctuated the shoreline; and the shimmering surface of the lake spread toward Wisconsin. At that time, expansive vistas were entirely new experiences for me, a young "flatlander" from the small city of Moorhead in far western Minnesota whose eyes had been conditioned by the Red River Valley—one of North America's foremost examples of a level landscape. Perhaps because of this early perspective, I eventually became a fan of high places and regularly sought out views from the upper stories of buildings; the overlooks from hills, cliffs, and mountain trails; and the window seats of airplanes. Many decades later, I found a postcard my mother wrote shortly after we had completed our adventure; it was sent to my father, who had been unable to accompany us because of his work schedule. She wrote that their son "had really enjoyed himself"—an apt description and prediction of my lifelong fascination with the North Shore, Lake Superior, and Duluth.

Within a year, we had moved from Moorhead to my grandparents' northeastern Minnesota farm. Then Duluth became a relatively commonplace destination for visits and major shopping excursions. At the age of thirteen, I took my first trip along the entire North Shore, this time in the company of a cousin, four years my senior, already the possessor of a driver's license, and the owner of a used Henry J—a four-cylinder automobile manufactured by the Kaiser–Frazer Corporation during the early 1950s. Our destination was the twin cities of Fort William–Port Arthur (now Thunder Bay), Ontario, where we visited several relatives, all of them recent émigrés from Finland.

Although many North Shore sights and stops from that trip remain imprinted in my memory, a few stand out: the exposed curve at Silver Creek Cliff, where, on my first "mountain" road experience, I peered 125 feet directly down at the lake below; Split Rock Lighthouse, perched on a precipice that seemed an impossible place to build such a structure; Gooseberry Falls State Park, its concourse constructed of monolithic rocks that even exceeded the size of the largest exposed boulders on our farm fields; and the vastness of Lake Superior, the iridescent inland sea that, mile after mile, extended to the distant horizon.

I also was fortunate that my eighth-grade art teacher was John Spelman III (1912–1969), a gifted artist who would later receive considerable acclaim for his stunning black-and-white lithographs of numerous North Shore sites, all produced during an all-too-brief lifetime and career. An excellent and perceptive instructor, he dispensed suggestions, praise, humor, and occasional exasperation as we labored over our student art projects, including the first, and only, woodcut I would ever produce. He also guided us on field trips, where we observed houses, sheds, storefronts, streets, sidewalks, clotheslines, utility poles, and railroad tracks. John Spelman III, in fact, was the first person to show me how to "read," understand, and appreciate vernacular or ordinary buildings and cultural landscapes—a subject that would become a central interest of my subsequent academic career.

I spent my first two years of collegiate life at the University of Minnesota Duluth, during which time I became much more familiar with the city, Lake Superior, and the North Shore. Especially memorable were the weekly, mile-long walks I made between the University of Minnesota Duluth's postwar campus and a historic building known as Old Main, where I volunteered at the KUMD radio station. Following my early-evening arrival, I spent several hours playing music from KUMD's record collection and reading public service announcements over the air before closing the station at 11:00 P.M. My return trip to campus offered fleeting glimpses of the moon's reflections on the lake (except during blizzards) and, in springtime and fall, sonorous sounds emitted by Duluth's foghorn. A direct encounter with the North Shore occurred during springtime, just as the recently melted, ice-cold water of rivers and streams poured into the lake. I then joined thousands of people in a nighttime, carnival-like ritual that involved the use of seines, dip nets, and even buckets to catch some of the massive numbers of small rainbow smelt *(Osmerus mordax)* as they swam upstream to spawn. For those of us who experienced the spectacle at its peak during the 1960s and 1970s, "smeltomania" remains a quirky, but nonetheless fond, North Shore memory.

The North Shore, Duluth, and Lake Superior became more geographically distant when I joined the faculty at the University of Wisconsin–Madison in 1974. Nevertheless, I maintained a direct connection with the Lake Superior region by devoting much of my research time and publication efforts to the cultural landscapes, vernacular architecture, resource-based company towns, agricultural and mining settlements, and immigrant groups of northeastern Minnesota, northern Wisconsin, and the Upper Peninsula of Michigan. This volume represents another excursion to northeastern Minnesota.

The book's genesis may be traced back to the late 1990s, when a former graduate student, Michael Koop, employed by the State Historic Preservation Office (SHPO) of the Minnesota Historical Society, began planning for the 2000 conference of the Vernacular Architecture Forum (VAF) that would be headquartered in Duluth. (The SHPO was transferred to the Minnesota Department of Administration in 2017.) Because each VAF meeting, which typically attracts well over one hundred participants, includes two full days of tours to different places in the local region, he asked if I might prepare a field guide for selected areas of Duluth, the Iron Range, and the North Shore.

In pursuing our initial survey work, we were able to explore many North Shore sites, some not accessible to the general public, for inclusion in the field guide. Among the most memorable were several elegant residences and buildings designed by architect Edwin Lundie during the 1940s and 1950s. But equally captivating were the North Shore's vernacular or "ordinary" structures and cultural landscapes that I encountered, both directly and in historic images. Through this study, I also discovered the rich and fascinatingly complex history of the North Shore Highway itself, which had evolved from a path, trail, and rudimentary roadway into a nationally recognized scenic drive.

Although the survey documented numerous North Shore places for inclusion in the field guide, there was insufficient time to consider the human stories tied to the development and evolution of the North Shore and its places. This book, therefore, also gives attention to the experiences and events associated with the lives and activities of numerous people who were and are an integral part of the North Shore narrative.

While I considered the North Shore as a possible book subject over several years, other obligations intervened, until 2014, when I began devoting more time to the project. The product of my efforts, presented in this book, represents thousands of miles of travel, by bus and car, between Madison and the North Shore and countless hours spent reading and reviewing reports, manuscripts, books, newspaper microfilms, online census documents, images, advertisements, directories, maps, and other sources, many held by historical societies, libraries, museums, and visitors' centers located in Duluth, St. Paul, Two Harbors, Grand Marais, Schroeder, Tofte, and Silver Bay. Equally important are the discussions and interactions I had with more than one hundred people who shared their knowledge of the North Shore with me; they are recognized in the acknowledgments and notes. The book is dedicated to them, as well as to the untold numbers of people who consider the North

Shore a place not only to enjoy and cherish but also to value, protect, and preserve so that others may appreciate its qualities and attributes well into the future.

Final caveats: It should be noted, of course, that any errors of interpretation or fact are entirely my responsibility. And, although this book seeks to offer a portrayal of the North Shore from 1856 through late 2023 and into 2024, it must be emphasized that changes in the built environment and cultural landscape are constant and relentless. What exists today may not be evident tomorrow.

Introduction

# From Footpaths and Mail Trails to a Scenic Byway

Among Minnesotans, you will often hear the names "Up North" and "Northwoods" (or "North Woods") to describe those places within the state where they look to find solitude, serenity, scenic views, and nature-based recreation. Such terms, however, seldom pinpoint a precise point on a map. Instead, Up North and Northwoods typically represent a concept or a perception of an idealized image of nature, forests, lakes, and wildlife that exists in our "hearts and imagination."[1] In contrast, mention "North Shore" and most Minnesotans will know it references a specific location, namely, the area of Lake Superior coastline that stretches between Duluth and the Canadian border.

Until the twentieth century's second decade, the vast majority of the North Shore could be viewed only from a Lake Superior watercraft, be it a canoe, sailboat, fishing skiff, or steamboat. This situation changed in August 1917 with the official opening of an overland road that made it possible for adventurous motorists to reach far northeastern Minnesota; a new wooden bridge over the Pigeon River even allowed them to travel an additional forty-five miles to the Canadian twin cities of Fort William and Port Arthur, Ontario. "Automobiles of every description have been seen here this week," wrote a Grand Marais correspondent for the *Duluth News-Tribune* in July 1918. "They range from flivvers [small cars] to eight-passenger limousines, while the outfits carried varied from wicker lunch-boxes with ice compartments, to trailers loaded down with everything required for a camp by the side of the road." Almost overnight, the North Shore's "front door" transitioned from Lake Superior to the new coastal roadway that would soon be called North Shore Drive. The once modest corridor, currently the state's most popular highway destination, is now identified as both North Shore Scenic Drive and Minnesota Highway 61.[2]

## The Lure of the North Shore

But why does the North Shore resonate so strongly among Minnesotans? Is it because the blending of "north" and "shore" occurs here, both in name and in the landscape? Do forests on one side of the road and a virtually endless panorama of water on the other create a magical experience that isn't replicated anywhere else in the state? Is it because the North Shore's waterfalls and cascades—with their rushing water and jagged outcroppings—appear exotic and even mystical to Minnesotans? Or does the astounding and magnificent presence of an inland sea within the North American heartland simply defy comprehension? When viewing Lake Superior from the North Shore, remarked St. Paul memoirist Patricia Hampl in a 1999 *New York Times* essay, "you're so full of superlatives you can only sigh with joy."[3]

Even earlier, in 1960, another well-known and prolific Minnesota author, Margaret Culkin Banning, stated that the North Shore didn't "depend only upon its looks." The former Duluthian believed that local residents, both past and present, also contributed to the North Shore's essence and attractiveness. "It has intellectual interest," she wrote. "It can earn a good living. It is as progressive as tomorrow because it has majored in history. It has primitive handwork to offer. . . . It is always ready for a rhapsody with a poet or to go on a picnic with the children. It is healthy and vigorous as well as handsome. There is no more well-rounded and intelligent beauty in the world than on the North Shore Drive."[4] Whatever the reasons, we can be certain that large numbers of Minnesotans, as well as many others from elsewhere, are inspired, stimulated, stirred, and invigorated by their involvement, encounters, and connections with the North Shore and Lake Superior.

Familiarity, awareness, and appreciation often are, of course, the products of experience. These factors were clearly at play in 1961 when a *Minneapolis Tribune* "Minnesota Poll" asked a representative cross section of the state's adult residents a simple question: which "points of interest"—six in Minnesota and one each in North Dakota and South Dakota—had they visited? The North Shore (73 percent) was the second most visited place, trailing only the Minnesota State Capitol (82 percent). Almost sixty years later, in 2018, a Minneapolis *StarTribune* online poll, intended "for entertainment purposes only," asked readers to choose their favorite Minnesota road destination from a list of eight popular places in the state. The North Shore, selected by almost 70 percent of all email respondents (1,995 of 2,825), was the overwhelming favorite.[5]

Simple surveys are interesting, of course, but they only serve as a snapshot in time, offer little more than anecdotal information, and provide no clear evidence as to *why* the North Shore is so meaningful to Minnesotans. It is quite surprising, therefore, that to date, only one major study—a 1981 survey conducted by University of Minnesota professors Timothy Knopp and Uel Blank—has employed rigorous research methods to identify the factors that underlie the North Shore's popularity. Among their clearest findings was the respondents' resounding appreciation of Lake Superior: 80 percent selected "watching the lake" (one of thirty-nine activities listed in the questionnaire) as their favorite pursuit. When asked which specific North Shore features were most attractive and inspiring to them, almost 50 percent of the entire group mentioned the views—of Lake Superior, of the Northwoods, and of natural formations. Such attitudes, wrote Knopp and Blank, demonstrate a recognition of what the North Shore offers—"a kind of opportunity that is becoming increasingly rare and valuable . . . namely, the chance to view unobstructed vistas, observe nature relatively unchanged, and simply enjoy peace and quiet." Then, and undoubtedly today, the North Shore "appeals to those seeking a place that stimulates the mind and challenges the spirit."[6]

These attributes were evident in 2020–22, when the greatest impact of Covid-19 was experienced throughout the North Shore and the entire world. When comparing 2019 to 2020 alone, the number of North Shore real estate transactions increased by 20 percent, with the most remarkable gains exhibited in the Cook County communities of Tofte (30 percent), Grand Marais (40 percent), and Lutsen (130 percent). The area is "so desirable," observed one local realtor, "because people are looking for a healthy, outdoor lifestyle, and that's exactly what we offer on the North Shore. We've got plenty of fresh air and lots of room for outdoor activities. It's a great place to social distance, that's for sure."[7]

## About This Book

Unlike many other books that, quite understandably, showcase the North Shore's outstanding natural attributes, this volume features its built environment and cultural landscapes. Hearing this, some might ask if there is any need for such a volume, given current and anticipated threats to the North Shore's waters, forests, and wildlife. Shouldn't all available attention, time, effort, and funds be devoted to protecting these precious resources? In fact, an outstanding 2015 book by Chel Anderson and Adelheid Fischer—*North Shore: A Natural History of Minnesota's Superior Coast*—clearly demonstrates just how vulnerable and fragile these environments are, especially in light of current and projected human impacts and climate change.[8]

It can be argued, nevertheless, that the role of humans, both good and bad, in shaping and forming the built environment and cultural landscapes of the greater North Shore area also is a subject worthy of attention. While we certainly lament the loss of North Shore animal species and natural habitats, so too can we bemoan the disappearance of much historical and contemporary evidence associated with a human presence along Lake Superior. Virtually no indications of a very early Paleo-Indian existence remain today, and much of the material culture tied to subsequent Cree, Dakota, and early Anishinaabe (Ojibwe) occupancy has also vanished. Only limited signs of the eighteenth-century fur trade era are apparent, although those with interests in this subject can visit Grand Portage National Monument, where interactions between the Anishinaabe and early Euro-Americans are interpreted within a remarkable set of reconstructed fur trade–era structures and a modern National Park Service visitor center. Even the history of commercial fishing, a significant activity along Lake Superior until the 1950s, is represented only sporadically in the contemporary North Shore landscape. Just a few of the humble but nonetheless evocative structures that once characterized the district's fishing industry—fish houses, boathouses, net reels, docks, and so forth—still dot the coastline. Once again, it is a more recent structure—a Tofte museum built in the form of a historic fish house—that documents and interprets the rise and demise of this once important activity. Equally evident is a steady loss of twentieth-century mom-and-pop resorts, cabins, and motels that once were ubiquitous features along the Lake Superior shoreline. Even when these properties are replaced, often by new forms of expansive and expensive commercial tourist development, access is limited to visitors who can afford them. And, of course, the sale and conversion of former resorts and rental cabins into private homes, for either year-round or seasonal use, eliminates any possibility of public access.

Also provided in this discussion are definitions for the built environment, the cultural landscape, and other related terms. Additional attention is given to various names that have identified the North Shore roadway as it evolved from a mid-nineteenth-century trail into a twentieth-century highway, and then, immediately after the millennium's arrival, into a National Scenic Byway and All-American Road. Further overviews are given of North Shore geology and ecology, of major population and ethnic groups, and of three resource-based activities—fishing, forestry, and farming—that supported many late nineteenth- and early twentieth-century residents and communities. Greater consideration is then given to tourism, the primary engine that has driven most local economies since the end of World War II.

Following the introduction are two separate parts. Part I provides an overview of almost seventeen decades of North Shore history (1856–2024), a period that covers the Lake Superior corridor as it evolved from a simple mail trail into a highway and, eventually, a nationally recognized scenic drive and byway. Part II, a significantly lengthier section, serves as a field guide to the North Shore's sites, places, and attractions. Much of this narrative is based on the stories and accounts of numerous residents and visitors who have experienced the North Shore throughout its history. Indeed, it is such stories that link past and present on the North Shore. As the distinguished American historian William Cronon has commented, it is through the never-ending telling of stories that the "past is reborn into memory to become living history, over and over and over again."[9] Stories, in fact, provide much of the background, meaning, and context for the people and places featured throughout this book.

## Defining the Built Environment and Cultural Landscape

The built environment may be succinctly defined as those features that have been "conceived and constructed by human hands." Structures and buildings come to mind immediately, but equally representative and important are the cultural landscapes that emerge and develop when natural features and areas are converted into parks, waysides, gardens, cemeteries, fields, lawns, yards, ponds, paths, streets, roads, and, of course, the North Shore highway itself, a place where the material actualities of the roadside may be viewed and considered. More recently, a term with ancient roots, *palimpsest,* has been used by Lovisa Kjerrgren and others to describe "the over-written layers of information that we may discern from the landscape." The North Shore trails created by generations of Indigenous people, for example, may have been "erased" by the subsequent actions of successive Euro-American groups, but those sections of the North Shore highway that follow the original pathways still serve as a palimpsest of the past—even if most people are not aware of this phenomenon as they travel along the Lake Superior shoreline.[10]

The built environment and cultural landscapes of the North Shore are additionally represented by its *places,* which range in scale from small sites and properties to settlements and cities. Equally important are the less tangible concepts of *place* imbued in such attributes as means of livelihood, religious and political beliefs, and ethnic and cultural practices, all of which offer numerous insights to the people connected with them. A related term, *sense of place*, refers to the emotional "bonds and attachments people develop or experience in particular locations and environments."[11] The appreciation, devotion, and love that many people have for the North Shore most certainly reflect these sense of place connections.

## What's in a Name?

An untold number of place-names have identified the Lake Superior shoreline through time. We will never know what terms Indigenous people used, many millennia ago, to describe the paths they formed and followed along the lake's northern shore. Later Euro-American explorers, trappers, prospectors, surveyors, land-lookers, and mail carriers often employed these earlier paths, thereby contributing "over the years to the making of a trail [that] would later become the Lake Shore Road."[12]

Numerous names, in addition to "Lake Shore Road," were used to describe the paths and routes during the nineteenth and early twentieth centuries—North Shore Trail, North Shore Indian Trail, Grand Portage Trail, Old Road, Mail Trail, Old Dog Trail, Beargrease Trail, and others. Since 1917, when the first roadway suitable for vehicular travel between Duluth and Canada was completed, the route has been known as North Shore Road, North Shore Drive, Minnesota Constitutional Highway 1, Minnesota State Highway 1, Lake Superior International Highway, U.S. Highway 61, Minnesota Highway 61, and North Shore Scenic Drive. Commonly recognized as both North Shore Drive and Highway 61 since the late 1920s and early 1930s, the Federal Highway Administration, during the early 2000s, designated the route a National Scenic Byway, one of eight in Minnesota; it also was identified, at this same time, as an All-American Road, one of two in the state. The North Shore road, through time, has achieved significant regional, state, and national recognition since the first vehicles rumbled over its length in 1917.[13]

## North by Northeast

Although the name "North Shore" is familiar to Minnesotans and knowledgeable visitors, most seldom think about its seeming geographic incongruence: only a very few sections of the road actually proceed directly north (and south). Much of the roadway, in fact, is generally laid out in a northeasterly–southwesterly direction along the northwestern side of the lake. Why, then, is it called the "North Shore"? This conundrum is quite easily solved if one disregards the international border between Minnesota and the Canadian province of Ontario. When viewing early maps dating to the 1600s, or contemporary satellite images that are devoid of political and governmental boundaries, Lake Superior stands out as a mid-continent jewel with two easily recognizable borders. One is a lengthy northern coastline that extends between Duluth to the west and the twin cities of Sault Ste. Marie in Ontario and Michigan to the east. Likewise, and quite obviously, the coastline that forms the Michigan–Wisconsin Lake Superior boundary is identified as the South Shore. Those

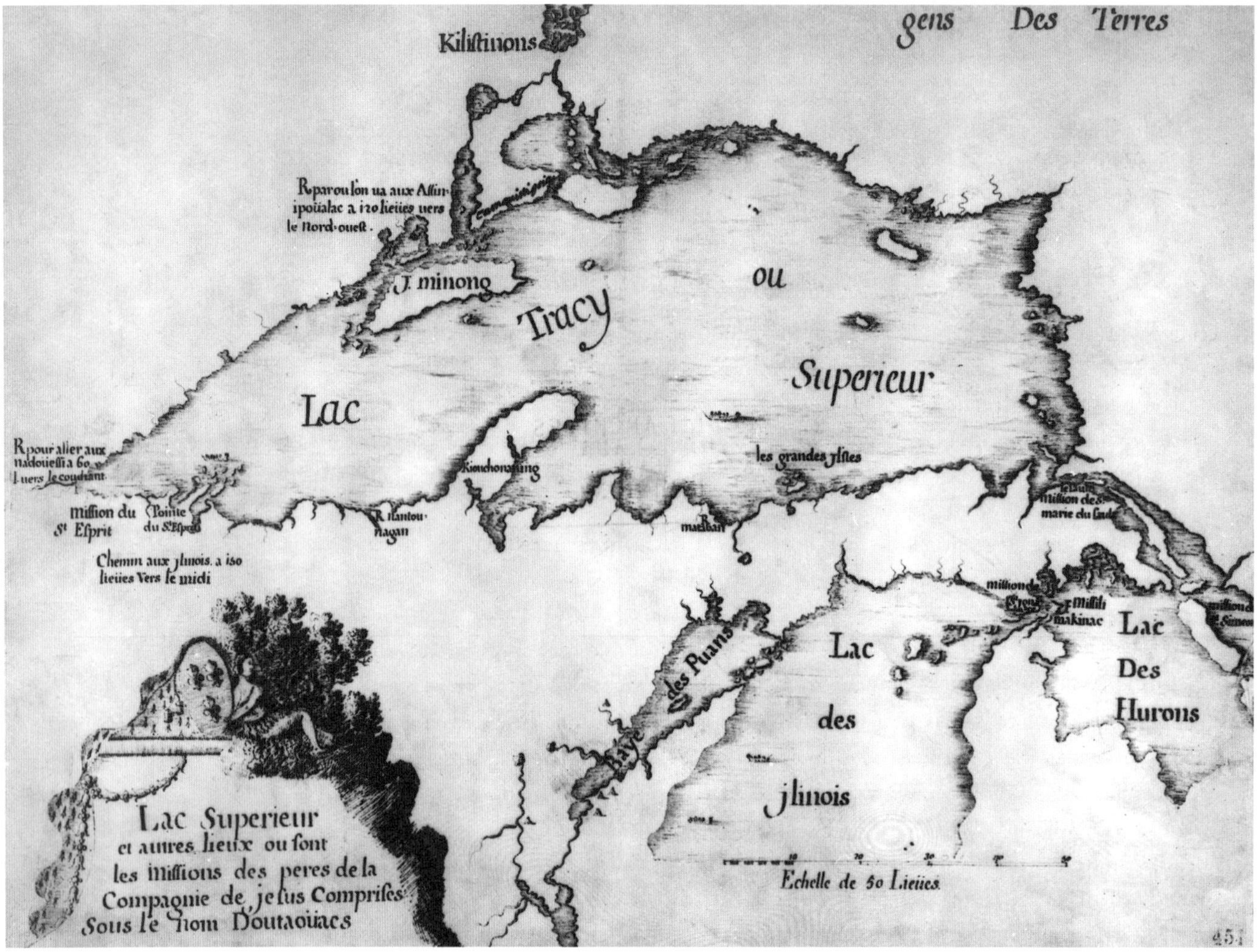


**A remarkable French Jesuit map from 1620 to 1622, attributed to cartographer Claude Dablon, depicts Lake Superior and parts of Lake Michigan and Lake Huron without any international or state boundaries. The entire expanse of Lake Superior's North Shore includes the coastline that extends between what is now Duluth to the west and Sault Ste. Marie to the east. Courtesy of Library and Archives Canada and the Map and Data Library, University of Toronto.**

having greater familiarity with the North Shore know that "lower" identifies the lakeshore side of the highway, whereas "upper" defines its inland side.

Besides Duluth, the 154 miles of Minnesota's North Shore highway pass by or through numerous governmental, cultural, and natural sites, including three counties; four incorporated cities; six incorporated townships; seventeen unincorporated settlements; four unincorporated territories; eight state parks; five state waysides; two Minnesota Department of Transportation (MnDOT) visitor centers; an Anishinaabe reservation; a National Historic Landmark; a National Monument; large sections of federal, state, and county forest land and recreational areas; and many rest areas, campgrounds, historic sites, and explanatory markers. As will be discussed later, some former incorporated villages and townships in Lake and Cook Counties were dissolved decades ago because of small populations and limited monetary resources; the governmental needs and obligations of these places continue to be handled by their respective counties.

## Revisiting Highway 61

Although the North Shore roadway, over time, has had several names, a single word and number, "Highway 61," have been used by federal, state, and local transportation authorities since the 1930s. And untold numbers of rock music aficionados have at least some familiarity with the road because of Bob Dylan, a native of Duluth and Hibbing, a recipient of the 2016 Nobel Prize in Literature, and the creative force behind the album (and song) *Highway 61 Revisited*. Soon after its 1965 release, numerous music critics and musicians identified *Highway 61 Revisited* as a breakthrough in contemporary music and even as "the most important and revolutionary album ever made."[14]

Minnesotans will point out (and sometimes complain) that Highway 61 is not mentioned in the album's namesake refrain. But because it is a Dylan song, the lyrics describe a mysterious and surrealistic "highway" inhabited by characters ranging from the biblical Abraham to a "roving gambler" who wants "to create a next nuclear war." Dylan would later write that Highway 61 was part of his early heritage: "It begins about where I came from . . . Duluth to be exact. I always felt like I'd started on it, always had been on it, and could go anywhere on it, even down deep into the Delta country."[15]

## Geology and Ecology: A Synopsis

The geology of northeastern Minnesota, which is "impressive both scientifically and aesthetically," has been a source of study since 1848, when geologist J. G. Norwood embarked on three successive years of fieldwork along Lake Superior. Because Norwood's efforts commenced soon after the existence of rich copper deposits had been confirmed on Michigan's Keweenaw Peninsula, geologists and financiers anticipated that the ore might also extend underneath Lake Superior to the North Shore. The publication of Norwood's 1852 report, which mentioned the existence of copper at the mouths of several North Shore rivers, was followed by a frenzy of exploratory and prospecting activities along several areas of coastline; none of the findings, however, proved commercially viable.[16]

Since then, several geologists—notably John Green and Richard Ojakangas, both of the University of Minnesota Duluth (UMD)—have developed an impressive body of evidence that explains the processes of rifting, glaciation, and postglacial erosion that formed and shaped the North Shore's diverse physical landscapes. An understanding of North Shore ecology has also been enhanced by the detailed investigations of numerous biological scientists; their findings have been described, summarized, and interpreted by Anderson and Fischer in their aforementioned volume *North Shore: A Natural History of Minnesota's*

*Superior Coast.*[17] The following discussion offers only a brief glimpse of the North Shore's very complex natural world.

**Geology.** During the Middle Proterozoic era, 1.1 million years before present (BP), sections of the mid-American continent began turning "inside out" when a mid-continental horseshoe-shaped split ("rift") developed. This action resulted in the emergence of a massive rift valley, a portion of which became the Lake Superior Basin. For the next twenty-five million years, enormous amounts of molten lava (magma)—probably one hundred times greater than Lake Superior's present volume—poured out of the rift's fissures. "The eruptive scene," wrote geologist Preston Cloud many years ago, "is unimaginable! . . . The searing heat of a blast furnace across the whole of it. Literally, hell on Earth."[18]

Two types of rocks, extrusive and intrusive, were created by the volcanic action. Extruded rocks emerged when the magma "squeezed" onto the surface as basalt—a material, black or dark gray in color, that composes 90 percent of the North Shore's lava flows. The shoreline of Temperance River State Park is a fine example of a series of thin basalt layers. Rhyolite, "a magma of granitic composition, which erupted and cooled on the surface," is a much less common form of extruded rock: the vertical cliffs at Palisade Head and Shovel Point display some of the best examples of rhyolite flows on the North Shore.[19]

Intrusive rocks were formed by magma that remained below the surface, where it solidified into coarser-grained materials, such as gabbro, which has served as a foundation stone for numerous North Shore buildings. More resistant to the forces of erosion and glaciation were diabase and anorthosite. Both are evident at some prominent North Shore outcroppings and overlooks: Split Rock Lighthouse sits on a block of anorthosite, whereas diabase is the primary mineral component of Silver Creek Cliff and Lafayette Bluff. Both diabase and anorthosite blocks have been used as riprap at several North Shore harbors. Highly attractive to rock collectors are Lake Superior agates, with their brilliant bands of color, and thomsonite, a rarer stone that displays circular bands or "eyes" of alternating color combinations. Both formed when gas bubbles in the lava were filled with mineral-rich hot fluids.[20]

The center of the rift gradually subsided under the cooled lava's weight, causing the layers of flows to tilt an average of ten degrees—a phenomenon that may be observed in the angle of the lake-facing slopes of Cook County's Sawtooth Mountains. With the subsidence that occurred along the rift, the rough outline of a basin, now filled by Lake Superior, was created; it remains "the deepest healed rift yet discovered," even though the "healing" took some time. From about 1.8 million to 10,000 years BP, huge glaciers moved southward from Hudson Bay and covered much of the mid-continent with ice that was greater than one mile in depth. Today's Lake Superior Basin, scoured out even further by the expansion and retreat of glacial ice, eventually filled with meltwater when the climate warmed and the ice sheet of the most recent glaciation receded. Glacial Lake Duluth—the first of several lakes that filled the basin—covered the western one-third of present-day Lake Superior at a depth that was 1,085 feet above sea level, or almost twice the current average of 602 feet. Duluth's Skyline Drive follows some of the beach ridge formed by the wave action of Glacial Lake Duluth, whereas several sections of the North Shore highway are built on lower beaches created during later proglacial lake stages. Superior, the world's largest lake, covers 31,700 square miles and contains more than 10 percent of the world's fresh water. Just eighteen miles east of Grand Portage, but officially part of Michigan, is Washington Island on Isle Royale, "the largest island on the largest lake in the world."[21]

Twenty major North Shore rivers and numerous smaller streams and creeks empty into Lake Superior. Most are little more than ten miles long, but the rushing water that cut through ancient bedrock fractures has created several gorges and numerous waterfalls, rapids, cascades, and potholes. Not surprisingly, almost all of the North Shore's eight state parks are centered primarily on rivers, gorges, and valleys.[22]

The Lake Superior coastline also includes several small bays and coves with cobble beaches and one extended stretch of a gravel and sand beach situated northeast of Grand Marais between the Kadunce and Brule Rivers. The coastline, overall, is quite linear and primarily rocky; it also has just nine islets and islands and a few "rocky patches to hamper the onslaught of waves." Because the exposed coastline poses dangers to anglers and boaters who encounter storms and inclement weather, safe-harbor advocates have been active since the late 1930s. Nevertheless, it was not until the 1990s that the Minnesota Department of Natural Resources (MDNR) allocated funds to develop a limited number of small boat harbors, even though some critics question the impacts these developments have upon the fragile coastline.[23]

The coastline consists of bedrock and sediments, such as clay, silt, and sand, that were left behind as the ice retreated. Most prevalent is the "sticky red clay," one to one hundred feet in depth, which extends one to five miles inland from the lake. Unfortunately, sixty miles of clay embankments in St. Louis County and southwestern Lake County are at risk of erosion. "As waves undercut the toes of [clay] bluffs, weakening their structural support," write Anderson and Fischer, "whole sections of hillsides can collapse into the water." Another one-fourth of the North Shore's bedrock bluffs are exposed to the water and "battering waves" that occur during periods when lake levels are especially high.[24]

**Ecology.** The North Shore's old-growth forest, prior to Euro-American settlement, comprised largely conifers (pine, spruce, cedar, and fir) and some hardwoods. The forest, after the 1850s, however, was changed dramatically—the result of intensive logging, uncontrolled fires (notably in 1908 and 1910), drought, insect infestations, white-tailed deer browsing, and the development of buildings and transportation systems. Highway 61 itself, which consumes at least twenty-one hundred acres of land, has also created an "extensive and permanent open edge" that increases sun exposure and reduces humidity levels along the corridor. The highly visible demise of the North Shore's birch trees, which, by the early twenty-first century, were approaching the end of their normal lifespan of seventy to eighty years, may very well have been hastened by the highway's presence. The highway also serves as a "de facto fence" to amphibians that find refuge in the forest but need to reproduce in shoreline pools. Birds that feed on insects attracted by the road's heat are killed by trucks and automobiles, although the white-tailed deer that migrate across Highway 61 are the most noticeable victims of vehicle encounters.[25]

The Lake Superior Highlands, located five to seven miles inland from the shoreline, are generally outside the scope of this book but assume great importance because of their outbursts of autumn colors, which draw thousands of "leaf peepers" to the North Shore each September and October. In fact, close to 25 percent of Cook County's annual tourist receipts are generated during these two months. The source of attraction is the highlands ridge, some six to ten miles wide, which has bedrock protrusions, swooping hills, and waterlogged lowlands. Growing on the lower, lake-facing slopes and in river valleys are aspen, birch, white spruce, cedar, and balsam fir. On the tops and upper south-facing slopes of the ridge and hills are the extensive stands of sugar and red maples and yellow birch that prove especially attractive to "peepers." The first observers arrive during early fall to see the maple forest, while later lookers come for the birch and aspen "show."[26]

Many of these North Shore–related pursuits, ranging from active recreation to leaf watching, are and will be influenced by climate change, a phenomenon that has become more evident on Lake Superior with increasing surface water temperatures and shrinking evidence of ice cover. Indeed, a survey of 2,545 North Shore residents and visitors, conducted in 2015 and 2017 by investigators from the University of Minnesota and other institutions, revealed that almost 80 percent of the respondents believed that climate change is occurring along the Lake Superior shoreline. The respondents' most important concerns were the impacts a changing climate could exert on native fish, wildlife, and forest health, while accelerating the presence of nonnative species and pests. The survey also addressed the likelihood that a recent downward trend in North Shore nature-based recreation participation will continue because of climate change, "thereby altering the behavior of outdoor recreationists and tourists and, subsequently, the economies of local communities." Upon hearing this, one owner of a North Shore tourist enterprise felt, for the first time, "fear from climate change [because] it could literally put this place out of business."[27]

## The People of the North Shore

A human presence has been evident in the western Lake Superior district for more than ten thousand years, but distinctive American Indian tribal alliances were not apparent until the 1500s and 1600s. It was also at this time that interactions between Native peoples and European explorers, fur traders, and missionaries commenced. Except for two Anishinaabe reservations, at Grand Portage and Fond du Lac, the 1854 Treaty of La Pointe resulted in the transfer of virtually all territory in northeastern Minnesota to the federal government. "The changes brought by this new pattern of imposed confinement," observe Anderson and Fischer, "as well as the ecological transformation of the North Shore watershed by Euro-American newcomers, would change the character of the land and its people as dramatically as the retreat of the ice sheet thousands of years before."[28]

### From Indigenous People to the Anishinaabe

Relatively few archaeological sites have been discovered along the North Shore, but excavations undertaken at nearby locations provide signs of a nomadic Paleo-Indian presence that coincides with the initial retreat of glacial ice from the district. These prehistoric peoples used stone-tipped spears to hunt caribou and also gathered wild plants that appeared in the formerly frozen environment.[29]

As the climate began stabilizing during the Archaic Period (10,000–7000 BP), the Indigenous population engaged in shaping the trunks of white and red pines into dugout canoes that were used for fishing activities. Tools and ornamental items were also crafted out of native copper derived from Isle Royale and Michigan's Keweenaw Peninsula. The Early Woodland Period, beginning around 500 B.C., was marked by an upsurge in the growth of wild rice *(mano'min)*—a plant that served as a reliable and nourishing food source. (The shallow rice beds were accessed by birchbark canoes.) Wild rice contributed to commensurate increases in population numbers and "likely revolutionized the prehistoric subsistence economy."[30]

It was during the subsequent Middle and Late Woodland Periods, which extended to the time of initial European contact during the mid-1600s, that two distinctive cultural groups emerged in the vicinity of Lake Superior: the Cree to the north and the Dakota to the west and south. Following the Cree and Dakota in their migration from eastern North America to the mid-continent were the Anishinaabe. These inhabitants, previously called the Chippewa and Ojibwe, but who now prefer to call themselves Anishinaabe (plural Anishinaabeg), were ensconced in the eastern district of Lake Superior (Gichi Gami), where they would be among the last Native groups contacted by French fur traders. In 1679, soon after making their appearance around western Lake Superior, the Anishinaabe entered into a mutually beneficial alliance with the Dakota, a relationship that was maintained until 1736, when the first of several major battles broke out between the two groups. Following the establishment of a basic peace in 1770, the victorious Anishinaabe controlled most of the Lake Superior region and a significant part of the territory that later became Minnesota.[31]

Because of environmental constraints, the Anishinaabe did not always establish or reside in permanent settlements. Instead, as Theresa Schenck has written, their nomadic existence was based on a "seasonal round" that required movement to different camps where the "bounty of the lakes and forest" could be utilized. Winters were spent hunting game in forest encampments, while early spring was spent tapping maple trees for sap that would be converted into sugar; late spring was a time for fishing in lakes and streams. Early summer marked the period when different Anishinaabe bands came together, often at a common fishing site, to reestablish relationships by way of marriage or religious rites. The groups dispersed at summer's end to different autumn hunting and fishing locations.[32]

The 1837 Treaty of St. Peters, informally known as the White Pine Treaty, did not include the North Shore but proved especially harmful to the Anishinaabe overall, given that it was the first pact that precipitated the transfer of Native lands in east-central Minnesota to the U.S. government. Although the treaty included a key provision—namely, that access to fishing, hunting, and wild rice opportunities would be assured to the Anishinaabe—the huge influx of white settlers soon denied them "both access to and use of the land." The 1854 Treaty of LaPointe forced the Anishinaabe to surrender their land and water in northeastern Minnesota, including the North Shore, and relegated them to two reservations: one at Grand Portage, the other at Fond du Lac. (The two reservations represented traditional Anishinaabe territories that met on the North Shore: Grand Portage's domain extended southwest past the location of present-day Beaver Bay, whereas Fond du Lac's went northeastward beyond what is now Two Harbors.) The Anishinaabe, following the 1854 treaty, "became wards of the federal government," wrote Carolyn Gilman. "Culturally

Anishinaabe members of the Grand Portage Band gathered next to the annuities ("goods") they acquired from the nearby U.S. government warehouse in June 1889. On the right is Indian Agent M. A. Leahy. Photograph by George A. Newton. Courtesy of Archives and Special Collections, University of Minnesota Duluth. S2381 George A. Newton photographs.

they became targets of a government project aimed at wiping out Indian identity and assimilating the Ojibwe into the life-style and beliefs of Euro-Americans."[33] Grand Portage, some of which is now part of a National Historic Monument, continues to serve as one of Minnesota's most important cultural sites and mirrors the often conflicted and complicated relationship between Indigenous people and Euro-American colonists.

### Euro-Americans and the North Shore: A "Voyageurs' Highway" and a "Nordic Riviera"

A very small number of European explorers, some seeking riches and treasure, others searching for a northwestern water passage to the Pacific Ocean, appeared in the Lake Superior region by the mid-1660s. Whereas the quest for a northwestern route proved elusive, the countless number of pelts supplied by the region's fur-bearing animals—especially beaver, which were virtually eliminated by trapping—provided immense wealth for French and British interests. Of these two groups, the French *voyageur* (traveler) served as the primary transporter of furs from the far-flung inland domain to Montreal's warehouses and shipping facilities and is still memorialized in the region's folklore and history. The voyageurs' vast water "highway," including Lac Supérieur, but especially its tributary streams and a maze of inland lakes and rivers, was centered at Grand Portage. (Much earlier, of course, Indigenous people used the same waterways.) The French were followed by the British, who maintained power over the fur trade until the War of 1812, when the United States assumed control of present-day northeastern Minnesota. The American Fur Company continued operating for a brief period thereafter, but because of a severe decline in fur-bearing animals, it functioned only as a fishing business from 1836 to 1842.[34]

The North Shore was still part of the Anishinaabe domain until 1854, but some prospectors and adventurers established illegal exploratory pits and built cabins between

Knife River and French River as early as 1846–47. The 1854 LaPointe Treaty—termed a "miners' proposition" by historian William Watts Folwell, the University of Minnesota's first president—quickly attracted more prospectors, land speculators, surveyors, and townsite promoters to the North Shore: within four years, numerous preemption claims and almost two dozen townsite plats were filed along Lake Superior and its tributary streams and rivers. Methodist missionary James Peet, who rowed along thirty miles of Lake Superior coastline in 1854, wrote that "nearly all the land is claimed and a shanty built nearly every half-mile. . . . Some of the 'townsites' have one or two families on them, others a few single men, others are not inhabited at all." Only a few locations produced very limited amounts of copper, and most claims were abandoned during the nationwide Panic of 1857.[35]

It was not until the 1880s that a significant influx of permanent Euro-American settlers—most from Norway and Sweden, with smaller numbers from Finland and Canada—arrived on the North Shore, where they established fishing, logging, and farming enclaves. (Greater ethnic diversity was evident in the iron ore shipping port of Two Harbors.) By 1920, a total of 7,410 people (almost 200 listed as Anishinaabe) resided along or proximate to Lake Superior between Duluth Township and Canada. Overall, 2,500 of these inhabitants were foreign-born, among them 2,010 Nordics: 1,020 Swedes (775 in Two Harbors alone), 750 Norwegians, 190 Finns, 135 Finland Swedes (immigrants born in Finland but who spoke Swedish), and twenty Danes. The 245 Canadians composed the only other large foreign-born contingent, whereas the remaining 140 immigrants represented more than a dozen nationality groups.[36] At least two dozen North Shore businesses, between the 1920s and 1970s, employed Nordic names or themes—Bit of Norway, Sweden House, Niolina's Pensionat, Linnea Woods, Finlandia, and others. Today a Nordic presence is recognizable in local surnames, place-names, and cultural traditions. No wonder that the North Shore was, and is even today, occasionally called a Norwegian, Finnish, Nordic, or Scandinavian "Riviera."

### Making a Living: Fishing, Forestry, Farming, and Tourism

The North Shore's earliest settlers sustained themselves by utilizing the region's resources—especially the fish in Lake Superior and the forests situated proximate to streams and rivers. Some pioneers secured homesteads from the federal government, while others purchased land for small-scale, part-time farms. (Two Harbors was an exception because it served as an iron ore shipping port.) A limited number of nineteenth- and early twentieth-century visitors also made their way to the North Shore on steamships, but the district would not become a popular tourist destination until the first road opened in 1917 and Minnesota Highway 1 was completed during the early to mid-1920s. Tourism, currently the primary driver of the North Shore economy, generates an annual combined total of almost $120 million in Cook and Lake Counties—where all but seventeen miles of the North Shore highway are located.[37]

**Fishing.** Scientists have determined that Lake Superior has served as the natural home for thirty-two native fish species and twelve that have been introduced either intentionally or accidentally; another thirty-nine species inhabit the lake's tributary rivers and streams. Three fish were extremely important as a food source for Native people—lake trout

*(Salvelinus namaycush)*, whitefish *(Coregonus clupeaformis)*, and lake herring or cisco *(C. artedi)*. Because of its high fat content and nutritional value, the Anishinaabe favored siscowet, a subspecies of the lake trout that literally "cooks itself."[38]

Commercial fishing operations on Lake Superior were initiated in 1834 by the American Fur Company, which had previously participated in the exploitation and near extinction of North America's beaver population. The firm utilized the skills and knowledge of the Anishinaabe residing at Grand Portage, one of its primary fishing stations. Unfortunately, the American Fur Company continued to pursue the nonsustainable practices of its previous fur-trapping operations: not only did the company harvest huge quantities of fish but its small mesh nets didn't discriminate between mature adults and the younger specimens that typically had been rejected in favor of larger specimens. Because the demand for fish declined precipitously during the nationwide financial panic from 1837 to 1842, American was forced to close its operations.[39]

The copper prospectors and land speculators who arrived on the North Shore in 1856–57 were sustained by a relatively small number of commercial fishermen. The demand for fish declined when most fortune hunters departed following the Panic of 1857. Only two North Shore fishing camps remained—at Grand Portage and Beaver Bay—after the mineral claims and other townsites were abandoned. Sportfishing for coaster brook trout *(S. fontinalis)* in the lake's tributaries, however, became popular after the 1865 publication of *Superior Fishing*, written by Robert Barnswell Roosevelt, an uncle of future president Theodore Roosevelt. Thereafter, Lake Superior's "coasters" would attract a relatively small but steady stream of anglers from throughout the world. Unfortunately, the species was almost eliminated within a half century because of several factors, including overfishing and the loss of habitat caused by extensive logging.[40]

Norwegian immigrants began arriving during the late 1870s and quickly dominated Minnesota's Lake Superior fishery. The 1895 Minnesota census listed a combined total of sixty-nine North Shore fishermen in Duluth Township and the counties of Lake and Cook: forty-two were born in Norway (twenty-seven of them residing in Cook County alone), thirteen in Sweden, six in Finland, three in the United States, and five in three other countries. The actual number of Norwegians who pursued fishing was appreciably higher, however, given that many who listed their primary occupation as farmer, laborer, or carpenter also owned a boat.[41]

The early steamers that transported supplies to isolated fishing camps picked up barrels of salted trout and whitefish for delivery to Duluth wholesalers like the Cooley–Laveque Fishery, established in 1871—just one year after the Lake Superior & Mississippi Railroad connected St. Paul and Duluth. Cooley–Laveque was sold, in 1886, to Alfred Booth & Sons, a huge Chicago-based wholesale fish enterprise that operated in Duluth and throughout much of the western Lake Superior region. Booth established a virtual monopoly over most of the fisheries, thereby creating a relationship between fisherman and wholesaler that has been described as similar to the confrontational relationship between management and labor in industry and business. Longtime North Shore–Isle Royale resident Ingeborg Johnson Holte offered a firsthand account of the dilemma faced by fishing families at this time. "Each fisherman's supplies and freight were delivered on account at the beginning of the season," recalled Holte in a 1973 interview. "As the fisherman sold fish to the [Booth] company through the season, his credit was merely deducted from his account. Rarely did the fisherman or his family see cash."[42]

Before 1910, the most common fishing craft used by the North Shore's Euro-Americans was the Mackinaw boat. With its flat bottom, pointed bow and stern, and one or two sails, the open Mackinaw proved especially appropriate for Lake Superior's "short, steep choppy water, variable and quickly changing winds, alternating shoal and deep water." Another popular boat was the skiff, a double-ended craft, sixteen to seventeen feet in length, that had a flat bottom and sides. Typically rowed by one fisherman, the skiff included a spar sail; by cutting off about a foot of the stern, a small outboard motor could also be attached to the boat. The "ultimate evolution" of a North Shore vessel was the gas boat, used on Lake Superior until major commercial fishing activities ended during the 1950s. Although the design of each gas boat often reflected the preferences of a specific fisherman, it usually included "a semi-traditional Mackinaw hull and inboard power." During the early decades of the twentieth century, one group of North Shore fishermen formed a "Mosquito Fleet" of gas boats that competed successfully with major wholesalers, such as Booth & Sons. The Mosquito Fleet succeeded because its boats could access small coves and harbors and outrace the Booth's vessels to sites that had fish ready for shipment. Also found on the North Shore was the totally enclosed tug, often used for wintertime herring fishing.[43]

Commercial fish-production figures dropped precipitously on the North Shore and Lake Superior after World War II. While overfishing played a role in the decline, a major factor was the 1956 opening of the Welland Ship Canal between Lakes Erie and Ontario, which allowed oceangoing vessels to enter Superior and the other Great Lakes. Unfortunately, the massive engineering project also gave increased access to the sea lamprey *(Petromyzon marinus)*, an invasive and ancient predatory fish that decimated Superior's fisheries. Most seriously affected were the lake trout, killed when the parasitic lampreys attached themselves to the bodies of the fish and drained them of their body fluids. The fishery entered into a slow recovery by the 1970s after various measures were introduced to impede the movement of lampreys into fish-spawning areas. Of more recent importance is the biologically based Lake Superior Management Plan, introduced in 1995 and updated in 2017 by the MDNR. Among its provisions are limitations on the number of non-Anishinaabe commercial fishing licenses (currently twenty-five) allocated annually by the MDNR. In selecting applicants, the agency evaluates a prospective applicant's Lake Superior fishing experience, previous work as an apprentice with a licensed fisherman, and possession of necessary equipment. Herring, as they have since the 1940s, continue to provide a foundation for the North Shore's limited number of commercial fishing operations.[44]

**Forestry and farming.** Logging activities that commenced during the 1890s had a highly noticeable impact on the North Shore's natural landscape for several ensuing decades. Whenever possible, the companies involved in this work used rivers and streams to direct the harvested logs toward holding facilities on the lakeshore, where they were then shipped to sawmills, most located in Duluth and Ashland. A web of railroad lines that connected remote logging camps to the small North Shore settlement of Knife River was also in place from 1898 to the early 1920s. The last phase of large-scale logging occurred from 1923 to

1972 at Schroeder, Grand Marais, and Pigeon River, where huge pulpwood rafts were organized and then towed to sawmills.

Unlike logging, farming left a limited imprint on the North Shore landscape. Because of soil and climatic constraints, most farms never developed beyond small-scale subsistence units that included modest plots of cleared land where potatoes and other vegetables and some small grains were grown; hay was also harvested for a few cows and perhaps a horse. Farming-related obligations, nevertheless, could even trump fishing at key times during summer and autumn. "Folks have been putting in their crops," wrote a Hovland correspondent in early June 1891, "and now will resume fishing operations." Booth & Sons manager John Coventry defined the immigrants' practices as "mixed farming"—an approach he deemed similar to their fishing activities. Rather than relying solely on a pricy "gillnetting rig," Coventry observed that North Shore fishermen often employed inexpensive hooks and lines: if one apparatus didn't work, the other often did.[45]

## Mom-and-Pop Tourism and "Hay Fever Havens": Early Cabins, Cabin Courts, Resorts, and Motels

While sportfishing attracted some adventurers to Lake Superior by the mid-1860s, even they were preceded by a limited number of hardy tourists who heeded New York journalist John R. St. John's recommendation: anyone interested in the "pursuit of pleasure," wrote St. John in 1846, should travel to the Lake Superior area and view its "grand scenery, waterfalls, lakes, and mountains." Completion of the Soo Locks at Sault Ste. Marie in 1855 allowed steamboats carrying both cargo and passengers to pass much more easily between Lake Superior and the other Great Lakes.[46]

A succession of steamers that connected Duluth, Isle Royale, and Port Arthur were stopping at several small North Shore sites and harbors by the 1880s. Those tourists, hunters, anglers, and land-lookers wishing to make an extended stay could secure food and lodging with two of Cook County's pioneer couples: Anna and Carl Nelson of Lutsen and Anna and Ole Brunes of Hovland. After the North Shore road opened in 1917, motorists typically packed their vehicles with provisions and pitched a tent close to the road; sleeping in one's automobile was not out of the question either. Some visitors stayed in tourist rooms or small hotels found in Two Harbors and Grand Marais, but most motorists sought out cabins provided by fishing families—the earliest examples of mom-and-pop tourism on the North Shore. A number of these tiny units were occupied for several weeks by people who hoped to find relief from hay fever—an allergic reaction to pollen that once was a scourge faced by millions of Americans. (By the early twentieth century Duluth's Park Point was being advertised as a "far famed hay fever and summer resort.") Because large water bodies were considered an ideal antidote for this affliction, Lake Superior's North Shore would also become known as a "hay fever haven." Among the hay fever sufferers seeking relief from their "annual complaint" was Minnesota governor J. A. O. Preus, who, during the 1920s, made mid-August retreats to Beaver Bay.[47]

The cabins, typically located close to the owner's fish house, were constructed either

Lake Superior served as a front door to the North Shore's settlements until an overland road opened in 1917. Shown here are many well-dressed tourists on the SS *Ossifrage*, docked at Knife River during the 1880s. Courtesy of Archives and Special Collections, University of Minnesota Duluth. S2381 George A. Newton photographs.

of logs or of frame and board. Round logs, often scribed to fit closely together, and locked together with saddle notch corners, existed at many places along the North Shore. Some cabins displayed dovetailed corners—a feature that distinguished the finest log structures built by Nordic immigrants. Later, as the supply of large trees dwindled and became increasingly scarce and expensive to acquire, vertical split-log construction was often used. Many vertical log cabins were constructed of stray cordwood, typically eight feet long, that had washed up on the shoreline while being towed to mills for conversion into paper pulp.[48] Splitting a vertical log into halves also doubled the amount of available construction material; a larger log could provide four vertical slabs and a square center post. Almost all cabins were built of frame and board after World War II.

Early cabin owners who had sufficient lakeshore property often organized the units in a linear row that conformed to the outline of the shoreline—a practice that provided all guests with direct views of Lake Superior. The interiors typically included some or most of the following: one or two iron bedframes; a cast-iron stove; an icebox; a washstand and pitcher; a dresser; two chairs; several dishes, plates, and pieces of silverware; a few pots and pans; and a sink that drained directly onto the ground. Outside were a single hand pump, a privy or privies, and a crude building with showers, all of which served the entire cabin

A 1930s North Shore cabin at Lockport in the Lutsen area, constructed of closely fitted horizontal logs that were locked together at the corners with saddle notches. A small tool, called a scriber, guided the builders as they cut out a concave spline or groove along the bottom length of each log. This incised section, when placed over the round (convex) form of the lower log, created a very tight fit. The smooth logs of the Lockport cabin's front wall were hand-hewn with a broadax; the sidewall logs were round.

grouping. During this early period, recalled resort owner Claude Midlam of Duluth Township, "tourists were content with almost any cabin" and would willingly "walk out to the outhouse, or plug walls with wads of paper to keep out the mosquitoes."[49]

A number of resort operators, almost immediately after the end of World War II, began improving and modernizing the interiors of their rental cabins by adding innerspring and Beautyrest mattresses, propane gas stoves, electric lights, hot shower baths, and "inside toilets." Reading materials, games, outdoor fire pits, and a few other amenities might also be provided. Some operators sought to attract visitors with wild-animal attractions, such as a few fenced-in deer or, occasionally, one or two bears that were chained to a post or tree. Also emerging by this time were a number of resorts, typically with six or more cabins, that served as destinations for guests who stayed on the site for several days or more. Many early resorts operated on the "American plan," meaning that all or some meals were included in the charge; guests at "European plan" resorts paid only for the room or cabin.

During the 1920s, another form of accommodation—usually described as a "cabin court," "motor court," or "auto court"—was emerging in Florida and southern California. By 1934, the "courts" were so evident throughout the entire nation that the editors of

Some of the vertical split-log cabins, built during the mid-1920s by Emil Edisen at his Camper's Home Resort in Castle Danger. Considered the North Shore's first cabin resort, Camper's Home also had several units constructed of horizontal logs and of frame and board. An expansive resort, dating to the late 1990s, now stands on the site. Photograph by Harold Youngren, 1929.

**Camper's Home was one of Minnesota's first cabin resorts when it emerged, during the early 1920s, at Castle Danger, situated eleven miles northeast of Two Harbors. Camper's Home was also distinctive because of its twelve lakefront cabins; all but one was removed when a large resort complex, Grand Superior Lodge, was built on the site during the late 1990s.**

*Fortune* commissioned celebrated author James Agee (1909–55) to prepare a ghostwritten article, "The Great American Roadside," for their magazine. Agee chose to celebrate the courts because of the freedom they provided when America's citizens ventured out onto the nation's highways. "Casually yet eagerly this American people has spun away the summer length of day, in cars, along the great road," he wrote. "The lifted dark brings them down like sea birds, wherever night finds them to rest along their line of flight."[50]

**A 1930s interior view of a cabin at what is now Island View Resort in Knife River. Island View's utilitarian furnishings were typical of many mom-and-pop cabin resorts located on the North Shore until the post–World War II years. Courtesy of Island View Resort.**

The North Shore's first motor court, dating to 1929, was built by Finnish immigrants Victor and Hilja Elmgren in Lakewood Township, situated just beyond Duluth's northeastern boundary. The majority of motor courts, however, appeared along Duluth's Congdon Boulevard and in Duluth Township shortly after World War II. Their defining feature was a horseshoe-shaped plan, with closely spaced cabins grouped around the central open area. Some courts had cabins that were joined together and covered by a common roof, which heightened the sense of visual integration and also sheltered the entrance to each unit. The shared open space at the center, often similar to a well-maintained lawn, typically included playground equipment, lawn chairs, picnic tables, and, occasionally, a portable swimming pool.[51]

Although motor courts allowed travelers to park their vehicles by a rental unit, it was

Roadside attractions, ranging from reconstructed trading posts and logging camps to caged deer and chained black bears, were on display at a few North Shore resort sites, primarily from the 1930s to the 1960s. Daring (and perhaps foolhardy) tourists could feed marshmallows to the bears, such this bruin, tethered to a post at Finch's Resort, located three miles northeast of Little Marais along the Manitou River.

**Elmgren's Motor Court (now the Gardenwood Resort and Motel), 1930s. Situated a short distance from the northeastern end of Duluth's Congdon Boulevard, the twenty-unit complex, built in 1929, was the earliest example of a courtyard layout on the North Shore. Although seven cabins at the left were later removed and replaced by a four-unit motel, the overall courtyard pattern has been retained to the present. Courtesy of the Gardenwood Resort and Motel.**

the postwar motel (a combination of the words *motor* and *hotel*) that would forever change the nation's roadside landscape. Indeed, the growth in motel construction that occurred between 1946 and 1954 has been termed "almost unprecedented in American history." The North Shore's first two motels appeared during the late 1940s in Larsmont and Tofte. One, the Sea Breeze (surprisingly, not named the Lake Breeze), was built northeast of Larsmont by Two Harbors railroad engineer David M. Anderson, after he traveled through several southwestern states during the immediate postwar years. Anderson initially planned to build several separate cabins on the property but decided that interconnected motel units were a more suitable choice. Identifying the Sea Breeze as an example of "Spanish architecture," Anderson constructed a row of nine separate, flat-roofed units connected by narrow carports; each had stucco-covered walls that sought to replicate the appearance of adobe. (Other Southwestern-themed motels that emerged throughout the United States during this period were often termed examples of "Spanish Adobe" or "Indian Pueblo.") Each compact Sea Breeze unit included a combination living/sleeping room, but Anderson claimed that all were "modern in every way" because of their gas heaters and stoves, shower baths, and kitchenettes. He later painted the exteriors pink and purple before removing the entire complex from the site during the late 1960s or early 1970s.[52]

The other North Shore late-1940s motel was built by Thomas and Madeline Jacobsen Hansen of Tofte. Each of the Hansens' units included a slightly sloped roof with four relatively large perpendicular gables, which offered more interior space than the majority of motels that soon appeared along Highway 61. A typical North Shore motel generally had four or more connected units, a common roof, and shared interior walls. This compact design and plan proved attractive to owners, who, for a relatively small monetary investment, could construct, maintain, and heat an entire building situated on a small plot of land. Most early North Shore motels, however, were torn down or removed during ensuing decades. Several have been replaced by much larger facilities, some of which are financed and built by national companies or "chains" that provide standardized design and management guidelines for the franchise owner or operator.

The mom-and-pop resorts that had proved so popular on the North Shore since the 1920s began closing or changing by the 1950s—a process that accelerated during the 1970s and 1980s and has continued into the present. Although a significant number of these properties have disappeared altogether, some were replaced or transformed into large facilities that offer amenities and services typical of upscale destination resorts and lodges throughout the United States. Another major transition appeared during the early 2000s when *fractional ownership*, a practice that emerged a decade earlier at Rocky Mountain ski resorts, became evident on the North Shore. This ownership model allows buyers to acquire a fraction (often one-fourth) of a townhouse, cabin, or condominium unit, thereby reducing the purchase price, as well as costs related to the upkeep and maintenance of a singly owned property. A one-quarter share, for example, provides the titleholder with thirteen weeks of annual access to the property and its amenities. The unit may also be used to secure rental income when not occupied by an owner. The titleholders pay fees to a membership association that covers taxes, insurance, and upkeep; a manager or company administers the association's regulations and oversees the property and rental program.[53]

Also transforming the contemporary North Shore tourist scene is a recent and increasingly popular practice: advertising private cabins and properties on Airbnb, Vrbo, and other listing services. Distinguishing between cabins that serve as a "personal retreat" and others

**The Sea Breeze, with nine separate units linked together by automobile breezeways, was one of the first examples of a motel on the North Shore when it emerged between Larsmont and Two Harbors in 1949. A residence now stands on the property.**

**Maintaining an equitable balance between private and public landownership, as demonstrated by this 2020 Lake County sign, can pose difficult and controversial issues in highly popular areas such as the North Shore.**

that "pull in extra income by listing them as short-term rentals" is of considerable concern to assessors and tax officials, as well as the owners of nearby properties who have to cope with the arrival of new neighbors on an irregular basis. A question posed by Minnesota governor Tim Walz in late 2019—"Is it a lodge or is it a family cabin?"—will undoubtedly generate considerable debate along the North Shore for many years.[54]

Some current tourists certainly prefer the small number of traditional mom-and-pop businesses that remain along the North Shore, but others who have sufficient monetary resources choose "to unplug from everyday lives," even if they "don't want to disconnect." These visitors prefer the newer complexes that have many or at least several of the following features: high-speed Wi-Fi and internet access; cable television; modern heating and air-conditioning systems; king-sized beds; around-the-clock front desk service; spas, saunas, massage therapy, and exercise rooms; heated swimming pools; full-service restaurants; activity directors; and so forth. Furthermore, fewer people are choosing to work long hours and pay the high taxes that a family-owned resort or tourist business requires.[55] The field guide section of this volume (Part II) offers numerous examples of places that represent decades of transition and change along the North Shore.

# PART I

## A History of Minnesota's North Shore Highway

Anyone who has traveled over this Lake Superior–International Highway will agree that its native beauty and grandeur finds a parallel only in the Columbia River Highway, or in the Amalfi Drive, of European fame. Two hundred miles of exquisite driving, penetrating a nearly untouched wilderness, and most of the way presenting a full view of the water of Lake Superior. It is Minnesota's greatest attraction, and thousands of people yearly will come to this section of the state to enjoy its attending health and beauty.

—Thomas Owens, president of the Lake Superior International Highway Association, 1925

Chapter 1

# Dogs, Horses, and Mail along the North Shore Trail

A 1792 federal law that empowered the U.S. Congress to establish post offices and post roads was responsible for launching mail service along the North Shore in 1856—the same year a settlement emerged at Beaver Bay, situated fifty-two miles northeast of Duluth's harbor. Mineral prospector Robert B. McLean, appointed Beaver Bay's first postmaster during summer 1856, served only until November, when postal duties were assumed by Albert Wieland, who had recently arrived in Beaver Bay with his six German immigrant brothers. Wieland often contracted with numerous carriers who delivered mail between Superior (the small Wisconsin settlement that bordered Duluth) and early North Shore post offices situated in French River, Buchanan, Beaver Bay, Grand Marais, and Grand Portage.[1]

At the beginning of each spring season, when Lake Superior's ice was melting and the narrow trail became excessively soft and muddy, carriers used a horse to transport the mail or packed it on their own backs. Rowboats equipped with sails were employed on the lake from April into November, but when sufficient snow accumulated during winter, the mail was delivered by dogsled. Once adequate ice formed along the shoreline, the mushers and their dogs moved onto Lake Superior's frozen edge, although they often found it necessary to go back and forth between lake and shore during the journey. Because of the isolation and darkness that prevailed during much of the winter season, the arrival of a North Shore mail sled, pulled by three or four dogs with small bells festooned to their collars, was an event of a festive quality: the "jingling sleigh bells, U.S. mail, and toboggan," wrote a reporter who described Louis Plante's late December arrival in Grand Marais, "resembled old Santa Claus coming to town."[2]

Several subcontractors who delivered mail during the late nineteenth century were Anishinaabe men, the most famous being John Beargrease (1858–1910), the son of a tribal leader and a highly proficient hunter, trapper, and fisherman. Beargrease made his deliveries by rowboat during the summer season but achieved legendary status for his daring and reliability when transporting up to seven hundred pounds of mail on wintertime dogsled runs between Two Harbors and Grand Marais, which typically required four to six days of travel.

"Day or night or good weather or bad made no difference with John Beargrease," wrote Cook County historian Willis Raff. "He was sure to arrive some time with the mail intact." Since 1980, the annual three-hundred-mile-long John Beargrease Sled Dog Marathon has commemorated and memorialized the mail carrier's name throughout northeastern Minnesota. The race participants, stated one recent observer, are drawn to the race by "a steely family bond, a religious-like zeal for dogs, or the mysterious call of John Beargrease."[3]

Local contractors were hired to maintain a narrow pathway for the dogs and mushers, as in 1872, when St. Louis County's commissioners authorized the payment of $1,000 to McKenzie & Company, a Duluth firm, to engage in "cutting and grubbing" eleven miles of winter road between the city's eastern limits and the Lake County border. St. Louis County commissioners also made an unrealistic request of Lake County officials at this time, namely, that they appropriate $10,000 to develop the roadway as far as the Canadian border. (Lake County extended to Canada until Cook County was organized in 1874.) The *Duluth Minnesotian* revealed the sarcasm that often colored the competitive relationship between the two counties: "Lake County has always been represented to us as rich in her agricultural and mineral lands," wrote the *Minnesotian*'s editor in 1872, "but they remain undeveloped because of their inaccessibility. Build a road through the county and their value will be enhanced ten-fold—and the people of the county must be near-sighted, indeed, not to see it." Only later, however, was it determined that the "rich mineral lands" of St. Louis County barely extended into Lake County.[4]

The Canadian government, in 1873, authorized funds for the development of a trail from the Minnesota–Ontario border at Pigeon River to Fort William–Port Arthur, which opened one year later. The State of Minnesota responded immediately by financing improvements for the Beaver Bay to Grand Marais section, with a possible extension to Grand Portage. Securing the contract were the Wieland brothers, who received twelve dollars per mile to clear a trail that was six feet wide. The 110-mile-long trail, by 1874, had been sufficiently "brushed out" between Duluth and Grand Marais to serve as a wintertime road for one-horse sleighs and dog trains. But when the money gave out in Grand Marais, the remaining thirty-five miles to Grand Portage and the Pigeon River had not even been surveyed.[5]

A stage line opened between Duluth and the new settlement of Agate Bay (later called Two Harbors) in 1883, although poor road conditions and "rotten ice" made it difficult to transport passengers and supplies during some periods of the year. The situation improved considerably in early 1887, when the Duluth & Iron Range (D&IR) Railroad opened twenty-six miles of track on its Lake Line. Despite the relatively flat terrain traversed by the railroad, construction crews needed to build several large bridges and trestles and numerous smaller structures over the North Shore's rivers, streams, and marshy areas. A heavy mid-December 1886 snowstorm delayed the train's inaugural journey, but a D&IR engine with a few cars in tow pushed its way into Duluth two days later. "Farewell dog trains and United States mails on one-horse sleds," announced a reporter following the train's arrival, "farewell, a long farewell to the old trails and [crossing] streams on fallen logs, and farewell too, to days of tramping through the snow and nights of frozen sleep, with feet in

Horse-drawn sleighs and coaches began making mail deliveries and carrying passengers between Two Harbors and Grand Marais in late 1899. Courtesy of Lake County Historical Society.

the campfire and head in an atmosphere forty below."[6] Most important to Two Harbors' citizens, however, was the dependable, year-round, mail, passenger, and freight service that the Lake Line provided.

In 1890, a passenger steamship, the SS *Hiram R. Dixon,* replaced the summer-season rowboats that, for several previous years, had served the settlements located northeast of Two Harbors. Owned and operated by Alfred Booth & Sons Packing Company, the Duluth-based *Dixon,* for six to seven months of the year, made twice-weekly trips along the North Shore before it was destroyed in a 1903 fire. The *Dixon* was replaced by the SS *America,* which sank by Isle Royale in 1928.[7]

As the nineteenth century ended, Cook County residents issued calls to convert the Two Harbors–Grand Marais trail into a road that could handle either sleighs or stagecoaches pulled by teams of horses. That stretch of the trail, noted one exasperated 1898 critic, "is only to be traveled in winter by dog-train and even then with much hardship and difficulty." If suitable improvements were made, contended the writer, horse-drawn sleighs could traverse the entire route in just two days. "We want it [the road] badly, and are determined to get it," implored the correspondent.[8]

In 1899, the counties of Lake and Cook provided more funding for roadbuilding purposes. An improved roadway, much of it located inland from Lake Superior, was completed to Grand Marais in December. One week prior to Christmas Day, a group of Grand Marais citizens welcomed the first horse-drawn postal sleigh into their village. The trips were divided into three relays. After departing with mail from Two Harbors' railroad depot, the team went as far as Beaver Crossing, where fresh horses were secured for the next leg of the journey and the driver and passengers could eat and rest at the Half-Way House. Another stop occurred at Little Marais in eastern Lake County before the final run was made to Grand Marais. Making their way simultaneously from Grand Marais to Two Harbors were other teams and drivers. As 1899 drew to a close, a group of eight men, several of them Cook County officials, made a three-day trip from Grand Marais to Duluth in a horse-drawn sleigh—the first such journey in North Shore history.[9]

## Carriages and Bicycles in Duluth

Meanwhile, road improvements were advancing quite rapidly at the Duluth end of the North Shore. New London Township, platted east of Duluth's developed area in 1871, was soon connected to the city by London Avenue (now London Road). The township and nearby subdivision of Lester Park, including the mouth of the Lester River and a federally sponsored fisheries station, were incorporated as the Village of Lakeside in 1889, then as the City of Lakeside in 1891—two years before being annexed by Duluth. London Road, described by the Duluth Board of Park Commissioners as the city's "Lake Shore Boulevard" in 1894, would ultimately proceed to the Lester River. London Road, opined the board members, is "to Duluth what the Lake Shore Drive is to Chicago."[10]

London Road in 1892, close to its current intersection with Fortieth Avenue East. Three horse-drawn carriages (one horse at the right is drinking from a water tank) and two bicyclists are visible along the recently paved road. Courtesy of Archives and Special Collections, University of Minnesota Duluth.

London Road quickly became a popular pleasure drive for Duluthians, who ventured to the Lester River in horse-drawn carriages and sleighs; less affluent residents could reach the destination by streetcar. A path, one-half mile long, extended from the river's mouth to the Lakewood Pumping Station, which began providing Duluthians with drinking water in 1896.[11] The road that headed from the Lester River to Two Harbors followed the D&IR railroad tracks to Clifton, where it veered inland toward the Lake County boundary; from there the road moved back to the shoreline and paralleled Lake Superior and the D&IR tracks.

In 1892, when London Road was paved with macadam, local bicyclists affiliated with the League of American Wheelman organized a race from downtown Duluth to Lester Park. It was "the concept of speed that made bicycles popular with the young sports," reminisced pioneer Duluthian David Naymark many years later. During summer and autumn, bicycle enthusiasts also peddled along the unpaved road between Duluth and Two Harbors. "The wheeling is rough in many places," acknowledged one rider engaged in organizing a July 1896 cycle club run from Duluth's Board of Trade Building to Two Harbors; participants who didn't wish to face the rigors of a round-trip journey could return by boat. Two months later, Duluthian G. E. Booth set a record for the twenty-six-mile "wheel" to Two Harbors by covering the distance in a "neat" one hour fifty-seven minutes. Bicyclists also emerged as the earliest Duluth voices in the nationwide good roads movement, which advocated for better transportation routes throughout America. (Minnesota's Good Roads Association appeared in 1896; Duluthians formed their club two years later.) Interest in bicycling waned once automobiles appeared in greater numbers during the second decade of the twentieth century. Nevertheless, the good roads movement, including chapters in Duluth and Two Harbors, played a major role in promoting highway improvements until the 1930s.[12]

Chapter 2

# A Road and a Bridge to Canada, 1900–1917

Duluth's first automobiles, powered either by steam or by gasoline, appeared in 1901, about a half dozen years after a few vehicles had ventured onto the streets of Minneapolis. Among the earliest was a lightweight Studebaker-Stanhope owned by E. J. Filiatrault, who opened Duluth's Mutual Electric and Auto Company in 1901 and began selling cars one year later. The early motorized vehicles that entered the city's treacherous streets failed to generate much acceptance or enthusiasm among residents. "The automobile is neither present nor practicable in Duluth," claimed one 1903 contrarian, while another attributed the lack of vehicles (only thirty-five in 1905) to the city's steep hills and poor roads. Just two years later, however, local resident Peter Wahlin wrote a brief but prescient letter to the *Duluth News-Tribune*, predicting that automobiles would soon replace horse-drawn carriages on London Road, the city's "only real driveway." Wahlin also argued that extending London Road some miles along Lake Superior would provide Duluth with "one of the grandest and most picturesque drives in the world." The *Tribune*'s editors agreed, anticipating that a connection between the lakeshore boulevard and Duluth's emerging skyline drive atop the hill would have "double charm for the tourists, and spread the fame of the city."[1]

Two Harbors residents joined the ranks of North Shore automobile owners after businessman Henry Bryan purchased a 1903 gasoline-powered Curved Dash Oldsmobile. Motorists could soon drive, with some difficulty, between Two Harbors and Duluth, but by summer 1910, a one-way trip still required about one hour and thirty-five minutes; the average speed, sixteen miles per hour, was only slightly faster than that of a well-conditioned bicyclist. When travel was impossible because of the deep ruts left by vehicles during a springtime thaw or after periods of heavy rainfall, horses pulled heavy steel drags that smoothed out the surface.[2]

Because of limited private vehicle ownership and unpredictable road conditions, both the D&IR and Knife River–based Duluth & Northern Minnesota (D&NM) railroad companies operated Sunday "Fishermen's Specials." Early-morning D&IR trains departed Duluth and dropped off anglers at the mouths of several North Shore streams and rivers.

Early twentieth-century travelers who braved the North Shore trail faced challenges during the spring snowmelt and periods of heavy rainfall. Courtesy of Lake County Historical Society.

FISHING EXCURSION

Sunday, May 17th

VIA

DULUTH & NORTHERN MINNESOTA RAILWAY.

Special train connecting with Duluth and Iron Range leaving Duluth 7:45 a. m. Returning 6:45 p. m. stopping at Knife River, Stewart River, Encampment River, Gooseberry River, Split Rock River, Beaver River and Schauff Lake. Fine fishing at any of these points. For further information call at 512 Lonsdale Bldg. or phone 708 Old,

Fishing enthusiasts during the early 1900s could board a special D&IR train in Duluth and travel to Knife River. From there, a D&NM train transported them closer to the inland headwaters of several North Shore streams and rivers. Courtesy of the *Duluth News-Tribune*, 14 May 1908, 8.

Others disembarked at Knife River, where they transferred onto a D&NM train that transported them inland and a few miles closer to the rivers' headwaters. The participants, with creels often filled with fish, returned to Duluth on a late-afternoon train. The same process occurred in November when hunters from Duluth and Two Harbors traveled to the Knife River depot, where they boarded another train that transported them "into the deer country."[3]

## Promoting a North Shore Road

The Duluth–Two Harbors roadway continued to experience weather-related problems during the early 1900s, but at least it could be traversed by motorized vehicles and was a virtual thoroughfare compared to the inland track that eventually reached Schroeder, where the existing lakeshore route continued to Grand Marais. Despite some improvements that occurred during the late 1890s, the section of road that extended beyond Two Harbors remained essentially inaccessible to vehicles throughout the early twentieth century. "It is in extremely bad condition and is impassable most of the year," fumed a Lake County commissioner in 1903, whereas another commentator lamented that other than in midwinter, "it is well-nigh impossible to get from any place to anywhere in this section. The people here, nevertheless, must travel in summer as well as in winter."[4]

Springtime could also present significant problems for steamship travel, as in mid-April 1907, when numerous people were stranded along the North Shore because of excessive ice that made it impossible for the Booth Company's steamer, *Bon Ami*, to depart Duluth's harbor. Mail carriers faced other challenging and often dangerous conditions after periods of rapid thawing or when heavy rainfalls washed out makeshift bridges; the carrier then had to choose whether to ford the roiling water. The experience of Caleb Carlson, a Swedish American mail carrier from Two Harbors, illustrates the dire consequences of making an incorrect choice. When high water tore away the Poplar River bridge by Lutsen in April 1908, Carlson asked a local Anishinaabe resident, White Sky Gesik, to walk the mail over a fallen tree that spanned the river. Carlson and his steed then attempted to ford the Poplar, but its strong current pulled both of them into Lake Superior, which was buffeted by northeastern gale-force winds. The twenty-two-year-old carrier was swept away by a wave and drowned; his body was recovered several days later, about a mile from the river's mouth. Ironically, both the horse and the mailbag eventually arrived safely in Grand Marais.[5]

Mail carriers actually welcomed the winter season because the snow would "fill the pitch holes, cover the smaller stumps, and level the roughness." Oscar Beckman, who, along with his brothers, delivered mail between Two Harbors and Grand Marais from 1903 to 1911, remarked that a horse-drawn sleigh would ride on top of the brush when snow depths were adequate. Twenty years after Beckman's final delivery, the hardy "knight of the road" recalled his exploits with typical Nordic modesty: "of course it got bitter cold and there was bitter storms, but I got used to them and didn't mind weather very much no matter what it was." Even when improvements did occur, the springtime thaw posed constant problems. "The roads are in bad condition and getting worse," wrote a North Shore resident in April 1905. "The stage came through from Little Marais on wheels last trip, while on the Two Harbors and Grand Marais route [there] were short stretches of soft sleighing." During the spring breakup, travel often occurred entirely at night, when colder temperatures froze the tracks.[6]

## Inland to Finland

Huge rock outcroppings and difficult river crossings between Two Harbors and Schroeder proved insurmountable to early twentieth-century road builders. Therefore the initial North Shore roadway headed inland from a point close to the mouth of the Stewart River, then continued a considerable distance from Lake Superior, for some fifty-five miles. The road passed through several tiny enclaves—Buell, London, Beaver Crossing, Freedom, Lax Lake, Safford, Finland, Silver, Cramer, and others—before it bent southward toward Schroeder and Lake Superior. All of these inland hamlets served, from 1898 to 1923, as station stops along the D&NM Railroad—the Knife River–based subsidiary of Alger, Smith & Company (also Alger–Smith), a Michigan logging and lumber firm.

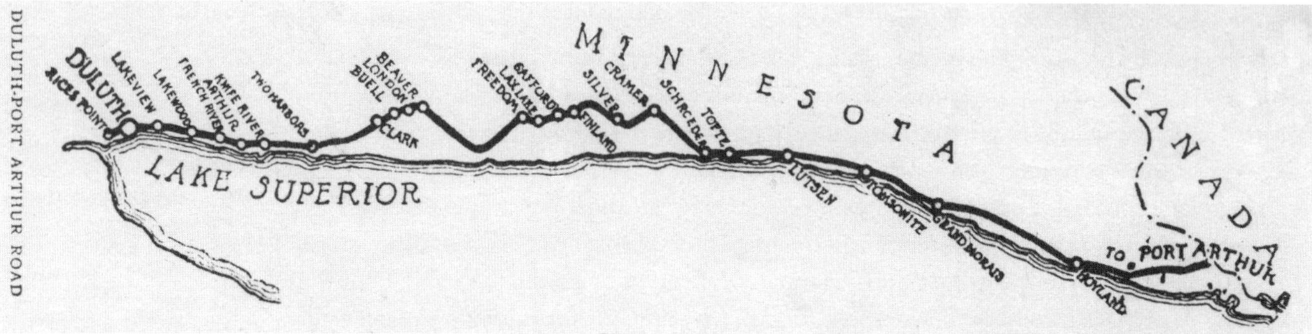


**A 1916 map of the North Shore road that would be completed, one year later, between Duluth and the Canadian border. The road went inland at the Stewart River (about three miles northeast of Two Harbors), then continued for fifty-five miles until it once again reached Lake Superior at Schroeder. *Duluth Herald*, 1 April 1916, 17.**

While most of these places included little more than a small railroad station and some houses and cabins, a few had additional buildings. One was Beaver Crossing, a point of call on the stage and sleigh mail route that emerged between Two Harbors and Grand Marais in 1899. Two years later, Alger–Smith would establish its summertime horse stables and pastures nearby. Beaver Crossing's only business was the Half-Way House, which initially provided travelers with food and lodging but began catering to loggers searching for "entertainment" and a "sporting atmosphere" in 1904. The business closed in 1919, when Alger–Smith ended its timber-harvesting operations.[7]

**The inland bridge that spanned the Gooseberry River, with a 1916 Dodge convertible on its deck. The structure was typical of several bridges built in northeastern Minnesota before the mid-1920s. Note the cutover landscape. Photograph by William Roleff.**

The Scientific Ranch, one year after Rudolph and Mary Illgen opened their Beaver Crossing tourist business in 1921. The tar paper–covered structure (formerly known as the Half-Way House) had a store, gas pump, and diner that served motorists. Courtesy of Lake County Historical Society.

Finnish immigrants, in 1913, opened a consumers' cooperative store in Finland, one of more than seventy similar outlets organized by Minnesota's Finns. Now just one of two Finnish-sponsored consumers' cooperatives remaining in the state, the Finland store continues to serve a small but progressive community of organic farmers, loggers, tourist providers, commuters, and retirees, as well as motorists, truckers, and vacationers.

Rudolph and Mary Illgen acquired the vacant structure in 1920, shortly after responding to a sales advertisement for eighty acres of land at Beaver Crossing. A 1905 émigré from Germany, Illgen married Mary Pauli, the daughter of Swiss German parents who had recently moved from Wadena, Minnesota, to an Oklahoma farm. Although the Illgens intended to develop a "scientific ranch" at Beaver Crossing, they soon discovered that serving tourists and railroad crews was far more profitable. Therefore they transformed the former Half-Way House into the Hotel Scientific Ranch, which offered a store, diner, gas pump, and bus stop; a few cabins also stood nearby. But when Minnesota Highway 1 was under construction along the North Shore in 1923, the Illgens and their children closed the hotel and moved to Crystal Bay on Lake Superior, where they launched a larger business.[8]

After Beaver Crossing was Lax Lake, named for Finland Swedes Johannes and Wilhelmina Kronman Waxlax, who settled on their homestead in 1894. During the 1920s, other Waxlax family members would build a store and cabins (owned by non–family members since 1973) along the Lax Lake shoreline. Six miles northeast of Lax Lake is Finland, the only surviving settlement on the early inland road. Originally a mail stop, Finnish immigrants who arrived in the area during the early 1900s worked as trappers and loggers before establishing subsistence farms, where, as one settler colorfully recalled, they raised their families "between the rocks and strawberries." Years later, a north–south highway (now Minnesota Highway 1) that connected the North Shore and Ely passed through Finland, thereby assuring its long-term viability. The Finland area is also distinctive because of its topography. Just west of the boundary separating Lake and Cook Counties are the tallest hills of the Lake Superior Highlands; some that rise 1,950 feet above sea level represent the greatest elevation change in Minnesota.[9]

Cramer dates to 1905, when Joseph Cramer established a homestead claim eleven miles northeast of Finland. The Pennsylvanian pursued farming, taught school, and opened a store and post office following the D&NM's arrival in 1910. Soon, a hotel and seventeen residences emerged in Cramer. For just over a decade, the settlement would serve as an important Cook County mail stop: once the train arrived, the mail was picked up by carriers and distributed to several of the county's settlements. In April 1916, Fred Winger and George Robertson, the operators of a Grand Marais livery firm, purchased two vehicles, a Ford and an Overland Eight, which they used to provide daily postal service between Cramer and Grand Marais. "It will be a little strange to have mail every day," wrote a resident, "but it will be a great convenience to the people of this county." The railroad tracks were removed in 1923, and all of Cramer's buildings had vanished by 1928.[10] Much of the remaining inland route is now called Cramer Road.

## Completing a Highway

Amendments to the Minnesota Constitution in 1898 and 1906 authorized the establishment of a very limited state road and bridge fund that was financed with a small general tax and distributed to counties by the recently formed State Highway Commission. Cook County's voters also approved the sale of bonds that funded limited road construction efforts during the late nineteenth century; Lake County followed some years thereafter. Because the improvements were so minimal, Grand Marais residents continued issuing pleas calling for the development of an improved road that would connect them to the "outside world." Nevertheless, by October 1911, residents of both counties were still bemoaning the inadequacies of a road described as "passable for teams in ordinary weather, but not for machines."[11]

Despite the inland road's inherent limitations, it was the only passable route that led northeast of Two Harbors. The old shoreline trail, nonetheless, still attracted a few adventurers, among them Daniel Naymark and Ben Crystal, two Jewish European immigrants from Duluth who made a horse and buggy trip to Grand Marais in 1911. The corduroy-covered route between Duluth and Two Harbors required only one day of travel, and the dirt road that extended four miles northeast of Two Harbors was also traversed quickly. From there, however, the lakeside track quickly became a narrow trail that eventually disappeared. It was covered with brush, recalled Naymark in 1940, and "the only semblance of a road was when you gazed up in the air and you could see how the timber was cut to accommodate the road." The deadheads and windfalls were so prevalent that the men had to saw off the branches, cut the logs into sections, and use a chain and tackle and their horse to clear the former trail. Because it had taken the men more than two weeks to "get out of the jungles and into civilization," Naymark and Crystal decided that the difficulties of a return trip were too great to consider; therefore the men and their helpful steed traveled from Grand Marais to Duluth by steamship. Naymark was one of Duluth's oldest pioneers when he died at the age of ninety-eight, in 1984.[12]

In 1913–14, after Lake and Cook Counties issued bonds to improve the inland road,

Duluth commentators deemed their actions worthy of praise. With additional funds provided by the one-mill state tax, efforts were then made to develop an upgraded roadway in both counties. Clearing much of the right-of-way required significant work—primarily cutting through heavy forests, pulling stumps, and filling in or draining swampy soils. "Old roads were rebuilt [and] connected," commented the *Two Harbors Sentinel*, "and new roads blazed through the wilderness." A. D. Stephens, a former state senator from Crookston in northwestern Minnesota, gave full-throated support to the emerging highway, claiming that it "would develop settlement and scatter outside wealth, not only along its whole length, but in all the byways to be reached from it."[13]

Until late 1914, no motorized vehicle had yet made a trip from Duluth to Grand Marais. This situation changed in November, when Edward J. Filiatrault and his friend S. B. Kirby Sr., each accompanied by a son, completed a round-trip journey between the two places. In addition to his role as Duluth's earliest auto dealer, Filiatrault was a well-known, colorful, and often flamboyant promoter of Duluth, the North Shore, and himself.[14]

The *Duluth News-Tribune* unabashedly described the excursion undertaken by Filiatrault and his companions as "the wildest trip in America." Kirby identified the Duluth to Beaver Bay section as relatively adequate but described the subsequent thirty-six miles along Lake Superior as "simply fierce." By engaging the transmission of his Model T Ford in four hours of "continuous grinding," Filiatrault was able to drive around many large boulders, thereby avoiding "tearing out an axle or breaking some other part." He also maneuvered through brush that was two to three feet high and crossed over a bridge that was ready to break through; the four adventurers also removed or cut away fifteen to twenty windfalls and drove over or around others that proved too large to dislodge. Although Kirby may not have understood the geological origins of the narrow glacial beaches their Model T followed, he was awed by the view: "high perpendicular walls often appeared on one side, with a sheer drop of several hundred feet on the other side down to some roaring trout stream emptying into Lake Superior." The steepest hills were surmounted by going up the inclines in reverse, which placed the gas tank above the engine so fuel would flow into it. The banks of the Manitou River provided the greatest challenge: there Filiatrault, without his passengers, locked the brakes and "slid the entire way down that hill."[15]

Ten hours after departing Duluth, the weary travelers arrived in Grand Marais. Because Filiatrault had telegraphed the local Ford dealer just before setting out on the venture, a large crowd of townsfolk gathered to welcome the first motorized vehicle that had successfully followed the entire lakeshore from Duluth to Grand Marais. The travelers decided to return along the inland route, which, quite obviously, was a much less daunting and challenging journey.[16]

Filiatrault continued to praise the North Shore following his adventure. "There is no place in North America that can excel the beauty and grandeur of the North Shore of Lake Superior," he raved, "and as soon as the roads are opened up sufficiently, undoubtedly the state of Minnesota, assisted by the counties of St. Louis, Lake, and Cook, will immediately take the necessary steps to educate the world at large as to the advantages of the scenic beauty of the north shore of Lake Superior." After making a second North Shore trip in June 1915, this time proceeding beyond Grand Marais to the Pigeon River, Filiatrault declared the road significantly improved. Once the project is finished, he claimed, "the north shore boulevard can then take its place among the famous highways of the world."[17]

During the early twentieth century, several citizens in the Ontario cities of Port Arthur and Fort William began issuing calls for a road that would link their cities to Minnesota. Among their complaints was a four-week-long communication gap that often separated them from major Canadian cities like Toronto and Ottawa. A road connection to Minnesota, they argued, was the only possible way "to get out of the woods." Soon, representatives from both northeastern Minnesota and Fort William–Port Arthur were promoting the highway as an international project. Building such a road, asserted a Canadian official, would prove attractive to motorists and draw both tourists and capitalists to the region. When the highway is completed, urged N. G. Neal, Port Arthur's industrial commissioner, two large touring cars, one representing his city, the other Duluth, should embark on a trip from Lake Superior to New York, "advertising in every county and village on the way . . . that a great automobile highway has been opened up to one of the most beautiful stretches of country in the world."[18]

Work on the road between Fort William–Port Arthur and the Pigeon River had progressed to such an extent by August 1916 that the three owners of Port Arthur's Central Garage—William Foot, W. S. Blanchard, and Bert Skeels—sought to gain some publicity by completing the first successful automobile journey from Canada to Duluth. Most of the problems encountered on their adventure, undertaken in a 1911 Cadillac Roadster, occurred over the final eight miles in Canada, where the roadway was not yet graded. They successfully forded the Pigeon River at a place that had low water and used axes and crowbars to open a pathway through the first two miles in Minnesota that were not cleared. Upon completing the five-day-long journey to Duluth, the three men, along with their automobile and a dog, returned to Port Arthur on a Lake Superior steamer.[19]

## The Congdon Legacy

As roadbuilding occurred beyond Two Harbors, the section connecting eastern Duluth to the Lake County boundary was also receiving considerable attention from attorney and industrialist Chester Congdon, who had moved to Duluth with his wife, Clara, in 1892. The Congdons, in 1905, purchased twenty-two acres of London Road property that had significant frontage on Lake Superior and about one-quarter mile of adjacent land extending northwestward along both sides of Tischer Creek. The lakeshore land would be used for Glensheen, the Congdons' massive mansion, built from 1905 to 1908, whereas the Tischer Creek holding, with subsequent additions, was donated to the city and named Congdon Park in 1908. The design for Glensheen's grounds was undertaken by well-known New York landscape architect Charles Leavitt, with the on-site assistance of his employees Anthony Morell and Arthur Nichols. The two men, in 1909, established their own business, Morell & Nichols, in Minneapolis, which soon became Minnesota's largest landscape architecture and town planning firm. One of the partner's first commissions, funded by Congdon, was a design for his namesake park. The Morell & Nichols firm would later prepare designs and plans for several other major projects throughout Duluth.[20]

In addition to his demanding business and personal schedule, Congdon served two terms (1909–13) in the Minnesota House of Representatives. During his first year as a legislator, the Duluth Republican sponsored a bill that allowed "any city to lay out, build and maintain, outside of its limits, any road, street, avenue boulevard, parkway, or other public highway." The bill, which became law later that year, also approved the methods for condemning any envisioned parkway or public property. Soon, one of Congdon's agents was purchasing land for a boulevard that, after crossing the Lester River on a new bridge, would extend along Lake Superior, typically one hundred to four hundred feet from the shoreline, as far as the Lake County boundary. In May 1913, Congdon explained that his efforts had been intended "to get for the city, while land is cheap, a lakeshore driveway, which . . . can be properly improved when the time arrives." Realizing, nevertheless, that he alone could not acquire all of the desired properties, Congdon requested the City of Duluth to pursue condemnation of the remaining parcels for the development of his envisioned dream, the Lake Superior International Highway. He also agreed to pay for all costs associated with condemnation and land acquisition. The *Duluth New-Tribune* supported Congdon's plans, stating that the development of such a boulevard would make it suitable for both summer homes and suburban residences. The city approved the condemnation and construction proposal in June 1913.[21]

In March 1914, proceedings were initiated against fifty-three properties, owned by more than 150 individuals, all deemed necessary before highway construction could proceed. Several sites included small houses and fishing camps, some occupied by people who had never acquired legal title to the land. Boulevard development was delayed, however, when numerous owners expressed dissatisfaction over the appraised value of their properties. Another year would pass before the cases were settled in district court. Finally, in June 1915, Duluth mayor William Prince placed his signature on an agreement that accepted the terms of the gift—to pay for the "condemnation of lands, by the City of Duluth, for road, highway and boulevard purposes, along the shore of Lake Superior." The agreement's most important stipulation included language that remains in force today—"the land so acquired shall be forever used by the City for the purposes for which the same was condemned, and that the City of Duluth shall never use the same for any purpose other than as a road, highway or boulevard, and shall never dispose of the same or any part thereof." Once obtained, the properties were commonly, if not officially, identified as "Congdon Trust land," a term that continues to the present.[22]

Landscape architects Morell and Nichols had, already in 1910, prepared an initial design for the envisioned boulevard. The entire right-of-way would have had two pedestrian walkways, a single bridle path, and separate drives, each two lanes wide, for automobiles and carriages. Providing a pair of well-constructed automobile lanes, Congdon argued, would prevent any possibility of a collision—even at one hundred miles per hour.[23] But, because of Congdon's untimely 1916 death, the development of a boulevard, albeit not as wide and less ornate than originally envisioned by Morell and Nichols, would be delayed until late 1922. Today, most of Duluth's shoreline beyond the Lester River remains free of development because of the stipulations established in 1915.[24]

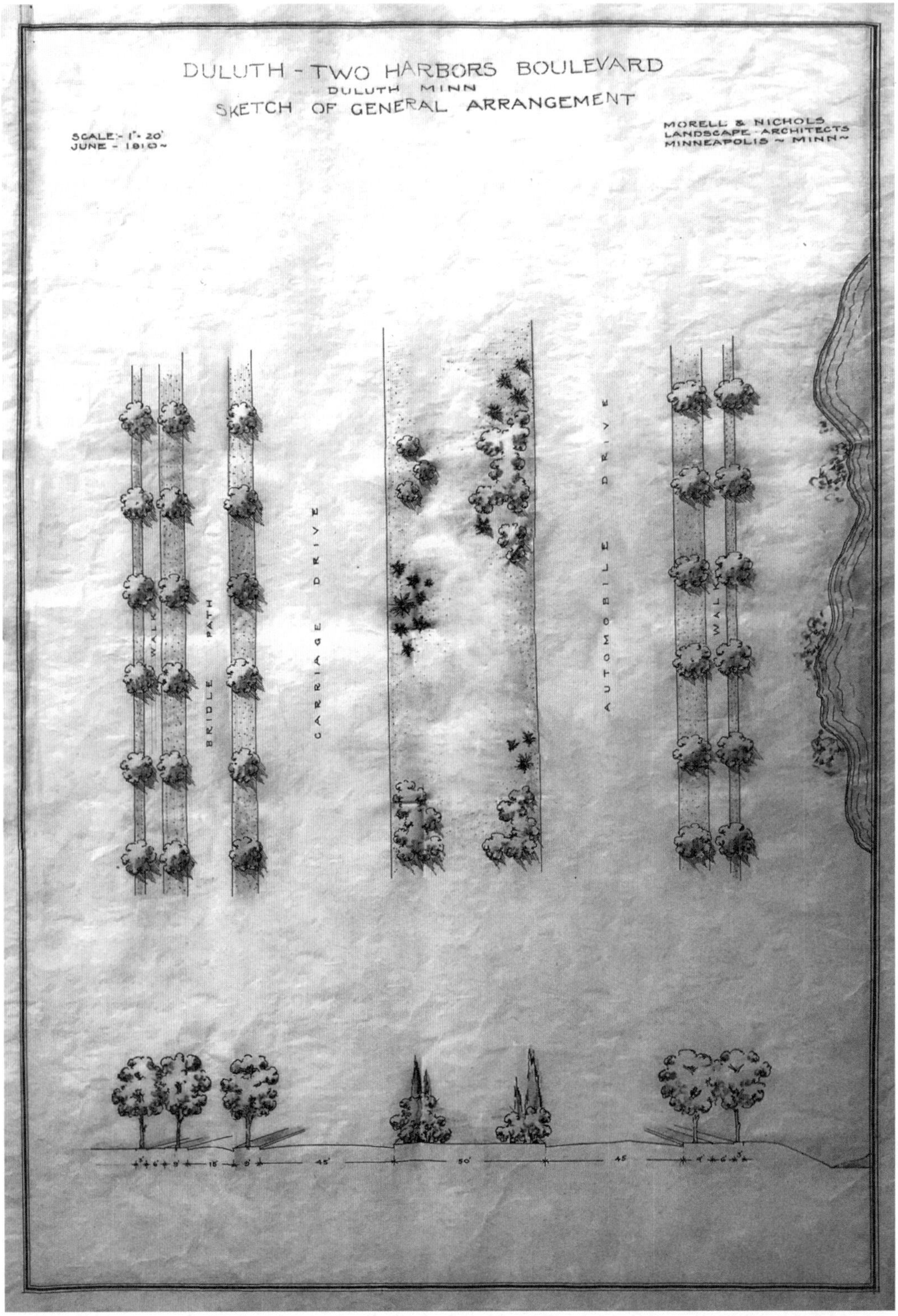


An early design for a section of boulevard at the eastern end of Duluth, prepared in 1910 by landscape architects Anthony Morell and Arthur Nichols. Their grand proposal, which had two pedestrian walks, a bridle path, and separate drives for carriages and automobiles, was modified extensively before boulevard construction began in 1916. Congdon Family Papers, U6192, Archives and Special Collections, Martin Library, University of Minnesota Duluth.

## On the Way to Grand Marais

Among the first automobiles that plied the streets and roads of Grand Marais and nearby areas of Cook County was a 1911 two-seat, two-cylinder Sears, Roebuck Motor Buggy "Highwheeler"—one of only thirty-five hundred vehicles the company sold nationwide from its catalog between 1908 and 1912. Because Grand Marais was still difficult to reach at this time, the initial vehicles purchased by its citizens and other residents of Cook County arrived on Lake Superior steamers. By August 1916, however, Cook County motorists were exploring North Shore settlements and sights as distant as Two Harbors and Duluth. When a group of Cook County officials returned from a two-day trip to Two Harbors, one participant commented that the road "is bound to be a self-advertiser, becoming famed as among the great driveways in this or any other country." The inland route between Two Harbors and Beaver Bay was even claimed to be in better condition than the road leading out of Duluth. To celebrate the occasion, Two Harbors' automobile club organized a Labor Day caravan to Beaver Bay. "The purpose of the trip was not to make any record time," announced club officials, "but to maintain a reasonable rate of speed during the entire distance so as to enable all to keep up with the pace and to be able to appreciate the splendid road and to get a good view of the magnificent scenery."[25]

The journey between Two Harbors and Grand Marais could now be covered in five to seven hours during good weather. Motorists, nevertheless, still needed assistance when they were stalled in mud between Finland and Cramer. Theodore Wirth, the Minneapolis park system superintendent, described much of the landscape along the inland route as a "dreary hinterland" that had "very uninteresting, burned-over rugged country." But when Wirth reached Schroeder, the stunning view of Lake Superior appeared once again. "From there on," he raved, "the scenery was most picturesque and highly attractive and inspiring, awakening in us a desire that the road would keep in view the rugged, rocky shoreline most of the way to our destination." Minnesota Department of Highways (MDH) engineer J. H. Mullen was even more effusive, claiming that "the mountain scenery, which is not surpassed anywhere for wild beauty, is in Lake and Cook counties."

The *Cook County News-Herald,* in 1916, started making note of visitors who arrived from considerable distances, including a party of four from Kalamazoo, Michigan, who had passed through Grand Marais in their Cadillac Eight. An adventurous New Orleans motorist informed the *News-Herald* that because of the inspirational and rugged scenery, the road trip he had just completed along Lake Superior was one of the best in his experience. Cook County officials also began warning drivers that they would enforce the maximum speed of eight miles per hour within Grand Marais and twenty-five miles per hour in sparsely settled areas.[26]

Although a relatively good road was now available for warm-weather travel, wintertime conditions still bedeviled drivers. In late 1916, the Winger & Robertson firm purchased fourteen horses in anticipation of the snow their Grand Marais–Cramer service would encounter that winter. In February 1917, when the company's buses could not surmount the snowdrifts, Winger & Robertson was forced to use horses along the road's entire length for several weeks.[27]

A 1917 view of the inland road between Two Harbors and Beaver Bay. Photograph by William F. Roleff. Author's postcard collection.

As the August 1917 North Shore road dedication approached, members of Duluth's automobile club were marking the route with diamond-shaped black-and-white signs, a task that represented "the end of years of labor and varied effort to connect Duluth by a series of improved highways to important cities within a radius of 300 miles or more." The club's efforts extended the already existing national Black and White Trail that started in Kansas City, Missouri, and continued northward to the Twin Cities and Duluth; the Duluth to Fort William–Port Arthur section represented a 220-mile-long scenic route expansion of the trail. Five additional trails connected Duluth to several other cities. Three were Green and White Trails: one stretched westward through Brainerd to Fargo–Moorhead, another went northward to Biwabik on the Mesabi Range before turning westward toward Hibbing, and the third headed directly to Hibbing and the western Mesabi. A Red and White Trail traveled in a northwesterly direction through Floodwood and Grand Rapids before culminating at Bemidji.[28] The use of colors to identify major highways would be replaced by a more rational system of numbered routes during the 1920s.

## Reaching the Outlaw Bridge and Canadian Border

Except for a small inland diversion at Hovland, the road that headed northeastward from Grand Marais followed the Lake Superior shoreline quite closely until reaching the Reservation River. From there it turned northward for fourteen miles to the Pigeon River crossing and Canadian border. This final leg of the route was chosen because state and federal officials did not wish to impinge upon the Anishinaabe community in Grand Portage. The final section of the road, before reaching the Pigeon River, passed through the diminutive rural colony of Mineral Center, where a few white farmers and timber workers had settled in 1909. Although the land that composed Mineral Center and its surrounding area was originally held by the Grand Portage Band of Anishinaabe, some of the holding was divided into smaller parcels at a time when the Native people had limited power and authority. Therefore several early twentieth-century Euro-American settlers had gained a foothold in the area.[29]

Both the American and the Canadian roads that culminated at the Pigeon River were passable by August 1916, but it was impossible to connect them because a bridge had not yet been constructed. (Small chartered boats did cross the river once or twice a week during the warm-weather months.) Because the construction of an official span required an agreement between the two national governments, community leaders in northeastern Minnesota and Fort William–Port Arthur quickly recognized that a lengthy and wearying process lay before them. Realizing that it would be simpler and less troublesome to bypass official governmental procedures, a small group of citizens from both Minnesota and

Ontario launched a campaign to raise private funds and construct the bridge themselves. The effort was led by two public-spirited men: William Scott, president of the Pigeon River Timber Company and Thunder Bay's most respected highway advocate, and E. J. Filiatrault, the colorful Duluth automobile dealer and Rotary Club president who had driven the first vehicle along Minnesota's North Shore in 1914. After engaging a Minnesota Department of Highways (MDH) engineer to prepare a design for the bridge, financial donations were secured from several sources, including Duluth's automobile dealers; the key contributions, however, came from the Rotarians of Cook County, Duluth, and Fort William–Port Arthur. Building materials, donated by Scott's timber company, arrived on the Canadian side of the river during the early months of 1917. In May, when the approaches at each end of the bridge were still incomplete, a Ford truck owned by Grand Marais's Winger & Robertson Company was the first American vehicle to rumble over the span. Because the structure had been built without any authority from the government of either the United States or Canada, it was initially identified by residents on both sides of the border as an "outlaw bridge."[30]

Though considered a temporary structure, the Outlaw Bridge, 110 feet long, was called "a very substantial affair" by the Two Harbors *Journal Herald*. It utilized a wooden Howe truss—attributed to Massachusetts millwright William Howe—the most common type of truss employed by nineteenth-century railroad bridge builders. As described by the late Minnesota Historical Society (MHS) historian Denis Gardner, the Pigeon River truss was "a rectangle with webs formed by a multitude of crossed diagonals in compression, interrupted by vertical members in tension." Although most of Minnesota's early twentieth-century bridges were constructed of steel, the Pigeon River span was one of the last to use wood.[31]

The grand opening of what, by this time, was occasionally termed "North Shore Drive" occurred in Grand Marais on 18 August 1917. On that morning, a total of 240 Fort William–Port Arthur residents, including a group of bagpipers, piled into sixty-five vehicles and headed for Grand Marais. Because of uncertain road conditions, the caravan even included a "mobile tire and engine repair shop." Once the entourage arrived in Grand Marais, seventy-five Duluth–Superior Rotarians and their wives greeted the Canadians. The crowd, which reportedly reached five hundred people by that afternoon, gathered on the grounds of the Cook County courthouse, where they heard the mayors of Duluth, Port Arthur, and Fort William describe the highway as a bond that would strengthen the friendship between Canada and the United States. The keynote speech, given by George Howard Ferguson, Canada's minister of lands, forests, and mines—and later the premier of Ontario—also included a somber message: the scourge of World War I and associated threats posed to Canada and the United States by several European adversaries. With the armed forces of the United States having entered the war effort only four months earlier—almost three years after Canada had joined Britain and her allies in the conflict—Ferguson assured his audience that democracy was certain to triumph over tyranny and autocracy. Upon hearing from several other dignitaries, the audience listened to the bagpipers, watched dancers who performed in Scottish kilts, engaged in singing, and participated in a community dance. During the late afternoon, several Duluthians, including mayor C. R. Magney, drove to the Pigeon River, where they viewed the Outlaw Bridge. "Located on the boundary line, the

**Several of the sixty-five Canadian vehicles that crossed the decorated Outlaw Bridge on 18 August 1917. They were headed to Grand Marais, where the grand opening of the completed roadway between Duluth and Fort William–Port Arthur would be celebrated. Courtesy of the Brodie Resource Library, Thunder Bay Public Library.**

bridge was decorated to suit the occasion," reported Magney. "On our side American flags lined the railings. On the Canadian side the flags of the Maple Leaf country were everywhere in sight. The bridge itself is a wonderful structure and a credit to the men who built it." And, declared the mayor, "the roadway is a wonder."[32]

Because Grand Marais's small hotels could not accommodate all the visitors who remained in the village over Saturday night, the overflow was welcomed into private homes. The success of the celebration, which concluded on Sunday, demonstrated that the citizens of a small North Shore community could successfully organize an event attended by hundreds of people from two nations. The residents were also pleased that the visitors had discovered "what a pleasant place Grand Marais is." The community had, in fact, established a high standard for many North Shore celebrations that would occur over subsequent years and decades.[33]

Chapter 3

# A State, Federal, and International Highway, 1918–1929

The recently completed North Shore roadway, by summer 1918, had quickly emerged as a popular tourist destination. Travelers were assured by reports that gasoline was available at several filling stations along the road, and anyone experiencing a mishap would not be stranded for more than an hour before receiving assistance.[1] Many travelers may have been discovering the North Shore's delights for the first time, but local residents were even more appreciative. These patient citizens, after decades of frustration and delays, finally had a relatively reliable land route that linked their communities and also provided access to the rapidly growing state and national highway network. The North Shore roadway, by the late 1920s, would be identified simultaneously as Minnesota Highway 1, U.S. Highway 61, and the Lake Superior International Highway.

In 1918, MDH engineer J. H. Mullen claimed that increasing numbers of vehicles were visible along the North Shore's "magnificent gravel-topped highway." Most of the roadway, nevertheless, remained a narrow corridor flanked by parallel ditches that often were spaced no more than sixteen feet apart. Many sections also remained inaccessible throughout the spring thaw and during periods of heavy rainfall and snowfall. In mid-April 1919, when L. A. Simonson and his son made the year's first trip between their Duluth home and Grand Marais, the pair succeeded despite experiencing several flat tires and having to plow through mud and a foot of snow on much of the journey. Simonson, nonetheless, was pleased that he had "negotiated" the first North Shore trip of the season. A carload of Fort William residents also experienced numerous challenges when returning home from a North Shore trip during the third week of April 1920. The group had easily negotiated most of the road, but after encountering a "muddy and greasy hill" northeast of Grand Marais, they realized that it was not possible to go any farther. After spending the night in their automobile, the Canadians were assisted by local residents, who jacked up the vehicle and laid down planks "to run the car over," which allowed the group to reach Fort William.[2]

Just one month later, road crews from both Minnesota and Ontario worked vigorously to repair the numerous washouts that had occurred along the road. Following this, Grand

In 1922, while on a camping trip at Silver Creek Point, Two Harbors photographer William Roleff took this image of his wife, Josephine; five of their seven children; and the family's new Chevrolet truck. Roleff's family is at the right, but the identities of the other couple and their two children are unknown. Courtesy of Minnesota Historical Society.

Marais's residents eagerly awaited the steady stream of motorists they hoped would arrive from the northern side of the border. The *Cook County News-Herald* mirrored this anticipation by listing the names and cities of origin for all seventy-eight Canadians who crossed the Pigeon River and entered Minnesota during a single week in May. The account even identified the sixteen automobiles that accommodated them: fourteen had been manufactured in the United States (nine Chevrolets, two Fords, two MacLaughlin–Buicks, and one Dodge), while two were Canadian made (an Overland and a Gray-Dort). The Outlaw Bridge was crossed by 10,410 people in 1919 and by 12,035 during five months (April–August) of 1921.[3]

Because the North Shore road had been built at various times by different units of government, several segments were linked together with poorly defined intersections. Motorists who began their venture in downtown Duluth were told, by one of the city's newspapers in 1919, to maintain a sharp eye for several landmarks and mile markers as they ventured out on a convoluted journey to Knife River and Larsmont:

> Duluth, Superior Street & 5th Avenue, 0.0. Go east with trolley on Superior Street. Pass golf links on right, 4.0. Left-hand diagonal road, just before the railroad, 4.6; bear left with trolley. Pass LAKESIDE [RR] STATION on right, 4.9. Through Lester Park, 6.1. Avoid left-hand diagonal road, 9.5. Fork, sign in center, bear right, 13.0. Cross [railroad] switch, 19.4. Left-hand diagonal road, 19.5; bear left across railroad tracks; 4-corners; beyond small bridge turn right, 19.6. KNIFE RIVER,

> 19.7; fork, Post Office on left. Bear right, 21.4. End of road, just beyond RR; turn right across RR. Pass LARSMONT STATION on left, 22.5.[4]

Farther northeast in Cook County, the directions for drivers who were negotiating the road from Grand Marais to the Pigeon River bridge and Canadian border were also given detailed directions and clearly informed about the need for proper documentation:

> GRAND MARAIS. 4-corners, store on left, 126.5. Turn left, one block. BE SURE TO GET YOUR PASSPORT HERE. 4-corners, turn left, 126.6. End of road, at large stone school, 126.8 . . . travel close along shore of lake. Cross iron bridge, 141.5. End of road, at large stone school, turn right, 144.2. PASS HOVLAND, MINN, town hall on right, 147.1. End of road, store on left: turn left, 159.5. Cross wooden bridge over Pigeon River, 166.1, which is international boundary line; now on [Canada's] Scott Highway.[5]

Public officials, by this time, were calling for road improvements and modifications that would exceed anything proposed or undertaken in the past. The most important recommendation was a shoreline alternative to the inland trek that passed through Beaver Crossing, Finland, and Cramer. Norwegian immigrant Hans Engelsen of Tofte, chairman of the Cook County Board and a leader in the good roads movement, spoke in 1922 about the need for "agitation" before an improved North Shore route could be developed. Such a road, he prophesied, would "shorten the distance considerable [*sic*] and get away from the heavy snowfall in winter, besides presenting a much better view to the tourists."[6] Unlike in the past, when less ambitious projects took many years to complete, Engelsen's expectations would be accomplished between 1922 and 1925.

## Duluth's Lakeshore Boulevard

Simultaneous attention was given to Duluth's section of the North Shore, where progress on the proposed lakeshore boulevard had remained relatively dormant following Chester Congdon's 1916 death. Although several people whose land had already been condemned were "counting on its reversion to their ownership," Congdon's widow, Clara, gave new life to the boulevard plan in 1920. When the Congdons' son Edward made a May appearance before the Duluth City Council, he read a letter from his mother that confirmed the family's willingness to provide funding for a paved boulevard that would begin at the mouth of the Lester River. The boulevard, previously identified by Congdon as the entrance to an envisioned Lake Superior International Highway, was projected to follow the lakeshore for some fourteen miles. Once the Duluth City Council approved the plan in October 1922, the St. Louis County Board agreed to extend the boulevard along Duluth Township's lakeshore to the Lake County boundary.

Later that year, as potential rights-of-way were under consideration, Duluth mayor Samuel Snively and commissioner of public works J. A. Farrell stated that the proposed routes should be studied "as religiously in winter as in summer." To do so, the men made their own detailed assessment of how snowdrifts formed along the lakeshore throughout the winter of 1922–23. Using descriptive language honed on decades of wintertime experience, Farrell astutely noted that before planning a road in northeastern Minnesota, one had "to learn the lay of the snow as well as the lay of the land."[7] The boulevard would be dedicated in September 1925.

## Minnesota Highway 1

The majority of North Shore highway-building projects undertaken during the early 1920s were woven together by a series of federal and state actions that had commenced during the previous decade. First was a 1916 federal bill that made funds available to states with official highway departments. In 1917, when the MDH replaced the former State Highway Commission, Elk River businessman and good roads proponent Charles Babcock was appointed the first commissioner. Voters, three years later, approved a change to the Minnesota Constitution, recommended by Babcock, that authorized the development of seventy numbered highways that would link all of the state's county seat towns and major cities. The "Babcock Amendment" was quickly ratified by the Minnesota legislature in 1921. The longest road, Constitutional Route 1 (later called Minnesota Highway 1), would start at the Iowa border and proceed northward through Albert Lea, St. Paul, Hinckley, Sandstone, and Moose Lake until reaching Duluth, where it turned toward the northeast and progressed through Two Harbors and Grand Marais to the Canadian border.[8]

State highway engineers and surveyors immediately began implementing the Babcock Plan, colorfully described as an effort "to pull Minnesota out of the mud." North Shore residents, in 1921, were pleased to learn that the future highway, whenever possible, would parallel the lakeshore. Of special note was the proposed section of shoreline highway scheduled to replace the existing inland connection between Two Harbors and Schroeder. Equally important were recommendations for twenty-six new bridges, several with ornamental concrete features, which would supersede the wooden structures deemed too narrow and unsafe for the anticipated volume of traffic.[9]

Although America's early twentieth-century roadbuilding projects were almost always guided by practical and utilitarian requirements, some engineers and landscape architects viewed new highway construction as an opportunity to make scenic sites and recreational opportunities more accessible—primarily by highlighting the outstanding natural attractions of an area or region. Among the few American scenic drives that preceded Minnesota's North Shore highway was the Bronx River Parkway in Westchester County, New York—planned and developed between 1907 and 1923—which followed a meandering route along the river's wooded areas and meadows. Even better known was Oregon's Columbia River Highway, a rural scenic route that emerged between 1913 and 1922. Because of its well-designed bridges, fortified rock walls, and easily negotiable highway grade that never exceeded 5 percent, motorists were provided with superb views of the Columbia's gorge, cliffs, and waterfalls. In 1925, Two Harbors resident Thomas Owens, who had been elected president of the Lake Superior International Highway Association (LSIHA), claimed that the North Shore's "native beauty and grandeur finds a parallel only in the Columbia River Highway, or in the Amalfi Drive, of European [Italian] fame."[10]

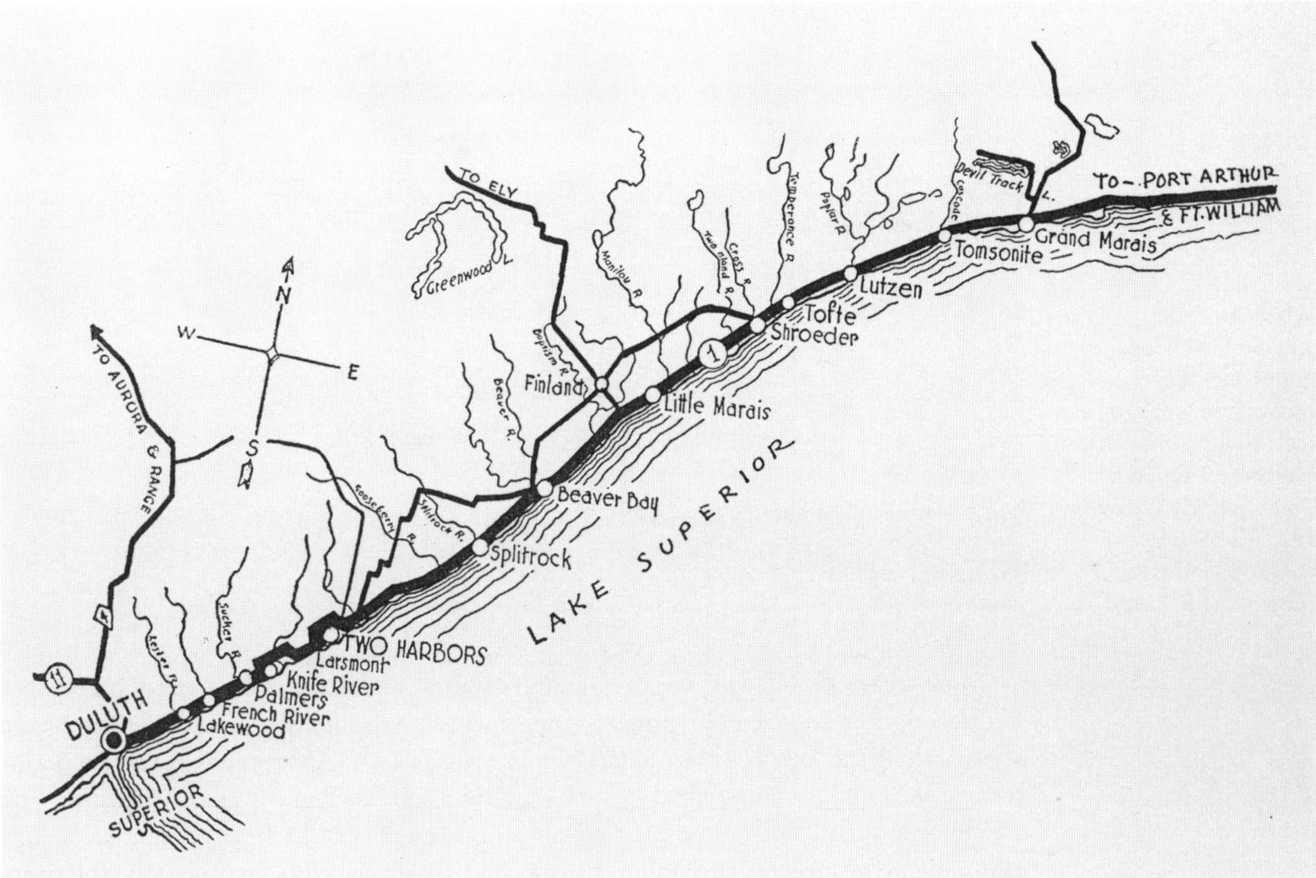


A map showing the North Shore section of Minnesota Highway 1 that was dedicated in 1925. Also depicted is the earlier inland road that began three miles northeast of Two Harbors and extended to Schroeder. Courtesy of the *Duluth News-Tribune*, 7 April 1930, C1.

Previous North Shore road builders did not have sufficient financing or adequate equipment to cope with the rock outcroppings that existed along many sections of the shoreline. This situation changed dramatically in 1922, when MDH began providing significant funds for major construction programs throughout the state. By June, work was under way at a few North Shore sites, including the first of three hundred culverts that would eventually appear along creeks and small rivers and under the road at places prone to washouts. The need for culverts was obvious, as demonstrated at Beaver Flats in May 1922, when one to five feet of water covered one thousand feet of the site. MDH officials initially dealt with the issue by making a team of mules available to pull out any flooded vehicles that were stalled in the water.[11]

In September, engineers and supervisors employed by one of Minnesota's largest construction firms, A. Guthrie & Company of St. Paul, established their headquarters in Lake County's courthouse. The firm eventually employed seven hundred workers, but because of constant labor turnover, the total was much higher. Seven subcontracting firms, throughout fall and winter 1922–23, performed the "grading and grubbing" that preceded bridge and culvert construction. The workers were housed in several camps, most located at the mouths of rivers and streams. Sadly, longtime North Shore highway proponent E. J. Filiatrault, who died at Rochester's Mayo Clinic in November 1922, could not observe the activities.[12]

Workers and a steam shovel engage in preliminary excavation work for a section of Minnesota Highway 1 in Cook County, early October 1922. Courtesy of Cook County Historical Society.

More steam shovels and several "dinkey engines" and dump cars arrived at the Two Harbors dock in March 1923. Soon, twenty steam shovels and three hundred horses were at work along the Two Harbors–Little Marais route, which Guthrie construction superintendent W. L. Johnson described as "very rough and solid rock nearly all the way." Building a highway in such a demanding environment, MDH engineer Charles Forbes reported, was realized only by incising "shelves" in the towering, solid rock cliffs and spanning the rivers that separated them. Although most of the large outcroppings were previously deemed insurmountable, Forbes reported that laborers and engineers employed on the project in 1924 had been able to blast and dig through many boulders and rock ledges, all of which was possible only because of their willingness to engage in "slow, tedious, and persistent work through all seasons of the year and in all kinds of weather." The most expensive and demanding project by far occurred at Silver Creek Cliff; there the work was deemed equivalent to the removal of an entire side of a small mountain. Although the massive rock cut allowed the road to bypass the outcropping, the heavily altered site immediately posed problems because of rock falls and a dangerous curve. Split Rock and Palisade Head, two insurmountable obstacles located farther northeast of Silver Cliff, forced the road to diverge away from the lakeshore and bypass both sites—just as it does today.[13]

MDH engineers, like their Columbia River counterparts, demonstrated an awareness of early twentieth-century scenic design principles. Many stretches of the roadbed were built on "benches"—actually the beaches of early glacial lakes that stood 75–130 feet above Lake Superior. "From these points," commented Forbes, "one has wonderful views of the winding road itself and the rocky shoreline up and down the lake for miles in both directions until they fade away on the horizon." The unobstructed views, he remarked, were visible because the road was designed and cut to follow the topographic contours. Even when the road bent away from the lakeside route, the chosen elevation provided complete views of the lake and landscape. And, as a *Duluth Herald* newspaper reporter pronounced, the new highway didn't just offer glorious views of Lake Superior; it also provided access to "thundering" rivers and waterfalls, "staunch bridges," and "hospitable villages and towns."[14]

From 1922 to 1925, motorists were forced to cope with a plethora of impediments caused by highway construction: driving on detours, dealing with ruts and rocks, and maneuvering around labor crews and road construction equipment. Several drivers who ventured onto the highway during this period experienced accidents, both major and minor. At least six motorists lost their lives in Lake County during the construction period, but no incident received more attention than the one that Minnesota governor Jacob A. Preus and his family experienced at a bridge washout located three miles southwest of Grand Marais. "There was no lantern or other sign of danger," stated a description of the late July 1922 event, "and the governor brought his car to a stop barely in time to avoid plunging into the deep ravine below." Preus quickly exerted his influence and authority by calling for the discharge of the worker who oversaw that section of highway. "A state employee who will permit such a situation to exist without at least putting up a warning sign," stated an obviously infuriated Preus, "is clearly unfit for highway work."[15]

As a flurry of construction activity occurred throughout summer 1924, local newspapers supplied their readers with a steady stream of updates. The *Lake County Chronicle* described the road as "a scenic highway, thirty feet wide, with grades and curves conforming to federal standards, and permanent bridges and culverts," while a *Duluth News-Tribune* editorial expressed appreciation for the progress that was increasingly evident along the entire Lake Superior shoreline: "One link after another is being completed," enthused the writers, and "little by little the new North Shore boulevard is being opened to traffic." When a

During the 1920s, engineers employed by the Minnesota Department of Highways often followed the contours of former glacial lake beaches when laying out rights-of-way for the North Shore section of Minnesota Highway 1.

twenty-mile-long segment opened northeast of Two Harbors in July 1924, motorists were finally able to reach Split Rock Lighthouse, which, since its 1910 inception, had been accessible only to Lake Superior vessels.[16] Soon the lighthouse would become one of Minnesota's most popular tourist attractions.

When most of the upgrades were completed by the end of the 1924 construction season, MDH crews worked long hours to keep the road open during the winter season. After an immense January 1925 storm halted mail service for a single day, three tractors and several trucks, all equipped with snowplows, quickly cleared Highway 1. The feeder roads, however, did not receive the same attention, which led Two Harbors' school board to recommend that buses should be abandoned throughout the remaining winter season. "The wear and tear on the buses in bucking snow," reasoned the board members, "is out of proportion to the service rendered by teams [of horses] for which they already have the equipment ready to be put into service."[17]

The North Shore highway's grand opening was celebrated on two different occasions in 1925: the first in Two Harbors and the second in Duluth. The initial event, sponsored by Two Harbors' Rotary Club, occurred on July 11. Attending the huge gathering was a caravan of cars organized by Duluth's Good Roads Association. An inexpensive option, the SS *Montauk*, a large steamboat, transported seven hundred people, many of them from Superior, to Two Harbors. The crowd assembled in Lakeview Park, where they heard a Naval Reserve band perform, feasted on "an old-time barbecue" of two steers, and listened to the featured speaker, MDH commissioner Charles Babcock. The new road represents a progression from the "old overseer's guess" to the "modern highway engineer's blueprint," proclaimed Babcock, and it also offers access to anyone "seeking God's great outdoors." It is a scenic highway, he continued, which "climbs the rock-bound shore of Lake Superior to the top of the world." The businessman-turned-commissioner became even more passionate when discussing the road's monetary benefits. Declaring that "every shovel of earth and

Minnesota lieutenant governor William Nolan dedicated a plaque at Silver Creek Cliff that marked the official North Shore opening of Minnesota Highway 1 on 11 July 1925. Courtesy of Lake County Historical Society.

every foot of rock on this undertaking was handled on an economy basis," Babcock asked the audience to "prize the highway" for the million dollars of value it would bring to the North Shore. "You will find yourselves fixing time according to the years this road was improved," he predicted. The next speaker, Lieutenant Governor William Nolan, concluded the celebration with lavish praise for Babcock, identifying him as "the greatest road builder since Claudius Pompeianus of the Roman Empire." Later that afternoon, many attendees drove to Silver Creek Cliff, where they observed Nolan dedicate a bronze plaque that described the site's historical significance.[18]

**A 1929 view of Congdon Boulevard about two miles northeast of the Lester River. Photograph by F. Rodney Paine. Courtesy of St. Louis County Historical Society.**

The second 1925 celebration was held in Duluth during late September, about twelve years after Chester Congdon had announced his vision for the North Shore boulevard and Lake Superior International Highway. Work on the Duluth end of the roadway, which started in 1922 and continued throughout 1923 and 1924, persisted at a feverish pace during summer 1925. Although the September event recognized the entire highway, most attention was given to the Lester River Bridge and boulevard that extended through eastern Duluth to the Duluth Township border. The boulevard was not as formal and ornate as the one proposed by landscape architects Morell & Nichols in 1910, but the *Duluth News-Tribune* affirmed that the completed project exhibited "many landscape and artistic features not ordinarily associated with highway or street improvements." Shortly after the celebration's conclusion, the Duluth City Council passed a resolution naming the completed section Congdon Boulevard.[19]

Duluth mayor Snively later determined that $335,425 (equivalent to approximately $6 million in 2024) had been spent on the construction of bridges and eleven miles of road situated between the Lester River and Stoney Point. The overall figure, which included land acquisition expenditures, construction costs, and legal and design fees, was shared equally by the Congdon Trust, the City of Duluth, and St. Louis County.[20]

## The Lake Superior International Highway Association

The early North Shore roadway, following Congdon's 1914 recommendation, was occasionally called the Lake Superior International Highway. Eleven years later, in March 1925, Two Harbors Rotary Club officials called for the official adoption of the name because it would "stand the test of time in advertising one of America's most picturesque highways." In July, the Rotarians submitted a petition to Commissioner Babcock, requesting that the North Shore segment of Minnesota Highway 1 receive approval as the Lake Superior International Highway. Included with the petition was another request, namely, that Babcock authorize the incorporation of LSIHA, which would allow the organization to publicize and "beautify" the North Shore roadway. Babcock rejected both requests in late January 1926, informing the petitioners that plans were already under way to have the road jointly designated as Minnesota Highway 1 and U.S. Highway 61. (Babcock's comment referred to an anticipated action of the American Society of State Highway Officials, which, in September 1926, approved a rational system of numbered highway routes, including the cosigning of Minnesota Highway 1 with U.S. 61.) Babcock was equally concerned over LSIHA's plans, which called for the placement of several informational signs along the highway. Especially disquieting to the commissioner was a huge Lake Superior International Highway sign proposed for the Lester River Bridge entrance. Two Harbors resident Thomas Owens, LSIHA's tenacious president, quickly followed up with a letter to Babcock, avowing that the association never intended "to place any obnoxious signs along this road or do anything that would in any way injure the beauty of the highway." Instead, wrote Owens, the purpose of LSIHA was to continue the fine work that Babcock and the MDH were pursuing. In March 1926, Babcock finally agreed to both requests—the incorporation of LSIHA and the tri-part designation of the North Shore roadway as Minnesota Highway 1, U.S. Highway 61, and the Lake Superior International Highway.[21] Although Minnesota Highway 1 remained the most commonly used term throughout the 1920s and into the early 1930s, motorists could now claim that they traveled simultaneously on a state, federal, and international highway.

Babcock may have approved the LSIHA requests, but his letter also included an important caveat, namely, that Owens provide a drawing of the proposed lettering, shape, and color of the signs and an indication of their placement in the landscape. Despite Babcock's clearly voiced concerns, Owens again called for a very large sign (six by ten feet), designed in the shape of an arrowhead, for placement by the Lester River. (The sign's shape referenced the Minnesota Arrowhead Association, formed in 1924 to promote tourism throughout northeastern Minnesota.) Owens even intimated that LSIHA might erect a large electric sign at the river crossing. H. Rodney Paine, Duluth's parks director, echoed Babcock's concerns. "One of my main objections to the signpost is the size," wrote Paine in his critique, and "I do not feel that the sign proposed is any better looking than most of the commercial advertisement signs which the city is trying to prohibit in such locations." Paine did agree, however, to work for the placement of a more reasonable and respectable sign that would not blemish the landscape.[22]

**The letterhead for the Lake Superior International Highway Association, which appeared in 1926, included a large arrowhead that would be used to promote tourism throughout the counties of northeastern Minnesota. The "Arrowhead Region" remains a familiar term today, although it is not used as extensively as in previous decades. Courtesy of Lake County Historical Society.**

Following further recommendations from Paine and the MDH, an agreement reached during summer 1927 led to the selection of a bronze metal sign with lettering sufficiently large that it could be observed from the highway. Owens, by early 1928, was praising the sign for its striking qualities and urging people "to look for it when you go by."[23]

The misunderstandings that preceded the design and placement of the Lester River sign pale in com-

This sign, placed by Lester River and U.S. Fish Hatchery in 1927, identified the Duluth entrance to the Lake Superior International Highway for several ensuing years. Courtesy of Lake County Historical Society.

A brochure cover, dating to the late 1920s, included several idealized features that were used to advertise the Lake Superior International Highway—Split Rock Lighthouse; a steamship; a Northland Transportation Company bus; and two large sedans, one moving along the road, the other pausing so its passengers could view the scenery.

parison to a July 1926 incident that took place northeast of Tofte. Earlier in the year, several verbal confrontations occurred between local farmer John Westblade, who had posted some illegal land-sale signs along Highway 1, and MDH officials charged with enforcing the law that banned such intrusions. These incidents culminated in tragedy when Westblade accosted two local state highway patrolmen, Sigurd Ide and Alvin Tofte, as they removed his sign. The irate forty-seven-year-old bachelor (described as a "Winchester farmer" because of his affinity for rifles) opened fire on Ide and Tofte, killing both. Westblade then burned his cabin to the ground, cut down several prized apple trees he had planted many years earlier, and fled into the woods. Three days later, Westblade was shot and killed by Cook County sheriff's deputies who found him hiding in a thicket close to the murder site.[24]

## Riding the "Hound"

George Robertson, by 1918, was sole owner of the North Shore Transportation Company, which had provided two years of mail service between Cramer and Grand Marais. Later in the year, Robertson acquired a pair of twelve-seat buses, both fabricated from truck bodies, which were used to offer daily round-trip passenger service between Grand Marais and Duluth. Each bus made nine stops on what would soon be called Minnesota's "longest motor truck line." Robertson ended his business in 1922, a decision undoubtedly influenced by the arrival of Orville Caesar's White Bus Lines Company, which had better equipment and greater access to financial resources.[25]

Caesar formed the bus company around 1916 while working for a truck sales agency in Superior, Wisconsin. He initially operated the buses only between Superior and Duluth but soon provided separate routes along the North Shore and Wisconsin's South Shore. Passengers appreciated Caesar's buses—especially those built by the Fageol Motor Company of Oakland, California—because they had five doors and twenty-two seats and were much more comfortable and accessible than the modified truck bodies that formed Robertson's fleet. A Fageol Safety Coach also had air brakes and a sixty-four-inch-wide wheelbase; the floor, placed twenty-one inches above the ground, gave the coach significant stability when negotiating curves and turns at highway speeds. The coaches were nicknamed "greyhounds" or "hounds" because of their ability to travel at fifty miles per hour, a feat that was possible because of their transmissions, which had four-speed gearboxes and "overdrive"—the latter an extra gear that allowed the engine to attain a faster velocity without excessive fuel consumption or wear.[26]

The daily bus schedule that Caesar provided on the North Shore Limited between Duluth and Port Arthur–Fort William in 1924 marked an appreciable improvement over

**The White Swan, one of several vehicles in Orville Caesar's White Bus Lines fleet that began providing service along the North Shore in 1922.**

the often erratic service that other companies had offered for a few previous years. The 1925 merger of the White Bus and Mesaba transportation companies (the latter organized in 1915 on Minnesota's Mesabi Iron Range) led to the formation of the Northland Transportation Company. Northland, by 1930, was part of the Chicago-based Greyhound Corporation, which employed Caesar as president from 1946 to 1955. Greyhound and other companies would operate buses along the North Shore for much of the twentieth century.[27]

The Northland Transportation Company, formed in 1925 with the merger of the White Bus Lines and Mesaba Transportation Company, was headquartered in Duluth. Northland's regular service, following the merger, was immediately extended to Fort William and Port Arthur, Ontario. *Cook County News-Herald*, 24 September 1925, 17.

## Life at the Border

Once the Outlaw Bridge opened, residents of Cook County and Fort William–Port Arthur, often led by Rotary Club members, gathered along the international border. One July 1921 event attracted participants who ate heartily and listened to Jens Flaaten's musical troupe of Duluth, who had trucked their piano to Minnesota's side of the Pigeon River. Another highlight was a tug-of-war between young men from Cook County and Fort William–Port Arthur. The fifteen Canadians were, reported a Grand Marais newspaper, "all tall, husky, handsome men, but . . . too soft to be put up against our team, who were all hardened to the task." After engaging in several minutes of vigorous struggle, the Americans won the competition.[28]

Mineral Center Township was, in 1920, home to approximately one hundred year-round residents, twenty-one of them Anishinaabe; most of the men worked as farmers, trappers, and loggers. Peter and Nellie Linnell's general store and post office, and a nearby schoolhouse that served, at most, twenty children, identified the nucleus of Mineral Center.[29]

Somewhat north of the settlement, and flanking the Pigeon River bridge, was the S-Curve Inn, which opened in 1920. Named for a slight curve as the road approached the bridge, the S-Curve had a café, gas pump, and dance pavilion, all operated during the tourist season by the wife of U.S. Customs agent Malcolm Arnold. The business was acquired, in 1925, by Norwegian immigrants Sextus and Martha Bugge Lindahl, some years after they married in Duluth. Lindahl had operated the often rowdy Rex Hotel saloon on Duluth's West Superior Street before he and his wife moved, around 1910, to Virginia, on Minnesota's Iron Range; they departed ten years later, when Prohibition forced the closure of Lindahl's saloon. After settling in Superior, Wisconsin, Lindahl sold soft drinks, worked as a laborer, and immersed himself in Republican politics. When running for a Wisconsin State Assembly seat in 1922, Lindahl called attention to his interests in hunting, fishing, and protecting wild game in northwestern Wisconsin and promoting "the ski sport" throughout the western Lake Superior district. Lindahl won the relatively close election, but lost in 1924, and also failed in a bid to become mayor of Superior. During the more than twenty years that followed the couple's 1925 acquisition of their Pigeon River property,

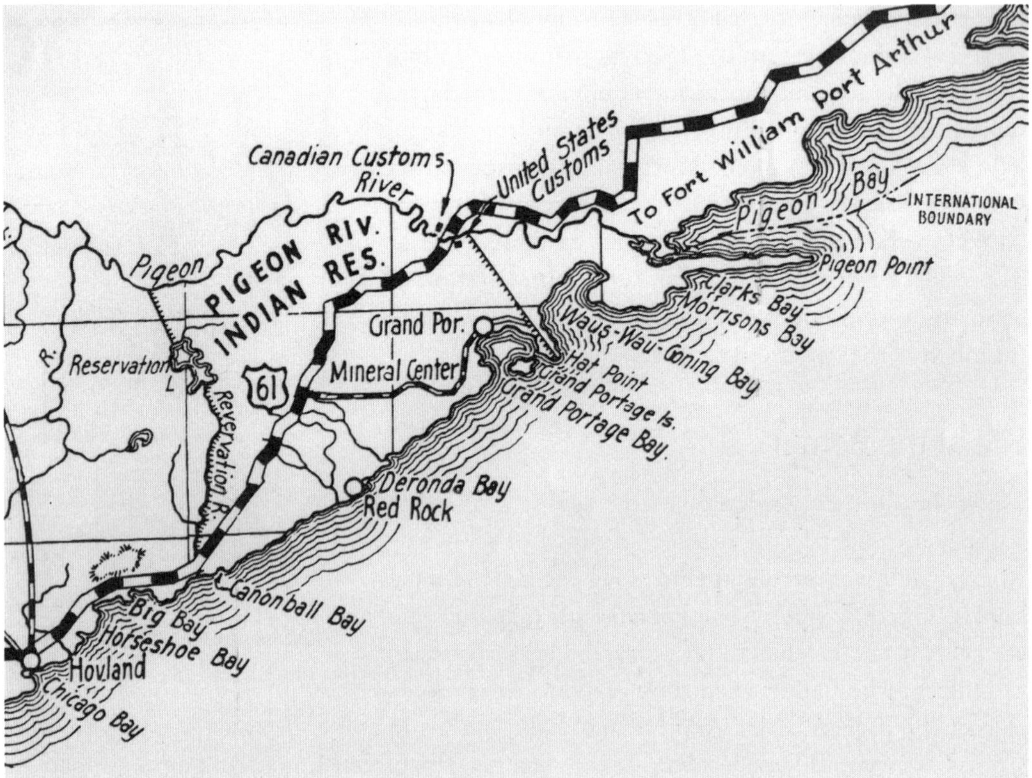


**Minnesota Highway 1 veered away from Lake Superior at the mouth of the Reservation River and continued through Mineral Center to the Pigeon River crossing at Sextus City, where a U.S. Customs station was located. A "tote road" connected the Grand Portage Indian Reservation to Mineral Center. Adapted from a North Shore tourist map, late 1920s/early 1930s.**

which they named Sextus City, the Lindahls typically resided at the site from mid-spring to mid-autumn.[30]

The couple's primary Sextus City building was a log hotel where Martha Lindahl prepared home-cooked meals in its restaurant. Nearby was the Sextus City Garage, which had gasoline pumps and a tire service station—the latter a vital business, given local road conditions. The Lindahls' property also included fourteen cabins, most built of logs. None had indoor plumbing, but all were equipped with electric lights provided by a gasoline-powered generator. One cabin, named Volkstead, was an ironic reference to Minnesota U.S. representative Andrew Volkstead, who had played a major role in preparing and passing congressional legislation that carried out the Eighteenth Amendment's Prohibition objectives. Two pairs of adjacent cabins were called Bachelor and Honeymoon and Oslo and Hollywood, while the names of a trio of nearby units—Jiggs, Maggie, and Dinty Moore—referenced the major characters in *Bringing Up Father,* a popular newspaper comic strip of the era. Lindahl also boasted that because of Sextus City's border location, he and his wife owned "the first and last hotel in America." After selling their business during the late 1940s, the Lindahls retired to San Mateo, California, where they passed away, respectively, in 1951 and 1972.[31]

The final segment of the North Shore highway had purposely avoided Grand Portage by passing through Mineral Center before it reached Sextus City. Because some Anishinaabe

**Sextus and Martha Lindahl's hotel and restaurant, shown here during the late 1920s, were located close to the Pigeon River bridge, which linked the United States and Canada. An automobile service station with an adjacent grease rack (partially visible at the left) was nearby. Next to the service station was an electric generator that provided power to the Lindahls' buildings, including its fourteen cabins. The caption, "driest city in the U.S.A.," was Lindahl's humorous reference to Prohibition, which existed from 1920 to 1934.**

tribal members wished to engage in tourist-related businesses, a four-mile-long "tote road" (now Cook County Road 19) was blazed through the woods between Grand Portage and Mineral Center. The road, predicted the *Cook County News-Herald,* "will be a great drawing card to the tourists and should be kept pretty full of sightseers all season for it is an ideal spot for campers." Completion of the road, which occurred during autumn 1921, was termed an important accomplishment because visitors would finally have access to Grand Portage and its numerous historical and cultural properties. Most tourists, however, were content to interact with those members of the Grand Portage Band who sold blankets, baskets, jewelry, curios, berries, and other items from two birchbark-covered stands and a tepee that stood in Mineral Center.[32]

Because the first two U.S. Customs agents assigned to the border crossing had no nearby housing, they resided in Grand Maris and maintained an office in the Cook County Courthouse. The Canadian agent and his family, however, were almost immediately ensconced in a "handsome bungalow" located close to the Pigeon River. Both the American and Canadian agents reportedly were careful "to see that all of the tourists are bona fide or that they carry papers which indicate that they have legitimate business on one side or the other of the boundary."[33]

Tourists could stop and purchase items that members of the Grand Portage Indian Reservation displayed in Mineral Center. Courtesy of Cook County Historical Society.

The U.S. agents were also engaged in enforcing local Prohibition laws passed by several Minnesota communities and counties between 1917 and 1919. Because of these regulations, which banned the sale, transport, and manufacture of alcoholic beverages, the agents reportedly were "emphatic in declaring that whiskey flasks do not constitute a passport." Passage of the Eighteenth (Prohibition) Amendment to the U.S. Constitution in 1919 made the Pigeon River crossing an even more important outpost. Once enforcement of the nationwide ban on alcohol was initiated in early 1920, U.S. Bureau of Prohibition agents engaged in a never-ending search for illegal home-brewed liquor—often known as moonshine, hooch, white lightning, and other colorful terms. One 1921 situation led to the arrest of twelve men from Grand Marais, Two Harbors, and other North Shore settlements, who were charged for having four stills, four hundred gallons of moonshine, and two thousand gallons of mash—a fermented mixture of ingredients used to make alcohol—in their possession. Pigeon River agents also paid special attention to "rum running" from Ontario into Minnesota. (Ontario experimented with prohibition, but enforcement was not nearly as rigorous as it was in the United States.) A highly publicized example of such illicit liquor transfer occurred in July 1920, when Duluth's police chief, a deputy federal marshal, and nine other Minnesota men were arrested and indicted for bringing 1,236 quarts of Canadian whiskey into Duluth over the Outlaw Bridge. The defendants, nonetheless, claimed they were transporting only homemade beer with an alcohol content lower than the federal minimum. Because the grand jury that heard the case in Duluth's federal courthouse failed to agree on a verdict, none of the men were charged with a crime, although both the police chief and the federal marshal lost their jobs. Once a deputy U.S. Customs agent was permanently stationed at Pigeon River in 1922, Canadian motorists were issued cards that allowed them to stay as many as thirty days on the American side of the border. The primary reason for the cards was clear—to gain "closer control of the government's interest against liquor smuggling."[34]

As traffic numbers increased throughout the 1920s, the structural inadequacies of the Outlaw Bridge became increasingly evident. Accessing the ramps at each end of the bridge required careful attention from drivers, and the wooden railings were hardly able to stop a vehicle from plummeting into the Pigeon River. Such an accident did occur in July 1929, when Mary Stark, the postmistress at Buffalo, Minnesota, was killed. Stark's sister-in-law was seriously injured in the accident but survived because of the heroic rescue efforts rendered by a Port Arthur motorist who was passing through Sextus City. The bridge was quickly repaired after the accident and replaced the following year.[35]

## One More Celebration

Northeastern Minnesotans would once again celebrate Highway 1, this time in September 1929, with an event that recognized the paving of the road between Lake County's western boundary and Two Harbors. An estimated five thousand people attended the Two Harbors–based festival. Termed an "elaborate program" by its organizers, the events began with a parade headed by the Two Harbors band and a color guard. Following them were twenty-five units that depicted the progression of transportation from "packsack to airplane" on the North Shore. Forming the entourage were many people on foot; some sitting in dogsleds, oxcarts, and horse-drawn buggies; and others riding in vintage or modern automobiles and trucks. Charles Forbes, the MDH engineer who had played a pivotal role in supervising the construction of Highway 1, served as the primary speaker. Beginning with a brief synopsis of Lake Superior's human history, Forbes claimed that Two Harbors not only served as an important center for America's steel industry but had become a "headquarters of romance and adventure." He then launched into a summary of MDH facts, accomplishments, and plans: Minnesota had seven thousand miles of state highway, almost 679,600 registered vehicles, a five-year highway construction budget of $44 million, and a state traffic patrol staffed by thirty-five men.[36] But both the practical and symbolic meanings of the new concrete highway must have been most appealing to the people who gathered on that September day in 1929. Forty-five years after Two Harbors had emerged along the Lake Superior shoreline, a well-built, all-weather road finally connected the small industrial city to Duluth and the outside world.

Chapter 4

# The North Shore during Depression and War, 1930–1945

The economic depression that commenced with the stock market crash of October 1929 quickly engulfed the nation, the state, and every locality on the North Shore. Even though very limited funds may have been available for highway improvements, the outmoded and unsafe Outlaw Bridge was replaced in 1930. The original bridge had been funded by private donations, but the highway departments of both Minnesota and Ontario shared equally in supporting the new, $20,255 structure. MDH officials insisted that the steel span would make an incident like the fatal 1929 accident "virtually impossible."[1]

Much more important for the North Shore over the decade were several significant highway, wayside, and state park projects, most sponsored and financed during the first two

Shortly after the June 1930 opening of this new steel truss structure, the older Outlaw Bridge on the left was torn down. The view looks northward from Sextus City toward the Canadian Customs station. Courtesy of Cook County Historical Society.

terms (1933–40) of President Franklin D. Roosevelt's New Deal administration. But when America's attention, from 1942 to 1945, was focused completely on the demands of World War II, highway construction work came to a virtual standstill.

## Coping with the Great Depression

Duluth residents undoubtedly were startled by an ominous February 1930 announcement reporting that a nearby section of Lake Superior was under consideration as "an ideal drill and practice site" for a U.S. Army squadron equipped with twelve antiaircraft guns, 144 machine guns, and fifteen searchlights. The lake was deemed highly suitable for such drills, explained military officials, because it avoided "the danger of firing into a wooded area."[2] The proposal was never implemented and soon forgotten once the North Shore, and the entire United States and world, faced the travails of the Great Depression.

The North Shore community that immediately experienced the most significant consequences of the economic downturn was Two Harbors, where dockworkers were impacted by precipitous declines in America's steel manufacturing output and corresponding reductions in Minnesota's iron-mining activities. When comparing the 1920s to the 1930s, for example, the state's ore shipments fell by more than 35 percent, and in the especially bleak year of 1932, virtually all Iron Range mines were shut down. As unemployment figures rose in 1931, Two Harbors mayor Michael Brickley asked the city council to approve policies similar to those already occurring on the Iron Range, namely, the development of publicly financed projects that offered jobs for men who were either unemployed or working part-time. Two Harbors had adequate funds, argued Brickley, "which in all Christian spirit it should lay out in labor at this time." The council members approved several "sewer work" projects that provided some men with part-time employment, primarily repairing streets and sidewalks. Many North Shore families also suffered because of an extreme decline in the demand for fish, the severity of which was highlighted by a drastic September 1931 action: the dumping of twenty-five thousand tons of gutted herring back into Lake Superior. "Fish Galore, Market Shy," reported a brief but telling newspaper headline. Nonetheless, those North Shore residents who engaged in fishing and part-time farming were at least able to sustain themselves by utilizing the products of their own labors.[3]

## Tourism and a "Hay Fever Haven"

Tourism, throughout the Depression, served as one bright spot along much of the North Shore. The economy, noted the *Cook County News-Herald* in 1931, "is dependent almost entirely on the tide of summer visitors attracted by the unique recreational features of the region." The *Two Harbors Chronicle* also reasoned that people who traveled to northeastern Minnesota's resorts and cabins served as an antidote to the "din of calamity" and gave reason for the "citizenry to throw their hats in the air, and dance." Because many visitors were interested in sportfishing, some North Shore residents opened "deep-sea" charter craft operations that plied the waters of Lake Superior. An ambitious promotional scheme occurred during summer 1931 when the Lake County Development Association sought to lure visitors with "big fish bait." After a few of the best local fishermen had been hired to catch several species of fish, the prime specimens were quickly transferred into unique General Electric refrigerators equipped with high and wide glass windows. The tanks were then sent to several Midwestern cities for display in department stores, hotel lobbies, and other commercial venues. Very limited information is available to determine fish survival rates and the campaign's success, although Charles Johnson, a sports reporter for the *Minneapolis Star*, wrote enthusiastically about the "dandy" specimen he saw in one display tank—a large salmon that came from Lake Superior's North Shore area.[4]

Although the area's health-giving qualities had been touted for decades, these attributes received greater national recognition soon after February 1935, when the Minnesota Hay Fever Association was organized in Duluth. The association's board of directors touted the findings of a recent study by the Minnesota Department of Preventive Medicine and Health that asserted that "the north shore of Lake Superior [is] the only place comparatively free from ragweed, and with a climate condition so advantageous to the relief of hay fever that it has no competition on the North American continent."[5] Soon, many resort and cabin owners would advertise their properties as "hay fever havens."

## Improving the Highway and Local Economies

MDH engineers begam making traffic counts along Highway 1 as early as 1920. The organization's annual August surveys revealed that the number of vehicles traveling between Duluth and Two Harbors, extremely modest when compared to current counts, grew from 1,110 per day in 1925 to 2,490 in 1930. The respective figures for the Two Harbors–Grand Marais section were 465 to 675 and 175 to 725. Other onlookers occasionally made their own observations, such as one resident who counted license plates from fifteen states and three Canadian provinces on a single June day in 1928.[6]

Motorists and highway officials, by 1930, realized that the North Shore highway required repairs—even if very limited funding was available for such work. The most immediate concern was Silver Creek Cliff, where thirty-five men worked for two and a half months to clear and repair the roadway after a huge November 1929 rockslide blocked the road. Despite an obvious shortage of funds, MDH officials also made plans to improve several other sectors of the highway. North Shore residents followed these plans very closely, not only because of the envisioned improvements that would ensue but also for the employment opportunities that road construction might offer. In late 1930, MDH commissioner Babcock announced that rather than waiting two or three years, the clearing of a new right-of-way between Schroeder and Grand Marais would begin in a matter of months. The project, he noted, was seen as a way to relieve the critical unemployment problems experienced by settlers and fishermen who resided along Lake Superior. In April 1931, the A. Guthrie & Company, once again, received the highway construction contract, this time for $232,000. The firm would build several new sections of roadway, some of which situated Highway 1 closer to Lake Superior between Little Marais and Schroeder. Concrete barrel-vaulted bridges were also planned for the Cross, Poplar, and Temperance Rivers. Minnesota's Farmer-Labor governor, Floyd B. Olson, just five months after his November

The barrel-vaulted Cross River bridge has been photographed countless times, but few images are more evocative than this view, taken by William Roleff shortly after the span was completed in 1931. Similar vaulted bridges were constructed over the Poplar and Temperance Rivers.

1930 election victory, decreed that the minimum wage for the state's highway laborers would be raised to forty-five cents per hour.[7]

Large shipments of road construction machinery arrived at Two Harbors' docks in April and May 1931; once there, the cargoes were transferred onto trucks and hauled to several worksites. A tug and scow that encountered numerous problems when delivering large equipment to Grand Marais during a late November storm eventually entered the protective confines of the local harbor without any damage, but only because of the skills displayed by both captains. Unlike in the 1920s, when several North Shore labor camps housed many men who were employed along the North Shore, the early 1930s workforce either boarded with local citizens or resided in their own homes and traveled to and from the construction sites in private vehicles. While North Shore residents believed that local men would fill the workforce, their hopes were dashed by a July 1931 statement in the *Two Harbors Chronicle* that warned that anyone hoping for a highway job was "chasing rainbows." Rather than employing a sizable labor force to clear and grade the roadway, the *Chronicle* noted, the presence of large machinery was making the need for men "merely incidental." Furthermore, the open job positions were being filled by experienced equipment operators, a majority of whom came from areas other than the North Shore and northeastern Minnesota. The *Chronicle* gave the reconfigured landscape mixed reviews as construction activities proceeded in 1931. "Juggernaut steam shovels are biting savagely through the cuts," observed the reporter; "the new road abolishes the scenic beauty of the winding road, but it makes for efficiency in the movement of traffic." As work progressed, however, other onlookers insisted that the changes were providing Minnesota with one of the Midwest's best examples of modern highway construction practices.[8]

## Speeding, Safety, and the End of Prohibition

It would not be long before some vehicle drivers realized that the North Shore highway offered opportunities to determine how "one's motor leaps to the gentle touch of the foot." *Duluth News-Tribune* automobile editor P. A. ("Doc") Coulter even used the North Shore roadway as a test track where the speed and roadworthiness of different vehicles could be evaluated. In April 1930, when Coulter and Duluth automobile dealer J. O. Leveille sped along a relatively straight stretch of highway northeast of the French River bridge, the speedometer on their three-ton, sixteen-cylinder Cadillac "hovered" at one hundred miles per hour. "At high velocities," raved Coulter, "this car rides with an ease that is nearly unbelievable." Three months later, Coulter was aboard a six-cylinder, fifty-horsepower Chevrolet, this time with Charley Cannon, the sales manager for a Duluth automobile dealership. Although their vehicle was rather modestly powered, the men still "received a thrill" when they rounded a curve at seventy miles per hour: the "car clung to the road," exulted Coulter, "and we rode in surprising comfort."[9]

Perhaps Coulter felt relatively comfortable while driving at high speeds because of several safety features that began appearing along Minnesota's highways during the late 1920s and early 1930s. Among the most important were the three-quarter-inch, tensile steel cable guardrails, all placed two feet above the ground and fastened to white cedar posts spaced twelve feet apart along the highway. (The cables replaced a former system of wooden barriers that were intended, but which often failed, to keep snow from drifting onto the road.) A Two Harbors newspaper reporter even asked readers to consider how many times the cables had stopped vehicles from careening into a ditch or the number of accidents that had been prevented by the posts' white-painted tops, which indicated where the "danger line" existed along the road's edge. The posts also were vital in keeping vehicles on the road during foggy and stormy conditions and when nighttime drivers faced a line of bright headlights coming toward them.[10]

Meanwhile, designation of the North Shore section of Minnesota Highway 1, which had been cosigned with U.S. Highway 61 since late 1926, was eliminated from state transportation maps in May 1934. The decision, made by MDH officials, "expanded and consolidated the trunk highway system, fully incorporating the U.S. routes and eliminating the old

Steel cables connected to white cedar posts, shown here southwest of Grand Marais, were commonplace along the North Shore and throughout Minnesota by the early 1930s.

**When Prohibition ended in 1934, several North Shore tavern and restaurant operators were once again able to dispense alcoholic beverages. One was Sextus Lindahl, who soon opened his beer garden at Sextus City. At the right is the U.S. Customs building; in the background are the Canadian Customs building and a hotel. Courtesy of Cook County Historical Society.**

redundant state routes." U.S. Highway 61, which stretched for 1,715 miles between New Orleans and the Pigeon River, would serve as one of America's major north–south transportation corridors for more than a half century. Soon, many North Shore communities and businesses gave prominent attention to "U.S. 61" or "Highway 61" in their promotional materials. Another early name, Lake Superior International Highway, had remained relatively popular throughout the 1920s but seldom appeared thereafter.[11]

A major change that affected the North Shore and entire nation was the December 1933 ratification of the Twenty-First Amendment to the U.S. Constitution, which rescinded the Eighteenth Amendment and thereby ended America's experiment with Prohibition. (Minnesota had approved the amendment in October, the twenty-sixth state to do so.)[12] When the calendar turned to 1934, many North Shore taverns, along with some restaurants and resorts, once again began providing alcoholic beverages for parched customers who hadn't made a legal purchase since 1920. The change was clearly obvious at the Pigeon River bridge crossing, where Sextus Lindahl readied his tavern for the tourist season. Gone were the U.S. Prohibition agents who had checked motorists' vehicles for fourteen years; now boldly evident on the Sextus Hotel facade was a sign that invited patrons to Lindahl's beer garden.

## The New Deal on the North Shore

Major construction work had occurred along Minnesota Highway 1 during the 1920s, but the scope and scale of those efforts pale in comparison to the many projects undertaken during President Franklin D. Roosevelt's first two terms in office. During the four months between Roosevelt's November 1932 election and March 1933 inauguration, the president and his advisers prepared large numbers of bills, most intended to break the back of the

Depression and assist large numbers of Americans who needed economic assistance. Then, with lightning speed from 9 March to 16 June (known as the Hundred Days), the U.S. Congress passed an unprecedented number of bills, thereby establishing the foundation for what is defined as the New Deal era of American political history.[13] Several programs that grew out of this period had an immediate impact along the North Shore because of the employment opportunities they generated for local citizens. Much longer lasting, and still highly visible today, are many of the impressive projects that several New Deal agencies implemented or influenced.

The federal program that had, by far, the most significance on the North Shore was the Civilian Conservation Corps (CCC), which offered "employment on conservation projects—in forestry, erosion and flood control, and parks—for needy, jobless young men between the ages of eighteen and twenty-five." Although federal funds provided monetary resources for work carried out by the CCC and other New Deal agencies, many projects were supervised and implemented in partnership with state and local governments. One key agency that sponsored and supervised several CCC endeavors was Minnesota's Roadside Development Division (RDD), formed within the MDH in 1932. The success of the partnership between federal works projects and roadside development has been termed an outstanding and even "ideal" example of early New Deal–era cooperation. The RDD and CCC also collaborated with the Division of State Parks, organized by the Minnesota Department of Conservation (MDC) in 1936, to ensure that the locations of parks and wayside rests were complementary.[14]

Six CCC camps, some accommodating more than two hundred young men (often called "CCC boys"), were involved in highway-related work along the North Shore. The members of Lakeshore Wayside Park, a CCC camp situated at Stoney Point close to the small St. Louis County settlement of Palmers, engaged in several nearby North Shore projects. Established by the RDD, the camp's enrollees constructed Stoney Point Drive and a nearby wayside and monument that commemorated the 1850s townsite of Buchanan. Nearby, in Lake County, was the Knife River Nursery, maintained by enrollees from the Spruce Lake Camp, who traveled some forty miles to the facility. Farther northeast in Lake County was the Gooseberry Falls Camp, sponsored by the Division of State Parks, where a large group of CCC enrollees was engaged in the construction of several stone buildings and a large highway concourse. The property would be designated as the North Shore's first state park in 1937. Two other North Shore CCC camps emerged in Cook County: the Spruce Creek Highway Wayside CCC Camp, located close to the Cascade River's mouth, and the Temperance River Camp, whose members worked on a highway bridge and built stairways and small overlooks along the waterway.[15]

Other important CCC work, carried out on the Grand Portage Indian Reservation, was sponsored by the Bureau of Indian Affairs (BIA) and overseen by the Consolidated Chippewa Indian Agency. (All BIA-sponsored facilities were called "CCC-ID camps.") Anishinaabe enrollees at the Grand Portage CCC-ID camp performed archaeological excavations; cleared a major voyageur-era portage; reconstructed historic fur-trade buildings; and built a new school, a bridge, a ranger station, and other structures. Historian Douglas Brinkley has noted that when images and descriptions of Grand Portage reached the White

A 2007 sculpture, the CCC *Worker*, located within Gooseberry Falls State Park, commemorates the eighty-six thousand young Minnesota men who carried out natural resource conservation and building projects on the state's public lands from 1933 to 1942.

House, President Roosevelt was "particularly elated about the work the Indian CCC had done in Minnesota."[16]

National Park Service (NPS) personnel—primarily architects, landscape architects, engineers, inspectors, naturalists, geologists, and foresters—oversaw the CCC's largest North Shore projects, a practice that was adopted to ensure that the workmanship would be of the highest quality. Additional expertise and skills were provided by a few "local experienced men" (LEMs)—most of them stonemasons, construction tradesmen, and other skilled workers—who had knowledge of the area's building traditions, plant materials, and weather conditions. Park and roadside development along the North Shore and throughout the entire United States was inspired and guided by NPS architectural and landscape design standards known as the "rustic style." NPS architectural consultant Albert Good, whose 1938 three-volume work summarized many of the nation's most outstanding New Deal park projects, wrote that the rustic style was accomplished "through the use of native materials in proper scale, and through the avoidance of rigid, straight lines, and over sophistication, [which] gives the feeling of having been executed by pioneer craftsmen with limited hand tools. It thus achieves sympathy with natural surroundings and with the past."[17] Stone and wood, of course, served as the primary construction materials along the North Shore.

A number of architects, landscape architects, and civil engineers designed the New Deal projects that emerged throughout Minnesota during the CCC era, which extended to early 1942. No single designer, however, influenced the North Shore and entire state more significantly than did RDD landscape architect Arthur Nichols (1881–1970), who was based in the agency's St. Paul office. Nichols began his long Minnesota career in 1909, when he established a Minneapolis-based partnership with Anthony Morell. Following Morell's unexpected death in 1924, Nichols continued to operate the firm but moved into public work during the early Depression years, when he served as a consultant to the MDH and RDD (1932–44), and later, the State Parks Division (1953–60). Much of Nichols's activity with the latter organization featured the preparation of site plans for parks originally proposed or developed during the New Deal era, including several on the North Shore. When Nichols retired in 1960, his half-century-long career included hundreds of projects that shaped the built environment of Minnesota and the Midwest. Although he is considered the most prolific landscape architect in Minnesota history, Nichols's name, quite surprisingly, is not included on any North Shore marker or plaque.[18]

Several other New Deal agencies, in addition to the CCC and NPS, appeared on the North Shore. One was the Public Works Administration, which dates to 1933. The agency employed professional architects, landscape architects, engineers, and well-established construction firms to design and erect large buildings and structures, including the Lake County High School in Two Harbors. Several Grand Marais projects initiated in late 1932 and early 1933 by the short-lived Civil Works Administration—a sewer system, an airport, and street improvements—were completed by the Works Progress Administration (WPA), which provided jobs for large numbers of less-skilled laborers. Other activities, such as the construction of tourist parks and golf courses, the repair of culverts and bridges, and the "graveling, ditching, and brushing" of roads in Lake and Cook Counties, were also undertaken by the WPA. The National Youth Administration (NYA) was involved in a few projects, and artists affiliated with the Federal Artists Program of the WPA worked in Two Harbors, where they created murals for the city's new high school.[19]

The CCC and WPA also implemented several North Shore highway plans that MDH officials proposed during the early 1930s. One project, undertaken during mid-decade, resulted in significant improvements to the section of highway that extended between Duluth's Congdon Boulevard and the eastern boundary of St. Louis County. Another major effort that involved moving the right-of-way between Lutsen and Grand Marais closer to Lake Superior shortened the road's length by almost two miles: twenty-two sharp turns or "kinks" were eliminated in the process, including one northeast of Grand Marais called "Devil's Turn" because of the dangers it had posed to motorists since 1916. Once the realignment was completed, MDH engineers announced that "new ideas in highway beautification and safety will be carried out along the new roadway. . . . Steep side ditches and sharp, ugly cuts will be reduced to safe, gentle slopes." And, rather than "being a raw gash through the woods," the redesigned highway would "harmonize with the scenery so that the edge of the right-of-way will blend imperceptibly with the wilderness." These projects, reported the *Duluth Herald*, were providing Minnesota with one of the Midwest's finest examples of highway development. The latter years of the decade were devoted to paving the highway's gravel-covered sections with a bituminous and asphalt mix—a notable improve-

**Several men employed by the Works Progress Administration are shown rebuilding a portion of the Grand Marais seawall in 1933. Photograph by Milford J. Humphrey. Courtesy of Cook County Historical Society.**

ment over former oil and tar treatments. The final project, completed in 1939, surfaced the road that extended from the Reservation River to Mineral Center and continued to the Pigeon River bridge at Sextus City. When completed, the long-anticipated paved highway that would connect Duluth and Canada was a reality.[20]

Visitor counts revealed that motorists from at least forty American states, four Canadian provinces, and three other countries had passed over the Pigeon River bridge at Sextus City in 1937 and 1939. Already in 1935, however, MDH officials were advocating for the replacement of the Pigeon River span with a new structure a quarter mile below High Falls, four miles downriver from Sextus City. The envisioned bridge also meant that Highway 61 would be rerouted along Lake Superior and situated much closer to the Grand Portage Indian Reservation. Local business owners, notably Sextus Lindahl of Mineral Center, opposed the proposal because they realized that any highway relocation effort would result in the demise of their ventures. The bridge project, delayed by several judicial decisions and the onset of World War II, was not initiated until 1958.[21]

## Just before and during the War

The North Shore, by summer 1939, was showing signs of increasing economic vitality. The Labor Day weekend of that year, reported tourist officials, "registered the greatest volume of traffic since the popular highway was built fifteen years ago." By Saturday evening, all 240 cabins and every tourist home and hotel room between Knife River and Two Harbors were filled. Members of Two Harbors' tourist board telephoned residents until two o'clock Sunday morning, asking if they might have a room or bed to spare. All of the "citizens were patient in being called out of their sleep," reported a local observer, "and generous in their willingness to discomfort themselves in providing shelter for the unfortunate late vacationists." Those motorists who could not find a room slept in restaurant booths or in their cars. A number of visitors, when returning home from the North Shore on Monday, stopped at the tourist bureau to thank the employees who had provided assistance.[22]

North Shore resort operators, also during the late 1930s, reported that tourists were expressing a nine to one preference in favor of cabins over hotels and expressing some hesitancy in renting residential rooms. A few resort, tavern, and dance hall operators also capitalized on the big band craze of the 1930s and 1940s by booking musical groups from the local area and Midwest. One group, the Cliff Kyes Orchestra, a Twin Cities swing band that typically performed in large venues, played at Russ Kendall's Knife River tavern in 1940. While those people who were able to crowd onto Kendall's small dance floor certainly appreciated the group's music, many were also impressed by the orchestra's customized "Dream Bus": it had, marveled a Two Harbors newspaper reporter, all the luxuries of the best hotels, namely, electric fixtures, telegraph and telephone connections, hot and cold running water, spacious wardrobes, and full-length mirrors.[23]

At this same time, however, ominous newspaper and radio reports were informing North Shore residents and Americans about military actions and civilian casualties and displacements in Europe and Asia. Nevertheless, the upturn in economic conditions continued to bring hope to many North Shore communities. In April 1940, when Republican governor Harold Stassen addressed a Duluth conference of the Minnesota Arrowhead Association, he predicted that the forthcoming tourist season would be "unusually successful." But, cautioned Stassen, future success depended "on whether 1940 and its tourist business will be an opportunity for immediate cash return, or whether we make it the opportunity for a long-range investment for the years to come." Achieving that goal, he emphasized, would require bringing an awareness of northeastern Minnesota's advantages to all American states, especially those closest to the region. The Arrowhead organization also passed a resolution calling for communities to "arouse public opinion against promiscuous placarding of natural beauty spots and roadways." Of immediate concern were the political signs and billboards that would appear during the fall 1940 election campaign. Less than a month later, the North Shore Resort Operators Association (NSROA) was formed at a meeting in Beaver Bay. Organized to assist the economic situation of people involved in North Shore tourism, the members agreed to improve their properties, advertise extensively, promote beautification, gain a greater understanding of vacationer "ethics," and educate resort operators about increasing the North Shore "up to the standards found in other tourist sections."[24]

Conditions obviously changed dramatically following the Japanese bombing of Pearl Harbor on 7 December 1941. Virtually overnight, many of the North Shore's young men were mustered into the armed services by way of the military draft or enlistment. Because of their Lake Superior experience, several joined either the U.S. Navy or the U.S. Coast Guard. Two Harbors native James Wilber, who had already enlisted as a coastguardsman in 1928, became a local celebrity when he rose to the rank of lieutenant commander and led an assault transport ship on several amphibious invasions. Another high-profile serviceman was Cook County resident Robert Gapen, a colonel and pilot in the U.S. Army Air Force, who received the French Legion of Honor in 1943 and five American medals in 1945 for participating in fifty combat missions over Burma. At least sixteen young women from Lake County, and a smaller number from Cook County, also joined the military ranks. Many more women, however, replaced men who were no longer available to perform vital defense-related work on northeastern Minnesota's iron ore trains and docks. "Ladies not only kept the home fires burning," wrote Lake County historian Hugh Bishop, "but also kept the fires burning and the steam up in the locomotives that wailed their mournful song day and night in the countryside between the Iron Ranges and Two Harbors."[25]

Throughout the wartime period, which ended in early August 1945, the tempo and rhythm of North Shore life changed noticeably. Nonessential travel was severely limited by gas rationing and a shortage of tires and vehicle parts. Several resort owners involved in the war effort announced that they had closed "for the duration." Because Two Harbors and Duluth were vital links in the movement of Minnesota's iron ore to eastern steel mills, the bridges located along the railroad tracks that connected the two cities were monitored by civil defense workers, who looked out for possible saboteurs.[26]

Seventeen Lake County servicemen, and eight from Cook County, gave their lives to the war effort. No wonder that Victory in Europe (VE) Day on May 8, and especially Victory in Japan (VJ) Day on August 15, were celebrated on the North Shore with loud

Women railroad workers in Two Harbors, who replaced many of the men who were serving in the armed forces during World War II. Courtesy of Lake County Historical Society.

blasts from boat whistles, car horns, and fire sirens. Once the residents had gotten their "fill of the good news" on the radio, they greeted one another with "laughter and shouts," hung out American flags, and expressed gratitude at well-attended church services. Two Harbors mayor Gust Kragseth undoubtedly summed up everyone's feelings with a modest but succinct comment: "Very glad it's over. Hope we never have to celebrate the end of another war." The events continued into late August when a crowd gathered at the Lake County Fairgrounds, where National Guard troops engaged in a "sham battle" that concluded with fireworks. But it wasn't until the Labor Day weekend of early September, the first public holiday in almost four years with "unlimited gas," that many Minnesotans and Americans were able to enjoy a carefree break from many of their previous fears, worries, and tensions. Among the North Shore visitors was a group of twenty-five motorcyclists who attracted substantial excitement when they rode through Two Harbors on their noisy machines. Several thousand spectators also gathered to watch eight lighted iron ore carriers anchored in Agate Bay on a clear September evening. Not only did the occasion offer a beautiful scene, recounted one observer, but with the war having ended just a few weeks earlier, it also was "somewhat very peaceful."[27]

As had occurred during the Labor Day weekend of 1939, local food and lodging facilities were poorly equipped to handle the deluge of people who descended upon the North Shore for the 1945 holiday. The operators of many restaurants, cafés, and diners simply closed their doors on Friday evening after they had no food left to prepare and serve or when the staff became overly fatigued. Again, however, it was the lack of lodging facilities that caused the greatest chaos. After all the cabins, hotels, and tourist homes were filled, desperate motorists knocked on the doors of residences late into the night, hoping the owners might have a bed to spare. One Wisconsin family of six even spent the night in Lake

County's jail. Many people, nevertheless, were once again forced to sleep in their vehicles: First Avenue in Two Harbors, remarked one onlooker, "was lined with cars filled with sleeping families—legs, arms, and heads hung out of windows."[28] Although local residents may not have recognized the full significance of what was happening at that time, the 1945 Labor Day holiday served as a portent of the substantial popularity the North Shore would experience over subsequent years and decades.

Chapter 5

# On the Road Again, and Again, 1946–2024

The 1945 Labor Day holiday was a clear indicator of just how popular the North Shore would become during subsequent years and decades. The immediate postwar period also was a time of readjustment for North Shore residents, especially those who returned to their communities after engaging in military or civilian service throughout the nation and world. New residents also made their way to the area, where they pursued employment, opened businesses, or retired. Optimism was clearly evident, given that the North Shore stood to benefit from the pent-up demand for travel opportunities and recreational experiences that had been suppressed during the Depression and wartime years. The booming postwar economy would also provide more American workers and their families with greater disposable income and paid vacations. But despite this optimism, the ominous presence of the Cold War, fostered by geopolitical divisions and the possibility of military conflict or nuclear war between the United States and its primary adversary, the Soviet Union, loomed in the background. North Shore residents would even have a front-row seat to some national defense preparations that were conducted throughout the 1950s.

Highway safety concerns also led state, county, and local transportation agencies to implement a host of improvements, some of which began almost immediately after World War II. Most of the upgrades, nonetheless, have occurred since the 1990s, which has allowed ever larger numbers of people to access the North Shore's outstanding natural, scenic, historical, and cultural features. The Federal Highway Administration recognized these qualities during the early 2000s, when the agency named North Shore Drive both a National Scenic Byway and an All-American Road.

## Postwar Tourism on the North Shore

In June 1946, the Grand Marais Chamber of Commerce started planning for the deluge of tourists expected to descend upon the North Shore during the ensuing tourist season. Residents with spare rooms, including those in rural locations, were asked to fill out forms that listed the number of beds they had available for visitors. In late August 1947, Two Harbors tourist bureau attendants worked until midnight finding rooms in private homes for two hundred visitors; another fourteen were housed in the jail. Recognizing that the approaching Labor Day weekend would be even more chaotic, Ralph Elmgren, president of the North Shore Resort Operators Association (NSROA), quickly wrote a letter for publication in the *Two Harbors Chronicle and News*. Anyone with "a room to spare," implored Elmgren, should inform the tourist bureau and tell them about it, "so it will be possible to find accommodations for all of these visitors. . . . Let's not send them back by lack of accommodations to knock our area." Two months later, the 175 people who attended the NSROA's annual meeting celebrated one of the North Shore's most impressive tourist seasons. The members also discussed the possibility of expanding the tourist season beyond the early June through September months, but listened with some skepticism as incoming NSROA president Alfred Lorntson sought to impress them about the potentially significant advertising benefits a proposed Lake County project—a low-grade iron ore (taconite) beneficiation plant for the Beaver Bay area—could bring to the North Shore.[1]

Another major announcement, this one in late July 1948, reported that the first major venture aimed at making the North Shore "a year-round playground" would occur at Lutsen, where a ski hill was under development. It opened in December and was followed, one month later, by another facility on the outskirts of Grand Marais. Greater access to the North Shore was provided during summer 1951, when Northland Greyhound Lines collaborated with the International Transit Company of Canada to offer round-trip service between Duluth and Port Arthur–Fort William.[2]

In 1952, when 230 resorts, cabin businesses, and motels existed along the North Shore, NSROA's new president, Claude Midlam, owner of the Lakeview Castle just outside of Duluth, looked back at the numerous changes he had witnessed since the end of World War II. Both the "tired wife and breadwinner," declared Midlam, want to stay at resorts that provide the comforts and benefits of home. A veteran of World War I, Midlam also recognized that modern-day servicemen no longer were interested in "roughing it," as they had during their military duty, or in "bedding down in any old two by four [structure] that kept out the rain." The contemporary tourist, Midlam observed, wants "indoor plumbing with bath or shower, modern furnishings, radio, and maybe a kitchenette." Pleased that his own Fish Fry Resort was receiving record numbers of reservation requests, Midlam claimed that Americans had become "the greatest gypsies in the world."[3]

The North Shore was also becoming well known throughout the nation because of newspaper and magazine coverage that touted the area's attributes. The *Cook County News-Herald*'s editor claimed that the best portrayal of the North Shore ever given was a well-illustrated article by James Liston in the September 1952 issue of *Better Homes and Gardens*. "If it's spectacular scenery you're seeking," wrote Liston, "if it's the industrial might and the brawn of the North Country, the awesome solitude of the wilderness, and the constant companionship of America's largest fresh-water lake—you'll find it all on the North Shore Drive of Lake Superior."[4]

## Traffic, Safety, and Signs

Because highway maintenance had been deferred during the war, transportation issues were of immediate concern to several North Shore organizations. One group was the Lake County Safety Council, which, already in August 1945, predicted that future traffic gains on the North Shore would lead to an alarming increase in vehicle accidents. Four years later, MDH and Duluth city engineers developed and presented two preliminary plans for an expressway that would bypass the section of North Shore Drive connecting Duluth and Two Harbors. The resort association's membership voiced immediate opposition, stating that major construction work would "overload the highway, scaring away tourists." Rather than an expressway being built, only the existing highway and a few bridges were widened slightly in 1951–52.[5]

North Shore traffic and accident numbers continued to increase during the 1950s. Summertime conditions were often so perilous that MDH engineers considered the establishment of a rigorously enforced speed zone of sixty miles per hour—except at places where lower speeds were necessary for safety reasons. The limits were deemed essential because of heavy traffic volumes at some locations, the dangers posed by curves and sight limitations, and the temptation to speed on open sections of the roadway. Many problems, observed the engineers, were caused by the differences that arose between regular highway users who only wanted to reach their destinations and a growing number of sightseers and tourists whose major objective was viewing and experiencing the North Shore's numerous scenic attractions. In 1957, the Minnesota Highway Patrol began experimenting with measures to curtail the growing number of North Shore vehicle accidents, including one brief effort to detect speeders from two Piper Super Cub airplanes flying at an altitude of five hundred feet.[6]

Another highway-related dispute arose in June 1955 after MDH workers began citing and marking for removal all illegally placed advertising signs that disfigured one of the Upper Midwest's most attractive highways and posed numerous maintenance problems and travel hazards. Highway officials and local business owners were soon engaged in impassioned arguments over the issue, including MDH engineer Victor Benson, who attended a November 1955 meeting of seventy-five resort owners. Benson opened his presentation by noting that the North Shore was one of the Upper Midwest's primary scenic highways and a major tourist attraction. But, as he quickly noted, the presence of four hundred signs—most encroaching on the highway right-of-way, and typically of a nonstandard size—compromised the North Shore's beauty. While the resort owners would not accept the request for uniform signage, Benson and his MDH colleagues did convince them that only a single sign located fifty feet from the centerline of Highway 61 should mark each entrance road. The problem, nonetheless, reared its "ugly head" once again, this time in 1961, when the St. Paul Garden Club passed a resolution that demanded the removal of all unattractive billboards between Duluth and Canada. A sign company supplier responded immediately, insisting that the club's restrictions would bring significant hardship to the North Shore's tourist businesses. Most opposition would disappear, he argued, if the advertisers themselves chose to "coordinate and exercise self-control on the quality of all North Shore signs."[7]

## The Cold War on the North Shore

While the hustle and bustle of everyday life occupied North Shore residents after World War II, they would, from 1950 to 1953, follow the actions of American military forces on the distant Korean Peninsula. Direct evidence of the Cold War with the Soviet Union could also be seen and heard on the North Shore throughout the decade because of the presence of U.S. Air Force bombers and fighter planes engaged in training exercises over Lake Superior. Just before the first flights were initiated in mid-February 1950, North Shore residents received a brief, seemingly innocuous mailing, assuring them that "the bombing operations will be of a very light type." Duluth's chapter of the United Northern Sportsmen quickly lodged a complaint with the MDC, asserting that the bombing operations would be "hazardous to fish life in the bombed area"; a state fisheries supervisor responded immediately, claiming that it was highly unlikely any negative consequences would result. Only minimal warnings were issued just before the bombing runs occurred. "It is recommended," noted a brief but telling U.S. Air Force memorandum, that "fishermen and all other persons keep out of the . . . described area during the period of the scheduled operations." One February 1952 incident, though not related to the Lake Superior training exercises, brought a few moments of terror to Lutsen's residents when a Duluth-based P-51 Mustang fighter plane, flying at an altitude of eighteen thousand feet, crashed to the ground, killing the pilot on his return from a distant "ordered defense mission."[8]

The military exercises resumed from May through October 1953, when several fighter-interceptor squadrons entered North Shore airspace. Residents and boaters received assurances that no firing would occur if any vessels were nearby at the time, although a stronger warning was issued to anyone who might venture out onto the lake while the runs were taking place: one was "requested to cooperate with the training program," admonished the advisory, "and navigate with extreme caution when necessary to enter the danger area." A similar notice occurred just before another round of bombing started in 1956, but now the zone was identified with greater military precision—as an "Air-to-Air Gunnery Range and Rocket Impact Area." Unlike in 1950 and 1953, when the firing took place only from sunrise to sunset, the 1956 actions occurred during both daytime and nighttime hours. The twice-a-day schedule resumed in July 1960, this time with six B-47 and eight B-52 bombers that conducted low-altitude runs close to Grand Marais. Apparently, the military ended most, if not all, of its Lake Superior operations after 1960.[9]

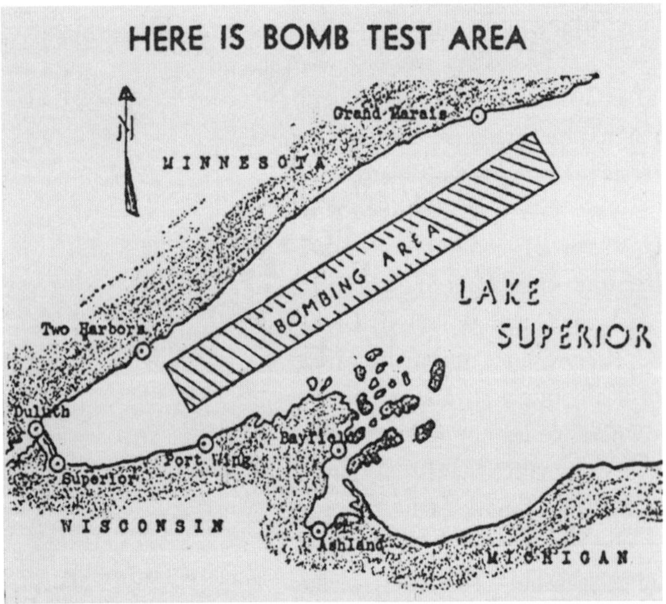


**A simple newspaper map informed North Shore residents of the U.S. Air Force bombing range that would extend between Two Harbors and Grand Marais in early 1950. Courtesy of the *Duluth News-Tribune*, 16 February 1950, 13.**

Other than the United Northern Sportsmen's complaint, very little, if any, opposition was directed toward the bombing and gunnery practices. At that time, of course, military training and national defense received widespread support from the American public. Furthermore, Duluth was on a direct line between Soviet air bases, where nuclear bombing strikes would be launched, and potential population and industrial targets in the American Midwest. The city also was among the Soviet Union's first-strike targets because of Duluth's strategic Semi-Automatic Ground Environment (SAGE) facility, completed in 1955, one of America's most secretive defense installations. Nearby was Duluth's 343rd Fighter Group, a unit in the nation's Air Defense Command, which equipped, administered, trained, and provided defense forces for Minnesota and several nearby states. A BOMARC supersonic long-range surface to air missile base also existed in Duluth Township from 1961 to 1975.[10]

## The Demise of Sextus City and Mineral Center

Sextus and Martha Lindahl, who had established their Sextus City hotel, restaurant, tavern, cabins, and automobile service station at the Pigeon River crossing in 1925, sold the complex in 1947 because of the patriarch's ill health and retired to San Mateo, California; Lindahl died there in 1951, his widow in 1972. The buyers, Ed and Mabel Ryden, from Hill City in nearby Aitkin County, renamed their holding the Pigeon River Resort and dubbed its main building the Ryden Hotel. Tourists and local residents continued to frequent the tavern and beer garden, where the jukebox and an occasional live band provided music for dancing. Now, however, it was Canadians who made Sunday the busiest day of the week at the Pigeon River site. Since Ontario allowed no beer or liquor sales on Sundays, even the low alcohol content (3.2 percent) of Minnesota beer was sufficient to attract large numbers of thirsty Canadians. The Sunday before Labor Day 1955 set an all-time record when fifty-two hundred Canadians either walked or drove over the Pigeon River bridge to Minnesota. One of the Rydens' sons later reminisced about the arrival and departure of Ontario residents during the 1950s: large numbers of Sunday patrons "would leave their cars on the Canadian side," he recalled, "walk across, drink all day, and go back again. And smuggle cigarettes back if they could."[11]

A March 1959 fire destroyed the Rydens' hotel, combination store and tavern, and two large storerooms, although their residence, cabins, and a building leased to the U.S. Customs Service did survive the conflagration. The family reopened the store in one cabin but soon replaced it with a new building; the hotel and tavern were also rebuilt. In 1963, however, the Rydens began moving their business to a new site, located about five miles to the east, where, one year later, a new U.S. Customs Station and international bridge would open at the terminus of a rerouted Highway 61.[12]

Nathaniel and Joanne Velz Hart, he an English professor, she a poet and author, purchased the Rydens' abandoned, forty-seven-acre property in 1968. Six years later, the couple and five of their eight children moved from Morris, Minnesota, to the Pigeon River, where they constructed two new buildings and rehabilitated some of the existing cabins. They had no running water but did secure access to electric power generated in Ontario. Joanne Hart spent considerable periods of time, often alone, at the Pigeon River site, where she wrote

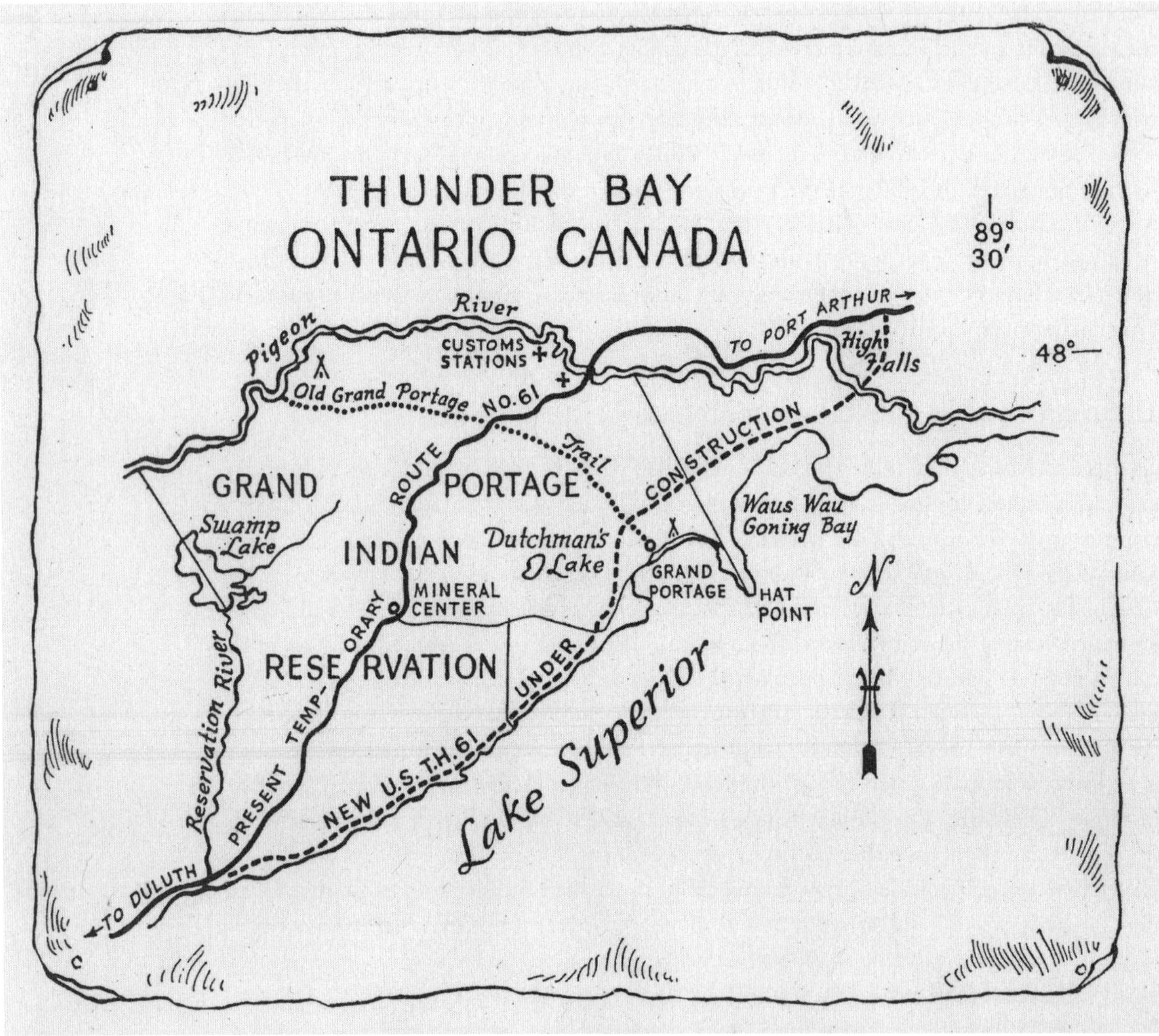


**The rerouting of Highway 61, completed in 1964, extended from the Reservation River to a new border crossing located in the vicinity of Grand Portage. Courtesy of Cook County Historical Society.**

essays for several journals; published three poetry chapbooks and a collaborative poetry and art book, *Witch Tree*, about Lake Superior's mystical Little Cedar Spirit Tree (Manidoo-giizhikens); and prepared a column, "View from the Border," for the *Women's Times*—a monthly Cook County newspaper that appeared during the late 1970s. Well before her 2018 death at the age of ninety, Hart sold the property to the Grand Portage Reservation Tribal Council, which provided the Pigeon River denizen with a lifetime lease. The agreement called for the eventual return of the property to its "natural state," a satisfactory solution, Hart observed in 2001, given that "the rocks, the trees, and the river are indeed alive and changing, long before and long past my time."[13] All of the structures had been removed from the area by 2023–24.

During the 1940s and 1950 motorists could purchase basic necessities and supplies from the Kawakanig Cabin, a small log structure situated in Mineral Center. Courtesy of Cook County Historical Society.

Several of Sextus and Martha Lindahl's log cabins, constructed during the 1920s, were later used by the Ryden and Hart families. Lindahl's original Honeymoon Cabin, the largest and best-built unit, once stood at this site on the left; it was replaced by the smaller cabin shown here. At the right is Lindahl's original Bachelor Cabin, later converted into a sauna by the Hart family. Both cabins were removed in 2013–14. Photograph 2012.

**The final five miles of Old Highway 61 between Mineral Center and Sextus City are no longer maintained by the Cook County Highway Department. Photograph 2015.**

At nearby Mineral Center, only the birchbark tepee and two stands, which attracted tourists during the 1920s and 1930s, remained on the site after World War II. The picturesque structures included many sale items, notably the Anishinaabe baskets. Close to the stand was the Kawakanig Cabin, where motorists could purchase refreshments and flowers made from wild fibers and pay for Shell gasoline that an attendant pumped into their vehicles. The original Mineral Center settlement site, vacated after the new section of Highway 61 opened in 1964, is currently identified only by a single relocated log cabin. The small Mineral Center Cemetery, maintained by the Grand Portage Reservation Tribal Council, is located nearby along County Road 17.[14]

## Circling the Lake

The idea of developing a continuous highway in Minnesota, Wisconsin, Michigan, and Ontario that would encircle Lake Superior gained momentum during the 1950s. The concept had been promoted by the LSIHA as early as the 1920s and early 1930s, but the organization was no longer active as the 1940s approached. A new version of the LSIHA emerged in 1957 when representatives of several tourist organizations from the greater Lake Superior region gathered at Sioux Ste. Marie, Ontario. The association was immediately involved in promoting the tourist facilities and services that would be available to motorists once the missing sections of the thirteen-hundred-mile-long Lake Superior Circle Route were completed.[15]

In September 1960, more than four thousand people, including several hundred Duluthians, gathered in Wawa, Ontario, to celebrate the Circle Route's completion. Despite many long-winded speeches and a heavy rainfall that turned Wawa's streets into "rivers of mud," Duluth Chamber of Commerce president Erling Berg was in good humor and spirits as he presented local officials with the Minnesota city's gift: a replica of a golden egg that was five feet long. The egg recognized both the linguistic origins of "Wawa" (Anishinaabe for "large goose") and the roadside structure that would become one of the Circle Route's most popular landmarks—an outsized Canada goose, fabricated of chicken wire and plaster. (A much more substantial steel goose, twenty-three feet high, which supplanted the original version in 1963, was itself replaced by a rustproof, bronze-plated goose in 2017.) After leaving Wawa, the Duluth celebrants traveled to Sault Ste. Marie, where they turned west and headed home. Having spent almost five days on their venture, the Duluthians were among the first motorists to circumnavigate the entire lake. After the LSIHA awarded them "Admiral of Lake Superior" certificates for their participation, one enthusiastic

Duluth and other cities announced their presence on the Lake Superior Circle Route following its 1960 opening.

recipient predicted that the Circle Route would "become the finest scenic highway on the North American continent." The route's popularity was immediately evident: whereas 43,345 vehicles entered Ontario from Minnesota in 1957, the number departing Ontario for Minnesota during the first eight months of 1962 rose to 126,000. It was not until 1985, however, that tourist officials in Ontario and the three American states developed and approved a uniform system of signposts marking what is now termed the "Lake Superior Circle Tour."[16]

## Building an Expressway and Moving a Border Crossing

MDH officials, already in 1955, declared their intentions to start work on the four-lane Duluth–Two Harbors expressway that had been proposed during the previous decade. Following the 1955 announcement, one of Duluth's highway engineers made a rather brazen prediction: "It probably won't be many years before the four lanes will be extended to Beaver Bay," he stated, "and possibly to the Canadian border." Construction of the Duluth–Two Harbors section, nevertheless, was delayed once again, this time to 1965—almost twenty years after local officials and organizations had issued their initial proposals. The expressway, now part of Minnesota Highway 61, is also identified as the Arthur V. Rohweder Memorial Highway, which recognizes a former Duluth railroad executive and member of both the Minnesota Safety Council and National Safety Council who "worked tirelessly towards preventing accidents and saving lives." The original two-lane lakeside road that now constitutes North Shore Scenic Drive is cosigned with St. Louis County 61 and Lake County 61.[17]

Work on a new international bridge, U.S. Customs station, and rerouted highway was also under way at the northeastern end of Highway 61 by the early 1960s. Although the three projects were related, the highway proposal had been postponed since the 1930s, primarily because of financial limitations, wartime demands, and concerns over the possible environmental and social impacts the Grand Portage Indian Reservation might experience. Several Minnesota critics, notably attorney Ernest Oberholtzer—an original 1934 member of the Quetico–Superior Committee, a founder of the Wilderness Society in 1935, and a "guiding hand" in federal designation of Minnesota's Boundary Waters Canoe Area in 1964—was an especially adamant opponent of the highway realignment. Writing in May 1958 from far northern Minnesota, where he maintained homes close to the Canadian border at Ranier and on Rainy Lake's Mallard Island, Oberholtzer sent an impassioned letter to the *Minneapolis Tribune*, railing against the "invading highway" that would despoil "a panorama for the gods." Undoubtedly aware that his cause was already lost, Oberholtzer concluded the letter with a wistful observation: "When all the blasting at Grand Portage is done and all the miles of causeways and gradings are completed and the costly machine work paid for and the freight trucks go whizzing by," he lamented, "the living area of today will be as dead as the hundreds of millions of wild pigeons that gave Pigeon River its name." The rerouted highway, along with a new international bridge and U.S. Customs Station, opened in 1966.[18]

Canadians cross the Pigeon River bridge and enter Minnesota in far larger numbers than do Americans who venture into Ontario—a phenomenon that has been evident for decades. In 1990, when 385,110 Canadians passed over the Pigeon River, only 182,175 Americans (a difference of 202,935) made their way into Ontario. By 2014, the Canadian figure had grown to 460,915, whereas the American total dropped to 78,620 (a differential of 382,290). Although the number of Canadians declined to 359,000 in 2018, and the American figure increased slightly to 86,450, the difference (273,450) was still considerable. Some commentators have reasoned that Americans became more hesitant to cross the border during the early twenty-first century, perhaps because of greater scrutiny by border officials and the imposition of additional regulations following the terrorist attacks carried out against the United States on September 11, 2001. (Americans entering Canada have also needed a valid U.S. passport since 2007. And, of course, the Covid-19-related regulations and restrictions that resulted in a complete shutdown of the border during 2020–21 obviously had a significant economic impact on the entire Grand Portage community.) Fluctuations in monetary exchange rates and prices for gasoline and goods influence the total numbers, but the high Canadian figures are more closely linked to the attractions of Minnesota's Grand Portage Casino and a large border store. Also important are the single-day trips that residents of the Thunder Bay region make to one of Grand Portage's parcel pickup services, which offer a low-cost alternative to the high postal rates charged for mailing goods directly from the United States to Canada. After an item arrives at one of the delivery service facilities, the Canadians "come down and pick up packages, get cheap gas, and cheap duty-free items." A minimum charge is levied on each package, but the costs increase with greater weight.[19]

## A Safer Highway, a National Scenic Byway, and an All-American Road

Despite numerous road improvements, North Shore residents, by 1999, were becoming more impatient and vociferous in voicing their concerns over the dangers they encountered on Highway 61, where traffic counts had doubled in only four years. One respondent addressing a highway safety meeting attended by Minnesota's Democratic-Farmer-Labor (DFL) governor Rudy Perpich reported that he had counted 329 signs between Duluth and Tofte, all of which delivered some sort of "be careful" message. Another resident, who bravely ventured out for daily walks along the highway's twenty-four-inch-wide shoulders, expressed greater apprehension over the drop-off, which was eighteen to twenty inches above the eroded earth below.[20]

Even the *New York Times*, in early 1990, made note of the two-lane North Shore road that stretched between Two Harbors and Grand Portage, calling it "one of America's most beautiful and treacherous highways." Not only had six fatalities happened along the "killer" corridor from 1986 through 1988, reported the *Times*, but the 185 traffic accidents in 1988 alone—twice the number experienced on all of Minnesota's other rural highways—were of a "spectacular variety": seventy-one collisions between vehicles and animals (primarily deer), fifty-five vehicles going off the road, and fifty-nine crashes involving two or more vehicles. The North Shore's precipitous roadside topography and ditches were specifically problematical, given that any action taken to avoid a deer was "dangerous if not lethal." Another issue bedeviled residents who had to cope with the large number of trucks and vacationers' recreational vehicles: "local drivers face an unnerving combination of truckers trying to beat the clock, and tourists in Winnebagos so spellbound by the scenery that they sometimes stop in the middle of the highway to snap photographs."[21]

Because of the highway's unsafe and hazardous situation, MnDOT soon allocated $108 million for a host of improvements that would be carried out into the early 2000s. Receiving immediate attention were two very dangerous sites—the rapidly eroding sections of highway at Lafayette Bluff and Silver Creek Cliff, both deemed so fragile that they might "slip into Lake Superior." The concerns at both sites were resolved by employing a road construction technique seldom practiced in Minnesota—mining a tunnel through the huge rock formations.[22]

The majority of highway improvements, which continue to the present, include smoothing curves and hills, widening shoulders and rights-of-way, developing passing lanes, making cuts through rock outcroppings, rehabilitating and replacing bridges, upgrading intersections, placing rumble and "mumble" strips on and along the road, reconfiguring drainage systems, and engaging in the seemingly never-ending process of highway repaving. All of these efforts, which occur over the brief construction season, are accompanied by noise and traffic delays that receive complaints from residents and visitors alike. Any road construction worker who starts "banging away" on the bedrock at 6:30 in the morning is "like a bad dentist," exclaimed one Tofte resort owner in 2002. "When he hits a nerve, it affects your whole body! Boom!"[23]

**The road sign for North Shore Scenic Drive. Photograph 2017.**

The North Shore highway, since the early 1990s, certainly has become a safer and more efficient corridor (twenty-five deaths, an average of about one per year, occurred between Two Harbors and the Canadian border from 1988 to 2011)—even though a few veteran motorists and travelers still believe that the improvements have removed several of its charms and interesting challenges. The highway engineers and landscape architects who design the new segments seek to maintain the visual and environmental qualities that form the North Shore driving experience. These "character-defining features" typically are dependent on the width of road cuts and shoulders, the steepness of the swales that slope away from the shoulder, and the sense of enclosure provided by flanking vegetation and rock cuts.[24]

## Minnesota Highway 61 and North Shore Scenic Drive

In 1991, as Interstate 35 was nearing completion in Minnesota, U.S. Highway 61 between the northern Twin Cities metropolitan area and Canadian border was decommissioned; the North Shore section, however, was maintained as Minnesota Highway 61. One year later, when the last leg of Interstate 35 was finished between downtown Duluth and Twenty-Sixth Avenue East, the avenue's intersection with London Road was designated as the entrance to Minnesota Highway 61 and North Shore Scenic Drive. This action occurred shortly after the North Shore route was identified as a Scenic Byway, one of eight Minnesota roadways now included in the Federal Highway Administration's National Scenic Byway program. The North Shore corridor was additionally designated an All-American Road, a recognition limited to the small number of national highways that demonstrate two or more "intrinsic qualities"—scenic, recreational, natural, historic, cultural, or archaeological—deemed "unique and important enough to be tourist destinations unto themselves."[25] North Shore Scenic Drive obviously has several of these qualities.

The North Shore Scenic Drive Council, part of the Duluth-based Arrowhead Regional Development Commission (ARDC), is involved in providing tourist-related information but also gives attention to "the quality of the route, while preserving its cultural, social, and natural integrity." Receiving specific consideration are the North Shore's seventy public sites, which range from several with well-designed interpretive displays and numerous visitors' services to others that serve as little more than simple pull-offs.[26]

## State Parks and a National Monument

Because of the financial constraints posed by World War II and, to a lesser extent, the Korean conflict, none of Minnesota's state parks received any development and maintenance funds from 1942 to 1953. Once MDC officials acknowledged that its overtaxed facilities were "literally falling apart at the seams," legislators addressed the predicament, in 1953, by passing a Sticker Act, which imposed an annual tax of one dollar on each vehicle entering a state park. At that time, MDC managed just two North Shore state parks—Gooseberry Falls and Baptism River (now Tettegouche)—and had responsibility for the operation of four much smaller state waysides.[27]

Significant land donations resulted in the designation of four more North Shore state parks during the 1950s: George H. Crosby Manitou, Judge C. R. Magney, Cascade River, and Temperance River. The former Split Rock Wayside was also enlarged and renamed Split Rock Lighthouse State Park in 1967; the MHS, in 1976, assumed ownership and management responsibilities of the lighthouse and its associated buildings, which, in 2011, were also designated a National Historic Landmark. The most recently authorized state park, Grand Portage, approved in 1989, is owned by the BIA and managed jointly by the MDNR and the Grand Portage Reservation Tribal Council. Overall, the North Shore's state parks are highly popular tourist destinations. The North Shore includes three of Minnesota's five most popular state parks—Gooseberry Falls, Tettegouche, and Split Rock

Lighthouse—which were visited by a total of 1,890,600 people in 2021. Another major cultural property, Grand Portage National Monument, has been operated and managed by the NPS since 1960.[28]

## Other Tracks and Trails

Several different tracks and trails mirror the linearity of Highway 61/North Shore Scenic Drive. The oldest, originally called the Lake Line, was built between Duluth and Two Harbors by the Duluth Missabe and Iron Range (DM&IR) Railroad in 1885–86. When the line was put up for sale during the 1980s, Duluth's Lake Superior Railroad Museum (LSRM) called for the establishment of a public association that would secure a title to the tracks and "interpret history in a dynamic way." Formation of the St. Louis and Lake Counties Regional Railroad Authority in 1985 precipitated a refurbishing of the tracks and equipment, which were subsequently leased to LSRM. The organization's highly popular May–October tours that run between Duluth and Two Harbors have been offered since 1990.[29]

Another major project, the Superior Hiking Trail (SHT), initiated in 1986 and completed in 2017, extends northeastward from the Minnesota–Wisconsin state line to the Pigeon River, which also serves as the boundary between Minnesota and Ontario. More than three hundred miles long, SHT passes through four counties; eight state parks; forty miles of Duluth; seventy miles of the Superior National Forest (SNF); and, remarkably, forty-five miles of private land. The terminus occurs at the 270-Degree Overlook, an apt description of the astounding, panoramic view offered from that point. Strictly a hiking (and, in winter, a snowshoeing) trail, the SHT was completed with funding provided by the State of Minnesota but is primarily supported with private donations. Volunteers affiliated with the Superior Hiking Trail Association perform most of the required on-site maintenance work. In 2019, SHT was also officially cosigned as part of the North Country Trail, which eventually will connect the states of Vermont and North Dakota.[30]

During the 1980s, a number of North Shore resort operators and organizations began advocating for the implementation of another major project—a nonmotorized recreational trail dedicated to bicyclists, in-line skaters, walkers, and joggers. MnDOT, in 1999, authorized construction of the envisioned eighty-nine-mile-long Gitchi-Gami State Trail (GGST), including some sections that would follow former Highway 61 rights-of-way. Work soon began on a seventeen-mile-long section of the Gitchi-Gami, completed in 2017, which connected Gooseberry Falls State Park and Silver Bay. A twelve-mile-long section of the trail, with the exception of a half-mile gap in Tofte, has also been completed between Schroeder and Lutsen. The most recent addition, opened in 2017, is a five-mile-long link between Grand Marais and the Cut Face Creek State Wayside. A very short segment, just one-half mile long, also exists at Silver Creek Cliff. Completion of the entire GGST system is expected to occur slowly because of high land acquisition and construction costs.[31]

Another transportation corridor that caters to kayakers is the Lake Superior Water Trail (LSWT). Authorized by the MDNR in 1993, the trail extends between Duluth's harbor and the Grand Portage Indian Reservation boundary. The most problematic issue faced by LSWT advocates is securing permissions to establish a sufficient number of campsites and access points for paddlers. Managing the LSWT jointly are the MDNR and a support group, the Lake Superior Water Trail Association; the two organizations provide information about water access and safe harbors, campsites, maps, and safety considerations. Because similar water trails are found in Wisconsin, Michigan, and Ontario, much of the Lake Superior coastline is now a safer place for paddlers.[32]

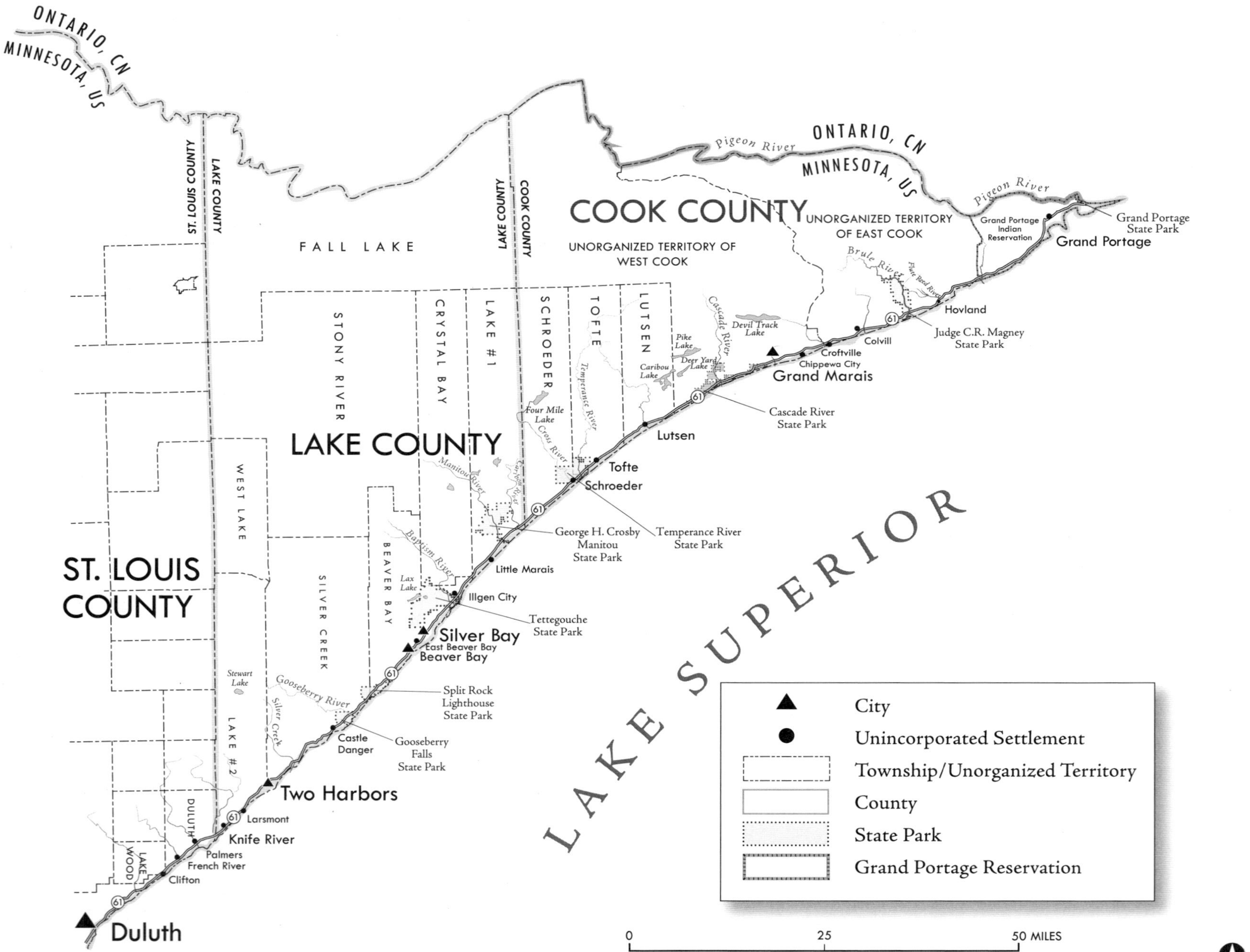

ONTARIO, CN
MINNESOTA, US
Pigeon River
COOK COUNTY
UNORGANIZED TERRITORY OF EAST COOK
UNORGANIZED TERRITORY OF WEST COOK
Grand Portage Indian Reservation
Grand Portage State Park
Grand Portage
Brule River
Flute Reed River
Hovland
Judge C.R. Magney State Park
Colvill
Croftville
Chippewa City
Grand Marais
Devil Track Lake
Cascade River
Pike Lake
Deer Yard Lake
Caribou Lake
Cascade River State Park
Lutsen
Tofte
Schroeder
Temperance River
Temperance River State Park
Four Mile Lake
Cross River
LUTSEN
TOFTE
SCHROEDER
LAKE COUNTY
COOK COUNTY
ST. LOUIS COUNTY
FALL LAKE
LAKE #1
CRYSTAL BAY
STONY RIVER
WEST LAKE
SILVER CREEK
BEAVER BAY
LAKE #2
DULUTH
LAKE WOOD
Manitou River
Carlton River
George H. Crosby Manitou State Park
Little Marais
Baptism River
Lax Lake
Illgen City
Tettegouche State Park
Silver Bay
East Beaver Bay
Beaver Bay
Split Rock Lighthouse State Park
Stewart Lake
Gooseberry River
Silver Creek
Castle Danger
Gooseberry Falls State Park
Two Harbors
Larsmont
Knife River
Palmers
French River
Clifton
Duluth
61
ST. LOUIS COUNTY
LAKE SUPERIOR
City
Unincorporated Settlement
Township/Unorganized Territory
County
State Park
Grand Portage Reservation
0
25
50 MILES
0
50
100 KILOMETERS

# PART II

## A Guide to Highway 61

The remainder of this book serves as a field guide that provides information about more than two hundred places and properties along Highway 61. The discussion begins with Duluth's London Road entrance to Highway 61 and continues along the Lake Superior shoreline through St. Louis, Lake, and Cook Counties before culminating at the Pigeon River and Canadian border.

### Highway 61 as a Transect

This guide follows Highway 61 on its route from Duluth to the Canadian border. As such, it employs the concept of a *transect*—a term originally used by ecologists to define "a path along which one counts and records occurrences of the species of study." The transect has been subsequently adopted and adapted by many investigators in several fields of inquiry. To cultural geographers, for example, the transect serves as "a route along which a survey or observations are made," whereas urban and regional planners employ the transect when "organizing the components of the built world: building, lot, land use, street, and all of the other . . . elements of the human habitat."[1]

Considerable time and effort are typically required when choosing and laying out a transect, especially when it follows a circuitous route or path. The linearity of Highway 61, however, clearly presents itself as a logical transect for any study of Minnesota's Lake Superior shoreline. But selecting a transect route is only the beginning step in a long process: numerous observations are required, and considerable information, data, and material—much of it provided by local informants, historical societies, libraries, government offices, organizations, and so forth—must be located and evaluated.

Grady Clay, a keen observer of the cultural landscape, provided some of the most useful directions and approaches for using a transect, which he called the "cross-sectional" method, in a place or region. "To come to an understanding of places, requires . . . maps, documents, histories, interviews, photography [and] careful observation," he wrote in 1994. "But above all, understanding depends upon the continuity of moving self-consciously and completely through a place—in-one-side-and-out-the-other—and then repeating that process over time."[2] This North Shore guide represents my efforts to follow these suggestions.

## Visiting the Sites and Rules of the Road

This book, as is typical of most guides that are grounded in a specific place, uses addresses to identify the locations of individual sites. Although this approach makes the guide much more useful to readers, it must also be emphasized that the rules and rights associated with privately owned property must be followed and respected. Most, but not all, commercial and public properties are accessible to visitors—as long as established rules are respected and observers do not interfere with the activities and wishes of owners, customers, or guests. Private homes and residences should be observed only from a public walk or street. Unless access is granted by an owner, those private properties not visible from a public vantage point are typically off-limits. For this reason the guide does not provide specific addresses for these places. Photography, of course, must also be pursued with great discretion: people who might be identifiable in an image should be asked for permission before their image is captured.

# St. Louis County

The first seventeen miles of North Shore Scenic Drive/Minnesota Highway 61 are situated, almost entirely, within two of St. Louis County's jurisdictions—the city of Duluth and Duluth Township. The Duluth entrance to Scenic Drive is located at the intersection of Twenty-Sixth Avenue East and London Road. From there, the route continues along London Road for slightly more than three miles to the Lester River Bridge, where the name transitions to Congdon Boulevard; it then proceeds another five miles to the city's eastern boundary. After passing through a very short section of Lakewood Township, Scenic Drive enters Duluth Township and is cosigned with St. Louis County Road 61 for almost nine miles, until it reaches the Lake County border.

## Duluth: London Road

London Road, already called Duluth's "Lake Shore Boulevard" by the late nineteenth century, accommodated carriages, sleighs, and bicycles before automobiles and motorized vehicles appeared in the early 1900s. Throughout this early period, numerous Victorian-era mansions and residences emerged along London Road and other streets and avenues in East Duluth. Because of their monumentality, symmetrical order, and eclectic details, architectural historian Paul Clifford Larson has called them examples of a "Duluth style." Among the most visible characteristics of these residences are their extensive front porches and foundations and walls built of dark Duluth gabbro.[1]

Although London Road has served as a prestigious Duluth address since the nineteenth century, its upper side includes a number of relatively modest post–World War II homes. Also located along the lakeshore, and close to the Scenic Drive entrance, is a notable cultural landscape feature, Scandia Cemetery (3200 London Road), one of the city's oldest burial grounds. Sponsored in 1881 by members of Duluth's First Danish Norwegian Evangelical Lutheran congregation, the cemetery now includes about fifteen hundred burial sites and remains in active, but limited, use. Nearby, on the upper side of London Road's 3700 and 3800 blocks, is London East, a housing complex, initiated in 2020 but not yet completed, which currently includes some twenty townhomes.[2]

### Glensheen: Chester and Clara Congdon Residence
3300 London Road

No London Road, or Duluth, mansion is more massive and impressive than Glensheen, built from 1906 to 1912 for Chester and Clara Hesperia Bannister Congdon. Born in Rochester, New York, Congdon studied law before moving to St. Paul in 1875; by 1892, the ambitious attorney was in Duluth, where he accumulated significant wealth through professional associations with several iron and copper mining and commercial endeavors. In 1902 the Congdons commissioned Clarence H. Johnston Sr.—a St. Paul architect whose firm designed some four hundred homes, churches, and public and commercial buildings throughout Minnesota—to provide plans for their residence, which would be constructed on part of a twenty-two-acre land parcel located between London Road and Lake Superior. The Jacobean revival style mansion (sometimes termed Jacobethan revival), based on seventeenth-century English manor houses, was constructed of steel beams and reinforced concrete and faced with reddish brown Flemish bond brick walls

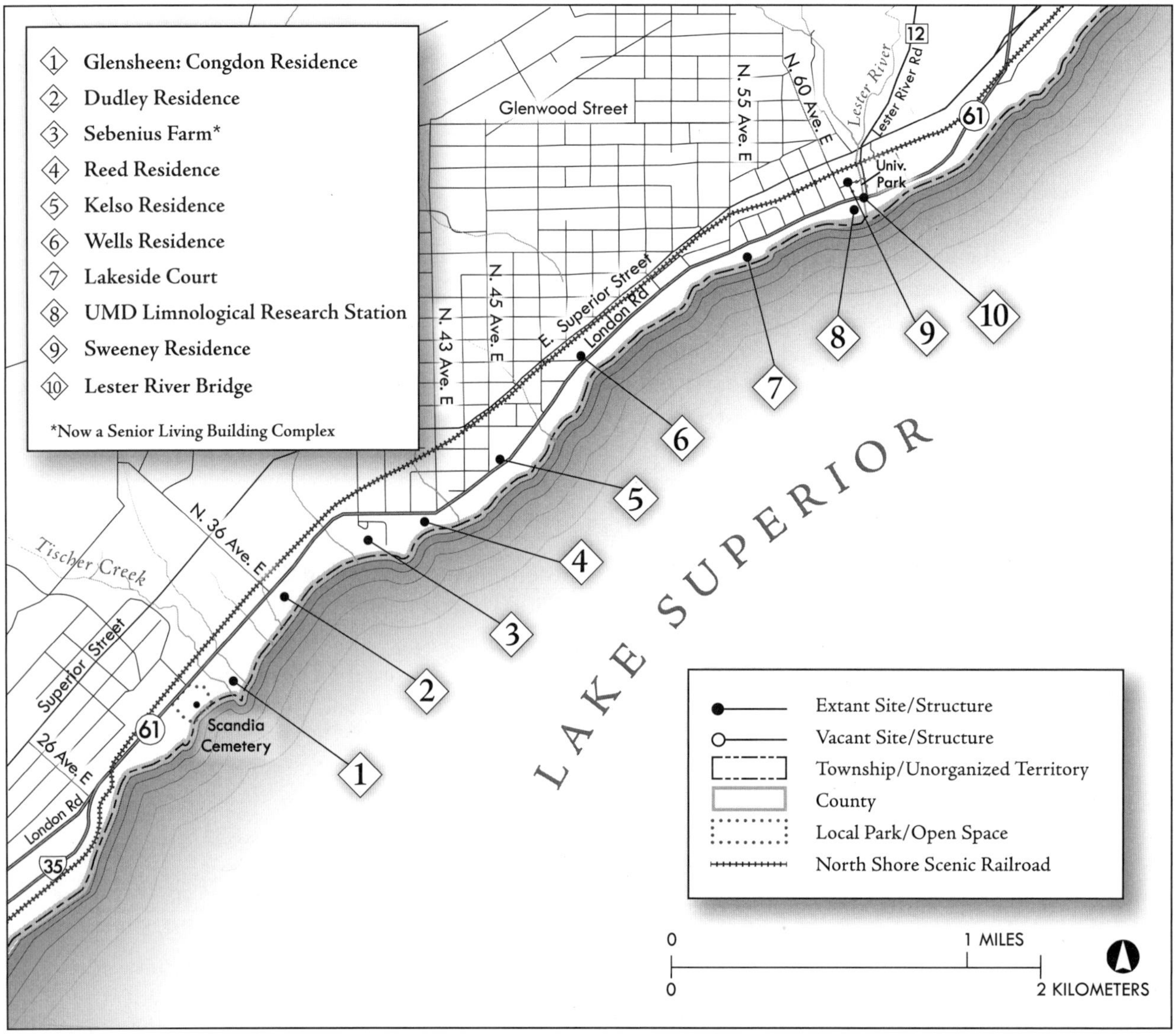
1 Glensheen: Congdon Residence
2 Dudley Residence
3 Sebenius Farm*
4 Reed Residence
5 Kelso Residence
6 Wells Residence
7 Lakeside Court
8 UMD Limnological Research Station
9 Sweeney Residence
10 Lester River Bridge
*Now a Senior Living Building Complex
Glenwood Street
N. 55 Ave. E
N. 60 Ave. E
Lester River
Lester River Rd
12
61
Univ. Park
N. 45 Ave. E
N. 43 Ave. E
E. Superior Street
London Rd
N. 36 Ave. E
Tischer Creek
Superior Street
26 Ave. E
London Rd
35
Scandia Cemetery
LAKE SUPERIOR
Extant Site/Structure
Vacant Site/Structure
Township/Unorganized Territory
County
Local Park/Open Space
North Shore Scenic Railroad
0
1 MILES
0
2 KILOMETERS

and Vermont granite trim. Built into a slight hillside, the mansion's southern elevation, which faces Lake Superior, is distinguished by three, full-height gable projections, four hipped dormers, and five corbeled brick chimneys that protrude from the roof. Extending across the mansion's western side is a balustrade that overlooks nearby Tischer Creek and its glen.[3]

Altogether, the mansion's four floors provided the Congdons with thirty-nine rooms, fifteen fireplaces, and twenty-seven thousand square feet of living space. Located on the first floor were the public spaces: reception, living, dining, and sunrooms, as well as a library and kitchen. The upper two floors, with fourteen bedrooms and eleven bathrooms, afforded private quarters for the family and their five servants—a butler, a maintenance man, a cook, and downstairs and upstairs maids. The lower level or basement, a place of "work for the staff and play for the family," had space for billiards, toys, and amusement, along with utility, milk, laundry, and storage rooms. The utility room was originally equipped with a semiautomated steam boiler that provided heat for more than one hundred radiators; also in the home were a centralized vacuum cleaner system and several other innovative features. William French of St. Paul and John S. Bradstreet of Minneapolis designed most of the arts and crafts and art nouveau features found throughout the interior: gold-leaf ceilings; silver light fixtures; walnut, oak, and cypress woodwork; Rockwood tile; Italian and Algerian marble; hand-carved railings; and art glass windows fabricated by Chicago's Linden Art Glass Company. Each bedroom reflected the personal tastes of the Congdons and their six surviving children.[4]

**A 2016 overview of Glensheen, Chester and Clara Congdon's mansion, which overlooks its formal garden to the south. At the right, but obscured by vegetation, are the Carriage House and former Gardener's Cottage. Congdon Family Papers, U6192, Archives and Special Collections, Martin Library, University of Minnesota Duluth.**

Several smaller buildings also compose the estate, most noticeably a 1909 two-story, brick and false half-timber Carriage House that has three sections. The building once included several stables, with walls covered by white subway titles, which sheltered the family's horses and small herd of cows. The building also had storage areas and a "full-service repair shop" for carriages, sleighs, and vehicles; space for hay, feed, and outdoor furniture; a clubroom where workmen could relax; and living quarters for the coachman or chauffeur. The 1906 Gardener's Cottage, located east of the house and adjacent to the vegetable garden, was originally built as a small-scale version of a Jacobean revival house. In 1927, however, when the cottage proved too small for the head gardener and his family, Clara Congdon commissioned Duluth architects Harold Starin and A. Reinhold Melander to convert the building into an English Tudor style house with a distinctive saltbox roof. Subsequently renovated and renamed the Bridal Cottage, the building is now used for catered wedding events that occur on the Glensheen grounds. South of the house and adjacent to Lake Superior are a boathouse and a pier.[5]

Providing context and setting for Glensheen are its remarkable landscape features, an outstanding achievement given the climatic and environmental challenges posed by Lake Superior's immediate presence. Designed in 1908 by New York landscape architect Charles Leavitt and two key assistants, Anthony U. Morell and Arthur R. Nichols, Glensheen is one of the state's foremost examples of a landscape dating to the "country place era"—generally the period from 1890 to 1930, when "wealthy Americans commissioned extensive gardens at their country estates, [by] emulating European gardens." Glensheen is typical of country place landscapes, especially in its use of "symmetrical and . . . formal geometries" organized around a central axis that extends southward from the residence, passes through the formal garden, and terminates at Lake Superior. The garden, fifty by one hundred feet in size, includes two major features—a simple rectangular plane of grass and a pool with a fountain at its center. Both elements are clearly articulated by a geometrically precise system of brick walkways, low retaining walls, and ten adjacent flower beds. The formal garden also serves as a transition to Glensheen's extensive natural landscape.[6]

Leavitt's planting list for the entire grounds included 266 species of shrubs, trees, perennials, and annuals. (The latter were grown in Glensheen's greenhouses before being transplanted to the garden.) His design for the formal area, also preferred by Chester Congdon, replicated the rigid symmetry and organization of an Italian Renaissance garden. Clara Congdon, however, favored the more informal and "bountiful look of an English cottage garden," which relied on a lusher and more colorful plant palette. George Wyness began implementing the changes after starting his career as Glensheen's head gardener in 1921. When Wyness retired in 1945 at the age of eighty-two, he was immediately followed by his son Bob, who held the position until 1985. Together the two men served as Glensheen's gardeners for sixty-four years.[7]

Over time, many plant varieties disappeared, and numerous overgrown trees sheltered the garden. This situation changed in 2004 when a group of volunteers formed the Glensheen Garden Guild and developed a detailed restoration plan and program for the site. Using a 1916 plan prepared by Morell and Nichols as their guide, the guild's members introduced plantings that resulted in the more informal look of an English garden. The overall composition "has a billowy, full look, lots of color and plants tightly massed," noted the Garden Guild's 2004 description, "where you don't see individual clumps but waves of plants." The success of their efforts quickly made the garden area one of Glensheen's most admired and visited spaces.[8]

East of the residence are symmetrically organized flower and vegetable gardens and the site of former greenhouses (razed in 1971), all formerly tended by the Wyness father-and-son team. Above the gardens is a clay tennis court. Also leading eastward is a pathway system that provides access to Bent Brook, a diminutive creek formerly crossed by several small wooden bridges. The brook is channeled through a stone-faced culvert that passes under London Road. Before it empties into Lake Superior, the brook is spanned by three bridges: one built of wood and two that are incorporated into the driveway (one near the mansion, the other by the boathouse). West of the residence is a more substantial stream, Tischer Creek, approached by a tree-lined path. Straddling this creek is a graceful stone arch bridge that leads to a network of other paths, one of which continues along the shoreline, where it presents an outstanding overview of the house and formal garden.[9]

An infamous July 1977 incident that occurred at Glensheen is deeply etched into the history of criminality in Minnesota: the murders of the last surviving Congdon child, eighty-seven-year-old Elisabeth, and her nurse, Velma Pietila. Elisabeth Congdon's adopted daughter Marjorie and her husband, Roger Caldwell, were immediately identified as suspects. Roger Caldwell was convicted and sent to prison in 1979 but released four years later in exchange for an admittance of guilt. Although Caldwell refused to implicate his wife, many believe she was involved in "aiding and abetting and conspiracy to commit murder."[10]

A philanthropist like her parents, Elisabeth Congdon had bequeathed Glensheen to UMD in 1968. She was given a life estate and resided there until her untimely death. Now comprising twelve acres, Glensheen opened to the public in 1979, was listed in the National Register of Historic Places in 1991, and subsequently emerged as Minnesota's most visited house museum. An especially ambitious restoration and preservation program, initiated in 2015 following a major 2012 flood that damaged several areas of the property, utilized $6 million—supplied by donors, ticket sales, and state funds—to restore fifteen interior spaces, protect several valuable art and craft collections, rebuild the clay tennis court, repair several structures, and convert the Gardener's Cottage into the Bridal Cottage. Numerous pine and cedar trees planted under the direction of Clara Congdon have been removed to provide historically accurate views from and toward the house. Additional fundraising and repairs have occurred since October 2017, when another significant storm severely damaged Glensheen's boathouse and three-tiered shoreline. Indeed, a major project that involved the rebuilding and restoration of Glensheen's gardens and fountain in 2021 was undertaken to keep the entire property "from sliding closer to the lakeshore."[11]

Despite these challenges, it is remarkable that so much of Glensheen—comprising buildings, furnishings, collections, and landscapes—has survived for over a century. "Of all the mansions in Minnesota," observed architectural historian and writer Larry Millett in 2014, "none is more elegantly appointed, more beautifully sited, nor more deeply connected to its place than Glensheen."[12] And of course, Glensheen serves as a highly visible reminder of the tremendous private wealth that northeastern Minnesota's natural resources generated for a single Duluth family.

### Harry C. and Marjorie Dudley Residence
3600 London Road

Harry Dudley, an internationally renowned exploration geologist, married Chester and Clara Congdon's daughter Marjorie in 1917. The couple, several years later, commissioned Howard Shaw & Associates, a Chicago architectural firm, to design their residence, built on six acres of land adjoining Glensheen's eastern boundary. The Dudleys and their two sons moved into the three-story, twenty-four-room Tudor Revival residence in late 1930. Constructed of half-timber and light-colored rubble stone and topped by a red slate roof and tall chimneys, the mansion is often described as one of Duluth's finest homes. Three large gables project outward from the front facade, while an exquisitely detailed bay window distinguishes the central gable. At the rear are two bay windows that provide exquisite views of the grounds and Lake Superior. A commanding entryway opens into a gallery that is fifty feet long and supported by stone columns and oak beams. Found throughout the interior are carved Swedish pine paneling, teak and pegged-oak floors, and brass chandeliers. The grounds were designed by Jens Jensen, one of the Midwest's most prominent landscape designers, who was based in Chicago at the time. Following the severe flooding event of 2012, which caused considerable damage to the building and landscape, owners Lee and Penny Anderson oversaw a major restoration of their property, an effort that was recognized, one year later, with an award from the Duluth Preservation Alliance.[13]

**A view, probably dating to the 1940s, of the Harry and Marjorie Dudley residence, one of Duluth's finest Tudor style buildings. The property is partially visible from London Road. Courtesy of St. Louis County Historical Society.**

### John and Susan Sebenius Residence and Farm (*now* Ecumen Lakeshore)
4000 London Road

In 1890, thirty-three-year-old mining engineer John Sebenius emigrated from Värmland, Sweden, to Marquette, Michigan. He departed for Minnesota's Iron Range in 1892, three years before marrying Marquette resident Susan Manning. In 1907, while Sebenius was employed in Duluth by the U.S. Steel Corporation, the couple and their two sons moved into a commanding, two-and-a-half-story residence distinguished by its two imposing corner towers. Sebenius also used the property, which had a thousand feet of Lake Superior shoreline, to pursue his hobby—experimenting with the raising of dairy cattle and agricultural crops. (Sebenius named the model dairy on his property, Trianon Stock Farms.) Susan Sebenius died in 1918, but her husband spent the remaining fourteen years of his life on the estate before Duluth's Lake Shore Lutheran Home acquired the property and razed the residence in 1933. The site is now occupied by Ecumen Lakeshore, a health provider that offers independent retirement, assisted-living, and memory-care services.[14]

The John and Susan Sebenius residence, shown here, probably during the 1920s, included one thousand feet of Lake Superior shoreline. The extensive holding also allowed Sebenius to pursue his hobby: raising crops and cattle. Courtesy of Duluth Public Library.

### David and Effie Reed Residence
4218 London Road

In 1887, David and Effie Wheelock Reed moved from New York State to Duluth, where David would soon serve as the city engineer. The couple and their three daughters lived on London Road in this three-bedroom, Victorian house, one of the earliest residences built by the Lakeside Land Company in 1888–89. The home's notable features are its classical columns; spindle work details; decorative front-gable ornamentation; and steeply pitched, irregular rooflines.

Both the exterior and the interior of this Victorian-era house, which dates to the late 1880s, were carefully restored during the late twentieth century.

Although Reed died in 1919, his widow continued to reside in the home until 1929, when it was sold to the first of several subsequent purchasers. Mike and Cindy Bayer, who owned the residence from 1986 to 2016, undertook an exceptional restoration and maintenance program during their tenure. The couple restored the interior hardwood floors, paint, wallpaper, plaster, and fireplace; rebuilt the chimney and porch; applied new cedar shakes to the roof; and carefully selected the exterior paint colors, including the highlighted decorative front-gable ornamentation. The Bayers' efforts were recognized, in 1998, with an award from the Duluth Preservation Alliance.[15]

### Daniel and Pearl Kelso Residence
4631 London Road

One of only a relatively few art moderne homes in Duluth, the Kelso residence reveals several features of the style: rounded corners and windows, a flat roof with a parapet, two horizontal wall bands, and a stucco exterior. Designed in 1938 by Duluth architect Hugo Wold, the house was built for Daniel and Pearl Swartz Kelso, who owned a successful roofing business. (The couple would donate a triangular acre of open space, located along an alley behind the residence, to the City of Duluth for Kelso Park.) The residence was called Kelso's Tourist Home during the early 1950s when a pair of air-conditioned

**Daniel and Pearl Kelso moved into this art moderne house in 1938. Two of the upper-floor bedrooms were rented to tourists during the 1950s.**

bedrooms—one of the first times this feature was advertised on the North Shore—were available for rent to travelers. Sold in 1966 following Daniel Kelso's death, the dwelling still retains many of its original exterior design details.[16]

Another residence, also designed by Wold at 4901 London Road, combines elements of both the moderne and colonial styles and represents, as architectural historians David Gebhard and Tom Martinson have stated, "the best of the past and the near future." Wold's interpretation of the streamlined moderne style (a variation of art moderne) stands at 4631 London Road, while architect Otto M. Olson's version appears at 4920 London Road.[17]

### Benjamin and Charlotte Wells Residence
4811 London Road

This Queen Anne style house, the most imposing structure on London Road's upper side, was built in 1889 for Benjamin and Charlotte Bullen Wells and their four sons. The family had recently departed Clinton County, New York, for Duluth, where Wells assumed the vice presidency of a major wholesale grocery business. The frame-and-board house would be altered and converted into an assisted living facility, Lakeside Manor, during the 1990s. The front facade still displays several of its original elements, including an open porch that wraps around much of the southern and western facades and twin towers—one covered by an "octagonal cone," the other by a "bulbous mushroom cap," both of which establish and announce the movement and variety that serve as hallmarks of Queen Anne style buildings.[18]

**Sixty-five years of time and design styles separate Benjamin and Charlotte Wells's large, 1889 Queen Anne style residence and its neighbor at 4843 London Road, a ranch style house dating to 1954.**

### Lakeside Court

### Lower Side of London Road at the Intersection with Fifty-Fifth Avenue East

Large homes on single lots clearly predominate along London Road's lower side. In 1920, however, the London Land Company prepared a much different layout for Lakeside Court—a block of eight moderately sized residences that would be grouped around three sides of an oblong area of open space. Such a plan, claimed the developers, offered several advantages for prospective residents: improved circulation of light and air, opportunities to develop gardens and lawns within a "homelike" setting, and sufficient space "for children to romp and play without fear by their parents of being hit by a passing automobile." The eight six-room bungalows, all designed by Duluth architect Arthur Hanford, were also intended to create a "harmonious" residential grouping within the landscape. The central open space, now called Lakeside Court Park, is listed as an official park by the City of Duluth, even though it has no public access. What Lakeside Court continues to offer, more than a century after completion, is a park-like setting for its two parallel rows of residences.[19]

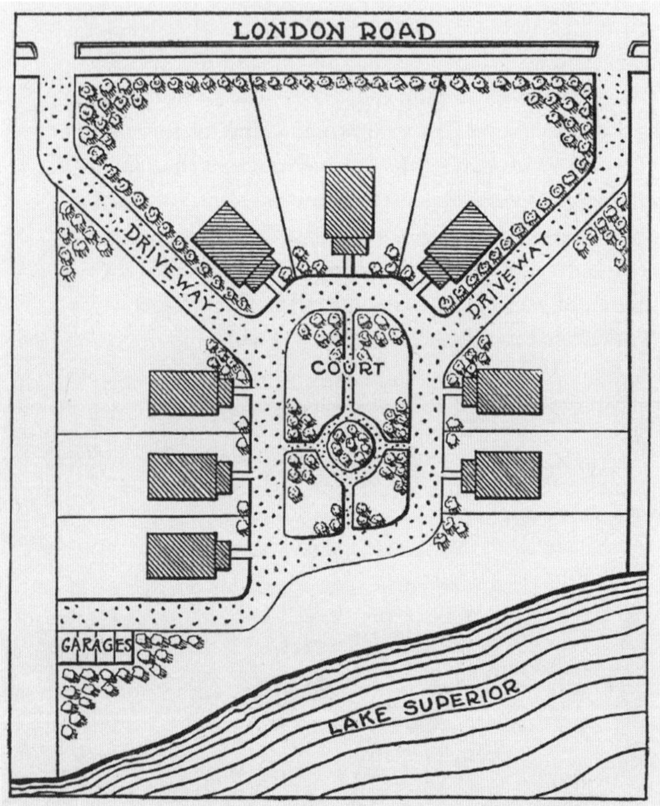


**The 1920 Lakeside Court plan called for the placement of eight dwelling units around three sides of a central open space. The completed layout, however, eliminated both diagonal driveways and the road that was planned to encircle the court. Entrance to the site is now provided by two parallel roadways, each of which accesses a row of four residences that extend southward from London Road. Courtesy of the *Duluth News-Tribune*, 11 January 1920, 3.**

### U.S. Fisheries Station–Duluth (*now* UMD Limnological Research Station)

### 6008 London Road

This former U.S. Fisheries Station hatchery, located at the Lester River's mouth, remains one of Duluth's outstanding late nineteenth-century structures. The idea for such a facility was launched during the mid-1880s by the recently formed Duluth Fishery Association, which sought "the promotion of the welfare of its members; the preservation of whitefish of Lake Superior waters; the restocking of the old spawning grounds with fish fry; the better understanding of the state laws concerning the preservation of fish; and abolishing the using or making of any kind of nets with less than three and one-half inches." (The larger net openings allowed immature fish to pass through them.) When Minnesota's U.S. senator Knute Nelson secured federal funding for the project in 1886, a U.S. Fish Commission official announced that the Duluth building, the first of its kind on Lake Superior, would hatch fifty million whitefish eggs annually and serve as the largest and best facility on the Great Lakes.[20]

Leading the project was Robert O. Sweeney, who had served as a Union Army pharmacist in the Civil War before becoming a nationally known fish propagation expert and director of the Minnesota Fisheries Association (MFA). Also an artist, Sweeney prepared and illustrated a proposal for the envisioned hatchery, which the *Lake Superior News* termed a "cradle for finnies" in 1886. Sweeney's design, however, was deemed excessively large, elaborate, and expensive and failed to receive approval from MFA officials. A less ambitious proposal, accepted in early 1888, was followed by the onset of construction activities in June and the naming

The former U.S. Fisheries Station, restored by the University of Minnesota Duluth, remains one of the city's most impressive late nineteenth-century structures.

of Sweeney as superintendent just before the hatchery's October opening. Samuel P. Wires assumed the superintendent's position in 1894, but Sweeney remained an active participant in hatchery operations until his passing in 1902.[21]

The two-story hatchery, constructed on land donated to the federal government by Duluth's Lakeside Land Company, still sits on its original gabbro foundation. Termed a "successful [architectural] marriage of the stick and shingle styles," the structure displays a combination of decorative gable fanlights, brackets, sunbursts, scalloped shingles, and pierced ornamentation along the gables and eves. It is situated within a park-like setting that also accommodates three other structures. Nearby is the one-and-a-half-story superintendent's residence, sheathed with clapboard siding and covered by a gabled, jerkinhead (clipped) roof; its one-story porch wing has a single Tuscan column at the entrance. Located immediately behind the hatchery is a two-story carriage barn with a catwalk access. Completing the building ensemble is an octagonal well house that includes a "spear-like" finial atop its roof.

An especially important feature of the hatchery's operations was the constant availability of cold water provided by the Lester River. Just north of the hatchery was a dam, which allowed fishery workers to control the river's flow as it passed through a sluice and underneath the D&IR railroad tracks. Superintendent Wires, in 1917, reported that the facility had collected forty-five hundred bushels of fish eggs during its three decades of operation. Unlike in earlier years, when whitefish predominated, the hatchery was raising significantly more lake and brook trout fry by 1917. The fry, Wires noted, received as much "tender care as a baby"; but after reaching a desirable size, they were "set free and allowed to shift for themselves."[22]

In late 1946, following almost six decades of steady activity, the U.S. Fish and Wildlife Service announced that its Duluth hatchery would be closed for "economy reasons" and an inadequate supply of water. Despite the protestations of local fishermen and fishery officials, the entire property was sold, in 1947, to UMD, which subsequently used the hatchery as a warehouse and converted the residence into temporary faculty housing. In 1955–56, however, the facility was renovated and renamed the UMD Limnological Research Station. UMD investigators, during the 1960s and 1970s, would collaborate with scientists at Duluth's nearby U.S. Environmental Protection Agency (EPA) facility to study the impacts of acid rain and mercury contamination on Lake Superior and northeastern Minnesota's inland water bodies. The research program, nevertheless, was closed in 1977 following funding cutbacks.[23]

The 1978 nomination and listing of the entire complex in the National Register of Historic Places gave primary attention to the hatchery's architectural features. By 2010, when the building's outstanding exterior elements were displaying significant deterioration, a UMD facilities management crew began a two-year-long restoration project that would address these issues. The crew's efforts included rebuilding numerous windows and uncovering others that were boarded up. The crew also installed new shingles on the roof, replaced the deteriorating wooden gutters with ones constructed of reclaimed cedar, fabricated a missing weathervane that had a decorative whitefish at the top, and replaced the delicate finials that once graced each end of the gabled roofs. After the front and rear entrances were rebuilt, the entire structure was painted with colors that reflected its late nineteenth-century origins. The results were recognized in 2013 by the Duluth Preservation Alliance, which honored UMD for going "above and beyond" the expectations of typical restoration projects. The main building's lower level now provides meeting space for some UMD departments and functions, while the overall property is used by instructional programs that offer training in outdoor recreation, surfing, and kayaking.[24]

**This vertical log building, originally a playhouse when constructed in 1915 at 6019 London Road, was later expanded into a tourist cabin. At the rear of the lot, but not visible in the image, is a garage that also served as a seasonal rental unit for several years.**

## Robert and Helen Sweeney Residence

### 6019 London Road

In 1852, Robert Sweeney, a Philadelphia Quaker, moved to St. Paul, where he established the first pharmacy in Minnesota's territorial capital; Sweeney married Helen Benezet in 1864, following the completion of his Civil War service. The couple moved into their recently finished Duluth home in 1890, two years after Sweeney was named superintendent of the nearby hatchery. The residence, which is situated one block north of the facility, had a 6019 Delaware Avenue address at that time and also accommodated the couple's son and his family. It stood only some seventy-five feet west of an earlier Lester River Bridge that was removed when the current London Road span emerged in 1925.[25]

Following Sweeney's 1902 death, his widow, son, daughter-in-law, and five grandchildren remained in the house until 1909. The subsequent owners added a log cabin (termed a "child's playhouse") to the grounds in 1915—some years before newlyweds Linus and Florence Wallberg acquired the property. A watchmaker who emigrated from Sweden to Minnesota in 1909, Wallberg served in World War I prior to his marriage to Florence Erickson, a teacher and the daughter of Swedish immigrants from Brainerd, Minnesota.[26]

The Wallbergs began renting out tourist rooms during the late 1930s. In 1948, shortly after her husband's death, Florence Wallberg expanded the log playhouse and a garage into housekeeping cabins that were identified, for several years thereafter, as "havens for hay-fever sufferers." In 1981, shortly before she sold her property, the Duluth Preservation Alliance noted that the home's exterior may have been extensively modified but its interior still expressed the "interests and personality" of the cheerful eighty-one-year-old owner. Until her death at the age of ninety-three, Wallberg remained committed to the same social causes she had pursued throughout her lifetime: service as an officer in local Baptist, temperance, and welfare organizations and as a drug and health education teacher in several Minnesota schools.[27]

## Lester River Bridge

Travelers who proceed northeastward along London Road gain their first close-up view of Lake Superior at the Lester River Bridge. Completion of the span in

1925 left a half-block square (2.75 acres) of open space on the upper side of the hatchery grounds. Named University Park sometime after UMD's 1947 acquisition of the facility, a portion of the lawn-like space still serves as a manicured feature along London Road.[28]

The Lester River span, despite its modest $9,000 construction costs, represents the North Shore's most sophisticated and aesthetically accomplished example of bridge design. Several highly regarded professionals were involved in its initial development: landscape architects Morell and Nichols served as the primary designers, with assistance provided by Duluth City engineers William Cruikshank and John Wilson and the Minneapolis architectural partnership of William Tyrie and George Chapman. The bridge includes several classical revival details, notably random courses of ashlar (stone worked or "dressed" into square or rectangular shapes) that are mortared onto both reinforced concrete arches. The dressed gabbro stones, observed historian Denis Gardner in 2008, exhibit "sharp lines to top and bottom and left and right; the facing is a series of carved rectangles of various dimensions that offers a clean appearance." Another striking feature is the archivolt (a contrasting band of light-colored granite supplied by a quarry in Rockville, Minnesota) that follows the bridge curvature on each of its sides. Stone railings also distinguish the structure, although its most outstanding highlights are the graceful lanterns and standards, designed by Morell, that "harmonize with the delicate yet substantial lines of the bridge." The span was widened in 1939 with the addition of a new concrete arch on its northern side, but the details are very similar to those of the original bridge design.[29]

Although the deteriorating lighting elements were removed in 1973, the integrity of the bridge was deemed sufficient for National Register of Historic Places designation in 2002—three years before a semitruck veered into the lakeside railing and destroyed it. MnDOT officials could have argued for demolition of the bridge and replacement with a modern structure, but the agency collaborated with Minnesota's State Historic Preservation Office (SHPO) to maintain the span's historic appearance, while simultaneously making needed safety improvements. The concrete arches were rehabilitated, new stones were matched with the recovered originals, a historically compatible mortar mix was developed, and the rebuilt railing reflected the original design, including replacement of the missing

**The Lester River Bridge, completed just before the North Shore section of Minnesota Highway 1 opened officially in 1925, continues to make an attractive aesthetic statement at the junction of London Road and Congdon Boulevard.**

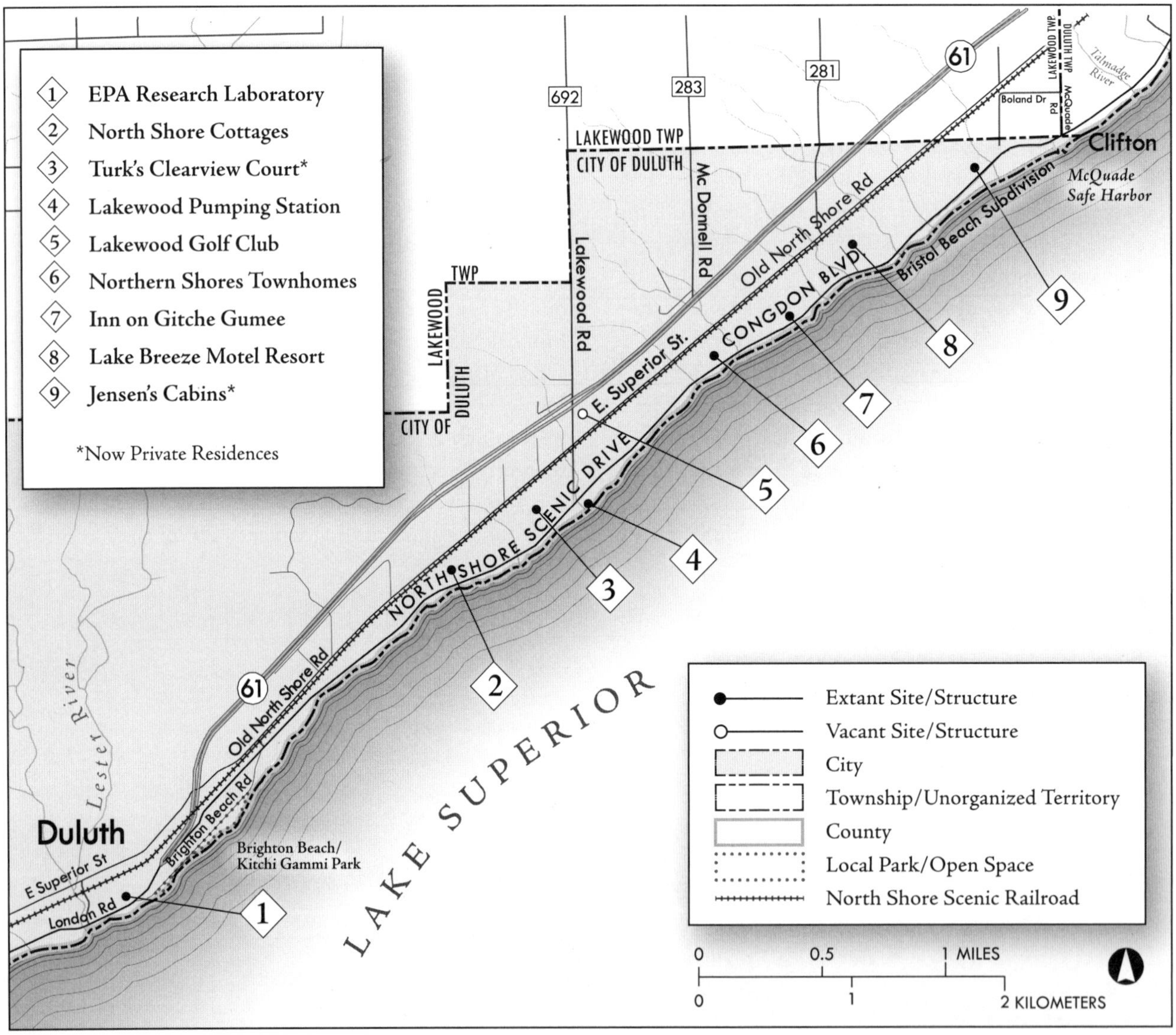

1 EPA Research Laboratory
2 North Shore Cottages
3 Turk's Clearview Court*
4 Lakewood Pumping Station
5 Lakewood Golf Club
6 Northern Shores Townhomes
7 Inn on Gitche Gumee
8 Lake Breeze Motel Resort
9 Jensen's Cabins*
*Now Private Residences
Extant Site/Structure
Vacant Site/Structure
City
Township/Unorganized Territory
County
Local Park/Open Space
North Shore Scenic Railroad
0 0.5 1 MILES
0 1 2 KILOMETERS
LAKE SUPERIOR
Duluth
Clifton
McQuade Safe Harbor
Brighton Beach/ Kitchi Gammi Park
Lester River
Talmadge River
NORTH SHORE SCENIC DRIVE
CONGDON BLVD
Bristol Beach Subdivision
Old North Shore Rd
E. Superior St.
E Superior St
London Rd
Brighton Beach Rd
Lakewood Rd
Mc Donnell Rd
Boland Dr
McQuade Rd
LAKEWOOD TWP
CITY OF DULUTH
DULUTH TWP
61
692
283
281

lighting standards and lamps. Zinc anodes were placed at the top and bottom of both arches to prohibit further corrosion and ensure that the bridge would remain functional for many ensuing years. The Duluth Preservation Alliance saluted the rehabilitation effort in 2006, as did the Preservation Alliance of Minnesota, which also acknowledged MnDOT's important role in leading the state's overall bridge preservation efforts. When the International Concrete Repair Institute recognized the project with an award of merit for transportation in 2011, specific attention was given to the quality of the repairs, all of which sought to "replicate the structure's original appearance."[30] Today, both the bridge and the former fish hatchery serve as exceptionally well-designed and maintained historic structures at an important point of entry along North Shore Scenic Drive.

## Duluth: Congdon Boulevard

London Road transitions to Congdon Boulevard at the Lester River Bridge. The boulevard then proceeds for about one-half mile before intersecting, on the left, with the Minnesota Highway 61 Expressway. It is here that travelers are offered a choice between two routes: the four-lane expressway that proceeds toward the left is used by the vast majority of motorists who wish to reach Two Harbors and other North Shore destinations as quickly as possible; Congdon Boulevard, which extends toward the right, provides travelers with an opportunity to pursue a more leisurely paced journey that offers intimate, close-up views of Lake Superior and its shoreline. A small North Shore Scenic Drive sign, which appears shortly after the Lester River Bridge crossing, informs motorists that the official federal scenic byway begins there.

An even earlier roadway, now called Old North Shore Road, parallels the railroad tracks built by the D&IR Railroad in 1885–86. Several fishing families who lived along the shoreline during the twentieth century's early decades were connected to this early road by narrow paths and driveways. The entrances to some holdings included fish sales stands and homemade signs that advertised the availability of a room, cabin, or hot meal. By 1936, virtually all of the lakeshore properties had been acquired by the Congdon Trust through purchase or condemnation, although leasing agreements allowed several "fishermen's establishments"—primarily cabins, fish houses, net reels, and smokehouses—to continue. H. Rodney Paine, the director of Duluth's Park Board who was involved in planning and supervising several projects carried out by the MDH, NPS, and CCC during the 1930s, praised the "rugged character" of the fishing enclaves. They "add a feature of value to the scenery by their presence and value," Paine declared, and repay "the city for the space they occupy." Members of Lakeshore CCC Company 1751, whose camp was at Stoney Point in Duluth Township, were also told "not to disturb [the] fishermen's huts" since they provided Congdon Boulevard with "a complete beauty treatment." (Additional roadwork during the 1950s would remove most of the remaining camps.) CCC workers, who focused their efforts on several projects situated between the DM&IR railroad tracks and Lake Superior, expanded the road's right-of-way to forty feet (eighteen feet of pavement, with shoulders of eleven feet on each side); removed brush along the lakeshore, while retaining many of the most desirable conifers and birches; and developed a number of turnouts that offered parking spots for motorists who wished to stop and view Lake Superior and several of the streams that feed into it.[31]

Today Congdon Boulevard is bordered by several public sites and spaces, including a popular beach, and numerous turnouts and waysides. At least fifteen automobile-oriented businesses appeared on the upper side of the roadway between the mid-1920s and the late 1950s; some disappeared rather quickly, whereas others prevailed for three or four decades. Only four exist today, albeit in modified and renamed forms. The majority of the built environment now consists of more than one hundred residences, most constructed after World War II. Other than fourteen residences that border Lake Superior at Duluth's far eastern end, all are on the boulevard's upper side.

### Brighton Beach Tourist Camp (*razed, now the Great Lakes Toxicology and Ecology Division Laboratory of the U.S. Environmental Protection Agency*)

6201 Congdon Boulevard

In 1921, as construction of Congdon Boulevard was under way, several Duluth organizations and recently elected mayor Samuel F. Snively advocated for developing sites where motorists could get "close to nature

[and] rough it with comfort." Snively, and Duluth's park superintendent, Henry Cleveland, quickly selected and acquired three places within the city that, by spring 1922, would be available to tourists. One of the three, Brighton Beach Park, located along Congdon Boulevard, was seen as "promoting a spirit of good fellowship among visiting motorists, and co-operation of the park department."[32]

Initially, the camp offered only a water spigot and some space for freestanding tents and "lean-tos" that motorists attached to their vehicles. A flagpole, fifteen feet high, identified the site to prospective campers as they drove along the boulevard. Soon the facility would be equipped with running water, toilets, and a covered pavilion. After the campground's boundary was extended to Sixty-Third Avenue East in 1926, space was provided for eight additional cabins and a larger number of travel trailers. At least twelve more cabins appeared during the next decade, nine of them built in 1938 by workers affiliated with the National Youth Administration, another New Deal agency. In August 1941, the *Duluth News-Tribune* termed the campground a "tourist colony" because several visitors had spent up to six weeks at the site during successive summer seasons. Receiving most attention was a group of motorists from St. Paul, Omaha, and Kansas City who had met at the camp during the previous decade and returned for an annual reunion with their "steadfast friends." We like the city, people, and climate, they exclaimed.[33]

A few workers employed in Duluth's vital industries occupied the cabins during the midst of a severe World War II–era housing shortage. When the tourist camp reopened at war's end, it became an even more popular destination. Attendance figures reached a record high in 1948 when the trailer and tenting sites were respectively claimed 3,840 and 225 times; the eighteen cabins were rented out on 2,425 occasions. Also stopping by were 18,080 day visitors from thirty-six states. Custodian George Hogue commented that he had to make a careful daily count of trailers because anything exceeding forty-five units caused the electrical circuits to overload.[34]

The thirteen-acre campground was leased to a private operator in 1955, before its 1964 transfer from the City of Duluth to the federal government, which constructed a national water quality laboratory on the site. Northeastern Minnesota's DFL congressman John A. Blatnik—who played a major role in securing funding for the building, designed by architects Melander Fugelso and Associates of Duluth—invited U.S. secretary of the interior Stuart Udall to speak at the August 1967 dedication. Udall acknowledged the growing environmental consciousness of the period and

**The Brighton Beach Tourist Camp, by the late 1920s, included several tent sites and a few cabins. Courtesy of St. Louis County Historical Society.**

lauded America's "conservation community, which has alerted the people to the dangers of water pollution and helped bring laboratories and research facilities such as that dedicated here today." Current staff members, now affiliated with the EPA's Great Lakes Toxicology and Ecology Division Laboratory, use Lake Superior to study "the ecological effects of water pollutants on fish, wildlife and ecosystems."[35]

### Brighton Beach and Kitchi-Gammi Park
#### Congdon Boulevard and Sixty-Third Avenue East

The separation of Congdon Boulevard and the Minnesota Highway 61 Expressway occurs less than a half mile beyond the EPA building. Before this point is the boulevard's first public site: Brighton Beach and Kitchi-Gammi Park. Initial discussions about the property had commenced in 1921, when Mayor Snively and other Duluth officials expressed concern over the possible ramifications of a recent subdivision proposed for the site. Snively was totally opposed to the development and favored acquiring the land for public use. He also argued that the linear site should be designated a park because Congdon Boulevard would soon parallel the property and the London Road terminus of Duluth's streetcar line was nearby. Other city officials chimed in with their concerns and observations, claiming that preservation of "the choicest strip of land on the North Shore of Lake Superior" would protect Duluth's water supply (the city pumping station was located only a short distance to the northeast) and rule out "the erection of shacks in that locality." The sixty-nine-acre holding was acquired for $46,200 in September 1921.[36]

In 1926, Duluth park superintendent Henry Cleveland named the property Kitchi-Gammi Park, an unofficial title that continues to the present. The federal government's Civil Works Administration, in late 1933, authorized funds to hire several unemployed men who would construct the park's most visible feature—a stone fireplace shelter that still provides a protected, semicircular bench where as many as six people can sit. The beach and park served as popular destinations for Duluthians over several subsequent decades. Much of the site was overgrown with vegetation by the early 1980s, when Duluth mayor John Fedo launched a campaign to improve several public areas throughout the city, including Brighton Beach and Kitchi-Gammi Park.

**The fireplace shelter located along the Brighton Beach shoreline, constructed in late 1933 by men working for the Civil Works Administration, was restored during the 1980s.**

Public works employees and volunteers labored several years to restore the site and its deteriorating fireplace shelter.[37]

Because of the site's rocky shoreline and frigid water, Brighton Beach obviously differs from its more famous counterpart in Brooklyn, New York, which served as the locale for Neil Simon's popular Broadway play *Brighton Beach Memoirs*. Duluth's Brighton Beach, nevertheless, is an extremely popular public place where residents and visitors pursue numerous activities, including strolling, jogging, biking, and dog walking; picnicking and outdoor cooking; beachcombing, birdwatching, wave watching, and painting *en plein air* (in the open air); sunrise, moon, ore boat, and storm watching; kayaking, canoeing, and paddleboarding; and splashing, jumping, and even swimming and surfing in the cold water. The property also serves as a venue for weddings and art fairs. But when strong northeastern winds and gales prevail—formerly only about once every ten years—Brighton Beach suffers from the lake's fury and destructive force. The situation worsened during the 2017–21 interim, when Brighton Beach experienced five relentless storms. The first, a late October 2017 outburst, left "boulders, giant chunks of trees, sand and gravel . . . piled onto the beach by 20-foot Lake Superior waves" and an entrance road that "looked like it had been shelled by artillery."

It was only through the considerable dedication and effort of city employees and volunteers that the beach reopened within two months. But, given the increasing frequency of subsequent storms, city engineers and park planners, in 2021, adopted and began implementing a "mini–master plan" that transferred the roadway farther inland, removed nonnative vegetation from the site, replaced damaged landscape and turf materials, and provided infrastructure to "armor and protect" the beach.[38]

### Loneyville Motel (*now* North Shore Cottages)
7717 Congdon Boulevard

A quarter mile after the Brighton Beach Road intersection is Congdon Boulevard's first tourist business, originally known as the Loneyville Motel, which Jim and Lois Loney opened in 1949. Although identified as a motel, Loneyville was laid out as a large, U-shaped auto court; however, only six double cabins, all placed at the upper end of the property, were constructed. Early advertisements for Loneyville's "modern, restful units" cited the private showers and toilets, innerspring mattresses, vented heat, kitchenettes, and double or twin beds. To a child, however, Loneyville served as a delightful playground because of its miniature farm, built of wood and plaster, and a "children's fairyland," which included a windmill, lighthouse, church, and other objects, such as a large shoe that referenced the English nursery rhyme "There Was an Old Woman Who Lived in a Shoe." The property was so appealing, recalled longtime North Shore resident Duane Madison, that he and his sister would compete for a seat on the Loneyville side of the car whenever their mother drove by the site. Called North Shore Cottages since 1988, only a few changes have been made to the original property—the addition of outdoor decks to the double cabins and the conversion of the former owner's residence into a two-bedroom rental unit.[39]

### Turk's Clearview Court *(now residences)*
8015 Congdon Boulevard

Palm's Cabins and Turk's Clearview Court were constructed a short distance beyond Loneyville, but only the latter remained open into the 1970s. Turk's Clearview Court was initiated during the early 1950s by Joe and Claudia Turk of Minneapolis, who built seven two-unit cabins, all located a considerable distance from the highway to ensure that travelers would acquire a quiet night's rest. The Turks touted the cabins' wooden knotty walls and picture windows that overlooked Lake Superior; each unit also had an electric refrigerator, a shower bath, vented heat, and "free radios." Some cabins were eventually supplied with a "TV." When Turk's closed around 1974, the cabins were converted into private residences and outbuildings.[40]

**The former Loneyville Motel, now North Shore Cottages, was popular with children because of its play area, which included miniature buildings and structures.**

The cabins at North Shore Cottages, now painted in vivid and varied colors, have experienced very few changes since they appeared in 1959. A remnant of the original Loneyville children's castle is in the background. A wooden train, built before 1988 by an owner who followed plans published in *Popular Mechanics* magazine, stands in the foreground.

The Lakewood Golf Club operated just north of North Shore Drive from 1931 to 1936, and briefly as the Hook and Slice Clinic after World War II. *Duluth Visitor,* 15 July–2 August 1947, 17.

### Lakewood Golf Club and North Shore Hook and Slice Clinic *(razed)*

North of the Highway 61–Lakeview Avenue Intersection

Congdon Boulevard intersects with Lakeview Avenue a short distance from the former Clearview Court property. Situated slightly north of the Congdon Boulevard–Lakeview Avenue intersection was the Lakewood Golf Club, a privately owned facility that operated from 1931 to 1936. Although designed as an eighteen-hole course, only nine holes were developed, along with a small clubhouse. Lakewood's tenure was limited because of the economic problems encountered by Depression-era golf courses as well as the competition offered by Duluth's five public facilities. The site experienced a brief rebirth after World War II, when it was converted into a "hook and slice clinic" for golfers. The grounds remained open until midnight, a pail of balls cost just thirty-five cents, and all of the golf clubs and lawn chairs were free. The driving range and putting green soon closed, and the land was eventually acquired for construction of the Highway 61 Expressway. The clubhouse was moved elsewhere and converted into a residence.[41]

### Lakewood Pumping Station
8130 Congdon Boulevard

No Congdon Boulevard structure is more architecturally distinctive than the Lakewood Pumping Station (also called the Lakewood Pumphouse), which appeared along Lake Superior's shoreline in 1896. The pumping station was built in response to a typhoid outbreak that public officials believed had originated at a polluted site, located close to the central area of Duluth, where the city secured its drinking water. In 1895 alone, Duluth experienced more than fifteen hundred cases of typhoid and at least one hundred deaths. By December 1895, a few years before it was determined that the spread of typhoid could be curtailed by adding chlorine to the water, "fear of the disease reached a frenzy." With the backing of new mayor Henry "Typhoid" Truelsen, the Duluth Common Council authorized the issuance of more than $1 million in public bonds for the construction of a pumping station.[42]

**The Lakewood Pumping Station, which opened in 1898. A water treatment plant, dating to 1976, stands on the opposite side of the historic structure.**

Duluth City engineers probably designed the two-and-a-half-story Romanesque revival structure, constructed of reinforced steel, sided with brown brick, and placed on a foundation of brownstone quarried at Iron River, Wisconsin, and barged across Lake Superior to the site. A round tower with battlements stands at its right front corner, while corbeled brickwork accentuates the facade's uppermost sections. Skylights, a smokestack, and a conical roof tower were removed in 1932, and glass blocks replaced the original windows throughout the main building in 1941. Located on the opposite side of Congdon Boulevard is the Lakewood Water Treatment Plant, dating to 1976. The facility was built in response to concerns that a mid-1950s taconite processing plant, located forty-seven miles to the northeast at Silver Bay, was depositing carcinogenic fibers into the lake.[43]

### Horace L. Johnson Residence and Memorial Camp and Duluth Tent and Trailer Camp (*razed, now* Northern Shores Townhomes)
8351–8411 Congdon Boulevard

A twenty-acre site, situated about a quarter mile northeast of the pumping station, served as a longtime retreat for Horace L. Johnson, who retired as president of the D&IR Railroad in 1931. Johnson's property included a brick-and-frame residence, a private water system, "modern plumbing," and three outbuildings; the grounds comprised a spruce grove and a large lawn with plantings. In 1943, the eighty-seven-year-old, London-born Johnson donated his holding to Duluth's Boy Scouts, who had been searching for a site that would be accessible to and from the city by both train and bus. The Scouts used the property—named the Horace Johnson Memorial Camp following the donor's 1946 death—for about a decade, until their new facility opened at Island Lake, located north of Duluth. The Congdon Boulevard buildings eventually reverted to residential use before the property was converted into the Duluth Tent and Trailer Camp. Following the camp's closing in 2007, the site was platted for a multiunit residential complex, Northern Shores Townhomes, which soon opened with a pair of two-unit residences. Three more double units were completed from 2018 to 2020.[44]

The entrance garden to the Inn on Gitche Gumee, 2022.

### Wilkinson's Cabins and MacDilles Motel (*now the* Inn on Gitche Gumee)
8517 Congdon Boulevard

Three closely spaced cabin and motel businesses emerged just northeast of the Boy Scout camp during the 1950s—Grant's Cabins, Pelander's Motel, and Wilkinson's Cabins. Grant's and Pelander's closed within two decades and were converted into residential properties, but Wilkinson's, dating to 1953, continues today as the Inn on Gitche Gumee. The initial development was initiated by longtime Duluth grocer Eugene Wilkinson and his Swedish wife, Gudrun Olson Wilkinson, who managed their "new fully modern cabins" until retiring in 1967. The property soon became Mack's Motel following its purchase by Donald and Dorothy MacMillan, who were joined, in 1969, by a business partner, Philip Dille. The renamed MacDilles Motel was a familiar site to Duluth residents and North Shore motorists throughout the 1970s and early 1980s.[45]

After Butch and Julie Sievert acquired MacDilles in 1986, the couple and their children "completely reconfigured and renovated" the motel. Sievert, an experienced contractor, used his construction equipment to lift up the motel and erect a structure below. The completed nine-unit project, renamed the Inn on Gitche Gumee in 1996, was provided with stone fireplaces, double whirlpool baths, a second-floor overview of Lake Superior, and a three-season garden. The intimate, small-scale enterprise, which competes successfully with the North Shore's larger, corporate-owned resorts, was sold, in late 2023, to new owners, who immediately announced their plans to maintain the Gitche Gumee's features and amenities into the future.[46]

### Chippewa Club *(now a private residence)*
Old North Shore Road

In 1914–15, some five hundred "devotees of motoring," most residents of Duluth and Superior, but a few from the Iron Range, formed a social organization, the Chippewa Club. After purchasing ten acres of land proximate to both the D&IR railroad tracks and what is now Old North Shore Road, the members commissioned engineer Fred Waldron to design their clubhouse. When completed, the two-story, rustic style log building provided a wide prospect of Lake Superior and the nearby landscape from large verandas that looked toward the east and south. A stone fireplace spanned much of the western wall in the thirty-by-fifty-foot interior "grillroom," used for dining, dancing, and

**The former Chippewa Club, shown here as it appeared in 1915, opened on land situated between the Old North Shore Road and the D&IR railroad tracks. The heavily modified building now serves as a residence. Drawing by Dean Proctor.**

socializing. Ten second-floor dormers identified the "stag" rooms available for overnight visitors. Just before the September 1915 clubhouse opening, the members hired a manager, W. P. Adams, to oversee "a high-class year-round outing place." Because of Adams's previous work on the summer resorts of Long Island, New York, it was anticipated that he would hire an experienced chef and caterers and offer an outstanding cuisine for the club's members. Adams also predicted that the grounds could possibly include tennis courts and a golf course and might even be improved by a landscape designer.[47]

Little is known about the ensuing history of the Chippewa Club, but it was, during the 1930s, converted into the Woodbine, a supper club operated by Modder and Ellen Cox of Duluth. Because Cox was from England, the name may have referenced the woodbine plant, a common form of honeysuckle in Britain. The Woodbine closed several decades ago and was extensively remodeled into a residence.[48]

### Lake Breeze Motel Resort
9001 Congdon Boulevard

Opened in 1952 by Donald and Ruth Bohn, the Lake Breeze Motel originally had eight two-unit cabins arranged in an L-shaped form at the northwestern corner of its site. Located a relatively long distance from Congdon Boulevard, the expansive, eleven-acre complex still has many units with unobstructed views of Lake Superior. A heated outdoor pool as well as volleyball and badminton courts and a nine-hole "mini-put" course were added during the 1980s. Now called the Lake Breeze Motel Resort, the site includes eighteen units and a large rental Cabin by the Lake, which is situated on the property's wooded southwestern corner.[49]

### Bristol Beach Subdivision
Congdon Boulevard, between Ninety-Second and Ninety-Sixth Avenues East

The only private residences that remain along the shoreline section of Congdon Boulevard are found in the Bristol Beach subdivision, platted at the far eastern end of Duluth in 1922. The upper side of the subdivision includes the largest number of homes; the buildings that once composed a popular cabin resort were recently razed and replaced. Most of the structures within the subdivision were constructed during the immediate post–World War II period, although a few date to the twenty-first century.[50]

### Jensen's Cabins and Anchor Away Motor Lodge *(razed, now undergoing development)*
9439 Congdon Boulevard

The far northeastern section of Bristol Beach once included a cabin resort that was developed in 1947 by George and Ruth Krans Jensen, the former owners of a Duluth printing company. When advertising their rental units, the couple gave prominent attention to the "quiet atmosphere" that anglers would experience when returning from Lake Superior fishing expeditions. Following the 1973 purchase of the Jensens' property by Archibald Kausch, a former German ship captain, and his wife, Hilda, the cabins were upgraded, winterized, and renamed the Anchor Away Motor Lodge. When Cynthia Donner acquired the holding in 1998, the Duluth social worker and college instructor established her residence in the main building and rented out the cabins to college students and people in need of short-term housing. Also on the site was a studio used by Donner's husband, Carl Gawboy, a

Finnish Anishinaabe artist whose vivid illustrations of northeastern Minnesota and the North Shore are well known throughout the region. All of the existing structures were removed following a 2022 property sale; a new residence and other buildings were under construction at the time of this writing.[51]

## Lakewood Township

Congdon Boulevard/Scenic Drive exits Duluth's eastern boundary and passes through a very short section of Lakewood Township before entering Duluth Township. Despite the limited area, two important North Shore properties are associated with Lakewood: one a venerable tourist court that has remained open without interruption since 1929, the other a former, highly popular lodging and dining establishment that was replaced by a large public "safe harbor" during the early twenty-first century. Postal addresses in both Lakewood Township and adjoining Duluth Township are identified as North Shore Drive.

### Elmgren's Tourist Court (*now* Gardenwood Resort and Motel)

5107 North Shore Drive

Elmgren's Tourist Court, later renamed the Gardenwood Resort and Motel, has been available to travelers, without interruption, since 1929. It is the North Shore's earliest and only remaining version of a tourist or motor court and the oldest commercial business still operating between Duluth and Knife River. The original establishment was built by Victor and Hilja Lampinen Elmgren, who were married in 1907, shortly after both migrated separately from Finland to Duluth. Elmgren worked as a clerk in Two Harbors' Finnish cooperative store before the couple and their two children moved to Cloquet during the 1920s. Although the Elmgrens launched their business in 1929, they initially frequented Lakeview Township only during the tourist season. By 1940, however, the Elmgrens and their son and daughter-in-law were residing on the North Shore and managing the cabin complex. Two features were advertised regularly—"innerspring" mattresses and indoor toilets. Bathing occurred in a few shower room stalls and the Finnish sauna (now a storage building). Groceries, ice cream, Orange Kist carbonated beverages, souvenirs, and novelty items were available for purchase in the small store, and customers with spare change could play one of the slot machines sequestered in a back room. Hilja Elmgren also prepared "dinners at all hours." By the early 1950s, when each of the twenty cabins was equipped with a private shower, the units could still be rented for as little as three dollars per night. By this time, the couple was spending their winters in Douglas, Arizona, where Victor Elmgren died in early 1955, his widow in 1965.[52]

Oscar and Esther Kyromaki, also Finnish immigrants, purchased Elmgren's in 1955. Kyromaki, a skilled carpenter, acquired additional land next to the motor court and moved a Finnish log cabin from rural St. Louis County to the site. The cabin, furnished with items that Esther Kyromaki imported from Finland, soon became a popular field trip destination for school children. A 1962 sale resulted in the removal of seven cabins, which were replaced by a four-unit motel. (The name change that occurred at this time—to Gardenwood Resort and Motel—has been maintained throughout two subsequent ownership transitions.) The current owners, Dan and Darcy Motschenbacher, purchased the business in 2002; identifying themselves as "stewards of the property," the couple believes that maintaining Gardenwood's "connection to the past is vital." To respect that history, the Motschenbachers discontinued TV and Wi-Fi service; encouraged outdoor cooking fires; and maintained the size, scale, and "quirky" features of the original cabins. And, perhaps most remarkably, the Elmgrens' original horseshoe-shaped auto court, although somewhat modified, is the only remaining example of such a layout on the entire North Shore.[53]

### Fish Fry Lodge (*now* McQuade Small Craft Harbor)

Intersection of North Shore Drive and McQuade Road

Also in Lakeview Township was Claude and Beatrice Midlam's Fish Fry Lodge, a very well-known North Shore establishment for almost four decades. Claude Midlam, from Oneida County, New York, arrived in Duluth during the mid-1920s, where he worked as a dairy products company salesman and a truck driver. He married Beatrice Borup, a teacher, in 1926—five years before they invested fifty dollars in opening the Fish Fry, a simple, shed-roofed diner that also had two nearby gas pumps. The business, by the late 1930s, had evolved into a "lodge" that included a restaurant, trailer camp, and twenty-four overnight and housekeeping cabins. The Midlams closed the Fish Fry during the latter years of World War II, but when the business reopened in 1946, the couple sought to attract young families by providing a miniature golf course, hayrides, and even free childcare. The restaurant also served as a beacon for motorists because it remained open eighteen hours a day throughout the tourist season. The menu featured fish from Lake Superior and Minnesota's inland lakes, but unlike in most diners and supper clubs, the Midlam's advertisements informed patrons that "NO BEER" was for sale. In 2016, more than seventy years after working as a summertime handyman around the lodge, cabins, and campground, Merle Norgren could still recollect the importance of Beatrice Midlam's business acumen and managerial skills in ensuring the Fish Fry's success. Especially vital, observed Norgren, was her ability to recruit and train the many female employees involved in operating the restaurant and cleaning the cabins.[54]

Both entrance roads that provided access to the restaurant and cabins were spanned by a skeletal-like log structure constructed of four tall, vertical posts and a pair of horizontal connecting poles. Diagonal and vertical braces, some with advertisements nailed to them, provided stability. A community fire alarm topped the northeastern entry, while the southwestern structure displayed a huge fish—for many years one of the North Shore's best-known roadside features.

**The Fish Fry Lodge entrance sign became a highly recognizable North Shore roadside attraction immediately after World War II. Next to the diner in the background is a long wagon, pulled by a mid-1930s International truck, which Claude Midlam used to provide his guests with hayrides.**

The Midlams closed the Fish Fry in 1968, thirty-seven years after its opening. The owners of Lakeview Castle, a nearby business, eventually purchased the property and operated its campground until 1999, a year before the former Fish Fry restaurant and a few vacant structures were reduced to ashes by vocational school trainees engaged in a firefighting exercise. (Ironically, the fire alarm formerly attached to one of the Fish Fry's entrance sign was no longer available to wail out a warning.) Removal of the buildings, however, was only the first step in an arduous and often contentious process that preceded construction of what became the McQuade Small Craft Harbor. Supporters of the project emphasized its envisioned contributions to small watercraft safety, given that the proposed location was about halfway between similar facilities at Duluth's Park Point to the southwest and Knife River to the northeast. Critics listed numerous concerns, including the environmental consequences, high monetary costs, and use of Congdon Trust land. Even Chester and Clara Congdon's great-granddaughter, Emily Ann Evera, who was residing in England, weighed in with her misgivings: any effort to remove control over land "given explicitly to the city in perpetuity," she wrote in 2001, "would clearly be wrong." Finally, after several state and local units of government hammered out an agreement, construction proceeded on the McQuade Small Craft Harbor, which opened in 2008. Almost a decade later, a Duluth Township supervisor commented that many local residents and officials may have not been ready to give McQuade their overwhelming approval but appeared to agree on one point: "the safe harbor did not turn out as badly as everyone feared." In 2019, however, when one breakwater required extensive repairs after suffering extensive damage from severe storms and rising lake levels, some early critics wryly commented that "their money is on the lake in the long run."[55]

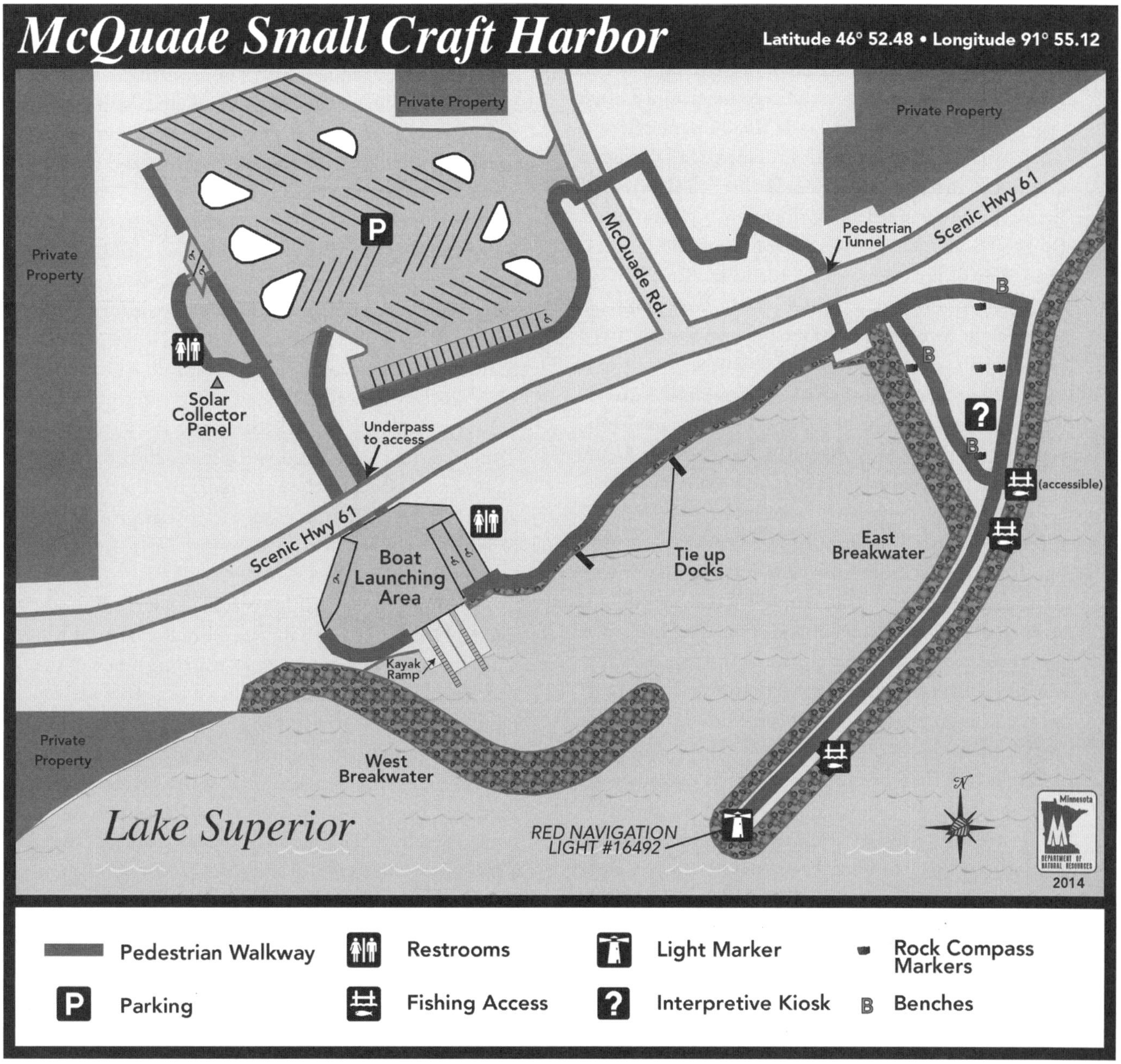


**The site plan for McQuade Small Craft Harbor, posted by the MDNR at the site.**

McQuade was Minnesota's first solar-powered boat landing and now provides boaters, anglers, and motorists with numerous services: a three-acre harbor for small craft, an almost equally large area for parking vehicles and boat trailers, fishing platforms, boat launching ramps, a pedestrian tunnel, information kiosks, and public restrooms.[56] Nevertheless, the magnitude and scale of McQuade's facilities, especially its huge, paved parking lot, can be somewhat jarring to first-time North Shore visitors who have just experienced Congdon Boulevard's intimate lakeshore waysides, spacious residential lots, and small tourist facilities, all of which stand before a backdrop of trees and vegetation.

## Duluth Township

The Duluth Township section of North Shore Scenic Drive, which is cosigned with St. Louis County Highway 61, begins at the McQuade Road intersection. Three small, unincorporated settlements, all dating to the nineteenth century—Clifton, French River, and Palmers—are located along the township's shoreline. By 1930, some 300 people, 115 of them immigrants, resided by or proximate to the roadway. Almost 90 percent (105) of the residents had Nordic backgrounds: thirty-eight Swedes, thirty-four Finland Swedes, twenty Norwegians, and thirteen Finns. No other sector of the North Shore included such a relatively similar distribution of the four Nordic groups. Duluth Township was, in fact, one of only a very few North Shore fishing districts where Norwegians did not predominate.[57]

Old North Shore Road, which also meanders through Duluth Township, proceeds northeastward between North Shore Drive and the Highway 61 Expressway before it is interrupted about one-half mile after the McQuade Road intersection. Thereafter Old North Shore Road continues along the expressway's northern flank until reaching Alseth Road, where it veers to the southern side and continues as far as the Lake County border.

At least thirty-five tourist-oriented establishments, along with several public and institutional structures and properties, and scores of fish houses, fish sales stands, and boathouses, have existed along or proximate to the Duluth Township section of Lake Superior's shoreline. A significant number of lakeshore properties were acquired by the City of Duluth at the time Chester Congdon was encouraging and financing their purchase during the early twentieth century. These sites are still owned and managed by the City of Duluth. The transformation of several small farms and undeveloped land parcels into residential sites was also under way by the mid-1950s. These changes, noted a *Duluth News-Tribune* reporter, were occurring because "the ideal suburban character of the area appealed to city dwellers intent on settling out of town." Well over one hundred of Duluth Township's residences currently access the lakeshore roadway, but its semirural character remains evident.[58] Ten businesses, one church, and a former federal fish hatchery (now owned by the MDNR) are located on the drive's upper side.

Duluth Township is also a noteworthy example of how a North Shore unit of government began resolving a number of long-standing environmental and pollution issues that had become especially severe and troublesome by the late twentieth century. Because many of the township's private shoreline septic systems had failed by this time, the granting of new building permits was banned until plans were developed to address the problem. A solution emerged with the formation, during the late 1990s, of the Duluth North Shore Sanitary District, an agency that would be funded with assessments on all homes and businesses located between the shoreline and the Highway 61 Expressway. The sewer line work, completed from 2001 to 2003, has been followed by the enactment of other township zoning and subdivision regulations that protect the township's many sensitive shoreline areas, wetlands, and stream banks.[59]

The Duluth Township section of North Shore Scenic Drive may not have the dramatic natural features that one experiences when traveling much of the shoreline between Two Harbors and the Canadian border. Nonetheless, the township does include several examples, both historical and contemporary, of the built environment that defines much of the North Shore. And, because the nearby expressway funnels off so much high-speed traffic, Duluth Township's section of Scenic Drive allows motorists to enjoy the North Shore at a safer and more leisurely tempo.

### Clifton

The intersection of North Shore Drive and McQuade Road identifies the western side of an early plat for the townsite of Clifton, one of several similar, and unsuccessful, ventures that arose during the North Shore's mid-nineteenth-century copper frenzy. The 1855 plat, which centered on the Talmadge River, was surveyed by Richard Reif, who filed the document one year later in Duluth's courthouse. Sponsored by Ohio land speculator John S. Watrous, the first speaker of Minnesota's House of Representatives during his single legislative term (1857–59), Clifton was intended to have seventy-two square blocks, eleven of them bordering on Lake Superior.

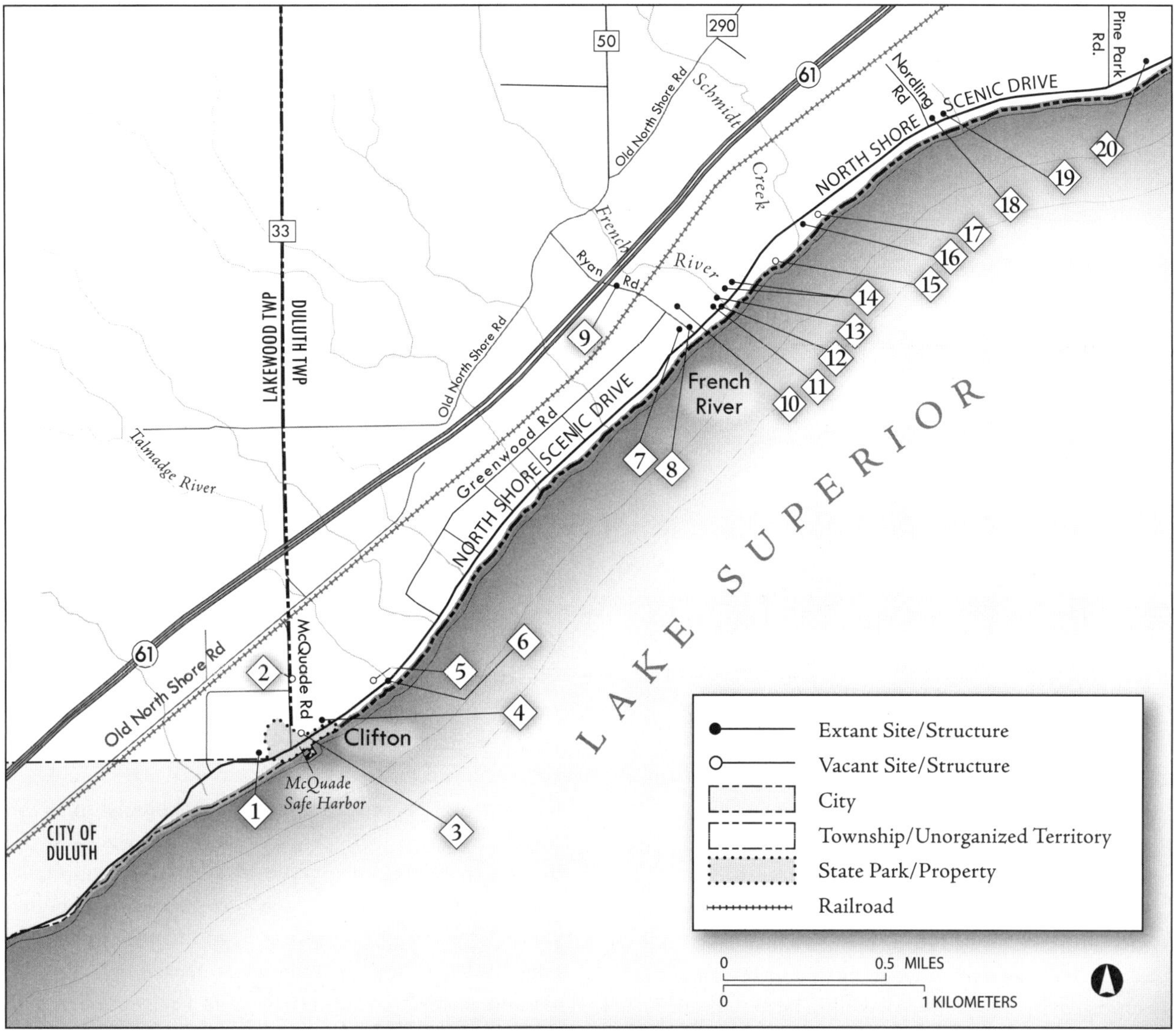


1 Gardenwood Resort and Motel
2 Boland's Lumber and Supply
3 Beachway Motel and Cabins
4 Clearwater Catering and Event Center and former Lakeview Castle
5 Forrest Inn
6 Talmadge River Bridge
7 Stromgren's Modern Motor Court*
8 Anderson's Store*
9 Clifton–French River Historical Marker
10 French River Lutheran Church
11 Snyder Log Cabin Residence
12 French River Bridge and Wayside Park
13 Lake Superior Fisheries–MN DNR
14 Chalet and Swissota Residences
15 Mattson Fishing Camp
16 Wonderland Tourist Court and Lodge*
17 Gilmore Comedy Theatre
18 Falk Boat Works and Nordic Inn*
19 New Scenic Café
20 Ironstone

*Now a private residence

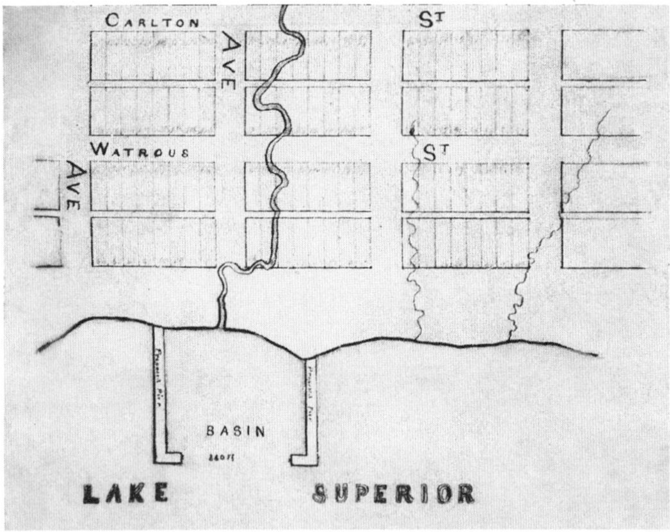


**The lower section of the unrealized mid-nineteenth-century townsite plat for Clifton reveals the large, protected harbor that was envisioned for the mouth of the Talmadge River. Courtesy of the Register of Deeds, St. Louis County, Duluth.**

(Watrous Street, of course, would have served as the primary lakeside road.) Each block was bisected by an alley and subdivided into sixteen 50-by-150-foot lots. But because no viable copper deposits were discovered in the nearby area, Clifton failed to advance beyond its status as a "paper town."[60]

In 1857, British émigré Scargall Wakelin, assisted by his brother Edwin, preempted the Clifton claim and developed a farm and logging operation along the Talmadge River. By 1886, Wakelin's farm had several cattle and horses and a "three-story hennery." He and his wife, Mary, also operated the Wakelin House, a forty-room Duluth hotel. British immigrants Smith and Hannah Croft, along with four of their children, later settled on Wakelin's farm before moving several miles northeast to a fishing camp at Stoney Point. Several of the Croft's twelve children would later play formative roles in establishing other North Shore settlements and enterprises.[61]

Clifton reemerged in 1886 when it became a stop on the new D&IR Railroad that connected Two Harbors and Duluth. Eventually, the Scott and Holsten Company built a railroad siding and section house for its log rafting and loading operations at Clifton. Anglers were also camping on the property by the late 1890s, the same time that Clifton received some consideration as a summer resort site. (The proposal was never initiated.) A small waiting station that appeared along the railroad tracks around 1917 was sold and moved elsewhere after passenger service ended in 1961.[62]

Another property that disappeared even earlier than the depot was the so-called Log Cabin University, where classes were offered to Clifton-area workers and farmers during the 1920s and 1930s. The school was inspired and funded by Russian immigrant Louis Hoffman, once described "as a pioneer friend, idealist inventor, green-thumbed gardener, and man of goodwill . . . [who makes] our communities better places in which to live."[63] Nothing remains of Hoffman's unique school today.

One distinctive business, a teahouse known as the Chateau, was opened in Clifton during the late 1930s by two of the North Shore's most cosmopolitan residents: Arthur and Madeleine (Ada) Neeb. Although little is known about the history of Ada Neeb, a native of France, her husband's background is easier to trace. Originally from the southeastern Minnesota community of Lewiston, Neeb received a medical degree before becoming a St. Paul pathologist in 1913. He met his future wife while serving with the U.S. military in France during World War I. The couple, following their 1920 marriage, moved to Minneapolis, where Neeb became a partner in an insurance company. By 1928, however, Neeb's professed love of "art and things" led to his career as a self-employed sculptor. During the latter 1930s and early 1940s, he taught a summer art course at Duluth State Teachers College and supervised several WPA art projects in northeastern Minnesota. It was at this time that the couple established their "elegant" Chateau tearoom in Clifton. Neeb's artwork and personally designed fine chinaware were on display in its two rooms, along with examples of "distinctive and functional furniture." Ada Neeb was in charge of the menu and food preparation. The Chateau's "atmosphere made it," declared Neeb in a 1954 interview. "It was different and there just wasn't anything quite like it on the North Shore at that time." Following America's entry into World War II, the Neebs sold their Chateau property and moved back to Minneapolis. (They would return to Duluth Township during the 1950s and develop another North Shore dining establishment—Shorewood Terrace.) Subsequent owners used the Chateau as a residence until it was torn down following a destructive storm and flood in June 2012. Several other buildings, most catering to motorists, also stood in Clifton until the early 2000s, when they were either removed or burned down to make way for the McQuade Safe Harbor walkway, pedestrian underpass, information kiosk, and overflow parking lot.[64]

### Boland's Lumber and Supply Company *(razed)*

#### Boland Drive–McQuade Road Intersection

A structure that once housed John W. Boland's lumber and supply company flanked the eastern side of McQuade Road until 2023. Boland, the son of German immigrants, had, by 1916, claimed a homestead and established a sizable logging operation in St. Louis County's Industrial Township. In 1920, he and his wife, Beatrice, were also operating a boardinghouse that served nineteen timber workers, a majority of them foreign-born. The couple moved, around 1924, to the state of Washington, where Boland worked as a logging contractor. He would return to Minnesota during the early 1930s, settle in Clifton, and establish a business that, until 1957, provided local contractors and residents with lumber, paint, and building supplies. All evidence of the unused structure was removed in 2023.[65]

### Midnight Ramble and Beachway Motel and Cabins *(vacant)*

#### 5119 North Shore Drive

Immediately east of the McQuade Road intersection is the site of what was the Midnight Ramble, a dance hall and "bring-your-own-bottle" supper club opened by two Black Duluth men sometime after Prohibition ended in 1930. A subsequent owner, during the early 1950s, converted the Ramble into an eight-unit motel, the Beachway, and also added six separate cabins to the property. When Marland ("Skip") and Shirley Hildebrandt acquired the Beachway in 1983, they already were managing another motel located along the South Shore of Lake Superior at Herbster, Wisconsin. Over the ensuing three decades, the Hildebrandts moved from their home in St. Bonifacius, Minnesota, to the Beachway, where they resided from May through October, and also made brief, daily trips to oversee the Herbster property. They undoubtedly were the only North Shore business owners whose business cards could advertise a distinctive facet of Lake Superior's geography: "See the sunrise on the North Shore. Watch the sunset on the South Shore."[66]

Until 2015, the Beachway remained a throwback to the mom-and-pop businesses of previous decades. The Hildebrandts had made some improvements to their property during the early 2000s in response to Duluth Township's increasingly stringent sanitary regulations, but the motel retained its paper-thin

**Until it was razed in 2023, John Boland's long-vacant lumber and building supply company served as a lonely reminder of several businesses that once existed along or proximate to the Duluth Township section of North Shore Scenic Drive.**

walls, sloping floors, antiquated plumbing fixtures, dim lights, makeshift heating system, and office cluttered with years of accumulated brochures, notes, receipts, photographs, and other paraphernalia. Some tourists and travelers certainly found the Beachway's motel and cabins too basic, too small, and too outdated for their tastes, but other patrons who returned year after year, some for more than two decades, termed it charming, rustic, cozy, homey, and "the best bargain on the North Shore." A 2014 California guest admitted that her Beachway cabin may have been "a bit run down" but also described the interior as "cute and comfortable" and "all you need."[67]

Although Hildebrandt expressed uncertainty about the Beachway's future in 2013, he reflected on the positive attributes of pursuing a North Shore business. "The Beachway never made us rich," he confided, "but all the work has been worth it because of the people who return year after year." To him, the Beachway's regular guests were members of the couple's extended family. The eighty-one-year-old Hildebrandt died in May 2016, just days before the opening of Minnesota's fishing season. The Beachway operated only intermittently that year, but in 2017, his resolute widow returned to the site, where she oversaw the razing of the antiquated motel and construction of a new two-story building on the former foundation. Because of sanitary and environmental issues, however, Duluth Township officials soon shut down all construction activities. The incomplete building, its exterior still covered with eroding construction paper during the mid-2020s, remained a stark reminder of an unrealized North Shore dream.[68]

### Lakeview Castle (*now* Clearwater Catering and Event Center)
#### 5135 North Shore Drive

Proximate to the early Midnight Ramble was a "modern cabin court" that Duluthian Harry Fagel, the son of Russian Jewish immigrant parents, opened in 1933. Fagel, soon joined by his new wife, Laura, claimed that each of the Castle's patrons was treated "like a King." Serving as the centerpiece of Fagel's business was the Lakeview Castle, which exhibited some elements of the 1930s streamline moderne style, namely, a horizontal building form; rounded walls at each end of the structure; minimal ornamentation; a flat roof with an

**Harry and Laura Fagel's Lakeview Castle, shown here during the early 1940s, displayed a number of streamline moderne features. Parked in front of the Castle is a late-1930s Chevrolet. Courtesy of Alvine Sternberg Shatto.**

edge defined by a thin band of contrasting material; smooth, white wall surfaces; and vertical window openings, accentuated by a steel framework of linear bands that wrapped around the building. A pyramidal dome capped the Castle's entrance tower.[69]

Fagel closed the Castle in 1958, one year before Frederick and Daphne Sternberg purchased the property. Sternberg—born in Germany, raised on an Otter Tail County farm in west central Minnesota, and a decorated veteran of World War II—married Daphne Tembeli in 1948, shortly after she arrived in Minnesota from Greece. (Her sister, the wife of Sternberg's best friend, served as matchmaker.) A few years later, the couple and their young son and daughter, Andrew and Alvine, settled on a small Clover Valley farm in Duluth Township, where they supported themselves by selling eggs and Greek cheese.[70]

The Sternbergs made several changes to the Castle following their 1959 purchase of the property and also built a motel and residence nearby. After they replaced the main building with an entirely new structure in 1978–79, the Sternbergs' version of Lakeview Castle emerged as one of the North Shore's largest restaurant and dining facilities. Duluth architect Ray Blesener offered structural and design assistance, but Sternberg provided many of the conceptual ideas for the Castle's "touch of royalty," namely, its two huge, rock-faced

**Some twenty years after their 1959 purchase of the Lakeview Castle, Frederick and Daphne Sternberg constructed this new building on the original site. The rock wall and a nonfunctional drawbridge were later removed and replaced with an outdoor deck.**

fireplace chimneys; three large dormers; and low rock wall and faux drawbridge at the entrance. When completed, the structure's twenty-five thousand square feet of interior space included a stage for musical performances, a lounge that seated as many as 130 customers, and a dining room for 250 people. The Castle could simultaneously accommodate several events, including wedding and birthday parties, high school proms, class reunions, and small conferences. A deejay who appeared at the Castle during the 1970s and 1980s later recalled its "glamorous" interior, "large gleaming dance floor," and "good shows." But most memorable, he noted, were the "quasi-famous local celebrities and their various trophy wives and hangers-on," all of whom made the Castle a "very fancy, high-class destination for dressed-up Duluthians."[71]

The Sternbergs' children acquired the Castle in 1985 and managed the business until 2003. The changes made to the Castle by another buyer in 2010 included replacing some of the "medieval" rooms with a "lighter and brighter look" and changing its name to the Clearwater Grill, Red Swan Catering & Event Center. The business closed in 2021 during the height of the Covid-19 outbreak, and has, since its subsequent reopening, focused on catered events.[72]

### Talmadge River Bridge

The six-mile-long Talmadge River is named for pioneer Josiah Talmadge, who settled at a nearby location in 1856. Because the gorge carved through the river's bedrock is relatively narrow, the first highway bridge, constructed in 1922, was only forty feet long. Designed by MDH engineers, the single-barrel arch of the reinforced concrete structure also displayed considerable ornamental stonework. When the bridge was widened from nineteen to thirty feet in 1951, metal railings with minimal art deco details replaced the original concrete, open-panel railings. Galvanized steel guardrails were added several years later as a safety measure.[73]

### Forrest Inn *(razed)*

#### Both Sides of the Talmadge River

Once adjacent to the Talmadge River was a "roadhouse," called the Forrest Inn, which Herbert and Anna Forrest opened during the 1930s. Because of Forrest's demanding work schedule as a locomotive engineer for the D&IR Railroad, his wife oversaw the restaurant, tavern, and dance floor, all of which made the inn a popular local hangout for several years. A number of cabins were also located on each side of the river. The inn burned down in 2005, and just one cabin remains on the property.[74]

### French River

The transition to the unincorporated settlement of French River begins only a few miles northeast of Clifton. Located in the area is a thirteen-mile-long river known as Angwassago-zibi (Floodwood River) to the

Anishinaabe and as the Rivière des Français to the French. When surveying the Lake Superior coastline from 1848 to 1850, geologist Joseph G. Norwood claimed that the area revealed evidence of the best copper vein on the North Shore. He also reported that a mining company agent had already built a few cabins close to the creek's mouth, "for the purpose of securing a pre-emption claim to the veins which occur here." While the claim was quickly abandoned, two families were still ensconced in well-built dwellings prior to ratification of the 1854 La Pointe Treaty.[75]

Prospectors, surveyors, and speculators descended on French River once the North Shore was officially opened to settlement. The Panic of 1857 brought all activities to an end, but a revived demand for copper during the Civil War saw the French River Mining Company undertake extensive explorations in 1863. Although these ventures also proved unsuccessful, several "abandoned shafts, artesian flows, and shallow pits now overgrown with trees, but marked unmistakably by nearby waste piles," remain faintly evident within the current landscape.[76]

It was commercial fishing, not mining, that led to the establishment of a permanent settlement at French River. Once the site became a D&IR Railroad stop in 1886, an adjacent station house, boardinghouse, and post office were built at the point where Ryan Road now crosses the tracks. Timber cutting, much of it undertaken by the Lesure Lumber Company, provided more employment opportunities from the 1890s to the early 1920s. Nordic immigrants who established inland farms during the early twentieth century would, over time, come to share a common identity with the fishing families who resided along the shore. The completion of Minnesota Highway 1 also led to the establishment of several businesses that catered to tourists. Except for the railroad tracks and bridge, relatively little evidence of early French River remains today.

### Stromgren's Modern Motor Court *(razed, now private residences)*
### 5335 North Shore Road

Motorists who drove northeastward on Highway 61 during the 1950s knew they were approaching French River when the Idle-A-While Cabins came into view. Although Idle-A-While closed quickly, Stromgren's Modern Motor Court, located nearby, had a longer tenure. Located just west of the Ryan Road–Scenic Drive intersection, the cabins sat on farmland that Swedish immigrants Gust and Garda Larson Stromgren had cleared around 1910. The couple's daughter and son-in-law, Myrtle and Henning Carlson, opened the tourist facility shortly after World War II. Although laid out as a motor court, the cabins were placed only along two sides of its U-shaped road. The central open space offered a clear view of Lake Superior and served as the location for a business office and large playground. The buildings were moved away when Stromgren's closed during the 1960s; part of the site was later converted to residential use.[77]

### French River Motel and Anderson's Store *(razed, now a private residence)*
### 5339 North Shore Road

Carl R. and Ethel Bergquist Anderson, who moved from Duluth to French River, opened a pair of two-unit tourist cabins at the intersection of Ryan Road and North Shore Drive in 1941. The couple also oversaw a small store that included their residence and two second-floor rental apartments; elsewhere on the property were a few buildings that Anderson used for his bulk petroleum delivery business. Although the grocery store and gasoline pumps were a well-known North Shore stop, the Andersons closed their business during the 1960s, some years before the buildings were destroyed by a 1972 fire. A private home now occupies the site.[78]

### French River Lutheran Church
### 5310 Ryan Road

French River Lutheran Church, a prominent landmark, stands slightly north of the Andersons' former business site. The roots of the church date to 1924, when local Swedes and Finland Swedes organized the Immanuel Swedish Evangelical Lutheran Congregation of French River. The members of Bethel Lutheran Church, a large congregation of Finland Swedes from West Duluth, assisted in building the initial French River edifice, located four miles north of the railroad tracks. Services were soon held in the partially finished building, even though a shortage of funds delayed its completion for a decade. Finally, after years of serving their "famous fish dinners"—an event "anticipated by

**Carl and Ethel Anderson's store and motel, looking northward along Ryan Road during the late 1950s or early 1960s. Prominently displayed in front of the two Skelly gasoline pumps is a free-standing telephone booth—a common feature once provided by many small North Shore businesses. To the north are Anderson's motel units and the French River Lutheran Church.**

people for miles around"—the "ladies" of Immanuel Lutheran raised sufficient funds to complete the church, which was dedicated in 1944.[79]

Soon after World War II ended, the congregation's membership gave their approval to the construction of a new church that would be located closer to Highway 61. Designed by the Duluth architectural firm of Melander and Fugelso, the church was dedicated in 1957, but only after volunteers once again devoted countless hours of work to its completion. Additions and several remodeling projects have expanded the structure, which now has some 320 members—making it the North Shore's largest rural congregation. Ironically, Bethel Lutheran, its West Duluth "mother church," closed in 1989 because of a sharp decline in congregational numbers.[80]

### Clifton–French River Historical Marker
Intersection of Ryan Road and Highway 61 Expressway

North of the church and railroad tracks is a free-standing lectern-style marker similar in appearance to a speaker's platform or pulpit. The inscription on its attached plaque describes Clifton's unrealized 1855 townsite plat, the unsuccessful efforts to find merchantable copper deposits in the French River area from 1864 to 1866, and the major logging operations that started during the 1880s. The tan, roughly cut limestone marker, designed in 1959 by MDH engineers, was built one year later by members of Minnesota's Youth Conservation Commission and restored during the early 2000s.[81]

### Edward C. and Mary Snyder Log Cabin Residence
5345 North Shore Drive

One of the North Shore's most distinctive log cabins, a prefabricated structure built for Edward and Mary Snyder, arose on a lot overlooking Lake Superior and the French River in 1934. Snyder, a Pennsylvania native, resided in Texas before his 1889 move to Two Harbors, where he found work as a D&IR fireman and locomotive engineer. In 1913, Snyder married Mary Seaman of Duluth, who, from 1924 to 1932, served as the boardinghouse matron in a Two Harbors "teacherage."[82]

The Snyders purchased their prefabricated building from the Page and Hill Company of Minneapolis, which, in 1930, had hired architect Chilson D. Aldrich to design a number of prototypical cabin plans for inclusion in catalogs the firm distributed throughout the

United States. Aldrich, two years earlier, had received nationwide recognition for his book, *The Real Log Cabin*—a volume that demonstrated how the combination of beauty and prime building materials could produce functional and aesthetically pleasing structures for a generation of young urban residents who believed they had "lost much by not being pioneers." Asserting that "the genuine American is going back to the good old ancestral custom . . . [of] building himself a log cabin away from the honks of man," Aldrich believed that achieving this goal required the skills of both an architect and a woodsman. "Beauty of structure must harmonize with the sturdy material in which it is wrought," he wrote.[83]

Page and Hill not only provided their clients with an Aldrich plan but also supplied the western red cedar logs, as well as the doors, windows, hardware, and built-in cupboards. A trained log builder supervised the local construction crew. Unlike the handcrafted log walls of most North Shore buildings, Page and Hill provided logs that were mechanically "milled top and bottom with grooves to receive [a] spline"; a majority of the company's cabins displayed saddle notches with jagged, protruding ends. The east–west axis of the T-shaped floor plan included the kitchen, bedroom, and bathroom. A trapdoor offered access to the partial basement, constructed of poured concrete, where the furnace and hot water heater were located. Extending southward was the dining room and living room wing. A rustic fireplace, beautifully crafted of local stone by a North Shore mason, graced one living room wall; an upright window with thirty panes of glass afforded a view of Lake Superior.[84]

The 1936 Page and Hill catalog included a testimonial from an obviously pleased Mary Snyder, two years after she and her family had moved into the cabin. "We marveled when the temperature registered 44° below zero, to find ourselves so snug and warm," she wrote. "Without a doubt we have been more comfortable in our log house these last two winters than in any home we have been in during the winters in Minnesota. . . . And, in summer it is just as comfortable, always cool."[85]

Despite its modest size, the cabin had a relatively high valuation of $7,500 in 1940. The couple resided in their cabin for a total of seventeen years, until Mary Snyder's 1951 passing. Her widowed husband remained there until ill health forced him to leave some months before his 1958 death. The Snyders' son and daughter-in-law moved into the cabin one year later and remained there until 1971, when it was sold. During the 1980s, another owner attached a poorly built pine log bedroom to the eastern wall of the living room—an action that resulted in sawing off some log corner log extensions and covering a lower exterior section of the fireplace chimney.[86]

Current owners Mike Lazaretti and Tim Counts of Minneapolis purchased the cabin in 1993. They later contracted with two log builder/historic preservation specialists who brought "the cabin back to life" by going over "every inch inside and out." The contractors rebuilt

**The Snyder log cabin after its restoration under the current owners' direction. Photograph by Tim Counts, 2014.**

**The outstanding interior log and stone details of the Snyder cabin are clearly evident today. Photograph by Tim Counts, 2018.**

the 1980s addition with western red cedar logs that matched the original material and building style; replaced the missing log extensions; removed and restored all of the windows, doors, and hardware; and carefully crafted replacements for any broken or deteriorated features. The project's success was recognized in 2016 by the Duluth Preservation Alliance, which lauded Lazaretti and Counts for their efforts to restore and maintain the "cozy log cabin."[87]

### French River Bridge and Wayside Park

A reinforced concrete arch bridge, designed and built by the MDH, opened at the French River's mouth in 1921. The only open-spandrel bridge on the North Shore, the span's two curved concrete cribs and classical revival style railings were similar to a number of much larger Twin Cities–area structures that crossed the Mississippi River. A major 1951 remodeling of the French River Bridge, which added a third rib to its southern side, resulted in the expansion of its deck width from nineteen to thirty feet. Almost seventy years later, in 2019, St. Louis County's Public Works Department announced that the bridge required immediate attention because of numerous structural deficiencies. The agency's initial proposal, which called for the rehabilitation of its existing structure, was quickly shelved when the costs were deemed excessive. A public hearing also revealed that local citizens favored a replacement that did not mimic the former structure; instead, they expressed a strong preference for the "sense of security . . . and fresh new look" that a more contemporary bridge would provide. The $5 million concrete-beam, single-span bridge, with a twenty-two-foot-high, boulder-lined retaining wall, opened in late 2020—almost a century after the former structure's dedication. Extensive erosion control measures were also carried out on the nearby wayside, which had been heavily damaged by the relentless pounding of Lake Superior's storms and high waves.[88]

**French River Bridge and Wayside Park includes this a modernist structure that opened in 2021, and was designed by Aune Fernandez Landscape Architects of St. Paul; the wayside includes interpretive panels, an observation platform, and an easily accessible parking area. Photograph by Marlene Wisuri, 2023.**

### Lake Superior State Fish Hatchery and French River Cold Water Hatchery (*now* Minnesota Department of Natural Resources Duluth Area Fisheries)

5351 North Shore Drive

In early 1913, Minnesota legislators began discussing the possibilities of providing funding for a fish hatchery at the mouth of the French River. The new facility, proponents argued, would include "all necessary buildings, equipment, machinery, plant, conduits, dams, and apparatus, grounds, and dwellings requisite for the cultivation and propagation of fish and everything necessary to properly maintain and operate the same in the best and most efficient manner." Work began in 1918 after $30,000 was appropriated for the land and property. The hatchery opened one year later but was superseded by a larger structure in 1928. A major 1974–75 expansion resulted in the construction of several additional structures and facilities that emerged just north of the original facility. The enlarged complex was renamed the French River Cold Water Hatchery at this time.[89]

Throughout its early history, the hatchery's work was devoted to raising Chinook and Atlantic salmon; brook, brown, and lake trout; walleyes; northern pike; muskies; and catfish. All of these programs were discontinued decades ago. The focus, in 2007, shifted entirely to the production of two rainbow trout (*Oncorhynchus mykiss*) varieties: steelheads and Kamloops (the latter are also known as loopers). Steelheads, introduced from the Pacific Ocean into Lake Superior's rivers during the 1880s, quickly "naturalized" and thrived in the new environment.

**The original Lake Superior State Fish Hatchery, constructed close to the mouth of the French River in 1919, was replaced by this building in 1928. Photograph by Harold Youngren, 1930.**

Their numbers, however, declined drastically during the 1950s because of lamprey predation and overfishing. An effort to make up for the shortfall occurred in 1976, when Pacific Kamloops trout were introduced into Lake Superior, where they thrived and proved highly popular among anglers. The restocking program, nevertheless, was terminated in 2017 after numerous studies revealed that the wild steelheads' reproductive capabilities had been diluted, likely because of interbreeding with the Kamloops. It is anticipated that without a hatchery breeding program, the Kamloops will soon disappear from Lake Superior.[90]

French River Hatchery managers, by the early 2000s, faced a host of problems associated with an aging physical plant, equipment maintenance, and staffing reductions. The facility, reported one manager, "was held together with baling wire and duct tape." A 2013 study estimated that renovation costs would approach $8 million, while the funding of a fully staffed hatchery might require an annual budget of $700,000. Although Lake Superior sportfishing aficionados enthusiastically favored the upgrade, MDNR officials, in late 2016, announced the closing of the French River facility and its conversion into an egg-taking station for the agency's Crystal Springs Hatchery, located in southeastern Minnesota. Now, after hatching occurs at French River, the steelhead fry are sent to Crystal Springs until the age of one year; they are then brought back to the French River and imprinted to the stream. The steelheads spend the next three years in Lake Superior before returning to the French River, where they spawn. Licensed anglers who fish for steelheads may keep as many as three hatchery specimens, which are identifiable by their previously removed adipose fin.[91]

### Chalet and Swissota Residences
5359 and 5363 North Shore Drive

On the French River's eastern side is a pair of unique North Shore houses, the Swissota and the Chalet, both designed by John Mueller, an industrial chemist who had received some architectural training in his native Switzerland before immigrating to the United States in 1910. From 1913 to 1919, while employed on various Great Lakes iron ore carriers, Mueller discovered the attractions of Duluth. Vowing to make the city his home, Mueller soon returned to Duluth, where he worked as a paint and varnish specialist for the Marshall–Wells Company from 1921 to 1923. He then departed the city and eventually started his own lacquer and varnish company in Chicago Heights, Illinois. During the 1930s, Mueller once again began making trips to Duluth and soon purchased land by the French River, where he supervised the construction of a residence named the Swissota. In 1940, following the death of his first wife, Mueller married Winifred Gibson of Duluth; within two years, he would transfer the company to nearby Superior and move his family into the still-unfinished Swissota residence.[92]

In 1946, Earl Finberg, the *Duluth News-Tribune*'s building editor, described the completed French River house, one and a half stories high with three single-story wings, as "a North Shore log lodge patterned on Swiss models." Three wings that faced toward the east, south, and west gave the Muellers and their three children "a chance to follow the sun throughout the day," whereas the flat roof of the eastern wing, accessible from the second floor, offered unobstructed views of Lake Superior.[93]

By late 1943, Mueller was also supervising construction of the Chalet, a larger residence situated slightly west of the Swissota. Built of local stone and wood, the Chalet incorporated several Swiss style architectural features that had become popular in the United States at the turn of the twentieth century: gabled roofs with wide eaves, exposed roof brackets, decorative balconies, and carved entry posts. The Swissota was sold around May 1950, when the Mueller family, including their five children, relocated into the still-incomplete Chalet. From 1953 to 1955, Mueller's work as a textile lacquer and adhesives specialist caused the family, on two different occasions, to move between Duluth and Belleville, Illinois; nevertheless, he was able to oversee the Chalet's completion during these years.

**The Swissota, *right*, and the just-completed Chalet, *left*, early 1950s. The small rocks atop the Chalet's roof, a traditional Swiss practice, were soon removed for safety reasons. Courtesy of Jackie Mueller.**

Following Mueller's unexpected 1955 death, however, his widow sold the Chalet, thereby ending the family's connection to the French River area.[94]

Joe and Beth Alpert, who had acquired the Swissota in 1952, eventually added a two-room motel onto its eastern wing and later constructed two separate buildings, each with four motel units, on the grounds. Following the sale of Alpert's Motel in 1976, the Swissota transitioned into a well-known tearoom before it once again became a private residence. Because of major changes made to the Swissota over many decades, only a few of its interior details maintain John Mueller's original design intent. Subsequent purchasers of the Chalet, however, preserved much more of the original building, which also has served as a bed and breakfast business.[95]

### Louis, Selma, and Hjalmar Mattson Fishing Camp *(razed)*

Northeast of the French River outlet to Lake Superior

Little material evidence remains of the numerous fishing camps that were once found in the French River area. Some early occupants never secured title to the land they occupied, while others surrendered their property after it was condemned and purchased for inclusion in the Congdon Trust. A number of these sites have now remained free of development for almost a century.

One noteworthy fishing camp was established northeast of the French River by Finland Swedes Louis and Selma Bergendahl Mattson. After engaging in commercial fishing at Grand Marais, Isle Royale, and Duluth, Mattson was able to acquire the land in 1906. During September of that year, Selma Mattson and the family's four children, accompanied by a friend, departed Duluth for the French River railway stop. From there they walked to the small cabin that Mattson had constructed along the Lake Superior shoreline. Two neighbors, using a sailboat, soon transported the family's belongings, as well as a cabin door and pair of small windows, to the site. During their early years of residence, the Mattsons' team of horses hauled wicker baskets, filled with smoked fish, to buyers in Duluth. Later, a freight boat picked up as much as one and a half tons of fish that were packed into wooden boxes and kegs.[96]

**Louis Mattson chose, following his wife's 1918 death, to have her family name incised into its surface—an unusual practice for that era. The gravestone is in Duluth Township's Lakeview Cemetery, located along Old North Shore Road.**

Four more children were born in the cabin between 1907 and 1916. The family, however, experienced tragedy during the 1918 influenza epidemic when Selma Mattson died, leaving her husband as the sole parent of six daughters and two sons ranging in age from two to sixteen years. Inez, the oldest child and a surrogate mother for the other children, would quickly become, said her father, the "best hired hand he ever had"—both in the house and at the fishery. Mattson's sons, Hjalmar and Ted, assumed responsibility for all fishing operations during the 1930s, but their partnership ended in 1941 when Ted entered the U.S. Army. He was killed on the Italian battlefront during summer 1944 and buried in an American military cemetery near Florence.[97]

Louis and Hjalmer Mattson continued working at the family's fishing camp following the death of their son and brother. Mattson's Deep Sea Fishing business provided tourists and residents with powerboats, tackle, guides, and "speed-boat rides," while the fresh, frozen, and smoked fish they sold could be packed and shipped "to any location in the United States." The elder Mattson, bedridden with a broken hip for several years, died at home in 1958. Hjalmar, already termed a "genius" by some neighbors and acquaintances, was often featured in the pages of the *Duluth News-Tribune*. The newspaper's reporters and photographers were drawn to the quiet, unassuming, amiable, and sometimes idiosyncratic bachelor's musings; to his well-crafted boat, the *Rosebud*; and to Tipper, Mattson's obedient German shepherd. Nothing, however, drew more attention than his inventions, including "Mattson's Monster," a combination road grader and snowplow built of Chevrolet, Ford, and International Truck

**Hjalmar Mattson's dog, Tipper, waits patiently for the entrails of a fish that is being cleaned by his master. Courtesy of the *Duluth News-Tribune*, Cosmopolitan, 11 January 1948, 1.**

parts. Even more impressive was a dredge, powered by a Bucyrus–Erie engine salvaged from an Iron Range mine and anchored with cables to several nearby trees and six upturned car frames that had been welded together. Another "peculiar-looking contraption," termed both an iceboat and a snowmobile by Mattson, had an automobile motor (later replaced by a five-cylinder air-cooled airplane engine) with an attached propeller. Used "for fun and for checking the nets set on ice," Mattson reportedly attained a speed of eighty miles per hour on the frozen lake, although steering was somewhat counterintuitive because shifting the propeller to the right forced the machine toward the left.[98]

Because of the rapid decline in commercial fishing activities that occurred during the 1950s and early 1960s, Mattson started pursuing seasonal work as a Duluth boat mechanic—even while continuing to tinker with his inventions. One, a "smelt trawler," was intended to sort the fish by size: after a net trapped the smelt at the front of his boat, a wheel pulled the catch onto the deck, where the fish dropped into different-sized compartments. Mattson, nevertheless, could not use the trawler because it failed to receive approval from MDC officials. By 1977, the grounds of Mattson's fishery, still visible to motorists who traveled along Highway 61, had "the look of the old and rusty—cars, trucks, boats, shacks and an assortment of gadgets that appear to be out of the Depression era." While Mattson's "junk" probably did not offer "a pretty site" to most motorists, wrote *Duluth News-Tribune* reporter Jim Blubaugh, the accumulation represented "a story of functionalism, inventiveness, and thrift." To those "connoisseurs of the old and junky," Blubaugh concluded, "Mattson's yard may be a thing of beauty."[99]

Mattson departed his French River domain for a Duluth assisted-living facility in 1996, where he died in late December 1998, just three days shy of his eighty-seventh birthday. Eventually, when trees and vegetation totally blocked the highway view, knowledge of Mattson's unique environment faded from the collective memory of North Shore residents. Scavengers and the surging water and ice of Lake Superior subsequently removed much of the fishing and industrial landscape that Mattson had created along the Lake Superior shoreline, but some steel and concrete elements still provide evidence of his hardy and inventive spirit. Springtime anglers, among them Hjalmar Mattson's great-great-grandniece and great-great-grandnephew, also continue casting for coho salmon from the shoreline.[100]

**The mine engine that once powered Hjalmar Mattson's dredge was still evident on his former property in 2016.**

### Wonderland Tourist Court and Lodge *(razed, now a residence)*

5384 North Shore Drive

For several decades, the North Shore's first grouping of shoreline cabins appeared about seven miles beyond Duluth's eastern boundary. There, in 1938–39, Osmund (O. E.) Thompson opened a real estate sales office and store on land that had been harvested of its timber by the Lesure Lumber Company in 1895. Thompson, in 1902, at the age of sixteen, immigrated from Norway with his parents to Minnesota's Vermilion Range. He would later attend a Duluth business college, work as a jitney driver, and eventually serve as a leader in the Scandinavian Local of the Duluth Socialist Party; he also was heavily involved in Minnesota Farmer-Labor Party politics and mounted three unsuccessful Duluth mayoral campaigns. Thompson did, however, receive an appointment from Minnesota's Farmer-Labor governor Floyd B. Olson to serve as a dairy and food inspector and district supervisor for Minnesota's Department of Agriculture during the 1930s. He and his second wife, Johanna, also rented out tourist cabins, some of which had been originally built for Lesure Company employees. The Thompsons' unassuming tourist facility, and their two subdivision plats situated along both sides of Highway 61, were collectively called "Wonderland."[101]

Thompson's firm, North Shore Real Estate, was still selling lakeshore and highway frontage for homes and businesses during the late 1950s. By this time, his son and daughter-in-law, Vernard and Elvie Thompson, were running the Wonderland Tourist Court, which extended for five hundred feet along the Lake Superior shoreline. The Wonderland's cabins, all provided with "electric refrigeration and picture windows," were available for moderate rates. Because very limited space was available between the highway and the lakeshore, the twenty-two cabins were arranged in an irregular pattern. Also crowded on the property was a lodge that had a dance hall, bar, restaurant, and dining room with space for large numbers of patrons.[102]

**Unlike most North Shore motor and tourist courts that appeared on the upper side of North Shore Drive, the Wonderland was built along a constricted parcel of Lake Superior shoreline.**

Jack and Joan Bates purchased the Wonderland in 1968, but the Thompsons maintained ownership of the lodge for several years before it burned down in 1974. The guests who patronized the resort over the next three decades could select from three cabin types—rustic-primitive, semimodern, and modern—which reflected the period and quality of construction as well as the availability of furnishings and facilities. The rustic-primitive units had exposed ceiling joists and wall studs, a propane gas plate stove, an old refrigerator, and a black-and-white television set; because no indoor water or plumbing were available, guests used a common shower room for dishwashing and "personal" needs. The semimodern units had a few improvements, while the ten modern cabins were insulated and included a commode, shower, gas stove, newer refrigerator, and color television set. The Wonderland, recalled one former patron, was "known and cherished for its rustic nature" and also served as "a tradition for many families." After the Bates family ended their thirty-year-long affiliation with Wonderland in 1998, an ensuing owner kept a few creekside cabins for personal use, razed the remaining buildings, and constructed a large private residence on the site.[103]

**The Gilmore Comedy Theatre (later Theatre 61) brought a sense of Broadway sophistication to the North Shore during each summer from 1949 to 1957.**

### Gilmore Comedy Theatre *(moved)*

Immediately east of 5384 North Shore Drive

Slightly beyond the former Wonderland property is a row of three lakeside residences. At the eastern end of the row was a fourth structure, removed many years ago, its form and function quite unusual for the North Shore—a forty-by-eighty-foot Quonset building that accommodated the Gilmore Comedy Theatre from 1949 to 1957. Paul Gilmore, a well-known Broadway stage actor who began his career during the 1890s and was a pioneer in the American motion picture industry, established the comedy theater, which typically operated from mid-July to mid-October. Both he and his daughter Virginia Gilmore, also a performer, had visited Duluth on several occasions during previous summers in their search for hay fever relief. When

***As Husbands Go*, a comedy by Rachel Crothers, was performed on Broadway in 1931, filmed as a movie in 1934, and presented at the Gilmore Theatre in September 1949. *Duluth Visitor*, 1–15 September 1949, 19.**

announcing his plans for the theater, Gilmore claimed that the hundred-seat facility would serve as an example of "modern architecture." By "modern," Gilmore was referring to the more than 150,000 Quonset buildings that, over the span of a few earlier years during World War II, had been produced by American military manufacturers.[104]

The Gilmores' intention—to produce "legitimate plays, which have been Broadway hits"—came to fruition when a popular comedy, *This Thing Called Love*, was performed in July 1949. The play was a "great success," claimed one Duluth reviewer, "which indicates a good season for the cozy little Quonset theater just beyond French River." The second play, offered during the first two weeks of August, was an English comedy, *The Bishop Misbehaves*, whereas the next two weeks were devoted to *Angel Street*, a "Victorian thriller in three acts." Early September featured *As Husbands Go*, a Broadway play the Gilmores had performed during the winter season at the Cherry Lane Theatre in New York's Greenwich Village. The ambitious 1949 season was extended into mid-October with the addition of a fifth offering, *Family Upstairs*.[105]

Plays were presented for the next five years, but problems associated with advancing age and poor health forced the eighty-two-year-old actor and impresario to sell his theater prior to the 1955 season. Three Twin Cities men, after purchasing the Gilmores' venue, employed Actors Company of New York performers, who presented several plays, including *Tovarich*, a French comedy, and Oscar Wilde's *The Importance of Being Earnest*. The 1957 and final season, performed in the renamed Theatre 61, featured two nationally acclaimed plays: *Anastasia* and *Bus Stop*. The vacant Quonset building was removed from the North Shore not long after theatrical activities ended. Only a concrete slab marks the site today.[106]

### Falk Boat Works *(razed)* and the Nordic Inn *(now a private residence)*
5451 and 5457 North Shore Drive

At one time, at least five cabin businesses, all on the highway's upper side, were situated immediately northeast of the Wonderland and the Gilmore. Still operating as a commercial property in the former North Star Motel and Restaurant is the heavily remodeled Spinnaker Inn (5427 North Shore Drive), a small apartment complex. At the intersection of Scenic Drive and Nordling Road—named for early Swedish farmers Carl Sr. and Anna Nordling—and close to the eastern limits of the French River settlement were two businesses, both dating to the 1940s: Falk Boat Works and the Nordic Inn.

Albin Falk, a skilled patternmaker, built cedar fishing boats on the site, while his son, Roderick, maintained the tradition and business into the 1990s. The Falks' house still remains, but the boat works is gone. Immediately east of Falk's was the Nordic Inn, where visitors were offered "modern heated rooms," although greatest attention was given to preparing and serving fine food. Because no alcoholic beverages were allowed, the dining area was termed "a nice place for the family." The Nordic also sought to attract the Gilmore's theatergoers with a simple rhyme—"Just before or after the show, this is the place to go." The business closed many years ago, and the building was converted into a private family residence.[107]

### Johnson's Drive-In (*now the* New Scenic Café)
### 5461 North Shore Drive

Close to the former Nordic Inn is a building that began as a 1952 fast-food emporium and subsequently experienced several iterations before it was transformed into the current New Scenic Café, "a beloved place to eat" and one of the premier restaurants of the North Shore and Minnesota. The success of several dining ventures at this single site is certainly tied to the ready accessibility of Duluth and the scenic attributes of nearby Lake Superior. But perhaps most important has been the consistent ability of different owners to adapt to changes in culinary tastes and preferences, as they evolved from road food to the "adventurous cooking" included in the contemporary New Scenic menu, much of it "infused with eclectic, globe-trotting flavors."[108]

The initial business emerged at the site in 1952, when Hilbert and Catherine Johnson moved their London Road drive-in, located by Duluth's armory and auditorium building, to the current Highway 61 location. One of the North Shore's first rural drive-ins, the Johnsons' food emporium initially featured hot dogs, hamburgers, French fries, homemade chili, fountain service, and frozen custard; chicken, shrimp, and trout were added to the menu during the 1960s. The fast-food options, carhop service, jukebox, and pocket-sized dining area attracted an appreciative clientele, never more so than during the springtime smelt run. And, as might be expected, Johnson's Drive-In was a favorite gathering place for the "local hotrod generation" of teenagers during the 1950s and 1960s.[109]

**During good weather, the New Scenic Café's garden, which faces Lake Superior, is occupied by patrons as they wait for seating in the restaurant's dining areas.**

Art and Esther Turnquist maintained the drive-up service after purchasing Johnson's in 1972 but identified their acquisition with a new name, the Scenic Drive Inn. Because of limited space, some cooking was done outside. The ensuing owners, Bob and Jan Fox, ended window service following their 1980 acquisition of the business. The remodeled building, renamed the Scenic Café, included a lunch counter at the entrance and a small dining room with six tables. In 1990, when the Foxes' daughter and son-in-law, Polly and Charlie Merhar, assumed ownership, the Scenic would become a year-round business.[110]

The drive-in was sold, in 1998, to Scott Graden and his aunt, Rita Bergstedt ("Rita B"), who opened their New Scenic Café in April 1999. Graden, a native of northeastern Minnesota who possesses a degree in chemistry and a master's degree in business administration, lived in a nearby garage for four years while establishing the New Scenic and creating many new food offerings, which ranged from "rainbow trout Veronique with red grapes, bell pepper and asparagus" to "curly carrot salad with citrus vinaigrette." Rita B provided further enticements with her pies, cakes, and baked bread. The initial New Scenic menu, Graden later recalled, was "shocking for locals," many of whom had grown accustomed to the former drive-in's offerings of hamburgers and French fries. In 2019, following a rapid increase in customer numbers, Graden expanded the foyer and bar and constructed an additional dining room that is also used for wedding parties and private gatherings. The café's unassuming appearance represents a complex of interconnected spaces, including sections of all previous businesses that have existed on the site since 1952.[111]

Graden, who became sole owner of the New Scenic following Rita B's 2007 retirement, continues as its executive chef; he has also published two large cookbooks, one in 2014, the other in 2023. The North Shore restaurateur, for well over a decade, has consistently received high praise for his culinary abilities and achievements. James Norton—cofounder of the *Heavy Table*, a former, highly popular Minneapolis-based food website, and author of the 2014 book *Lake Superior Flavors*—lauds Graden for presenting "subtle snapshots of local food, reflecting farm, forage, and fish." More recently, Rick Nelson, the Minneapolis *StarTribune*'s primary restaurant critic from 1998 to 2021, observed that the New Scenic's attractions are not limited to excellent food but also represent the owner's numerous travels and a more reflective view of his Swedish ancestry. The New Scenic, he wrote, offers "a pinnacle dining experience" that is tied to Graden's "perseverance, ingenuity, craft, passion, and business acumen."[112]

**The international style features of Glenn and Edith Nelson's 1964 Ironstone residence and store remain clearly evident to the present.**

### Ironstone: Glenn C. and Edith Nelson Residence, Studio, and Salesroom *(now a private residence)*
5527 North Shore Drive

Glenn and Edith McIntyre Nelson, during the early 1960s, selected a prime parcel of North Shore real estate for their new residence and store. Nelson, a UMD professor of art from 1956 to 1975, was, at the time, gaining national recognition as a ceramicist, author, and art collector. The couple, in 1963, commissioned Duluth architect Donald Stanius to design their international style structure, which would serve as a combination residence, studio, and salesroom. Because of the high-quality ceramic products that Nelson created and sold, Ironstone became a well-known shopping destination for customers from the Duluth area as well as the entire Upper Midwest and Fort William and Port Arthur, Ontario.[113]

While the building that resulted from the collaboration of architect and artist is a somewhat modest example of the international style, it displays several hallmark characteristics of the genre: a flat roof and wall planes, linear windows, a lack of ornamentation, and utilitarian building materials—primarily glass, concrete, steel, and aluminum. Built on a concrete slab, the first floor included the retail salesroom and a separate office space, both of which faced toward the lake and road; the salesroom had a large fireplace with a mantel crafted of wood harvested from the property. Immediately behind the showroom was a studio where Nelson did his ceramic work. The building's central area had a two-stall garage and a small kitchen and dining area with a westward-facing patio. At the far northern end was a bedroom that provided living quarters for Nelson's mother. The second floor included the master bedroom with an attached balcony overlooking the lake and two smaller bedrooms at the rear.[114]

The couple closed their store around 1970 because of Nelson's demanding teaching schedule. After selling the property in 1975, the Nelsons moved to Garrison, New York, where they built a smaller retirement home. Ironstone's new owners soon converted the building into a residence for two adults and four children. Subsequent purchasers made several changes to the interior, but the overall integrity of its exterior has been retained. Although international style buildings were seldom intended to establish an intimate relationship with their local landscapes, Ironstone's understated features offer a sense of timelessness and stability. Furthermore, Ironstone serves as a fitting and appropriate tribute to Glenn Nelson, who, at the age of ninety-seven, was eulogized in 2010 for his aesthetic sensitivities, technical comprehension, and considerable grasp and understanding of international design.[115]

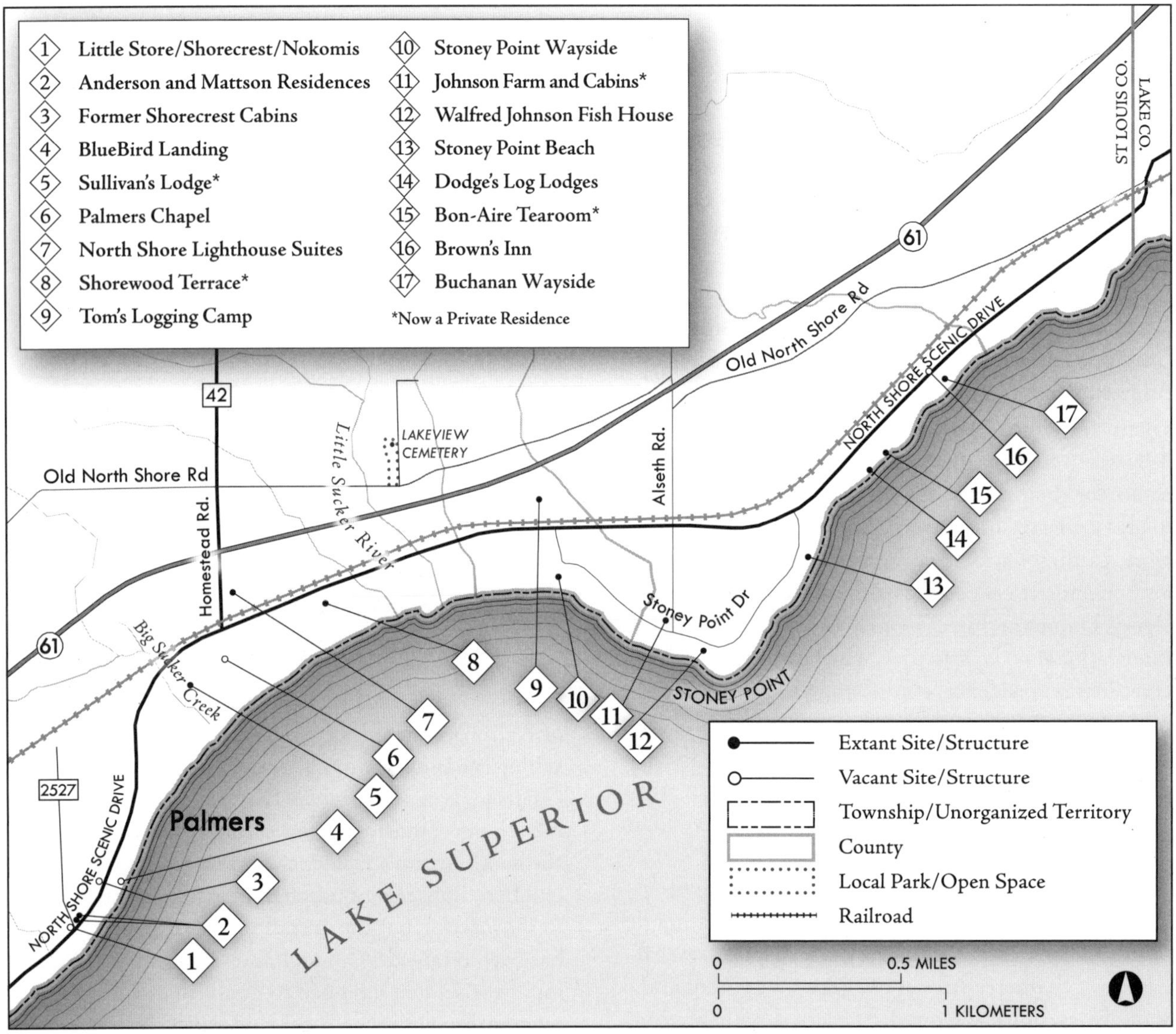

1 Little Store/Shorecrest/Nokomis
2 Anderson and Mattson Residences
3 Former Shorecrest Cabins
4 BlueBird Landing
5 Sullivan's Lodge*
6 Palmers Chapel
7 North Shore Lighthouse Suites
8 Shorewood Terrace*
9 Tom's Logging Camp
10 Stoney Point Wayside
11 Johnson Farm and Cabins*
12 Walfred Johnson Fish House
13 Stoney Point Beach
14 Dodge's Log Lodges
15 Bon-Aire Tearoom*
16 Brown's Inn
17 Buchanan Wayside
*Now a Private Residence
ST LOUIS CO.
LAKE CO.
61
42
Old North Shore Rd
Old North Shore Rd
LAKEVIEW CEMETERY
Little Sucker River
Alseth Rd.
Homestead Rd.
NORTH SHORE SCENIC DRIVE
Big Sucker Creek
Stoney Point Dr
STONEY POINT
2527
NORTH SHORE SCENIC DRIVE
Palmers
LAKE SUPERIOR
Extant Site/Structure
Vacant Site/Structure
Township/Unorganized Territory
County
Local Park/Open Space
Railroad
0
0.5 MILES
0
1 KILOMETERS

## Palmers

### Little Store, Shorecrest Auto Court, and Nokomis Restaurant *(vacant)*

5593 North Shore Drive

As Highway 61 curves slightly northward, an attractive view toward the south and southeast is enhanced by a subtle blending of Scenic Drive and the Lake Superior shoreline. The French River and Palmers settlements also merge imperceptibly in this area. (The original center of Palmers is discussed later.) It was here, around 1915, that Ernest and Santra Hendrickson, both turn-of-the-century immigrants from Finland, built a lakeshore cabin on land purchased from fisherman Tom Croft. Later, following the completion of Minnesota Highway 1, the Hendricksons constructed several rental cabins and also opened their Little Store, where groceries and refreshments were available for purchase. After their son and daughter-in-law, Clarence and Cora West Hendrickson, assumed ownership in 1935, the couple added a dance hall onto the store and provided a Red Cross rescue station along the shoreline.[116]

The business closed following Clarence Hendrickson's death from tuberculosis in 1940 and was open only sporadically until 1946, when Pasco ("Pat") and Ida Jorgenson Valentine (Valenti) acquired the property. Valentine was five years old in 1913, when he and his family emigrated from Italy to the United States; his wife was the daughter of Norwegian immigrants who had settled in North Dakota. The couple operated

**The Shorecrest Auto Court, developed by Pat and Ida Valentine after World War II, included twenty-four cabins. By 1956, as shown here, the Valentines already had removed seven cabins and were in the process of replacing them with an eight-unit motel (note the piles of lumber at the rear). At the lower left is the Valentines' store, supper club, and dance hall. Close to the dock is Alphonse and Gertrude Anderson's original fish house; their fish sales stand and residence are along the road at the far right. Toward the upper end of the road was a cluster of small buildings that composed a small tourist business, Ida Anderson's Modern Cabins.**

a West Duluth diner from the 1930s to 1944, when Valentine was drafted into the U.S. Army. In early 1946, immediately after Valentine received his military discharge, the couple purchased the Little Store and quickly transformed it into the Shorecrest, which became a popular supper club. The Valentines offered home-cooked dinners, reestablished the Hendricksons' Saturday night dance tradition, and improved the cabins, which were advertised as "strictly modern, heated with showers." Known as the Shorecrest Auto Court by the early 1950s, the complex had twenty-four small cabins, all organized in a pronounced horseshoe-shaped pattern. The couple removed ten cabins from the property in 1956 and replaced them with an eight-unit motel; eventually, all of the fourteen remaining cabins would be supplanted by five two-unit structures. Souvenirs, groceries, and sporting goods were available in the store, while a heated swimming pool, added to the center of the courtyard during the late 1950s, was available for guests and local children. Valentine also gave rides in his boat, the *Ida V*, but this service ended when the dock was washed away by storms. The couple's thirty-year-long affiliation with the Shorecrest—a place that many tourists and year-round residents termed their "favorite spot along the Scenic Drive for dining and entertainment"—ended when the property was sold in 1977.[117]

Several other owners maintained the Shorecrest's restaurant and resort services until 2005, when Sandy Lewis and Rondi Erickson, a couple with considerable business experience and acumen, assumed ownership. The Ericksons sold the motel and several two-unit cabins to buyers who moved them from the site and also added twenty-four acres of adjacent woodland to the original nine-acre holding. The most noticeable change was their remodeling and upgrading of the supper club into the renamed Nokomis Restaurant and Bar, where a grandson, Sean Lewis, served as chef. Almost immediately, food connoisseurs from the Twin Cities and elsewhere identified the Nokomis as "a prominent gastronomic stop" along the North Shore "culinary highway." The Nokomis had the North Shore's "best food and fanciest views," claimed one reviewer, while another called the menu "a cunning hybrid of local and cosmopolitan." Despite its popularity, Lewis and Erickson closed the restaurant at the time of their 2012 retirement and later proposed a planned-unit development for the property. The project failed to attract buyers, and the land and building were put up for sale in 2017. Other than the vacant Nokomis, the site remained undeveloped in 2023.[118]

### Alphonse and Gertrude Anderson Residence and Fishing Camp and Ida Anderson's Modern Cabins *(now private residences)*

**5597 and 5599 North Shore Drive**

Adjacent to the original Little Store site are two properties, both still owned by descendants of original settlers Alphonse and Gertrude Amundson Anderson. A Finland Swede who immigrated to Duluth Township in 1912 at the age of sixteen, Anderson found work with a local fisherman, but in November 1917, six months after the nation entered World War I, he was drafted into a U.S. Army artillery unit and later experienced combat in France. Discharged in late 1918, Anderson used his military bonus to purchase ten acres of land along Lake Superior and began pursuing the life of a commercial fisherman. (Anderson later called a small peninsula that juts into the lake "Bonus Point.") Anderson's Swedish wife sometimes ventured out onto Lake Superior with him, although she more commonly waded into the water and hooked their boat,

**Gertrude and Alphonse Anderson smoke herring along the Lake Superior shoreline, circa 1940s. Courtesy of Lake Superior Commercial Fishing Museum.**

the *Alvera A* (a fishing skiff named for the Andersons' daughter), onto a winch line, used to pull the vessel along a log skid into the fish house.[119]

The Andersons shipped most of their catch to Duluth but also opened a small fish sales stand close to the highway during the late 1930s. Their fresh and smoked fish obviously attracted most buyers, but soda pop, beer, and a few groceries were also available for sale. A slot machine was available for those who wished to engage in minor gambling. Twelve years after Anderson's 1953 death, his widow married Leif Osbakken and moved to Two Harbors. The original dwelling was eventually razed and replaced by a new residence that housed the Andersons' daughter and her family. Now, more than a century after Alphonse Anderson purchased land at Bonus Point, a grandson and his family own the house and property.[120]

Close to the residence was a modest tourist business, Ida Anderson's Modern Cabins. Known as Ida Smith when she migrated to Minnesota in 1921, the twenty-five-year-old Finland Swede was employed as a cook and maid by Isle Royale's wealthy summer residents. After marrying fisherman Emil Anderson (Alphonse Anderson's cousin) in 1927, the couple built a bungalow on an adjacent parcel of land. Following Emil Anderson's 1936 death, his widow began renting out two small "hay fever cabins." The number expanded to five following her marriage to Arthur Mattson, who converted a blacksmith shop and two sheds into cabins; all five would be described as "thoroughly modern" following the addition of electric hot plates. The cabins were sold and removed during the 1960s, well before Ida Mattson's passing in 1987. Her charming bungalow remains on the property and is owned by family members.[121]

### BlueBird Landing *(razed)*
### 5630 North Shore Drive

BlueBird Landing was a favorite destination for many North Shore residents and visitors who engaged in sportfishing, pleasure boating, dining, and lake watching from 1940 to the late 1950s. The property was acquired by Swedish immigrants John and Anna Sandberg, who settled along the Lake Superior shoreline during the early twentieth century; however, after their dwelling was twice destroyed by storms, the couple chose to relocate and build somewhat farther inland. A portion of the shoreline property was taken for the construction of Minnesota Highway 1 during the 1920s, but the Sandbergs were able to maintain their commercial fishing activities along a remaining area of lakefront. The Sandbergs' holding eventually included a large dock, dating to 1937, which had a cedar log crib filled with small boulders that was covered by a concrete cap.[122]

**After acquiring a pair of Shorecrest cabins in 1956, one buyer moved both units to a nearby highway location and joined them together to form this small, seasonal residence. The structure, although vacant for many years, remains evident along the upper side of Scenic Drive.**

In April 1940, the Sandbergs' daughter Evelyn and son-in-law Tim Lukkonen (who, at the age of one year in 1911, had departed Finland with his family for the North Shore) built a thriving business, BlueBird Landing, on the shoreline property. When the Lukkonens opened the Landing with a "shoestring" budget of $1,000, they only had three vessels available for rent, including "a Norwegian sailing boat with a set of sails for fun, and a Briggs & Stratton motor for trolling." As BlueBird Landing thrived, the Lukkonens' fleet grew to eleven boats, all painted blue and white. A former Duluth streetcar, trucked to the site during the early 1940s and placed on concrete piers at the edge of the beach, was converted into a popular café and lunchroom, the Flagship. A galley was situated at one end of the streetcar; filling the remaining interior space were the counter and several booths that could seat a

Although limited shoreline space was available at BlueBird Landing, Tim and Evelyn Lukkonen's business, which operated from 1940 to 1957, included a large dock; a former Duluth streetcar that was converted into a diner, the Flagship, *right*; a boathouse, *left*; a bunkhouse; and other ancillary buildings. Very little of the shoreline remains visible today. Photograph courtesy of Mary Ann Sironen.

total of sixteen customers. Blue-and-white colors maintained the nautical and bluebird themes, while prints of small sailboats decorated the curtains and menus. Evelyn Lukkonen, assisted by her mother, sister, aunt, and several young women from the local area, operated the business. The Flagship's lakeside location also allowed customers to observe the hustle and bustle of activities on and around the dock, but the most popular attraction was the owner's culinary skill, which made her diner "the best place to get a piece of pie anywhere along the shore." Also on the property were a boathouse and a bunkhouse that accommodated several young men who assisted the family with their charter boat service.[123]

Shortly after World War II ended, Lukkonen commissioned master boatbuilder Reuben Hill of Larsmont to design and construct the *Blue Bird*, which became one of the area's best-known all-purpose fishing vessels. Hill and several assistants spent almost two years working on the *Blue Bird*. Because of its significant size and two marine gas engines—one for powering the boat, the other for running the trolling equipment—the *Blue Bird* was an ideal charter fishing vessel. Around 1950, Lukkonen also acquired the "eminently rugged and seaworthy" *Blue Jay*, a completely enclosed fishing tug, constructed of steel, that had doors and hatches that could be bolted down when storms brought high winds and waves to Lake Superior. Because of its powerful diesel engine, five trolling lines, and a large rear door that allowed the mechanical lifter to pull an entire netload of herring into the hold, the *Blue Jay* was one of the North Shore's most efficient commercial fishing vessels. One person in a typical fishing boat seldom caught more than a few hundred pounds of herring during a single day, whereas two people working on the *Blue Jay* were able to harvest a significantly greater quantity.[124]

The demise of Lake Superior's fishing industry that began during the 1950s ushered in a chain of significant changes at BlueBird Landing. The deteriorating streetcar succumbed to the battering of Lake Superior's storms and was torn down during mid-decade. A disabling stroke suffered by Tim Lukkonen in 1959 brought a complete end to BlueBird Landing's tourist services and fishing operations. Eventually, all of the family's boats and fishing equipment were sold to pay for some of his medical expenses. Lukkonen's widow would later move to the western United States, where she remarried and pursued different employment opportunities. The hardy BlueBird Landing cofounder passed away as a California resident in late 2018, at the age of 104.[125]

After the Landing's remaining structures had been razed during the 1960s, the property was used as an unofficial public beach where tourists and local residents launched their boats and gained access to the water from a dock remnant that extended into Lake Superior. By 1997, however, following several years of high water and the constant forces of ice, wind, and waves, evidence of the dock, access road, and most of the beachfront had vanished. Today, it is difficult, if not impossible, to believe that a very busy and thriving recreational and commercial property once existed at the location. Grandma's Rock, located just west of the former BlueBird Landing property, is now used as an unofficial access site by tourists and locals who engage in wading, picnicking, morning yoga exercises, and "raucous bonfire gatherings."[126]

**A 1940s interior view of the Flagship, the diner that attracted customers to BlueBird Landing for almost two decades. Photograph courtesy of Mary Ann Sironen.**

### Montezuma Townsite *(undeveloped)*
Mouth of the Big Sucker River

The Big Sucker River outlet, which appears shortly after BlueBird Landing, was intended to serve as the location for an 1856 townsite named Montezuma. The site was platted two years after the R. B. Carleton Land, Mineral, and Mining Company had established copper claims in the vicinity. One of the members, Vose Palmers, made his claim at the northeastern corner of the river's mouth, where he and three assistants built a cabin and laid out the townsite plat. Although no town ever appeared, Palmers and several members of his family later engaged in logging, farming, and other activities throughout the area. The Palmers surname also identified a small railroad stop that appeared during the mid-1880s.[127]

### J. Daniel Mahoney Summer Estate and Sullivan's Lodge and Cabins *(razed, now a private residence)*
5708 North Shore Drive

J. Daniel Mahoney, around 1938, established a summer estate on twenty-three acres of land close to the Big Sucker River's mouth. A Canadian who was raised in Michigan, Mahoney moved to Duluth in 1888. There the ambitious twenty-year-old immediately secured work as a messenger boy for the American Exchange National Bank and quickly rose through the ranks as a clerk, teller, bookkeeper, cashier, and vice president. He continued serving as a vice president following the 1929 merger that led to the formation of Duluth's First and American National Bank. Mahoney also moved into Duluth's Kitchi Gammi Club, where he resided until his 1956 death.[128]

Mahoney's single-story North Shore residence included a large fireplace that fronted on an interior space where programs and small dances could be staged. Outside were another fireplace, a garage and horse stall, a pedestrian bridge that spanned the river, and two stone entry posts, one with "3rd Avenue West" carved into it. (Both banks that employed Mahoney were located at Third Avenue West and Superior Street.) Noted for his hospitality and philanthropy, Mahoney supported local 4-H clubs and other organizations and invited "hundreds" of Duluthians to visit his domain. Mahoney was equally generous when interacting with the local North Shore community:

the 1944 Clover Valley High School prom occurred within the house, as did programs presented by students enrolled in the nearby Palmers American Sunday School.[129]

Frank and Anne Sullivan moved onto the site in 1947. Originally from Two Harbors, Sullivan noticed the residence while working as a DM&IR Railroad conductor. The couple opened six tourist rooms in the residence, where guests were provided with access to its fireplace and "lounge" room. They also built several cabins just above the lakeshore. The Sullivans touted the "restful, homelike atmosphere" of their establishment, the attractive pine forests that bordered Lake Superior, and the trout fishing opportunities afforded by the river. Because of Sullivan's interest in winter sports (he was an instructor at the Duluth Skating and Curling Club), their business was among the first to advertise the North Shore's skiing and skating possibilities.[130]

The Sullivans, in 1969, sold their property, which was later acquired, in 2005, by a purchaser who razed the deteriorated residence and replaced it with a new home that has expansive views of Lake Superior. Mahoney's fireplace was taken apart and reassembled next to the outdoor patio; also overlooking the lake is a large, rehabilitated flagpole. Most visible and historically significant, however, is the pair of stone entry posts that still stand where J. Daniel Mahoney placed them in 1938.[131]

### Palmers School *(razed)* and Lighthouse on Homestead (*now* North Shore Lighthouse Suites)
5730 Homestead Road

The center of Palmers was formerly located at the intersection of the D&IR railroad tracks and Homestead Road. Situated halfway between Two Harbors and Duluth, the site was selected as a staging area and supply center for railroad construction activities in 1885–86. The name was derived from members of the extended Palmers family, who established themselves throughout the area after 1856. Palmers, over time, has included a school, a store, a restaurant, railroad buildings, and a few other structures. None, however, remain at their original locations today.[132]

Two contemporary buildings now flank the eastern side of Homestead Road: one, a log structure, includes medical offices, while the other, which occupies the former school site, might be mistaken for a landlocked lighthouse. The latter building opened in 2007 as the Lighthouse on Homestead, a restaurant that was owned and operated by four local women—three sisters and one daughter. The "food and ambiance," coupled with the building's distinctive architectural features and interior furnishings, attracted a devoted following of customers who congregated at the "friendly neighborhood restaurant." Many of their recipes came from the Shorecrest's former restaurant owners, who gave the women permission to use them in their new venture. (The three sisters had worked at the Shorecrest for several years.) The Lighthouse reportedly "filled in the great vacuum" that existed following the Shorecrest's closing; it also appealed to foodies who lived beyond the North Shore. The *Heavy Table* reported, in 2009, that the Lighthouse was a worthy contributor to the North Shore "culinary highway."[133]

Unfortunately, the Lighthouse closed in July 2011, a victim of greater-than-anticipated construction costs and the lingering effects of the 2008 economic recession. After it had stood vacant for almost three years, new owners converted the building into the North Shore Lighthouse Suites, a vacation rental property. Its thirty-six hundred square feet of interior space are divided into two well-appointed suites, each of which can house as many as six people; a separate wood-fired sauna adjoins both suites. The former forty-vehicle parking lot has also been reworked to provide an appropriate landscape setting for the building's current use.[134]

### Palmers Chapel *(vacant)*
South of the Homestead Road–North Shore Drive Intersection

On the lower side of North Shore Drive is a former chapel, built in 1950 by Palmers-area residents who had affiliated with the American Sunday School Union (ASSU)—an organization, dating to 1824, that focused on the organization of Sunday schools in rural areas. A visiting pastor officiated at monthly chapel services, but members of the Palmers Ladies Aid taught the Sunday school classes, while young women preparing for missionary work provided additional summer Bible school instruction. (The ASSU, in 1974, would join with the American Missionary Fellowship—now

**Religious services were conducted, from 1950 to the 1990s, in the Palmers Chapel, currently a vacant building on the lower side of Scenic Drive.**

InFaith—which continues to focus on evangelical work in underserved areas of the nation.) When the Palmers congregation disbanded during the early 1990s, the chapel was sold and converted into a storage building and workshop. The structure still remains in its small clearing but is steadily deteriorating.[135]

### Shorewood Terrace *(razed, now residences)*
5746 North Shore Drive and Adjacent Properties

Among the outstanding dining establishments that have distinguished the North Shore was Shorewood Terrace, which opened a short distance from the Big Sucker River around 1953. It was built, owned, and managed by Arthur and Ada Neeb, who, during the late 1930s, had operated the Chateau, a teahouse in nearby Clifton. The Neebs sold the Chateau during the early 1940s and moved to Minneapolis but returned to the Palmers area about a decade later, where they operated the Shorewood from mid-May to mid-November for almost fifteen years. Neeb designed the building, which displayed a combination of both flat and gabled roofs and an interior that included several examples of his art and craftsmanship. Ada Neeb was in charge of the most important functions—developing a sophisticated menu, overseeing food preparation, and managing the staff and business. Already advertised as a "nationally known restaurant" by 1957, the Terrace offered its patrons a fashionable dining opportunity—a novel experience for that period of North Shore history. Carolyn Tuominen Marino, one of many local women and UMD students who waited on tables at the Shorewood, could still recall, in 2016, some of the favorite items that Ada Neeb included in her "continental cuisine": leg of lamb, roasted duck (prepared during the fall hunting season), Vichyssoise soup, and a crab salad piled so high that it was dubbed the "Tower of Babel." Many of the Shorewood's well-heeled patrons tipped generously and could, by 1960, pay their bill with an American Express credit card (the Shorewood was one of the first North Shore establishments to accept this form of remuneration). Besides catering to tourists, Ada Neeb also gave special consideration to local

**Shorewood Terrace, developed and operated by Ada and Arthur Neeb, was a premier North Shore dining establishment from the early 1950s to the mid-1960s. *Duluth Visitor*, 1–15 July 1960, 12.**

residents who wished to hold parties, wedding celebrations, and other events in her restaurant.[136]

The "beautifully situated" Shorewood was located on eighteen acres of lakeshore land. The dining room offered a direct view of Lake Superior, but customers could get even closer to the water by walking along pathways that meandered through an attractive and meticulously maintained garden, also designed by Arthur Neeb. Because some local residents believed that the owner was stern, aloof, and unapproachable (he maintained that an unclaimed noble title and chateau awaited him in France), they dubbed him "Baron von Neeb." Soon after Neeb's 1966 death, his widow sold the restaurant and moved to Duluth. The Shorewood building would house at least one other business before it was burned down, perhaps by people engaged in smelt fishing, during the 1970s. Several residences are now situated on the site.[137]

### Tom's Logging Camp and Trading Post
5797 North Shore Drive

One of the North Shore's few remaining 1950s-era roadside tourist attractions—a re-created logging camp and trading post—is positioned north of Scenic Drive and the railroad tracks. Established by Thomas Deebach of Hinckley, Minnesota, the lumber company salesman initially moved five buildings to the site—a bunkhouse, cookhouse, blacksmith shop, Finnish logging-camp sauna, and horse barn—before he expanded it into a "museum" that also included a horseshoeing stall and harness and shoemaker's shops. A wagon, "pulled by real logging horses," was also available for visitors. Deebach would later add another structure, built of white pine timbers, that he called the Old Northwest Company Trading Post.[138]

Following Robert Fisher's purchase of Tom's during the 1960s, the roadside attraction was described as "an authentic duplicate of a typical Northern Minnesota logging camp, built as in days gone by." Fisher expanded his complex with three more structures: an old-time transportation building, a "gravity" house, and a structure that included a collection of miscellanea (including an old electric chair from Colorado) called "odds, ends, and a peek into the past." Lining the trading post walls were furs, traps, the heads of trophy animals, and examples of "Indian craftsmanship."

**The entrance to Tom's Logging Camp, 1950s.**

Available for purchase were imported Scandinavian items, local maple syrup, and Lake Superior agates. When Fisher's daughter Lauren Weckman assumed ownership of Tom's during the 1980s, she developed a nature walk along Hell's Creek; added a trout pond; and populated the property with llamas, pygmy goats, and chickens. "We push hard to keep it the kind of tourist attraction that was around when we were kids," commented Weckman in 2015. "We try to stay away from anything too modern." Even the most recent addition to Tom's, a diner, is constructed of two 1920s-era cabins that Wekman's husband, Steve, moved to the site in 2015 from nearby Stoney Point. He joined the units together, remodeled the expanded structure, and operated the diner until it closed in 2019.[139]

### Lakeshore Wayside Park CCC Camps 2753 and 1751 *(removed and razed)*

East of the Stoney Point Wayside

The linear profile of Lake Superior's shoreline changes noticeably at Stoney Point, which marks the termination of an anorthosite shelf that extends underwater for three hundred miles. Because the Point is one of only a few naturally sheltered places along the lower North Shore, it provided Indigenous inhabitants with a haven from storms, whereas late nineteenth- and early twentieth-century timber companies used the site for their log-rafting operations. Because of its scenic attributes, Chester Congdon identified Stoney Point as the terminus for his envisioned lakeshore boulevard. Stoney Point, predicted the *Duluth News-Tribune* already in 1913, was where "the boulevard will take a turn from the lake shore and circle around a 165-acre tract, which will be converted into a park."[140]

In September 1935, a group of young men from Company 2753, all affiliated with the CCC's Lakeshore Wayside Park Camp, set up their tents on thirty acres of Stoney Point's public land. They were replaced, in April 1936, by a contingent of 156 enrollees from CCC Company 1751, most of them former Twin Cities and southern Minnesota residents. While at Stoney Point, the enrollees constructed numerous buildings, including a kitchen and dining hall, an education building and library, a hospital, a recreation hall, and a washroom and latrine. Also on the site were several barracks and separate water and power plants. In May, the commanding officer, Lieutenant B. O. Rogers, informed his CCC contingent that "every spare hour of daylight will be devoted to the improvement of the appearance and convenience, utility, and comfort of the campsite." By this time, several new buildings were ready for painting and staining, tree planting was under way, a garden plot had been seeded, and a "hotbed" of plants was ready for enrollees who wished to pursue courses in horticulture and gardening. Rogers also insisted that full attention be given to the site's natural attractions. One month later, Rogers was complimenting the CCC enrollees in his command. "Every individual in this camp," he noted, "has shown me and the other officers an exhibition of how immature boys become real men under the cooperating guidance of appointed leaders. Resourceful futures are waiting for that type of young man who goes out with aching back and tired limbs to dig holes, plant trees, paint and beautify the barracks, lay company streets and sidewalks, and always remain in a joyful mood."[141]

Lakeshore was an MDH State Park Camp, with crews supervised by NPS staff members. Following Camp 2753's completion, the young men spent several months before April 1936 broadening the shoulders of Highway 61 and "replacing the square cut and ragged ditches with smooth rolling slopes." These projects, claimed the supervisors, would allow a vehicle "to descend into the shallow ditch with little or no damage to itself." During their relatively brief stay, Camp 2753's enrollees only had spades for digging into the earth and wheelbarrows for transporting the soil to other sites. Camp 2753's enrollees were soon followed by a group of young men from Camp 1751, who had the benefit of a gasoline-powered steam shovel that arrived in May 1936. They were asked, nonetheless, "not to disturb [the] fishermen's establishments along the shore or to detract from the rugged character of the little coves in which they nestle."[142]

When Camp 1751 closed abruptly in 1937, the enrollees were transferred to Jay Cooke State Park in Carlton County before the year ended. During November, a few Stoney Point buildings would be opened to timber workers engaged in a months-long labor strike that occurred throughout northeastern Minnesota. Some private

**The buildings at Stoney Point Lakeshore Wayside Park Camp, including this kitchen and diner, were completed in 1936 by members of CCC Company 1751. In the background is the Stoney Point Wayside, also constructed by the same CCC group. Courtesy of the John Pawlek CCC Collection photographic collection, Iron Range Research Center.**

property owners later purchased and moved several smaller CCC buildings to their own landholdings, but the larger structures were torn down or dismantled. The land remained vacant until the early 2000s, when the City of Duluth sold a portion of the acreage to a purchaser who eventually built a large residence on the land. The city, in exchange, secured ownership to property situated directly north of the area undergoing development.[143]

### Stoney Point Wayside

#### Southwestern Corner of Stoney Point Drive

Also constructed by Camp 1751's enrollees in 1936–37 was a horseshoe-shaped "loop road," which eventually intersected with North Shore Drive at both ends. The road, one and a quarter miles long, and later named Stoney Point Drive, continues to provide travelers with close-up views of the shoreline's natural and cultural features. Several parking areas, walls, waysides, overlooks, and hiking trails were also planned for much of Stoney Point, but only a single wayside, designed by MDH engineers and built by Camp 1751's enrollees, appeared south of the drive's western intersection. The project included a turnout and parking plaza paved with flagstone, although the most notable feature was its "ornamental wall of masonry"—250 feet long, eighteen inches wide, and about three feet high—constructed of semi-dressed stone and punctuated with several equally spaced pilasters.[144]

Stoney Point Wayside was, for several decades, a popular lake-watching and picnicking spot, where children entertained themselves by walking and running along the wall's top surface. Eventually the structure experienced major deterioration because of erosion, shoreline subsidence, and minimal maintenance. Soil and grass covered much of the concourse plaza by 2005, when it was deemed "in poor condition" by St. Louis County highway officials; most seriously damaged, however, was a collapsed section of the concourse wall, seventy feet in length, which had not been adequately anchored to the bedrock situated forty feet below the surface. Huge boulders placed at the edge of the exposed opening were meant to keep people and vehicles from plummeting over the steep slope, where nine-inch-diameter trees grew on the surface. Basic repairs were made to the wayside during the early 2000s by St. Louis County's Public Works Department: much of the existing stonework was tuck-pointed, a few eroded segments were rebuilt, and a new section of wall was constructed of concrete and covered with stone veneer similar in appearance to the original materials.[145]

**This wall section at Stoney Point Wayside, constructed by CCC Company 1751 in 1936–37, was rehabilitated during the early twenty-first century.**

### John, Gertrude, Edwin, and Adeline Johnsen Farm and Gladys Johnsen Cabins *(now seasonal residences)*

#### 1351 Stoney Point Drive

At the center of Stoney Point is Alseth Road, a north–south roadway named for early Norwegian settlers Albert and Elizabeth Alseth. During the early twentieth century, Norwegian immigrants John G. and

Gertrude Johnsen secured a large tract of land along both sides of the road, which extended northward from the lakeshore toward and beyond the railroad tracks. Johnsen had been a fisherman and farmer in Norway, but after arriving on the North Shore, he and his family devoted themselves to agriculture. The farm and farmstead eventually were passed on to the couple's son, Edwin O. Johnsen, a DM&IR night watchman who also sold milk, produced by his small herd of cows, to area residents. Unlike most farm-based dairies of the 1950s, however, Johnsen provided only pasteurized milk because his wife, Adeline, a trained dietician employed in Duluth, insisted upon this sanitary practice. Four nearby cabins were the responsibility of Edwin Johnsen's sister Gladys, a registered nurse who worked in Duluth. The arrival of summer precipitated her return to Stoney Point, where she managed the small tourist business. The Johnsens' original house was torn down some years ago, but an area of land that includes the original barn and well house remains with their descendants; two nearby cabins and a new seasonal residence are owned by non–family members.[146]

**Walfred Johnson's former fish house. In the background are two of the cabins that Gladys Johnsen rented to tourists decades ago.**

### Walfred Johnson Fish House

### Lakeshore Side of 1341 Stoney Point Drive

Adjoining the farm on its eastern side is a forty-acre tract of land, deeded by John Johnson to his fisherman brother and sister-in-law Ole and Oline Johnson, during the early twentieth century. The couple was childless but assumed responsibility for raising Walfred Johnson, whose mother had died shortly after his 1910 birth. Upon joining the ranks of North Shore commercial fishermen as a teenager, Johnson constructed a fourteen-by-sixteen-foot board and batten fish house and a smaller net house between Stoney Point Drive and the lakeshore. Children often congregated at the fish house, where they were also enthralled by the genial fisherman's speed and skill when cleaning and filleting his catch; they were further entertained by the feral cats that gorged themselves on the fish entrails Johnson tossed onto the ground. Johnson, typically accompanied by a black Labrador dog, drove his truck to several areas of Duluth Township, where numerous customers purchased the fish he had caught that morning.[147]

In 1952, two years after marrying Evelyn Elmberg, Johnson moved to northwestern Wisconsin, where he also worked as a crew laborer for the Chicago & Northwestern Railroad Company. The former North Shore denizen died in 1990, but his fish house, which is maintained by a nearby property owner, still stands on land owned by the City of Duluth.[148] It remains one of the North Shore's most picturesque vernacular structures.

### Stoney Point Beach

### Northeastern End of Stoney Point Drive

A beach at the northeastern terminus of Stoney Point, termed "THE best surf spot on the Great Lakes" during the early twenty-first century, continues to attract adventurous and hardy individuals from as far away as Milwaukee and Thunder Bay. The participants, members of the unofficial Stoney Point Surf Club, monitor weather websites carefully to determine when ideal surfing conditions are approaching. While September and October offer the warmest water, the best waves typically occur during November, when northeastern winds can bring two to three days of swells and temperatures that range between zero and fifteen degrees Fahrenheit. Any participant, quite obviously, must always be vigilant and aware of the potential dangers that Stoney Point poses: because of the waves' pitch, surfers can find themselves being pulled down to boulders spread out at the bottom of the lake. "You

A surfer rides the waves at Stoney Point Beach in November 2016. Photograph by E. J. Klepinger.

become encrusted with this ice layer in just a matter of an hour or less," exclaimed sixty-three-year-old surfer Erik Wilkie in 2022, "and feeling like you're pushed to a survival level that you haven't been to before." Despite the obstacles and challenges, Stoney Point's surfers describe their experience in sublime and awe-inspiring terms. "The full brunt of open sea swells release on the rock shelf," enthused Twin Cities surfer Brian Stabiner. "It is powerful, beautiful, and very humbling."[149]

## Dodge's Log Lodges
### 5852 North Shore Drive

This small tourist facility, dating to 1932, retains one of the North Shore's more euphonious names—Dodge's Log Lodges. Dodge's is also the first lakeside business that present-day motorists encounter after departing Duluth and traveling northeastward along Scenic Drive. Chester and Alice Dodge, both educators from Mondovi, Wisconsin, developed the small cabin grouping as an economic hedge against the negative impacts of the Great Depression. Dodge, who had physics and mathematics degrees from the University of Wisconsin in Madison, moved, sometime before 1925, to Mondovi, where he became the high school principal and married Latin teacher Alice Wilkinson.[150]

The couple's five modest cabins, constructed of small horizontal logs, were aligned atop a section of Lake Superior shoreline known as Greenwood Cliffs. Each cabin had a single window and a narrow deck with space for one or two chairs. Behind the five cabins was a two-story building (now called the Lodge) that offered basic automobile services on its lower level and an upstairs room for tourists. The Dodges, around 1937–38, replaced the small units with several well-

Five cabins at Dodge's Log Lodges have overlooked Lake Superior from the top of Greenwood Cliffs since 1932. These units replaced the original cabins during the 1990s.

built cabins acquired from the nearby, recently vacated Lakeshore Wayside Park CCC Camp.[151]

The resort was sold sometime before Chester Dodge's 1953 death. Subsequent owners made changes and improvements to the site, including constructing a manager's residence in 1980. Among the owners were Bruce and Nancy Von Riedel, who initiated a major cabin-replacement program throughout much of the 1990s. They were followed, in 1997, by Dale and Cathy Krueger, who later formed a management company that allowed buyers to acquire fractional cabin shares in the resort. The Kruegers also completed the cabin-rebuilding program initiated by the Von Riedels. Each of the five units, constructed of tightly fitted cedar logs joined together by saddle notch corners, was built on an original cabin footprint. The management company's owner maintains the association's property and handles the booking schedule for each cabin.[152] All of Dodge's cabins, as they have since 1932, offer direct access to the sights and sounds of Lake Superior.

### Bon-Aire Tearoom *(now a residence)*
5856 North Shore Drive

Adjacent to Dodge's Log Lodges is a Cape Cod style residence, situated ten feet above Lake Superior, that Olive Davidson opened as the Bon-Aire Tearoom in 1946. "It's unique, it's homey," stated Davidson, who kept the establishment open ten hours a day, seven days a week, from May to December. The business became the Bon-Aire in 1953, following its acquisition by Esther Boberg—an Iron Range native of Swedish American descent who had earlier worked as a Duluth business college teacher and manager of the city's Hamilton Hotel. Known for her entrepreneurial skills, fine food offerings (especially Scandinavian cooking and pastries), and high-quality service, Boberg operated the Bon-Aire until 1977. Used as a short-term rental property for many years thereafter, the Bon-Aire is currently a private residence.[153]

### Brown's Inn *(razed, now a residence)*
Opposite Side of the Buchanan Historical Marker

Brown's Inn, once the northeasternmost business in Duluth Township, was operated on the upper side of Scenic Drive for some twenty years. Clifford Brown, a U.S. Customs agent at the Pigeon River international border crossing, built a cabin on the site during the early 1940s. He soon added a gift shop and diner, both of which were operated by his parents, Paul and Olga Brown. The couple resided in crowded quarters above the diner and rented out the cabin. The diner and its outdoor deck could accommodate fourteen customers, but because the property lacked a well, Brown carried water to the site from a spring located one-quarter mile distant.[154]

**Brown's Inn, shown here during the 1950s, had a diner on its lower floor and living quarters above; a single rental cabin was nearby.**

The diner, open year-round, provided customers with breakfast, refreshments, short orders, and alcohol. Fresh and smoked trout, herring, and whitefish—some supplied by Walfred Johnson of nearby Stoney Point—were also available for purchase. Brown's was sold during the 1960s and converted into a residence before a fire destroyed the original building some twenty years later; the remaining structures were removed by the 1980s. A private home now stands close to the site.[155]

### Buchanan Historical Marker and Wayside
5878 North Shore Drive

On the opposite side of what was Brown's Inn is a lakeside monument that commemorates the 1856 settlement of Buchanan. The original townsite and current monument, however, are not geographically congruent. Most of the original Buchanan townsite was located along the western bank of the Knife River in Lake County, although a small section may have extended

**The Buchanan Historical Marker and Wayside during the 1940s, soon after members of CCC Camp 1731 completed the monument, which was designed by landscape architect Arthur Nichols.**

into St. Louis County. The monument location undoubtedly was selected because of its ready accessibility to motorists.[156]

The townsite was named for James Buchanan, the nation's eighteenth president. Unlike the unrealized townsites of Palmers and Montezuma, however, Buchanan developed into a viable, albeit short-lived, settlement. William Cowell, a land speculator involved in early North Shore development activities, sponsored the plat, which had been surveyed by Christian Wieland of Beaver Bay. The 316-acre property was divided into blocks, all 150 by 400 feet in size. The streets, each eighty feet wide, paralleled the lake, while fourteen avenues were named for several regional rock formations: Amygdaloid, Greenstone, Granite, and so forth.[157]

Cowell astutely realized that naming the townsite for a sitting president might result in political and financial rewards. Therefore, in 1856, he traveled to Washington, D.C., and successfully lobbied for the designation of Buchanan as northeastern Minnesota's official U.S. Land Office. A number of log structures, five of them two stories high, soon emerged at the townsite. They included one hotel; three boardinghouses; two buildings with offices and quarters for land agents; a few saloons; some private cabins for "miners, loggers and workmen"; and a newspaper office, where the *North Shore Advocate* was published in 1858–59. A pier also allowed a steamboat, the *City of Superior*, to access Buchanan during the ice-free months.[158]

By the end of 1857, Buchanan was already doing a "land office business" serving copper prospectors, land and timber speculators, and a few would-be farmers. During summer 1858, the Minnesota Legislature authorized the incorporation of Buchanan Township (later disbanded); most of the officers were speculators and prospectors. Buchanan, however, would be severely impacted by the nationwide Panic of 1857. From January to May 1858, only six cash transactions occurred at the land office, and in June, its functions were transferred to Portland in the Duluth area. Soon the abandoned Buchanan pier succumbed to the spring ice breakup, and the buildings were later consumed by a forest fire.[159]

The Buchanan wayside and historical marker, designed for the MDH by landscape architect Arthur Nichols, was built in 1936–37 by young men enrolled in Lakeshore Wayside Park CCC Camp 1751. Because Nichols sited the marker and plaque so carefully, motorists are able to view the rustic native stone memorial when approaching either from the southwest or the northeast. The wall, 184 feet long, provides observers with different vantage points from which to observe the monument and Lake Superior; they can also sit on the wall, lean against it, or pose for photographs. Two staircases lead down to the flagstone platform, where a projecting bay highlights the rectangular, "shrine-like" marker and its plaque.[160]

Ownership and management of the wayside were transferred from MDH to St. Louis County in 1965. The site remained in relatively good condition for the ensuing three decades, but numerous maintenance problems were evident by the early 2000s. The "deteriorating, yet lovely historical site," noted one 2009 account, "rises grandly above the tangled weeds and wildflowers, made more stately by the disrepair and neglect of the benches and small plaza." St. Louis County's Public Works Department restored the wayside one year later and added a nonobtrusive handicapped access ramp to its southwestern side.[161] Because of these improvements, motorists are still able to observe and enjoy the wayside and Lake Superior views that landscape architect Arthur Nichols astutely envisioned in 1936.

# Lake County

The border separating St. Louis and Lake Counties occurs just after Scenic Drive passes under the North Shore Scenic Railroad Bridge. From there, fifty-three miles of highway extend through Lake County and its three incorporated cities (Two Harbors, Beaver Bay, and Silver Bay), two organized townships (Silver Creek and Beaver Bay), and six unincorporated settlements (Knife River, Larsmont, Castle Danger, East Beaver Bay, Illgen City, and Little Marais). Also within Lake County are two "unorganized territories"—a U.S. Census Bureau term that identifies sections of counties not located within a legally designated civil division or incorporated place. Lake No. 1 is at the far eastern side of the county, Lake No. 2 on its westernmost side.[1]

In 1890, most of Lake County's thirteen hundred residents were concentrated in Two Harbors, which had emerged as a Lake Superior iron ore shipping port just six years earlier. The county's population grew to 4,655 people in 1900 and then to 8,250 in 1920—a total that would not be exceeded until 1960, when the figure peaked at 13,700. The significant gain occurred because of the workers and families who populated a new town, Silver Bay, located next to an industrial plant that opened along Lake Superior during the 1950s. (The facility converted taconite, a low-grade iron ore, into high-quality pellets that were shipped to steel mills in the eastern United States.) Although Lake County's population figure had declined to 10,425 by 1990, the count would remain remarkably stable over the next thirty years: 11,060 in 2000; 10,855 in 2010; and 10,905 in 2020.[2]

## Unorganized Territory Lake County No. 2

The western border of Unorganized Territory Lake County No. 2 separates St. Louis and Lake Counties, while its southern boundary follows the Lake Superior coastline between Knife River and Two Harbors. Because of its proximity to Two Harbors, the 2020 population count of 2,210 residents is unusually large for one of Minnesota's unorganized territories. Within the territory's boundaries are the unincorporated settlements of Knife River and Larsmont, which have a combined population of almost four hundred residents.[3]

### Knife River

Knife River, a place name that identifies both a river and a settlement, is a close translation of an Anishinaabe word, *makomanzi-zibi* (sharp stones standing on edge in the streambed). Because the river has no natural barriers that prevent fish from migrating upstream, it supports the North Shore's only naturalized population of wild steelhead trout. American Fur Company (AFC) officials recognized the river's significance by employing local Anishinaabe natives, who fished at the site from 1834 to 1839. The North Shore's first shipwreck occurred close to the Knife River mouth in April 1838, when pack ice crushed an AFC schooner, the *Madeline*. Unsuccessful explorations for copper ore would also occur close to the river in 1854, and again in 1864 and 1929.[4]

During the late nineteenth and early twentieth centuries, a number of Norwegians were attracted to the river's fishery, where Knife Island offered some protection from

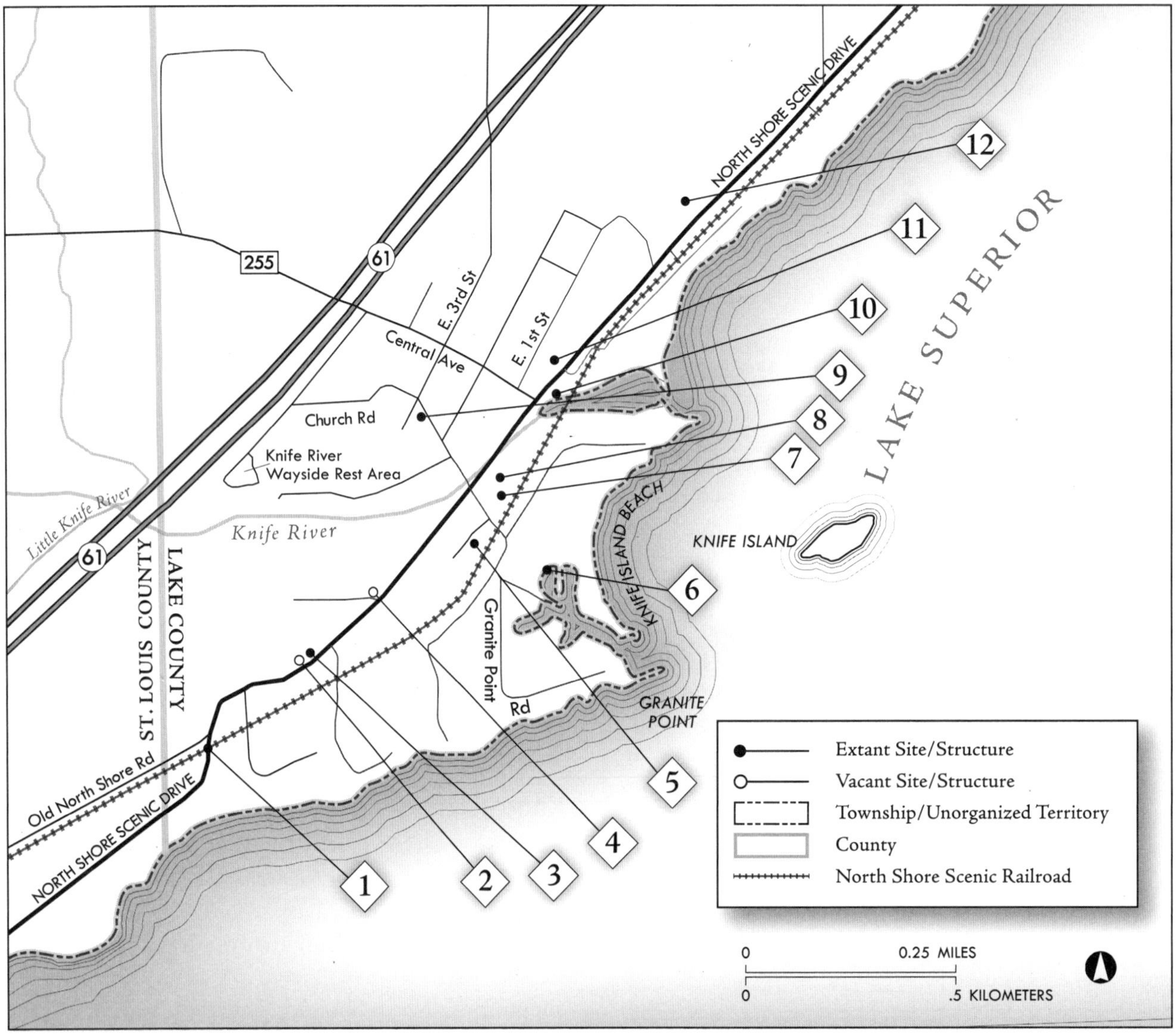


1. North Shore Scenic Railroad Bridge
2. Former Ronning's Store
3. Russ Kendall's Smokehouse
4. Former Coolidge Brothers Garage
5. Marina View Townhomes
6. Knife River Marina and Access
7. Knife River Heritage and Cultural Center
8. Knife River Campground
9. Knife River Lutheran Church
10. Emily's Store/Lighthouse at Emily's*
11. Great! Lakes Candy Kitchen
12. Island View Resort

*Now a private residence

winds and storms. The first Norwegian immigrant to secure a foothold along the river and North Shore was Charles Anderson, a Civil War veteran and Great Lakes ship's captain. After acquiring land in 1869, Anderson engaged in fishing and logging; constructed a log house for his wife, Serene, and their three children; and sold building lots to other Nordic fishermen. Once logging activities expanded during the late 1890s, Anderson opened Knife River's first tavern and an adjacent hotel. In 1905, he started developing a farm on 160 acres of cutover land outside of Knife River. By 1912, Anderson's "ideal farm" had a three-story barn that sheltered his horses and twelve head of cattle; the ambitious Norwegian also cleared twenty-five acres of land, where he cultivated wheat, oats, and potatoes. Inside the attic of Anderson's two-story model farmhouse was a 225-gallon tank filled with water pumped from the river, which provided his family with some conveniences, such as indoor plumbing. The "father of the town of Knife River" would later deem farming a "great money maker" that was much preferable to fishing and logging.[5]

While most early settlers pursued fishing, some found employment opportunities with the D&IR Railroad, which opened between Two Harbors and Duluth in 1888. The railroad also offered an alternative to the vessels that transported fish to Duluth wholesalers, although the foundation for Knife River's two-decades-long period of greatest economic prosperity was provided by the Alger, Smith & Company's logging activities. Late nineteenth-century timber operators recognized that significant wealth could be derived from northeastern Minnesota's pine forests, but the region's swift, narrow, and rocky streams and rivers posed a major hurdle, because most were unsuitable for transporting logs from inland logging camps to North Shore harbors. Although some firms attempted to control the rivers with dams, these efforts often failed. By 1901, it was clear that railroads were "the only way" to transport logs within the region.[6]

**An early twentieth-century D&NM train engine pulls more than twenty railroad cars, loaded with logs, to the Alger, Smith & Company docks in Knife River.**

Alger, Smith & Company, which would become one of the North Shore's leading logging firms, relied heavily on an extensive network of railroad lines after its headquarters and shops were moved from Michigan's Upper Peninsula to Knife River in 1898. The company's railyards were located about one-half mile upstream from the river's mouth—approximately where the Highway 61 expressway now skirts the settlement. A railroad, the Duluth & Northern Minnesota (D&NM)—also known as the Alger Line—connected the firm's timber holdings to Knife River. From there, the D&IR Railroad transported the logs to Alger–Smith's Duluth mills. By 1919, the D&NM had one hundred miles of main line and about 350 miles of branches, spurs, and temporary tracks. As many as 120 men were employed at the busy Knife River rail center, which included machine and blacksmith shops, separate passenger and freight depots, a seven-stall roundhouse, and a warehouse. The harbor also had a dock, built in 1909, for shipping pulpwood and receiving coal.[7]

The small townsite of Mellie, platted on the eastern side of the river in 1899, and renamed Knife River in 1903, attracted residents, who established homes and businesses in the booming settlement. Knife River's commercial district, at its peak, included three hotels, four stores, and several boardinghouses and saloons. Most impressive was the general store owned by Archibald ("Archie") McPhee, a Scottish Canadian who arrived in Knife River with Alger–Smith but quickly exited the company and became a well-known businessman. His two-story building, "a favorite with virtually the entire town," had groceries, hardware, dry goods, glassware, crockery, boots and shoes, cigars and tobacco, stationery, and confectionary items for sale; a nearby warehouse stored flour, feed, and hay. McPhee was actively involved in real estate and received an appointment, in 1907, as Knife River's postmaster. In 1922, McPhee and his family departed the settlement for Los Angeles, where he became a grocery merchant.[8]

Close to McPhee's establishment was a ten-room residence that housed Barbara Craven's hotel. Craven, also a Scottish Canadian, supplied her guests with "clean beds and plenty of towels" as well as "snowy white table linens and three good meals a day"; the building was, observed a reporter for the *Duluth News-Tribune* in 1915, "a desirable hotel for the most elite to stop at." Another business owner was Michael Di Marco, a night agent for the D&IR who ran a small depot store at the end of the railway platform, a place where fishermen's lunches, soft drinks, ice cream, and a full line of smoker's supplies were available.[9]

Following its 1909 incorporation as a village, Knife River's six councilmen typically were Alger–Smith and D&NM officials. In 1910, the population reached 490 people—170 of them foreign-born residents who represented a dozen ethnic and nationality groups. The seventy-two Canadian émigrés formed Knife River's largest single assemblage of residents, although the eighty-seven Nordic immigrants—forty-eight Norwegians, sixteen Swedes, fifteen Finns, and eight Finland Swedes—comprised more than one-half of the entire foreign-born population.[10]

The small enclave soon faced financial problems, so much so that in early 1917, after struggling for several years, Knife River citizens "voted to suspend the village organization." The vote may have been a portent of the dramatic change that occurred just two years later, when Alger–Smith crews loaded the company's last load of logs onto a D&NM train. The rail line was abandoned in 1921; most of the tracks and facilities were torn up and removed within two years. The shut-down was a "thunderclap" to Knife River residents, wrote Lake County historian Hugh Bishop. "From a huge enterprise with hundreds of miles of rail lines, hundreds of railcars, a dozen or more locomotives and hundreds of workers in the woods, rail and yard jobs, little but the wandering right-of-way remained within a span of only three years." Knife River's population also tumbled, from 330 in 1920 to 195 in 1930. The former boomtown of Knife River is gone, observed a Duluth reporter who drove through the settlement in 1930. "Where the old railroad yards stood is filled with scars of trackage ripped up and moved. The main thoroughfare is barren, many of the stores having been torn down or closed."[11]

Commercial fishing again emerged as a major factor in the economy, but it was tourism that fueled Knife River's subsequent revival as a viable North Shore community. Today Knife River is unlike any other unincorporated North Shore settlement, because its streets, building density, and population numbers (an estimated 255 residents in 2020) give the appearance of a small village. Within Knife River are numerous dwelling units, one of the North Shore's oldest Protestant churches, a safe harbor and marina, and a few businesses that cater to tourists and motorists. Its residents are also known for embracing their Nordic heritage, which is exemplified by a Norwegian holiday event, Julebyen (Christmas Village), initiated and organized by the Knife River Recreation Council in 2013. The Knife River version of Julebyen features a Gnome Dome and Troll Village and several huts—most decorated with conifer branches and pinecones—where vendors sell handcrafts, honey, smoked fish, and other locally produced items. Carolers and other participants dressed as Nordic mythological characters add music, color, and humor to the weekend event, as does a Troll Patrol, which keeps watch over the "infestation" of these fictional creatures. Providing more excitement and sounds are the engine and cars of the North Shore Scenic Railroad that travel the tracks between Duluth and Knife River.[12]

Also within the settlement is an access point to the Knife River Trail, which begins as a rough and narrow path that follows the stream's southern bank, crosses over exposed lava flows, passes by a fish ladder and small waterfall (First Falls), and goes under the Highway 61 Expressway. Much of this northern section is very well built because it served as the original southwestern terminus for the Superior Hiking Trail during the 1990s; it was converted into the Knife River Trail when a new section of the Superior Hiking Trail, situated farther inland, opened between Duluth and Two Harbors. Located along the trail, now maintained by the Knife River Recreation Council, are an abandoned 1863 copper mine site and the diminutive but charming Second Falls. Also proximate to the expressway is the Knife River Rest Area, a MnDOT wayside. The site displays a plaque that recognizes Arthur V. Rohweder, a Duluth railroad executive who served as president of the Minnesota Safety Council for twenty-five years.[13]

### North Shore Scenic Railroad Bridge No. 19A
Overpass on Highway 61 (Knife River)

The original DM&IR Knife River Railroad Bridge, built in 1922, separated the company's trains from vehicular traffic that passed below on a recently completed section of Minnesota Highway 1. Termed a deck-plated girder bridge, the structure used its own railroad tracks to form the deck. As traffic counts increased over succeeding decades, however, the bridge posed several risks to motorists, including a reversing horizontal curve that was encountered when passing through the opening; protruding concrete abutments that encroached on the entrances; and a limited vertical clearance of fourteen feet, which restricted passage to standard-sized vehicles only. Nevertheless, the bridge endured until 2009, when it was finally torn down and replaced by a new structure that opened one year later. The viaduct, designed by the Duluth engineering and architectural firm of Krech Ojard & Associates, was commissioned by the St. Louis and Lake Counties Regional Railroad Authority.[14]

**The North Shore Scenic Railroad Bridge is located at the western entrance to Knife River. Rebuilt in 2009, the bridge now provides a much improved and safer passageway for motorists, bicyclists, hikers, and runners.**

The company's engineers resolved the horizontal curve problem by skewing the new bridge an additional twenty-two degrees; the limited vertical clearance was raised by lowering the roadway; and the narrow width of the sight distance was improved by increasing the number of spans from two to three and significantly expanding the length of the central section. The installation of a curb and gutter also gave the bridge the "feeling of an urban setting" that would suggest slower speeds to motorists. Widening, paving, and striping the shoulders along both sides of the bridge approaches has provided a "refuge" for the growing numbers of people who bicycle, walk, run, or Rollerblade along this section of Scenic 61.[15]

### Ronning's Store and Residence *(now a storage building)*
147 Scenic Drive

Ronning's Store, which closed long ago, was one of many highway-oriented businesses that developed along the North Shore during the 1920s and early 1930s. Thor Ronning, the store's namesake and founder, immigrated to Minnesota from Norway in 1891 at the age of sixteen. A commercial fisherman, Ronning moved to Beaver Bay in 1901 and, in 1911, to Knife River, where he became well known for shipping smoked fish, by rail, to Duluth markets. After his 1925 marriage to Bertha Tews Sunde, a widow from Red Wing, Minnesota, the couple established Ronning's Store in a building attached to their residence. The dwelling, characterized by its steeply pitched roofline and front-gable entrance, contrasted with the adjacent store, which had a rectangular false front with the family's name emblazoned on it. A large neon sign on the facade, placed perpendicular to the highway, was highly visible to motorists who approached from afar. Sales items at Ronning's Store were quite similar to those of many North Shore stores of the era—groceries, cigarettes and tobacco, soft drinks, and other sundry items—although the most prominently marketed product, spelled out in large letters on the front window, was "FISH." Advertisements also assured travelers that "snappy curb service" was available at the gasoline pump. Within the store was a small tavern that had two slot machines, both prominently situated next to the bar. Ronning was involved in business operations virtually up to the time of his death in 1959, at the age of eighty-four. His widow opened the store for brief periods of time thereafter but eventually closed the business. Russ Kendall, who owned an adjoining commercial establishment, later purchased both of Ronning's buildings, which are now used for storage.[16]

### Russ Kendall's Smokehouse
149 Scenic Drive

Russ Kendall's Smokehouse—a long-lived, highly successful, and very well known North Shore business—now marks the southwestern entrance to Knife River's built-up area. The family name has been synonymous with Knife River's history since 1908, the year William ("W.T.") and Anna Brandt Kendall, respectively the children of English and Swedish parents, arrived from Michigan's Upper Peninsula. Kendall worked as a local railroad machinist until 1924, when the couple opened a small grocery store, and also acquired Charles Anderson's former tavern and hotel, which they converted into a warehouse and garage. The Kendalls smoked fish in a small log building situated behind the store and sold them from a stand located along Highway 1. Kendall also began using his REO Motor Car Company truck to pick up and deliver fish and freight along the entire North Shore highway.[17]

The family soon opened a diner that specialized in "fish dinners and short orders [and] smoked fish." Once Prohibition ended in 1933, Kendall added a tavern and dance hall that featured inexpensive beer, slot machines, and local and midwestern bands, such as Mumma's Orchestra, which played for dances on four nights a week during summer 1940. By 1947, Kendall's Boat Service was also offering an array of services, including rental cabins and boats, daily charter trips, "deep-sea" fishing excursions, evening cruises, and speedboat rides. When wrestling became popular on television during the early 1950s, Kendall hired professional grapplers, who performed in a room adjacent to the tavern.[18]

Following Anna Kendall's death in 1938, three of the family's six children—Sarona, Lowell, and Russell—spent long hours helping their father run the businesses. A U.S. Census enumerator noted, in 1940, that all four Kendalls, including sixteen-year-old Russell, had worked ninety-eight hours during a typical week—an average of fourteen hours per day, Monday through Sunday. After graduating from Two Harbors

High School in 1941, Kendall sailed on Great Lakes ore boats for two seasons, joined the U.S. Merchant Marine, served in the Pacific theater during the final months of World War II, and then signed on as an Atlantic sailor. Following his return to Knife River in 1948, Kendall began a thirty-six-year-long career as a DM&IR fireman and engineer. Besides working on the railroad, the tireless young man assisted his father in operating the family's fish market. And, over subsequent years, Russ Kendall "built a name for himself" by delivering countless truckloads of smoked fish to communities between Knife River and the Twin Cities. When W.T. died in 1958, ownership of the store was assumed by siblings Russ and Sarona, who informed customers that anyone who purchased Kendall's smoked trout, whitefish, herring, cod, and salmon could "eat them here or take them along." Some time after 1965, the store was renamed Russ Kendall's Smoked Fish, which attracted more customers from throughout Minnesota who were familiar with the former truck driver's products. Kendall continued working at the store after his daughter Kristi and her husband, Gordy Olson, assumed ownership in 2000. The still-active eighty-five-year-old Knife River legend passed away in 2007.[19]

Since the species and availability of Lake Superior fish vary so greatly, the Olsons now rely on a wide network of suppliers to stock their smokehouse and store. Minnesota's North Shore fishermen are given priority, but they cannot satisfy the huge demand. Therefore numerous suppliers based in Wisconsin, Michigan, and Canada, several with Anishinaabe backgrounds, also stock the store with herring, trout, and whitefish. Only the salmon, caught on fishing lines in Alaska's Bristol Bay, come from outside the region. After arriving at Kendall's, the fish are soaked for twenty-four hours in a brine made of salt and water. Following this process, they are placed into a concrete-block smokehouse where the fire, fueled by locally harvested maple wood, is carefully tended for twelve hours. The "secret" of Russ Kendall's Smokehouse—opined Andrew Zimmern, the Twin Cities–based host, cocreator, and consulting producer of the Travel Channel's popular *Bizarre Foods with Andrew Zimmern* from 2006 to 2018—comes from the maple wood.[20]

The Kendall business and secret, however, were severely threatened in mid-May 2014, when a Sunday-morning conflagration destroyed the smokehouse and caused smoke damage to the store and bar. Immediately after hearing about the devastating loss, Olson thought he might have to "give it all up." But upon arriving at the scene, where scores of vehicles were lined up along Scenic Drive, he realized that large numbers of local residents and friends were willing to offer voluntary and monetary support. A new retail area emerged within just five weeks, and another Knife River smokehouse was used until the

**The retail store for Russ Kendall's Smokehouse adjoins Thor and Bertha Ronning's former store and residence (now a Kendall storage building). A separate smokehouse, rebuilt in 2015 following a fire, stands at the rear.**

**Russ Kendall's daughter and son-in-law, Kristi and Gordy Olson, have operated the renowned Knife River business since 2000.**

new facility opened in October 2015. Also involved in the current enterprise is Cody Olson, Russ Kendall's great-grandson. Given the family's work ethic and commitment to their business, Russ Kendall's Smokehouse will likely remain a Knife River "destination for tourists and a regular stop of locals."[21]

### Coolidge Brothers Garage *(vacant)*
171 Scenic Drive

Another long-standing Knife River business, which existed for almost a century, was the Coolidge Brothers Garage. The family's Knife River origins may be traced to the early 1900s, when Ai and Mary Coolidge departed Gladwin County, in east-central Michigan, for the tiny northeastern Minnesota settlement of Cramer, where Coolidge worked as a sawmill timekeeper and lumber camp foreman for Alger, Smith & Company. By 1922, following the family's arrival in Knife River, their sons Lloyd and Francis (Dutch) began operating the Coolidge Garage, which catered both to local residents and to tourists. The brothers initially sold tires and tubes, gasoline, and oil but soon opened a service station, where vehicle repair and tow truck assistance were offered. During the 1940s and 1950s, the family's nearby residence also included the Coolidge Inn, which provided meals to tourists and residents.[22]

The Coolidge brothers were recognized as having an uncanny ability to "fix most anything people brought to them" and for performing "miracles on some vintage vehicles, from Model Ts to a Scripps-Booth car" (the latter a luxury automobile manufactured from 1913 through 1923). They also invented, patented, and fabricated their version of a trolling plane, a common fishing lure. The Coolidges' 1940 U.S. Patent Office application claimed that their device could function in water at the deepest level but also allow anglers to "raise the lure [quickly] when struck by a fish, the advantage of which is well known to all fishermen." Despite competition offered by other manufacturers, the Coolidge

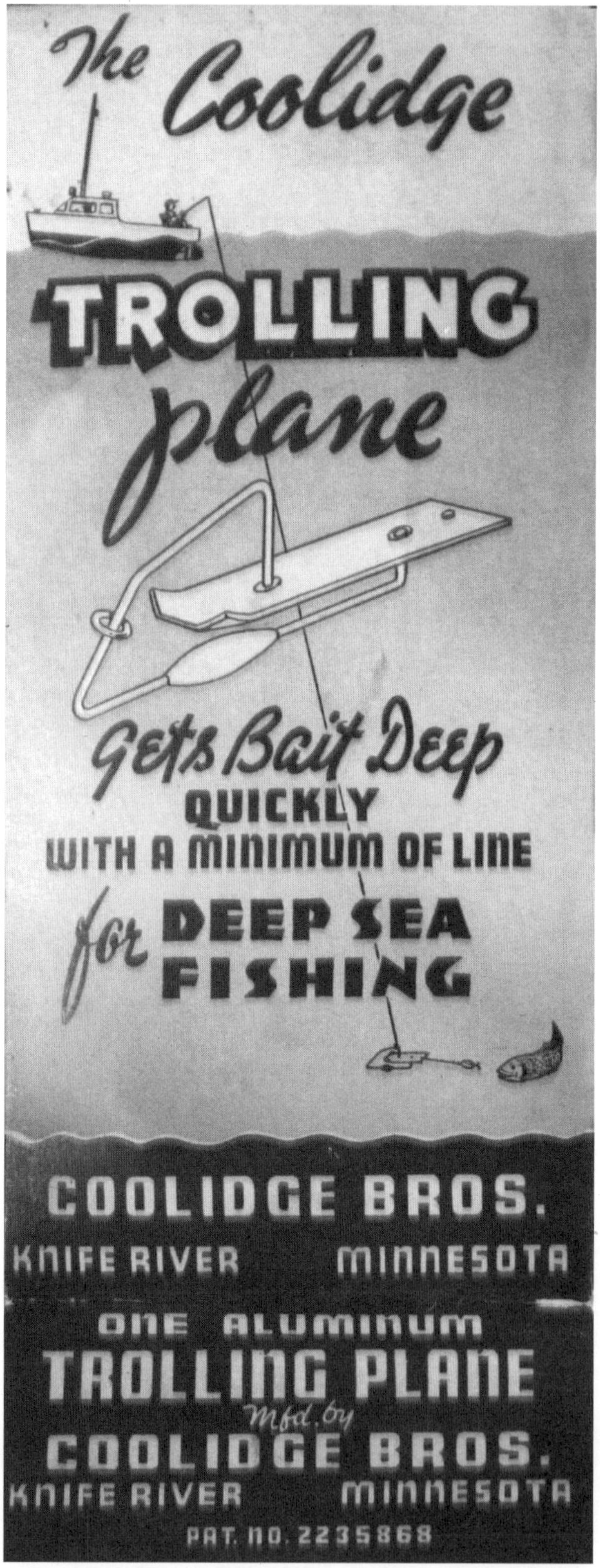


**Advertisements for the Coolidge Trolling Plane, fabricated in Knife River during the 1940s and early 1950s, claimed that even distant fish would be enticed by its "novel attractive properties," primarily the thin sheet of polished aluminum on both sides of the lure.**

Trolling Plane soon received official U.S. Patent Office approval. The device was fabricated and marketed quite successfully, but the decline of Lake Superior fishing during the 1950s brought an end to its production. Coolidge Machine, however, would continue as a third-generation business before closing around 2020. The building was then sold to Randy Ellestad, a local entrepreneur and owner of the Knife River Campground, who purchased the structure because of its "great potential for a variety of businesses that cater to the increasing number of visitors traveling the North Shore." It remains vacant at the time of publication.[23]

**Marina View Townhomes, one of Knife River's more recent structures, reveals subtle Nordic architectural influences.**

### Marina View Townhomes
Marina View Drive

This eight-unit townhouse complex, which opened on a three-acre site in 2006, was designed to reflect the characteristics of a fishing village in Scandinavia, while simultaneously maintaining Knife River's "small-town feel."[24] The two-story structure parallels the North Shore Scenic Railroad tracks and is within easy walking distance of Knife River's beach, marina, and harbor.

### Knife River Marina and Access
115 Marina Road

The mouth of the Knife River served as a harbor and staging area for commercial fishing as early as the 1870s, but it did not offer much protection from Lake Superior's unanticipated gales. Heavy rainfalls could send "high water roaring down the river out into the lake to tear boats away from their moorings," and the river's mouth was often blocked with sand generated by lake currents. Local organizations and officials issued numerous calls for the development of a safe harbor at the river's mouth, but it was not until 1937 that the U.S. Army Corps of Engineers received congressional funding and authority to conduct a comprehensive review of potential sites along the tristate Lake Superior shoreline. The survey eventually considered Knife River, but only after several North Shore groups agitated for its inclusion. Despite the tacit approval, no federal funding was authorized for the harbor.[25]

Finally, in 1946, Joseph Liberty, a local merchant and president of the Knife River Harbor Association, convinced his fellow citizens to form a cooperative and raise funds for the facility. Two years later, after securing $20,000 through the sale of individual $100 shares, the cooperative acquired twenty-nine acres of lakeshore land located between two rocky points west of the river's mouth. Once volunteers had cleared eight acres of the site, a contractor built a dock, breakwater, and entrance road. Unfortunately, a December 1959 gale delivered a severe blow to the still-incomplete project. The storm's huge waves, some twenty feet high, toppled the breakwater's boulders in every direction within the harbor, smashed and tore away pilings, and severely damaged or wrecked ten fishing boats; at least one hundred nets, all laden with fish worth a total of $25,000, were also lost. The damage would have been even greater had not ten brave Knife River fishermen ventured into the roiling water and pursued the "awful job" of keeping the boats within the harbor. Additional problems occurred only a few months later, in early April 1960, when a thick accumulation of ice barred access to large numbers of herring nets. The frozen barrier was eventually broken, but only after the fishermen tied dynamite onto long birch poles, inserted the explosives into holes that had been drilled through the eight-inch ice with an augur, and discharged the volatile packages. Once the ice was cracked, boats were pushed or rowed through the broken floes until they could be "beached" on stable ice; after repeating the "blasting-ramming technique" several times, the nets were finally freed.[26]

The current harbor and its marina, rebuilt with $800,000 in funding supplied by county, state, and federal agencies, was called a "spectacular" site by local contractor Edward Drill, who oversaw the project

An aerial overview of the Knife River harbor at the time of its 1974 dedication.

during the early 1970s. Rudy Perpich, Minnesota's DFL lieutenant governor at the time, dedicated the facility on a rainy Saturday in August 1974. (Perpich later served as governor from 1976 to 1979, and again from 1983 to 1991.) The MDNR acquired the site in 2001, which allowed the agency to expand its North Shore small craft and safe harbor system and also assure boaters that public access to Lake Superior would be maintained at Knife River. The privately operated marina provides one hundred boat slips, a launching ramp and boat lifter, fuel docks, a pumping station, potable water, space for winter storage, and other services. But, because of numerous deferred maintenance issues, the future status of the facility remains unclear.[27]

### Knife River Motel and Helen's Campground (*now* Knife River Campground)

196 Scenic Drive

South Dakotan Helen Ehlen Meriam opened her small Knife River Motel in 1954, three years after marrying Duluth pharmacist Arthur Meriam. By the early 1960s, she was also operating a campground, described as a "small, friendly" facility that included complete or partial hookups, clear well water, hot showers, fire pits, and picnic tables. The majority of Meriam's patrons arrived in recreational vehicles and trailers, but a few sites were also available for tent campers. After the nearby Knife River Marina opened in 1971, Meriam directed her advertisements toward two types of clients: anglers and boaters, who ventured out onto Lake Superior from the harbor, and trout fishing and smelting enthusiasts, who remained close to the river's outlet. Known as an enthusiastic promoter of both Knife River and North Shore tourism, Meriam renamed the business Helen's Campground following her husband's 1972 death. She would maintain ownership of the campground until the late 1980s.[28]

Randy and Deanna Ellestad, who purchased the facility in 2003, initially called their new acquisition the Depot Campground, which recognized the structure that had appeared along the nearby railroad tracks more than a century earlier. Later named the Knife River Campground, the Ellestads' thirty sites are proximate to one of the North Shore's "best-kept secrets"—a beach where campers enjoy picnics, sunbathing, sunrises, moonrises, and, yes, even swimming. In 2017, the couple announced the transformation of their facility into a seasonal campground that leases sites, for an entire summer, to owners of "RVs, park model RVs, tiny houses, cabin tents, micro-campers, and yurts."[29] Acknowledged as one of Knife River's most ardent supporters, Ellestad also possesses significant woodworking skills, a talent he has employed when restoring several classic North Shore fishing vessels.

**The D&NM Railway depot in Knife River, early 1920s. The restored building currently serves as the Knife River Heritage and Cultural Center.**

### Knife River Heritage and Cultural Center
South Side of the Knife River Campground

A D&NM Railway depot, built in the Lester Park neighborhood of Duluth during the late 1880s, was transported on railroad flatcars to the bustling Knife River settlement in 1899. The depot closed in 1961 after passenger service ended and was on the verge of collapse by 2018, when community and county citizens formed an organization that raised funds to restore and convert the former station and its nearby freight building into the Knife River Heritage and Cultural Center (KRHCC). Over the next two years, a group of local volunteers, among them several skilled builders, carpenters, and artisans, worked to stabilize the depot, reinforce its chimney, pour concrete footings and a new foundation slab, level the roof, cover a large hole on the ridgeline, replace most of the siding, and restore the electrical system. Interpretive panel boards and artifacts now provide information about the depot's history.[30]

Nearby on the KRHCC property is a storied fishing tug, the *Crusader II*, completed in 1939 by well-known boatbuilders Charles and Reuben Hill, a father-and-son team from nearby Larsmont. The vessel was commissioned by Carl Erickson, a Knife River fisherman and resort owner. In June 1939, Erickson even succeeded in having the still-incomplete vessel christened by Crown Prince Olav (later King Olav V) of Norway, who had arrived in Duluth while on an official tour of the United States. The tug, launched into Lake Superior three months later, served as a fishing and charter vessel before it was put on display, in 1990, next to the Two Harbors lighthouse entrance. The *Crusader II* finally returned "home" in 2016, when a group of local boat-preservation enthusiasts expressed their willingness to bring the vessel back to Knife River, where it would be restored and protected. The project acquired new life in 2023, when Florida resident Douglas Hill, a great-grandson and grandnephew of the original boatbuilders, moved to Knife River for the summer and fall months and worked on the restoration and replacement of the *Crusader II*'s deteriorated hull and ribs. (He would use some of the family's original boatbuilding tools in the effort.) Construction of a shelter that protects the boat, and also provides a viewing deck with interpretive displays, was completed in 2024.[31]

Also situated on the KRHCC grounds is another remarkable vessel, the *Leif Erickson*, a Viking ship replica built in 1925–26 by craftsmen from Korgen, Norway. The *Erickson*, just forty-two feet long, and equipped with nothing more than oars and a square sail, was navigated across the North Atlantic in 1926 by a crew of four men, including the captain, Gerhard Folgero. The twentieth-century Vikings would cope with fog, icebergs, and hurricane-force winds on their voyage, which began in Bergen and skirted the Shetland Islands, Faroe Islands, and Iceland before reaching Newfoundland in July and Boston and Philadelphia in August. While in Philadelphia, the *Erickson* was transported to the site of the nation's Sesquicentennial Exposition and put on display for three months. The crew then spent three winter months in New York City, until March 1927, when they continued their venture along the Hudson River and Erie Canal, sailed through Lakes Huron and Ontario, and entered Lake Superior. The boat and its crew reached Duluth on 23 July 1927, having traveled sixty-seven hundred miles. During their Duluth sojourn, Folgero accepted an invitation to sail the boat thirteen hundred miles to Chicago, where it was put on display for the city's 10 September Leif Erickson celebration. Because of the high winds and snowstorms that the vessel experienced on its return voyage, the *Erickson*'s October arrival in Duluth, reported Folgero, "surprised the city, which had given up hope of seeing us again."[32]

The boat was later displayed in Duluth's Leif Erickson Park, where it quickly became one of the city's major attractions. The vessel, however, experienced considerable deterioration over ensuing decades, even after a 1985 grassroots campaign, Save Our Ship, raised $200,000 for its rehabilitation. When subsequent calls for the construction of a protective shelter proved unsuccessful, the *Erickson* was put into storage,

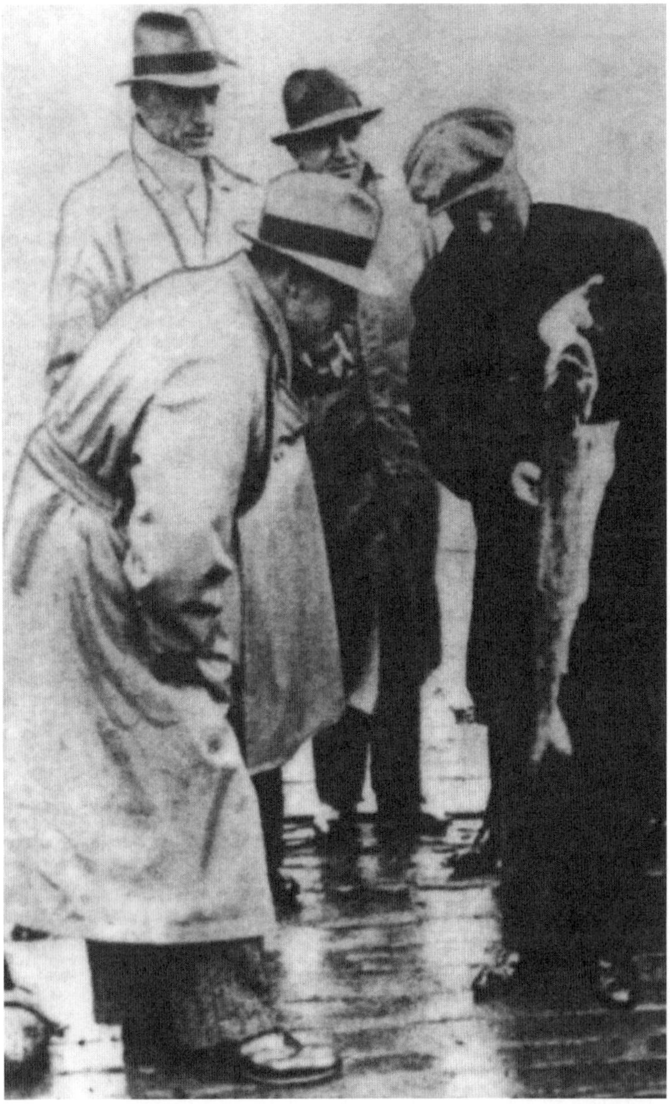

**Crown Prince Olav of Norway inspects a lake trout caught by one of Knife River's fishermen in 1939. The royal visitor, marveled a *Duluth News-Tribune* reporter, kept "a cigarette aglow in his mouth during most of the time he spent in the outdoors with Knife River fishermen." Courtesy of the *Duluth News-Tribune*, 17 June 1939, 3.**

**Douglas Hill, a descendant of the two men who built the *Crusader II* in 1938–39, works on the restoration of the fishing tug in September 2023.**

where it remained for many years. In August 2022, KRHCC officials agreed that the organization would provide funds and expertise to restore, shelter, and display the Viking-era replica in Knife River. The *Leif Erickson,* stated the *Duluth News-Tribune*'s editorial board shortly thereafter, had avoided a "Norse funeral" by finding its "forever home" in Knife River.[33] The community's talented and dedicated volunteers, who began restoring the vessel in 2024, are expected to complete their work in the near future.

### Knife River Lutheran Church
158 Church Road

One of the North Shore's oldest Protestant churches, built by a Knife River Presbyterian congregation sometime before 1907, is situated two blocks north of Scenic Drive. In 1927, the Presbyterians gave Knife River's Norwegian Lutherans permission to use the church for every-other-Sunday religious services conducted by a visiting Two Harbors pastor. But when the Lutherans announced their plans to organize a Sunday school and ladies aid group, "the Presbyterians objected to [such practices] in their place of worship." The Norwegians then moved their services into the village hall, even while admitting that the building and its facilities were less than adequate. In early 1928, after raising $186 from a Norwegian dinner of fishcakes, meatballs, vegetables, apple pie, and coffee, as well as the sale of "fancy work," the Lutheran group made a down payment on a house that seemed appropriate for church services. Once the congregation was officially organized in June, its members immediately affiliated with the Norwegian Lutheran Church of America. In 1937, when the small Presbyterian congregation was no longer able to support a church, Knife River's Lutherans purchased the building for $350.[34]

The wooden-frame structure is quite similar to many churches that emerged in small towns and rural areas of late nineteenth- and early twentieth-century America: the central tower has two entry doors that open into a small narthex, a pyramidal steeple and a cross top the bell tower, and both sidewalls have four equally spaced Gothic windows. Before dedicating their acquisition in late 1938, the congregation remodeled and insulated the interior, painted the entire building, added electricity, and attached an open entrance porch onto the narthex. The members looked well beyond Knife River's borders during World War II when they organized fish dinners and smorgasbords that raised funds for civilian relief efforts in Norway and Finland. The immediate postwar years, which focused on the creation of "a more presentable place where all may come and worship," included raising the sanctuary and tower to accommodate the construction of a lower story. (A salvaged section of railroad track stabilized the structure.) The exterior was covered with stucco in 1960, and a major building project, completed in 2002, resulted in further remodeling, additions, and improvements. The congregation currently has some 165 members.[35]

### Emily's Store/Lighthouse at Emily's *(now a private residence)*
218 Scenic Drive

In 1905, thirteen-year-old Constance Emily Hanson and her widowed aunt emigrated from Norway to Knife River. In 1929, a few years after Emily married Sigwald Erickson, also a Norwegian immigrant, the couple salvaged lumber from Archie McPhee's former retail establishment and constructed a building and living quarters that became Emily's Store. The ever-industrious Emily informed a U.S. Census enumerator, in April 1940, that she was spending eighty-four hours per week running her business. Renamed Liberty's General Store after its 1947 sale to a new owner; Emily operated the Riverview Coffee Shop in her nearby residence until 1953.[36]

Carol and Stephen Carlson, the original owner's granddaughter and her husband, acquired the building in 1989 and opened Emily's General Store, Inn and Deli, which included a bed-and-breakfast business. When the Knife River Post Office moved out of Emily's in 2000, the vacant space was converted into a kitchen for an expanded restaurant. Then, in 2011, the four local women who had recently closed the Lighthouse on Homestead in nearby Palmers leased the Knife River building. Calling their new venture the Lighthouse at Emily's, the women offered "good food, great people, and a great local tap beer list" and created a "nautical atmosphere" where Knife River's fishing heritage was honored. Unfortunately, when the owner failed to arrange a sale to a buyer who would maintain the lease, the restaurant shut down in October 2015.

Emily's, which served as a Knife River store, diner, and residence from 1929 to 2018, is shown here as the Lighthouse at Emily's, two years before it closed.

New owners opened the renamed business Emily's Eatery on Knife River in July 2017, but it, too, closed, in late 2018, much to the consternation of residents, visitors, and travelers. The entire building, after standing empty for some time, is now used as a residence.[37]

### Loining's Store *(razed)* and Mel's Fish (*now* Great! Lakes Candy Kitchen)
223 Scenic Drive

Norwegians Rasmus and Alma Loining immigrated to the Keweenaw Peninsula of Michigan's Upper Peninsula in 1889 before settling in Duluth. They and their five children joined the ranks of Knife River's Nordic fishing community in 1910. During the 1930s, their business-savvy son Thomas established Loining's Store along the upper side of Highway 61, where he sold groceries, refreshments, and Texaco gasoline and motor oil; the building also included a tavern and living quarters. About a decade later, Loining built fifteen one- and two-room cabins that provided direct access to Lake Superior and the Knife River beach. The cabins were eventually torn down, and the store, closed sometime prior to Loining's 1971 death, was also razed.[38]

Mel Bugge ran this small store from the 1960s to the 1990s. The name was maintained by the following owner until 2007, when it became the Great! Lakes Candy Kitchen.

The site was later occupied by a small fish-sales outlet owned and operated by Melvin and Sophie Marbach Bugge. Born in Knife River in 1913, Bugge, as a teenager, began fishing with his Norwegian father and also helped run the family's fish stand. During the 1960s, Bugge moved his stand to the vacant Loining site, where it once was described as "an exceedingly modest establishment, a small square building with an inviting front porch and a gravel parking lot with a capacity of maybe five cars, a herring's toss from the rocky Knife River on the North Shore Scenic Drive." In 1991, Bugge sold his wooden-hulled boat, the *Nels J*, to a buyer who reconditioned and moved the vessel to Duluth's Canal Park, where it would serve as a fish-sales stand. Following Bugge's 1994 death, a succeeding owner operated the Knife River outlet as Mel's Fish for several years.[39]

When Mel's was sold once again, this time in 2007, the building soon reopened as the Great! Lakes Candy Kitchen—owned by Patricia Canelake and Pamela Canelake Matson, twin sisters who trace their origins to the Iron Range city of Virginia. It was there that the sisters' Greek grandfather, Gus Canelake, started selling candy and fruit to customers in 1905. (The "lakes" in the store's name represents its presence in the Great Lakes and in their surname.) Among the current recipes used are some developed by Gus Canelake, whose great-grandson, Andy Matson, now manages the business, which is open from April to December.[40]

### Pine Ridge Cabins (*now* Island View Resort)
249 Scenic Drive

At the eastern end of Knife River is a picturesque grouping of cabins built by Carl and Roseina Erickson some ninety years ago. In 1899, at the age of seven,

Erickson, along with his mother and brother, departed Norway for Knife River, where they joined their fisherman father and husband. In 1913, Carl Erickson married Roseina Sutton, who, as a young girl, had moved from Michigan to Knife River with her French Canadian parents. During the 1930s, while Erickson continued working as a fisherman, the couple established Pine Ridge Cabins on their property. Later renamed Erickson's Cabins, and then Island View Resort, the facility is still operated by family descendants.[41]

The Ericksons' early advertisements announced that five housekeeping cabins were available for rent; all faced the lake and included ice, fuel, electricity, and artesian well water. Ten cabins and a shower building (now the resort office) were in place by the late 1940s. Numerous improvements would be made to the cabins throughout the following years: indoor plumbing and bathrooms were added to each unit, sheetrock was placed over the interior wall studs, and propane gas heaters replaced the wood-burning stoves. When the original screened-in porches were enclosed, Pine Ridge became a year-round resort. The cabins' yellow exterior color has been maintained from the beginning, although the doors were painted red for a time during the 1950s, when Erickson sought to attract the attention of passing motorists. Also appealing to early resort guests was Erickson's "deep-sea" fishing vessel, the *Crusader II*, designed and built by acclaimed boatbuilders Charles and Reuben Hill, of nearby Larsmont, and dedicated by Norway's Prince Olav in 1939.[42]

The Ericksons' daughter and son-in-law operated Island View from 1969 until 1988, when the resort was sold to longtime friends. The business, however, returned to the family in 2005, once the original owners' grandson and his wife, Bob and Sheryl Erickson, acquired the property. Their presence, along with a daughter who now resides nearby with her family, represents the third, fourth, and fifth generations of Ericksons at Island View.[43]

Located on the crest of a gradual hillside slope and some distance from the road, Island View still provides guests with a panoramic view of Lake Superior. Likewise, motorists who observe the resort from Scenic 61 can experience the pleasing visual qualities of several well-sited cabins, each standing before a backdrop of spruce, pine, and birch trees. Because the cabins' diminutive scale and ample spacing have remained intact for nine decades, Island View conveys a unique sense of timelessness and stability on the North Shore.

**The picturesque cabin row, established during the 1930s, has been maintained to the present at Knife River's Island View Resort.**

## Larsmont

A short distance from Knife River is Larsmont, originally identified as Milepost 22 by the D&IR Railroad in 1888. Also arriving around this time were three Norwegian brothers—Theodore, Louis, and Tollef Thompson—who secured their boats nearby, cleared some land for subsistence farming, and engaged in fishing. Other Norwegians followed them, but Finland Swedes, who initially appeared in 1909, eventually surpassed their numbers. When Larsmont's total population peaked at 120 residents in 1920, the group included eighteen foreign-born Finland Swedes (plus their fifty American-born children), twelve Norwegians, and eight Swedes. The Finland Swedes had, already in 1915, submitted a petition to rename Milepost 22 as Larsmo, the home village in Finland for many of them. But when postal and D&IR officials insisted on the more Americanized name of Larsmont, the Finland Swedes reportedly "had to take it the railroad way."[44]

Fishing served as the mainstay of Larsmont's economy for several decades. The railroad depot was even equipped with special facilities that facilitated the speedy shipment of herring to Duluth wholesalers. Larsmont was closely linked to Tobin Harbor on Isle Royale, where many families spent their summers at fishing camps. The harvesting of timber and pulpwood

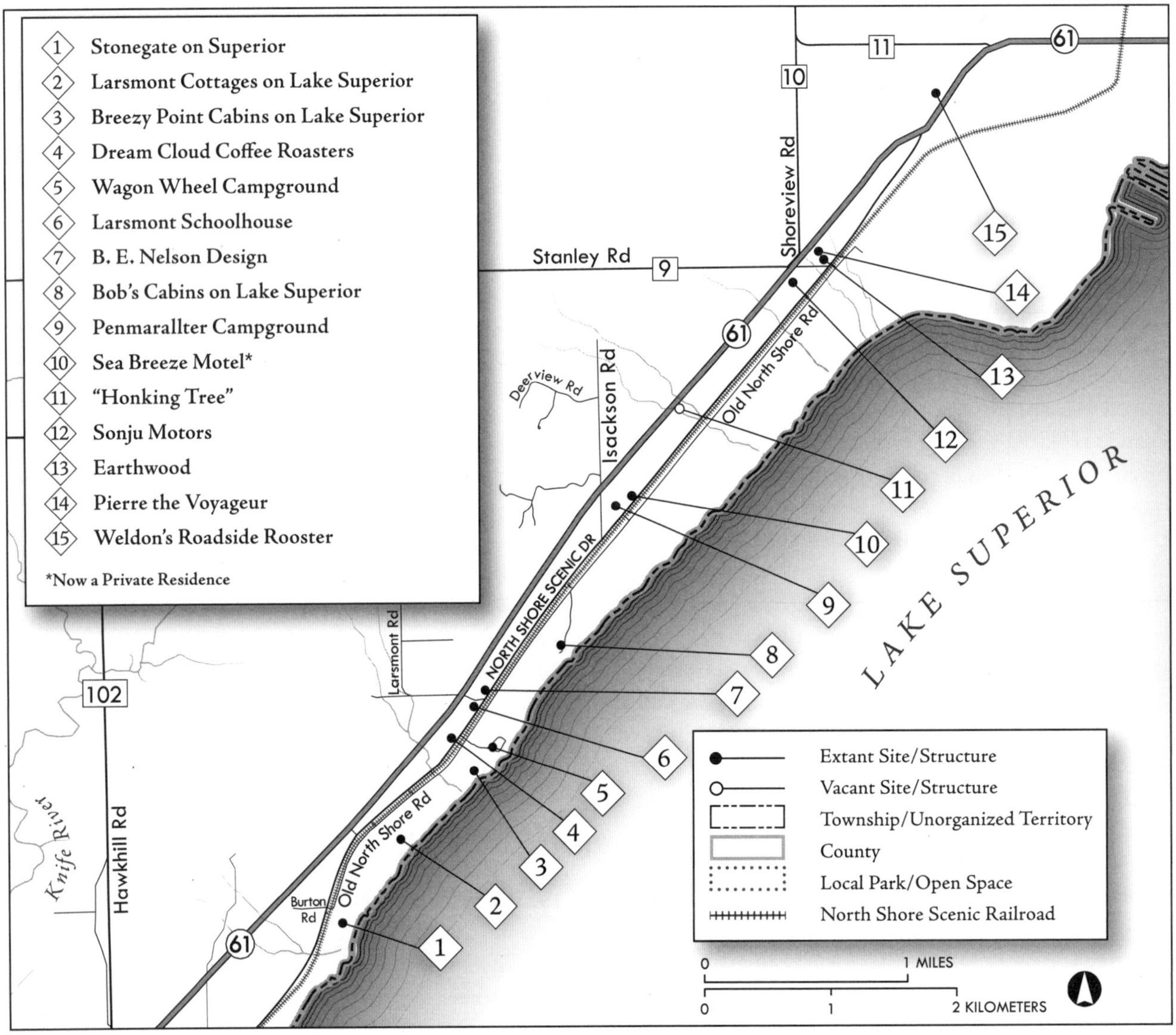

1 Stonegate on Superior
2 Larsmont Cottages on Lake Superior
3 Breezy Point Cabins on Lake Superior
4 Dream Cloud Coffee Roasters
5 Wagon Wheel Campground
6 Larsmont Schoolhouse
7 B. E. Nelson Design
8 Bob's Cabins on Lake Superior
9 Penmarallter Campground
10 Sea Breeze Motel*
11 "Honking Tree"
12 Sonju Motors
13 Earthwood
14 Pierre the Voyageur
15 Weldon's Roadside Rooster
*Now a Private Residence
Extant Site/Structure
Vacant Site/Structure
Township/Unorganized Territory
County
Local Park/Open Space
North Shore Scenic Railroad
LAKE SUPERIOR
Stanley Rd
Shoreview Rd
Isackson Rd
Deerview Rd
Larsmont Rd
Hawkhill Rd
Burton Rd
Old North Shore Rd
NORTH SHORE SCENIC DR
Knife River
61
102
11
10
9
0
1 MILES
1
2 KILOMETERS

also occurred during the early 1900s. And, for almost three-quarters of a century, Larsmont was home to the North Shore's best-known and most prolific boatbuilding family: Charles Hill and his four sons, notably Reuben, the second youngest.[45]

Charles Hill emigrated from Finland to Michigan's Upper Peninsula in 1893 and was later employed by a Duluth boatworks. In 1899, he married Maria Mattson, who had arrived from Larsmo nine years earlier. While living on Encampment Island, located by the Lake County settlement of Castle Danger in 1902–3, Hill built the *Thor*, which became part of the legendary Mosquito Fleet—a group of small, independent North Shore vessels that competed successfully with large freight and fish haulers. The family, eventually including nine children, settled in 1910 at Larsmont, where Hill established his boatbuilding business.[46]

Reuben Hill was just ten years old in 1913 when he began assisting his father with simple boatbuilding tasks. At the time of the elder Hill's 1950 death, his son had already established a reputation as one of the North Shore's "premier builders of gas boats"—even though he was simultaneously employed by DM&IR's bridge and building department. During the more than four decades that Reuben Hill was involved in boatbuilding, the Larsmont denizen gained renown for the "innate sense of form" displayed by his vessels and the attention he gave to each of them. Folklorist Timothy Cochrane has stated that Hill believed in his "responsibility to understand the basic needs of a customer and then find the best way to meet those needs." Rather than preparing plans or drawings, Hill glued pieces of pine and mahogany together and carved an exact, small-scale half model of the envisioned craft. He then began the tedious task of laying out each boat, at the scale of three-quarters inches to one foot, on paper spread out over the floor of the family's crowded home. Hill possessed, said longtime acquaintance Alvera Pierson, "the mind of an engineer, mathematician, carpenter, draftsman, and artist all rolled into one, [along] with much humor and patience."[47]

When Reuben Hill died at age ninety-two in 1997, it was determined that he, either by himself or with his father and other family members, had constructed at least 120 boats. The Hills' armada included gasboats, rowboats, tugboats, freight boats, sailboats, and, most remarkably, five antisubmarine boats completed for the U.S. Navy during World War II. The family built "very good boats," remarked veteran North Shore fisherman Walter Sve at the time of Hill's passing. "I've been in some pretty rough weather on their boats," he recalled, "and they always pulled me through." A few of the Hills' boats remain today, including the *Viking*, now on display at Tofte's North Shore Commercial Fishing Museum, and the aforementioned *Crusader II*, in Knife River.[48]

Another form of economic activity was initiated at Larsmont during the late 1920s when a few modest tourist cabins were built along Old North Shore Road by John and Anna Hendrickson. Both Finland Swedes, the couple and their three children moved, in 1912, from Duluth to Larsmont, where Hendrickson worked as a commercial fisherman. The Hendricksons rented out the cabins for some twenty years, but seldom, if ever, advertised their business. Operated as Fitch's Cabins for a brief time following Hendrickson's 1949 death, the units were eventually sold and converted into private homes.[49]

At least seven other cabin and resort complexes have appeared along Larsmont's section of the North Shore since the 1930s. Three of the four that remain retain much evidence of their original appearance and layout. Also standing along Scenic Drive are two early twentieth-century structures: a former store that later became a popular coffee shop and a cherished schoolhouse, currently a community building. Although the settlement is unincorporated and has no official boundaries, the Burton Forge & Gallery (443 Scenic Drive) might be considered Larsmont's southwestern "entrance." The forge and gallery were started some thirty years ago by local craftsman and resident Dale Burton, who creates and sells his handcrafted metal and wooden items from a timber-frame gallery building that is sheathed with board and batten siding.

### Stonegate on Superior
#### 412 Scenic Drive

Only a few feet before the Scenic Drive–Old North Shore Road intersection is an entrance to Stonegate on Superior, opened as Stone-Gate Cabins during the late 1930s by Esther Vinquist Erickson, a Finland Swede who had immigrated to Duluth in 1899 at the age of sixteen. She was assisted by her Swedish American husband, Charles, a locomotive fireman and "cement finisher," and some of their nine children. Erickson's advertisements emphasized Stone-Gate's eight "completely modern" cabins, each of which had "beautiful" lake views and "secluded spots for sunbathing." Because of limited space, the cabins' placement did not follow the Lake Superior shoreline. Instead, the small structures were strategically sited in a free-form pattern that allowed each cabin to overlook the lake. Although all of the units have been upgraded or rebuilt since the 1930s, they still maintain their original footprints and vistas. Also standing at the entrance are two original concrete gateposts, both of which reveal the resort's name and Charles Erickson's masonry skills. When current owners Brook and Kendra Wright purchased Stonegate in 2017, they became the third generation of a family who, for more than eight decades, has owned and managed several businesses at the western end of Larsmont.[50]

### Wright's Cabins/Big Blaze Campground (*now* Larsmont Cottages on Lake Superior)
596 Larsmont Way

In 1939, Franklin Wright, just twenty-two years of age, moved from Duluth to Larsmont, where he began building cabins on a recently acquired tract of prime Lake Superior property; Wright's Cabins would open to tourists within two years. Since Wright served as a U.S. Army Air Corps navigator and bombardier during World War II, Charlotte Boynton Wright, whom he married during the early 1940s, operated the business throughout his absence. Although gasoline rationing restricted the number of tourists who arrived by automobile, the resourceful woman informed prospective patrons that buses running between Duluth and Canada still stopped at the resort. Following Wright's return from military service, the couple advertised the "private and quiet" qualities of their cabins and also opened a commercial nursery that was tied to another similar family business in Duluth. They later established the Big Blaze Camp and Trailer Park on the property, which was eventually operated by their son and daughter-in-law.[51]

In 2004, Odyssey Resorts, a North Shore company, acquired the forty-four-acre Big Blaze holding and its thirteen hundred feet of shoreline. Within a year, Odyssey opened the first phase of what became a large, full-service resort, Larsmont Cottages on Lake Superior. Modeled on the physical appearance of Nordic fishing villages, the buildings exhibit steeply pitched roofs, extensive use of wood, and muted colors. The centrally located lodge has a full-service restaurant and covered outdoor veranda; nearby are a heated swimming pool, an outdoor whirlpool, an exercise room, a lakeside massage cottage with two therapy rooms, and a wood-fired Finnish sauna converted from a former cabin. The forty "cottages" include thirty-six that are sited along the lakeshore and four located in a semisecluded, wooded area. The majority are apportioned into fractional, one-quarter shares; those with second-floor bedrooms also have separate "lockout" entrances that allow them to be rented out even when the lower floor is occupied by another renter. Odyssey Resorts was sold to the Minnesota-based Blackburn Investment Management and Madison Hospitality Group in 2019, but the original name and business model have been retained.[52]

### Barthell's Cabins *(now private residences)*
Old North Shore Road

Andrew Barthell, a Finland Swede, immigrated to the mining town of San Juan, Colorado, in 1899. By 1909, a few years after arriving in Butte, Montana, the twenty-eight-year-old copper miner had married Hannah Happala, a Finnish boardinghouse servant. In 1914, the couple and their two children departed Montana for Larsmont, where three of Barthell's sisters resided. The Barthells acquired forty acres of land from boatbuilder Charles Hill and constructed their residence close to the lakeshore. Sadly, Barthell died suddenly in 1919, five months before his wife gave birth to their sixth child.[53]

In 1935, the always-resilient Hannah Barthell borrowed $500 from a member of her church and opened five shoreline cabins, all constructed of vertical logs; another five were added later. Advertisements for Barthell's "new seaside log cabins" began appearing in North Shore tourist brochures by 1937. When Hannah retired from the cabin business in 1964 (eighteen years before passing away at age ninety-seven), the matriarch's widowed daughter and six children moved from Illinois to manage the resort, which they did until 1976. The property was then divided among the three surviving Barthell children. Daughter Mille retained the original resort and home, where a grandson resided until 2019; one son, Milton, moved some cabins onto his land and rented them out until the property was sold following his 2004 death; and the eldest son, Walter of Two Harbors, retained the property where, many years earlier, he had constructed a boathouse and smokehouse. A CCC enrollee during the late 1930s, Walter Barthell served in the U.S. Navy throughout much of World War II and was then employed by the DM&IR for more than thirty years. Despite the demands of a full-time job, Barthell, using his skiff, the *Zsa Zsa*, also engaged in commercial fishing and ran a charter boat service. "Walt worked on the docks at night and fished during the day," recalled a neighbor in 2006. "There wasn't much sleeping time." Throughout the winter months, Barthell, assisted by his wife and children, smoked, pickled, packaged, and weighed the fish, which he trucked to different places in Minnesota and Wisconsin. Until his passing at age ninety-seven in 2010, Barthell continued renting out a few tourist cabins. His children still own the property, but none reside there.[54]

### Breezy Point Cabins on Lake Superior
540 Old North Shore Road

Sophia Ostrom and John Sjoblom, both Finland Swedes, emigrated separately to Duluth, where they married in 1903. Working as a shoemaker until 1910, Sjoblom, along with his wife and children, moved to Larsmont, where he began pursuing commercial fishing and also served as Larsmont's postmaster from 1919 to 1935. The origins of John's Breezy Point Cabins date to the mid-1930s, when Sjoblom and his three sons constructed twelve small, minimally furnished lakeshore cabins. Each cabin sat atop the shelf of Larsmont basalt that protected them, "even as the winds whipped up and pummeled the land." The Sjobloms termed their property "an ideal place for hay fever sufferers" and a prime "bathing and boating" location.[55]

The couple's son and daughter-in-law, Lester and Martha Sjoblom, assumed ownership of the resort in 1951. A Duluth fireman, Sjoblom, in 1940, had married Martha Nygard, who taught in rural St. Louis County's school system for several years. The couple and their three daughters resided in Duluth, but because of his fireman's schedule—twenty-four hours on, twenty-four hours off—Sjoblom was often free to work at the resort; Martha Sjoblom, however, was totally in charge whenever her husband was fulfilling his fireman's duties. The Sjobloms' daughter and son-in-law, Marilyn and Richard Loining, acquired the resort in 1974 and ran the business until it was sold to Odyssey Resorts in 2015.[56]

Odyssey's acquisition of the twelve cabins, twelve acres of land, and one thousand feet of shoreline occurred several years after the company had purchased the nearby Big Blaze Campground and developed Larsmont Cottages on Lake Superior. The company sought to maintain Breezy Point's "original form," along with its "northwoods feel" and "rustic charm"—even as the cabins simultaneously received "a good dose of the modern era to wake them up." Odyssey's $3 million investment in Breezy Point included enlarged windows, which make the most of several striking lake views; furniture fabricated of cast iron and driftwood; reclaimed wooden cabinets and tables; stainless steel appliances; new kitchens and bathrooms; reconfigured floor plans; and cabin winterization. The underlying concept, claimed Odyssey's development team, was the implementation of a "rustic chic aesthetic." Purchasers may acquire a one-quarter share in a single Breezy

**The cabins at Breezy Point on Lake Superior closely follow an irregular section of the Larsmont shoreline. Google Maps, 2018.**

Point cabin, which is available for rent when not being used by the owner.[57]

### Keinonen's Cheese House Market, Mocha Moose Coffee Café (*now* Dream Cloud Coffee Roasters)
543 Scenic Drive

On the upper side of Scenic Drive is Larsmont's oldest remaining commercial building—the former Cheese House Market, which Ray and Pearl Keinonen, both children of Finnish immigrants, opened in 1950. Keinonen, a native of Waukegan, Illinois, worked as a butcher in the city's Finnish cooperative store during the 1930s. He married Pearl Vanhala, a Duluth native who, in 1935, had moved to the Chicago area, attended Northwestern University in Evanston, and also found employment in the accounting office of Abbott Laboratories. She would move back to Duluth in 1944 while her husband was serving with the U.S. Army in Europe. Upon his return, the Keinonens opened their Larsmont store in a one-and-a-half story building that had living quarters above and an attached flat-roofed addition, which served as a walk-in cooler and freezer for meat products. During the late fall, hunters brought their deer to the store, where Keinonen butchered and processed the venison and carefully wrapped and labeled each package before placing it into the freezer. Keinonen served as Larsmont's postmaster from 1965 to 1977, when James Kinslow bought the property. Kinslow's tenure as postmaster was short-lived, however, since the office closed one year later—a "sad day" for Larsmont's residents. The settlement is now served by Two Harbors' post office.[58]

The Kinslow building, following its 2013 purchase by a mother-and-daughter team, Micki and Penny Agar, was converted into the Mocha Moose Coffee Café. Almost immediately, travelers and residents were attracted to the Moose because of its selection of coffees, homemade baked goods and food, and locally produced gifts and artwork. Once the former cooler was converted into overflow seating for special events, the Moose emerged as a community center where local residents could interact with one another, use the internet service, pursue arts and crafts classes, bring their children to programs, and listen to or engage in both organized and spontaneous musical events. Because of Micki Agar's wish to retire, however, the Moose was put up for sale in early 2020 and purchased, three years later, by Charlie and Emily Comnick, the former owners of a Duluth specialty coffee shop that had offered programs and opportunities for bakers, painters, ceramicists, photographers, and "craft process enthusiasts." The Comnicks' Dream Cloud venture, which opened in 2024, is intended to accommodate changes and "new interpretations" that both they and their patrons may wish to pursue in the future.[59]

### Wagon Wheel Campsite
552 Old North Shore Road

Immediately south of the Dream Cloud, but with access provided from Old North Shore Road, is the Wagon Wheel Campsite, positioned on land acquired in 1909 by Victor and Sophia Barthell Sjoblom. Also a Larsmo immigrant, Sjoblom worked as a Duluth shoemaker before he and his wife established a small farm at Larsmont; however, most of the income for their family, which included nine children, was secured from Sjoblom's commercial fishing activities. Two subsequent owners occupied the acreage before it was acquired by the couple's niece and her husband, Leonard and Judy Sjoblom Beardsley, who immediately established the Wagon Wheel Campsite on the grounds in 1967.[60]

The Beardsleys ran Wagon Wheel as a full-service campground with thirty-four sites that catered to both short-term and long-term renters until 2006, when it was limited to campers who parked their recreational vehicles and trailers for an entire tourist season. The campground, in fact, soon became a second-home community for many clients who, year after year, occupied the sites from May through October.[61] The Wagon Wheel, which marked its fifty-fifth anniversary in 2022, is one of only a few North Shore businesses to have been owned and operated by the same proprietors for more than a half century.

### Larsmont Schoolhouse and Community Club
701 Larsmont Road

The center of Larsmont is located at the intersection of Larsmont Road and Scenic Drive, where two distinctive buildings, their origins separated by almost eighty years, are located—one a former schoolhouse, the other a contemporary gift shop. No existing build-

**This former schoolhouse, now a community building, has been a fixture in Larsmont since 1914.**

ing better defines Larsmont's history than does the schoolhouse, built by Charles Hill and John Strom in 1914, two years after students started attending classes in local homes. The building was also used by Larsmont's Baptists for religious services and Sunday school classes, Christmas and musical programs, weddings, and funerals. Memorial Day picnics, Fourth of July celebrations, and baseball games occurred on the grounds. The school closed in 1932, shortly after consolidating with the Lake County School District. Larsmont's Gospel Mission Society acquired the building in 1938, followed by the Larsmont Volunteer Fire Department in 1959. The building is now owned and managed by the Larsmont Community Club.[62]

Constructed on concrete piers, the building is a simple but well proportioned, an almost square, one-story structure with a small entry porch. A kitchen occupies the former library and cloakroom, while the classroom area is identified by a hipped roof and windows on the southwestern wall. The exterior still retains its original wooden lap siding, which was painted "schoolhouse red" with white trim during the 1990s.[63]

Since opening more than century ago, the one-time schoolhouse has maintained its position as a Larsmont landmark and social center—even as the vast majority of early twentieth-century one-room schoolhouses in Minnesota, and Lake County in particular, have been razed or considerably altered. The listing of the schoolhouse in the National Register of Historic Places, already in 1992, confirmed its uniqueness, significance, historic integrity, and high level of maintenance.[64]

### B. E. Nelson Design Silversmith
583 Scenic Drive

Another important Larsmont building, Ollie's Store, was located close to the schoolhouse until the 1990s. Opened in 1929 by Oliver and Vera Hill Isaacson, Ollie's served as a general store, although the staff was also kept busy "waiting on tourists, pumping gas, and scooping out ice cream cones." Besides operating the store, Isaacson was well known for his participation in civic affairs and efforts to conserve the Lake Superior area's environmental and scenic values. After Isaacson sold the business in 1966, several owners occupied the building until 1980, some years before it was razed.[65]

Larsmont artist and silversmith Bradley Nelson, whose grandparents had emigrated from Sweden to the Two Harbors area in 1885, acquired the vacant property during the 1990s. Nelson constructed a new building on the site, but one that is rooted in a centuries-old Norwegian building tradition, the *stabbur*, originally used to store grain, food, and important household items. In Norway, a *stabbur* was typically two stories high and placed above the ground on posts or pillars. The lower floor was constructed of logs, whereas vertical staves were often used to build the upper floor. The sidewalls of the second story jutted somewhat over the lower section, which made it more difficult for rodents to access the upper level; the roof, sometimes covered with sod, had wide overhangs. Decorative carvings often appeared on the corner posts, railings, door- and window frames, and roof brackets.[66]

Nelson was fascinated with children's fairy-tale books, many based on Nordic themes, including those written and illustrated by Jan Brett, an American writer and illustrator. Later, when consulting sources on Norwegian folk architecture, Nelson determined that it would not be possible to construct an exact replica of a *stabbur* because of excessively high costs. Instead, he combined three different styles to establish the building's proportions and the decorative design details that are visible on its corner posts and entrance doorframe. Especially indicative of the building's timber-frame components are the large main beam

**Silversmith B. E. Nelson's Norwegian-inspired *stabbur*, dating to 1997, is complemented by the gardens and stone walls that he also designed and built. Photograph by Marlene Wisuri, 2016.**

and supporting members. Since opening in 1997, the building has served as a studio where Nelson designs and creates jewelry and maintains a sales shop that also includes the work of several Nordic artists.[67]

### Jacobsen's New Lake Front Cabins (*now* Bob's Cabins on Lake Superior)
664 Old North Shore Road

Bob's Cabins is one of relatively few remaining North Shore resorts that maintains many of the features and traditions guests once experienced in mom-and-pop businesses of the immediate postwar period. Norwegian immigrants Ingvald and Bertha Jacobsen built the original cabins in 1928—sixteen years after their move from Two Harbors to Larsmont, where they joined the community's Nordic fishing and farming families. The couple eventually opened Jacobsen's New Lake Front Cabins, which included seventeen one-room lakeside cabins. The exteriors were covered with varnished siding and rolled roofing, while the interiors had bare wooden floors and wall studs. Iron bedframes (still in use today), a washstand and pitcher, and a wood-burning stove constituted the interior furnishings. Before 1940, the Jacobsens' advertisements mentioned little more than the "clean and cozy" cabins and modest rental charges, which began at $1.50 per day. In 1942, the recently widowed Jacobsen noted that all of his units were equipped with electric lights and screened-in porches, while water for the shower room was pumped in from Lake Superior.[68]

Jacobsen sold the property to Duluthians Robert and Doris Sansom in 1948. Renaming their acquisition Bob's Cabins, the Sansoms operated the "modest but widely respected resort" until 1977. During their period of ownership, the couple maintained the basic character of Jacobsen's cabins, although they did make a few changes and additions: some cabins were enlarged by joining smaller units together, porches were rebuilt, and the bare interior walls were covered with plasterboard. The pump that brought Lake Superior water into the shower room was replaced by a new well that also served the cabins' kitchens and recently installed indoor bathrooms. The numerous pine and spruce seedlings planted by the Sansoms have grown and now tower over the grounds. Peg Morris and Ed Landin, after purchasing Bob's in 1977, attached decks onto the cabins and added more trees and vegetation to the grounds. The couple ran Bob's until 1993, when it was sold to Bill Guse.[69]

A carpenter, plumber, painter, electrician, and overall handyman, with knowledge of geology, ecology, civil

**Bob's Cabins during the 1930s. The linear cabin layout established by Ingvald and Bertha Jacobsen during the late 1920s has been maintained to the present.**

engineering, history, and economics, Guse traced his management philosophy to the German-born architect Ludwig Mies van der Rohe (1886–1969), who later moved to the United States, where he popularized the aphorism "less is more." While Guse informed guests that the "cabins and their furnishings are simple," he also reminded them that such "simplicity can remind us that we can have intense satisfaction and enjoyment without a luxurious built setting." Among those assisting Guse was Jim Goodman, who began doing lawn mowing and other basic work at the resort when he was fourteen years old. In 2020, Goodman and his wife, Laura, purchased Bob's, thereby assuring that the resort will continue into the foreseeable future as it has for decades—"neat and tidy, a bit old-fashioned in appearance, and well maintained."[70]

### Penmarallter Campsite
725 Scenic Drive

Shortly after retiring from the U.S. Navy in the late 1960s, Two Harbors native Cliff Hanson and his wife, Lee, amassed several small parcels of adjacent land situated between Scenic Drive and the Highway 61 Expressway. In 1968, the couple opened a campground on the property, which they named Penmarallter—a word formed from the first three letters of their children's names: Pennie, Marilyn, Allen, and Terry. The Hansons operated the campground until 1992, when it was acquired by their daughter and son-in-law, Pennie and Stan Burton. The Penmarallter property continues to provide space for twenty-four recreational vehicles during the tourist season.[71]

### Sea Breeze Motel *(razed, now a residence)*
735 Scenic Drive

The Sea Breeze Motel, which had nine imitation adobe units linked together by carports, was built in 1949 by Two Harbors railroad engineer David M. Anderson, who had been inspired by the motels he'd observed while traveling through the American Southwest shortly after the conclusion of World War II. The Sea Breeze, one of the North Shore's two earliest motels, had simple one-room units that included a kitchenette and shower bath. Anderson operated the Sea Breeze until the late 1960s or early 1970s, when it was torn down and replaced by a residence.[72]

### Honking Tree *(removed)*
Highway 61 Expressway

Until 2009, a white pine, affectionally known as the Honking Tree, stood along the inside lane of the expressway that connects Larsmont to Two Harbors. Located about three miles southwest of Two Harbors, the tree was the largest of several that survived construction activities during the early 1960s, but only because an MnDOT inspector lobbied for its protection. Eventually, many Two Harbors residents established a tradition—honking when passing by the tree on their return to the city. When the pine, with an estimated age of 107 years, was mysteriously cut down in April 2009, local residents were outraged, although no one was ever charged for the act. MnDOT, in 2010, authorized the creation of nine medallions from slices of the trunk—each with a silhouette of the tree and the years 1902–2009 inscribed on it. Most of the medallions are now on display in several public offices throughout Two Harbors.[73]

### Sonju Motors
893 Scenic Drive

Scenic Drive and the expressway merge just southwest of the boundary that separates Unorganized Territory No. 2 and the city of Two Harbors. Less than one mile before the intersection is Sonju Motors, a large automobile dealership. Tourists who encounter the intersection on a busy Friday or Sunday afternoon often contend with high traffic volumes as they enter or exit Two Harbors. Most, however, very likely do not realize that equivalent or even greater vehicle densities, albeit of a stationary nature, exist on Sonju Motors' thirty-acre "car campus."

The company dates to 1925, when Alfred Sonju, the son of Norwegian immigrants from Lake County's Finland settlement, opened a Ford dealership within Two Harbors. Sonju kept the business open around the clock, from 1931 to 1945, by selling gasoline, offering towing service, and providing storage space for Greyhound buses and other vehicles. After his son-in-law Alder Johnson assumed leadership of the company in 1966, the inventory of vehicles was expanded to such an extent that Sonju's operations were moved to a Seventh Street site in Two Harbors, and then to its current Scenic Drive location during the 1980s. Later, a few non–family members who had invested in Sonju acquired the company, which maintains its position as one of northeastern Minnesota's largest automobile dealerships. Also linked to the site is Grandma's Marathon, an internationally recognized race that dates to June 1977. The race participants (seventy-five hundred in 2024) start the marathon on the section of Scenic Drive that parallels Sonju Motors' large vehicle lot, proceed to and through Duluth along the Lake Superior shoreline, and end in the city's Canal Park district. The race course, observed Volha Mazuronak of Belarus, who won the 2024 women's marathon, is "beautiful with scenery."[74]

### House of Sweden (*now* Earthwood Inn, Restaurant & Bar)
#### 933 Stanley Road

Just before the western boundary of Two Harbors is the former House of Sweden, opened in 1948 by Walter J. and Karin Johnson Grant of Duluth. Grant was the son of Swedish immigrants; his wife emigrated from Sweden as a teenager in 1915. The couple remained in Duluth following their 1924 marriage but began building the House of Sweden during the immediate post–World War II period. While the single-story hip-roofed restaurant, constructed of cinder blocks and wood, appeared quite similar to many North Shore residences, advertisements for their new business boldly announced one of the building's high-tech features—large "Thermopane" (double-pane glass) windows. When announcing the restaurant's June 1948 grand opening, the Grants claimed that their patrons would "dine in a pleasant Swedish environment and enjoy delicious foods prepared for the most discriminating taste." The Swedish smorgasbord also became popular among Two Harbors' large Nordic population. A flat-roofed addition was later attached to the rear of the restaurant, and a separate ten-unit motel appeared nearby.[75]

Duluthians Tony and Margaret Lubina Radosovich purchased the House of Sweden in 1971. The owners, both children of Croatian and Slovenian immigrants, changed the name to Radosovich's Earthwood Inn, Restaurant, Bar, and Motel and transformed the former Nordic cuisine into one that emphasized traditional American fare. The Radosoviches ran Earthwood until late 2010, when Eric Potts and Sandra Fritz bought the business. Besides remodeling and upgrading the property, Potts and Fritz purchased and transferred a nearby roadside attraction, Pierre the Voyageur, to the Earthwood grounds.[76]

### Pierre the Voyageur
#### Stanley Road, Slightly North of Earthwood

Until it was moved in 2011, Pierre the Voyageur loomed above the Voyageur Museum and Motel, located about two miles east of Earthwood along Highway 61. The idea for both the museum, which closed years ago, and Pierre came from Voyageur Motel owner Stanley Nelson. In 1960, Nelson hired Art Carlstrom, a Two Harbors "master plaster and stucco man," who designed and supervised construction of the statue. Built of railroad ties, wire mesh, and stucco, with telephone poles for legs, Pierre stood twenty feet high and weighed an estimated five thousand pounds. Much to the delight of children, Pierre originally spoke with a resounding voice and moved his head and eyes. The Duluth construction crew that transported Pierre to the Radosoviches' Earthwood location in early 2011 began their "surgery"

**Pierre the Voyageur, built in 1960, was moved, fifty years later, to its current location.**

by sawing off the voyageur's head, cutting his legs at ground level, and using a crane to lift the disparate parts onto a flatbed truck. After being slowly transported, disassembled, to Earthwood, Pierre was "refurbished" and soon put back together. Although a March 2017 windstorm blew off the statue's paddle and one arm, repairs were made, and Pierre still greets motorists who travel along the expressway.[77]

### Weldon's Gift Shop and Roadside Rooster
1065-MN 61

About one-half mile northeast of Pierre is another popular, albeit much smaller, roadside attraction—a rooster. The fiberglass fowl, which is only about eight feet high, has stood at the entrance to Weldon's Gift Shop since 1965, two years after Weldon and Marion Johnson established their business on the property. According to family lore, it was an awareness of Finnish traditions that led the Johnsons to select and purchase the rooster from a collection of fiberglass animals—including a bear, horse, and Sinclair Oil Corporation dinosaur—all displayed on a flatbed truck. (The rooster, in Finnish folklore, acts against negative forces, serves as a symbol of morning light, and represents cosmic order and the cyclical nature of time.) Vandals, on three occasions, have removed and deposited the rooster elsewhere, including one especially damaging event, in 2003, when the roadside bird was pitched off a bridge situated twenty feet above Duluth's Amity Creek. Johnson's rooster, nevertheless, was quickly repaired by several fiberglass artisans, all of them Northwest (now Delta) Airlines employees who volunteered their services for the project.[78]

## City of Two Harbors

Minnesota Highway 61 coexists with Seventh Avenue in Two Harbors. Several residences still remain along the avenue, but both sides of the corridor are dominated by diners, restaurants, automobile service stations, motels, and similar commercial establishments. Some motorists, in fact, don't even realize that Two Harbors' downtown business district is situated just a few blocks south of Seventh Avenue. A noticeable exception to the strip development pattern is Lakeview Cemetery, a large expanse of open space that appears on the avenue's southern side. Designated a cemetery already in 1884, Lakeview now includes from eight thousand to nine thousand burials, although an unknown number are unmarked.[79] Lakeview is, by far, the largest cemetery along Highway 61, and other than Duluth, it has a "population" greater than any North Shore city.

The ensuing discussion provides a broad overview of Two Harbors' evolution from its nineteenth-century origins to the present and then turns to an examination of specific sites within the city. At least three structures that date to Two Harbors' mid-1880s origins as an iron ore port are among the North Shore's oldest buildings.

### Two Bays: Agate and Burlington

Hundreds of years before the earliest appearance of Europeans, the Anishinaabe called the Two Harbors area *Wasswawinig,* "a place to spear fish at night by torch light." The major physical features are its two bays, respectively termed "Agate" and "North Agate" by early white observers, before the latter name was changed to Burlington Bay. A very small Euro-American presence may have been evident during the 1840s when a few AFC employees possibly settled by the waterfront; rumors of copper deposits also attracted prospectors, who built shanties along Agate Bay in late 1854. The next year, Thomas Sexton, an Irish Canadian, ventured to the area and established a claim for 154 acres of shoreline land. While Sexton found no copper, the pioneer settler did clear twenty acres of land, some of which he cultivated. Sexton also built two small structures, one of them a cabin, "14 by 16, with a good roof," before acquiring title to the property for one dollar per acre in 1863.[80]

In 1856, J. J. Hibbard and his brother platted the townsite of Burlington along the eastern bay, where they established two steam-powered sawmills. The Hibbards' small workforce and some other inhabitants who pursued fishing, prospecting, and fur trading resided in a few small houses. Most of Burlington's settlers dispersed after the sawmills closed in 1859, and the entire townsite was abandoned five years later.[81]

Agate Bay experienced a dramatic transformation following the arrival of agents employed by industrialist Charlemagne Tower Sr., who had been funding iron ore exploration efforts in northeastern Minnesota since 1872. Once Tower's agents confirmed the commercial viability of deposits on the Vermilion Range in 1882, the Philadelphia financier organized the Minnesota Iron Company (MIC). The natural Agate Bay harbor, sixty-eight miles south of the Vermilion, was selected as the location for the company's railroad and shipping activities. The site was also favorable because of the bay's clay bottom, a rare feature along the rocky shoreline. In April 1883, Sexton sold all but four of his 154 acres to George Stone, Tower's primary agent. Throughout summer 1883, workers employed by MIC and the D&IR Railroad, the latter a recent Tower acquisition, began transforming Agate Bay into "a bustling hive of industrial activity." D&IR's labor force converted the property's remaining timber resources into lumber, beams, and railroad ties, all used to construct numerous buildings and structures, most notably two ore docks that extended into Agate Bay. Because no road existed between Duluth and Two Harbors, all supplies were brought by steamer to the bay, where "horses and men, rails, barrels of railroad spikes and blasting powder and a myriad [of] other materials were unloaded."[82]

## Whiskey Row

The Minnesota Iron Company's workers were quartered on the four acres of land that Sexton astutely subdivided into thirty-nine small lots. The holding would serve as the locus for "Whiskey Row," a name that referenced its early establishments, most of which offered lodging, food, spirits, entertainment, and ample material for Two Harbors' most colorful period of history. The number of men arriving is significant, wrote one observer in June 1883, while another account claimed that nine of Agate Bay's twenty-five hastily constructed structures and tents were saloons, all of them crowded along the waterfront landing. Numerous observers and reporters lost no time in portraying Whiskey Row as a center of vice and debauchery. John L. Morrison, writing in 1900, identified the workers as "masters in the art of celebrating pay day," while George Rock, D&IR's freight and passenger agent and a committed Presbyterian, termed Whiskey Row "the vilest of vile resorts." N. C. Nelson, who ran D&IR's sawmill in 1883 and later became a Two Harbors businessman, even claimed that "dead bodies were thrown into any convenient hole without the least semblance of a funeral ceremony." The seeming decadence, however, did not deter sightseers from boarding steamships in Duluth and making their way to the busy construction site. Among them were members of a Duluth Baptist Sunday school, who engaged in a search for Lake Superior agates. Whiskey Row's tenure, nevertheless, was very brief. An 1884 fire destroyed some of the structures, but the transfer of buildings that occurred after Sexton sold his property to Tower for the "princely" sum of $20,000 was primarily responsible for its demise: Whiskey Row's remaining structures were quickly razed or transferred to new sites. Several other businesses were established in a more "respectable" area farther north of the docks, where MIC officials had platted the new townsite of Two Harbors in 1885.[83]

Accounts of Whiskey Row's brief but turbulent social history have been repeated and embellished so many times that they now form the core of Two Harbors' early folklore. Hal Bridges, the author of a 1952 biography of Charlemagne Tower, even created a new term for Whiskey Row: "Hell's Four Acres." Archaeologist Timothy Tumberg's review of Two Harbors' early years, however, revealed no evidence that Hell's Four Acres was ever used to describe the site. Tumberg also oversaw a team that excavated and analyzed material culture evidence gathered from a three-year-long investigation (2008–10) of Whiskey Row. Their study determined that the "sinful" nature of the site had very likely been overstated ever since 1883. The paucity of "saloon-related artifacts," concluded Tumberg, "overwhelmingly support[s] the notion that it was a typical frontier community."[84]

## Ore Docks and a Townsite

Crews of laborers were working feverishly to complete wooden Dock No. 1 during summer 1884, before the first iron ore shipment arrived by rail from the Soudan Mine. All activities quickly shifted to Dock No. 2 after a section of the still-incomplete Dock No. 1 collapsed when its clay footings shifted. Once the *Three Spot* locomotive and ten accompanying railcars arrived at Agate Bay on 31 July, the iron ore was dumped into the holds of the steamer *Hecla* and its tow schooner-barge the *Ironton*; both vessels proceeded, in early August, to steel mills in Cleveland, Ohio. The eventual completion of Dock No. 1 allowed MIC to handle the

**Many of the tents and hastily constructed buildings at Two Harbors' Whiskey Row in 1883 were located proximate to the Agate Bay shoreline. Courtesy of Lake Superior Maritime Collections, UW–Superior.**

increasing volume of ore that arrived during ensuing years. Three more docks would be built before the new century dawned. With the D&IR's docks, railroad shops, twenty steam locomotives, and five hundred ore cars, Two Harbors soon became a major Lake Superior transportation and shipping hub. And, once the huge iron ore deposits of the recently opened Mesabi Range were linked to Agate Bay during the mid-1890s, the D&IR was able to compete with Duluth-based docks operated by the D&NM Railroad.[85]

The elderly Tower, who was personally involved in the development of Two Harbors from his distant Philadelphia office, called for "wide streets, public squares, a reliable water supply and the complete elimination of real estate speculation." He also sought to establish a "civilized" setting for workers and their families by appointing constables and a justice of the peace. Lake County's governmental functions were moved from nearby Beaver Bay to Two Harbors in 1886, two years before the settlement's official incorporation as a village; Two Harbors' city charter would be approved in 1907. Steady growth led to the platting of additional subdivisions in 1889, 1895, and 1900; collectively, they extended the original 1884 grid pattern. The platted area, by 1900, approached the D&IR Railroad shop and rail lines to the west, extended eastward to Burlington Bay, and proceeded northward beyond Seventh Avenue.[86]

## Population, Politics, and Economics

Only 545 people populated Two Harbors in 1885, but the total grew to 1,225 in 1890 and then to 3,280 by 1900. The census count, which peaked at 4,490 in 1910, never fell below 4,000 for the next seven decades. In 1990, however, the figure declined to 3,650; since then, the totals have remained appreciably steady: 3,615 in 2000; 3,745 in 2010; and 3,830 in 2020.[87]

Because of the steady employment opportunities provided by the early railroads and ore docks, Two Harbors' workers and their families could patronize a relatively wide range and large number of businesses, including grocery stores, restaurants, pool halls, taverns, hardware and clothing stores, banks, pharmacies, photography studios, newspapers, and attorneys' offices. Several early business owners were already one generation removed from their families' immigrant origins, but the city's working-class population included a significant representation of European émigrés. In 1910, Two Harbors' 2,035 foreign-born inhabitants constituted just over 40 percent of all residents. By 1920, when 1,470 immigrants represented one-third of the entire population, the vast majority (1,165) were Nordics: 775 Swedes, 335 Norwegians, 105 Finns, 38 Finland Swedes, and 12 Danes. The 140 Canadians formed the only other group with a sizable number of residents.[88]

Two Harbors' Nordic denizens also sponsored several religious and fraternal institutions, and much of its early twentieth-century political life was shaped by the progressive attitudes of these citizens. In fact, the Two Harbors City Council was controlled by Socialists from 1911 to 1917. One notable politician, Ernest Strand, a Swedish barber who immigrated to Two Harbors in 1901, was elected as the Socialist Party's candidate to three different positions: alderman (1911–16), mayor (1916–17), and three-term legislator in the Minnesota House of Representatives (1917–22). Another politically active Nordic resident was Ida Pasanen, a 1903 Finnish immigrant who lived in Two Harbors for several years. She would serve as a regional and national organizer for two left-wing political organizations: the Finnish Socialist Federation and the Finnish Industrial Union—the latter affiliated with the Industrial Workers of the World (IWW). Lake County clearly expressed its political views in the presidential elections of 1908, 1912, and 1920, when its voters were among the nation's strongest supporters of Eugene Debs, the Socialist Party of America candidate. The city and county also served as a stronghold for Minnesota's Democratic Party in 1936 and 1940, when President Franklin Roosevelt received, respectively, 80 and 73 percent of the entire vote; the same pattern was maintained after the 1944 merger that created the state's DFL Party. Lake County's citizens, from 1948 to 2012, continued giving strong support to Democratic Party presidential candidates. The political dynamics changed dramatically in 2016: Democrat Hillary Clinton lost the national election to Republican Donald Trump, but won in Lake County, albeit by only 269 votes. In 2020, Joseph Biden defeated Trump, both in the United States and Lake County, although he received just 254 more votes in the latter election. And, when Trump won nationally in 2024, he lost Lake County to Kamala Harris by 289 votes.[89]

Two Harbors experienced the first of several economic changes in 1898, when the MIC was purchased by the Illinois Steel Company; this firm, only three years later, would be absorbed by the gigantic U.S. Steel Corporation. The D&IR, however, didn't merge

**The primitive streets, scattered houses, cattle fences, and cutover landscape indicate that Two Harbors had not yet progressed beyond the frontier stage of development when this photograph was taken in 1886. At the upper right is the first Lake County Courthouse, which burned down in 1904. Courtesy of Lake County Historical Society.**

with U.S. Steel's railroad until 1938, following formation of the DM&IR Railway. Control of the DM&IR was assumed, in 2004, by the Canadian National Railway, which merged, seven years later, with another of its subsidiaries, the Wisconsin Central, and operates Two Harbors' docks and rail lines.[90]

The tremendous depletion of Minnesota's high-grade iron ore deposits caused by World War II and the Korean conflict caused significant change and disruption to the city's industrial ventures. All of Vermilion's mines were exhausted and closed during the 1950s, along with several Mesabi operations. Then, on 18 January 1963, an infamous day that Two Harbors residents would identify as "Black Friday," the city's docks were completely shut down. The docks would reopen in 1966, but only after Minnesota voters approved a 1963 constitutional amendment guaranteeing tax benefits to companies that developed facilities for the conversion of low-quality taconite ore into high-grade pellets used to manufacture steel. Since that time, Two Harbors has maintained its position as a taconite port for the Mesabi Range, even though annual shipments fluctuate because of changing national and global market conditions. (The majority of taconite pellets that arrive in Two Harbors come from Minntac, a processing plant operated by U.S. Steel at Mountain Iron on the Iron Range.) The Black Friday experience also spurred efforts to transform Two Harbors from a single-industry city into one with a more diverse economy. These efforts resulted in the development of an industrial park during the late 1960s, an action that attracted a few small businesses and manufacturing firms to its environs.[91]

Another important event occurred in 1992, when the extension of Interstate 35 reached eastern Duluth, thereby making the North Shore expressway much more accessible to motorists. "Suddenly," noted one observer, "travelers could hold out for gas and snacks until they hit Two Harbors." (No McDonald's or other franchise drive-in diners existed between Duluth and the Canadian border prior to this time.) Unfortunately, the "unplanned development" that emerged along Seventh Avenue and at the city's borders resulted in the loss of "acres of trees" and a decline in the economic health of downtown Two Harbors.[92]

Because of these problems, Two Harbors' residents have been discussing and debating the future direction of their city for decades. Michael Creger, a former editor of the *Lake County News-Chronicle*, observed that the community was still struggling with a major question in 2019, namely, "is Two Harbors a working town or a tourist town"? Despite numerous debates concerning this question, Creger observed that "it's got only a small portion of either." The question that must be answered, he concluded, is whether Two Harbors can make the "leap from a place to begrudgingly pass through with traffic jams on weekends into becoming more diverse economically for residents and tourists." Respondents who participated in a 2018 Two Harbors "quality of place" survey recognized this issue when expressing their wish to maintain a balance between residents and visitors. The city, they hoped, will neither become a version of Grand Marais, a North Shore settlement that is highly dependent on tourism, nor turn into a bedroom community of Duluth, where many services are offered but any small-town character is missing.[93]

Two Harbors' built environment continues to play an important role in linking the city's past, present, and future. The following assessment focuses on the southernmost section of Two Harbors, which extends between Agate Bay at the south and Seventh Avenue to the north. Included within this area were and are Two Harbors' iron ore docks and railroad facilities, as well as its downtown district, where numerous commercial, public, and institutional buildings still remain. Much of Two Harbors' housing stock is also located here, a subject of interest because, other than Duluth, the city has the North Shore's largest inventory of late nineteenth- and early twentieth-century vernacular dwellings—several of which still offer glimpses of Queen Anne, Craftsman, and other stylistic details. Most were constructed for officials and highly skilled workers employed by the D&IR as well as business owners and a small cadre of individuals who provided professional services. The smaller, less-ornate residences situated throughout the city were built or purchased by married dock and railroad workers and other laborers with families. Many of these dwellings have been modified over the decades, while others require maintenance. Nonetheless, the appreciable number of historic residences that remain in Two Harbors serves as a tangible reminder of the tastes and aspirations of its early citizens.

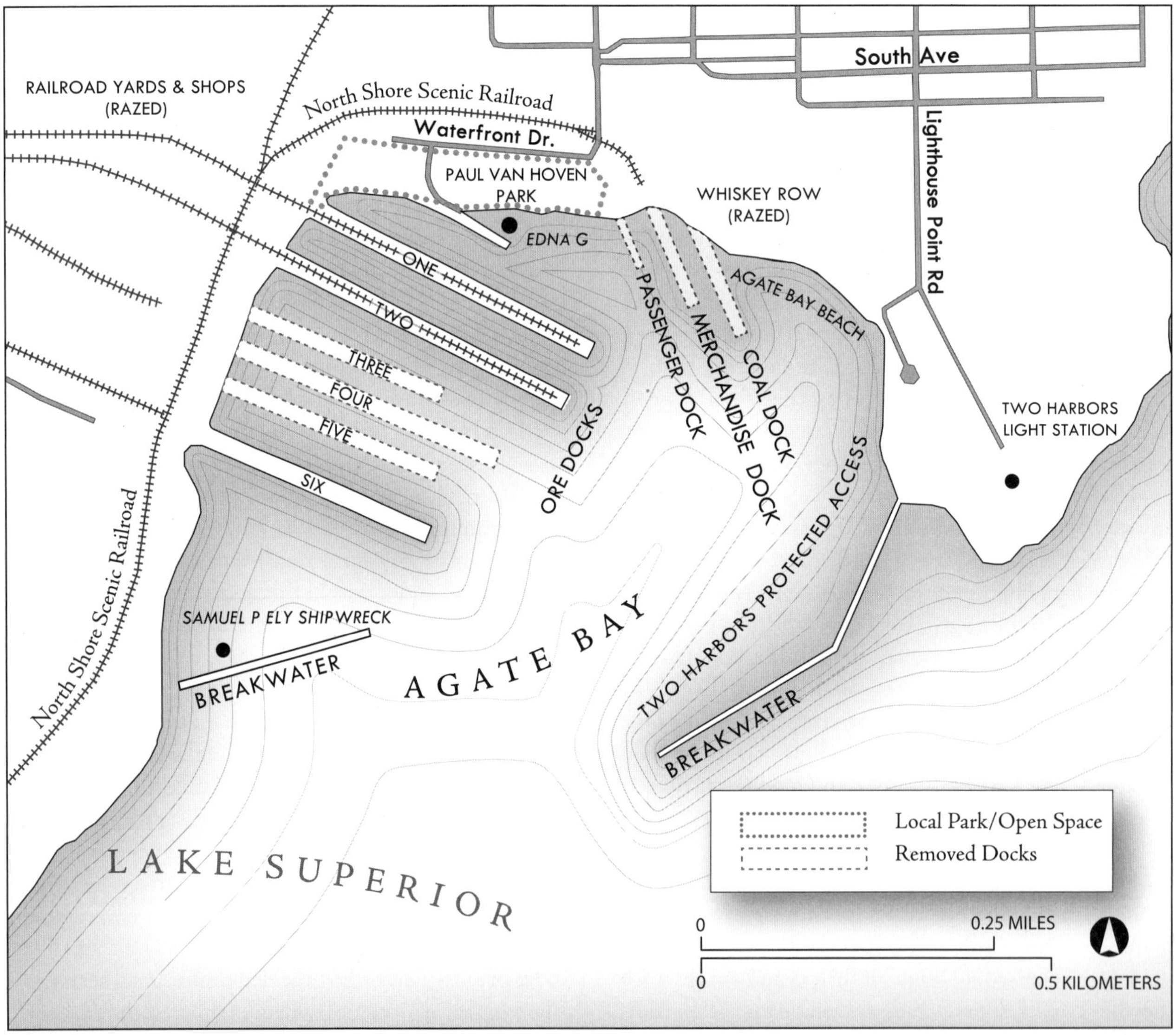

RAILROAD YARDS & SHOPS (RAZED)
North Shore Scenic Railroad
South Ave
Waterfront Dr.
PAUL VAN HOVEN PARK
Lighthouse Point Rd
WHISKEY ROW (RAZED)
EDNA G
ONE
TWO
THREE
FOUR
FIVE
SIX
ORE DOCKS
PASSENGER DOCK
MERCHANDISE DOCK
COAL DOCK
AGATE BAY BEACH
TWO HARBORS LIGHT STATION
TWO HARBORS PROTECTED ACCESS
BREAKWATER
SAMUEL P ELY SHIPWRECK
BREAKWATER
AGATE BAY
North Shore Scenic Railroad
LAKE SUPERIOR
Local Park/Open Space
Removed Docks
0
0.25 MILES
0
0.5 KILOMETERS

The ensuing depictions begin with sites on or proximate to Agate Bay's shoreline and then proceed to the city's avenues, each of which is described from west to east. Because fewer properties are situated on the shorter north–south streets, these places are discussed wherever the nearby avenue is given consideration. Two Harbors' streets and sidewalks offer access to these sites, and the Sonju Trail provides a path for bikers, hikers, and walkers who wish to follow a designated route through the city.

## Agate Bay Harbor and Shoreline

The Agate Bay harbor and shoreline include a number of maritime structures—two breakwaters, a shipwreck, a public park and beach, a tugboat, protected water access, and, most noticeably, three huge iron ore docks. No longer evident are three other ore docks; coal, passenger, and merchandise docks; a railroad and roundhouse complex; several hotels and boardinghouses; and a "fish house row."

### Canadian National Railway Ore Docks

Western Side of Agate Bay

The construction of Two Harbors' first pair of D&IR company ore docks began here in 1883. Throughout this early period, most workers lived in a company boardinghouse, managed by "Ma Blake," which was situated on a lot close to Dock No. 1. The "thin board partitions between the rooms," wryly commented one veteran D&IR supervisor, made it "possible to hear snoring in at least five languages." Dock Nos. 3 and 4 were ready for the 1886 shipping season, and the largest wooden dock, No. 5, just over a thousand feet long, was completed in 1896. (Dock Nos. 3, 4, and 5 were removed during the mid-1920s.) Dock No. 6, finished in 1908, introduced steel and concrete dock construction technology to the Great Lakes. Despite the higher costs, steel and concrete proved more economical than wood because of long-term durability, ease of repair, reduced fire risk, and eventual value as scrap material. Dock Nos. 1 and 2 were rebuilt of steel, with concrete decks, in 1911 and 1916, respectively.

Dock Nos. 1, 2, and 6 still jut into Agate Bay, but only Nos. 1 and 2 are in use. Dock No. 6 has not been active since 1976, when a new storage area for taconite ore was under construction at Dock No. 2; the latter project, completed in 1978, made Dock No. 6 inaccessible to railway cars. The $36 million modernization of Dock No. 2 was undertaken in response to new ore carriers, more than a thousand feet long, that began plying the Great Lakes during the 1970s. Because these vessels cannot be filled with typical gravity chutes, the

Three iron ore carriers wait to be loaded along one of Two Harbors' docks during the early 1920s.

upgraded system runs the ore cars through an unloading station where taconite pellets are dumped into a forty-acre storage area that has a capacity of two million tons; from there, an elaborate conveyor system transports the pellets into the ship. Dock No. 1, however, still has a traditional gravity feed that allows railcars to unload ore directly into Great Lakes vessels.[94]

### D&IR Railroad Company Shops and Roundhouse *(razed)*

West of the Ore Docks

Because of the harbor's importance as a bulk transfer point, the D&IR erected a rail repair complex just west of the docks and slightly outside Two Harbors' boundary. The original wooden buildings were quickly replaced, first by bricks, later by concrete blocks. The primary unit, a roundhouse with a turntable of one hundred feet, was used for inspecting, maintaining, and storing locomotives. Another imposing structure was the 88-by-288-foot machine shop—a three-and-a-half-story structure with a metal gable roof that had numerous ventilators and skylights; inside the building were a 600-ton hydraulic press and a 130-ton traveling crane that had a 30-ton auxiliary trolley. Blacksmith, tin, steel car repair, carpentry, and paint shops were used to perform an amazing array of functions, ranging from fabricating caboose windows and upholstering chairs to sandblasting and lettering railway cars.[95]

**The D&IR roundhouse, by the early 1900s, had numerous locomotive bays grouped around a central turntable. Each locomotive, when undergoing inspection and repair, was placed in a separate bay and lined up under a smokestack that projected through the roundhouse roof. Courtesy of Lake County Historical Society.**

The facilities were abandoned in 1962–63, following consolidation of the company's railroad repair functions with similar operations in Proctor, located just west of Duluth. A few short-lived business ventures—among them a company that manufactured fiberglass components for three-wheeled mail cars being built for the U.S. Postal Service and another that forged diesel cylinder heads for use in the railroad industry—were established in several buildings during the 1960s and 1970s; no active businesses have been at work on the property since the late 1980s. All but a few small structures were torn down several years ago, and the site remains unused today.[96]

### *Samuel P. Ely* Shipwreck

Western Agate Bay Breakwater

The *Samuel P. Ely*, an 1869 single-deck ore schooner with three sails, was converted into a tow barge after an 1885 storm sheared off its topmasts and jib boom. In late October 1896, the *Ely* and another barge were being towed by a steamer, the SS *Hesper*, to Two Harbors, where both would be filled with iron ore. An extremely severe storm arose on that journey, which forced the *Hesper*'s crew to abandon the towline that linked it to the *Ely*. The barge foundered for some time before crashing against Two Harbors' western breakwater. The crew of the tugboat *Ella G. Stone* braved considerable danger to save all ten men from almost certain death.[97]

Many artifacts were removed from the *Ely* once recreational divers discovered the well-preserved wreck during the late 1950s: a large wooden anchor appeared as a lawn decoration in Superior, the deck capstan was donated to Duluth's Canal Park Museum, and the bell is now on display in the Lake County Depot Museum. By the time the *Ely* was listed in the National Register of Historic Places in 1992, it had already experienced considerable vandalism and deterioration. In March 1994, a group of preservation-minded divers went under the ice, hoisted the deck by drilling holes into the frozen surface, and installed steel rods that stabilized the hull; the deck was then returned to its original setting. Further work in 2001 resulted in the installation of stronger tie rods, equipped with adjustable turnbuckles. Members of the Great Lakes

Preservation Society continue to monitor the *Ely*, one of the North Shore's most visited shipwreck sites.[98]

### Paul H. Van Hoven Park
Northern Agate Bay Shoreline

The northern shoreline of Agate Bay was already used as a public space before being improved, during the late 1940s, by the Lake County Civic Council and DM&IR Railroad. Dedicated in 1950, the park honored a company president who had overseen the DM&IR and D&IR merger in 1930. Despite the park's rather minimal landscape design features, its lawns and benches served as the only place in Two Harbors where one could "get a complete unobstructed view of ore carriers being loaded."[99] A few small changes have been made to the original layout, but the park still offers a direct view of Dock No. 1 and serves as a venue for summertime events; until recently, it provided access to one of Two Harbors' major attractions, a tugboat, the *Edna G*.

### Tugboat *Edna G*
Paul H. Van Hoven Park Walkway

The *Edna G*, a steam-powered, coal-burning tugboat, was built for the D&IR in 1896 to assist iron-ore carriers that entered and departed Two Harbors' docks. Named for a daughter of J. L. Greatsinger, president of the D&IR from 1892 to 1901, the steel-hulled *Edna G*, 112 feet long, included a small galley, passengers' salon, captain's cabin, and crew quarters. The *Edna G* saw continuous service at Two Harbors from 1896 to 1981, except for two years during World War I (1917–19), when it was commandeered and based at the port of Norfolk, Virginia. Both before and after its military service, the *Edna G* was used to rescue sailors caught in Lake Superior's storms, such as the November 1905 calamity that sank or disabled numerous ships. Before the tugboat was retired in 1981, three crews, comprised of four members, worked eight-hour shifts to operate the *Edna G* around the clock during each shipping season. In 1975, while still a hardworking vessel, the *Edna G* was listed in the National Register of Historic Places.[100]

Following the tug's 1981 retirement, the *Edna G* was moored at its original 1896 location. Although the city had no specific post-retirement plans for the vessel, the tugboat was opened periodically for public tours.

**The tugboat *Edna G* assists an iron ore carrier, the *Benjamin F. Fairless*, in the 1960s. Named for a president of U.S. Steel (1938–55), the *Fairless* transported iron ore on the Great Lakes from 1942 to 1982; the decommissioned vessel was sold for scrap metal in 1988.**

Some minor repairs were made to the boat, but subsequent storm damage and the ongoing effects of aging prompted a recent decision: the eventual removal of the *Edna G* from Lake Superior. A local nonprofit organization, Friends of the *Edna G*, is currently raising funds for the construction of a "dry cradle mounting" system to protect the iconic tug from Lake Superior's impacts; repairs, maintenance, and tours will also be simplified and safer to conduct. Among the group's fundraising efforts is a "Christmas Tea," when the *Edna G* is decked out in lights and holiday finery. If these efforts prove successful, visitors and Two Harbors residents will be able, once again, to learn much more about the "tough little boat that helped build and defend America, and that could get things done."[101]

### Whiskey Row/Coal, Merchandise, and Passenger Docks/Coal and Pulpwood Storage Yard *(razed)*
Northeastern Side of Agate Bay between Fourth and Fifth Avenues

Vacant land now characterizes the majority of what was Whiskey Row, the four-acre land parcel that Thomas Sexton retained after selling 150 acres of his property to the D&IR in 1882. Three years later, when some of "Whiskey Row dissipated into smoke and memories," all of the remaining buildings were removed. The site would be used for coal and pulpwood

**Two steamboats at Two Harbors' passenger dock in 1906. On the left is the SS *America*, which also carried mail and freight. A sign, hidden from view, states that teams of horses are not allowed on the dock. Farther to the left are Two Harbors' merchandise and coal docks.**

storage during subsequent decades. The coal dock that projected into the bay from the shoreline could, by 1907, handle three hundred thousand tons of the fuel, most transported to the Iron Range. Also nearby were merchandise and passenger docks. Then, in 2001, long after the storage yard and docks had been abandoned and removed (a very small section of the coal dock foundation still remains), the U.S. Army Corps of Engineers authorized a study that called for the conversion of the site into a North Shore marina and harbor of refuge. Although the city's 2015 comprehensive plan also called for such a facility, no work has occurred to date.[102]

**Boxes of frozen fish, many provided by the Lind brothers of Castle Danger, wait on Two Harbors' merchandise dock at the end of the shipping season, late 1920s or early 1930s. Courtesy of the Lind family's Castle Danger Photograph Collection.**

### Fish House Row (*now* Agate Beach Park and Two Harbors Protected Access)

#### Eastern Agate Bay Shoreline

The D&IR leased lots along Agate Bay to commercial fishermen, who found the harbor quite ideal following completion of the eastern and western breakwaters in 1901–2. Soon the shoreline would be dotted with numerous fish houses and boathouses. Some structures were scattered along the western side of the bay, but the greatest concentration bordered the more protected eastern shoreline. Many were abandoned when commercial fishing underwent its major decline during the 1950s and 1960s; this was well before 1985, when the DM&IR leased a portion of the eastern shoreline to the MDNR, which proposed to "beautify and upgrade" the property. The remaining fish houses and boathouses, most in a deteriorated condition, were reduced to ashes in June 1985 when the Two Harbors Volunteer Fire Department burned all but one as part of a training exercise. Unfortunately, just a few years later, a fire of unknown origin consumed the single remaining structure, which had been spared to memorialize the once-thriving fishing industry.[103]

East-southeast of the coal dock foundation remnant is Agate Bay Beach, a narrow section of shoreline that attracts rock hounds during warm weather. From there the beach extends southward to the Two Harbors Protected Access, built and operated by the MDNR in 1981 and reconstructed in 2011; its three ramps, a 150-foot-long crib dock, and an adjacent paved parking area with space for vehicles and boat trailers are maintained by the City of Two Harbors. Nearby is the eastern breakwater, which extends thirteen hundred feet into Agate Bay. Since 1972, when a thirty-foot-wide concrete cap was added to the rock-filled, boulder-lined timber cribs, the breakwater has served as a popular walkway that offers exceptional vantage points of the city and its ore docks.[104]

**A gas-powered boat passes by several boathouses and fish houses once situated along the eastern shoreline of Agate Bay. In the distant background is the Two Harbors Light Station. Photograph by Harold Youngren, 1930.**

### Two Harbors Light Station (*now* Lighthouse Bed & Breakfast)

#### 1 Lighthouse Point

The light station that guards the entrance to both Agate and Burlington Bays is the oldest still-functioning facility of its type on the North Shore. The need for such a structure was evident once boat traffic rose following the first shipment of iron ore in 1884. Although the U.S. Congress, in 1886, allocated $10,000 for the construction of a light station atop the rocky promontory on Agate Bay's eastern side, work did not commence until 1891. The tower emitted its first white beacon of light in 1892.[105]

The keeper's house, two stories high, is built of bricks and covered by two gabled roofs that face toward the south and west. Rain from the roof was collected in a basement cistern that provided fresh water for the keeper and his family. The square light tower, tucked into the space formed at the intersection of the L-shaped residence, stretches upward for almost forty-four feet from its base to the top of the ventilator ball, while the focal plane of the lens is situated seventy-eight feet above Lake Superior's average low water level. The light was electrified in 1921, and two diaphonic horns tuned to an F chord replaced the steam-powered fog whistles in 1923. The original fourth-order Fresnel lens is now on display in the station. Also on the grounds is the two-story assistant keeper's residence, converted from a barn dating to 1895, and a fountain that was transferred to the site from Thomas Owens Park in downtown Two Harbors.[106]

The need for a keeper was eliminated in 1981 when the U.S. Coast Guard fully automated the station. Following this action, the Lake County Historical Society (LCHS) received permission to lease the property and conduct tours of the facilities. The entire complex—light station, keeper's house, and assistant keeper's house—was listed in the National Register of Historic Places in 1984. After its official transfer to LCHS by a 1999 U.S. congressional act, the facility opened as the Lighthouse Bed and Breakfast. LCHS secures funds for maintenance and management from the rent of its four rooms, but the organization also depends on the efforts and skills of numerous volunteers, some of whom perform very specialized tasks. One crew of four, the Light Keepers, maintains the beacon, which typically flashes at regular intervals throughout the night. In doing so, the crew members have often engaged in "patch and repair" operations that rely on parts "cannibalized" from other sites throughout the United States. A late 2019 malfunction that proved beyond repair wasn't resolved until June 2021, thanks

**The former Two Harbors Light Station, now the Lighthouse Bed and Breakfast. In the foreground is the *Crusader II*, completed at Knife River in 1938 by boatbuilders Charles and Reuben Hill and placed on the lighthouse grounds in 1990. The tug was moved, in late 2016, to the Knife River Heritage and Cultural Center, where it has been restored and is on display.**

to the U.S. Coast Guard, which provided a temporary light for the facility. Finally, in 2025, sufficient funds were raised to purchase a new, rotational LED beacon from Finland, thereby ensuring that a permanent flashing light will once again illuminate the Two Harbors night sky.[107]

Despite its idyllic setting, much of the land and shoreline that constitute Lighthouse Point served as the setting for a contentious and prolonged land-use dispute during the early twenty-first century. The controversy arose after DM&IR officials announced their plans to sell the company's landholdings, most of which had been accessible to the public for many years. Two Harbors officials immediately sought to acquire the property, but DM&IR's directors, in late 2002, reported that 155 acres of the most valuable land had already been sold to a Twin Cities developer, who announced his plans to construct condominiums on some of the most attractive sites. Following a public outcry, Two Harbors officials stalled the project after determining that the city's zoning code did not permit such developments. Both parties worked together to form a revised proposal in 2006, but further disputes and lawsuits delayed any construction activities. An agreement was forged in 2013, when a district court judge issued a ruling that required the developer to surrender all but five heavily wooded acres, located by the lighthouse, to the City of Two Harbors. It was not until 2023 that the developer issued another proposal, this one calling for a much smaller planned-unit development of two dozen townhouses and a commercial building; the plan was immediately rejected by the Two Harbors City Council, but the land parcel's ultimate future remains in doubt.[108]

## South Avenue

Bordering the northern edge of Two Harbors' former Whiskey Row is South Avenue, one of the city's earliest roads. Located along the avenue are a former D&IR depot and two locomotives as well as one of the city's oldest residences. Two Harbors' former "Finntown" emerged along two city blocks located between South and First Avenues during the early twentieth century; the district included a workers' hall, a cooperative store, a public sauna, a few private saunas, and at least two boardinghouses.

### Duluth and Iron Range Railway Company Depot (*now* Two Harbors Depot Museum)
### 520 South Avenue

The D&IR depot, listed in the National Register of Historic Places in 1983, and featured in the 1992 Disney Studios film *Iron Will*, occupies a key location in Two Harbors: to the south are Lake Superior and the ore docks; the city's downtown lies to the north. A March 1907 newspaper account predicted that Duluth architect Peter Olson's design would result in "a handsome station, embracing all modern conveniences," including a "commodious ticket office," separate rooms for baggage and express items, "one of the most complete and comfortable suites of waiting rooms . . . for both ladies and gentlemen," and a pair of "handsomely appointed lavatories." Railroad operations were headquartered in second-floor offices, while the full basement provided space for a heating plant, telegraph batteries, storage room, and vault. Most of the work was completed by October 1907.[109]

The rectangularity of the two-story brick exterior is visually reinforced by the repetition of thirteen bays along its length and four that span its width. The depot also displays several Romanesque revival features, among them stone corbels, brick belt courses above and below the second-story windows, and stone quoins that

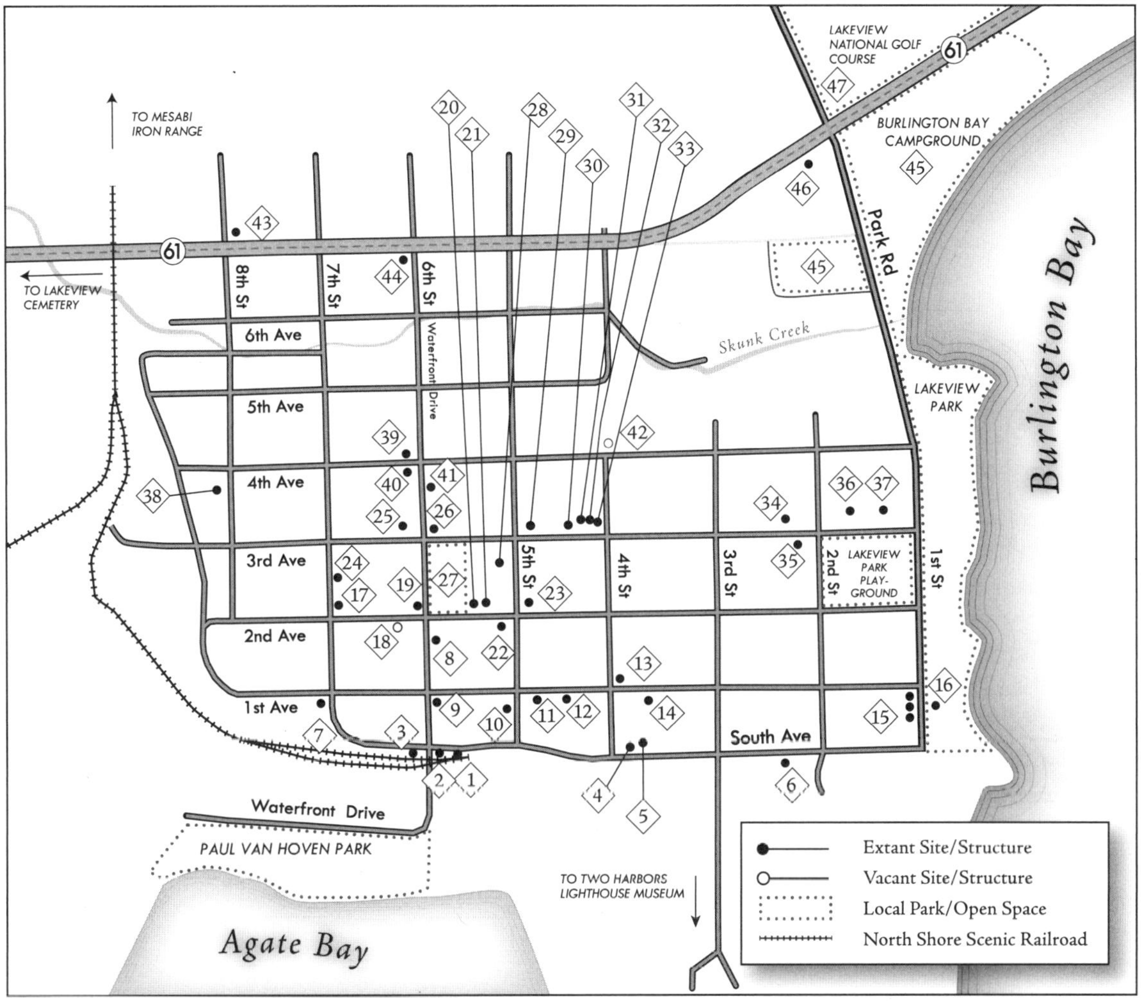


1. Two Harbors Depot Museum
2. D&IR Engine No. 3
3. Yellowstone Mallet No. 229
4. 1883 Residence
5. Falu Hus
6. Koskinen–Joki Finnish Boardinghouse
7. Castle Danger Brewery
8. Salvation Army Corps Building
9. Agate Bay Apartments
10. Shea Residence
11. Budd House Board and Lodge
12. Barross Manor
13. Pelto Residence
14. "Finn-Hop"/Apartments
15. "Hay Fever" Cabins
16. Lakeview Park entrance and Veterans' Memorial Gate
17. Fortitude Masonic Lodge No. 188
18. Old City Hall
19. 3M Birthplace Museum
20. Headley Residence
21. Owens Residence
22. Dwan Residence
23. Park Lane Chateau
24. North Shore Architectural Antiques
25. Lake County Courthouse
26. United Church of Two Harbors
27. Thomas Owens Memorial Park
28. Holy Spirit Catholic Church and Rectory*
29. Spurbeck Residence
30. Former Episcopal/Lutheran Church
31. Rock Residence
32. James Residence
33. Shea/Jones Residence
34. Haugen Residence
35. Falk Residence
36. Bryan Residence
37. Harbor House Apartments
38. Lakeview Apartments and Lodging
39. Bethlehem Lutheran Church
40. Emmanuel Lutheran Church
41. Two Harbors Carnegie Library
42. Former Two Harbors High School Site
43. Anderson Residence
44. Blackwoods Grill and Bar
45. Burlington Bay Campground
46. R. J. Houle Information Center
47. Lakeview National Golf Course

*Now a private residence

top the upper stringcourse. No longer in place is the former full-front promenade, which had a projecting gable that faced the railroad tracks and a shed roof with wooden ornamental supports.[110]

The D&IR's management activities were transferred to Duluth in 1937, and passenger service ended in 1961. The depot, after its 1960 acquisition by LCHS, was converted into a museum and store within a year. The society's membership was confident that the growing "vacationist interest" in museums would make the site a "local asset" for Two Harbors. The North Shore Scenic Railroad's excursion train also makes weekend round trips between Duluth and the depot from May through October and provides additional tours during the fall color season.[111]

### D&IR Engine No. 3 ("Three Spot"), Ore Car No. 251, and Caboose No. 22

Western Side of the Depot

Prominently displayed on the depot grounds, and protected by a metal-roofed shelter, is Engine No. 3, the legendary railroad locomotive that dates to the early 1880s. Affectionately known as the Three Spot, the small engine was constructed by the Baldwin Locomotive Works in Philadelphia, shipped by rail to Duluth in July 1883, and then transported by scow and tugboat to Agate Bay, where it became the first locomotive put into service by the D&IR. The Three Spot also transported the initial shipment of iron ore from the Vermilion Range to Two Harbors in 1884. Fifteen years later, in 1899, the Alger, Smith & Company's railroad, the D&NM, acquired the Three Spot. It was later owned by a series of buyers before being acquired by a scrap dealer during the early 1920s; in 1923, the D&IR's Thirty-Year Veterans' Club bought the Three Spot and put it on display by the depot. Ore Car No. 251, built in 1893 and scheduled for the scrapyard during the early 1930s, and Caboose No. 22, which was in use until 1932, were both acquired and added to the display in 1934 as part of the D&IR's "50 Years of Ore Celebration."[112]

### Yellowstone Mallet No. 229

West of the Three Spot

This Yellowstone Mallet, one of the last steam locomotives employed at Two Harbors before all were replaced with diesel engines, was donated to LCHS and put on display in 1969. (It supplanted two other Mallets that had been successively exhibited at the site since 1960.) The Mallets were imposing specimens of engine power: each was 128 feet long; weighed in at more than four hundred tons without the tender, could carry twenty-six tons of coal and twenty-five thousand gallons of water, and generate a tractive effort of 140,000 pounds. A major restoration of Locomotive 229 was completed in 2011.[113]

**The D&IR's historic locomotive the Three Spot, hitched to an iron ore car and caboose, was put on view by the Two Harbors depot in 1924. They are now protected by an overhead canopy.**

### 1883 Residence
331 South Avenue

A pair of adjacent houses, both built in 1883 at the edge of Two Harbors' former Whiskey Row district, stood for almost 140 years at 333 and 331 South Avenue. The corner dwelling (333) was removed in 2019, but its counterpart (331) remains on the original lot. Although the extant residence has experienced significant alterations, its original rectangular form and two-and-a-half-story front gable entrance are still evident.[114]

### *Falu Hus*
323 South Avenue

At first glance, this residence might be considered a very well-preserved and -maintained example of an 1880s dwelling unit. The house was, however, constructed during the early 2000s, but its form, scale, and features sought to replicate a nineteenth-century Swedish farmhouse. Built and owned by a descendant of Swedish immigrants who settled in Two Harbors, the Falu Hus (Swedish for "Red House") has separate living quarters on its lower and upper floors.[115]

### Koskinen–Joki Finnish Boardinghouse *(now an apartment building)*
216 South Avenue

This two-and-a-half-story structure with a cross-gable roof, built in 1906 by Finnish immigrant Nestor Koskinen, was soon purchased by his ethnic compatriots, John and Mary Salo Joki, who opened a boardinghouse with rooms for six to nine lodgers. The Jokis' son and daughter-in-law ran the business from 1937 until the mid-1940s, when the building was converted into apartments. One of its distinctive features, later removed, was a wooden exterior stairway that provided access to the upper-floor rooms. Also nearby on South Avenue was a Finnish public sauna, owned by Hilma Lager. The immigrant woman announced, in a 1913 advertisement, that her "steam baths" were open to women on Wednesdays and Saturdays between 2:00 P.M. and 6:00 P.M., while the men's hours extended from 6:00 P.M. to 12:00 A.M. Tragically, the fifty-seven-year-old woman was murdered in 1920, and the sauna closed soon thereafter.[116]

**Two Harbors' oldest remaining residence, built in 1883, stands at 331 South Avenue. Also visible are the sidewalk steps that led to a similar, neighboring house, which was removed in 2019. In the background at the far right is the Falu Hus, built during the early 2000s and modeled on a rural nineteenth-century Swedish residence**

### First Avenue

First Avenue formerly served as the heart of Two Harbors' thriving downtown commercial district. It included one of the North Shore's premier hotels, currently an apartment building, and several traditional businesses, only a very few of which remain today. First Avenue does have, however, the city's newest and largest enterprise: a sizable brewery that has brought vitality to the downtown district.

### DM&IR Clubhouse and YMCA (*now* Castle Danger Brewery)
17 Seventh Street

A clubhouse, financed and furnished by the DM&IR Railroad Company, emerged at the southwestern corner of the First Avenue–Seventh Street intersection in 1897. Since the clubhouse was conveniently located on a primary path between Two Harbors' residential districts and the company's docks, shops, and railyards, workers heading toward their homes had an opportunity to "clean up" in its basement, which had twelve bathtubs, eighteen washbasins, and "two of the latest improved shower baths." Eight second-floor sleeping rooms were "occupied constantly," some by men who worked on the railroad for brief periods of time. The programs that occurred within the clubhouse confines were managed and supervised by the YMCA, which reportedly had one thousand members by 1909. The first floor, equipped with attractive reading rooms, gave the men access to the "best" periodicals and books, while a large social room and fireplace provided a setting where they could play checkers, sing tunes to the accompaniment of an upright piano, and "spin yarns to their hearts' content"; Sunday afternoon religious meetings and weekly Bible classes were also conducted in the room. Two wings, added on to the original structure after World War I, provided space for a swimming pool, gymnasium, kitchen, and dining room. As many as forty-eight unmarried or widowed men, among them retired and disabled employees, could be housed in its second-floor rooms. The YMCA-run facilities, also accessible to the public for a nominal fee, served as the "center of community life" in Two Harbors for several decades. The building and its programs were abruptly shut down in late August 1962, however, a precursor of the Black Friday event of January 1963 that saw the DM&IR close its Two Harbors operations for three years. The abandoned clubhouse was torn down in May 1963.[117]

The site remained vacant until 2013–14, when it would accommodate the most significant project in the previous half century of Two Harbors' downtown history—construction of the Castle Danger Brewery. The modest roots of the business were established in 2006, when Clint MacFarlane started experimenting with home brewing at his family's home and resort in Castle Danger, located eleven miles northeast of Two Harbors. In 2011, after completing a small, three-barrel brewery on the resort grounds, MacFarlane began distributing his products to thirteen local bars and restaurants. Three years later, when the products had become extremely popular, MacFarlane built and opened a taproom and thirty-barrel production and canning line in Two Harbors and began marketing the beers throughout Minnesota. Then, in 2017, the brewer and his partners initiated a major expansion project that required significant brownfield remediation before work could begin on the construction of a packaging hall that now has the capacity to can, keg, and cool forty thousand barrels of beer per year, which are distributed throughout Minnesota and in some North Dakota and Wisconsin border towns. The brewing company annually attracts tens of thousands of visitors to the city and downtown and also sponsors and supports Team Danger, a volunteer group of employees and others who perform "dangerously good deeds around Two Harbors."[118]

**The DM&IR Clubhouse–YMCA was one of Two Harbors' most important community buildings from the 1890s to the early 1960s. Photograph by Harold Youngren, late 1920s.**

The Castle Danger Brewery, which appeared on the former DM&IR Clubhouse–YMCA site in 2014, was expanded three years later.

### Salvation Army Corps Building *(now offices)*
### 116 Waterfront Street

In 1907, Swedish immigrants Nels and Greda Olson invited a Duluth Salvation Army officer to conduct religious services in Two Harbors. As the army's primarily Scandinavian membership grew, plans were made to construct a building that would provide space for religious services and residential rooms to accommodate staff members. The structure opened in 1920; it was financed by the estate of Lake County auditor John Olson, a Swedish émigré who also gave the organization three contiguous lots on Sixth Street, one of which would be used for the army's building.[119]

The rectangular, brick edifice was noticeably modified in 1950 when Two Harbors' new post office emerged on the two vacant lots. The most visible and severe change occurred at the original entrance, which was moved from its side gable location to one corner of the front facade. Nevertheless, some of the building's exterior arts and crafts details are still evident, namely, the hipped roof, two distinctive rows of windows, and brick facades accentuated by a pattern of raised bricks in square and diamond-shaped forms. The building, following its sale during the 1990s, initially included a store and a private fur trade museum but now accommodates offices.[120]

The arts and crafts details of the Salvation Army building were clearly visible from 1920 until 1950, when Two Harbors' post office was built on the two vacant lots in the foreground. This action eliminated the building's southern entrance and obscured the original facade. Photograph by Harold Youngren, 1927.

### Agate Bay Hotel (*now* Agate Bay Apartments)
530 First Avenue

Several lodging facilities—including hotels named the Lakeview, North Shore, Commercial, Svea, Central, and New England—were constructed in Two Harbors during the late nineteenth and early twentieth centuries. When the Commercial burned down in 1918, it was replaced by the "modern" Agate Bay Hotel—built in anticipation of the increasing numbers of visitors who would need lodging once Minnesota Highway 1 entered Two Harbors during the early 1920s. The Agate did, in fact, become Two Harbors' premier hotel following its 1924 completion. Several sources of revenue were used to finance the building, including donations from a number of U.S. Steel Corporation executives. The D&IR president also contributed funds for a fireplace, situated in the lobby, that memorialized Two Harbors' pioneer settlers; constructed of Agate Bay cobblestones, an exceptionally large, polished agate was fixed to its center. When Two Harbors' American Legion Post 109 moved into the basement in 1944, and purchased the entire building in 1957, the members claimed that they owned the "most modern" Legion lounge in Minnesota. The Legionnaires closed the hotel in 1974 and sold the building two years later; it would reopen in 1978, after being converted into the Agate Bay Apartments.[121]

The brick, rectangular, box-like structure is situated on a lot that slopes downward toward the lake. At the rear is a projecting second-story lounge, perched on two slender posts, that overlooks the depot and waterfront. The large fireplace still remains in one unit, but several interior changes occurred when the hotel was converted into apartments. Although the exterior retains its original Waterfront Drive entrance, the two recessed storefronts that once faced First Avenue have been infilled and covered with contemporary windows and vertical siding; the Italianate metal cornice has also been removed. A few original design details still remain, such as the regularly spaced concrete medallions between each second-floor window. And, because the overall footprint of the Agate Bay hasn't changed, the building continues to serve as an example of former "state-of-the-art lodging in a small, remote city in the early twentieth century, and . . . a landmark from an important phase in Two Harbors' history."[122]

### John J. Jr. and Katie Shea Residence
502 First Avenue

In May 1883, John Shea Jr. (1865–1943), an Iowan, accompanied his Irish immigrant father to Agate Bay, where both worked on the construction of the D&IR railroad. After receiving rapid promotions to the posi-

**The Agate Bay Hotel, here during the 1920s, provided access to the Two Harbors Post Office and a First Avenue commercial business. The hotel entrance was on Sixth (now Waterfront) Street.**

**For many years, a pair of pharmacies owned by the James, *left*, and Falk families anchored the intersection of First Avenue and Sixth Street.**

tions of fireman and engineer, the younger Shea, in 1890, was named the D&IR's roadmaster, a position of considerable responsibility because it required "close contact not only with the men engaged in the maintenance of the roadbed, but every man who had anything to do with the rolling stock and movement of trains." When Shea retired in 1931 as an assistant superintendent, he had worked for a longer period of time than any other D&IR employee. Following the death of his wife, Katie (1873–1936), whom Shea had married in 1894, the longtime railroader moved into the Agate Bay Hotel, where he would reside until his passing seven years later.[123]

The Sheas' two-story residence, built in 1898, has a sandstone and concrete-block foundation, a cross-gable roof, and wooden shingle sheathing. An open front porch, with Doric columns and lattice railings, extends from the projecting front gable section. On the east is a small, one-story shed-roof addition with a scalloped overhang. One of the dwelling's distinctive features, a polygonal bay with a window and a stained glass transom, was removed during the early 2000s.[124]

### Budd Hospital (*now* Budd House Board and Lodge)
426 First Avenue

Because of "fearful accidents [that] often occur on the ore docks and in the woods and sawmills of the nearby country," wrote a local observer in 1896, the opening of Two Harbors' Budd Hospital "filled a long-felt want." The hospital was established by Dr. J. D. Budd, who had been hired as the D&IR's chief physician in 1888. (He would also serve as Lake County's medical examiner and coroner for many years and participate in forming the 3M Company in 1902.) The hospital, supported by small employee payroll deductions, provided D&IR (and later DM&IR) workers and their families with medical care. Duluth architect Oliver Traphagen, who had petitioned D&IR officials for the contract, designed the building. On the first floor were a general ward and reception room; nearby was the surgery room, with its large, southwestern corner bay window, which provided sufficient light for "any operation." The second floor had another general ward and a few private rooms. The Budd family's living quarters, later removed, were attached to the hospital. Two doctors who purchased the facility following Budd's 1915 retirement renamed it the Burns and Christianson Hospital.[125]

A group of cooperative-minded residents acquired the hospital in 1944. After raising $35,000 for its purchase, the members organized a health cooperative and hired physicians and other medical staff. Funds for hospital operations were secured from a voluntary prepayment plan managed by the nonprofit cooperative's Community Health Center. The group's pioneering efforts were soon recognized as a new form of hospital ownership and management that was unique to Minnesota and much of the nation. The National Conference on Cooperative Health Plans acknowledged the hospital's status in 1946, when Two Harbors was selected as the site for the organization's first meeting, which attracted two hundred representatives from seventeen states. The conference, covered by the *New York Times* and other media outlets, resulted in the formation of the Cooperative Health Federation of America (renamed the Group Health Federation of America in 1952). The Two Harbors cooperative, a precursor of the health maintenance organizations that would burgeon throughout the United States some decades later, functioned into the early 1950s, when it became obvious that the outdated and unsafe hospital required replacement. Contentious disagreements arose within the ranks of local citizens, however, when another group advocated for a hospital that would follow a more conventional corporate financing and management model. The compromise eventually forged between the two groups resulted in the formation of the North Shore Memorial Hospital Association and the 1957 opening of a new, nonprofit facility, Lake View Memorial Hospital, situated north of Highway 61. The original hospital building was eventually converted into a thirty-room nursing home, the first of its kind on the North Shore. Renamed the Budd House Board and Lodge in 2016, the facility now provides housing for people with special needs and requirements.[126]

### D&IR General Office Building and Finnish Boarding Club (*now the* Barross Manor)
414 First Avenue

This two-and-a-half-story structure, originally located close to the merchandise dock, was built by the D&IR in 1883. It served as the D&IR's first office building until the company moved to First Street during the early twentieth century. The building was then converted into two housing units following its purchase by local attorney John Dwan; it was acquired, sometime between 1910 and 1920, by the Finnish Boarding Club, which had been formed by a group of unmarried immigrant men. (Management of the club was similar to that of several hundred cooperative ventures, most of them retail stores, that were organized and operated by Finns throughout the Lake Superior region during the first half of the twentieth century.) The men paid a weekly fee to Finnish immigrant Amalia Oksanen Moisio, who served meals in the common dining area. She and her dockworker husband, Kalle Moisio, and their daughter Tyyne resided on the first floor, while a few men rented the second-floor rooms. The boardinghouse was transformed into apartments during the 1940s, before becoming the Barross House, then the Barross Manor, which continues to function as an assisted-living facility for the elderly. The building has been substantially modified, but the upper story of the front facade still has its five evenly spaced windows. The original, centrally placed bay remains at the lower level, although it has been extended to cover one window.[127]

### Charles and Sanni Pelto Residence
335 First Avenue

During the late 1880s, Charles Pelto (1862–1950) emigrated from Finland to Ely, where he found work as a carpenter. In 1890, Pelto married Sanni Maki (1858–1944), also a recent Finnish émigré. Around 1912, the couple and their three children moved to Two Harbors, where Pelto secured a space in the Kinsela Building; he would soon open the Two Harbors Bottling Works, which produced and sold cider, seltzer water, ice cream, and soda. In 1923, the Finnish immigrant assembled a Sears, Roebuck & Company kit house on a recently purchased residential corner lot. The Peltos' daughter and son-in-law, Esther and Carl Nordlund, resided with them during the 1930s. Esther Nordlund remained in the home for many years following the deaths of her parents and husband between 1944 and 1951.[128]

The six-room, three-bedroom residence appeared in the Sears Company's 1913 and 1917 catalogs as "Modern Home No. 155," where it was described as "a two-story house with a bungalow effect." The plan featured

Charles Pelto assembled this Sears, Roebuck & Company kit home for his family in 1923.

several details that emphasized light and ventilation—numerous windows; a screened-in, full-length entry porch; a second-floor front gable dormer/sleeping porch that opened onto a balcony; and another second-floor sleeping porch attached to a rear bedroom.[129] Some changes have been made to the century-old residence, but its original exterior features are still clearly evident.

### Finnish Workers' Hall/"Finn-Hop" *(now apartments)*

322 First Avenue

Finnish Socialists residing in the Two Harbors area founded a workers' society in 1907. Over the next ten years, the society's members sold shares and raised funds for the construction of a hall that would operate as a "home for the toilers . . . where their unions and political organizations can meet and feel at home." The hall would, in fact, serve as the primary social center for Two Harbors' Finntown over a span of almost forty years. The rectilinear auditorium had a stage where plays and performances occurred and a large space with a hardwood floor that was used for seating, dancing, receptions, and gymnastics. A lending library provided members with Finnish-language books, magazines, and newspapers. The kitchen was in the basement, while a second-floor apartment housed the caretaker. The hall calendar was filled with a busy schedule of Finnish-language plays, political events, musical performances, and movies. Although Two Harbors' Swedish and Norwegian residents had their own halls—respectively, the Scandia and the Nordia—both groups also rented

Well-known Swedish and Norwegian performers, none more famous than Olle i Skratthult, often appeared at the Finnish Workers' Hall during the 1920s. From 1923 to 1931, the Swedish humorist, musician, and entertainer owned a North Shore cabin in Hovland. *Lake County Chronicle*, 24 June 1929.

the Finns' building for events that generated large audiences. Later called the "Finn-Hop" because of the highly popular public dances that occurred within its confines, the building was sold and converted into apartments in 1958.[130]

### "Hay Fever" Cabins *(now residences)*
Park Road south of First Avenue; First Street between South and First Avenues

Two Harbors, by the 1920s, was attracting hay fever sufferers from the entire Midwest. Most of the "hayfeverites" found rooms in hotels and resorts during the summer season, although a few built their own cabin retreats, including three families from Illinois and Iowa who constructed a "colony" of separate cabins in 1928–29. The location, on First Street above South Avenue, was considered ideal for hay fever relief because it overlooked Lakeview Park and Burlington Bay.[131] The three cabins now serve as seasonal and year-round residences.

### Lakeview Park and the Veterans' Memorial Gate
Sonju Trail in Lakeview Park

In August 1902, the Village of Two Harbors purchased land along Burlington Bay that, five years later, would become Lakeview Park. At the time of its 1907 grand opening, the park was designated alcohol-free, except for some occasions when the village council granted a special permit that allowed imbibing. Lakeview immediately became the focal point for numerous public events, including the annual Scandinavian Midsummer festivals that attracted large crowds to their "interesting programs of sports and music and dancing." In October 1921, after Thomas Owens assisted in securing additional Burlington Bay land from the D&IR, several hundred "public-spirited residents," who represented "every walk of life, turned out with picks and shovels to clean up Lakeview Park." The citizen workers, organized with the exactitude and precision of a military operation, were supervised by two directors, ten crew leaders, and ten labor foremen. All of Two Harbors' businesses were closed during the work period. In July 1925, when thousands of people gathered in Lakeview to celebrate the opening of Minnesota Highway 1, the *Lake County Chronicle* claimed that there was "no more beautiful natural park in Minnesota." Two years later, while on a transcontinental tour, the Oriole Club Review Orchestra of Baltimore stopped in Two Harbors and performed at the grand opening of Lakeview's new pavilion.[132]

**The Sonju Trail passes by the Veterans' Memorial Gate in Lakeview Park.**

Although the pavilion no longer exists, a former entrance gate, moved from the Lake County Memorial Forest in 1999, now stands at the southern end of Lakeview Park. The Memorial Forest was established in 1931 when five thousand white spruce tree seedlings were planted on land located northeast of Two Harbors along County Road 3. Specific trees were marked with the names of each Lake County soldier killed in either the Civil War, the Spanish–American War, or World War I; the later deaths of other veterans—including those who fell in World War II and the Korean and Vietnam conflicts—were recognized in subsequent decades. By 1999, when "the trees were dying, and the Memorial was in disarray," a crew of workers moved the gates to their new Lakeview Park setting, situated along a section of the recently opened Sonju Trail, where fifty-one white pines had been planted much earlier. Before the project was completed in 2012, it was decided that only those men and women killed in military action (currently forty-six males) would be recognized at the site.[133]

## Second Avenue

Second Avenue, now a relatively quiet downtown street, was the location for Two Harbors' first city hall. Also on the avenue is a still-active Masonic lodge, which remains an important landmark, as does another building that, more than a century ago, housed the Minnesota Mining and Manufacturing (3M) Company during its formative years. A few of Two Harbors' most important citizens also resided along Second Avenue, notably D&IR president and civic booster Thomas Owens and one of 3M's founders, John Dwan.

### Fortitude Masonic Lodge No. 188, AF & AM
631 Second Avenue

Two Harbors' Fortitude Lodge No. 188, AF & AM (Ancient, Free & Accepted Masons), organized in 1889, is one of the city's oldest institutions. Its members met at different locations for thirty-five years before the current building was completed in 1924. By this time, the Masons, "without embarrassment and without borrowing any money," had raised sufficient funds to construct and furnish their building. The most distinguishing feature of the rectangular, two-story brick structure is the entrance, flanked by paired columns that support a pediment festooned with decorative scrollwork. Adding further detail are its double entrance doors, stained glass sidelights, and a semielliptical transom. Also evident is the belt course—here represented by continuous rows of brick inserted between the first and second floors. Although some of its windows have been covered, Fortitude Lodge remains one of the best-preserved institutional buildings in Two Harbors.

### Old City Hall *(vacant)*
610 Second Avenue

Local governmental operations were established at Agate Bay by D&IR and MIC representatives in 1885, an action that preceded official organization of the village by just a few months. Planning for a structure that would house village functions, nonetheless, did not commence until 1905. Duluth architect Austin Terryberry prepared a design for the building later that year, while local contractor George Spurbeck served as the construction supervisor. In 1907, one year after the building was completed, Two Harbors received its city charter. Attached to the brick, flat-roofed, neoclassical structure is a two-story brick and cement-block addition that expanded the original building footprint around 1916. The first floor had an office for the city's water and light collectors and space for Two Harbors' first public library. The entire building has been altered over the years, most noticeably with window replacements and the removal of a balustrade from the front facade. Several businesses occupied the building after a new city hall was constructed at 522 First Avenue during the 1990s; however, the original structure has not been used during most of the current century.[134]

### John Dwan Law Office Building (*now the* 3M Birthplace Museum)
201 Waterfront Drive/Sixth Street

Bordering Second Avenue, but with an entrance that opens onto Waterfront Drive (Sixth Street), is the only Two Harbors commercial building currently listed in the National Register of Historic Places. The structure was deemed historically significant because of its direct associations with the formation of 3M, one of the world's largest and most recognizable firms. The company was organized in June 1902 by five Two Harbors men who met on the second floor of the building, which John Dwan used as a law office. By pooling their resources, the partners sought to raise sufficient capital for mining corundum—a rare and valuable abrasive mineral used in the manufacture of grinding wheels. The men hoped their results would be more successful than those of other firms that had engaged in fruitless efforts to discover corundum and other marketable minerals in northeastern Minnesota. They focused their efforts on nearby Crystal Bay, where a brief flurry of corundum fever had occurred in 1901.[135]

Shortly after forming their organization, the men acquired a potential Duluth-based competitor, the Minnesota Abrasive Company. The new firm opened its operations at Crystal Bay in 1903 and established a sales office and warehouse in Chicago one year later. It was quickly determined, however, that the material was not corundum but anorthosite, a low-grade, virtually worthless mineral. Following their corundum misadventure, the board of directors concluded that they should focus on sandpaper production—even though the company was $14,000 in debt and still required an additional $25,000 to establish the new enterprise. The bleak prospects changed when St. Paul businessman Lucius Ordway offered to finance the venture in exchange for 60 percent of the company's outstanding stock. In 1905, when adequate dockage space could not be found in Two Harbors, 3M established its sandpaper-manufacturing venture in a former Duluth flour mill. Five years later, the factory moved to St. Paul because of Duluth's unfavorable climate and Ordway's wish to have direct oversight over manufacturing operations. Dwan insisted on maintaining 3M's headquarters in his Two Harbors office building but was outvoted in 1916 by other board members, who chose to move all of their business activities to St. Paul. Just three months after the transition, 3M paid its first quarterly dividend—the first of many that have continued to the present.[136]

Dwan's twenty-four-by-thirty-six-foot building, constructed in 1898, was situated one block south of the current location before being moved in 1909. A low parapet with a plain fascia board now conceals three sides of the building's flat roof, while a restored single fixed-pane window fills a large section of the front (eastern) elevation. The building housed various functions, including a dentist's office, before its 1991 acquisition by the LCHS, which converted the interior into a first-floor museum depicting 3M's early history. The 3M Company sponsored a total redesign of the interior space in 2002 and continues to partner with LCHS in operating the museum.[137]

### Albert and Robina Headley Residence
#### 517 Second Avenue

The western entrance to the residential section of Second Avenue occurs at the site of Albert and Robina Headley's 1903 home—a two-and-a-half-story house that sits on a stone foundation. It has a steep cross-gable roof and a porch with Eastlake style features, including rope-patterned columns and brackets. Wooden shingles still cover much of its facade.[138]

Headley (1855–1935), a British Canadian, began working as a carpenter in the Duluth area after moving from Ontario in 1880, the year he married Robina McKenzie (1850–1935). In 1883, the couple and the first two of their five children arrived in Agate Bay, where the D&IR put Headley in charge of its dock-building crew; he also supervised the construction of railway water tanks, section houses, and bridges. Soon, Headley was heading D&IR's car construction department, a position that he held until retiring in 1930, at the age of seventy-five. Once described as having "a conscientious efficiency, which made his department a model to follow," Headley worked forty-seven years—one of the longest careers in D&IR history. He also served as a local judge of probate and held other civic offices. A very religious man, Headley was especially proud of his Presbyterian Sunday school classes, where, for many years, he sought "to inculcate . . . a desire for Righteousness in the hearts of a number of young men."[139]

### Thomas and Sarah Owens Residence
#### 509 Second Avenue

Thomas Owens (1856–1944) was one of eleven children born to Welsh immigrants in the vicinity of Oshkosh, Wisconsin. In 1882, Owens married Sarah Roberts (1860–1941), who, in 1870, had emigrated from Wales to Oshkosh in the company of her aunt, a domestic servant. Owens arrived at the D&IR construction site in 1883, one year before serving as the chief locomotive engineer on the Three Spot, which hauled the first load of iron ore to Agate Bay. Named general superintendent of the D&IR in 1892, Owens was vice president from 1920 until his 1931 retirement. He also served as an officer in numerous religious and civic endeavors, not least of which was Owens's 1925 selection as the first president of the LSIHA.[140]

The 1888 residence, displaying some Craftsman style details, was described as "a comfortable but not overly pretentious house" in 1910, when it accommodated the Owenses' two daughters, Sarah Owens's aunt, and one to two female (typically Swedish) servants. The residence still has some Craftsman ornamentation at the top of its side gables and on the projecting front dormer, but several additions and remodeling projects, some undertaken as early as 1916, have resulted in significant changes. Most noticeable is the expansion of the home's front porch that removed a lower-floor bay window and resulted in the elimination of the original curved column posts and rooftop balustrade. A fountain, once located on the family's front lawn, was transferred to Thomas Owens Park in 1940; the decorative feature, which has the figures of two children huddled under an umbrella, later became the property of LCHS. It is now on the grounds of the Two Harbors Light Station.[141]

### John and Helen Dwan Residence
### 508 Second Avenue

In 1889, John Dwan (1862–1920), a Michigander, married Helen Stockwell (1869–1945), who, in 1875, had emigrated from England to the United States with her family. The young couple moved to Two Harbors in 1891, just after Dwan earned his law degree from the University of Michigan. By 1910, the family included six children (five sons and one daughter); two sons still resided with the Dwans in 1920.[142]

Besides his successful legal career, Dwan, at different times from 1903 to 1920, served as the attorney for both Lake County and Two Harbors and ran unsuccessfully as the 1908 Democratic Party candidate for Minnesota attorney general; he also assisted four governors with their staff work. Dwan participated in numerous civic activities and was involved in local business enterprises, most notably as secretary-treasurer of the five-man organization that founded the 3M Company in 1902. Despite Dwan's objections, 3M moved to Duluth in 1907, then to St. Paul in 1916. After Dwan's 1920 death, his widow departed for Minneapolis, where she lived the remainder of her life.[143]

The Dwans' two-and-a-half-story Queen Anne residence, constructed around 1900, still retains several of its original features: an irregular roofline, a wrap-around veranda with turned posts, an arched frieze, an open balustrade at floor level, and an oriel window on the front facade of the second floor. The most noticeable change is the partial filling in of a three-part Palladian window that once distinguished the upper level of the house. The first floor now serves as a dental office, while an apartment is located on the second level.[144]

### Two Harbors Teacherage (*now* Park Lane Chateau)
### 431 Second Avenue

This large building, formerly a boardinghouse dating to the late 1800s, offered living quarters for twenty-seven residents in 1900. Hannah Bury, a middle-aged, recently widowed Canadian, managed the facility, which accommodated twenty-two residents in 1910 and fifteen in 1920. (A live-in female servant was also present during the latter year.) The Two Harbors School Board, after acquiring the boardinghouse in 1924, converted it into a "teacherage." Mary Snyder, who immediately moved into the building with her husband and young son, served as the "matron" for eighteen unmarried female teachers in 1930. The building, however, was sold in 1932, when the school board voted to "get out of the boarding house business." The Snyders would move, two years later, into a new log home by the French River. The large Second Avenue building, now the Park Lane Chateau, houses several residents in its apartments.[145]

## Third Avenue

Third Avenue, one of Two Harbors' most important roadways, is flanked by the Lake County Courthouse, by a church that was sponsored and built by the members of Two Harbors' oldest religious congregation, and by the primary entrance to a downtown city park. Also located on Third Avenue, which is part of the East Two Harbors subdivision, are many of the city's finest turn-of-the-century homes, most built for railway officials and successful businessmen. Lakeview Park, located at the eastern end of the avenue; was acquired for public use when Two Harbors secured its city charter in 1907.[146]

### Scandinavian Co-operative Mercantile Company (*now* North Shore Architectural Antiques)
224 Seventh Street

Slightly south of Third Avenue is a Seventh Street structure, dating to 1894, that housed one of northeastern Minnesota's oldest consumers' cooperatives. Established by members of Two Harbors' large Scandinavian community, the cooperative was open to everyone, although an individual share of stock could be acquired only by someone with a Nordic background. Eventually, anyone, regardless of ethnic heritage, could become a shareholder. (Two Harbors' Finnish residents also formed their own Workers and Farmers Cooperative Company in 1917.) While the Scandinavian Company's large inventory initially included groceries, dry goods, and clothing, it began attracting buyers from a wider area following the addition of a furniture showroom in 1923. With twenty-nine thousand square feet of interior space, twenty-two clerical workers, 325 stockholders, and annual sales of $358,000, the cooperative was Two Harbors' largest commercial enterprise.[147]

When the Scandinavian cooperative closed in 1957, it had served the retail needs of Two Harbors' residents for more than six decades. A new proprietor remodeled the building and operated the New Scan Store for a brief period of time, before it was used as a private grocery business, an auto parts salesroom, and a lumberyard. In 2013, environmental consultant John McCarthy purchased the structure and transferred his business, North Shore Architectural Antiques, from Duluth to Two Harbors. McCarthy obtains his large inventory of materials—primarily windows, doors, wooden trim, hardware, fixtures, tin ceilings, bathtubs, and sinks—by securing the salvage rights to houses and buildings, most constructed from the 1850s to 1950s, that are being renovated or razed. As the only northeastern Minnesota business that offers a complete line of vintage building materials, the store also attracts restoration enthusiasts and architects from the Twin Cities and entire Upper Midwest.[148] The original two-story frame structure has experienced several alterations since the initial 1957 sale, most noticeably to the interior and to window and door openings.

### Lake County Courthouse
601 Third Avenue

Beaver Bay served as the initial seat of government when Lake County was organized in 1856. Once the court system moved to Two Harbors in 1888, a two-story Queen Anne style courthouse emerged within the incipient community; nearby was the two-story jail and sheriff's residence, designed as a simplified Queen Anne building.[149]

A 1904 fire that consumed the original courthouse led, two years later, to the construction of the present building. Designed by architect James Allen MacLeod, the Beaux Arts structure has been termed a "sophisticated version of a City Beautiful courthouse" by architectural historians David Gebhard and Thomas Martinson. Given the pioneer appearance of Two Harbors at the time, the structure was a remarkable expression of civic pride that anticipated a bright future for both county and city. Built of brick and stone, the courthouse is square in plan and sits on a high, limestone-faced foundation. At the top is a low, semicircular dome with a metallic fish scale pattern. Also distinguishing the structure are its brick quoins, stone window surrounds, and a projecting cornice that has modillions situated above a wide frieze. The most outstanding Beaux Arts features are its two-story columns, which frame the imposing entrance staircase. Inside the courthouse is a large mural, *Liberty and Justice*, painted in 1906 by Swedish artist Axel Edward Soderberg, who worked for the Odin Oyen interior decorating firm of La Crosse, Wisconsin. Soderberg also painted three smaller murals that illustrate commerce, forestry, and mining. No longer visible is the dome's interior, enclosed in 1945 because of acoustical issues.[150]

The original sheriff's residence and jail were torn down during the 1990s and replaced by the Law Enforcement Center. An extensive restoration was also carried out in the original courthouse interior: period light fixtures and paint colors were replicated, *Liberty and Justice* was restored and moved to the atrium of the Law Enforcement Center, and the three smaller murals were transferred to the second-floor boardroom. When air-handling systems were installed on the upper floor in 2002, the stairway, hallway ceilings, and two offices were also restored. Six broken skylights were discovered when the second-floor suspended ceiling was re-

Numerous automobiles were parked in front of the Lake County Courthouse and adjacent jail and sheriff's residence before the drivers and passengers set off on a Mother's Day excursion in May 1910. At the front is Henry Bryan's 1903 Curved Dash Oldsmobile, the first automobile in Two Harbors, which had a tiller rather than a steering wheel. Courtesy of Lake County Historical Society.

moved; the broken glass was replaced, but the skylights no longer open to the sky. The stairwell landing now displays a stained glass window, titled *Law and Justice*, done by local artist Ronald Benson. Another second-floor display features the impressive, early twentieth-century images of Two Harbors photographer William Roleff.[151]

### First Presbyterian Church (*now* United Church of Two Harbors)

#### 531 Third Avenue

Two Harbors' Presbyterians organized a congregation in 1887—only a few years after settlement activities began along Agate Bay—and soon constructed a small, wooden-frame church at the corner of Third Avenue and Sixth Street. During the early 1900s, when several prominent D&IR officials were members, the congregation voted to replace the existing church with a larger, more substantial brownstone structure that opened in 1906. First Presbyterian merged with two other congregations in 1969 to form the United Church of Two Harbors.[152]

Courthouse architects Frederick German and A. Werner Lignell of Duluth were already well known for designing many public, commercial, religious, and residential buildings throughout northeastern Minnesota. Before coming to Duluth in 1889, German had acquired considerable experience with several firms, including the prestigious McKim, Mead, and White office in New York City, while Lignell was the first Finland-trained architect to practice in Minnesota. The Presbyterians' fifty-eight-by-eighty-four-foot structure was constructed of cut brownstone shipped from a Port Wing quarry, located on the Wisconsin side of Lake Superior. Designed in an English Gothic style, the church is distinguished by its square corner tower, originally capped by a pyramidal roof. A pointed arch doorway marks the entrance, while large tracery windows, placed under Gothic arches, are located at each end of the high-vaulted nave, which can seat 275 people. Several art glass windows exist throughout the church, including one facing toward Lake Superior that memorializes the sailors who lost their lives in the massive storm of November 1905. The materials and workmanship evident throughout the church demonstrate an exemplary and sensitive use of Lake Superior brownstone in a small structure.[153]

**Thomas Owens Park in early 1931. At the far left is the Lake County Courthouse. The First Presbyterian Church, now named the United Church of Two Harbors, overlooks the park.**

### Thomas Owens Memorial Park
Sixth Street between Third and Second Avenues

This site, in 1927, was described as having ten dilapidated residences that posed, "not only a blot on the beauty of the city, but [also] a grave fire hazard." All of the structures were soon acquired by the city for $2,000 and "the cancellation of delinquent property taxes." After Thomas Owens, Two Harbors' always reliable public-minded citizen and fundraiser, secured the required sum in donations from retired D&IR employees, the houses were torn down or moved away, and the vacant land was converted into a public park. Initially called Courthouse Square, the property was termed "one of the city's beauty spots" at the time of its 1931 dedication as Thomas Owens Park. (It became Thomas Owens Memorial Park following his 1944 death.) The basic, nonelaborate layout included elliptical pathways that extended into the park from each of its corner entrances. Within the park were several randomly spaced conifers, a school bell, and a World War I German howitzer donated by the local American Legion Post; a row of saplings was also planted on each street terrace. The fiftieth anniversary of iron ore shipments from the Vermilion Range to Agate Bay was recognized with an elegant ceremony in 1934, when a ball-shaped monument, forged of ore from the first mine at Soudan, was unveiled in the park. Three years later, in 1937, WPA workers completed a band shell at the eastern side of the park. The Two Harbors City Band, organized in 1897, has used the Paul Gauche Memorial Bandstand (later named to honor a longtime band director) to present its weekly summertime concert series. Long-standing proposals to replace the band shell with a new structure that will include multiuse areas for the entire Two Harbors community were approved in 2024.[154]

### Holy Spirit Catholic Church and Rectory *(now a private residence)*
221 Fifth Street

This residence, built in 1888–89 somewhat south of Third Avenue on Fifth Street, served, for almost thirty years, as the Holy Spirit Catholic Church and Rectory. (There was no need for a rectory prior to the late 1880s because missionary priests served the parish.) The church, located just south of the residence, was dedicated in 1890 and removed sometime after 1921, when a new Catholic edifice emerged at the intersection of Third Avenue and Third Street; a private residence now occupies the former Fifth Street church lot. The Queen Anne style rectory was considered one of Two Harbors' finest homes when it appeared during the late 1880s. The front facade still has its tower and conical roof, a three-sided oriel window that projects outward from the second story, and fish scale siding on the front gable. The open front porch also reveals turned posts, a balustrade, and

**Holy Spirit Catholic Church and Rectory, early 1900s. The church was removed before 1921, but the former rectory, now a private residence, remains on the site.**

a triangular pediment above the entry. The rectory later served as a live-in adult-care facility before it was converted into a private home during the late 1990s.[155]

### George and Ella Spurbeck Residence
431 Third Avenue

In 1875, George Spurbeck (1856–1928), a Wisconsin native, moved to Mantorville, Minnesota, where he married Ella Van Ornum (1857–1914). When the couple and their two sons arrived in Two Harbors, Spurbeck worked one year as an assistant lighthouse keeper before becoming a prominent contractor. Spurbeck's firm constructed many of Two Harbors' homes, including his family's residence, and several major structures, among them the city hall, the D&IR passenger depot, and a large addition to the coal dock. After Ella Spurbeck died in 1914, her widowed husband remained in the house for fourteen years, until his passing in 1928. By this time, both of Spurbeck's sons were pursuing medical careers elsewhere in northeastern Minnesota. The two-and-a-half-story dwelling, constructed in 1902 on a corner lot, has a cross-gable roof, a wrap-around front porch, and a bay window that looks onto Fifth Street. Decorative shingles and garlands still remain on the facades that front toward the street and avenue. The residence, which sometimes housed a few lodgers when owned by the Spurbecks, was divided into three separate rental units several years ago.[156]

### Two Harbors Episcopal Church and Hope Lutheran Church *(vacant, privately owned)*
411 Third Avenue

East of the Spurbeck residence is a former church, sponsored and built by Two Harbors' Episcopalians in 1899. The congregation of Hope Lutheran Church acquired the church in 1960 and significantly modified the building two decades later. The most noticeable changes were the construction of a wide entryway that replaced the narrow vestibule's steeply pitched gable and the elimination of two Gothic windows on the front facade. Hope Lutheran's congregation changed its name to Shepherd of the Lake in 2004, sold the structure in 2006, and settled into a new church at 2014 Seventh Avenue in 2007. The Third Avenue building, now privately owned, has not been occupied for several years.[157]

**The Third Avenue residences owned, left to right, by the Rock (409), James (405), Jones (401), and Munford (333) families were portrayed in this late 1920s photograph. Courtesy of Lake County Historical Society.**

### George and Rachel Rock Residence
409 Third Avenue

George Rock (1860–1938), born in Philadelphia, was living in a city orphanage by 1870 and working as an Ohio farmhand ten years later. In 1883, Rock found employment on a telegraph construction crew working between the Soudan Mine and Agate Bay. He would have the honor, one year later, of sending the first message to Charlemagne Tower in Philadelphia, informing MIC's president that the initial trainload of iron ore had arrived at the Agate Bay dock. Appointed D&IR's freight and passenger agent in 1898, Rock held this position until retiring in 1931, having served the company for forty-seven years. A charter member of Two Harbors' Presbyterian congregation, Rock married Rachel Marr (1860–1911) in 1897, six years before their new Third Avenue home was completed. After her 1911 death, Rock remained in the residence with his two sons until they reached adulthood. During the early 1920s, he married Dora Madsen (1877–1964), a Two Harbors teacher and the daughter of Norwegian immigrants. Shortly after Rock's 1933 passing, she acquired a Duluth teaching position and sold the Two Harbors residence.[158]

Built in 1903 on a stone foundation, the dwelling displays a steeply pitched, two-and-a-half-story gabled roof with returns. Originally sheathed with shingles, the house has been covered with aluminum siding for several decades. The three vertical windows at the front-gable peak remain, although the original diamond pattern of the glazing has been replaced by small squares of glass; the shutters are also a later addition. A distinguishing feature of the house is the swan neck pediment over the front door.[159]

### Frank and Henrietta James Residence
405 Third Avenue

Frank James (1861–1926) was residing in Ely by 1890, when he married another Pennsylvanian, Henrietta Squier (1868–1952). After James apprenticed as a druggist in Ely, the couple and their two children moved to Two Harbors, where, in 1894, he opened a pharmacy that eventually was located at a prominent First Avenue location. The Jameses' son Lloyd, who had begun apprenticing as a pharmacist at a young age, ran the business from 1926 to 1949. The couple's daughter Harriet, who was the pharmacy's general business manager before she departed for medical school, later became a well-known Boston physician. The James dwelling sits on a cut-stone foundation and has narrow clapboard siding, exhibiting many features of a four square dwelling: hip roofs cover the house and dormers, and the open porch, which spans the entire front elevation, has a central stairway entrance and four, round Tuscan columns that support its roof and an upper balustrade. Also noticeable is a centrally placed square window at the second level.[160]

### James R. and Nellie Shea and George and Katherine Jones Residence
401 Third Avenue

While the exact ownership chronology of this house is difficult to trace, it can be determined that James R. (1872–1955) and Nellie Nolan Shea (1877–1935) were among the earliest residents. James Shea, the brother of John J. Shea, worked for many years as a traveling D&IR locomotive engineer. The house was acquired during the 1920s by D&IR rail supervisor George Jones and his wife, Katherine Mahady Jones. Their son Emmett (1904–87), who spent his younger years in the residence, later attended Georgetown University Law School before returning to Two Harbors, where he served, at different times over a forty-year career, as the attorney for Two Harbors and Lake County. The two-and-a-half-story residence, with a hipped roof and large gabled dormers, has a prominent front porch with Tuscan columns. Its triangular porch pediment and front facade have retained their original fish scale shingle siding. The addition of a square picture window that looks out onto the porch has changed the first floor to some extent.[161]

### Andrew and Theresa Haugen Residence
205 Third Avenue

Following their 1901 marriage, Andrew (1870–1957) and Theresa Erickson Haugen (1878–1955) settled in Two Harbors, where they opened a grocery store on 606 First Avenue. Haugen was a Norwegian immigrant, while his wife had departed Sweden as a very young child. In 1929, when Haugen retired from his highly successful enterprise, a Two Harbors newspaper reporter made a telling observation: after twenty-eight years in the business, it was obvious that Haugen "knew his groceries." Soon named president of the First National Bank of Two Harbors, Haugen's position gave him immediate insight into the grave economic problems many citizens experienced during the economic calamity of the 1930s. In 1932, the most trying year of the Depression, Haugen issued a plea to the greater Two Harbors community, imploring anyone who had "work of some kind" to hire those residents who were suffering most seriously during the "Great Gloom." The Haugens and their two sons moved into the new, two-and-a-half-story four square residence in 1915. The house still retains its hipped roof with a front dormer and flared eaves, as well as a full front porch with square pillars and a balustrade. The couple took pride in their lawn, which twice won city prizes during the 1920s for its "even stand of grass, of uniform color, kept closely mown, with the appropriate use of flowers, shrubs, and trees."[162]

### John and Matilda Falk Residence
202–204 Third Avenue

This large house was built in 1908 for John (1858–1924) and Matilda Falk (1862–1920), who, accompanied by their five children, departed Sweden for Two Harbors in 1890; five more children would be born in the city prior to the matriarch's death. Falk initially worked for the D&IR but was bequeathed considerable wealth from the estate of a relative during the early twentieth century. After sending a son and daughter to Sweden, where they collected their inheritance, the Falks formulated plans for a new house that would become Two Harbors' premier residence. The financial windfall must have been considerable, given that the Falks also bankrolled their oldest son, Charles, who established a pharmacy in the Norden Hall at Second Avenue and Seventh Street in 1908. Later, in 1924, he would move the pharmacy into the "Falk Block" at the corner of First Avenue and Sixth (now Waterfront) Street.[163]

The walls of the Falk house, one of only a very few historic Two Harbors dwellings constructed of a material other than wood, used fabricated concrete Miracle Hollow Blocks. The roughly textured foundation employed similar blocks, but of a different color. Still distinctive today are the quoins and lintels; the decorative features of the two-story bay window; and the hipped but slightly flared, slate-covered roof with gabled dormers. The interior originally had a large reception hall that provided access to the sitting/living room and dining room; the second floor had five family bedrooms, a maid's room, and an open porch, all accessed by a central hallway.[164]

After the parents' deaths during the early 1920s, their pharmacist son Charles (1882–1956) and his Norwegian wife, Barbara Kolberg Falk (1891–1981), acquired the residence. In 1929, they commissioned architect C. H. Smith to prepare a design that would convert the house into a duplex, or two-flat, with identical residential quarters on both floors. When local residents Jon and Deborah Robb Anderson purchased the house in 1978, the couple maintained the historic integrity of the residence but also made some changes and additions that upgraded both units. Most noticeable is the sun porch, added to the rear of the first-floor duplex, which used windows salvaged from the demolition of Duluth's historic Glass Block Department Store. (These windows required replacement in 2019.)[165] The exceptionally well-maintained dwelling remains Two Harbors' most outstanding historic residence.

### Henry and Millicent Bryan Residence
123 Third Avenue

Henry Smith Bryan (1836–1910), born in New York, worked as a railroad machinist and machine shop foreman in Illinois from the late 1850s to the early

**The northern elevation of the residence built in 1908 for John and Matilda Falk.**

1890s. Bryan's 1890 marriage, his second, to Millicent Wilson (1858–1945), was followed by their 1893 move to Two Harbors, where he initially worked as a D&IR master mechanic before becoming superintendent of motive power in 1904. He was named chair of the Two Harbors Library Board in 1897 and of the Lake County Republican Party in 1902, the same year he became one of the 3M Company's five founding members. Bryan, already in 1903, also was the first Two Harbors resident to purchase an automobile—the same year he and his wife and mother-in-law moved into their new residence. Already sixty-seven years old at the time, Bryan lived there for only seven years before his death. Millicent Bryan then moved to St. Paul, where she undoubtedly maintained an association with the 3M Company's founders. The Two Harbors residence was sold, shortly after Bryan's passing, to Iver and Alice Amundsen, who opened the nearby Rustic Inn in 1920. The roof and dormers of the Bryans' 1903 dwelling—one of relatively few bungalows in Two Harbors—are covered by hipped roofs. Four windows flank both sides of the recessed central entrance, which has a bracketed porch hood; the upper section of the interior chimney is visible at the rear of the dwelling. A wrought iron perimeter fence anchored by brick columns now surrounds the yard and bungalow.[166]

### Rustic Inn (*removed, now* Harbor House Apartments)

### 101 Third Avenue

The Rustic Inn, an attractive log structure that once overlooked Lakeview Park and Burlington Bay, was built by Iver and Alice Amundsen during the early 1920s. (This Rustic Inn should not be confused with two other North Shore businesses having the same name—one a former diner located just northeast of Grand Marais, the other still a very active restaurant in Castle Danger.) Iver Amundsen (1875–1961) had accompanied his family on their 1880 voyage from Norway to the southern Minnesota community of St. James. There, in 1896, he married Alice Anderson (1877–1967), the daughter of Swedish immigrants. After the couple and their five children moved to Two Harbors in 1900, Amundsen initially worked as a butcher and later in an automobile service garage. The Amundsens started building the Rustic Inn in 1920, as construction of Minnesota Highway 1 was under way. Initially a modest diner, the business eventually became one of Two Harbors' first sit-down restaurants. Eleven log-sided rental cabins also stood on the grounds.[167]

The Rustic Inn was able to thrive, reported the owners in 1932, because of its appeal to tourists, to Two Harbors residents, and especially to patrons from Duluth, who, after driving twenty-five miles, appreciated the Amundsens' outstanding dinners. Even during the depths of a severe economic depression, "the desire of the tourist for natural surroundings and wonderful home-cooked dinners" would not be denied. At this time, the Amundsens also upgraded the restaurant by replacing its former wood- and coal-fired stoves with butane gas ranges and by adding several "labor-saving devices" equivalent to those found in modern hotel kitchens. All of their improvements, noted the owners, assured customers that they "need not speculate as to the cleanliness and order which obtains in the kitchen." Several family members, and as many as twenty local teenagers, worked at the inn during the busy summer seasons. The family, nevertheless, closed their business in 1956, reportedly because of the competition posed by the North Shore's fast-food restaurants. The buildings were removed from the site and replaced in 1978 by Harbor Point Apartments, which now provides forty-five subsidized housing units for as many as seventy Lake County senior citizens.[168]

**Befitting its name, much of the Rustic Inn was constructed of horizontal and split upright logs; the frame and board sections were also covered with log siding. Photograph by Harold Youngren, 1929.**

A quaint setting was provided for patrons within the Rustic Inn's dining area. Photograph by Harold Youngren, 1929.

### Fourth Avenue

Facing each other on the opposite sides of Fourth Avenue is a pair of Lutheran churches, one Norwegian in origin, the other Swedish. Also proximate to Fourth Avenue are two important structures, both accessed from nearby streets—an early hotel that now serves as an apartment building and a public library. At the eastern end of the avenue is a large vacant area, the site of Two Harbors' former high school.

### Agate Hotel (*now* Lakeview Apartments and Lodging)

#### 319 Eighth Street

This structure, named the Agate Hotel when constructed by the D&IR in 1883, was located proximate to the future coal dock and just slightly west of the company's office building. Intended for dock- and railway workers, the plan for the horseshoe-shaped Agate structure, soon renamed the Lakeview Hotel, was created by joining its two L-shaped sections—one the original 1883 building, the other an 1887 addition. Moving the building to its current location was precipitated by the completion of D&IR's Lake Line between Two Harbors and Duluth in late 1886. Soon the company would construct its passenger and freight depots at the western end of Fifth Avenue. By 1896, most of the railroad-related buildings, including the Lakeview, had been moved to the area. Situated at the corner of Fourth Avenue and Eighth Street, the hotel could house eighty to ninety people, the majority of whom arrived or departed on trains that served Two Harbors. Some residents also lived year-round in the hotel. All of the railroad-related buildings were removed many years ago, but the hotel, converted into the present-day

The Lakeview shortly after its 1926 conversion from a hotel into apartments. The two wings that formed the original structure still remain today, but noticeably missing are the turned columns and angular braces that supported the open porch. Photograph by Harold Youngren, 1929.

Lakeview Apartments around 1926, remains on the same site it has occupied for some fourteen decades.[169]

### Bethlehem Lutheran Church
601 Fourth Avenue

### Emmanuel Lutheran Church
602 Fourth Avenue

Physical evidence of the once-strong identities expressed by Two Harbors' large Swedish and Norwegian immigrant populations is embodied in two Lutheran churches, respectively Bethlehem and Emmanuel, which face each other on opposite sides of Fourth Avenue. Both trace their origins to 1889, when the two ethnic groups organized separate congregations—First Norwegian–Danish Lutheran and Swedish Evangelical Lutheran Emmanuel. The two congregations then agreed to construct a single building at 601 Fourth Avenue—the Scandinavian Evangelical Lutheran Church—which was dedicated in 1891. Just four years later, however, the Swedish congregants sold their $1,200 share to the Norwegians, who changed the church's name to Bethlehem Lutheran. Following this transaction, the Swedes immediately began building their new church, Emmanuel Lutheran, on the opposite side of Fourth Avenue; it would open in 1896.[170]

Bethlehem, initially provided with a central narthex, bell tower, and steeple, is still in use today, although it was extensively modified at different times between 1939 and 1968: the narthex and bell tower were relocated to the southeastern corner of the structure, the Gothic windows were replaced, and the clapboard siding was covered with stucco. The original Swedish Emmanuel Lutheran Church, larger than Bethlehem when it emerged in 1895–96, was razed in 1960. The congregation used the site for their new church, a rectangular, brick-faced building that has narrow vertical windows, a high-ceilinged nave, an almost flat roof, and a free-standing spire. It is comparable to many postwar churches sponsored by midwestern congregations with relatively modest building budgets. The church and parish hall complex was expanded between 1970 and 1976 with the addition of an office, Sunday school rooms, and a library. The acquisition and demolition of two nearby residences preceded the development of a parking lot—another ubiquitous feature of postwar churches. Both congregations are now affiliated with the Evangelical Lutheran Church of America.[171]

### Two Harbors Carnegie Library
320 Waterfront Drive

Although Two Harbors' first public library was not completed until 1909, residents were able to read and borrow books as early as 1897, when officials and citizens voiced concern that the city's saloon and tavern culture exerted a negative impact on the community's predominantly male population. The village council sought to counteract these influences by establishing a small lending library that, over the next twelve years, was housed in various buildings. The city, in 1907–8, sought a donation from former steel industry magnate Andrew Carnegie, who had become nationally known for his sponsorship of public libraries throughout the United States. Once Two Harbors officials agreed to donate a site and ensure that funds would be made available for library maintenance, Carnegie offered a gift of $10,000, followed by an additional $5,000 contribution. Austin Terryberry, who had previously designed the city hall, was selected as architect.[172]

The forty-four-by-fifty-six-foot building, which reveals neoclassical influences, is constructed of Twin City pressed brick and trimmed with red cut sandstone. A low-pitched hipped roof covers the building, a projecting portico framed by two stone columns dominates the main facade, and an arched brick entrance, accessed by steps, defines the original point of ingress and egress. Quoins are evident on all corners, and thick stone lintels and thin stone sills frame the windows. The main floor of the interior, furnished in golden oak, was originally designed as one large room divided by bookcases. The basement, with its maple floor and walls finished in Georgia pine, included two clubrooms, a cloakroom, a toilet, and the furnace and coal room.[173]

A new, single-story addition, designed by Architectural Resources Inc. of Duluth, was attached to the basement level of the library's southern elevation in 1983. Constructed of light-colored brick and providing four thousand square feet of space for library services, the addition also offers a street-level entry to the building. The original central entrance has been closed, but the second level still retains its beamed ceiling and fireplace. The Carnegie section of the library was listed in the National Register of Historic Places in 1985.[174]

### Two Harbors High School *(razed)*
North Side of Fourth Avenue between Third and Fourth Streets

This Fourth Avenue location was selected as the site for Two Harbors' Central High School in 1901. When construction of a new Lake County High School was undertaken by two New Deal agencies (the PWA and the WPA) in 1939, residents were given the opportunity to purchase salvaged materials from the original building. The new school, constructed of buff-colored brick, with a decorative zigzag parapet trim and glass blocks on its projecting tower, served as an example of what is often termed "PWA moderne"; also within the school were several murals completed by three WPA artists. The New Deal–era high school and its facilities were deemed inadequate and outdated by the 1990s, but referenda calling for replacement of the complex were rejected by voters in 1999 and 2000. A successful 2002 referendum, however, led to the construction of a new school and community center on a seventy-acre campus located at the northern edge of Two Harbors, which opened in 2005. Efforts to find an alternative use for the abandoned structure failed before it was torn down in 2007; the vacant site was sold to a private party in 2020.[175]

## Seventh Avenue

Seventh Avenue, which coexists with Highway 61, is bordered by many of Two Harbors' newest commercial structures. Also located along or close to the corridor are a few historic buildings, including a well-maintained 1896 residence and an 1894 boardinghouse that was converted into a restaurant years ago. At the northeastern end of Two Harbors are two major open-space features: a campground and a golf course.

### Peter and Augusta Anderson Residence
731 Seventh Avenue

This residence, dating to 1896, was built by Swedish immigrants Peter (1860–1929) and Augusta Nelson Anderson (1864–1960). Anderson departed for the United States in 1884 and made his way, one year later, to Two Harbors, where he married Augusta Nelson, also a Swedish émigré. The couple, employed as "boarding masters" by the D&IR, supplied food for workers housed in the company's camps and railway cars. From 1901 to 1926, they also owned and operated the Lakeview Hotel, which accommodated guests, roomers, and boarders. The Andersons' monthly

**The Two Harbors Central High School, built by PWA and WPA workers, as it appeared at the time of its 1940 dedication. The entire structure was demolished in 2007.**

expenditure of $10,000 for "food stuff," noted a 1910 observer, was exceeded by no one else in the Two Harbors area. After Anderson's 1929 death, his widow continued supplying railway car workers with meals for many more years and maintained her Seventh Avenue home with a son and daughter-in-law and their three children.[176]

The Andersons' original kitchen and dining room were situated in the basement; the first floor included a parlor, a formal dining room, a library, and one bedroom; the second floor had four bedrooms. When Robert Anderson, a grandson, acquired the property in 1990, he converted the basement and second floor into rental apartments, while the first floor was rented to the Superior Hiking Trail Association (SHTA) for its headquarters. When the house was sold in 2020, following some 125 years of Anderson family ownership, SHTA moved its headquarters to First Street in downtown Two Harbors. The new owner converted her acquisition into three "quirky short-term rentals," all furnished and equipped with vintage signs, lava lamps, vinyl records, electric fireplaces, and other mid-twentieth-century memorabilia. The dwelling's well-maintained exterior continues to display its original full-width front porch, spindle work, and open balustrade with turned columns. The house has also served as a backdrop for Two Harbors' Under the Spreading Walnut Tree Art Festival—a three-day, summertime event that occurs along the sidewalk that parallels Highway 61 and spreads onto the home's large rear parking lot.[177]

### Martin Edwardson's Bakery and Boardinghouse and Oscar's Restaurant (*now* Blackwoods Grill and Bar)

612 Seventh Avenue

In 1894, shortly after his arrival from Norway, Martin Edwardson established a boardinghouse and bakery on Seventh Avenue. The business became Oscar's Restaurant in 1924, following its conversion into a tearoom and confectionary by new owner Oscar W. Anderson, an ambitious and diligent, twenty-four-year-old son of local Swedish immigrant parents. (In 1940, Anderson informed a U.S. Census enumerator that he worked 16 hours a day, a total of 112 hours per week, Monday through Sunday, in the food emporium.) Oscar's Restaurant would be known, some twenty years later, for its Norshore Room—Two Harbors' first version of a 1950s supper club—an eclectic combination of wood-paneled walls, linen tablecloths, colonial captain's chairs, and circular "Space Age" light fixtures. The business was renamed the Harbor House after its sale in 1974, and then as the Blackwoods Grill and Bar following its purchase by new owners in the mid-1990s. Few single properties better represent the century-long history and evolution of tearooms, cafés, diners, supper clubs, and restaurants on the North Shore.[178]

### Two Harbors Tourist Camp (*now* Burlington Bay Campground)

1328 Highway 61/626 Park Road

The City of Two Harbors established a tourist camp north of Lakeview Park shortly before the initial North Shore roadway opened to motorists in 1917. It was the completion of Minnesota Highway 1 during the 1920s, however, that introduced the campground's free features to large numbers of tourists. Because no boundary separated the campground from Lakeview, an "overflow" of tourists often extended into the park. In 1925, Two Harbors' *Lake County Chronicle* commented that anyone visiting the park could not help but be offended by "the smoke . . . from campfires, tents, and washings hanging on lines stretched between the trees." Although the editor suggested that protecting this "most beautiful spot" might require the development of a new campground elsewhere in the city, the site was retained and expanded over subsequent decades. It now offers more than one hundred campsites that are available throughout the tourist season.[179]

### R. J. Houle Information Center and the *Native American*

1330 Highway 61

Positioned along the lower side of Scenic Drive in eastern Two Harbors is a small log cabin—the R. J. Houle Information Center. Built by the CCC during the 1930s, the cabin originally stood forty-six miles north of Two Harbors at the Cloquet Lake Fire Station Lookout. Moved to its current location in 1975, and dedicated in 1977, the cabin now serves as a visitors' information center that is operated by the Two Harbors Chamber of Commerce. Standing just outside the cabin is a "giant" chair, a photographic attraction built

A former CCC cabin, left, moved to the far eastern border of Two Harbors in 1975, is now the R. J. Houle Information Center. At the far right is Peter Wolf Toth's wooden sculpture the *Native American*. Between them is a service building for the nearby Burlington Bay Campground.

by Two Harbors High School industrial arts students in 2017. Also on the grounds is a wooden sculpture, the *Native American*, carved from a pine tree trunk in 1977 by Hungarian American artist Peter Wolf Toth. About thirty feet high, the statue is the twenty-fifth of fifty (one for each state) of Toth's *Trail of the Whispering Giants* series, intended to "draw attention to the problems confronting descendants of the 'original Americans.'" In 2008, Toth returned to Two Harbors, where he spent several weeks restoring the thirty-one-year-old roadside attraction.[180]

### Lakeview National Golf Course and Two Harbors Curling Club
1349 Highway 61

Several of Two Harbors' golf enthusiasts developed a three-hole course on the upper side of Highway 61 in 1929. Efforts to expand the course into a nine-hole facility were encouraged because it was believed that the site's natural features "would obviate costly construction in the provision of artificial hazards." Expansion into a complete golf course was also viewed as a way to attract tourists and keep them within the city. The nine-hole facility, named the Lakeview Golf Course, was dedicated in 1932. The first clubhouse, a former toolshed located close to the ninth tee, was replaced with a log cabin located by the second tee; the cabin was later supplanted by a "picturesque but small and drafty" wooden-frame structure. The current clubhouse, which opened in 1993, provides participants with a golf shop, bar, and restaurant/grill. When it was expanded to eighteen holes and renamed the Lakeview National Golf Course in 1996–97, the property became one of the region's most attractive facilities, particularly because Lake Superior is visible from fourteen of its holes. Attached to the clubhouse is another structure that accommodates the Two Harbors Curling Club, constructed shortly after a 1991 fire destroyed the group's former headquarters. The curlers assumed ownership of the Lakeview building and its concessions in 2011.[181]

## Silver Creek Township

Minnesota Highway 61 enters Silver Creek Township just after the Lakeview Golf Course and proceeds almost twenty-one miles before it reaches Beaver Bay Township. Silver Creek includes just one unincorporated settlement, Castle Danger, but several well-known North Shore features—Gooseberry Falls, Lafayette Bluff, Encampment Forest, and others—are located within its borders. For almost seventy years, one site, Silver Creek Cliff, posed the greatest challenge to drivers who traversed Highway 61: until the cliffside drive was replaced by a tunnel in 1996, midwestern "flatlanders" could briefly imagine that they were encountering mountain-driving conditions.

The township's first Euro-American settlers arrived around 1890. By 1900, five years before the first official Silver Creek Township meeting, 155 people lived proximate to Lake Superior, among them seventy foreign-born residents, sixty-four of whom were Nordics—thirty-six Swedes, seventeen Norwegians, six Danes, and five Finland Swedes. The total population has grown slightly during recent decades, from 1,095 in 1990 to 1,180 in 2020. The number of seasonal residents is significant, however, given that just one-half of its 1,190 housing units were occupied year-round in 2020–21.[182]

### Scenic Point Cabins (*now* Superior Shores Resort & Conference Center and Burlington Bay Lakehomes)

#### 1521 Superior Shores Drive/1412 Burlington Bay Road

In 1936, Walfred and Clarence Pearson, owners of an automobile dealership and the sons of Swedish immigrants who settled in Two Harbors during the late 1890s, shipped a boatload of lumber to Burlington Point, a peninsula that separates Burlington Bay and Flood Bay. The Pearson brothers used the lumber to construct the first rental units at their new business, named Scenic Point Cabins. Located on the Flood Bay side of the peninsula, Scenic Point initially had ten cabins, a central shower, and a small lodge. A campground for "more rugged vacationers" was added after 1972. The rustic resort experienced a major transition from 1983 to 1985, when the next generation of family members built a small complex of townhouses overlooking the peninsula. A central lodge with guest rooms, a pool, and a restaurant were added in subsequent years. The business underwent an ownership change in 1994 when the Blue Waters Development Corporation assumed management responsibilities and a controlling interest in the expanded and renamed Superior Shores Resort. Its eighteen townhouses would eventually be available for purchase in unusually small, one-eighth fractional shares, which gives owners access to their unit and the resort's facilities for six to seven weeks per year.[183]

Another Blue Waters development, Burlington Bay Lakehomes, one of the largest residential projects on the North Shore when proposed in 2003, lies about one-half mile west of Superior Shores. Before development could occur, however, the twenty-two-acre site required access to Two Harbors' utility systems. The exteriors of the multibuilding complex are rather nondescript, but the interiors—ranging from one-bedroom units to five-bedroom "executive lodges"—are finished in an "upscale Northwoodsy décor," some with even more than one stone fireplace.[184]

Much of the combined holding—including several pools, a conference and event center with space for as many as 280 people, and 131 of 180 residential units (the remaining 49 are privately owned)—was purchased in early 2020 by the North Shore Resort Company for $15 million, believed to be, until then, the most expensive resort transaction in Minnesota history. The buyer, a family-owned, Ontario-based company, became a major player on the North Shore tourist scene in 2018 with the purchase of Lutsen Resort in Cook County. At the time of the Superior Shores sale, Bryce Campbell, the company's primary partner, remarked that what attracted him was its location—"close to Two Harbors yet up on the shore."[185] Despite these issues, Superior Shores continues to maintain a viable presence and identity within the greater North Shore area, primarily because of its striking and unsurpassed views of Burlington Bay and eastern Two Harbors. In July 2024, however, a Lake County District Judge issued an emergency order that placed Superior Shores into temporary receivership for failure to meet its financial obligations.[186]

### Flood Bay Cabins and Flood Bay Motel *(vacant)*

#### 1511 Highway 61

The Flood Bay site, situated on the upper side of Scenic Drive, was occupied by a few tourist cabins during the 1930s, but it is usually associated with Campman ("Campie") Anderson, the first white child born in Silver Creek Township. Anderson and his wife, Ebba, had previously worked as caretakers for the nearby Encampment Forest Association (EFA) before opening their Flood Bay Cabins soon after World War II. The cabins, termed "a good place to rest" by the Andersons, were moved away by another owner during the 1960s to make way for the ten-unit Flood Bay Motel. The shed-roofed structure, typical of other mom-and-pop motels of the era, remains on the site but has been closed for several years.[187]

### Flood Bay State Wayside
#### 1514 (144 MN-61) Highway 61

Crescent-shaped Flood Bay, named for an 1856 land claimant, lies a short distance from Burlington Bay. An unimproved, nineteen-acre property was opened to motorists by the MDH in 1963, but the Lake County Board of Commissioners requested a transfer to the MDC just two years later. The site, identified as Flood Bay State Wayside in 1985, was officially dedicated six years later, following completion of a shoreline erosion control project that used waste rock derived from the Lafayette Tunnel, then under construction several miles to the northeast. Now termed one of the North Shore's best beach walks by the MDNR, Flood Bay is well known for its black basalt shoreline, especially the Lake Superior agates, which are described on an interpretive sign erected by the Minnesota Geological Society in 2010.[188]

### Betty's Pies
#### 1633 Highway 61

Among the North Shore's most interesting personalities was Betty Christiansen Lessard, a Silver Creek Township wedding photographer who took over her family's small fish stand in 1956. Early customers who stopped at the bright red building, simply called "Betty's" at the time, ate "smoked fish and crackers served on wrapping paper" while seated at picnic tables; elsewhere on the grounds were two outhouses that reportedly leaned in "one direction or another." Lessard eventually added coffee, doughnuts, hamburgers, hot dogs, cookies, pies, and lunches to the menu; transitioned from smoked fish to fish dinners; and replaced the disposable paper cups and plates with her own china and silverware. She and her husband, Lloyd, soon constructed the first addition to the stand, which provided "enough space to enlarge the kitchen and install a lunch counter so customers could come in and sit down to enjoy their food." After four more additions, the renamed Betty's Café had evolved into a forty-one-seat restaurant.[189]

**A diminutive structure that housed the original Betty's in 1956 was expanded, one year later, into Betty's Café and eventually into Betty's Pies.**

**The expansion of Highway 61, completed in 2000, led to the removal of the original Betty's Pies and the construction of this much-expanded diner on a nearby site.**

Summertime Sundays drew overflow crowds, but the springtime smelting seasons of the 1960s and 1970s forced Lessard to stay open twenty-four hours a day. "Smelters would take anything that would burn for their riverside fires," she recalled in 2001, "and we lost the roof of our pumphouse, the front steps of the restaurant, and even caught them trying to take our flower boxes for firewood!" When her baked products became even more popular, many satisfied customers identified the location strictly by its product, "Betty's pies"—and "the name of the café was simply changed to that." The business, by the 1970s, had become one of the quirky places that patrons from throughout Minnesota and the Upper Midwest regarded as a "certifiable . . . North Shore landmark."[190]

Once addicted to cigarettes, Lessard quit her habit and initiated a no-smoking policy in 1978—well before a state law banned such practices in Minnesota's restaurants. A perfectionist, Lessard began each day at 3:00 A.M. by baking as many as a hundred pies. Although Lessard sold the business in 1984, almost thirty years before her passing at the age of ninety, ensuing owners maintained the original name. The threatened closing and razing of the building for a road alignment project in 1997, however, led two Twin Citians, practically on a whim, to purchase and continue operating the diner over the next three tourist seasons. The new owners soon selected a site just north of the original structure, where, in 2000, they opened an eighty-six-seat, $500,000 restaurant with a dining room that had blue-and-white tiles and an L-shaped lunch counter reminiscent of the former café. Betty's Pies, open year-round, remains a highly sought-out North Shore tourist stop.[191]

### Stewart River Bridge and Kelsey Beach
### 234–238 MN-61

The Stewart River, named for John Stewart, an 1856 land claimant, is proximate to Betty's Pies. A reinforced concrete-arch bridge crosses the river at this point, making it one of only a few rural places in the state with such a unique structure. Built in 1924, with a span of seventy feet and a width of nineteen feet (expanded to thirty feet in 1939), the Stewart River crossing received special attention from MDH officials because of its exposed rock formations, which provided opportunities to reduce overall construction costs. The river's scenic qualities and the North Shore's popularity as a tourist destination also influenced MDH engineers when they approved these out-of-the-ordinary measures. Among the structure's outstanding classical revival style details are the large vertical pilasters, each embellished with a rectilinear panel that stands on both sides of the arch opening; the open-balustrade bridge railings; and the different concrete surfaces that accentuate its design details—"coarse on the abutment walls, pilaster panels, and spandrel walls; smooth on the pilaster surrounds and archivolt."[192]

Upon completion, the normally staid highway agency expressed great pride in its new structure. Rural bridges are typically utilitarian, but the span's subtle classical features soon received acclaim as the "most aesthetically accomplished statement . . . produced by the state trunk highway program." Almost seventy-five years later, at the time of its 1998 listing in the National Register of Historic Places, the Stewart River Bridge was still termed "a striking ornament of the state's trunk highway system."[193] Kelsey Beach, a small public area along the southeastern side of the river's mouth, is comprised of small, dark cobblestones. Although several storms destroyed the pathway and steps in 2017–18, repairs were made, and Kelsey Beach is once again easily accessible to beachcombers.

Structural and safety issues posed by the historic bridge led MnDOT, in 2019, to conduct the first of several public meetings that addressed these concerns. Primarily because of its notable design features, agency officials determined that the bridge would not be replaced. Instead, MnDOT chose to provide a "one-way pair" of bridges over the Stewart. One part of the pair, a new bridge section on the highway's inland side, now carries traffic heading toward the southwest and Duluth and also includes turn lanes that provide motorists with a much safer connection to Betty's Pies. Motorists heading toward the northeast still use the historic bridge, which has been rehabilitated and restored. A new, separate right-of-way, eight feet in width and dedicated to pedestrians and bicyclists, is also part of the bridge.[194]

**The Stewart River Bridge, shown here in 2015, was one of the finest examples of 1920s highway design in Minnesota. The rehabilitation and restoration of the bridge, undertaken in 2022–23, maintained its original classical revival details. The steps to Kelsey Beach, which washed out in 2017–18, are at right.**

### Silver Creek Gifts and Gallery *(vacant)*
1825 Highway 61

A short distance northeast of the Stewart River Bridge is the entrance to Lake County Road 3—the fifty-six-mile-long inland route that motorists followed before the lakeshore section of Minnesota Highway 1 was completed during the mid-1920s. About one mile beyond the intersection, on the inland side of the highway, is a single-story log structure, built to commemorate the 1970 Sier du Lhut Tricentennial. (Duluth is named for Sier du Lhut, a French soldier who explored the area during the 1670s.) Students from Duluth Area Vocational Technical Institute's forest harvesting and building construction programs erected the horizontal log cabin, which was put on display in the city. The building was later taken apart, reassembled at 1825 Highway 61, and opened as a gift shop. The addition of three rooms also provided substantial space for the display of items that featured North Shore and Minnesota artists and themes. In September 2022, however, Silver Creek's collections and sales inventories were removed when the building was closed and vacated.[195]

## Silver Creek Bridge

Silver Creek (a close translation of an Anishinaabe term) was not visible to motorists for several decades because a box culvert, rather than a bridge, supported the highway crossing. The situation changed in 2022–23, when MnDOT removed the culvert and constructed a "typical North Shore bridge" with a pedestrian/bicycle crossing. The restoration of Silver Creek also received attention at this time.[196]

### Nick and Julia Nelson's Farm (*now* Silver Cliff Homes Association)
Silver Cliff Road

From 1910 to the early 2000s, Silver Creek Point, which juts into Lake Superior, was home to several fishing camps, a small farm, an overlook, a few tourist businesses, and some seasonal homes. The earliest permanent residents, Norwegians Nikolai Nilsen (Nick Nelson after his 1907 arrival in Minneapolis) and Julia Pedersen Nelson, established a farm and home at the base of the cliff in 1910. Nelson and two partners, in 1926, also platted Silver Cliff Park, a subdivision for cabins and summer residences; one of the homes, named Rockledge, was an "octagon lookout building" that stood at the tip of the point. Around 1936, the Nelsons and their six children opened Silver Cliff Resort, which had ten cabins equipped with electric lights and baths and a boat for "deep sea fishing and cruising." Nelson sold the property shortly after his wife's 1947 death.[197]

Bill Nauha, the son of local Finnish farmers, opened Mount Silver Cabins on some of Nelson's former land during the early 1950s. Renamed Bill's Silver Cliff Motel a few years later, Nauha claimed his new building was so close to the water that one could "sleep to the slap of the waves on the shore of Lake Superior." A similar business, Cliff n' Shore Motel and Cabins, was nearby, while the Pioneer Crafts Co-op Store, relocated to Castle Danger in 1992, paralleled Highway 61.[198]

In 2005, Kathleen Nye-Railing, the developer of International Market Square, an expansive commercial and condominium complex in downtown Minneapolis, purchased the two vacant motels and a few nearby buildings; all were either "cut up and moved to another location" or "removed and recycled to new owners." Eight of the envisioned thirteen units in Nye-Railing's $10 million project, called Silver Creek Homes, were constructed over the next two years. The units, each with 2,100 square feet of living space and priced from $775,000 to $925,000, were aimed at retirees who might wish to invest in a North Shore "luxury lakeside home." The purchasers, all members of the Silver Creek Home Owners Association, are provided with building and site maintenance and access to 560 feet of Lake Superior beachfront.[199]

### Silver Creek Cliff Tunnel
2025 Silver Creek Cliff Tunnel

The Two Harbors committee that oversaw the July 1925 dedication of Minnesota Highway 1 also selected a name for the specific section of new roadway that local residents often called "the point of rocks at Nick Nelson's farm." The committee was deluged with many suggestions—Gateway Cliff, Mount Silverlodge, Babcock Scenic Cliff, Owens Cliff, Morning Glory View, Inspiration Point, Panorama Ledge, Huge Ledge, Lookout Mountain, and others—before the members settled on a historically appropriate name: Silver Creek Cliff.[200]

**Rockledge, a summer home with an adjacent "octagonal lookout building," emerged on the Silver Creek Point shoreline in 1923. Photograph by Harold Youngren, 1931.**

**One of several dynamite blasts that tore down a section of Silver Creek Cliff in August 1923. Courtesy of Lake County Historical Society.**

Called one of the North Shore's "boldest places" by geologist G. M. Schwartz, the cliff proved impenetrable to early road builders. A dramatic change was initiated in March 1923, however, when crews began building a temporary rail line that transported a pair of large steam shovels, some small train engines, and numerous dump cars from Two Harbors to the cliff. In August, when two railcar loads of dynamite were ignited in a late-morning blast, the explosion tore down one side of the "noble mountain"—a sight "worth seeing," exclaimed an enthusiastic highway engineer. Another detonation, two weeks later, exceeded the expectations of MDH officials since the rock uplifted only slightly and was pushed to the side of the cliff, where it would be used as part of the roadbed. Once it was completed, North Shore travel brochures touted the cliffside's impressive features, especially the sixty thousand tons of rock that had been dynamited and moved to create the right-of-way and the sheer drop of 125 feet that existed between the road's outer rim and the lake below. One publication even claimed that it was now possible "to throw your cigarette butts into the lake, as you drive along in your car."[201]

**Sightseers traveling in a 1929 Model A Ford stop to gaze at Lake Superior from Silver Creek Cliff. The large rocks arrayed along the outer edge of the roadway were replaced, in 1931, by steel cables strung between posts. Courtesy of Lake County Historical Society.**

Although significant engineering expertise preceded construction of the cliff road, motorists and highway maintenance crews were still bedeviled by numerous rockslides, both large and small, over ensuing years. At

**The arch, shown here during the late 1920s or early 1930s, shortly after it was built over the highway along the southwestern section of Silver Creek Cliff. Bikers and hikers who now use the Gitchi-Gami Trail pass under a much smaller replica of the arch.**

least six major incidents occurred between 1926 and 1938, fortunately with no deaths or injuries. The first event took place in June 1926, less than a year after the official highway opening. An inspection of the slide, which filled the road to a depth of five to ten feet over a distance of seventy-five feet, led to a rather ominous conclusion. "The rocks are so seamed," observed the engineers, "that it is impossible to dynamite them except at a terrific cost, and the work of removing them by manual labor is a work that is most hazardous." After using half a railroad car of dynamite to bring down more rock and dirt, motorists were informed that the roadway was completely safe.[202]

Despite these assurances, a November 1929 episode caused an estimated twenty thousand tons of boulders to crash down from the embankment's summit. Included in the cascade was a single boulder weighing an estimated one thousand tons, which protruded four feet above the water after it tumbled into the lake. Several days of blasting were required to clear the huge accumulation of material that had piled on the road. The massive rockfall, concluded a MDH engineer one month later, demonstrated that the cliff was in extremely dangerous condition. Members of the local Castle Danger Farmers Club expressed even greater alarm and outrage over the immediate threats posed by the unstable cliffside. In May 1930, the club issued an impassioned petition to MDH commissioner Charles Babcock, pointing out that children who passed by the cliff on their twice-daily school bus trips faced "constant danger of death from falling rocks." The plea undoubtedly was motivated by the near-fatal experience, just two weeks earlier, of four Canadian men from Fort William who were forced to stop because of a recent rockfall. The men immediately turned around and sped off, just moments before a huge rockslide covered the spot where they had been standing. The cliff was deemed safe for travel seven months later, but only after highway officials conducted numerous investigations and workers dislodged thirty thousand tons of overhanging rocks and earth, which were dumped into the lake. A total of $50,000 was also expended in "facing off the slope," to eliminate any possibly dangerous conditions.[203]

Nevertheless, the cliff went on another "rampage" just two years later, as tons of rocks, some the size of an automobile, crashed onto the highway after being "pried off . . . by the frost." Work crews once again dynamited a narrow passage for vehicles before the entire roadway was cleared. The highway's outer rim, bordered by a linear row of boulders, all about three feet high, was also replaced by a steel guardrail. It is hoped, commented the *Two Harbors Chronicle*, that the new railing "will always keep even crazy drivers from jumping their cars into Lake Superior." Another

**The twenty thousand tons of rocks that hurtled down from the top of Silver Creek Cliff in November 1929 fell onto the highway and into Lake Superior. The rockfall blocked the roadway for several days before it was removed with explosives. Photograph by Harold Youngren, 1929.**

**Completion of the Silver Creek Cliff Tunnel in 1994 eliminated a dangerous site for North Shore motorists but also eradicated the famous cliff drive that both exhilarated and terrified travelers for seventy years. Because Highway 61 serves as an international route between Minnesota and Ontario, the volume of truck traffic is quite heavy.**

massive slide that covered the road in 1938 required the efforts of twelve workers, who toiled for three weeks on the challenging project, which demanded significant safeguards when the cliff top was "blasted to free it of protruding rocks." The severity of problems receded thereafter, although accidents still occurred, including a tragic March 1957 incident that claimed the lives of two Silver Bay workers who hurtled "through the guardrails and bounced down the . . . embankment and into the lake." Despite the efforts of the U.S. Coast Guard and several divers, the men's bodies were not recovered; miraculously, a third man survived the accident.[204]

The risks posed by rockslides and the blind corner at Silver Creek Cliff were finally resolved by "mining a tunnel" through 1,344 feet of core rock from 1991 to 1994. Eight years later, the project engineers, Charles Nelson & Associates of Minneapolis, received both an Excellence in Highway Design Award and a Rural Highways Merit Award from the Federal Highway Administration for their tunnel design, which includes a tile-covered interior, continuous lighted message signs, and a weather detection system.[205] The Gitchi-Gami State Trail (GGST), which utilizes the former highway right-of-way, allows bicyclists and hikers to enjoy the views of Lake Superior once experienced by motorists and also passes under a small arch, which replicates the larger structure that formerly spanned the cliff drive highway. Interpretive signs placed at the crest offer information about North Shore highway history.

### Halcyon Harbor Resort (*now* Cliff House Homeowners Association)

Richard Smiley, a Canadian-born engineer and manager of Duluth's U.S. Steel plant, and his wife, Edna, built a summer residence northeast of Silver Creek Cliff during the early 1930s. Lyle Oreck, the president of two major Duluth businesses—the Flame Restaurant and Oreck's Department Store—purchased the property in 1937. Oreck created a compound with five buildings that housed his guests, among them several celebrities, such as author Sinclair Lewis, boxer Joe Louis, and comedian Milton Berle. A succession of owners operated the property as a well-known resort, Halcyon Harbor, following Oreck's sale of the holding during the late 1940s.[206]

Halcyon's well-sited buildings, recalled one frequent visitor in 2016, provided a "simultaneous communal and private" experience in a "lovely enclave." A pair of small, two-story residences were identified as the Lake

**A 1990s brochure for Halcyon Harbor advertised the resort's "spectacular cliffside location where sky, water, and rock meet in an endless variety of change."**

House and Guest House, whereas another dual-level structure formed the Beach House and Studio. The signature building, a two-story structure called the Cliff House, was constructed atop a former wine cellar and linked to an adjacent outdoor fireplace and patio; a balcony that jutted outward from the upper story offered a spectacular prospect of Lake Superior. Four years after its 2004 closing, Halcyon was purchased by new owners, who maintained the Cliff House as their residence and sold the remaining buildings to other buyers. All are members of the Cliff House Homeowners Association and have equal shares in six and a half acres of land and six hundred feet of beachfront designated as the Cliff House Commons. The Cliff House Restaurant, a nearby, well-known diner, was removed prior to construction of the Silver Creek Cliff Tunnel.[207]

### Encampment Forest Association
#### Encampment Gate Roads 1–12

Almost one and a half miles lie between the northeastern end of the tunnel and the first of twelve consecutive "gates" that identify separate entrances to the EFA, one of the North Shore's largest private landholdings. Several entrance gates are linked by an early section of Highway 61 that became a private EFA road following a 1941 realignment. Flowing through the EFA's property, which covers more than two thousand acres, is the Encampment River, its mouth the site of an unrealized 1857 townsite proposal, also bearing the "Encampment" name. During the 1890s, Two Harbors attorney and philanthropist John Olson (whose estate funded the city's Salvation Army building in 1920) saved a significant tract of conifers from the lumberjack's axe when he secured 1,575 acres of land along the river and lake. Following Olson's 1919 death, three Twin Cities men—Thomas Winter, Edwin Hewitt, and Frances Shenehon—sought to acquire the unique holding, which "appealed to their imaginations and whetted their desires." In 1921, they and eighteen other

Twin Citians joined together to form the EFA. Each member contributed a minimum of $1,000 toward the purchase price of $27,500, while a bank loan, paid off in 1929, provided the remaining funds. Their acquisition included the river's rapids, two waterfalls (one forty feet high, the other twenty feet), two miles of Lake Superior shoreline, and a "forest of pine and spruce and cedar, much of it in almost primeval state." Geologist G. M. Schwartz deemed the EFA's white pine resources the primary reserve of these trees along the entire Lake Superior coastline.[208]

Development activities commenced in 1922 when Campman ("Campie") Anderson, the son of local Danish immigrant farmers, began working as the association's "camp man" and "forest foreman." Employed by the EFA for twenty years, Anderson was joined by his wife, Ebba, who served as the "efficient stewardess" at the main lodge. The longest walls of the lodge, constructed of horizontal spruce logs, were fastened together with saddle notches and wooden pins. Used elsewhere throughout the lodge were vertical logs, log siding, and milled lumber that had the appearance of logs. Other building materials were shipped to the site on a boat, the *Dagmar*, then hauled up in a large box attached to a cable pulled by a horse. The lodge, which had separate men's and women's sections connected by a covered porch, became a popular gathering place for EFA members following its May 1923 opening. Some members, around this same time, also began constructing individual cabins of both logs and milled lumber. In 1945, when twenty-five cabins stood on the grounds, the EFA's members could reflect on more than two decades of accomplishment. "The enterprise," wrote the obviously pleased directors, "has been a remarkable success as a cooperative effort." More recently, in 2010, the EFA acquired additional easements on almost one thousand acres of adjacent forested land.[209]

Today, when only 1–2 percent of Minnesota's white pines remain in a "primitive state," Encampment Forest constitutes a major part of the entire reserve. But virtually all of Encampment's pines, for a century, have remained totally inaccessible to the public: only those trees that border the highway may be easily viewed by motorists, who pass through a very small section of the property. Numerous "No Trespassing" signs that stand along more than a mile of both Highway 61 and the

**The Encampment Forest Association's massive acreage is home to several unique structures, including this timber king post bridge, identified by the late historian Denis Gardner as the only example of its type in Minnesota.**

Superior Hiking Trail also remind motorists and trekkers that Encampment is an "elusive, exclusive" place. Indeed, in 2015, when the Walker Art Center identified Encampment Forest as one of one hundred "exemplary places" that represent the best of Minnesota's built environment, the Minneapolis organization also pointed to the EFA's elite origins, isolation, collective ownership, and anonymous membership, all of which still "shroud the place in mystery."[210]

### Lafayette Bluff (*now* Lafayette Bluff Tunnel)
### 200 Feet Northeast of EFA Gate 12

The treacherous storm of 28 November 1905 damaged or forced almost thirty Lake Superior vessels to their watery graves; one gave its name to this landscape feature. On that day, the 5,115-ton steamer *Lafayette*, with the barge *Manila* in tow, stranded and broke up into sections while close to the bluff. The *Manila* remained afloat and was later salvaged, but one *Lafayette* crew member lost his life attempting to reach shore. The section of Lake Superior that borders Lafayette Bluff and nearby Castle Danger remains vulnerable to strong gales and storms, as in October 2018, when a record wind gust of eighty-six miles per hour created a wave that was twenty feet high.[211]

The problems faced by motorists at Lafayette Bluff certainly did not equal those experienced at Silver Creek Cliff. Nevertheless, highway engineers realized, by the 1980s, that significant roadside erosion occurring at the bluff could be resolved only by drilling a "mine tunnel"—a first for Minnesota. The $15 million project, completed in 1991, required the removal of more than two hundred thousand tons of material over a distance of 852 feet. Because of the sharp curve that resulted from the realignment, it was necessary to create an adequate sight distance of sixty-one feet at the entrance; when completed, Lafayette Bluff became one of the nation's widest hard-rock highway tunnels. It also includes walkways, continuous lighting, and a pavement-monitoring system that is crucial when icy road conditions occur.[212]

## Castle Danger

After exiting the tunnel, Highway 61 passes along the gracefully curved Crow Creek Bridge before reaching Castle Danger, featuring one of the North Shore's more captivating place-names. The etymological origins of "Castle Danger" are obscure, but one plausible explanation, among several, is the presence of a nearby reef that proved dangerous to early Lake Superior vessels. Castle Danger's first permanent white pioneers, Norwegians Ole and Lena Wick, arrived on a Duluth steamboat in 1893. They were joined by other settlers, most of them Norwegians who engaged in commercial fishing and part-time farming for several decades. A few cabins, built by Emil and Inga Edisen to house highway workers in the Castle Danger area during the early 1920s, were accommodating tourists by 1923–24; their business, Camper's Home Lodge, is considered the North Shore's first cabin resort. Not all Castle Danger residents were sanguine about the arrival of motorists, however. "With the influx of tourists into the country," wrote one local woman in 1931, "the time is approaching when outsiders will purchase the most desirable locations along the shore and settlers will be confronted with 'No Trespassing' signs all about." Nevertheless, the built environment of Castle Danger remained relatively intact until the 1990s, when several structures were moved into, out of, and within the settlement because of highway realignment and construction projects. Another major change occurred in 1998, when a large destination resort, Grand Superior Lodge, replaced Camper's Home.[213]

### Castle Danger Schoolhouse (*now* Our Savior's Lutheran Church of Castle Danger)
### 2176 Highway 61

This 1916 building, now a Lutheran church, originally was a schoolhouse situated one and a half miles northeast of Castle Danger. The school closed during the mid-1920s, but the building was transported close to the current location in 1931, where it would be used by the Castle Danger Farmers Club. The clubhouse, predicted local resident Agnes Stone, will "preserve for all time, a part of this community for themselves and their children." Although agriculture always was a marginal economic activity on the North Shore, several Castle Danger citizens were actively engaged in part-time farming during the 1930s and 1940s. State and federal agronomists, in 1931, even experimented with the propagation of a new variety of potato plant on the farm owned by Ole Wick, who was known as Castle

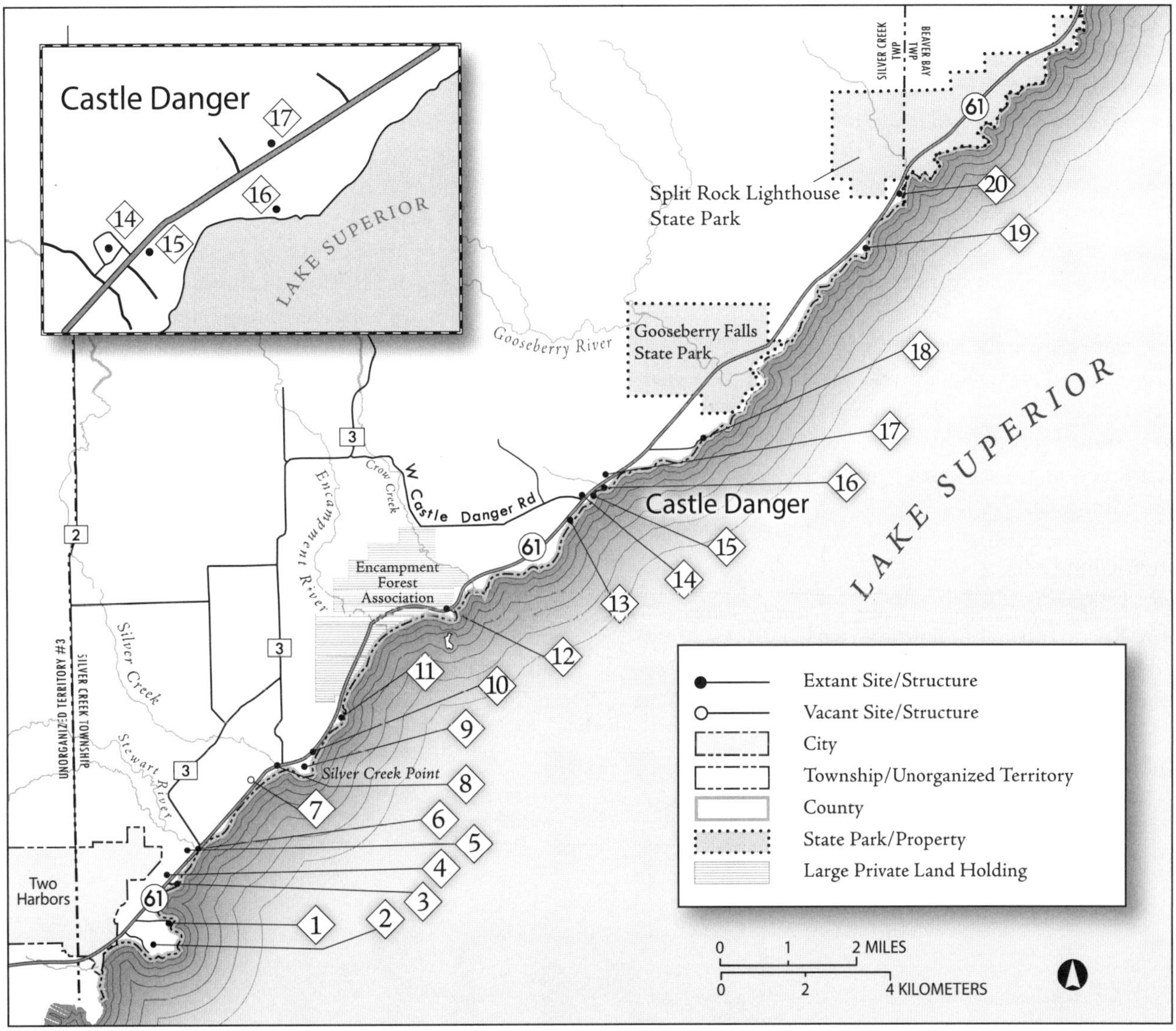


1. Superior Shores Resort & Conference Center
2. Burlington Bay Lakehomes
3. Flood Bay State Wayside
4. Flood Bay Motel
5. Betty's Pies
6. Stewart River Bridge and Kelsey Beach
7. Silver Creek Gifts and Gallery
8. Silver Creek Bridge
9. Silver Creek Resort*
10. Silver Creek Cliff Tunnel
11. Halcyon Harbor Resort*
12. Lafayette Bluff Tunnel
13. Our Savior's Lutheran Church of Castle Danger
14. Rustic Inn Café
15. Gooseberry Park Cottages and Motel
16. Grand Superior Lodge
17. Northwoods Pioneer Gallery and Gifts
18. Castle Haven Cabins
19. Iona's Beach Scientific and Natural Area
20. Split Rock Cabins

*Now a private homeowners association

Danger's most successful farmer. While the scientists hypothesized that "cool breezes blowing from Lake Superior over this jutting point [might] provide just the degree of moisture and temperature required by the potato plant for making seed," the experiments ended sometime after 1936.[214]

In 1950, Castle Danger's Lutheran congregation acquired and moved the clubhouse somewhat closer to the highway and transformed the building into their church. Simple Gothic arches were added to the windows during the late 1990s and early 2000s, and a large stained glass window was installed in the sanctuary. For several years, the congregation maintained a long-standing Norwegian tradition—serving fishcake dinners—which attracted people from a large surrounding area.[215]

### Rustic Inn Café
2773 Highway 61

The Rustic Inn Café comprises two historic buildings and a 1996 structure that connects them. The oldest unit originally served as the dining room for Inga and Emil Edisen's Camper's Home Lodge, situated about one-third of a mile to the northeast. When Beth and Jim Sullivan purchased the building in 1986, they named their acquisition the Rustic Inn Café. This action was followed, in 1988, by their purchase of a cabin—the former naturalist's residence at Gooseberry Falls State Park—which they moved to the property and converted into a gift shop. A 1995 realignment and upgrading of Highway 61, however, forced the Sullivans to move both the dining room and the gift shop to the present Rustic Inn site. The buildings were then linked together with a historically appropriate structure, designed by Blesener Dahlberg Architects of Duluth. That newer structure now serves as the café's entrance, waiting area, and second dining room.[216]

The Rustic Inn Café remains a popular North Shore dining destination, wrote one food critic, because "the core of its business is based on great, locally sourced food, and pies." Or, as a local aphorism proclaims, "come for the pie, and stay for the dinner."[217] Adding to the dining room's ambiance are its century-old vertical cedar log walls and birch floors.

**The Rustic Inn Café is composed of three structures. At the left is the original Camper's Home Lodge, built during the 1920s and moved to its current site in 1995; it now serves as the kitchen and dining room. At the far right, currently a gift store, is the former Gooseberry Falls State Park naturalist's residence, dating to the 1930s. Connecting the two units is a 1996 structure that serves as the café's entrance, waiting area, and ancillary dining room.**

### Gooseberry Park Cottages and Motel
2778 Highway 61

On the southern side of Highway 61 and the Rustic Inn are Gooseberry Park Cottages and Motel, built during the 1930s. Operated by the Rustic Inn's Beth and Jim Sullivan from 1991 to 1998, the property was purchased, in 2014, by former St. Paulites Kirsten Mohr and Ted Vanderbeek. "It was pretty run down," remarked Mohr when describing the condition of the six cabins and five-unit motel at the time of their purchase, "and we wanted to bring this 'Mom and Pop' resort back to life, as they are becoming fewer and fewer along the Shore." Sold again in 2021, Gooseberry's three original cabins remain its most popular units.[218]

### Camper's Home (*now* Grand Superior Lodge)
2826 Highway 61

In 1903, Emil Edisen, accompanied by his wife and three young children, emigrated from Norway to Duluth, where he found work in a lumberyard. After Edisen's wife and one daughter died in 1907, he and the two surviving children, along with a sister and her husband, sailed to the Split Rock River. The families engaged in commercial fishing and subsistence farming but moved to Castle Danger after a 1908 forest fire destroyed their Split Rock holding. Edisen married Inga Roen, a Norwegian immigrant widow with two children, in 1918—four years before the couple began renting cabins to highway construction workers. Once the highway opened, their cabin enclave, identified as Camper's Home, quickly attracted tourists. Although some of Edisen's neighbors called him "crazy" for borrowing money to expand the business, he later joked that "it wasn't long before they were trying to catch up with me."[219]

As the first cabin resort on the North Shore, Camper's Home eventually had as many as twenty-four

**Two of the Edisens' new, "elegantly furnished" cabins, which had prominent fireplace chimneys, opened at Camper's Home during the late 1920s. Available for three dollars per day, or fifteen dollars per week, each cabin had three rooms and beds and could house as many as six people. Photograph by Harold Youngren, 1929.**

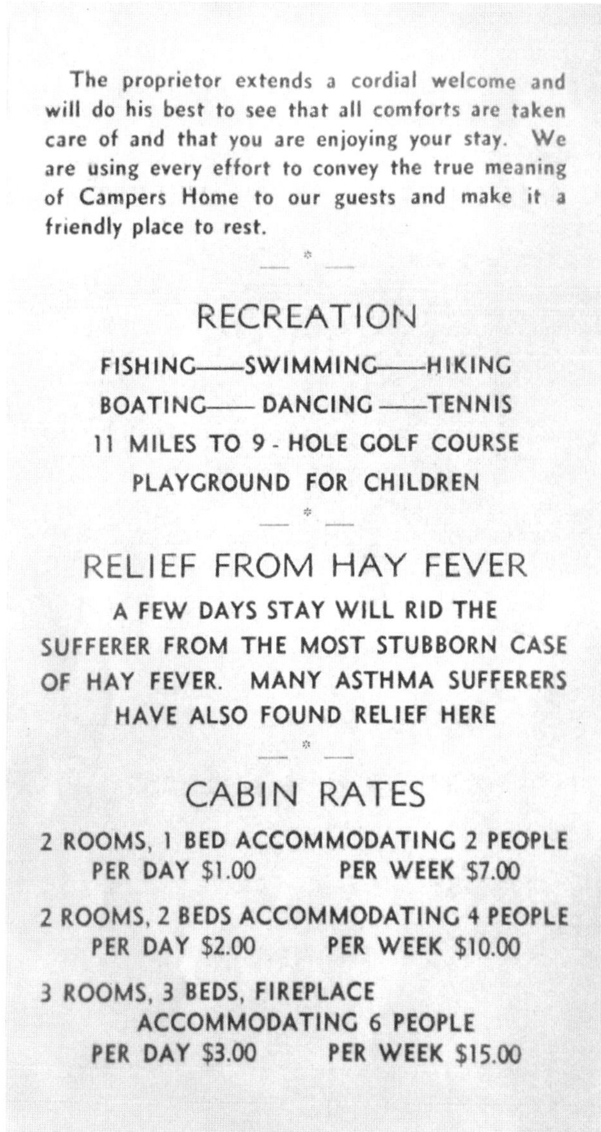


**A 1930s advertisement for Camper's Home described its attractions, cabin prices, and the Two Harbors golf course. Courtesy of Scott Roen.**

units, some built of horizontal or vertical logs, others of frame and board. About one-half were organized in a single row along the shoreline—one of the clearest examples of a linear cabin layout on the entire North Shore. Advertised as "an ideal place for hay fever sufferers," the cabins included electric lights and spring water. A few "modern" cabins, equipped with indoor showers by the late 1920s, were described as "elegantly furnished." Rental rates for the three classes of cabins during the 1930s ranged from one to three dollars per day and from seven to fifteen dollars per week.[220]

Following the 1963 death of Emil Edisen at age eighty-eight, and that of his eighty-nine-year-old widow two years later, the resort was purchased and operated by other owners. When Chicagoans Julia and Marty Byrnes bought the business in 1983, they renamed their acquisition the Star Harbor Resort. The Byrneses removed the oldest cabins, including one 15′ x 26′ unit that was donated to the MHS in St. Paul and placed in storage. The couple ran Star Harbor with a few original cabins and six new units and also gave consideration to the construction of a large lodge. In 1998, however, the Byrneses sold their holding to Odyssey Resorts, which erected a new complex—Grand Superior Lodge—on the property. Termed a "grand, authentic log resort"—equipped with a pool, hot tub, sauna, and workout room—the lodge rooms, cabins, and lakeside homes are available either for purchase or rent. Still standing at the far northeastern end of Grand Superior is the only remaining building dating to the Camper's Home era: Emil Edisen's original combination fish house and boathouse. Now called the Beach House, the structure retains its original footprint but has been completely modernized and may be rented for several hundred dollars per night.[221]

**Inga and Emil Edisen's son Palmer stands in the doorway of the family's store. Photograph by Harold Youngren, 1930.**

**One of the log structures at Grand Superior Lodge, which opened in 1998.**

### Edisen's Store and Tavern (*moved, now* Northwoods Pioneer Gallery and Gifts)
2821 Highway 61

Soon after building their Camper's Home complex, Emil and Inga Edisen expanded the business by adding a lodge and store on the highway's upper side. The lodge, described as Castle Danger's primary dining establishment and social center for many years, offered a menu that featured basic ingredients—primarily fresh milk, cream, butter, eggs, and meat—supplied by the Edisen's small farm. The modest prices charged for Inga Edisen's home cooking were quite typical of North Shore diners and restaurants throughout the 1930s: breakfasts, fifteen to forty cents; sandwiches, ten to twenty cents; and a complete lake trout or steak dinner, one dollar. Edisen sold groceries, confectionaries, fish, El Producto cigars, tobacco, oil, and gasoline from his store and added a tavern when Prohibition ended in 1933. Renamed the Rustic Inn following Beth and Jim Sullivan's 1986 purchase of the business, the building was moved to its current location in 1995. The struc-

**The businesses established by Emil and Inga Edisen, shown here during the late 1930s or early 1940s, served as the center of Castle Danger for several decades. At the left is the Camper's Home Lodge, later moved to its current Rustic Inn site; Edisen's store and an adjoining tavern are at the right. Attached to the rear of the store and tavern were living quarters. Northwoods Pioneer Gallery and Gifts currently stands on part of the site. Photograph courtesy of Scott Roen.**

ture that once housed Emil Edisen's store was relocated sixteen miles north of Two Harbors, where it exists in extremely poor condition.[222]

Now situated close to the site of Edisen's former properties is Northwoods Pioneer Gallery and Gifts. Organized in 1971 as the Pioneer Crafts Co-op, the association engaged in educational activities that highlighted the arts and crafts heritage of northeastern Minnesota's older residents. In May 1972, the cooperative opened a store at Silver Creek Point (seven miles to the southwest) that served as a sales outlet for items produced by the region's elderly and low-income residents. The store was moved to its current location in 1992, shortly before construction work began on the Silver Creek Cliff Tunnel. Because membership in the cooperative is no longer restricted by age or income, any area resident who produces "quality art and craft products" may participate. Because of its cooperative status, all members are required to share in some aspect of the store's operations, primarily as salesclerks, but also by offering painting, jewelry-making, beading, woodworking, and other craft demonstrations.[223]

### Castle Haven Cabins
### 3067 East Castle Danger Road

Highway 61 intersects with East Castle Danger Road, which also serves as the entrance to Castle Haven Cabins. The resort's origins are linked to Daniel and Ellen Carlson Lind (Lindjert), Norwegian immigrants who resided in Duluth and at an Isle Royale summer fishing camp following their 1893 marriage. In 1896, the family, along with Lind's brother Tom, moved to Castle Danger, where Ole and Lena Wick had settled three years earlier. Both brothers pursued commercial fishing and established small farms. In 1906, they launched Lind Brothers Fishing, one of the North

Shore's first mail-order frozen fish businesses, which later became a second-generation enterprise when two of Daniel and Ellen Lind's eleven children, Marcus and Edgar, assumed ownership.[224]

The two families also established separate cabin businesses in what they termed the center of the North Shore's "hay fever haven." Tom's Cabins closed many years ago, but Marcus and Edgar Lind's secluded shoreline resort, named Castle Haven Cabins by 1933, continues to the present. Ownership transferred, in 1975, to the succeeding generation, Dwight and Debbie Lind, who now assist their daughter and current manager Jamie Lind MacFarlane; her husband, Clint MacFarlane, and the couple's two sons also provide support.[225]

**Gambrel-roofed dairy barns were commonplace throughout the Midwest during the early twentieth century but seldom appeared along the North Shore. The barn on Tom Lind's farmstead, however, included a gambrel roof, as did one built nearby by his brother Daniel. Photograph by Harold Youngren, 1930.**

**The historic fish house at Castle Haven Cabins anchors a row of cabins that replaced seven older units between 1995 and 2000.**

Seven of Castle Haven's original seasonal cabins were moved and replaced by new, year-round units between 1995 and 2000. They are aligned in a tight row that extends toward the southwest from a centrally located fish house. Five older cabins, arranged in a more open pattern that spreads to the northeast, are limited to seasonal use. Clint MacFarlane also used the resort property, from 2011 to 2014, to establish the groundwork for what is now the Castle Danger Brewery in Two Harbors.[226]

### Nestor Logging Company and Gooseberry Falls Resort/CCC Company Camps 1720 and 2710 (*now* Gooseberry Falls State Park)
3206 Highway 61 East

In 2022, Gooseberry Falls State Park attracted 782,000 visitors—the highest number in Minnesota's state park system.[227] The seventeen-hundred-acre facility offers numerous opportunities for visitors who come to experience many of the North Shore's outstanding natural and cultural attributes at a single location. Lake Superior, five scenic waterfalls, and a river gorge are observable from different vantage points; numerous paths and trails provide opportunities for both leisurely and rigorous hiking; eighty stone and wooden structures, many built by CCC crews, are located throughout the park; and a full array of tourist-related information and items may be found in an award-winning visitors' center.

The Gooseberry River, much earlier, served as an Anishinaabe fishing site and subsequently attracted European explorers, among them Médard Chouart, Sieur des Groseilliers, of France, who traveled through the area in 1660. A French map of 1670 that marked the Riviere des Groseilliers was later called the Gooseberry River by American explorers, although it may have been from the translation of an even earlier Anishinaabe term. The efforts of nineteenth-century mineral prospectors and townsite promoters proved unfruitful, but wealthy sport fishermen who were attracted to the "almost untouched stream" experienced

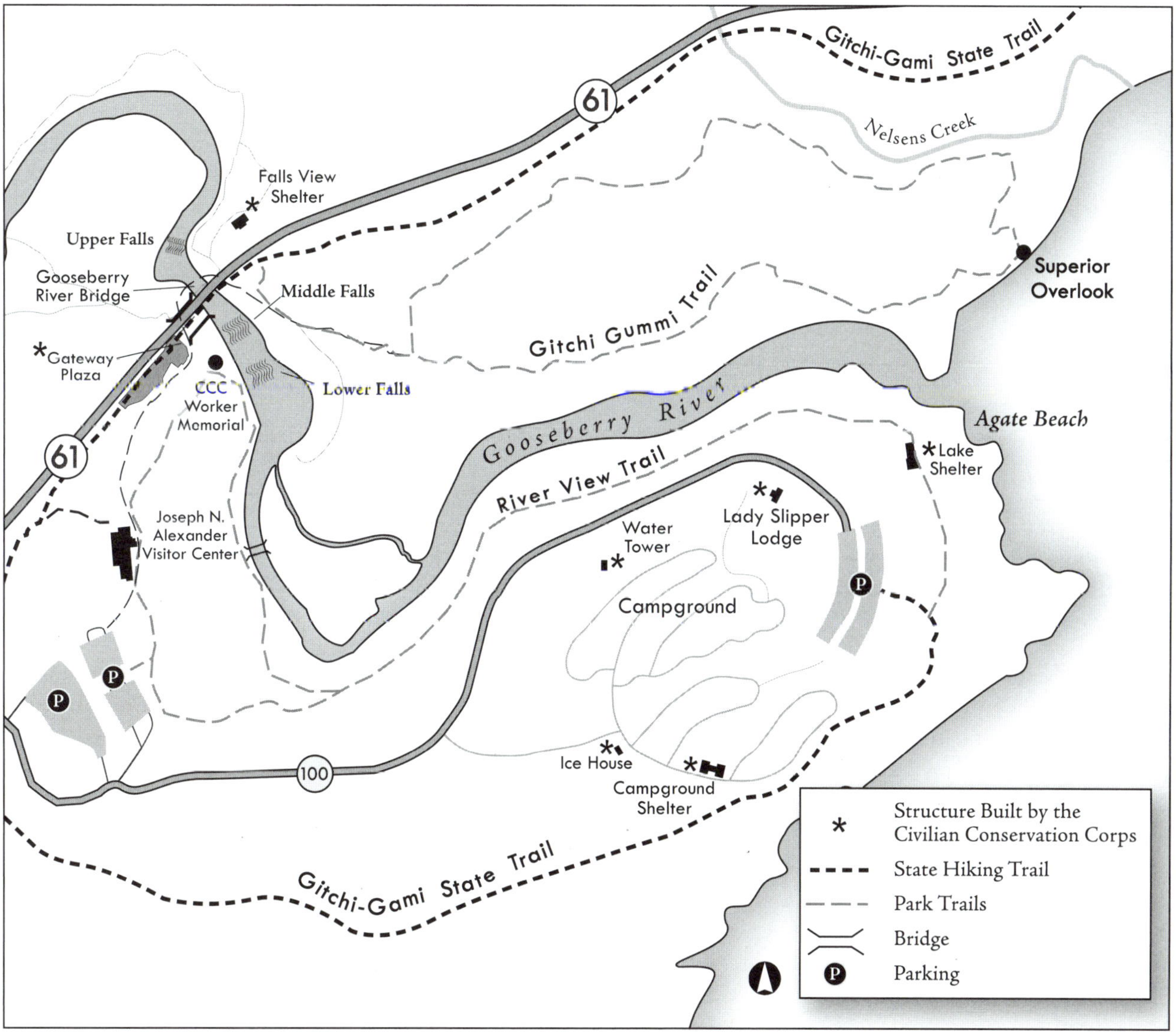

Gitchi-Gami State Trail
61
Nelsens Creek
Falls View Shelter
Upper Falls
Gooseberry River Bridge
Middle Falls
Superior Overlook
Gitchi Gummi Trail
Gateway Plaza
CCC Worker Memorial
Lower Falls
Gooseberry River
Agate Beach
61
River View Trail
Lake Shelter
Lady Slipper Lodge
Joseph N. Alexander Visitor Center
Water Tower
Campground
P
P
P
Ice House
100
Campground Shelter
Gitchi-Gami State Trail
Structure Built by the Civilian Conservation Corps
State Hiking Trail
Park Trails
Bridge
Parking

**These tents, during the May to September 1932 interim, were occupied by CCC enrollees affiliated with Gooseberry Falls Camp 1720. The much-expanded site, from 1934 to 1941, would accommodate the members of Camp 2710, one of Minnesota's largest and best-equipped CCC enclaves.**

considerable success. The Superior Lumber Company, formed in 1899 by Wisconsin's U.S. senator William Vilas and other investors, purchased several hundred acres of land along the river. One year later, the Nestor Logging Company acquired Superior Lumber's landholdings and purchased a sawmill in Ashland, Wisconsin. The company also constructed two rail lines that, from 1900 to 1909, transported logs from inland sites to the Gooseberry estuary. From there the logs were formed into rafts and hauled by tugboats to Ashland.[228]

The completion of a steel truss bridge over the Gooseberry River enabled tourists to access the site by 1925. A few years later, Duluthians Roy B. and Alice Lewis opened their Gooseberry Falls Resort (also called Gooseberry Bush), which had a few vertical log cabins, a store, gas pumps, and two Duluth streetcars, all situated on the eastern side of the river's mouth. In 1933, following approval by the Minnesota Legislature, the Lewis holding was included as part of a 640-acre property (most held by the Vilas Trust) that would form the nucleus for Gooseberry Falls State Park. After selling their property, the couple, around 1937, established the Roy B. Lewis Tourist Village in the Palmers area of Duluth Township, which closed sometime before the proprietor's 1945 death.[229]

One part of the state's Gooseberry land acquisition was classified as a scenic game preserve and public hunting ground by the MDC, but NPS officials, in 1934, recognized that its intrinsic qualities were suitable for state park designation. Work on the envisioned park was initiated in May 1934, when 240 young men enrolled in CCC Company 1720 (one of Minnesota's earliest) established a "tent camp" just west of the upper falls. They would transfer to southeastern Minnesota in October, when members of Company 2710, who also had been billeted in tents since July, moved into one of Minnesota's most fully equipped CCC camps. Its twenty-seven structures included ten barracks; administrative buildings; officer's quarters; and a mess hall, infirmary, and latrine. When the company's enrollees departed the site in 1941, they could claim the longest tenure of any Minnesota state park CCC camp.[230]

Gooseberry Falls became a highly popular destination for motorists, even as CCC enrollees were still transforming the former "wild area into [a] haven for visitors." Surveys between May and July 1937 revealed that Gooseberry's visitors came from all but three of Minnesota's eighty-seven counties and from thirty-five states. Today, the ensemble of more than eighty CCC structures and objects found within Gooseberry Falls State Park represents an uncommonly fine collection of 1930s rustic style design. The project work was overseen by architect Edward W. Barber, who collaborated with consulting landscape architect Arthur Nichols and other professionals employed in the St. Paul office of the NPS. Three local experienced men served as project stonemasons—John Berini and Joe Cattaneo, both Italians, and Axel Anderson, a Swede. The black-colored stone, identified as an "unusually iron-rich gabbro," along with significant quantities of blue granite, were secured close to Beaver Bay. The red granite came from a Duluth quarry, the logs from the Cascade River area.[231]

One of the most striking Gooseberry Falls State Park structures is the concourse, a "Castle in the Park," built from 1935 to 1940. Among its notable features is the retaining wall, three hundred feet long, which has a south-facing overlook bay that provides views of the river's lower waterfall. The concourse also serves as a barrier to the soil erosion that otherwise would be caused by the Gooseberry River when it passes underneath the Highway 61 bridge. When the span was widened from nineteen to thirty feet in 1935, the concourse provided parking areas along both sides of the highway. The concourse wall, which extends below grade to solid rock, is twelve feet wide at the base and twenty to twenty-five feet high; some rocks that weigh more than seven tons are the size of an automobile. Extending from the overlook to the bottom of the concourse is a large stairway, constructed of stone and poured concrete; "modern toilets" (closed long ago) were situated within the base. The overall design proved successful, wrote historic preservation consultant Rolf Anderson in 1994, because it separated "travelers who simply wanted to admire the falls from those intending to enter the park proper."[232]

A new bridge, which opened in 1998, employed steel arches similar in appearance to the original span. Several changes were also made to the concourse at this time, most noticeably the addition of stone planters and some "inappropriate vegetation" that had been introduced into an area that never had many plants and served as a parking area and highway pull-off. In 2019–20, some twenty years after the

**The steel truss bridge built across the Gooseberry River in 1924 was widened from nineteen to thirty feet in 1935. At the far left is the concourse, completed in 1940.**

**An architect's drawing of the concourse at Gooseberry Falls State Park, sometimes called the "Castle in the Park." Courtesy of the State of Minnesota, Department of Highways, "Stairway and Approach on Concourse at Gooseberry River," 1937.**

**Wood and stone are employed extensively as building materials throughout the Joseph N. Alexander Visitor Center, designed by architect David Salmela. Photograph by Peter Bastianelli-Kerze. Courtesy of David Salmela.**

changes had been introduced, an MnDOT-sponsored rehabilitation project eliminated the stone planters and vegetation, graded the site to its original level, and restored the stone walls.[233]

Another major structure, among the largest in Minnesota's state park system, is the former Combination Building, an H-shaped, forty-eight-by-eighty-four-foot edifice with a huge granite fireplace. Originally providing restrooms, showers, a laundry, a utility room, a kitchen, and picnic space, it now serves as a shelter for the park's seventy-two-unit campground. Elsewhere is the Refectory, a T-shaped building, constructed in 1934–36, which overlooks the Gooseberry estuary. One axis, constructed of stone and logs with saddle notch corners, originally had a heavily used concession area where visitors purchased refreshments. The other axis, built entirely of blue and black basalt and red rhyolite, includes a huge stone fireplace and a partially enclosed shelter. The Refectory was also used as an information center until the 1990s but is now vacant and shrouded by trees and vegetation. Proposals have been made to restore the structure and use it for displays of Gooseberry Fall's CCC legacy. Close to the former picnic grounds is one of the park's elegantly crafted jewels, a small, 1935 water tower encased in blue and red granite.[234]

The park's newest building is the Joseph N. Alexander Visitor Center, designed by Duluth architect David Salmela and completed in 1995. Design critic Thomas Fischer has observed that the building serves as a reminder of how architecture can "protect us from or link us to the four basic elements that have defined nature and reality since ancient times"—earth, air, fire, and water. The building's use of stone, wood, and post and beam construction also pays homage to Gooseberry Fall's CCC legacy. Recycled materials are apparent throughout the structure, including fir timbers from a San Francisco warehouse, built between 1895 and 1906, and redwood derived from Paul Masson wine vats, dating to the 1930s. The fireplace rocks were secured from the tunnel excavation at nearby Silver Creek Cliff, whereas the use of native vegetation throughout the site links the building to its greater landscape. The jury that gave the building a 1997 AIA Minnesota Honor Award identified it as "an architecture of great resorts and lasting design distinguished by texture, scale, and play of materials."[235]

### *Madonna of the Ice*

On 11 February 1939, following a severe northeastern Minnesota blizzard with winds clocked at seventy-two miles per hour, local tavern owner Roy E. Evans began taking photographs in the vicinity of Gooseberry Falls. Among the images was an ice formation, perhaps four feet high and resembling a standing Madonna, which the unabashed Evans termed a "miracle photograph" and the "greatest picture of all time." The feet of the robed figure were located just above the icy surface of Lake Superior, while the Madonna's head was tilted slightly downward and to the side, as if she were looking at a child held in her arms. Postcards and framed copies displaying *Madonna of the Ice* were published and distributed nationwide for several years thereafter by Evans's Split Rock Enterprises, which operated out of a small building situated along Highway 61.[236]

**Although *Madonna of the Ice* obviously was a very short-lived North Shore phenomenon, images of the February 1939 formation circulated widely for many years thereafter.**

### Twin Points Resort (*now* Iona's Beach Scientific and Natural Area)
#### 3548 Highway 61

In 1934, John and Iona Vähämäki Lind, Finnish immigrants who had met and recently married in Port Arthur, Ontario, moved to Duluth; once there, Lind would become the editor of *Industrialisti* (Industrialist), a Finnish-language newspaper affiliated with the IWW. Because of concerns over Lind's health, the couple, in 1938, moved to fifteen acres of recently purchased shoreline land located three and a half miles northeast of Gooseberry Falls. The Linds' acquisition included six cabins, but it was the "beautiful contrastive beach," comprising flattened, salmon-colored rhyolite pebbles, all chiseled out of Lake Superior's nearby cliffs, that especially attracted them. Under certain conditions, the deposited pebbles also make "a tinkling sound unique to this beach." Over the next year, the couple cleared brush, planted trees, and improved the cabins on their property, which they named Twin Points Resort. The arrival of power supplied by the Rural Electrical Administration (REA) during the 1940s, coupled with "Iona's extraordinary managerial and interpersonal skills," allowed the resort to flourish and expand. Eventually, Twin Points would have fourteen housekeeping cabins with knotty pine interiors and indoor water, a café and general store, two Standard Oil gasoline pumps, and a motel with "king-sized beds for tall guests." In 1950, *Minneapolis Tribune* columnist George Grim observed that the Linds "were absorbed in all things, Finnish," especially their sauna, which the newsman described as a "vapor bath" located in a small wooden building. Twin Points was also popular among the Linds' Finnish Canadian guests, who often termed the resort "Finlandia."[237]

Both Linds helped to organize the NSROA in 1940. Soon after retiring from the Finnish-language newspaper, Lind served as an early NSROA president and also employed his printing skills and publishing connections to print and distribute the association's brochures and advertising materials. But because Lind was a strong supporter of the Finnish American IWW movement, some neighbors erroneously identified him as a Communist during the 1950s Red Scare. Despite the animosities that arose from these allegations, the Linds attracted a steady stream of repeat guests to their resort, among them Judge C. R. Magney, the legendary proponent and benefactor of several North Shore state parks.[238]

**The Twin Points Resort restaurant operated by Iona Lind was known for its excellent food, high-quality service, and Finnish décor.**

In early 1969, Iona Lind and her two children, Alden and Arlene, joined with twenty other North Shore residents to form the Save Lake Superior Association (SLSA), an organization that grew out of their concern and outrage over the discharge of tailings into the lake by the nearby taconite plant at Silver Bay. The two siblings were later involved in several other progressive political and environmental causes in Minnesota and elsewhere. Arlene Lind Lehto, whose varied career included stints as a teacher, hairdresser, newspaper correspondent, and model, also served as the first president and executive director of the SLSA and organized three chapters in northern Wisconsin and Michigan. Duluth-area voters elected her to three terms in Minnesota's House of Representatives (1977–83), where she was the primary author of the state's acid rain law. Her brother Alden, who once said that it was his "responsibility . . . to stand on a soapbox and holler" about environmental issues, served as a political science professor at the University of North Carolina before returning to northeastern Minnesota in 1974. Lind was honored in 2001 by the Parks and Trails Council of Minnesota, which gave him its highest award in recognition of a lifetime of work as a persistent proponent of environmental protection.[239]

John Lind died in 1976, but his widow continued operating Twin Points until reaching the age of eighty-five in 1993. Her wish to convert Twin Points into a public site, an idea strongly supported by the matriarch's children and UMD geologist John Green, occurred within a year, when the property was sold to the Sugarloaf Interpretive Center Association (SICA). Following this action, SICA's director, former Minnesota governor Elmer L. Andersen, oversaw a complicated 1997 land transfer that led to the acquisition of the property by the MDNR, which then dedicated ten acres of land and shoreline as Iona's Beach Scientific and Natural Area. The MDNR also converted a section of shoreline where the cabins formerly stood into the Twin Points Protected Access; the facility opened with a small harbor and boat-launching site in 2002. The primary attraction, nonetheless, was and is Iona's namesake beach, the same "beautiful contrastive" shoreline that appealed to the Linds in 1938 and which now offers access to one of the North Shore's longest stretches (thirty-three hundred feet) of public lakefront. Iona Lind may have been only an ordinary citizen, noted a local reporter in 2022, but because of her great concern for "the lake and its stunning shoreline," she had "the power to save one of its most interesting beaches."[240]

### Split Rock Cabins
3668 Highway 61

One of Silver Creek Township's long-standing resorts is Split Rock Cabins, established by Ragnvald and Ragnhild Sve in 1932. The twenty-year-old Sve departed Norway, in 1922, for Edmonton, Alberta, where he worked on an uncle's farm. Two years later, after joining another uncle who resided in Lake County, Sve found employment as a dynamite blaster at Silver Creek Cliff but soon acquired a fifty-four-acre lakeshore holding following his 1926 marriage to Ragnhild Jacobsen. While working with his Norwegian father-in-law, Sve became an accomplished commercial fisherman.[241]

In 1932, when the couple opened two vertical log units at Split Rock Cabins, they and their four children would be confined to a combination home and office located on the second floor of a fourteen-by-eighteen-foot fish house. (The family moved into a more spacious residence in 1936, and a new fish house replaced the original structure in 1959.) As the tourist business expanded over subsequent decades, eight larger cabins were added to the resort. Sve's land provided pasture and hay for the one or two cows that produced milk for their children and also allowed the family to maintain a large garden.[242]

Walter, the oldest son, quit school in 1944 at age sixteen to join his father in the family's commercial fishing enterprise. By mid-century, they were among the first fishermen to express concern over the potentially negative impacts that a taconite processing plant—then under construction thirteen miles to the northeast—would have on the lake's water quality. Ragnar, Walter, and Carol Sve joined with their neighbors in 1969 to form the SLSA. Walter, in 2019, could still clearly recall the contentious sequence of events that had occurred almost seven decades earlier:

> During the early 1950s Reserve Mining and the State of Minnesota organized a meeting about the discharge of taconite tailings into Lake Superior. Although the meeting was not advertised in the news, the United Sportsmen's Club of Duluth heard about it. Since my dad, Ragnvald, belonged to the club, he was asked to call all of the fishermen he could, and ask them to attend the meeting. Only four went with him.
>
> At the meeting Reserve claimed that the tailings, some as fine as face powder, would be pulled to the bottom by a density current formed from the discharge of larger particles, and that all of the tailings would remain by Silver Bay at the bottom of the lake. But the fishermen stated that the wave action and lake current would keep the fine tailings suspended and carry them toward Two Harbors and Duluth and affect their drinking water. The warning was ignored, and Reserve received its permit.
>
> Minnesota's Department of Conservation organized two pollution meetings per year until the mid-1970s. My dad and I attended all of them and told what was happening to the clarity of the lake. By this time conditions had gotten so bad that a person could only see one foot down into the water. (Formerly the lake was clear to a depth of twenty-five feet.) Since the herrings' gills do not tolerate dirty water, the commercial fishermen were forced farther out onto the lake to find clear water, although several quit fishing and began working at other jobs.[243]

When engaged in fishing, Walter Sve tended three nets, each about five hundred feet long and weighted down by three hundred to four hundred pounds of concrete blocks. During the early-morning hours, from spring to late fall, the veteran fisherman departed his dock in a wooden skiff, which was eighteen feet long and powered by an outboard motor. After reaching the buoy that marked the location of a net, Sve engaged in a process that has not changed for ages:

Walter Sve removes a herring from one of his nets in 2014.

Steve, *left*, and Eric Sve, with their father, Walter, gutting and filleting herring.

while standing in his boat, he lifted one section of the net into the vessel, removed any herring caught in the mesh, dropped the fish into a container (plastic bins replaced wooden boxes years ago), and systematically inspected the entire net for holes or tears. The empty net then fell back into the water on the opposite side of the boat. Prior to the 1950s, a single fisherman could net several hundred pounds of herring per day; Sve's daily catch, in 2017, seldom exceeded one hundred pounds. Once his boat returned to the dock, the bins were loaded into a two-wheeled cart and pushed into the fish house. There he cleaned the herring with lightning speed, a reflection of long experience and skill in wielding his well-honed knife. Local residents, tourists, and operators of restaurants and smoked fish outlets eagerly purchased the boneless fillets.[244]

The North Shore denizen retired from commercial fishing in 2017 at the age of eighty-nine; Sve passed away five years later, but both of his sons have earned their licenses and are qualified to maintain the family tradition. When asked how he withstood the rigors of Lake Superior for seventy-five years, the veteran fisherman offered a simple but straightforward answer: "hard work, lots of fresh air, and a steady diet of fish."[245]

Walter and Carol Sve assumed ownership of Split Rock Cabins in 1974 and jointly operated the resort until her passing in 2000. Since then, Eric has served as manager. Gretchen Heath, who has stayed at numerous North Shore resorts for seven decades, observes that the Sves' cabins have changed very little through time: they are "true housekeeping cabins in the old sense," she notes. The "modest and traditional" furnishings include "well kept-up furniture," even though much of it dates to the 1940s, 1950s, and 1960s; "incredibly well-stocked kitchens—many dishes, pots, pans, and utensils"; and "very good beds," something that "is always important in cabin life now." There is "no television, of course, and cell service is almost never."[246] Split Rock Cabins is also one of only a few North Shore businesses that has not yet succumbed to the internet. But because of its long-standing reputation, Split Rock Cabins' entry signs almost always display a simple message: "No Vacancy."

## Beaver Bay Township

The boundary that separates the townships of Silver Creek and Beaver Bay occurs a short distance northeast of Split Rock Cabins. Beaver Bay Township, organized in 1885, is named for the townsite that was platted and settled at the mouth of the Beaver River in 1856. The number of permanent residents never exceeded four hundred until the 1950s, when major construction activities began at the nearby Silver Bay taconite beneficiation plant. Between 1960 and 2020, however, the township's population fell from 940 to 515 residents.[247] The twenty-one miles of Highway 61 located within Beaver Bay Township pass through the small cities of Beaver Bay and Silver Bay; two unincorporated settlements, Illgen City and East Beaver Bay; and two state parks, Split Rock Lighthouse and Tettegouche.

### Split Rock Lighthouse State Park
3713 Split Rock Lighthouse Road

The entrances to a pair of Minnesota's most outstanding and popular state parks—Gooseberry Falls and Split Rock Lighthouse—are separated by a distance of seven miles. The southwestern boundary for Split Rock Lighthouse State Park, a 2,075-acre holding, occurs just before Highway 61 crosses the Split Rock River. Three major sites are located between the river crossing and the Split Rock Lighthouse entrance: Split Rock Trail Head Wayside Park, Ellingsen Island, and the Split Rock Lighthouse Overlook. Overall, 544,500 people visited Split Rock in 2021—the fifth highest figure for a Minnesota state park.[248]

### Split Rock Trail Head Wayside Park
3978 Highway 61

The Split Rock River was called Gininwabiko-zibi (War Eagle Iron River) by the Anishinaabe. The current name very likely describes the river, which, when viewed from the lake, looks as if it splits a high rock formation. An 1850s proposal for the townsite of Waterville proved unsuccessful, but from 1899 to 1906, the Split Rock Lumber Company maintained a large log-rafting operation at the river's mouth. Three locomotives pulled railcars filled with logs along a ten-mile-long line to an estuary pond formed by a substantial dam constructed of log pilings and timbers; from there, a tugboat, the *Gladiator*, towed the log rafts to a West Duluth sawmill. A trestle and wharf—16 feet wide, 184 feet long—built atop rock-filled cribs, assisted in the log-rafting operations. The structure was also used by steamers that brought supplies to the long-vanished settlement of Splitrock, where a post office, a store, a warehouse, an icehouse, a dining room, two barracks, and seven dwellings existed for a few years. Some remnants of the dam and pilings are still evident in the estuary.[249]

Located on the highway's upper side is Split Rock Trail Head Wayside Park. In 2011, the new wayside was dedicated to the late Larry Moon, the first chair of the North Shore Scenic Drive Council upon its formation in 2000; Moon also played a key role in having Scenic Drive designated as an All-American Road. The wayside, which serves as a trailhead for the Split Rock River loop of the Superior Hiking Trail, includes a pedestrian tunnel that passes underneath Highway 61 and offers safe access to the river's mouth. From there hikers may proceed along the Gitchi-Gami Trail to Split Rock Lighthouse.[250]

### Ellingsen Island and Little Two Harbors
Between the Split Rock River Outlet and Split Rock Lighthouse Overlook

Located southeast of the Split Rock River mouth is Ellingsen Island—a small Lake Superior landform that includes a diminutive cove named Little Two Harbors. Also part of the cove is Pebble Beach, which has stones "worn smooth and flat by tumbling and rolling about in the waves for a long period of time." As many as fifteen Norwegian fishermen operated out of Little Two Harbors during the early twentieth century, but no more than four or five stayed year-round and braved the difficult winters. Some remnants of the cribs that supported the fishing dock still extend from the island into Lake Superior. A narrow land connection or tombolo, which connects the mainland and island, is visible only when water levels are low. Also on the mainland is Day Hill, an anorthosite knob that stands 250 feet above Lake Superior; in addition to the outstanding lake views that are available from its summit, the Day Hill knob has an intriguing cultural feature—"quite possibly, the only anorthosite fireplace and chimney in the world." Built by Duluth businessman Frank Day around 1900, the story and intent of the fireplace remain unknown.[251]

### Split Rock Trading Post and Overlook (*now* Split Rock Lighthouse Wayside)
Southwest of Split Rock Lighthouse Entrance

The Split Rock Gift Shop, opened by Clyde Adams in 1942, was renamed the Split Rock Trading Post around 1960. The kitschy roadside store had a treasure trove of trinkets, bric-a-brac, and other "stuff" for sale: gifts, agates, driftwood, imports, postcards, birchbark souvenirs, moccasins, Black Forest cuckoo clocks, wild rice, Canadian jams and candies, buckskin items, wild animal furs, and more. Other attractions were the tame deer and one or two chained bears that eagerly

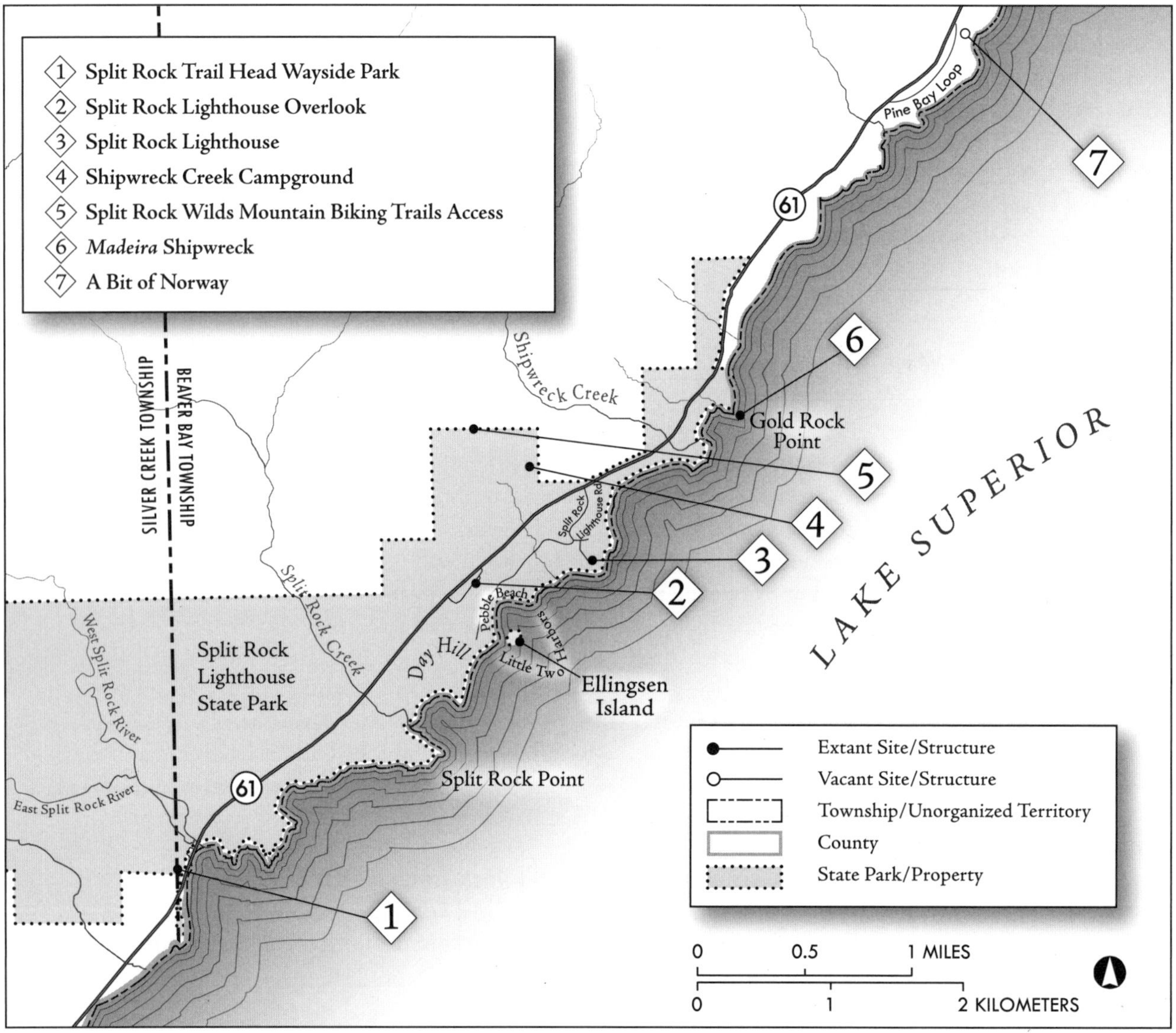

1 Split Rock Trail Head Wayside Park
2 Split Rock Lighthouse Overlook
3 Split Rock Lighthouse
4 Shipwreck Creek Campground
5 Split Rock Wilds Mountain Biking Trails Access
6 *Madeira* Shipwreck
7 A Bit of Norway
SILVER CREEK TOWNSHIP
BEAVER BAY TOWNSHIP
Shipwreck Creek
Gold Rock Point
LAKE SUPERIOR
Pine Bay Loop
61
Split Rock Lighthouse Rd
Pebble Beach
Day Hill
Little Two Harbors
Ellingsen Island
Split Rock Creek
West Split Rock River
East Split Rock River
Split Rock Lighthouse State Park
Split Rock Point
Extant Site/Structure
Vacant Site/Structure
Township/Unorganized Territory
County
State Park/Property
0
0.5
1 MILES
0
1
2 KILOMETERS

consumed the marshmallows fed to them by visitors. Behind the trading post was a wooden overlook stand, about fifteen feet high, that provided outstanding views of Split Rock Lighthouse and Lake Superior's ore boats. (Tourists paid ten cents to access the overlook platform.) Although the trading post closed before burning down in 1999, the moldering viewing stand remained on the site until it was removed in 2017.[252]

The site is now identified by the Split Rock Lighthouse Wayside, which comprises an overlook and two sections of curved wall that stand three feet above ground level. Constructed of multicolored native stone during the 1960s, the structure was inspired by earlier CCC projects. The wayside, from its outset, provided an excellent lighthouse outlook, but parking space was limited. Because of a slight highway rerouting that eliminated through traffic from the site in 2011, motorists are now able to park nearby and observe the lake and lighthouse from a safer and quieter vantage point.[253] A favorite spot at the wayside was recently identified as "Selfie Point."

**Several sightseers, shown here during the 1960s, enjoy the views from a lookout stand located next to the Split Rock Trading Post. On clear days, one could peer into the mounted telescopes and gain a distant impression of Wisconsin's Apostle Islands.**

### Split Rock Lighthouse
3755 Split Rock Lighthouse Road

### Split Rock Lighthouse State Park
3713 Split Rock Lighthouse Road

Split Rock was designated as the site for a lighthouse and fog signal in 1907—two years after the infamous Lake Superior storm of November 1905 damaged or sank eighteen ships. Approval for a lighthouse was quickly achieved when the national Lake Carriers' Association persuaded the U.S. Congress that such a facility would "do away with the serious danger to lives and property, which our experience has shown is due to the fact that there is no warning light or signal." Work on the $75,000, neoclassical revival style structure—constructed of brick, poured concrete, wood, and steel—began in 1909; Ralph Tinkham, a young architect-engineer, supervised the demanding and dangerous work. A derrick, powered by a steam engine and erected atop the 130-foot-high corundum rock dome, hoisted hundreds of tons of equipment and building materials from barges anchored below. Once the site was cleared of vegetation, building foundations were drilled and blasted out of the rocky base. Skilled carpenters and iron and concrete workers then moved onto the site. In August 1910, the first light from the tower—fifty-four feet high and equipped with an incandescent oil vapor lamp and bivalve lens—pierced across twenty miles of Lake Superior's nighttime sky. The light would flash at regular ten-second intervals for the next sixty years.[254]

Just west of the lighthouse and its adjacent foghorn are three identical, two-and-a-half-story Craftsman-influenced residences, all constructed of vitrified brick walls and metal "slate" roofs that offered protection from Lake Superior's harsh weather. Although each house had a nearby frame barn, the structures proved inadequate for domestic animals and were converted to automobile garages by 1934. (One garage burned down in 1969.) A tramway and car, constructed in 1916 and dismantled in 1934, connected the dock with a turntable located partway up the steps. Three tons of supplies and materials could be transported in the car; when it reached the turntable located by the tram house, the load was detached and pushed by hand up the remaining section of slope to the construction site.[255]

After Minnesota Highway 1 opened between Two Harbors and Split Rock in 1924, the picturesque location became one of the nation's most visited and photographed lighthouses. Because of new technological advances that eliminated the need for such a facility,

**A 1930s view of several structures that formed the Split Rock Lighthouse complex. Behind the lighthouse is the fog signal building; to the left are two of the three residences that housed staff members and their families.**

the U.S. Coast Guard closed the station in 1969, which, two years later, was acquired by the State of Minnesota. The light station and its grounds were listed in the National Register of Historic Places in 1971, five years before the MHS began managing the twenty-five-acre site. In 2011, Split Rock was also designated a National Historic Landmark—the highest form of federal recognition a historic property can receive in the United States. The complex was acknowledged not only for its architectural significance but also because "all major elements were built during its initial period of construction"—an uncommon feature among Great Lakes light stations.[256]

### Shipwreck Creek Campground and Split Rock Wilds Mountain Biking Trails

Upper Side of Highway 61, North of Split Rock

Although the 1980 Split Rock State Park master plan called for a drive-in campground, work on the project did not commence until 2019. Identified as Shipwreck Creek Campground at the time of its April 2022 opening, the site was developed for motorists who prefer campsites that are directly accessible to their vehicles. (All other Split Rock facilities are "cart-in campgrounds.") Also nearby is a trailhead for Split Rock Wilds, a new, twenty-two-mile-long mountain biking trail system that stretches to Beaver Bay. Several of its features are designed to challenge even the most accomplished mountain biker: a "rock garden" with 850 feet of boulders; a "flyover bridge," which leads down a steeply curved deck that has no railing; "jump trails with gaps"; numerous "rocks and drops"; and very steep technical climbs.[257]

### *Madeira* Shipwreck

Gold Rock Point

Northeast of the lighthouse complex is Gold Rock, a daunting outcropping that marks the remains of a shipwreck, that of the schooner-barge *Madeira*—one of many Lake Superior vessels to sink during the hurricane-force winds of late November 1905. On that auspicious night, the line broke between the *Madeira* and its towing steamer, the *William Edenborn*. The *Edenborn* went ashore close to the mouth of the Split Rock River, but the *Madeira* drifted away until it crashed into Gold Rock. Seaman Fred Benson managed to leap from the schooner's bow to the base of the cliff, where he rigged two safety lines that allowed eight shipmates to escape; only the first mate was not rescued. In 1955, shortly after a Duluth diving club, the Frigid Frogs, discovered the *Madeira*'s remains, a salvage company removed some steel from the 436-foot-long shipwreck. The anchor is now on display close to the Split Rock Lighthouse visitors' center, but the remaining sections of the bow and stern, and an extensive artifact field, have become a popular diving site. The shipwreck site was listed in the National Register of Historic Places in 1992.[258]

### A Bit of Norway *(moved)* and Gift and Antiques Store *(vacant)*

#### Northeastern End of Pine Bay Loop

One section of the five and a half miles between Split Rock Lighthouse and Beaver Bay is paralleled by a former segment of Highway 61, renamed the Pine Bay Loop following a 1996 rerouting. (The GGST is also cosigned with the Loop.) Located along the original highway was the A Bit of Norway, which, despite its relatively brief fourteen-year tenure, quickly became an acclaimed North Shore restaurant. The business was established in 1938 by Elsie Thingvold Schraa, nine years after she emigrated from Norway with her six-year-old daughter. The ambitious and talented woman, described as a "short, intense lady with a passion for everything Norwegian," was assisted by her husband, Henry Schraa, who had accompanied his parents when they departed the Netherlands for New Jersey in 1893.[259]

The one-and-a-half-story A Bit of Norway building, with a side-gable entrance, was covered with split-log siding. Steeply pitched roofs, somewhat reminiscent of Norwegian folk buildings, topped the small entry vestibule, as well as the three dormers that allowed sunlight to reach into the upper-story living quarters. Attached to the restaurant's eastern side was a single-story kitchen. Just west of the restaurant was a separate "only from Scandinavia" gift and antique shop; also faced with split-log siding, the building served as Elsie Schraa's version of a Norwegian *stabbur*.

A Two Harbors resident who visited A Bit of Norway in 1939, one year after its opening, expressed obvious

**The A Bit of Norway restaurant was operated by Elsie Thingvold Schraa from 1938 to 1952. To the right is the Norwegian-inspired *stabbur* that housed her gift and antique store.**

**The long-vacant *stabbur*, once located next to A Bit of Norway, still remains along Pine Bay Loop; the split-log siding that formerly covered the one-time gift and antique store was removed years ago.**

satisfaction with the quality and quantity of food he received while partaking of "what the Scandinavians call Smorgasbord":

> In plain English, that is a table laden with so many good things you don't know where to start. You take a sparse helping of deviled eggs, potato salad, then comes dainty imported sardines, a spiced ham in gelatin, and then come cheeses and sad to say your plate is full before you are a third way around the table. You are sorry you didn't wait to choose some of the things which look even more tempting as you pass around to be seated at your table where you are served coffee.
>
> The pile melts away on your plate and the little woman bustles around to make sure you are pleased, and if you are too polite to continue your prospecting, she insists you must try some of the other Scandinavian dainties all over again, and when your stomach has been distended to the point of rending your belt, you can go home and tell your friends that you have been to "A Bit of Norway" and you know your Smorgasbord.[260]

**The original building at A Bit of Norway was moved to the Lake Superior shoreline during the early 1990s and now serves as a vacation residence.**

Although A Bit of Norway closed in 1952 and was converted into residential units, the building stood vacant by 1989, when it was purchased by a St. Paul contractor. Three years later, after moving the structure down to the Lake Superior shoreline, he and his family devoted considerable time and effort to its repair. The relocation and restoration of this landmark structure represents one of the North Shore's impressive private preservation projects.

## City of Beaver Bay

The Beaver River, known as Ga-gijikensikag (Place of Little Cedars) to the Anishinaabe, passes through a rocky gorge before it empties into Lake Superior. At the mouth of the river is a tree-covered peninsula that divides the bay into western and eastern sections. Although the earliest Anishinaabe inhabitants didn't establish a permanent settlement along the river, they made fishing and hunting excursions to the site. In 1854, Thomas Clark, a surveyor from Superior, Wisconsin, explored the area for its timber resources, waterpower potential, and "agricultural possibilities and impossibilities." Two years later, after filing a plat for a townsite at the river's mouth, Clark built "two cabins to hold the waterpower and one to hold the site."[261]

Also arriving in 1856 on the steamer *Illinois* was a group of German immigrants from Ohio, among them the families of five Wieland brothers—Christian, Henry, August, Albert, and Ernst—who settled on the river's western side. Just six weeks later, a diary entry by Methodist minister James Peet noted that the industrious Germans had "made their land claims, built two shanties, seven houses, chopped twelve acres, four of which they have got into crops, made seven miles of road, and cut about twelve tons of wild hay; and they hope to find grass for fifty to one hundred tons."[262]

Unlike other North Shore townsites that were abandoned during the Panic of 1857, a solid nucleus of sixty-two people still remained in Beaver Bay by 1860: they included twenty-six American-born residents, along with thirty-two Germans, three Canadians, and one Briton. The community proved successful because of the Wielands' sawmill, located below the river's rapids, which provided lumber for shipments on their schooner, the *Charley*. The lumber was marketed at numerous places along Lake Superior, primarily in the emerging copper mining settlements of Michigan's Upper Peninsula. Several Anishinaabe workers found employment in the Wielands' logging and sawmill operations, but the *Charley* was their most popular worksite. The best-known Anishinaabe resident was the legendary John Beargrease, who, from 1879 to 1899, delivered mail with a dogsled during the winter months and by a boat or horse throughout the other seasons.[263]

In 1882, the four surviving Wieland brothers, after waiting for "the development that never came in the degree that had been anticipated," shut down their sawmill and moved to Duluth, where they resided for the remainder of their lives. (All four died between 1897 and 1899.) Nordic immigrants who began arriving during the 1890s soon built Beaver Bay into a small but thriving commercial fishing center. By 1910, the population of eighty-eight people included twenty-three Anishinaabe residents and twenty-three Norwegians, among them Martin Lorntson, who had migrated, in 1880, to North Dakota, where he found employment as a farmworker. After marrying Hannah Hansen in 1886, he returned with his wife to Norway but reimmigrated, around 1893, first to Superior, then to Two Harbors and, in 1896, to Beaver Bay. Tragically, Lorntson drowned during a December 1911 storm while tending his nets only a short distance from the family's fish house. Lorntson's descendants would play major roles in the ensuing development of Beaver Bay.[264]

Lydia Olsen Jacobsen, another Beaver Bay resident from Norway, was one of very few North Shore women to independently engage in commercial fishing. The twenty-one-year-old Olsen immigrated to Minnesota in 1906, the year of her marriage to Christian Jacobsen, a Norwegian fisherman who resided in Knife River. The couple, with their two sons, moved to Beaver Bay before 1920 and divorced during the 1930s. Nevertheless, wrote *Duluth News-Tribune* reporter Reginald Buck in 1943, Lydia Jacobsen "continued making her living as a fisherwoman who knows her business as well as the best fisherman on the north shore." Buck's profile of the "intrepid" woman also provided a vivid description of her demanding daily routine: rise before daybreak; don a heavy jacket, long scarf, rubber apron, and boots; walk to the boathouse; row four miles out onto the lake; locate six nets in water that was hundreds of feet deep; lift the nets onto the boat; remove three hundred

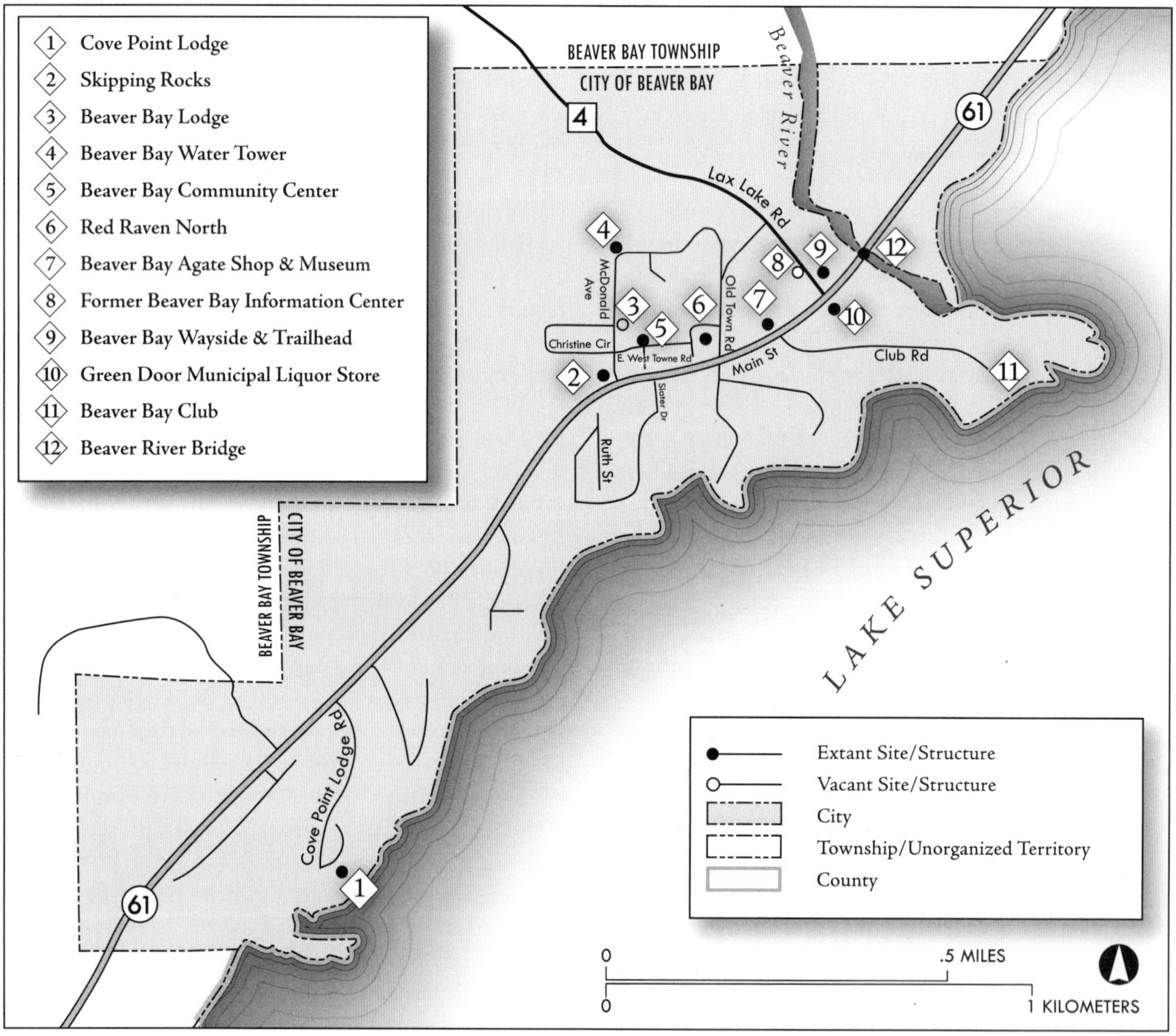

1 Cove Point Lodge
2 Skipping Rocks
3 Beaver Bay Lodge
4 Beaver Bay Water Tower
5 Beaver Bay Community Center
6 Red Raven North
7 Beaver Bay Agate Shop & Museum
8 Former Beaver Bay Information Center
9 Beaver Bay Wayside & Trailhead
10 Green Door Municipal Liquor Store
11 Beaver Bay Club
12 Beaver River Bridge
BEAVER BAY TOWNSHIP
CITY OF BEAVER BAY
Beaver River
Lax Lake Rd
McDonald Ave
Christine Cir
E. West Towne Rd
Old Town Rd
Main St
Club Rd
Slater Dr
Ruth St
Cove Point Lodge Rd
61
4
LAKE SUPERIOR
Extant Site/Structure
Vacant Site/Structure
City
Township/Unorganized Territory
County
0
.5 MILES
0
1 KILOMETERS

or more pounds of herring; row back to the fish house; and then clean, salt, and pack the fish for shipment and sale. Equally daunting was her monthly task: resetting six nets, each anchored down with rocks that weighed seventy to one hundred pounds. But it was Jacobsen's willingness to go out on Lake Superior in almost any type of weather that stands out as her most impressive feat. "The temperament and moods of Lake Superior," she mused in 1943, "are an old and well-known story to me." Jacobsen, by 1957, was residing in Duluth, where she died five years later.[265]

Early motorists could reach Beaver Bay by following the inland road that emerged just north of the settlement around 1916, but it was the arrival of Minnesota Highway 1, in 1923–24, that gave travelers and tourists improved access to its one hotel, two stores, and two diners; advertisements for Beaver Bay's three natural swimming pools also appeared during the 1920s.[266] Most of the early commercial businesses and other ventures that appeared before the 1950s have disappeared, but several of the sites now include newer structures that accommodate different functions.

Beaver Bay also served as the initial seat of government for Lake County from 1866 to 1888, before these functions were transferred to Two Harbors. And even though Beaver Bay is the oldest continuously inhabited white community on the North Shore, it was not officially incorporated as a village until 1953 and as a city until 1974. Population numbers have remained modest throughout Beaver Bay's history, even as some gains were experienced when the nearby Silver Bay taconite processing plant opened in the mid-1950s. Beaver Bay's population increased from 287 to 360 between 1960 and 1970, before a downturn in taconite production led to commensurate declines in population—283 in 1980 and 147 in 1990. Some growth, although slight, has occurred during the current century: 175 residents in 2000, 181 in 2010, and 173 in 2020.[267] Several Beaver Bay residences and buildings date to the taconite boom, but a number of vacant sites and structures await new owners and uses.

### Mickey and Pat Lorntson Residence and Fishing Camp (*now* Cove Point Lodge)
### 4614 Highway 61

Martin ("Mickey") Lorntson—the grandson of Beaver Bay's earliest Norwegian immigrant family—purchased an undeveloped property at the southwestern corner of the settlement in 1968. Lorntson, a longtime Silver Bay taconite plant worker, also pursued commercial fishing

**A lakeside view of Cove Point Lodge, looking north. Flanking the main lodge building on the left is Mickey's Fish House; to the far right is Fjord Village.**

from 1943 to 1993. Calling his 150-acre acquisition "an ideal location for a fisherman to make his home," Lorntson soon constructed a fish house and later, along with his wife, Pat, built a residence for themselves and their four sons.[268]

In 1994, the Lorntsons sold their property to a Twin Cities couple, Steve and Marcia Hillestad, respectively a health care executive and a teacher, both of whom "fulfilled a lifetime dream" by opening Cove Point Lodge just one year later. While the resort is easily accessible to Highway 61, a wooded hillside buffers the buildings, rocky outcroppings, and shoreline from the road's sights and sounds. The main lodge includes a spacious commons that has a large fireplace and adjacent dining room, an indoor pool with a lake view, a sauna, and other amenities found at several other North Shore destination resorts. All forty-five guest rooms, located within an adjacent wing, have lake views. The resort's "low-key Nordic" theme or "vibe" is expressed in its dining options, primarily the "Scandinavian breakfast," and in the building's exterior colors, which feature red- and yellow-painted wooden facades, white framing, and variegated rooflines. The Cove's forty cottages are organized into three groupings—Fjord Village, Coveside, and Ridge Line; many units may be rented when not occupied by an owner. (Also in the vicinity is Windsong, an upscale complex of twenty-six individually owned townhomes.) Still perched by the lakeshore is one of Lorntson's original structures, now called Mickey's Fish House, which serves as a quiet retreat space for Cove Point's guests.[269]

### North Shore Camping Company
### 4595 Highway 61

Directly north of Highway 61 and Cove Point Lodge is a facility, opened by the North Shore Camping Company (NSCC) in 2023, that caters to people who have interests in "glamping"—a form of outdoor recreation that provides participants with accommodations and facilities that are more opulent than those associated with typical camping. Swedish-language terms also identify the property's base camp, four hiking trails, and two overlooks. Each NSCC glamper also has access to Cove Point's grounds and services.[270]

### Spruce Point Diner and Motel (*now* Skipping Rocks/CCC Camp 721 Cabin)
### 700 MacDonald Avenue

Highway 61 coexists with Main Street as it enters the built-up area of Beaver Bay. On the northwestern side of the Main Street–MacDonald Avenue intersection is a relatively large area of land once occupied by several buildings that emerged when Silver Bay's taconite production plant was under construction during the 1950s. The earliest commercial structure was a former Duluth streetcar that Maybelle Wilson purchased for $400, moved to Beaver Bay in 1953, and converted into the Spruce Point Diner. Wilson also connected the diner to another streetcar that served as the kitchen and provided living quarters for her family. The staff, several of them Wilson's relatives, kept the diner open twenty hours a day during the busy construction period. Her daughter and son-in-law, Carmen and Edward Maki, completed the nearby Spruce Point Motel in 1957, the same year that Arnold Steffan opened his "variety store," where clothing, gifts, toys, and jewelry were available for sale in a trailer that was forty-three feet long. A developer who purchased the entire 3.2-acre site in 1974 converted the motel into apartments and also built several nearby rental units. The entire property, however, had been abandoned for several years when it was acquired by the City of Beaver Bay in 2010, ten years before the buildings were razed and the land prepared for development.[271]

The first new building and business appeared on a section of the cleared site in 2001—a twenty-four-by-fifty-foot cabin, constructed of vertical tamarack logs in 1933 for George Archibald, the superintendent of forestry at CCC Camp 721, located by the Baptism River in Lake County. Around two hundred young men, a majority of them from the local area, were enrolled in Camp 721 before it closed in 1938. The cabin was then purchased by Harold Menson, who transported it to the North Shore community of Schroeder. Later owners Minnesota DFL legislator Tom Berg and his wife, Margit, donated the cabin, in 1999, to the Bay Area Historical Society, an organization that represents the communities of Beaver Bay and Silver Bay. The cabin was moved, in 2001, to a site on the eastern side of the city, where it opened as the Beaver Bay Tourist

Information Center. Also situated within the building was a small museum that presented information and displays about Beaver Bay's origins and history.[272]

Owing to a persistent shortage of volunteers and maintenance funds, the visitors' center closed permanently after Labor Day 2019. The fate of the cabin would not be determined until 2021, when it was purchased by local businesswoman Tedi Kytola, the owner of Skipping Rocks, a local gift shop. After moving the cabin to a lot on the recently cleared site in western Beaver Bay, Kytola and her two sisters reestablished the business; some of Beaver Bay's historic items remain on display within the building.[273]

### Beaver Bay Lodge *(razed)*

Intersection of MacDonald Avenue and Upper Section of Christine Circle

In 1914, Minneapolis resident Mary Castner, described as "a bundle of energy with many interests," relocated to the Beaver Bay area following her acceptance of a teaching position at the nearby Lax Lake School. She married Hugh MacDonald in 1916, settled on a farm, and soon gave birth to two children. Mary's mother, who had moved to Beaver Bay in 1921 after purchasing some land along the new highway right-of-way, strongly encouraged her daughter to open a hotel that would cater to tourists, anglers, and hunters. The Beaver Bay Lodge (also known as Mary Macs) opened just before Minnesota Highway 1 entered the community in 1923. The establishment, described as "a new resort where meals and sleeping accommodations may be secured," included a two-and-a-half-story lodge with several housekeeping rooms; the lodge also had separate summer and winter kitchens—one equipped with a wood-burning range, the other with a six-burner kerosene stove. Also within the lodge were a large dining and fireplace room that could seat as many as forty people; it even had a library—an especially appropriate provision from the strongly committed public educator. The second building was a single-story wing-shaped structure with nine guest rooms. (Several rental cabins were also located nearby.) MacDonald encouraged her visitors to "come, stay, and play a while at Beaver Bay" and enjoy "delightful home-cooked meals, hiking through wooded trails, trout fishing, and everything." The lodge, during off-season months, also served as a boardinghouse for local teachers, construction workers, and hunters. MacDonald assisted in forming the North Shore Resort Operators Association but was best known for her efforts to improve local educational opportunities. She advocated for the consolidation of Lake County's small school districts during the 1930s, initiated the area's first children's lunch program, and served three terms on the county school board. The Beaver Bay Lodge burned down in the early 1960s, shortly after MacDonald's 1959 death; the still-vacant lot adjoins the appropriately named MacDonald Avenue. Just below the site, at 731 East-West Road, is a multipurpose building, dating to 2011, that houses the Beaver Bay Community Center, the Beaver Bay city and township halls, and three private businesses.[274]

**The two primary buildings at Mary MacDonald's Beaver Bay Lodge in 1930, seven years after her business opened. Photograph by Harold Youngren.**

### Beaver Bay Water Tower

Northwest of MacDonald Avenue–White Rock Road Intersection

Although no longer functional, a wooden water tower remains in Beaver Bay, reportedly the only such example still standing in Minnesota. (A number of others are constructed of materials other than wood.) The tower appeared in 1956, once it was determined that the town's individual wells, the source of water for all local homes and businesses, had an excessively high sulfur content. Financing for a centralized well and water tower, however, was not possible until Beaver Bay incorporated as a village in 1953. This action allowed the new village, two years later, to establish a municipal

Beaver Bay's wooden water tower, which served the community from 1956 to 1981, is now shrouded by birch, aspen, and spruce trees.

liquor store that provided sufficient revenue for the development of a community-wide water system.[275]

In 1956, the fifty-thousand-gallon tower was transported 110 miles to Beaver Bay from Markville, a small Pine County hamlet situated along Minnesota's eastern border with Wisconsin. The initial fifty-five miles of the tower's journey extended northward from Markville through northwestern Wisconsin to Superior, where the transport truck crossed over the bridge into Duluth, then proceeded along the North Shore to Beaver Bay. The tank began leaking during the 1970s, however, and was abandoned in 1981 when a new centralized water system opened. The future of the landmark tower remains uncertain, although proposals have been made to stabilize and maintain the structure as a Beaver Bay attraction.[276]

### Lorntson's Log Cabin Lunch and Camp 61 Restaurant and Motel (*now* Red Raven North)
1017 Main Street

Motorists who entered Beaver Bay in 1926 were greeted by a modest building, the Log Cabin Lunch, located in Arthur and Evelyn Mabie Lorntson's residence. (Lorntson, the son of Beaver Bay pioneers Martin and Hannah Lorntson, was a commercial fisherman who,

The Log Cabin Lunch, a diner opened by Arthur and Evelyn Lorntson in 1926, also had candy, ice cream, cigars, and Shell gasoline available for purchase. Photograph by Harold Youngren, 1930.

before his 1988 death at the age of ninety, served as Beaver Bay's first mayor, as a Lake County commissioner, and as chairman of the Silver Bay Bank.) Additions were made to the log-sided structure around 1931, when it became Lorntson's Inn, "the place to eat and meet your friends." The building burned down in 1937 and was replaced with Lorntson's Café, which also provided a few tourist rooms on the second floor.[277]

The sale of Lorntson's during the 1960s ushered in a series of ownership transfers and name changes, among them Berryman's Café, Steffan's Half-Way House, Beaver Bay Inn, Blue Heron, and the Inn at Beaver Bay. In 2010–11, local residents Todd and Carol Mealey Krynski, after engaging in considerable work and effort, brought "new life" to the "rundown building," which became the Camp 61 Bunkhouse and Restaurant. ("Camp 61" referenced the logging camps where Carol Krynski's grandfather and great-grandfather worked from the 1890s to the 1960s, and the iconic highway number.) Identifying themselves as an "eclectic sort," the Krynskis restored the original interior pine walls and bedecked them with historical furnishings acquired at auctions and from donors. Camp 61's primary attraction was the restaurant, although eight moderately priced motel units within the building maintained its longtime lodging traditions. The purchase of Camp 61 by new owners in late 2020 led to another name change (at least the tenth in its history), this time to Red Raven North. The business still includes an eight-unit motel and, since 2023, a bicycle rental and repair shop—an appropriate activity for Beaver Bay, given its importance as a hub for the GGST and as a terminus for the new Split Rock Wilds Mountain Bike Trail.[278]

## Beaver Bay Agate Shop and Museum
### 1003 Main Street

Clayton Lawson's automotive service garage, and a nearby a residence, appeared in Beaver Bay by the late 1920s. In 1941, four years after the structures were destroyed by a fire, Leo ("Rocky") and Lillian Quinn purchased the vacant property, where they "set up a tent and table with rocks for sale to see who else was as crazy as them." The Quinns constructed their modest Beaver Bay Lapidary Shop and adjacent residence in 1946, as well as a separate café and a building with six rental rooms. Jim Haase began managing the business in 1985, which his father had acquired following Quinn's death. An exceptional lapidarist and jewelry artist, Haase also established a museum in the shop before it was sold, in 1991, to the Quinns' son Randall, a retired taconite plant worker. He would expand the inventory of items in both the shop and the museum and also make improvements to the residence. After current owners Keith and Teresa Bartel of Aitkin, Minnesota, purchased the shop in 2003, the couple "remodeled the building several times [and] completely changed the museum." The business, still operated by the Bartel family, has large collections of agates and thomsonite that are on display and available for sale.[279]

**Rocky and Lillian Quinn's Beaver Bay Lapidary Shop, with its attached residence, late 1940s.**

## Beaver Bay Wayside and Trailhead
### Eastern Side of the Main Street and Lax Lake Road Intersection

Between the Agate Shop and the river is the Beaver Bay Wayside and Trailhead, which overlooks the falls and site of Wielands' former gristmill. Sponsored and built by the GGST association in 2015, the facility is one of the system's most important trailheads. The wayside, also accessible to hikers and motorists, includes a picnic shelter, tables and seating, a drinking fountain, and restrooms; several kiosks provide information about other nearby trails and the history of Beaver Bay.[280]

On the western side of the Beaver Bay Wayside and Lax Lake Road is the former location of a 1933 CCC cabin that was moved to the site in 2001. It served as an information center and small museum for the Bay Area Historical Society until 2019, when it was relocated to the western side of Beaver Bay and reopened as the Skipping Rocks gift shop in 2021.

### Beaver Bay Schoolhouse (*now the* Green Door Municipal Liquor Store)
1002 Main Street

Beaver Bay's school-age children were initially taught in the home of engineer Christian Wieland, who later served as the "schoolmaster" or superintendent. A small schoolhouse appeared by 1876, but after a fire destroyed the structure, Wieland replaced it for $250 in 1892. The one-room building accommodated grades 1–8 until 1928, when a multiroom structure was provided for Beaver Bay's students. Also used for Sunday services by local Catholic and Lutheran congregations, the schoolhouse was converted into Beaver Bay's Green Door Municipal Liquor Store in 1955, once a new school opened in Silver Bay. The basic form of the former hip-roofed schoolhouse is still evident, but a number of its original features have been changed or eliminated: all of the front windows are boarded over; the original entry porch, other than its pediment, no longer exists; and two large chimneys that once topped the roof are gone. The interior, also heavily altered, retains its original library bookshelves and a few blackboards. Still warmly recalled by residents are the annual, springtime "smelt fries," dating to the 1950s, that occurred in the basement kitchen. The events served as fundraisers for the Beaver Bay Volunteer Fire Department but ended in 1998 because of sharp declines in the numbers of both smelt and volunteer workers.[281]

### Albert and Magdalene Wieland Residence (*razed, now the* Beaver Bay Club)
201 East Club Road

Several of Beaver Bay's original settlers, among them Albert and Magdalene Wieland, acquired land along both sides of the river upon their 1856 arrival. Close to the Wielands' residence, which also served as Beaver Bay's teacherage, was a combination store and post office. Other residents occupied the Wielands' property following their 1882 departure from Beaver Bay, but the remaining buildings were consumed by a fire in 1922.[282]

By this time, a group of fifteen wealthy Twin Cities men were purchasing much of the land, where they proposed to organize an exclusive enclave, the Beaver Bay Club (BBC), which was officially incorporated in 1926. Because the BBC's members eventually owned the point of land that juts into Lake Superior, they were able to transform most of the Beaver River's lower section into "a private retreat." Although rather similar in both spirit and organization to the EFA, the BBC, with three hundred acres, is considerably smaller. A clubhouse, constructed of both vertical and horizontal logs, appeared on the site during the late 1920s. Because of its "modern kitchen and three bedrooms with a bath," club members termed the structure "incredibly comfortable"; several extensions were added during subsequent years. Ten log cabins also appeared before 1930, while others, most built of frame and board, emerged later. Joe and Elizabeth Shaaf Slater, who had occupied the Wielands' original buildings before they burned down in 1922, were the club's primary employees. Elizabeth Slater, a native of Germany, and the clubhouse manager and cook, reportedly served as the members' "mother [and] political and spiritual advisor"; she also was a midwife who delivered more than sixty babies in the Beaver Bay area. Her husband and their son John served as caretakers and assisted the BBC's membership with their building projects.[283]

The low public profile preferred by the association was interrupted in 2013 when its members demanded the removal of a fish house situated on BBC property. The original fish house, constructed in 1911 by two of Martin and Hannah Lorntson's sons, was destroyed during a 1943–44 storm. When the structure was replaced by the family's descendants, the BBC approved a "gentlemen's agreement," which allowed the fish house to remain on its property for ninety-nine years. Nevertheless, in 2013, twenty-seven years after another family had acquired the structure, the BBC's members called for its "immediate removal" because the organization had never received any rent for occupying the land. The plaintiffs, in turn, argued that the request was frivolous because the BBC had never prepared a lease or charged rent. Just before eviction hearings began in 2013, both protagonists agreed to a five-year lease, with the possibility of future renewals. Although defined by several residents as one of Beaver Bay's landmarks and "part of the North Shore experience," the unassuming structure was torn down in late 2022.[284]

### Beaver River Bridge

The first Beaver River Bridge, a log structure fastened together with wooden pegs and partially covered by vertical planks, was constructed just below the Wielands' gristmill in 1870. Built by Christian Wieland, the span demanded frequent repairs before it was replaced in 1909 by a steel truss bridge, jointly funded by the township and county. Anchored to both riverbanks by concrete piers, the new structure was constructed by the Joliet Bridge and Iron Company of Illinois. Once Minnesota Highway 1 reached Beaver Bay in the early 1920s, however, the bridge became a bottleneck because two vehicles could not meet on its narrow deck. A new steel-arch bridge was constructed closer to the river's mouth in 1924, but the deck, just twenty feet wide, also proved inadequate for the growing volume of traffic. Finally, in 1959, a larger steel bridge, situated atop concrete piers, was built over the river. Added to the structure in 2018 was a bicycle right-of-way that

**The privately owned fish house stood on the grounds of the Beaver Bay Club from the mid-1940s until 2022.**

A pair of Beaver River bridges, the one at the rear built in 1909, the other dating to 1924, coexisted for a few years before the older structure was torn down.

is ten feet wide and protected from the roadway by a low concrete retaining wall; it now serves as an important link in the Beaver Bay–Silver Bay section of the GGST.[285]

## East Beaver Bay

Highway 61 continues to skirt the lakeshore for about one-third of a mile within Beaver Bay before it once again meets the Beaver Bay Township boundary. One-third of a mile farther is the small, unincorporated settlement of East Beaver Bay, which sits high above Lake Superior. Initially settled by four Norwegian fishermen between 1902 and 1905, a few tourist-oriented businesses have also appeared and disappeared in the settlement since the 1920s. It was, however, the construction of the nearby Silver Bay taconite plant that changed the normal quietude of East Beaver Bay. Agnes Thorngren, who operated a local diner and bakery, later recalled her hectic daily schedule during the 1950s:

> Frank (my husband) got the idea to build a café/coffee shop when all these people were storming in here for work. My that was a job, I had three girls waiting for me. Talk about work. I had to get up at 4:00 A.M. to set bread and rolls because I baked all my rolls, and the boys were just crazy [for them] when they came from Duluth. They had to stop at the coffee shop and have sweet rolls, or doughnuts or cookies or cake or pie because we always had a lot of baked stuff.[286]

### Fonstead's Resort (*now* Beaver Bay Sports Shop) 4878 Highway 61

Most evidence of East Beaver Bay's early twentieth-century history was erased during the flurry of construction activity that occurred at Silver Bay during the 1950s. One such place was Fonstead's Resort, which included a lodge located along the highway and several cabins situated closer to the lake. Ole Fonstead, an 1885 Norwegian émigré, was working, fifteen years later, as a Duluth ship captain's mate and living on a barge moored in the city's harbor. In 1909, at the age of forty-seven, Fonstead married Mary McLauchlin, a French Canadian divorcée from Two Harbors with two children. While still engaged in fishing and farming during the late 1920s, the Fonsteads opened their lodge, where as many as twenty-five guests could secure a room and meals for three dollars per day. Three single- and double-unit lakeside cabins, each provided with a rowboat, were available for fourteen to eighteen dollars per week, while their small store offered basic supplies and a public telephone. Ole and Mary Fonstead, respectively seventy-seven and sixty-nine years of age, were still operating their North Shore resort in 1940. Fonstead died two years later, but his widow continued managing the establishment until 1950. The Beaver Bay Sports Shop currently occupies the former lodge site.[287]

### Mattson's Store and Service Station (*now* Second Hand Rose Antiques and Collectibles)
4898 Highway 61

Norwegian immigrants Edward and Lisa Mattson established a fishery and small farm at East Beaver Bay following their 1907 marriage. The couple also opened a roadside store in 1926 and rented out a few tourist cabins that overlooked the lake. The store was later operated by their son Milton, who also played a key role in establishing the SLSA; another son, Kermit, opened a nearby automobile service station that was transformed, some years later, into a plumbing and heating business. Now located on the site is Second Hand Rose, a quirky, tourist-season thrift and consignment outlet that has huge displays of vintage glassware and other previously owned items. The entire collection, arrayed on outdoor tables and in a nearby building, attracts visitors who are drawn to the North Shore's funky, eccentric, and "middle of nowhere" places.[288]

### Edward and Lisa Mattson Residence and Fish House
Fish House Road

While Edward and Lisa Mattson's East Beaver Bay store and cabins were situated close to the highway and well above Lake Superior, their residence and fishing operations hugged the Lake Superior shoreline. Mattson, a very successful fisherman, ventured as far as Isle Royale with his boat, the *Dagmar*; for one summer, he was even joined on the island by his wife, their three children, and the family's cow. Lisa Mattson also sold flour, butter, and meat from the family's house before the couple opened their highway store in 1926.[289]

The siting and placement of the Mattsons' residence and fish house still display a keen awareness of Lake Superior's vagaries and unpredictability: the buildings, tucked into the bay's upper side, are shielded from fierce northeastern storms, and tiny Wieland Island serves as a limited breakwater. The Mattson's sixteen-by-thirty-two-foot house, built in 1902 by an earlier Norwegian settler, is constructed of hewn logs held together by half-dovetailed corner notches. The gable roof was raised a half story in 1910, when seven courses of logs were added to the house; a stone

A water wheel with an attached rope connected Lake Superior to the lodge at Fonstead's Resort from the 1920s to 1950.

**Edward and Lisa Mattson's residence and fish house are among the finest remaining examples of early commercial fishing activity on the North Shore.**

chimney appeared in 1940. East of the residence is the fish house, constructed in 1930 as a replacement for an earlier structure. The twenty-four-by-twenty-nine-foot building was vital because it provided space for several important activities: cleaning and packaging fish, sheltering and maintaining boats, making net repairs, and storing ice and supplies. Situated on a high foundation, the fish house still retains its stone and concrete boat ramp.[290]

Mattson died in 1941, his widow in 1967. The property is now owned and used by a grandson, Clint Maxwell, who continues the family's commercial fishing traditions. The well-maintained residence and fish house, both of which still reveal many of their early features, were recognized with National Register of Historic Places designation in 1990. The buildings are on private property and should be observed only from a nearby public dock or Lake Superior.[291]

## City of Silver Bay

A stark landscape transition occurs when approaching Silver Bay from East Beaver Bay. Suddenly appearing on the landscape is a North Shore version of industrial America—a huge manufacturing plant that transforms low-grade taconite iron ore into high-quality pellets for shipment to steel mills in America's lower Great Lakes region. Standing along the Silver Bay shoreline are numerous structures and facilities—steel-enclosed buildings; large lots covered with stockpiled ore, pellets, and coal; a power plant and power lines; warehouses, trains, railroad shops, and tracks; docks, vessel-loading equipment, and ore boats. Dominating the complex are three structures (one 2,150 feet long), all constructed for the Reserve Mining Company during the early to mid-1950s: a "fine crushing" plant that grinds coarsely crushed taconite ore into small pieces, a concentrating plant that performs further "grinding, magnetic separation, and filtering" and creates a substance as fine as talcum powder, and a pelletizing plant where the "concentrate is rolled into balls and then burned hard to make the finished pellets."[292] On cold days and moonlit nights, ethereal billows of steam flow upward from tall chimney stacks, giving the entire scene an otherworldly appearance.

In 1945, Reserve's agents were quietly "acquiring land for a plant and a town on the north shore of Lake Superior," which, at the time, included about twenty cabins and a few small stores and business buildings. Residing at a key site were Norwegian immigrants Oscar and Hansina Pedersen, who had filed their homestead claim in 1915. The couple, ten years later, was renting cabins to motorists who drove along Minnesota Highway 1. Pedersen and his brother Hjalmer also opened a store and established two companies, Lake Superior Fisheries and North Shore Freight. Nearby was White Rock Cabins, operated by ore boat captain Nick Peterson and his wife, Dorothy. The rustic appearance of the lakeshore environment changed rapidly during the early 1950s, when the highway was moved a considerable distance inland from the shoreline and the infrastructure and foundations for Reserve's massive taconite processing structures were constructed on the vacated land. The initial features of a new town, later named Silver Bay, where housing and services would be provided for many Reserve workers, appeared north of the plant and relocated highway in 1952.[293]

Any overview of Silver Bay demands consideration of the taconite processing plant, which remains the most controversial industrial project in North Shore history. The facility, in fact, would serve as the centerpiece for a nationally significant environmental conflict

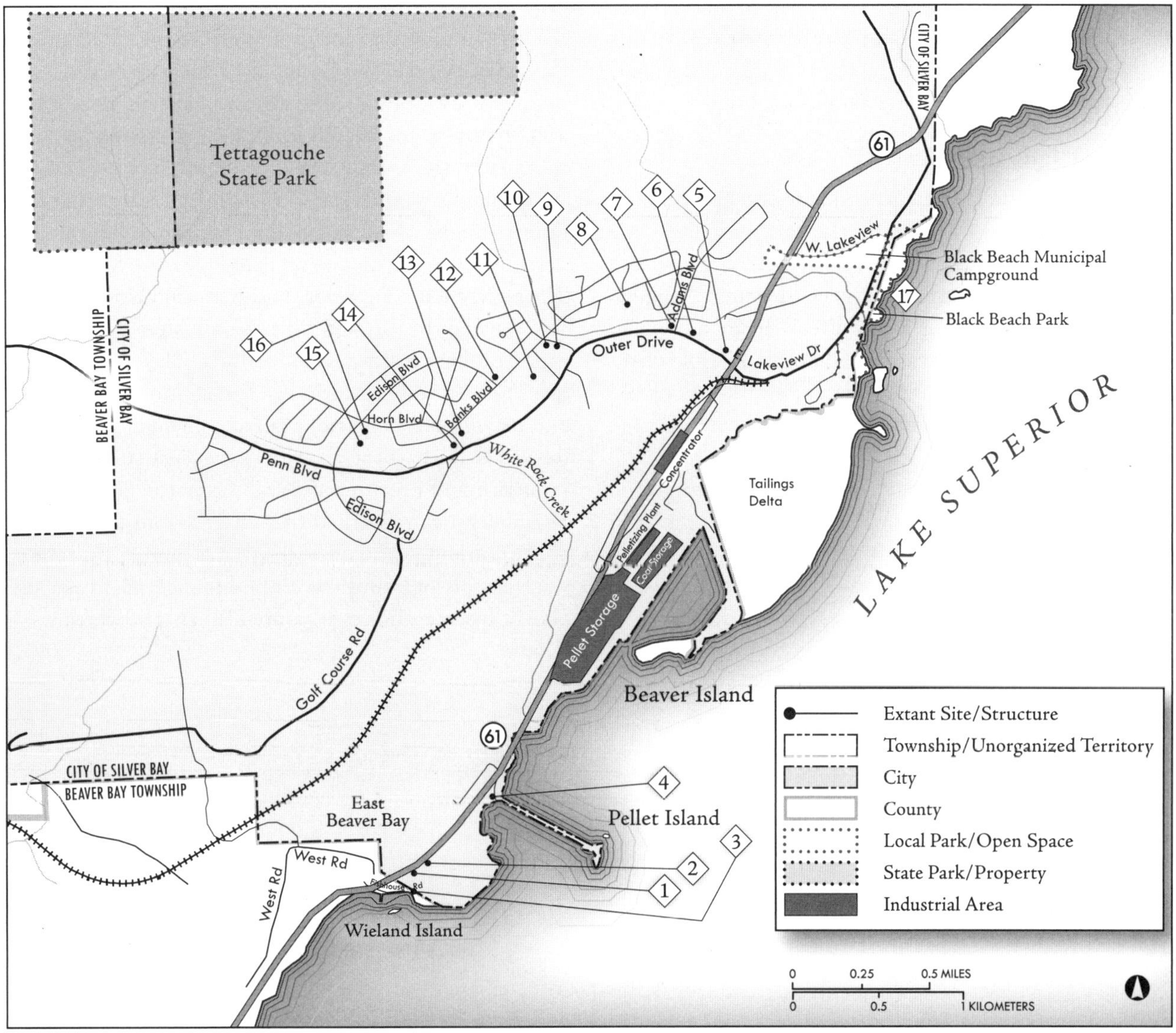


1. Beaver Bay Sports Shop
2. Second Hand Rose Antiques and Collectibles
3. Mattson Residence and Fish House
4. Silver Bay Marina, Protected Access
5. North Shore Adventure Park
6. Mariner Motel
7. Rocky Taconite
8. Minnesota Veterans Home–Silver Bay
9. Silver Bay City Hall
10. Silver Bay Public Library
11. Silver Bay Shopping Center
12. Sychar Lutheran Church
13. William M. Kelley Schools
14. United Protestant Church of Silver Bay
15. St. Mary's Catholic Church
16. Mary MacDonald Business Center

that played out during the 1970s. Although the issues were resolved after a prolonged legal battle, Silver Bay's subsequent taconite production figures and population numbers have been buffeted by the volatility of national and international steel markets.

## A Tale of Tailings

In October 1946, Reserve's president announced publicly, for the first time, that the company had purchased "certain lands on the shore of Lake Superior north of Beaver Bay and in that general vicinity." Eight months later, an advisory committee—headed by Chester S. Wilson, Minnesota's commissioner of conservation and chairman of the Water Pollution Control Commission—convened in Two Harbors, where its members conducted the first of eight hearings held in different parts of the state. The committee sought comments from parties who wished to speak either for or against Reserve's primary request, namely, securing permits that would allow the firm "to use Lake Superior water in its milling process and to discharge waste into the lake." The beneficiation process, which called for the annual dumping of millions of tons of finely ground waste rock (tailings) into the lake, raised immediate concerns among numerous conservation organizations, public officials, and fishermen. A July 1947 hearing, conducted in Duluth, gathered testimony from the United Northern Sportsmen, including fisherman Ragnvald Sve, who expressed alarm that the tailings might "cloud and pollute the lake water to the detriment of both commercial and pleasure fishing." The ad hoc Lake Superior Anti-pollution Committee also warned that no water filtration system could ever capture all the finely grained tailings. The city's public health director, Dr. Mario Fischer, commented that because of Lake Superior's currents, which flowed toward Duluth, there was worry that "the suspended tailings might prove a nuisance." City attorney Harry Weinberg also remarked that citizens and officials, at a minimum, wanted "reasonable assurance that the water supply of Duluth won't be endangered." Taconite plant advocates, however, contended that 99 percent

**Brothers Oscar and Hjalmer Pedersen opened this store along Minnesota Highway 1 in 1927 and also established a fish sales and freight hauling business. Their land would later be used for the Reserve Mining Company's plant. Courtesy of Bay Area Historical Society.**

**In 1953–54, the Reserve Company provided northeastern Minnesota newspapers with a series of cartoon-like drawings that illustrated progress on the new taconite plant.** ***Cook County News-Herald,*** **3 February 1955, 4.**

of the tailings would safely settle into the lake at the base of the facility, while the regional director of the U.S. Department of the Interior predicted the project would have minimal impact on Lake Superior's fish and wildlife. Reserve received its certification in late 1947, but only one permit stated that the tailings should not "result in material clouding or discoloration to the water, adversely affect fish life or public water supplies, cause other unlawful pollution of the lake water, interfere with navigation, or constitute a public nuisance outside the vicinity of the discharge."[294]

Surveyors were already evident along the lakeshore by 1947, when crews began clearing the right-of-way for a rail line that would connect the beneficiation plant to a taconite mine at Babbitt, located forty-seven miles north of Silver Bay. Workers began stripping vegetation and blasting one million tons of rock from the Reserve site in 1951. Two years later, a Grand Marais observer wrote that the rocky hills would soon be "taken down and shoved out into the water to form one of the [two] breakwaters" that protected the harbor, which itself had been carved out over two summers of round-the-clock dredging. "Gone are many of the tall trees between highway and lake," wrote another reporter. "Men and machines swarm over the area. The buzz of saws and pounding of hammers fill the air." While many area residents favored the new facility because of its perceived economic benefits, the massive transformation of the landscape as well as the size and scale of the emerging industrial structures were of concern to a number of people. Edward Schmid, Reserve's public relations director, sought to assuage the doubters, claiming that the one-mile-long stretch of reconfigured Highway 61 would no longer have "any trash, shacks, signboards, tourist cabins, beer joints, or taverns," and also predicted that Reserve's structures would be "clean, neat and attractive" and could even "add to the beauty of the North Shore drive rather than detracting from it." The overall effort, he prophesied, "should help, not harm, Minnesota's tourist trade." But, as later noted by Lake County historian Hugh Bishop, it was North Shore visitors who "viewed the operation as an intrusion on the pastoral lakeshore experience they were enjoying" and bemoaned the loss of the area's scenic qualities.[295]

The taconite ore mined at Babbitt went through a rock crusher before being loaded onto railroad cars and shipped southward to Silver Bay, where further crushing, grinding, concentration, pelletizing, and shipping occurred. Six pelletizing units went into production between October 1955 and February 1956; in April, the first shipment of pellets was loaded into the hold of the ore carrier *C. L. Austin*, which departed for a South Chicago steel plant. Once it was determined that taconite pellets were an ideal material for steel production purposes, a plant expansion, conducted from 1957 to 1961, increased the annual output from just under four million to six million tons.[296]

While Silver Bay's economic future initially appeared solid and stable, a major mid-1960s dispute over taconite tailings would soon "conjure a mixture of public perception and legal entanglement that threatened the very existence of this major new industry." Members of the aforementioned Lind, Sve, and Mattson families had already noticed the increasingly murky water that soon extended southwest of Silver Bay. Among others who expressed immediate concern over the conditions was Milton Mattson's nephew, attorney Grant Merritt, a Duluth native and descendant of a family whose name is synonymous with the history of northeastern Minnesota and the Iron Range. Merritt acted quickly and succeeded in formulating an antidumping resolution that was adopted as a plank in Minnesota's 1968 DFL Party platform. During that year, Merritt received an invitation to serve on the board of directors of the Minnesota Environmental Citizens Control Association, the first "environmental group to fight head-on Reserve Mining's daily dumping of 67,000 tons of taconite tailings in Lake Superior"; Merritt, in 1971, was also named executive director of the Minnesota Pollution Control Agency by newly elected DFL governor Wendell Anderson.[297]

**The completed taconite processing plant shortly after its 1955 opening. Courtesy of Minnesota Historical Society.**

By this time, water-quality scientists were warning that the tailings, which contained asbestos-like fibers, might be carcinogenic. In August 1973, more than a year after the EPA called for legal action to stop the dumping of tailings into Lake Superior, the U.S. Department of Justice launched a lawsuit against Reserve. (One *New York Times* reporter who covered the Silver Bay case was Jane Brody, later dubbed the "High Priestess of Health" because of the highly popular and influential articles she wrote for the newspaper from 1976 to 2022.) The trial stretched until April 1974, when the presiding federal judge, Miles Lord, issued a verdict stating that the asbestos-like fibers polluting Lake Superior were a threat to local populations. After more quarrelsome litigation, Reserve finally agreed to move its tailings disposal operations to an on-land site (called Milepost 7) that opened in 1980.[298]

The environmental impasse had been resolved to some extent, but the nationwide economic recession of the early 1980s caused severe cutbacks in the demand for steel and taconite and significant socioeconomic disruptions within Silver Bay itself. In mid-1986, Reserve and its partner, the LTV Steel Company, declared bankruptcy and shut down operations, which resulted in an immediate loss of 540 jobs. The plant did not reopen until 1989, when Cyprus Minerals of Colorado acquired the facility as part of its Northshore Mining Company division. Cyprus operated the plant until 1994, when it was purchased by the Cleveland Cliffs Company. Since then, Northshore's fortunes, and those of its employees, have been tied to the often-erratic health of the nation's steel industry. Increasing demands for steel in 2008 led to the opening of a Northshore furnace that had been idle since 1972; but then, in January 2013, two furnaces were shut down abruptly before starting up again in October. A more disruptive event occurred in late 2015, when the plant was completely idled for several months because of a steep drop in the demand for steel. Improved economic conditions,

**The *Mesabi Miner* takes on a load of taconite pellets at Silver Bay in 2014.**

however, led to a May 2016 reopening; a $100 million upgrade in 2019 made Northshore the nation's only taconite plant that could produce pellets for use by electric arc furnaces. Almost six hundred workers were eventually employed at the facility, before a royalty dispute led to another closing, this one in May 2022. The plant would not reopen until April 2023, when a limited number of employees began returning to work.[299]

## A Townsite and Housing

Already by the late 1940s and early 1950s, before any permanent residents moved into the new town that became Silver Bay, workers involved in taconite plant construction required housing. Many single men lived in barracks and secured their meals at a central commissary, while those employees with families utilized a trailer court that had a steel building equipped with washers, dryers, and showers. Cabins were also moved from throughout the area to Beaver Bay, where they could be rehabilitated and improved for year-round habitation. A 1948 announcement by Reserve officials, which stated that the company intended to build a new town for its permanent workforce, drew the attention of Robert Jones, a University of Minnesota professor of architecture. Jones, said to possess "a missionary zeal about community planning," was concerned that the town might grow in "a haphazard way" and become another mining town with little more than "a jumble of shacks and small houses." He implored Reserve officials to hire professional city planners and, during summer 1949, also supervised a group of architecture students who prepared three proposals and models for the envisioned town.[300]

Reserve officials, in fact, concluded that the state's existing mining towns displayed a "piecemeal and haphazard" appearance and were typified by a "considerable amount of aged and blighted housing." After determining that typical planning approaches would not be adequate in dealing with the sociological needs of future employees and their families, Reserve commissioned a Chicago-based planning and architectural firm, Pace Associates, to design the new town. The firm began by employing sociologists who conducted surveys and assessed the attitudes and needs of prospective workers and their families who resided in northeastern Minnesota. The results revealed that the most desirable employees could be "enticed" to the area only by providing them with satisfactory housing and "adequate, economical, and civilized amenities." One company official expressed a succinct assessment of what was required, namely, "attractively landscaped houses rather than shacks." Reserve gave significant attention to town planning and construction, stated company president W. M. Kelley in 1953; such an approach, he argued, would make Silver Bay a fine place to live and work and "not only attract, but hold, the highest type people." Pace's staff saw the project as "a planner's dream"—an opportunity "to start from scratch on a brave new world."[301]

Three other mining and ore-processing towns that emerged elsewhere in the Lake Superior region during the early 1950s—Babbitt and Hoyt Lakes, Minnesota, and White Pine, Michigan—all planned by Pace, were built on areas of level land. The Silver Bay site—two and a half miles long, a half mile wide, and situated in a natural "amphitheater" bordered by rocky hills on two sides—posed a more difficult challenge. The town layout, which displays curvilinear streets that

**A view of Silver Bay, looking toward the west during the late 1950s, reveals the town's curvilinear streets, single-family homes, and treeless lots. Highway 61, which passes diagonally through the community, is flanked on the left by a section of the taconite production plant and employee parking lot. Outer Drive intersects with Highway 61 and passes by the Campton School (now the Minnesota Veteran's Home) and Silver Bay High School. Photograph by Durant Barclay Jr.**

generally conform to the topographic features of the site, is rather similar to America's postwar suburbs and differs completely from the grid plans that typify the region's older communities. A single road, Outer Drive, provides access to the town from Highway 61; eight feeder roads lead from Outer Drive to residential "loop" streets.[302]

By late 1952, houses were available for the families of forty workers and supervisors engaged in taconite plant construction. Most had two or three bedrooms, picture windows (sometimes called window walls), vertical and horizontal siding, and five basic designs with "varied in room arrangements." In July 1953, plans were announced for three hundred ranch style homes (255 three-bedroom and 45 two-bedroom units), built of panels that could be combined in ten different exterior combinations. The panels, reportedly "designed for comfortable living in the severest winters," were constructed by the Harnishfeger Corporation of Two Rivers, Wisconsin, and trucked 420 miles to Silver Bay. Once the panels had been placed upon the already completed concrete foundations, the roofs were finished in one day. The exterior walls revealed one of several colors and treatments—including yellow, green, gray, and "fawn." A typical floor plan had a living room, a pass-through that connected the dining room and kitchen, three bedrooms with spacious closets, a bathroom, a utility room, and a garage.[303]

A smaller number of "stick-built" houses were constructed by the Modern Homes Manufacturing Corporation of Biwabik, located sixty-four miles north of Silver Bay. Unlike the prefabricated houses produced by Harnishfeger, advertisements for the Modern Homes residences claimed that their "assembly line techniques" would provide an exceptional product that was "designed and constructed to withstand the rigors of northern Minnesota's long winters and the extreme range of yearly temperatures." The finished houses, with painted interiors and exteriors, were transported by heavy-duty trucks to Silver Bay and completed "just four weeks from the day the first nail is driven." Prospective buyers could choose from five house plans—named Mary Ellen, Taconite, Babbitt, Reserve, and Erie. All were provided with steel cabinets, modern baths, and contemporary appliances and equipped either with forced-air furnaces or baseboard hot water heating systems. Isadore Cohen, writing for the *Duluth News-Tribune* in September 1954, was impressed with what she observed: "the houses, mostly ranch type, are the kind the average working man would give his eyeteeth to own."[304]

While hourly laborers and their families inhabited the smaller houses, salaried Reserve managers, supervisors, and executives lived in larger dwellings situated along a section of Arthur Circle called "Silk Stocking Row" by some residents; similar houses at the top of Outer Drive were located on what was dubbed "Snob Hill" or "Snob's Knob." During the town's formative years, Reserve financed most of the new housing, available either for purchase or rent. (Non-company employees, including teachers, were not allowed to purchase a Silver Bay house until 1963.) By April 1955, the town's 575 families were served by one elementary school and a shopping center that replaced the former Company Market. Overseeing the initial rental and sale of Silver Bay's dwellings, as well as management of the shopping center, was the John W. Galbreath Company of Columbus, Ohio. The Galbreath firm had considerable experience in operating and disposing of company town properties throughout the United States, including Morgan Park, a U.S. Steel community in Duluth that transitioned from corporate to individual ownership between 1942 and 1945.[305]

Commentaries that appeared during the initial decade of Silver Bay's settlement history ranged from pleased to critical. One reporter, after reviewing the town plan in 1952, foresaw "an ultra-modern little city" that would "far exceed even the wildest dreams of the earliest pioneers." Four years later, another correspondent chose to give a tongue-in-cheek description of Silver Bay and Babbitt: the towns have "no slums, no major crime, no juvenile delinquency, no serious traffic problems, no jails, no orphans, and no need for homes for the aged," he observed. "And although it's only temporary they also have no cemeteries." University of Minnesota architectural historian Donald Torbert, however, was not nearly as sanguine in his 1958 assessment. The opportunities to create well-designed buildings "were ignored or neglected on every hand" by Reserve and its architects, opined Torbert, especially the "undistinguished" houses and their "meaningless variations in color and sheathing materials." But it was mistreatment of the land, originally covered with conifers, birches, and aspens, that drew most of Torbert's ire: every tree, he lamented, had been removed from the townsite. Another reviewer made a similar observation in his portrayal of the surrounding hills, which were "stripped and bleak in mid-winter." A correspondent for the *Minneapolis Tribune* expressed some dismay over the small saplings that appeared on Silver Bay's residential lawns and yards in 1956. "The trees, all new," he observed, "have a lot of growing to do." But a writer for the American Iron and Steel Institute, who also visited Silver Bay in 1956, gave the new town a glowing appraisal. "There is a tailored look about the landscape," he commented, "that makes this midway point one of the most attractive along the 150-mile North Shore Drive."[306]

By 1960, when young families with several children filled most of Silver Bay's eight hundred houses, the population reached 3,725. At this time, U.S. Census standards revealed that almost 30 percent of the dwellings were overcrowded—a figure considerably greater than the state average. As family sizes declined somewhat during the next two decades, Silver Bay's population fell to 3,505 in 1970 and to 2,915 in 1980. The figure would shrink even more precipitously over the next ten years. Only 1,895 residents were counted in 1990—a direct reflection of the three-year-long taconite plant closure during the 1980s. By early 1985, almost 150 houses were on the real estate market, some for as little as $10,000. The low prices and a nationwide advertising campaign resulted in the sale of numerous residences, although most were used as retirement and seasonal properties. The population of 2,070 permanent residents in 2000 represented a gain of 175 since 1990, although the subsequent totals fell back to late twentieth-century levels: 1,885 in 2010 and 1,760 in 2020.[307]

The citizens of Silver Bay have basically adjusted to the new normal, but some recent part-time residents may not always understand the emotions and sensitivities that are linked to the community's eventful and often-traumatic past. Calling one's recently purchased property a "summer home" is acceptable, declared Silver Bay pioneer Ruth Koepke, but identifying it as a "hunting shack" is offensive.[308]

Silver Bay remains a unique community, not only because of its single-industry origins and economy, but also because of its residences: other than the Twin Cities area, this small North Shore city has one of the largest contiguous concentrations of postwar housing in Minnesota. Some modifications certainly have been made to Silver Bay's housing stock over several decades, but the overall scale, character, and appearance of its single- and one-and-a-half-story dwellings remain evident today. Likewise, Silver Bay's civic and institutional buildings reflect some of the features that characterized American construction practices during the 1950s and 1960s. Because of its relative remoteness, Silver Bay is often overlooked as a stand-alone prototype of the postwar building boom that occurred throughout many areas of Minnesota and the United States.

## Schools and Churches

Unlike most communities, where institutions emerge over many years or even decades, Silver Bay was an "instant city." The rapid emergence of three schools and three churches reveals the unique approach that was followed in providing Silver Bay with these services during a relatively brief and often hectic seven-year period from 1954 to 1961.

In 1950, just twenty-eight school-age children lived with their parents close to the construction site, but when the "mushrooming enrollment" figure reached eighty kindergarten and elementary students in 1952, four new houses on Banks Avenue were opened as classrooms. Within a year, 112 elementary students were enrolled in the makeshift classrooms; another 48 were accommodated in Beaver Bay's two-room schoolhouse; and 75 junior and senior high school students rode buses to Two Harbors. Silver Bay's first elementary school (Campton) opened in 1954, a junior–senior high school (Kelley) opened in 1958, and a second elementary school (MacDonald) opened in 1961. The Campton and Kelley schools were entirely funded by Reserve, whereas some three-fourths of the bonds issued for the MacDonald school were supported by company property taxes. Because of declining student numbers, Campton closed in 1978, MacDonald in 2000. All Silver Bay students, kindergarten through grade 12, now attend William Kelley.[309]

Also among Reserve's early practices was the allocation of lots for church construction, a process that began in 1953 when religious preference surveys were distributed among residents. The findings identified fifty-seven denominational groups, although many were represented by no more than a few individuals. Reserve, however, initially provided lots for just three religious alliances: Evangelical Lutheran, Roman Catholic, and "other" Protestant. All three groups opened churches between 1956 and 1958; buildings for Baptist and Lutheran–Missouri Synod congregations emerged a few years later.[310] But because of Silver Bay's subsequent population declines, the congregations have experienced significant membership losses.

### Silver Bay Marina, Protected Access
99 Beach Drive

Close to Silver Bay's southwestern entrance is a marina and protected harbor, constructed by the MDNR and the U.S. Army Corps of Engineers in 1999. Local officials hoped that the $8.2 million project would "tap into the tourist market that zips by every day on Minnesota Highway 61" and serve "as an antidote to the feast or famines . . . of an up-and-down taconite industry." Boating enthusiasts and MDNR officials also touted the facility as "a much-needed harbor of refuge . . . along a coastline that offers few shelters when Lake Superior turns angry." The site had already been stripped of its rocks and thin soils during the early 1950s when a breakwater, almost twenty-eight hundred feet in length, was constructed to protect ore carriers as they were loaded with taconite pellets. (The breakwater extends to a small landform, Pellet Island.) The marina, owned and managed by the City of Silver Bay and the MDNR, has 108 slips and also provides some on-land boat storage space for the winter months.[311]

Construction of the protected access started when more than ninety-two thousand tons of rocks and boulders, most from Babbitt, were trucked to Silver Bay and dumped into the water; they were then used to build a second breakwater situated perpendicularly to the older structure. The seven-acre "calm water basin" created by the L-shaped barrier has three docks—two for recreational boaters, the other for divers. Along the shoreline is the harbormaster's office and Bayside Park, which has a picnic area and opportunities to observe Great Lakes ore carriers as they take on cargoes of taconite pellets. Also nearby are kiosks with interpretive panels, one of which describes the *Hesper*, a wooden-hulled steamer that sank when a huge wave pushed it over a reef, with no loss of life, during a May 1905 storm. The *Hesper*'s remains, lying only three hundred yards east of the main breakwater, were listed in the National Register of Historic Places in 1994.[312]

### North Shore Adventure Park
43 Outer Drive

Since the mid-1950s, and for the next six decades, this key intersection at the northeastern corner of Highway 61 and Outer Drive was occupied by an automotive gasoline station. From 2017 to 2019, however, the site was converted into one of the North Shore's newest attractions—an adventure park with ten zip lines and seventy-five "elements." Advertisements for the facility emphasize the "endurance, confidence, [and] exhilarating experience" that participants can achieve when moving outside their "comfort zone."[313]

### Rocky Taconite
Intersection of Outer Drive and Adams Boulevard

The first commercial building that appears after the Outer Drive–Highway 61 intersection is the midcentury Mariner Motel (46 Outer Drive). Constructed of concrete, steel, and glass, the Mariner is an apt introduction to the predominantly single-story character of Silver Bay's built environment. Close to the Mariner is a smiling sculpture, *Rocky Taconite*. The cartoon-like character, placed on an irregularly shaped slab of taconite five to seven feet high, celebrates "the transition of taconite to steel" at Silver Bay as well as the "genius" of the people who succeeded in converting "a useless rock into a useful valuable product." The idea for such a unique figure came from Silver Bay dentist Otto Ringle, who promoted the sculpture as a symbolic equivalent of the famous Paul Bunyan and Babe the Blue Ox statues that stood in his hometown of Bemidji, Minnesota. Silver Bay officials agreed, anticipating that such a figure would draw attention and visitors to their community.[314]

Designed in 1961 by John Simrak, a Reserve Company sign painter, the statue was completed one year later for just $500 by the Star Iron Works, a Minneapolis metal fabricating company; ironworker Neil

***Rocky Taconite* was placed by the Silver Bay Post Office in 1962 before being moved to its current Outer Drive location in 1990.**

Forsberg oversaw the manufacturing process. Rocky's head and body, each formed from two pieces of one-quarter-inch metal, were hammered into spherical forms before being joined together. (The hammer marks give the piece a textured appearance.) The arms and legs, fashioned from pieces of pipe, connect Rocky's body to his hands and feet, which are covered by metal gloves and boots; one hand holds a pickaxe formerly used by Forsberg's grandfather, a Swedish immigrant miner. Placed atop Rocky's head is a saucer-like miner's hat, while a belt with a large buckle covers the welded seam that encircles his bulbous waist. Rocky's smile and facial features were chosen by the ironworkers after they used soapstone to sketch out several design possibilities. Though the statue was called "Mr. Taconite" for two years, a 1964 contest resulted in the name *Rocky Taconite*, which received many more votes than the other contender, "Petey Pellet."[315]

### Charles E. Campton School (*now* Minnesota Veterans Home–Silver Bay)
### 45 Banks Boulevard

Silver Bay's first school, named for Charles Campton, a longtime superintendent of Lake County's public education system, opened in 1954 and was dedicated in 1956. Students from grades 1–10 were initially in attendance, but the completion of a high school four years later allowed Campton to serve elementary-age children only. The single-story structure, with sixteen classrooms aligned along one wing, included a raised gymnasium roof at its center.[316]

Because of declining enrollments, Campton was closed before the 1978–79 school year began. The building successively housed several community organizations until 1988, when it was sold and converted, two years later, into a skilled nursing care facility for Minnesota military veterans and their surviving spouses. The Minnesota Department of Veterans Affairs oversaw the conversion of the former classrooms into four "neighborhood living spaces that combine the look and feel of a north woods lodge with all the comforts of a single-family home." Also emphasizing the Northwoods theme are displays of mounted fish and

**Located in a residential setting, the Minnesota Veterans Home was originally used as a Silver Bay elementary school.**

the heads of large game animals. Offices and a conference space occupy the former gymnasium. When the renovated building opened in 1990, Veterans Affairs officials pointed to its unique history. "The building was designed in 1953 to begin training and molding young Minnesota citizens," noted the first administrator, "and has now been remodeled and refurbished to provide for the health care of its elderly military veterans."[317]

### Silver Bay City Hall and Public Library
7 and 9 Davis Drive

Two simultaneous events occurred within the North Shore's "taconite town" during spring 1954: the designation of "Silver Bay" as an official place-name and the opening of a post office within the community. By October 1956, when 80 percent of Beaver Bay Township's population lived in Silver Bay, city residents sought "to benefit more directly from the flow of its tax money pouring into the coffers of the township" by voting, 531–251, to incorporate as a village. The initial village hall, police station, and library were situated in a former store building owned by Reserve. (That building, located by the shopping center parking lot, was later moved to Beaver Bay, where it serves as an Assembly of God church.) New buildings to accommodate the city hall and library opened along Davis Drive in 1967, as did a fire station on nearby Banks Boulevard.[318] The city hall and library, both constructed of brick-covered concrete, with infusions of steel, wood, and glass, are among the clearest North Shore expressions of the modest architectural modernism that typified many civic buildings in small-town America from the early 1950s to the mid-1970s.

### Silver Bay Shopping Center
Shopping Center Road

During the formative years of Silver Bay's development, workers and residents were able to purchase their necessities from a few small local stores and outlets. Only those merchants projected to generate an annual income of at least $5,000 were allowed to establish a business in the incipient community. Reserve was "very selective," stated one early business owner. "You had to follow just exactly the way they wanted it to be. There were a lot of regulations about things." The first business was a pharmacy that also served as a general store, where, other than groceries, residents could purchase just "about everything at that time"—gifts, clothing, flowers, yard items, and even television sets.[319]

In 1955, when Reserve opened a shopping center with 250 parking spaces, Silver Bay's citizens were informed that the selected site, while convenient to all areas of the community, would create very little traffic interference within residential districts. The single-story steel structure, with canopied arcades and glass fronts "all in a row," had separate grocery, jewelry, clothing, hardware, and drugstores as well as beauty and barber shops and a restaurant. The Norshore, a separate commercial building funded by local developers in 1957, housed medical providers, an attorney's office, the telephone company, a district office for the United Steel Workers Union, and a local Veterans of Foreign Wars post. Reserve, in 1958, sold the shopping center to the J. W. Galbreath Company, the same firm that managed the rent and sale of Silver Bay's residences. "We believe that towns which are free and independent of company ownership, direction, and influence are better towns," announced Reserve officials at the time. Galbreath would sell the structure a few years later, but the shopping center never achieved its envisioned outcomes. Even though "it was supposed to provide for all the needs of the people in the Silver Bay area," recalled Ed Maki, a longtime local citizen, "the great expectations of self-containment never materialized. There were still the frequent trips to Two Harbors and Duluth. These trips became family outings to escape the isolation of Silver Bay." Even fewer businesses are now located in the center, although various expansion and remodeling projects over the past seventy years have increased its overall footprint.[320]

### Sychar Lutheran Church
14 Edison Avenue

By 1951, Lutherans residing within the vicinity of the emerging taconite plant and townsite were holding services in homes and the Beaver Bay school; they would later gather in Silver Bay's temporary city hall and the Campton Elementary School. In June 1953, shortly after receiving designation as a "mission project" of the national Evangelical Lutheran Church, a group of residents in the Silver Bay area organized the Sychar Evangelical Lutheran Church congregation.

(The name "Sychar" was based on the biblical "Woman at the Well" parable mentioned in John 4:5.) One year later, Reserve donated a prime building lot—located at the intersection of Edison and Banks Boulevards—to the congregation. After a Duluth architect prepared a preliminary proposal for the structure, Evangelical Lutheran Church officials quickly urged the congregation's members to engage, instead, with Sövik, Mathre & Madson of Northfield, Minnesota—a firm well known for the high quality of its church design work. The principal partner, Edward Sövik, would later be termed "a theologian of space" for his extensive publications, which introduced new concepts "about the architecture of Christian worship and fellowship."[321]

A flat-roofed structure that opened in late 1955 would accommodate Sychar's large congregation over the next ten years. One feature of the building, considered vital in a congregation comprising almost entirely families with young children, was the insulated "crying room," which had a window that separated the "many fussy infants and toddlers" from ongoing religious services. The building was converted into an educational wing following the completion, in 1965, of a 320-seat sanctuary, a sacristy, and a choir loft, all covered by a triangular, steeply pitched roof that rests on the building's sidewalls. (Sychar differs from many of Sövik's mid-century churches, which have moderately sloping roofs.) Because of its form, Sychar is often termed an A-frame—a term, observes religious architecture scholar Gretchen Buggeln, that was "broadly and colloquially applied to [many] churches by postwar Americans." However, unlike a classic A-frame—"a rigid triangular frame in which the steeply pitched roof extends to the ground and doubles as side walls"—Sychar's structural system comprises several three-hinge arches, all constructed of glued laminated timbers ("glulams") fabricated from small pieces of wood.[322]

**The congregation of Sychar Lutheran Church, in 1954, was the first Silver Bay religious group to receive a building lot.**

Punctuating Sychar's sidewalls are thirteen multicolored stained glass windows, designed and fabricated by Universal Conway Studios of Winona, Minnesota, to create a "bold, sculptured, modern, and faceted glass style." Seven more windows were added to the narthex during the 1990s. The congregation, throughout Silver Bay's period of peak population and employment, accommodated "shift workers" by providing both Sunday morning and evening services. Today, the much smaller Sychar congregation faces many challenges as it strives to care for the large edifice while simultaneously offering programs and services that meet the needs of a smaller and aging membership.[323] Nevertheless, because of its prominent location, imposing scale, and unique fenestration, Sychar maintains its position as a highly visible landmark within a neighborhood of low-rise homes.

### United Protestant Church of Silver Bay
### 17 Horn Boulevard

The origins of Silver Bay's United Protestant congregation date to September 1953, when the Minnesota Council of Churches (MCC) sent a chaplain, the Reverend Cecil Hankins, to the emerging community. Because other Protestant groups, outside of the Lutherans, included relatively small numbers of members in the area, MCC addressed a question that was unique to the organization: "could several denominations together sponsor a local church?" Soon, representatives of at least eight groups agreed to organize a United Protestant Church congregation and build a church funded by its members and MCC. (At the time, Silver Bay was only the second Minnesota community

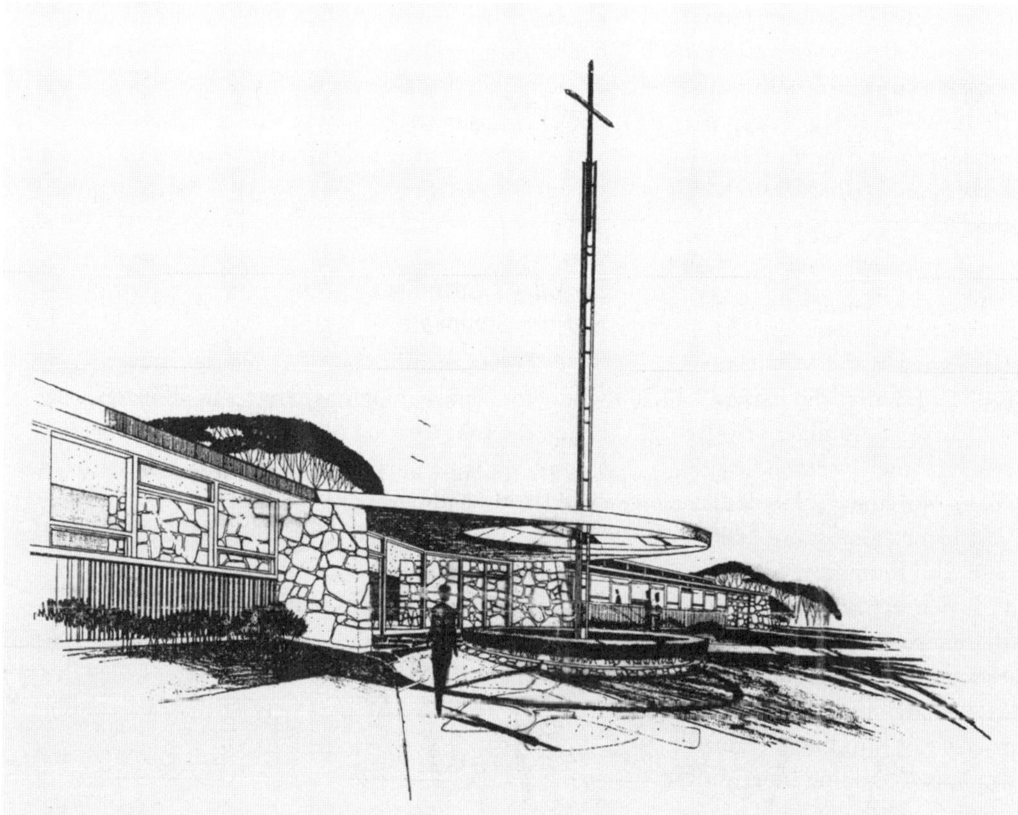

**Architect A. Reinhold Melander's 1955 drawing of Silver Bay's United Protestant Church. Courtesy of Duluth Public Library.**

to form a United Protestant Church; another congregation, established in 1922 with the same name and organizational philosophy, is still active in the former Duluth company town of Morgan Park.) When reporting on Silver Bay's United Protestant Church dedication in 1956, the *New York Times* termed the congregation "one of the nation's most unusual."[324]

Unlike Sychar Lutheran, the "modernistic design" prepared for Silver Bay's United church was not based on new concepts of religious fellowship, worship, and architectural space. Instead, reported Hankins in 1956, the choice of a contemporary design represented the congregation's wish to incorporate "the desires of all the denominations." Additionally, Duluth architect A. Reinhold Melander's proposal almost certainly was influenced by a change that began appearing in the religious landscape of suburban America by the early 1950s: the building of churches that would blend into their neighborhoods. The functional and rectangular features of United Protestant—built of stone, redwood, steel, and glass, with windows overlooking a creek and trees—mirror the horizontality and low profile of the city's houses. But because of the angularity displayed by its two wings—one for the nave, the other for a narthex, office, and the rooms used by the youngest children—Silver Bay's United church is not as "boxy" as many other religious structures of that period. (The fellowship hall, kitchen, and classrooms were built into a small slope located below grade.) Indeed, the United building might even be considered "playful," an observation shared by some congregants who termed it a "church for the Jetsons"—a reference to the futuristic animated television show of the 1960s.[325]

Befitting its name, the church includes several expressions of Christian unity. The cornerstone has a symbol for the World Council of Churches—a ship at sea enclosed by a circle, as well as a small Christian cross and the Greek word for "ecumenical," *OIKOUMENE*. Much more visible and dominant is the symbolic "unity circle" that stands at the church entrance: extending through the large ringlike form, which is about ten feet above the ground, are three steel shafts with a cross at the apex. United's congregation has, since 1985, maintained an affiliation with the MCC, and now represents five Protestant denominations: American Baptist, Disciples of Christ, Presbyterian, United Church of Christ, and United Methodist.[326]

### William M. Kelley Schools
137 Banks Boulevard

Silver Bay's high school, designed by the Minneapolis architectural firm of Bissell and Blaire, and named for Reserve's first president, occupies a prominent twelve-acre hillside location between Outer Drive and Banks Boulevard. At the time of its November 1958 dedication, the facility had 835 students, almost one-half of them pupils in grades 1–6 who soon moved into the new Mary MacDonald Elementary School. George Starkovich, Kelley's first principal, recalled that because of the high-quality materials used in the $4 million high school, it was "a model of architecture [and] model of sustainability." A University of Minnesota educator who evaluated the well-equipped building shortly after its completion also termed it "a combination of beauty and simplicity rarely achieved in large schools." In 2010, after a half century of use, Starkovich observed that the structure still remained as strong as the day of its construction. All Silver Bay students, from kindergarten through high school, are once again accommodated in the building, which is now called William M. Kelley Schools.[327]

### Mary MacDonald Elementary School (*now* Mary MacDonald Business Center)
99 Edison Boulevard

Because of the many elementary-age students who overcrowded both the Campton and Kelley Schools by the late 1950s, plans were made to construct a new school on Edison Boulevard. The building opened in September 1961 and was dedicated in May 1962 as the Mary MacDonald Elementary School, which honored the irrepressible Beaver Bay businesswoman and teacher who played such a major role in Lake County's public educational system prior to her passing in 1959. By 1985, however, student numbers had fallen to such an extent that plans were made to close the school. A public outcry delayed the shutdown, even as enrollment figures dropped from a previous high of 800 to 330 by 1990. Finally, because of continued declines throughout Lake County, the school closed in May 2004 and was later converted into the Mary MacDonald Business Center, which is now used for commercial and civic functions.[328]

### St. Mary's Catholic Church
57 Horn Boulevard

Silver Bay's Catholics began using the Beaver Bay school for Sunday religious services in 1954, one year before the congregation moved their activities into the Campton Elementary School. Following the dedication of Lutheran and United Protestant churches, respectively, in 1954 and 1956, Catholics expressed hope that they, too, could "erect a suitable house of worship." In 1957, the congregation approved the proposal for

**The taconite baptismal font at St. Mary's Catholic Church. Photograph by Lynn Bjorkman, 2017.**

St. Mary's Catholic Church, designed by Duluth architect Arthur C. Lucas Jr. Later that year, a Christmas Eve Mass was conducted in the still-incomplete $180,000 structure. The dedication of St. Mary's, which had space for 450 parishioners, occurred in 1958. (A catechetical center and rectory were added ten years later.) The gable ends of the church were enhanced by a series of stained glass windows, entitled *Litany of the Blessed Virgin Mary*. The windows on the entrance facade, however, were removed and replaced by a solid wall in 2018, an action deemed necessary because of construction flaws that occurred during a 2012 building project. The windows, which had been subjected to the direct impacts of northeasterly winds, rain, and snow for many years, were also removed in 2018; eventually, they will be framed, hung inside, and illuminated with back lighting.[329]

St. Mary's received considerable attention in 1958 when five tons of taconite rock were converted into the church altar and baptismal font. The process began with the quarrying of two large pieces of rock at Babbitt, which were then shipped to a granite company in Cold Spring, Minnesota. Once there, both pieces were carefully shaped into the altar and font, polished, and transported back to Silver Bay. "It is fitting," noted the congregation once both were in place, "that the very substance on which our community depends is also used in our religious life."[330]

### Black Beach Park and Campground
East Lakeview Drive

Black Beach Park, located at the eastern end of Silver Bay, stands out as an unusual North Shore landscape feature because of its fine sand, comprising tailings discharged by the taconite plant. Although official transfer of the thirty-two-acre site from Cleveland-Cliffs to the MDNR and City of Silver Bay did not occur until 2015, local residents had been visiting the site's three beaches (Black, Peach, and Agate) for several years. Since achieving official public status, the shoreline's jagged shoreline and protected cove have also become a "hotspot" for North Shore tourists. Most popular is Black Beach—a place where the forces of "time and nature have restored the beach's health" and simultaneously retained its black color. The fifty sites that compose the full-service campground, which opened in 2020, are typically filled throughout the tourist season.[331]

## Beaver Bay Township (Continued)

Beaver Bay Township appears once again, just over a mile northeast of the Outer Drive–Highway 61 intersection. From there, the highway passes through the lower section of Tettegouche State Park and a forty-acre parcel of privately owned land that, since 1924, has been known as Illgen City. Highway 61 then continues through Beaver Bay Township before entering Lake County Unorganized Territory No. 1.

### Palisade Head
5512 Highway 61

Palisade Head, a much-visited North Shore site, is an outstanding example of a rhyolite dome that towers more than three hundred feet above Lake Superior. Nonetheless, it would not be until spring 1936—after enrollees from CCC Company 721 in Finland spent a year working on the grounds—that Palisade was opened to visitors and tourists. George Archibald, a forester who served as Company 721's superintendent, did not find much to admire at the site before he and his CCC crew began working on the project. "Palisade Head was 80 acres of utterly worthless land," he reported, which could be accessed only by engaging in an "hour's stiff climb through the matted undergrowth. . . . Steep rock cliffs had to be blasted away and large valleys and cuts filled with rock debris." But, despite the conditions, Archibald concluded that the "marvelous views in all directions warranted this most difficult struggle to the top." The superintendent also pointed out how Palisade's natural qualities had been preserved by his CCC crew. "Where steps were necessary," he wrote, "they were arranged in such a fashion as to resemble natural rock outcroppings rather than the artificial work of man."[332]

Palisade is now part of but not contiguous to Tettegouche State Park, which lies about one and a half miles to the northeast. Virtually all motorists and hikers access the summit of Palisade Head along the narrow winding road that CCC Company 721's enrollees constructed during the mid-1930s. Now, however, a small but growing number of adventurous climbers

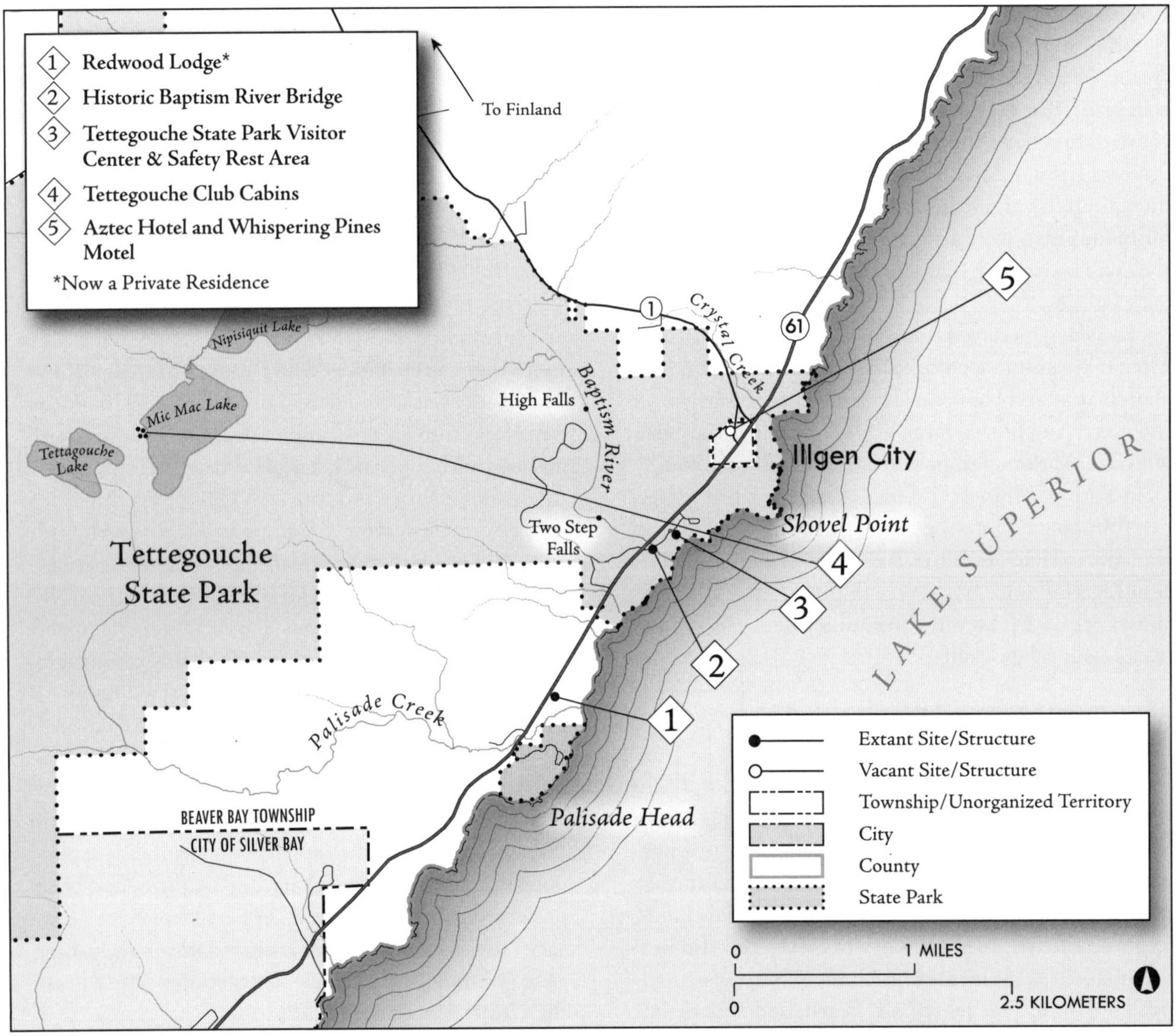

1 Redwood Lodge*
2 Historic Baptism River Bridge
3 Tettegouche State Park Visitor Center & Safety Rest Area
4 Tettegouche Club Cabins
5 Aztec Hotel and Whispering Pines Motel
*Now a Private Residence
To Finland
Crystal Creek
61
Nipisiquit Lake
Mic Mac Lake
Tettagouche Lake
High Falls
Baptism River
Illgen City
Shovel Point
Two Step Falls
Tettegouche State Park
LAKE SUPERIOR
Palisade Creek
Palisade Head
BEAVER BAY TOWNSHIP
CITY OF SILVER BAY
Extant Site/Structure
Vacant Site/Structure
Township/Unorganized Territory
City
County
State Park
0
1 MILES
0
2.5 KILOMETERS

A view of Palisade Head looking toward the northeast. In the distant background is another outstanding Lake Superior and North Shore natural feature: Shovel Point.

Between Palisade Head and the Tettegouche State Park Visitor Center is a former business, Redwood Lodge, dating to the 1950s, that provided meals and rooms for guests. The building became a diner, the Redwood Inn, following its 1960s purchase by Silver Bay teacher and athletic coach Lino Rauzi and his wife, Nancy Peterson Rauzi. Though the building is strictly a residence today, the Redwood Inn sign still stands by it.

consider Palisade Head the state's "crown jewel," a place that conveys "an air of seriousness not found at other Minnesota crags." Since most of Palisade Head is maintained in a seminatural state, only a short rock wall separates the cliff's edge from observation points at the peak, where stunning vistas of the Sawtooth Mountains and Split Rock Lighthouse are provided.[333]

### Tettegouche State Park Visitor Center and Safety Rest Area

5702 Highway 61

A total of 570,000 people visited Tettegouche State Park in 2021, the fourth-highest number for any Minnesota state park. The vast majority of people stop at the eleven-thousand-square-foot, $7 million, energy-efficient Tettegouche State Park Visitor Center and Safety Rest Area, which opened in 2014. Although the facility offers several services—exhibits, information, a gift store, and meeting spaces—perhaps none are more popular than its restrooms, which remain open year-round, twenty-four hours a day. The central offices for three state parks—Tettegouche, Temperance River, and George H. Crosby Manitou—are situated within the structure.[334]

### Tettegouche State Park

Tettegouche State Park, established in 1979, includes several important natural features— Palisade Head; a smaller rhyolite dome known as Shovel Point; the lower section and mouth of the Baptism River (named the River au Baptême by the French); four waterfalls, one of them the tallest waterfall (sixty-four feet) situated entirely within Minnesota; one mile of Lake Superior coastline; four inland lakes; and a rugged area of the Lake Superior Highlands. Also within the park are a historic bridge, several buildings that once composed a private wilderness camp, and the limited remnants of an unsuccessful corundum excavation at Crystal Bay. Because of its important natural and cultural features, Tettegouche is a prime section of the North Shore Biocultural Region and is one of Minnesota's "crown jewels."[335]

In 1886, Duluth Civil War veteran Charles Graves paid $440 for 352 acres of federally owned land at the river's mouth. Graves sold the acreage just six weeks later to the recently formed Baptism River Club, whose members proposed to breed, preserve, and propagate brook trout and other fish species in the river. In 1887, the group's forty members, most from Duluth and the Twin Cities, built a clubhouse overlooking Lake Superior; the caretakers were French Canadian Peter Pyette and his German wife, Anna.[336]

Baptist minister Myron Cooley, a club member from Detroit Lakes, Minnesota, described the array of items that were unloaded from steamers at the river's mouth in 1894: "trunks, boxes, bags, grips, bundles, baskets, guns in cases and out, ammunition boxes, trout creels, rods of half a dozen varieties, tackle boxes, [and] a water spaniel." Eventually, Pyette would build a wooden bridge over the Baptism, which made the transfer of people and goods much easier. By the early 1900s, however, the members were catching fewer fish; the charter was allowed to expire in 1916, and most of the holding was sold, in 1926, to the recently widowed Anna Pyette and her son George. Three years later, the Cliff Club, formed by a group of Twin Citians, secured a ten-year lease from the Pyettes, which gave them entrée to the land and clubhouse. In 1945, the State of Minnesota included part of the Pyettes' property within a five-hundred-acre land purchase designated as Baptism River State Park. Few improvements were made, however, until the entire property was renamed Tettegouche State Park in 1979.[337]

**The rustic style features of the Tettegouche lodge are revealed in this image, taken during the period when it was owned by Clement Quinn. Courtesy of Tettegouche State Park.**

Alger, Smith & Company of Knife River was also heavily engaged in logging a large area by the Baptism River from 1895 to 1905. The company employed Algonquin names to identify the lakes—Mic Mac, Nicado, Nipisiquit, and Tettegouche—on its property. In 1911, the Tettegouche Club, formed by a group of Duluth sportsmen, purchased about one thousand acres of the cutover holding. The members, by 1921, had constructed a lodge, kitchen/dining hall, and several other structures of unhewn pine and cedar logs, many overlooking Mic Mac Lake. The club managed the property "as if it were a park": fishing was allowed, but not hunting. When the club disbanded in 1921, one member, Duluth mining merchant Clement Quinn, acquired the acreage; he would, over the next fifty years, add more land and buildings to his "baronial estate." Serving as cook and caretaker from 1955 to 1971 was Maria Ostman, a colorful Croatian woman whose love of Tettegouche was surpassed by few others. "It was heaven to me," she later recalled. In 1977, six years after brothers John and Karl deLaittre acquired Quinn's 3,385-acre domain, the men offered an $880,000 option to The Nature Conservancy, which held the acreage until passage of a 1979 legislative bonding bill that allowed the MDNR to acquire the property for the purpose of developing Tettegouche State Park. The later addition of Baptism River Park and other adjacent properties would expand Tettegouche into a 9,350-acre holding.[338]

Included in the acquisition were the Tettegouche Club lodge and ten other structures, most constructed

**Six new Chandler automobiles cross over the Baptism River Bridge, 1928 or 1929. The vehicles, which arrived on a ship that docked in Duluth, were being driven to a dealership in Port Arthur, Ontario. Courtesy of Tettegouche State Park.**

between 1911 and 1925. Many have similarities with the rustic style popularized in the Adirondack region of New York from 1870 to 1930: horizontal and vertical log construction; open corner notching; overhanging roofs and wide eaves; simply proportioned, multipaned windows; screened-in porches; and native stone fireplaces and chimneys. The inherent qualities of the Tettegouche forest environment are also expressed in the natural color and grain of the buildings' interior wood surfaces, framing elements, and furniture. Four cabins and the lodge have been restored and are now accessible to hikers, bikers, skiers, and snowshoers. The lodge serves as a day-use shelter, whereas the rental cabins are open year-round.[339]

Close to the visitors' center is a five-span Baltimore steel truss bridge (identified by the extra diagonals on the bottom half of the span), constructed over the Baptism River in 1923–24. Because Baltimore trusses were typically employed when building railroad crossings, the Baptism River structure has been termed "a rare example of a deck-truss bridge in Minnesota." A new bridge, constructed nearby in 1969 as part of a highway realignment project, led to the acquisition of the older structure by the MDNR in the mid-1980s. The rehabilitated older bridge, now part of the Tettegouche State Park road system, includes two traffic lanes and a cantilevered deck that has a pedestrian walkway overlooking Lake Superior.[340]

At the northeastern end of Tettegouche State Park are Shovel Point and Crystal Bay. Shovel Point, accessed along a trail that follows ancient lava flows, has numerous well-built steps that culminate in a viewing platform where hikers gain superb impressions of Palisade Head and nearby sea caves. One of Shovel Point's best-known landmarks, however, disappeared in late 2019—a piece of volcanic rock, fifteen to twenty feet high, known colloquially as the Sea Stack. The free-standing vertical "stack," once connected to the mainland by a natural stone arch that fell into Lake Superior in 2010, crumbled and completely disappeared from view during the appropriately named Winter Storm Ezekiel of late November 2019. Shovel Point, like Palisade Head, is also popular with rock climbers, although ecologists lament the dieback of fragile vegetation that is occurring on the cliff top's staging area because of heavy foot traffic.[341]

Cave of the Waves, the longest sea arch on the North Shore, is located along a secluded section of the Crystal Bay coastline. Close to the mouth of Crystal Creek is a property once owned by the Minnesota Abrasive Company during its futile 1890s search for corundum, a mineral used in the manufacture of abrasive products. In 1902, the five Two Harbors men who later formed the 3M Company acquired the land, where they built a six-story crushing plant, a dock, a warehouse, and an aerial tramway that extended to the previous mine site. Once the men realized that the mineral was anorthosite, a worthless rock, the company turned its attention to the highly successful manufacture of sandpaper. The majority of foundations for 3M's operations are buried under Highway 61, although a few moss-covered footings and bricks remain elsewhere.[342]

## Illgen City

Situated along Highway 61 and within Tettegouche State Park is a forty-acre private landholding, identified as Illgen City in 1924. The unincorporated enclave was developed and named by Rudy Illgen, after the German émigré, accompanied by his wife, Mary, two children, and father, departed their "Scientific Ranch," the business they established along the inland section of roadway in 1921. Recognizing the new highway's potential economic opportunities, Illgen acquired some of 3M's Crystal Bay land, which he termed the "most unique place on the North Shore." For years thereafter, motorists were greeted by an entrance sign that proclaimed, "Illgen City Population 4, Room for Lots More." Although Illgen City is a century-old place-name, its population has never exceeded ten residents.[343]

### Aztec Hotel and Whispering Pines Motel *(razed)*
Intersection of Minnesota Highways 1 and 61

Rudy Illgen and his wife, Mary, known for "always working together," harvested the largest trees at Crystal Bay, used their sawmill to convert the logs into lumber, and began constructing the idiosyncratic Aztec Hotel on the highway's upper side in 1925. The hotel design reportedly was influenced by an earlier trip Illgen had

**A view of Rudy and Mary Illgen's Aztec Hotel during the late 1920s, shortly after its opening.**

The Aztec Hotel's interior revealed Rudy Illgen's interpretation of Mesoamerican iconography.

made to the Mayan archaeological site of Chichen Itza, Mexico, where he was impressed by its famous stepped pyramid, the Temple of the Warriors. It is quite likely, however, that Illgen also had some familiarity with the Mayan revival style that was gaining popularity in the United States during the 1920s. Although the term refers to the civilization established by the Mayans in Mexico and Central America, architects often borrowed from the decorative and artistic expressions of other Mesoamerican cultures, particularly the Aztecs.[344]

The Aztec's six third-story hotel rooms were set back from the first- and second-level platforms, which created a structure that slightly imitated a step pyramid. Although Illgen's hotel was constructed of lumber, the exterior walls were later covered with stucco and white paint, which, to Illgen, mimicked the stone and marble of Chichen Itza's ancient buildings. But the hotelkeeper most clearly expressed his interpretation of Mesoamerican iconography within the lobby and dining area, where there was a high ceiling as well as a lengthy, carved mahogany bar. Most noticeable, however, were two vertical columns festooned with symbols and connected by a large lintel, somewhat reminiscent of a Mayan doorway. The interior details were also visible at night and during periods of dim illumination because of the electricity derived from a generator powered by Illgen's Mack truck. The Illgens also showed movies, ordered from Columbia Pictures in Hollywood, to as many as 150 people, who could be seated in the dining room; they also organized basket socials and scheduled public dances where the Haveri Brothers band of nearby Finland often provided music.[345]

As a friend of Floyd B. Olson, Minnesota's Farmer-Labor Party governor, Illgen ran for a seat in Minnesota's House of Representatives in 1934, using the campaign slogan "My true intent—is for your delight." He lost the election, but only by forty-eight votes. In 1936, the always-innovative German émigré developed and patented his plans for a "cabinola"—a very small building furnished with only a bed and toilet—intended for motorists who sought out the most inexpensive overnight accommodations. Although Illgen intended to construct and name "a cozy cabin for every state in [the] union," his project ended at number thirty in 1941, when the Aztec closed because of a downturn in tourist business that occurred after the United States entered World War II.[346]

The Aztec's reopening was celebrated with a public gathering in June 1945. Mary Illgen's comments during the event recalled the positive impressions of visitors who had experienced the "enjoyment and happiness" of the North Shore and departed "with memories never to be forgotten." Her always visionary and optimistic husband, however, resolutely focused on the future, predicting that the North Shore would become America's "Silver Avenue," but only if "science, chemistry, imagination, and ingenuity" were applied to the development of its natural resources. The couple's daughter and son-in-law, Pauline and Leonard Peterson, moved to Illgen City in 1945 and acquired the property six years later, when the founders retired and moved to Florida. The Petersons also built Whispering Pines—a single-story motel—immediately west of the Aztec. After disposing of the Aztec in 1957, the couple began marketing the cabinolas before a scheduled highway rerouting occurred. The Aztec burned down in 1958, and Whispering Pines experienced a similar fate years later, well after the Petersons had sold both properties. A newer version of the Whispering Pines Motel opened on the site during the early 2000s but closed several years later. Only two original cabinolas remain in the Illgen City area.[347]

**Nine of the thirty cabinolas that Rudy Illgen built between 1936 and 1941 on the Lake Superior side of Highway 61.**

## Unorganized Territory No. 1: Lake County

The final eight miles of Highway 61 within Lake County are located in Unorganized Territory No. 1 (UT-1). Although the territory covers 190 square miles, it only has some 175 permanent residents, most of whom live along the highway. The entrance to UT-1 occurs by Kennedy Landing, a small cove where Scottish immigrants Charles and Mary Kennedy settled during the 1890s. Kennedy oversaw Alger–Smith's local log-loading operations and served as a supervisor when Crystal Bay Township was organized in 1904. (At that time, the township's boundaries extended well beyond Kennedy Landing.) Mary Kennedy provided meals for township officials who gathered at the couple's house for monthly meetings, fed the workers engaged in building nearby roads and bridges, and served as a custodian for Crystal Bay's first township hall, built adjacent to their house in 1905. The Kennedy Landing dock was used by early settlers who disembarked from steamboats and made their way to Finland and other inland outposts.[348]

The completion of Highway 1 in 1924–25 provided motorists with clear views of Kennedy Landing and Lake Superior, but a major 1969 realignment that created the "Kennedy Cut" eliminated its picturesque curves and vistas. (The parallel rock walls created by the incision are among the highest along Highway 61.) For several years thereafter, motorists could still experience the old road when driving by or stopping at Kennedy's Landing Campground. The campground was later removed, and the original highway now serves as a private driveway for some homes, including one that is perched on the former right-of-way.[349]

### Little Marais

Also located within UT-1 is a physical feature originally identified by the Anishinaabe as Waginokaning (Round Lodge). Later called "Little Marais," the name is often considered a French translation of "Little Marsh"

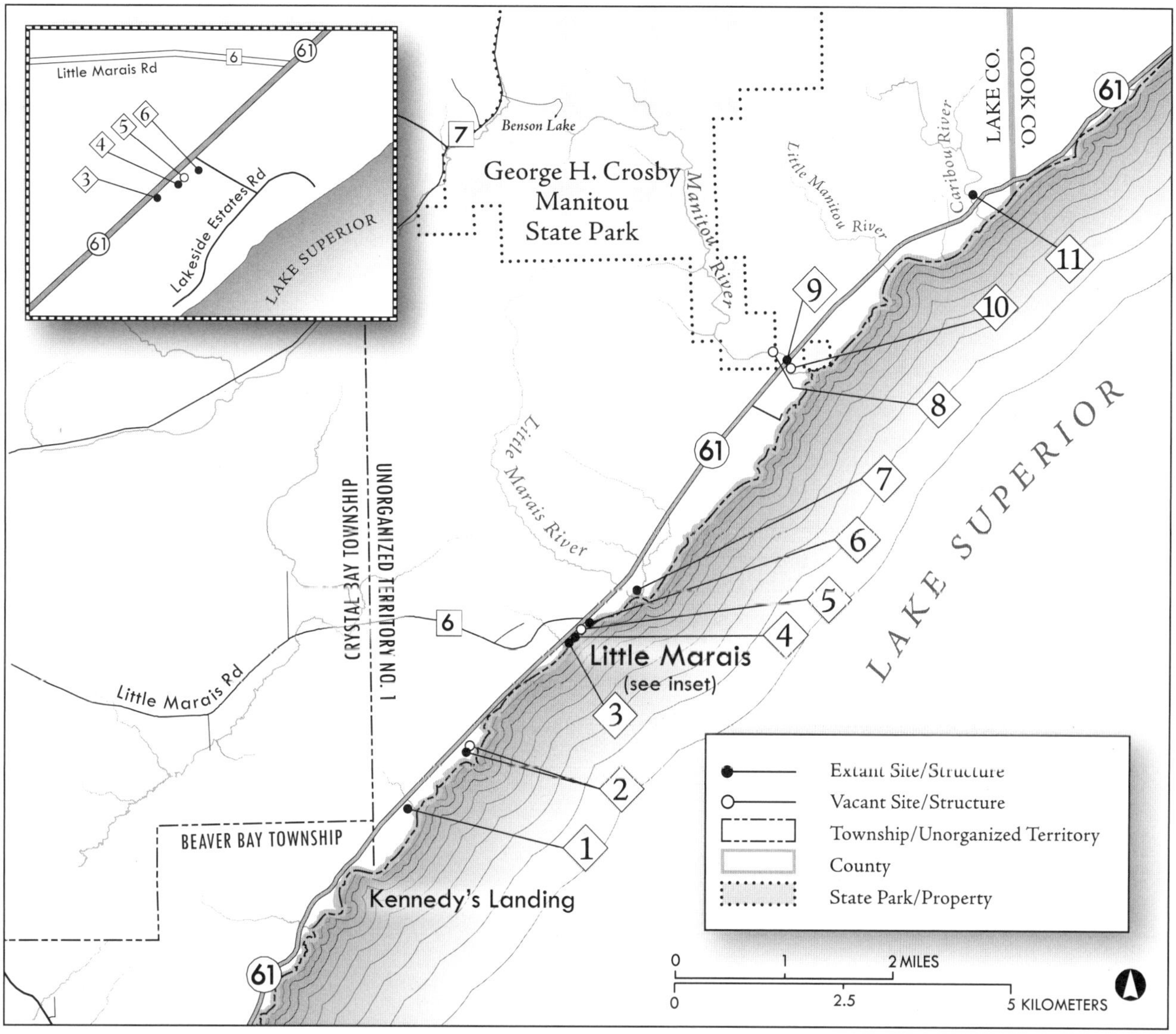


1. Fish Out of Water
2. Spirit of Gitche Gumee* and former Colonial Inn
3. Little Marais Community Club
4. Fenstad Brothers General Store/Eagles Nest Gifts*
5. Art Fenstad's Standard Service
6. Fenstad Homestead/Lake Side Inn/Stone Hearth Bed and Breakfast*
7. Fenstad's Resort
8. Historic Manitou River Bridge
9. Current Manitou River Bridge
10. Finch's Manitou River Resort
11. Caribou Falls State Wayside

*Now a private residence

or "Little Swamp." In 1943, however, the distinguished Minnesota historian Grace Lee Nute pointed out that French Canadian voyageurs had a "special vocabulary in which the word 'Marais' on a coast referred to a harbor of refuge, or a placid, protected cove or bay." A small trading post and a few sugar camps existed at the mouth of the Little Marais River by 1848, and log rafting occurred later in the century. The first Norwegian immigrants to arrive during the late 1880s and early 1890s developed fishing camps and farms and later provided facilities for overnight tourists. A post office operated from 1905 to 1964, a schoolhouse existed between 1905 and 1950, and a local telephone company was formed in 1915. Today, a single long-lived resort, several tourist cabins, a gift store, and a former one-room schoolhouse identify the small settlement. One Norwegian surname, "Fenstad," has remained a constant in Little Marais since the late nineteenth century.[350]

### Scandia House and Antilla's Gifts (*now* Fish Out of Water)
6146 Highway 61

Frank Antilla, the youngest of fifteen children (five of whom died in childhood) born to Finnish immigrants in 1927, described his North Dakota birthplace as "a lonely, unfriendly prairieland, with an incessant wind that blew most of the rich topsoil to other more fortunate places." Antilla later moved to Minnesota's Iron Range with his mother before joining the U.S. Merchant Marine, at age sixteen, during World War II. Following his discharge and subsequent 1952 marriage to Berdie Wivell, Antilla found employment at Silver Bay's taconite plant. The couple settled in Little Marais, where they established two stores in separate buildings—Scandia House and Antilla's Gifts—both of which offered "upscale gifts and a variety of them." Several other owners have followed the Antillas to the site since the early 2000s, when the couple sold their property. Now known as Fish Out of Water, the owners, who typically close the business during winter, entice prospective customers with their slogan "Nothing you need, everything you want."[351]

### Colonial Inn and Dining Room *(razed)* and Spirit of Gitche Gumee *(now a seasonal residence)*
6228 Highway 61

In 1934, North Shore enthusiasts Leonard and Evelyn Ryan Rudstrom moved from Illinois to Little Marais, where they constructed the first of more than a dozen rental cabins situated between Highway 61 and Lake

The lower story of the Little Marais Lodge was built of logs by Leonard and Evelyn Rudstrom in 1934.

**Soon after World War II, the Rudstroms covered their original lodge, *left*, with clapboard siding and renamed it the Colonial Inn and Dining Room. They also constructed the adjacent building, which had a store on the lower level and tourist rooms above.**

Superior. Soon the Rudstroms would add a building, the Little Marais Lodge, to their property. The lower level displayed round, tightly fitted horizontal logs with saddle notch corners, while the second floor, built of frame and board, had several tourist rooms, each topped by a small gable roof. An expansive dining area, attached to the rear of the lodge in 1939, could seat as many as seventy patrons, all of whom, the Rudstroms claimed, were served by "courteous and efficient waitresses." During the early years of World War II, the couple and their young daughter Rosemary moved to upstate New York, where Rudstrom worked for two years as a civil engineer. After the "Three Rudstroms" returned to Little Marais in 1945, the lodge was covered with white clapboard siding and renamed the Colonial Inn and Dining Room. Additional retail space and second-floor rental rooms were provided around 1950, when a new building, later described as "part store front, part mansion," was constructed just west of the lodge. Evelyn Rudstrom also gained a measure of local fame for the large number of antique lamps that she collected and displayed in the dining room. It was, however, the owner's array of services and offerings—ranging from exceptional cuisine to fine china, silverware, linens, and finger bowls—that made the Colonial Inn such a unique North Shore attraction.[352]

The Rudstroms wintered in Florida but returned to the Colonial Inn for the tourist season. Although Rudstrom died in 1964, his widow operated the inn until 1972. While several successive owners conducted

Mountain ash, birch, and aspen saplings crowded the long-abandoned Colonial Inn before it was torn down in late 2017.

tourist-related businesses on the property, the once-elegant inn was vacant and revealing signs of significant deterioration by the early 2000s. It was a forlorn, dilapidated ruin in 2013–14, when the adjacent highway and right-of-way were widened and upgraded. Although little more than a few feet of space separated the Colonial's sagging walls from vehicles that sped by on Highway 61, some motorists did slow down sufficiently to observe and photograph the poignant scene before demolition occurred in late 2017. The adjacent store building was used most recently as a bed and breakfast, the Spirit of Gitche Gumee, but closed during the early 2020s; it currently serves as a seasonal residence.[353]

### Little Marais Schoolhouse (*now* Little Marais Community Club)
6470 Highway 61

Among the students who attended the Little Marais schoolhouse at the time of its 1903 opening were the three oldest children of pioneer settlers Ben and Serine Fenstad. That building was replaced, in December 1930, with a new schoolhouse that appeared on land donated by the Fenstad family. Although the schoolhouse had but a single room, local residents described it as a "modern building" and "commodious structure." Typically used by nine or ten students who were enrolled in grades 1–8, the schoolhouse also provided space for church services, community events, and election voting. When the school closed in 1950, ownership was assumed by the Little Marais Community Club.[354]

### Fenstad Brothers General Store and Eagles Nest Gifts *(now a residence)*
6476 Highway 61

Once Minnesota Highway 1 was completed in 1924, motorists entering Little Marais from the southwest were greeted by the Fenstad Brothers General Store, a family business venture that gave "special attention to packing groceries for tourists." Ole and Josephine Haveri Fenstad—one of the family's seven sons and his wife—operated the store following their 1932 marriage. They were assisted by the Fenstads' youngest daughter, Sophie, identified in the 1930 U.S. Census as an "unpaid worker" who served as the store's initial bookkeeper, oversaw the Little Marais Post Office (situated in the building), and helped manage the family's fish sales and telephone companies. Her nephew Art Fenstad Jr. would later write that the indefatigable Sophie served as the "glue" who "held the family together" until 1940, when she and her husband, Jim Anderson, moved to

Idaho. The Fenstads' building was acquired in 1992 by Dean and Patty Carpenter, former Minnesotans who had moved to California before settling in Little Marais. The Carpenters used the building as their residence and a business, Eagles Nest Gifts, which featured local products, such as jewelry, regional books, and hand-turned wooden items. Eagles Nest was closed in 2022, but the couple continues to reside within one section of the building.[355]

### Art Fenstad's Standard Service *(razed)*
Immediately East of Eagles Nest Gifts

In 1927, the Fenstad brothers took advantage of increasing highway traffic volumes on Minnesota Highway 1 by opening a nearby "filling station" where motorists could purchase gasoline, oil, batteries, and tires and also have minor repairs performed on their vehicles. Art Sr., the youngest brother, acquired the business after his return from three years of duty with the U.S. Army during World War II. In 1956, he constructed a "new and even more modern station," which was removed in 1983. (The site remains vacant to the present.) He and his wife, Elsie Anderson Fenstad, an elementary school teacher, also ran Art's Modern Cabins, a group of four lakeside rental units that are now part of a cabin owner's association.[356]

### Benjamin and Serine Fenstad Homestead, Lake Side Inn, and Stone Hearth Bed and Breakfast *(now a residence)*
6572 Highway 61

Shortly after establishing a 127-acre homestead claim at Little Marais in 1884, Norwegian fisherman Benjamin Fenstad was joined by his Norwegian wife, Elen, who died just five years later. Fenstad then traveled back to Norway, where he married Serine Sandin before the

**An aerial view, approximately 1933, of several buildings constructed and operated by the Fenstad family. At the far right is the Fenstad Brothers General Store; Art Fenstad's filling station (now a vacant lot) is just left of center. The family's residence, which also served as the Lake Side Inn for several years, was approached on the road that passes under the entrance arch.**

couple sailed to Little Marais in 1890.[357] Over subsequent decades, the Fenstads and their seven sons and two daughters would play key roles in the development of Little Marais.

The Fenstads established an impressive grouping of buildings on the family's property, including a large residence that also accommodated mail carriers who rested and changed horses on their trips between Two Harbors, Grand Marais, and Grand Portage. Prospective settlers and a number of "wayfaring" men, most of whom arrived and departed on steamboats, partook of Serine Fenstad's "kindly hospitality" before proceeding to places within and beyond Little Marais. In 1926, when the Fenstads renamed their residence the Lake Side Inn, visitors could rent one of ten upstairs rooms for $1.50 per night; the dining room, which seated as many as sixteen people, offered Lake Superior trout dinners for seventy-five cents. Following the matriarch's 1945 death, a son and daughter-in-law, John and Clara Venberg Fenstad, acquired the residence. Although its rooms were no longer available for rent, the couple managed four rental cabins that retained the original Lake Side Inn name. The residence was sold outside the family in 1974 and opened as the Stone Hearth Bed and Breakfast; it has served as a non-Fenstad family retreat since 2005.[358]

## Fenstad's Resort
### 6572 Highway 61

In 1936, three years after commercial fisherman Ben Fenstad Jr. married Agnes Godin (a North Shore high school physics and mathematics teacher), the couple established a cabin resort east of the family's original homestead. More cabins were added during the subsequent tenure of their son and daughter-in-law, Blaine and Mary Fenstad, who ran the resort from 1968 to 2000. They were followed by the next and current generation of owners: David, Mark, and Susie Fenstad. The resort includes sixteen cabins, many built of logs; a vintage fish house; and spacious grounds. Advertisements for the resort consistently feature the fishing opportunities available at the site, which is located where the Little Marais River and a nearby stream meet and empty into Lake Superior. Because of its well-maintained buildings, exceptional views, and long-standing traditions (no credit cards, jet skis, pets, guns, fireworks, or slingshots), Fenstad's remains one of the North Shore's "great old family-owned resorts."[359]

**Fenstad's Resort, located by the Little Marais River, 1950s. Now owned by a third generation of the Fenstad family, the well-maintained resort has changed relatively little since its 1936 founding.**

**A 1939 Chevrolet sedan travels over the graceful but potentially risky Manitou River Bridge, which was removed and replaced in 1955–56.**

### George H. Crosby Manitou State Park
Lake County Road 7

The acreage for this state park, the one-time estate of mining magnate George Crosby, was donated to the State of Minnesota in 1955. Now embracing 3,320 acres of rugged, forested land, and ten miles of the Manitou River, the entire property has "a distinctly rustic, backcountry feel compared to other state parks on the North Shore." The first Minnesota state park designated and designed specifically for backpackers, Crosby Manitou barely touches Highway 61 and provides no direct access to Lake Superior; therefore the entrance road is located at an inland site on Benson Lake, about seven miles from Finland. The entire acreage is managed as a minimally developed, wilderness state park with backcountry campsites and several miles of steep hiking trails, including one that parallels the Manitou River's waterfalls, rapids, and cascades.[360]

### Historic Manitou River Bridge

Other than a sign that identifies the Manitou River, most motorists do not realize that an impressive, narrow canyon lies below the highway crossing. From 1924 to 1955, however, the Manitou River and its gorge were visible from a bridge—located about one-quarter mile north-northeast of the current structure—that had two narrow lanes, pipe guardrails, and a graceful midpoint curve. Motorists who crossed over the span during those three decades were treated to spectacular views, but because the structure offered minimal room for maneuvering, serious mishaps remained a distinct possibility. In 1955, MDH officials conceded that the bridge was "famous" but also noted that it represented a "dangerous point on the road." When the agency's engineers announced their plans to replace the existing span with a structure constructed of concrete box culverts, some North Shore civic groups expressed immediate displeasure, claiming that the change would "detract from the beauty of the road at that point." Agency officials, however, assured doubters that the proposed span would not only "enhance the beauty of the site, but also eliminate a dangerous point in the road." The picturesque bridge was torn down shortly after the new structure, located closer to Lake Superior, opened in late 1956.[361]

### Finch's Manitou River Resort *(razed)*

Southwestern Entrance to Manitou River Bridge

Duluthians Henry and Cleora Woods Finch established their residence, along with a "lunchroom," a combination bar and dining room, and several cabins, proximate to the original Manitou River Bridge. Another attraction was a chained black bear that eagerly consumed the marshmallows that tourists fed to them. When the new concrete culvert bridge was constructed closer to Lake Superior in 1955–56, the couple opened another resort and a campground close to its southwestern entrance. From there, guests could follow a steep path to the river's mouth and observe the only North Shore waterfall that drops directly into Lake Superior. The resort buildings were gone by the late 1970s, some years after the couple moved to the state of Washington. General public access to the river's mouth and waterfall was eliminated in 1987, when the property was purchased by a family that has large landholdings along the North Shore. For the present at least, Manitou Falls may only be viewed from a Lake Superior vessel.[362]

### Caribou Falls State Wayside

7232 Highway 61

Close to the border that separates Lake and Cook Counties is Caribou Falls State Wayside—one of five similar North Shore facilities currently managed by the MDNR. The ninety-two-acre property received recognition as a state park in 1947, but because of its small size, limited opportunities for expansion, and lack of Lake Superior frontage, the site was labeled a wayside in 1969. Caribou Falls, which has a drop of thirty-five feet, is a one-half-mile upriver hike from the wayside's recently renovated facilities and parking area.[363]

# Cook County

Cook County was carved out of Lake County in 1874, although another twelve years passed before the seat of government moved from Two Harbors to Grand Marais. Overall, 85 percent of Cook County's 3,340 square miles are within the public domain (70 percent federal, 15 percent state); another 5 percent are included in the Grand Portage Indian Reservation, while the remaining 10 percent are in private hands. Cook also has more surface water (1,888 square miles) than any of Minnesota's eighty-seven counties and ranks twelfth in land area (1,452 square miles).[1]

Cook County's population has remained relatively low throughout its history. Fewer than one hundred people were counted in both the 1880 and 1890 censuses, before the total grew to 810 in 1900 and to 1,335 in 1910. The 1920 figure of 1,840 included 195 Anishinaabe residents and 500 foreign-born immigrants, among them almost 400 Nordics—200 Norwegians, 135 Swedes, 50 Finland Swedes, 4 Finns, and 4 Danes. The 65 Canadians formed the only other immigrant group with a sizable presence. The 1980 population figure (4,090) represented slightly more than a doubling of the 1920 count. The numbers grew to 5,175 in 2010 and to 5,600 in 2020. The latter figure included 460 Anishinaabe inhabitants and another 380 residents with mixed heritage. While the 8 percent gain from 2010 to 2020 was the most significant relative increase, by far, among northeastern Minnesota's eight counties, Cook still remains one of the state's least populated places: only six of its eighty-seven counties had fewer inhabitants in 2020.[2]

Cook County's rugged terrain, limited transportation corridors, and paucity of productive agricultural land kept it "from being transformed by an influx of people and the trappings of modernity." During the twenty-first century, however, Cook County has experienced relatively more in-migration than other nonurban areas of Minnesota. The county's natural amenities, especially Lake Superior and the Northwoods, are often cited as the primary attractions, but so, too, is its vibrant cultural life, which embodies a blending of art, music, food, and history that often reflects Anishinaabe and Nordic traditions. Nevertheless, a number of people who wish to reside in this area of far northeastern Minnesota must often pursue two or more jobs simultaneously—a practice known locally as the "Cook County shuffle." Economic opportunity—primarily for the "educated, entrepreneurial, hardy, and artistic"—has recently increased with the introduction of broadband internet into many areas of the county. Also important is the growing acceptance of off-site or virtual work, which became a vital reality during the Covid-19 epidemic of the early 2020s. A complicating situation for new residents, nonetheless, is the limited availability of private land, which drives construction costs upward and creates an increasing demand for "tiny homes" and "small rustic properties."[3]

Cook County also emerged as one of Minnesota's most politically progressive strongholds during the early twenty-first century. While Democratic presidential candidate John Kerry received 52 percent of Cook County's votes in 2004, the party's next two standard-bearers—Barack Obama in 2008 and 2012 and Hillary Clinton in 2016—were favored by almost 60 percent of voters. The upward trend continued into 2020, when Democrat Joseph Biden garnered 66 percent of Cook

County's vote count—a figure exceeded in Minnesota only by the state's two largest counties, Hennepin and Ramsey, both part of the Twin Cities metropolitan area. The same pattern prevailed in 2024: Kamala Harris lost the national election to Trump but received 66 percent of the Cook County vote.[4]

Most of the county's permanent citizens, as well as some ten thousand part-time and seasonal homeowners, are concentrated within or close to several definable areas: Grand Marais, a half dozen unincorporated settlements, and the Grand Portage Indian Reservation. Other residents are situated along Lake Superior and Highway 61, numerous inland lakes, and four major north–south trails—Sawbill, Caribou, Gunflint, and Arrowhead. And, of course, Cook County serves as a destination for large numbers of visitors and tourists: each year, as many as two million people enjoy its attractions, primarily during the summer, fall, and winter seasons.[5]

Grand Marais is Cook County's only city and the site of its sole traffic light. Because of small population numbers and limited economic resources, the organization and maintenance of township governments often proved difficult in the past. Hovland emerged as the first township in 1894, but part of its area was taken, twelve years later, to create Colvill Township. The organization of three more townships—Grand Marais, Maple Hill, and Tofte Townships—occurred in late 1899. Two additional townships, Schroeder and Lutsen, were excised from Tofte in 1906, a tripartite division that occurred shortly after the annual supervisors' meeting was "split wide open between contending factions competing for control of the town government." Rosebush Township, bordering Grand Marais, emerged in 1907, while the Village of Grand Marais was incorporated in 1903.[6]

During the depths of the Great Depression, large areas of Cook County land, once privately owned, were abandoned and tax-delinquent. The Cook County Board of Commissioners sought to cope with the ensuing financial dilemma by invoking a 1927 Minnesota law that gave counties the power to dissolve any township having a tax delinquency rate greater than 50 percent. The commissioners ruled, in 1937, that the townships were already "at least de facto dissolved" because of their failure to carry out any functions and powers. Given the townships' lack of action, Cook County was forced to govern them as unorganized territories.[7]

Decades later, much improved economic conditions allowed the three southwesternmost townships to reorganize: Schroeder in 1971, Tofte in 1975, and Lutsen in 1984. Within the boundaries of each is an unincorporated settlement that also bears the township name. Other than the City of Grand Marais and the trio of townships, Cook County's remaining land comprises three areas, designated as "unorganized territories" by the U.S. Census Bureau—West Cook, East Cook, and Grand Portage. The unincorporated enclaves of Croftville, Colvill, and Hovland are located in East Cook, while the settlement of Grand Portage is included within the larger Grand Portage Indian Reservation.[8]

## Schroeder Township

Somewhat more than nine miles of Highway 61 pass through Schroeder Township. Both the township and its primary settlement were named for John Schroeder, a pioneer lumberman. Company agents claimed that the firm employed more than one thousand lumberjacks and timber workers from 1895 to 1905, although just seventy-two permanent residents—split evenly between American and foreign-born inhabitants (twenty-one of them French Canadians)—were counted in the U.S. Census of 1900. Only six women, the wives and daughters of two lumberjacks, resided in the township. The figure increased modestly thereafter. By 1920, the 118 inhabitants included seventy-five immigrants—twenty-eight Norwegians, fifteen Swedes, eleven French Canadians, and twenty-one members of six other ethnic groups. Schroeder Township's population hovered around one hundred until the mid-1950s, when the new settlement of Taconite Harbor appeared on Lake Superior's shoreline. A special 1977 Schroeder Township census counted 385 residents—a figure that dropped abruptly following the abandonment of Taconite Harbor during the late 1980s. While the U.S. Census of 2020 counted just 225 year-round Schroeder Township residents, the figure is appreciably higher during the tourist seasons: 245 of the township's 355 dwelling units (almost 70 percent) were not occupied year-round in 2020.[9]

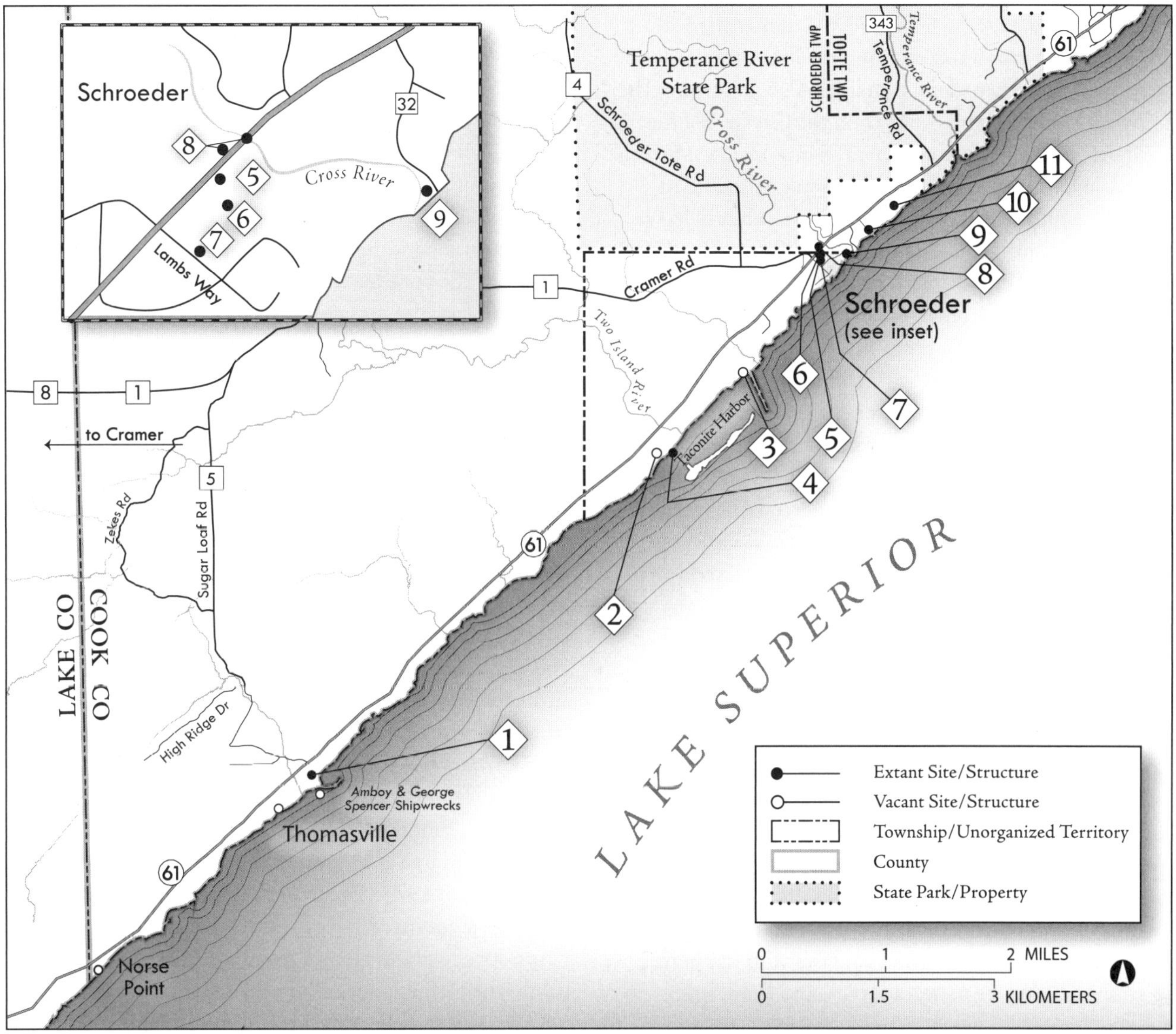


1. Sugarloaf Cove Nature Center
2. Taconite Harbor Townsite
3. Taconite Harbor Energy Center
4. Taconite Harbor: Small Craft Harbor
5. Cross River Heritage Center
6. Schroeder Baking Company
7. Lamb's Resort on Lake Superior
8. Cross River Falls Bridge, Safety Rest Area, and State Wayside
9. Father Baraga's Cross
10. Temperance Landing on Lake Superior
11. Gunderson's General Store and Cabins*

*Now private residences and cabins

### Norse Point and Thomasville

Two diminutive settlements—Norse (also Norris) Point and Thomasville—once served numerous fishing and logging camps situated along the first three miles of southwestern Schroeder Township. Also nearby are the shipwreck sites for the *Amboy* and the *George Spencer,* both driven ashore during the infamous Mataafa Storm of 26 November 1905 that either sank or stranded eighteen Lake Superior vessels; fortunately, all crew members on both the *Amboy* and the *George Spencer* were rescued. The completion of Minnesota Highway 1 in 1925 led to the emergence of some small tourist establishments, among them Birch Beach Cabins in Thomasville, initiated by Birgit Huseby Tveekrem, a young widow with two children. Tveekrem opened a few cabins soon after her husband and brother, respectively, Christian Tveekrem and Carl A. Huseby, were "lost at sea" while fishing during a fierce Lake Superior storm in April 1935. (Although the men's bodies were never recovered, both of their names are incised into a single Schroeder Cemetery headstone.) Her business began inauspiciously during the late 1930s when a woman seeking hay fever relief asked Tveekrem if she could rent a room for much of the summer. Birch Beach closed many years ago, as did the nearby Sugar Loaf Resort. More long-lived was the Kaffe Stuga, which opened on the upper side of Highway 61 during the 1950s, then became Satellite's Country Inn (9427 West Highway 61) following its purchase, two decades later, by a couple who also sold CB radios. Until closing in 2013, Satellite's remained a popular dining stop for "locals, truck drivers, and tourists who happened to stumble upon its fishcakes, pies, and homespun charm."[10]

### Gunderson Homestead and Sugarloaf Landing (*now the* Sugarloaf Cove Nature Center)
### 9096 West Highway 61

Sugarloaf Cove is one of very few significant natural harbors between Two Harbors and Grand Marais that offers protection from the direct impact of Lake Superior's storms. It was here that Norwegian immigrant John Gunderson, his Swedish wife, Martha, and their son Gilbert secured a 155-acre homestead in late 1899. The acreage was sold sometime after the senior Gunderson's 1927 death and purchased, in 1943, by the Consolidated Water Power and Paper Company (renamed Consolidated Papers, Inc. in 1962), which owned considerable Cook County forestland. The acreage supplied pulpwood for the company's Wisconsin paper mills, where much of it was converted into glossy paper used by several major American magazines, such as *Look* and *Time.* Throughout the fall and winter months, Consolidated's lumberjacks harvested spruce, balsam, and jack pine logs, which were hauled to Sugarloaf Landing for stockpiling. (Aspen was also used, but the bark had to be peeled off during the spring season before the logs could serve as pulpwood.) Once the lake ice melted sufficiently, the logs were dumped down a huge chute into the cove. There the logs were organized into booms, a demanding and often dangerous task. The booms were linked together to form rafts comprising three thousand to six thousand cords of logs, although one raft had a phenomenal seventeen thousand cords. A Consolidated tugboat, the *Butterfield,* spent all but two of thirty-four years from 1923 to 1957 slowly towing the rafts sixty-two miles to Ashland, where they were loaded onto railroad cars and shipped to paper mills. (The *Butterfield* was requisitioned for wartime duty at Alaska's Aleutian Islands from 1943 to 1945.) An all-time record of forty thousand cords were transported across the lake in 1962, shortly after independent contract loggers replaced the company's lumberjacks.[11]

Consolidated maintained the Sugarloaf Landing holding until 1971. The firm then removed most of its fourteen structures and planted several red pine and white spruce plantations throughout the property. (Only the former root cellar and a few raft remnants now provide visible evidence of Consolidated's activities.) In 1985, the company donated its sixty-five-acre property to The Nature Conservancy (TNC), which, three years later, traded one-half of the holding to Cook County in exchange for land northeast of Grand Marais and sold the other half to the MDNR for $250,000. Although the MDNR had no specific plans for its acquisition at that time, UMD geologist John Green and his wife, Jan, were successful in having 3.25 acres dedicated as the Sugarloaf Point Scientific and Natural Area (SNA) in 1995.[12]

The MDNR, by this time, was considering Sugarloaf as a potential safe harbor and marina site, and

**Consolidated Papers's log ramp at Sugarloaf Cove, 1950s or 1960s. The logs were towed by a tugboat to Ashland, then shipped by rail to Wisconsin paper mills. Courtesy of Sugarloaf Cove Nature Center.**

Cook County was proposing to sell some of its acreage for private lakeshore development. Former Minnesota Republican governor Elmer L. Andersen and his daughter Emily Andersen quickly recognized that the proposed sale posed significant threats to the site. Governor Andersen led the way in protecting the property by encouraging the MDNR to construct its safe harbor at Taconite Harbor, located 4.5 miles to the northeast, rather than using the Sugarloaf holding. Both father and daughter also bought shoreline acreage adjacent to Sugarloaf that was available for sale in 1986. Their acquisition was followed, some years later, by another purchase; overall, the merged properties created "an Andersen family buffer" that prevented nearby development along either side of their holding. In 1996, the Andersens, with assistance provided by Duluthian Lori Stromme and her husband, Steve Pihjala—both of them attorneys who had previous experience as environmental activists in Schroeder Township—formed a nonprofit organization, SICA. Dedicated to the restoration and protection of the site's outstanding natural features, the organization succeeded because of Governor Andersen's ability to gain bipartisan support for SICA and to recruit influential board members, such as former UMD chancellor Robert Heller, who served as the first president.[13]

Expansion of the Sugarloaf SNA to 10.3 acres in 1998 protected more of the site's natural features, primarily its tombolo, multicolored cobblestone beach, large cedars, basalt lava flows, lichens, and mosses. The restoration of an important wetland was initiated in 1999, and the dedication of SICA's interpretive center, built of locally harvested logs by a Grand Marais construction company, occurred one year later. The quality of the programs and expertise offered by Sugarloaf's staff members expanded the association's sphere of influence during the early twenty-first century. The SICA mission statement, modified and adopted in 2005, recognized the successful efforts that had been made "to inspire the preservation and restoration of the North Shore's unique environment through education and exemplary stewardship, especially at Sugarloaf Cove." Another revision was a name change, to Sugarloaf: The North Shore Stewardship Association. Among its primary offerings are forest stewardship learning opportunities for year-round and seasonal residents and visitors. Often mistaken as a state park, Sugarloaf receives the majority of its support from membership dues and visitor parking fees.[14]

## Taconite Harbor

Until the early 1950s this area of the Lake Superior shoreline was known as Two Island—a name derived from Bear and Gull Islands, both located close to the mouth of Two Island River. A plat for the townsite of Saxton was surveyed along the river in 1856 but failed to develop; only three properties were evident in the area by the late 1940s: a fishing camp with furnished cabins, operated by Tom and Mary Johnson; Armund and Lava Hovland's Two Island Lodge and Cabins; and the summer home of widower Clarence R. Magney, an associate justice of the Minnesota Supreme Court. All buildings on the three properties had been removed by 1953, one year after the Erie Mining Company, a subsidiary of the Cleveland-based Pickands Mather & Company, purchased the shoreline land. Erie would transform the property into its Two Island Project—which included a taconite loading facility, harbor, dock, breakwater, railroad, power plant, and townsite. When completed, the taconite pellets produced at a new beneficiation plant, located on the eastern Mesabi Range at Hoyt Lakes, were shipped seventy-two miles by rail to Taconite Harbor, then loaded onto Great Lakes ore carriers.[15]

## Taconite Harbor Townsite *(abandoned)*
### 4.5 Miles Northeast of Sugarloaf Cove

In mid-November 1953, Peter Kiewit Sons & Company, an Omaha-based firm, began working on the construction of a breakwater and four miles of railroad grade at the project site. Eighty men operated trucks, jackhammers, and large diesel-powered shovels throughout the ensuing winter. Although most employees were recruited on very short notice, the Kiewit Company official who hired them was "very happy to hear of the caliber of the local people, their experience in work in the far corners of the world, and their general stable character."[16]

Those construction workers who were not residents of the nearby area initially found housing at Birgit Tveekrem's Birch Beach Cabins, at Lamb's Resort in Schroeder, and at a few other places; nevertheless, some men had to live in their own vehicles for a brief time. Thirty men with families resided in a "trailer village" located west of the construction site during the winter of 1953–54. As 1954 came to an end, the encampment, officially known as the Hovland Trailer Park, had grown to 250 identical, closely packed units, each eight by twenty feet in size. Nearby was the Taconite Harbor Shopping Center, a T-shaped, steel-and-concrete structure: its central section, two stories high, had a thirty-bed dormitory on the second floor and a recreation room, administrative office, barbershop, and public restroom below. One single-story wing included a restaurant with 120 seats; a soda shop; and a stand where candy, magazines, and cigarettes were available. The supermarket, located in the other wing, had groceries, clothing, and pharmaceutical items and also offered a check-cashing service, a laundry, and a dry-cleaning facility. All business operators were required to sign an agreement that assured that their prices would be comparable to those in nearby towns. Among the other buildings was a dispensary where the company doctor treated patients and even delivered babies; parked nearby was an ambulance that could speed injured and seriously ill workers and residents to hospitals in either Grand Marais or Two Harbors. All units in the Hovland Trailer Park were removed soon after the taconite plant was completed in 1957; the supermarket and another two-story structure were transported to Grand Marais and converted into a bowling alley and an apartment building.[17]

A much smaller workforce was needed to operate the facility after construction activities ended. Some permanent employees were able to purchase or rent housing in the Taconite Harbor Subdivision, a small enclave situated adjacent to the trailer park. (All of the early trailers were soon removed from the site.) The subdivision plat called for three parallel roads, each one-third of a mile long, but only Brandon Avenue was developed. Seventeen single-story, three-bedroom homes were built along the avenue in 1957, while another five appeared over the next ten years. The residences may have been modest, but Taconite Harbor residents could claim that they had "million-dollar views" of Lake Superior. A community center and fire hall also appeared close to the housing area, as did a playground, a skating rink, and basketball and tennis courts. The residents paid a minimal fee for municipal services.[18]

Taconite Harbor's population peaked at some one hundred people during the 1970s. In 1986, however, the seventy-eight residents received word that their houses would be removed because of high maintenance costs and an impending sale of Erie Mining to the LTV Steel Company. The deadline was extended for a brief period after some residents quickly formed an ad hoc Save the Taconite Homes Committee; nevertheless, only four houses were occupied by 1987. All of the vacant dwellings were moved to new locations over the next three years.[19]

Vegetation has subsequently invaded the long-vacant residential lots and once-active recreational spaces. Only limited information about the townsite and Sugarloaf Cove is now provided at a small interpretive facility on the site. Also on display are the capstan from Consolidated Papers's tugboat, the *Butterfield*; the anchor from an ore boat; a huge bucket, formerly attached to a power shovel that extracted taconite ore on the Mesabi Range; and a tire, five feet high, removed from an off-road dump truck once used at the mine site. Other than some building foundations, several areas of badly cracked concrete pavement, a few rusting streetlight poles, and an abandoned basketball court, very little of Taconite Harbor is evident today; occasional first-time visitors, however, still post their impressions and images of the North Shore's "ghost town" on various social media sites. Schroeder Township officials and citizens continue to explore future options for the vacant townsite, now owned by the Minnesota Power Company. Some have argued that the site could

**From 1954 to 1957, the families of many Taconite Harbor construction workers were housed in 250 closely spaced trailers that overlooked Lake Superior. Courtesy of Cross River Heritage Center.**

be converted into a state park, but affordable housing, one of the area's most pressing needs, is more often mentioned as a possibility.[20]

### Erie Mining Company Taconite and Coal Unloading Facilities and Docks (*now* Taconite Harbor Energy Center, *on standby status*)

Southeast of the Former Townsite along Lake Superior

Although Bear and Gull Islands provided the project site with minimal protection from Lake Superior's severe northeastern storms, the engineers and contractors still faced a myriad of complex construction-related problems. Most daunting was the need to remove one million cubic yards of rock from the bottom of Lake Superior to deepen the cliff face by thirty feet. The massive effort required the construction of cofferdams fifty feet in diameter and filled with rocks and gravel, which held back the water of Lake Superior and created a construction space thirty-five feet wide and two thousand feet long. The largest excavated rocks, each weighing about five tons, were used to construct the pair of breakwaters that played an essential role in protecting the completed harbor: one breakwater linked Bear and Gull Islands, while the other extended outward from the power plant. Additional boulders weighing up to twelve tons each, termed "armor stone," were excavated from Carlton Peak in the Lake Superior Highlands and trucked to the site, where they offered further protection for the two breakwaters.[21]

The cliff, comprising layered rock or strata, was secured and reinforced by drilling huge rods, some more than thirty-five feet long, into the wall. After the surface was covered with concrete, the twelve hundred feet of Minnesota's "fastest, most efficient dock" could accommodate the simultaneous loading of two ore carriers. In late September and early October 1957, the *J. A. Campbell* and *A. B. Wolvin* inaugurated the Taconite Harbor facility. When operating at full capacity, the dock could handle fifty-eight thousand tons of pellets each day, all delivered by seven trains that operated around the clock. The trains passed through the Cramer

**When a Mesabi Range ore train approached Taconite Harbor, its descent to Lake Superior was slowed by the curvature or "looping" of the tracks. After the taconite pellets had been emptied into a Great Lakes ore carrier, the train completed a full circle and returned to Hoyt Lakes.**

Tunnel, the longest (1,810 feet) underground railroad passage in Minnesota, and crossed over numerous trestles, three of which spanned Highway 61. (One was hit by a truck and torn down in 2011.) Located by the power plant was another dock, 450 feet long, which handled the backhaul of coal that the ore carriers brought to Taconite Harbor; the coal fueled the power plant and was also shipped by train to the Hoyt Lakes beneficiation plant.[22]

In June 2001, an ore train, its last car renumbered "000," transported the final pellets from Hoyt Lakes to Taconite Harbor. The September departure of the ore carrier *William H. Donner* marked an official end to forty-four years of shipping activity, during which time 330 million tons of ore had passed through Taconite Harbor. The generating plant, also acquired in 2001 by Minnesota Power, functioned for the next fifteen years before it, too, was shut down. The ultimate fate of the plant, as of 2024, had not been determined.[23]

### Taconite Harbor: Small Craft Harbor
Northwestern Corner of the Large Harbor

When taconite shipments ended in 2001, the MDNR was already constructing a new, 1.7-acre small-craft harbor, with a depth of ten feet, at the northwestern corner of the large basin entrance. The MDNR project has two concrete ramps, two docks, a paved lower lot for five cars or trailers, a gravel upper parking lot for thirty-five cars or trailers, and a private charter boat service.[24] The pair of adjacent harbors at the site—one a former taconite shipping center, the other a functioning facility for small boats—offer a striking example of the massive differences in size, scale, and complexity that define industrial and recreational facilities along the North Shore.

## Schroeder

The settlement of Schroeder, originally known as Redmyer, recognized the name of a Norwegian family who settled close to the mouth of the Cross River in 1884–85. Also called Cross River, the current name of the settlement, dating to 1904, was derived from the John Schroeder Lumber Company, which operated in the area between 1895 and 1905.[25] The initial 1917 motor road, after exiting northeastern Two Harbors, turned inland toward Finland, Cramer, and a few other tiny settlements before it once again reached Lake Superior in the vicinity of Schroeder. Less than a decade later, the inland road would be supplanted by a newly built section of Minnesota Highway 1 that provided a direct lakeshore connection between Schroeder and Two Harbors. Schroeder would also serve as a commercial and residential center for many of Taconite Harbor's employees and their families during the latter half of the twentieth century.

### Redmyer Homestead, John Schroeder Lumber Company Headquarters, and Stickney's Inn and Store (*now the* Cross River Heritage Center *and* Lamb's Resort on Lake Superior)
7932 West Highway 61/61 Lambs Way

In 1888, Norwegian immigrants Henrik and Emilie Redmyer, joined by their adult son Hedley and daughter Nettie, settled on a 148-acre homestead claim at the mouth of the Cross River. The father and son, two of early Cook County's more colorful characters, engaged in fishing and farming and provided space for a post office in the family's residence from 1888 to late 1891. The men also built the *H. N. Emilie*, one of Lake Superior's largest fishing boats, which had two masts and was sixty-five feet long. (The *Emilie* was confiscated for a period of time in 1894–95, when the Redmyers were charged with possible opium smuggling; no evidence was found, but the men lost their boat to creditors.) The family departed Cross River for the San Juan Islands of Washington's Puget Sound in 1901. This was two years after the younger Redmyer led one Norwegian and five Sámi herders, with 135 reindeer in tow, on the final leg of a journey that had commenced in Nordic Lapland and culminated in Arctic Alaska. Redmyer's supervision of the epic reindeer drive, often conducted during extreme weather conditions, covered more than a thousand miles of difficult terrain between Alaska's southeastern coastline and the Yukon River. His efforts were acknowledged by Sheldon Jackson, a noted Alaskan official who oversaw the reindeer relocation project: the hardy Redmyer, "after great hardship and much personal danger," reported Jackson, had "fulfilled his mission."[26]

Hedley Redmyer returned briefly to the Cross River area in 1903, when he attempted to secure a liquor license and operate a saloon. But after his arrest for selling alcohol on Sundays, Redmyer journeyed to Alaska and participated in another reindeer drive before settling in Washington. The ever-restless Redmyer, however, once again made his way to Schroeder, this time in 1916—shortly after a new steel-truss highway bridge had been built upstream from the river's mouth, where Redmyer's narrow wooden span still stood. Redmyer continued using the wooden structure, one of the initial bridges in the area, to link his properties on both sides of the river; other residents and travelers, however, could gain access only by securing his permission. On 4 July 1916, while Redmyer was in Duluth, a group of neighbors, "after trespassing on his land, went in there with axes and cut and tore, and hauled away the best pieces, finally making a bonfire of the debris." Redmyer, who experienced considerable "consternation" over the incident, soon returned to Washington, where he spent the remainder of his life.[27]

Significant activities were occurring along the river as early as 1895, when the John Schroeder Lumber Company leased some of Redmyer's land for its headquarters. Schroeder had departed Germany for Milwaukee in 1846 and eventually developed a highly successful company that owned forestland, railroads, and mills throughout the Midwest. Schroeder's workers, from 1896 to 1905, harvested timber from a large area of the Cross River watershed, but only after heavily modifying the waterway, which facilitated the transfer of logs from the interior to Lake Superior: one waterfall was dynamited, and chutes, flumes, sluiceways, and seven dams (one a hundred feet long and fourteen feet high) were constructed along the waterway. Following the springtime snowmelt, the system was used to transport millions of feet of logs on their thunderous, downriver journey to the holding boom; once there, the logs were organized into rafts and towed to the Schroeder Company mill in Ashland.[28]

The company headquarters—comprising warehouses, docks, bunkhouses, and a store, hotel, and superintendent's house—were situated just west of the river. An infirmary, often referred to as the "pest house," as well as a saloon and bordello, or "sporting house," were on the eastern side. Following the Schroeder Company's departure in 1906, William Smith, a Canadian and former logging foreman, built the Smith House, which served as a roadside hotel and rest stop for the sleighs and stagecoaches that passed through the settlement. Although it was destroyed by fire in 1925, Smith soon constructed another hotel, this one for motorists, on the northeastern side of the bridge.[29]

In 1921, Horace Stickney of Clear Lake, Minnesota, purchased thirteen acres of land, just west of the river, which the Redmyers had previously leased to the Schroeder Company. Still located on the grounds were the superintendent's residence, an office, and a log bunkhouse. One year later, following Stickney's marriage to local teacher Nellie Fradenburg, the young couple moved into the one-time superintendent's dwelling. The building was so dilapidated, recalled Stickney, that his wife became "seasick" when it "weaved" in the wind. In 1922, three years before the official opening of Highway 1, the couple built a roadside store on the property. By 1928, the Stickneys also owned seventy acres of land, including the final parcel that remained in the Redmyers' possession.[30]

Although Stickney's Store burned down in late 1928, it was quickly replaced by a Tudor revival structure (a highly unusual architectural style for Cook County) on the southern side of Highway 61; the building still displays its steeply pitched, half-timbered gables and wood shingle and stucco cladding. Occupying the lower floor were the Stickneys' living quarters, with a large dining room and fireplace, as well as a grocery store, a confectionary, and a post office. The second-floor inn, with seven rooms for fifteen to twenty guests, had three bathrooms—one of the area's first lodging facilities that was supplied with indoor toilets, sinks, and a bathtub. Florence Page Jaques, a sophisticated New Yorker who wrote two classic books about the life she and her husband experienced while spending periods of time in a Gunflint Lake cabin during the late 1930s and early 1940s, made a brief visit to Stickney's "wonderful . . . half store and half home" in November 1942. After the couple had been escorted upstairs, Jaques marveled at the "clean, gay little room, with fresh flowered wallpaper and oh, a modern bathroom!! No snow sifting under the door, no windy cracks, no rough boards iced with hoar frost." Adding further allure to the Jaqueses' brief sojourn was "Mrs. Stickney's delicious dinner."[31]

The Stickneys opened a small Standard Oil gas station just west of the store during the 1930s. A log cabin

**Stickney's Inn and Store in Schroeder, a few years after the Tudor revival structure replaced an earlier building that had burned down in 1928. The lower level was occupied by the store and living quarters, while seven rental rooms were available on the second floor. The building now houses the Cross River Heritage Center. A small gas station was later built behind the Standard Service sign at the right side of the store. The barrel vault of the 1931 bridge still spans the Cross River, but the viewing platform and five steps in the foreground were eliminated during the late 1990s.**

that overlooked the Cross River was also available for guests by 1930, and another seven units, some with views of Lake Superior, opened later in the decade. When Stickney's nephew Harry Stickney Lamb and his wife, Doris, acquired the establishment in 1954, the couple began supplying food and groceries to the crew members who served on ore carriers that arrived at Taconite Harbor and also developed a campground on some of their acreage. In 1965, the business passed to their son and daughter-in-law, Horace ("Skip") and Linda Lamb, who continued operating the resort but sold the store to Bill and Gloria Jordan in 1976. Over the next two decades, Jordan's Cross River General Store would also include a refrigerated meat locker, barbershop, coin-operated Laundromat, and liquor store.[32]

Jordan's closed in 1998, when the property was condemned and purchased by MnDOT, which soon made major improvements to the Cross River Bridge, the roadside rest area, and an adjacent section of Highway 61. Fortunately, ownership of the building—the community's primary hub and oldest commercial structure—was transferred to Schroeder Township. This action allowed the Schroeder Area Historical Society to remove the noncompatible building additions and rehabilitate, restore, and convert the venerable structure into the Cross River Heritage Center. Creating functional areas for the center's exhibits, "story rooms," public gatherings, and a gift shop required the redesign of its interior layout, but as a 2015 assessment noted, the building's "integrity of location, design, setting, materials, workmanship, feeling, and association" were successfully maintained.[33] Because of the dedicated effort and work undertaken by a small number of volunteers and staff members, the Heritage Center offers displays, events, programs, and tours that attract visitors from a wide geographic area.

**This cabin, shown here shortly after its completion in the 1930s, is one of eight original log units that remain at Lamb's Resort.**

Slightly west of the Heritage Center is the former Pure Oil station, now housing the local post office and a popular diner, the Schroeder Baking Company. Farther southwest is Lamb's Resort, still owned and operated by the fourth and fifth generations of family members. As Twin Cities journalist Laurie Hertzel observed in 2011, Lamb's Resort cabins "were clearly designed for the days when nobody went to a resort and stayed inside." Instead, she wrote, Lamb's is "a place sweetly and deliberately stuck in the past"—a place where one can celebrate "the out of doors—the rushing waterfall of the Cross River, half a mile of rocky Lake Superior shoreline, [and] cedar- and pine-lined paths that crisscross its 60-acres." All eight of the original 1930s-era log cabins remain on the property, as do four newer units constructed of frame and board. With one hundred sites, Lamb's also has the North Shore's largest private campground.[34]

Also standing on its original site is the community's oldest structure—a Schroeder Company bunkhouse dating to the late 1890s. The building's walls are constructed of logs, and wooden shingles cover the frame and board gable ends. The interior, however, no longer has its original features: the bunks that formerly lined the walls are missing, as are the centrally located

**The former Schroeder Company bunkhouse, constructed during the 1890s, is the oldest remaining building in the Cross River area.**

**After his original hotel burned down in 1925, William Smith replaced it with this structure, located slightly northeast of the Cross River bridge. Named the Cross River Inn by a new owner in 1931, the building included a movie theater, roller skating rink, hotel, restaurant, and bar. The inn was torn down in the 1940s; only the fireplace and chimney, now shrouded by trees and vegetation, remain on the site. Photograph by Milford J. Humphrey, 1938. Courtesy of Cook County Historical Society.**

wood-fired stove that heated the structure and the web of ropes and wires once used to dry out the lumberjacks' malodorous clothing. Because well-maintained buildings of this type are so rare, the bunkhouse was listed in the National Register of Historic Places in 1986.[35]

## Cross River Falls Bridge, Safety Rest Area, and State Wayside

### Milepost 79, Highway 61

A steel truss bridge, constructed of prefabricated elements that arrived at the mouth of the Cross River on a Lake Superior barge, was erected in 1915 by the Foley Brothers Construction Company of St. Paul. The bridge, just wide enough for a single wagon or vehicle, was expanded to two lanes during the mid-1920s. It would be replaced, in 1931, by the current bridge, this one a solid concrete, barrel-vaulted structure with a span of fifty feet. Constructed by A. Guthrie & Company, also a St. Paul firm, each side of the bridge included a "catwalk" or platform that was accessed by five steps; the platforms provided observers with an intimate and even thrilling overview of the river and falls.[36]

The bridge was selected as the site for one of seventy official interpretive highway signs that appeared throughout Minnesota from 1929 to 1932. Shortly after MDH engineer Walter Rosenwald proposed the signs and markers program, he was joined by MHS museum curator Willoughby Babcock, who had observed that motorists traveling along the state's expanding highway network were failing "to reap the fullest benefits from their travels because they had no knowledge or awareness of nearby historic sites." The three-by-five-foot Cross River sign, with black lettering on a white background, described the arrival of Father Frederick Baraga, a missionary priest who landed at the stream's mouth during a severe October 1846 storm. Situated several hundred feet to the southwest and northeast of the sign were separate markers, both placed perpendicular to the highway and emblazoned with the words "Historic Site Ahead." Babcock believed that the markers would appeal to interested motorists and cause them "to slow down sufficiently . . . to read the principal inscription."[37]

During the mid-1930s, landscape architect Arthur Nichols developed a number of design details that sought to improve the appearance and functionality of the bridge and nearby site. The project was carried out by CCC workers, who covered the steps, platforms, and walkways with stone veneer; constructed a new stairway that connected the northwestern end of the span to a stone-lined river pathway; and built another pathway that extended from the northeastern bridge terminus to the river's eastern bank. Nichols also designed a unique lectern-style marker for the Cross River sign, which had edges "studded with small, round, carefully placed stones" pressed into wet concrete poured over a fieldstone core.[38]

By 1981, the wayside's deteriorating stairs and bridge paths were deemed "slithery" and in obvious need of considerable repair. Although some minor improvements were quickly made to the site, an extensive reconstruction project, undertaken during the late 1990s, eliminated much of the CCC work, including its viewing platforms and stairway. The wayside's rest stop and two parking areas, all deemed "disruptive and dangerous" because of their proximity to passing traffic, were improved by building a low wall of native stone that separated each site from the flow of vehicles. The Cross River marker, replaced by a stone monument faced with dark North Shore gabbro, has a raised central lectern topped by a polished granite pulpit that displays an inscribed, two-sentence description of Frederick Baraga's experience at Cross River; the lectern is flanked by flat pieces of granite, also polished, which provide travelers and hikers with places to sit.[39]

Extending inland from the bridge are 2,520 acres of undeveloped land once included with the original Cross River Wayside. Because the total acreage far exceeded that of another state park (Temperance River), located a short distance toward the northeast, the MDNR called for legislation that would consolidate both units into a single state park. The merger, accomplished during the 1990s, resulted in what is today's expansive Temperance River State Park.[40]

### Father Baraga's Cross
### 56 Baraga Cross Road

Baraga Cross Road, which intersects with Highway 61 a short distance from the bridge, is still flanked by a few small, long-abandoned buildings once associated with two businesses—Ella and Ara Smith's Pioneer Cabins and a resort owned by John and Florence

**The granite cross that commemorates Father Frederick Baraga's eventful 1848 voyage across Lake Superior was dedicated in 1952.**

Alnes. Close to the river's mouth is a granite cross that commemorates the experiences of Frederick Baraga (1797–1868), a legendary Slovenian priest and bishop whose accomplishments include several "firsts," notably the preparation of an Anishinaabe dictionary and a translation of the Bible into the Anishinaabe language. While serving a mission on Wisconsin's Apostle Islands in August 1846, Baraga heard of an epidemic at Grand Portage. The story of their venture reports that Baraga and an Anishinaabe guide, Louis Gandin, soon set off for the distant outpost by crossing Lake Superior in a small boat. Although a severe storm drove the men off course, they made a miraculous landing at the mouth of a small river, where Baraga displayed his gratitude by mounting a wooden cross on a nearby tree. (The "Cross River" name is linked to this event.) When the "crude original" was replaced by the current granite cross in September 1952, the dedication attracted delegates from virtually every parish in the Duluth Diocese.[41] The site is now maintained by Schroeder Township.

Catholics residing in the Lake Superior region began calling for the beatification of Baraga during the early twentieth century, a cause that was brought to the Vatican, in 1952, by Bishop Thomas Lawrence Noa of the diocese of Marquette, Michigan. The Vatican would deem Father Baraga a Servant of God in 1973 and Venerable in 2012—the first two of four steps that require verification before the "Snowshoe Priest" may be canonized as a Catholic saint.[42]

### Star of the North Resort (*now* Temperance Landing on Lake Superior)

Temperance Landing Road

The mile of Highway 61 between the Cross and Temperance Rivers was once flanked by eight resorts. One of the best known, Star of the North, was opened during the mid-1920s by Hazel Conkey Branson, a former Minneapolis stenographer. She would be assisted, after 1930, by her new husband, Joe Pecore, a Canadian who had arrived on the North Shore at the age of nineteen and later became one of the area's foremost building contractors. Star of the North, which could house thirty guests in its lodge and ten log cabins, operated on the American plan: guests paid a single fee for both their meals and lodging: four dollars per day or twenty-five dollars per week—although the daily rate went up to five dollars during the autumn duck and deer hunting seasons. The couple sold Star of the North in 1940, two years before Pecore joined the U.S. Naval Construction Forces ("Seabees"), where he achieved the rank of lieutenant while serving on a ship that assisted with World

**Guests who stayed at the Star of the North Resort could visit, read, and play board games in its inviting lobby and reception area and also gather within the space before being summoned to dinner. The lodge burned down in 1945 and was never rebuilt.**

War II military operations on Guadalcanal and several other Pacific islands. After operating a Schroeder hardware store from 1952 to 1958, the couple moved to Arizona, where both passed away in 1971.[43]

Star of the North was purchased in 1940 by two St. Paul women: Marie Aftreith, a regional director for the Girl Scouts of America, and Harriet Rust, a social worker. Guests were asked to redeem their World War II ration cards at the resort, which allowed Star of the North to remain open throughout the first half of the 1940s—even as many other cabin rental businesses closed during the conflict. When the lodge and all records of future reservations were lost in a catastrophic June 1945 fire, the owners quickly converted one cabin into a dining room, where they continued serving their "famous meals . . . recommended by Duncan Hines." The new dining situation, nevertheless, forced Aftreith and Rust to transform Star of the North into a European plan resort, which meant that guests paid separately for their lodging and food. Although both women also worked elsewhere during the off season—Aftreith as a school bus driver, Rust as a bookkeeper—they were unable to raise sufficient funds to rebuild the lodge before selling their resort in 1967.[44]

The seven-acre site was acquired in 2005 by Dennis Rysdahl and his business partner, Dennis Anderson. Rysdahl received strong support from the Schroeder Township Board when he presented the partners' proposal for Temperance Landing on Lake Superior, a planned unit development with "a distinctive upscale edge." The project was the third North Shore resort complex built by Rysdahl, who had formed the Tofte-based Bluefin Bay Family of Resorts in 1983. The Landing now comprises twelve two-and-a-half-story ponderosa pine log residences, all situated along four hundred feet of shoreline. Each individually owned unit has three thousand square feet of "style and space" and includes vaulted ceilings, three bedrooms, two fireplaces, an entertainment center, and several other amenities. When not occupied by their owners, the units are available for rent. Also on the grounds is a "classic" Finnish sauna, converted from a former Star of the North building.[45]

### Gunderson's General Store and Cabins
### *(now private residences and cabins)*
Gunderson Lane

A short distance separated Star of the North from Gunderson's General Store and Cabins. The business was started on property acquired by Fritjof ("Fred") Gunderson, an experienced fisherman who had emigrated from Norway's Lofoten Islands to Cook

**Two hunters, who were transporting a deer on the fender of their 1928–29 Ford Model A Sport Coupe, posed for this photograph shortly after Gunderson's General Store opened in 1930. Courtesy of Cook County Historical Society.**

County in 1910, five years before his marriage to Elen Olson. Gunderson and his Swedish father-in-law, John Olson, began developing the property by disassembling a nearby log house and rebuilding it on their lakeshore site. The family's business venture was established in 1923 when they started supplying food and lodging for a few workers involved in the construction of Minnesota Highway 1; a cabin originally built for Gunderson's friend, a Great Lakes sailor, housed some of the men. Once Gunderson's General Store opened in 1930, motorists were able to purchase general merchandise, camping supplies, Energy gas, and Puritan oil. Several free campsites were also available, and eight housekeeping cabins appeared a few years later.[46]

The Gundersons transferred the business to three of their daughters in 1962. The sisters attracted a steady stream of tourists, among them several authors who sought out the solitude, immediate lake access, "clean" cabins, and "comfortable beds" that characterized the resort. Gunderson's closed in 1994, following some sixty-five years of continuous operation; the property was eventually subdivided into separate lots and sold to individual buyers. Some cabins may still be rented, while the Gundersons' original log home, now covered with siding, continues as a private residence.[47]

### Temperance River State Park
### 7620 Highway 61

The Anishinaabe name for this thirty-nine-mile-long waterway, Kawimbash (Deep Hollow River), was used by American geologists David Dale Owen and J. G. Norwood, who surveyed the North Shore from 1848 to 1852. In 1865, fellow geologist Thomas Clark would write, perhaps in jest, that exhausted voyageurs searching for a sheltered landing were baffled by the lack of a gravel bar at the river's mouth; therefore they called it the "no *bar* or Temperance River." Although the exact origins of such an unusual but intriguing place name may never be known, there is no doubting the primary attractions of Minnesota's ninth most visited state park in 2019—a river with spectacular views of waterfalls and the rush of water along a narrow gorge that twists and turns through rapids for a quarter mile, just before it descends and enters Lake Superior. The river's sharp gradient allowed the water to wear through the site's lava flows for thousands of years, and the potholes formed from this action eventually connected together and created the gorge.[48]

In 1931–32, shortly after MDH acquired two hundred acres of land along both sides of the river's mouth, a concrete, barrel-vaulted bridge, very similar to the nearby Cross River span, was under construction. As the bridge neared completion in 1933, enrollees from Northern Light CCC Camp 1728 lined the viewing platforms and walkway edges with stones and small boulders and also covered the steps with a veneer of native stone. Camp 1728 was highly unusual for northern Minnesota in that its ranks were formed by Black enrollees who had arrived from St. Louis, Missouri, in June 1933. The men were transferred back to St. Louis one year later, after members of the Tofte Township Board asserted that local residents weren't "accustomed to live near any colored race" and requested relocation of the camp "further back in the interior or any other place where local whites will not object." (Such exclusionary attitudes were not universal throughout the area, however, as will be seen when viewing the Lyght family's experience in nearby Lutsen Township.) An all-white group of enrollees, members of Camp Temperance CCC Company 2705, reopened the outpost in 1934, where they remained until its 1936 closing.[49]

Among the state park's distinctive cultural landscape features are four sets of trail steps, all designed by Arthur Nichols and built by the members of CCC Camp 2705. One, a walkway (now closed) located beneath the bridge, allowed hikers to stroll along the river; it included a boulder wall that kept them "from falling into the gorge." Another feature, situated at the northwestern end of the bridge wing wall, reveals an elegantly curved set of eight gabbro steps set into concrete. Also part of the park are two parking areas, one at each end of the bridge. (The southwestern lot was labeled a "pedestrian outlook" in the original 1935 plan.) Two separate campgrounds were built close to the river's mouth in 1937–38, again by CCC enrollees. Here, declared a Two Harbors newspaper reporter in April 1938, "the camper not only has the convenience of this fine camp but is within five minutes of high falls . . . where the water falls over a high rock escarpment and down into Lake Superior."[50]

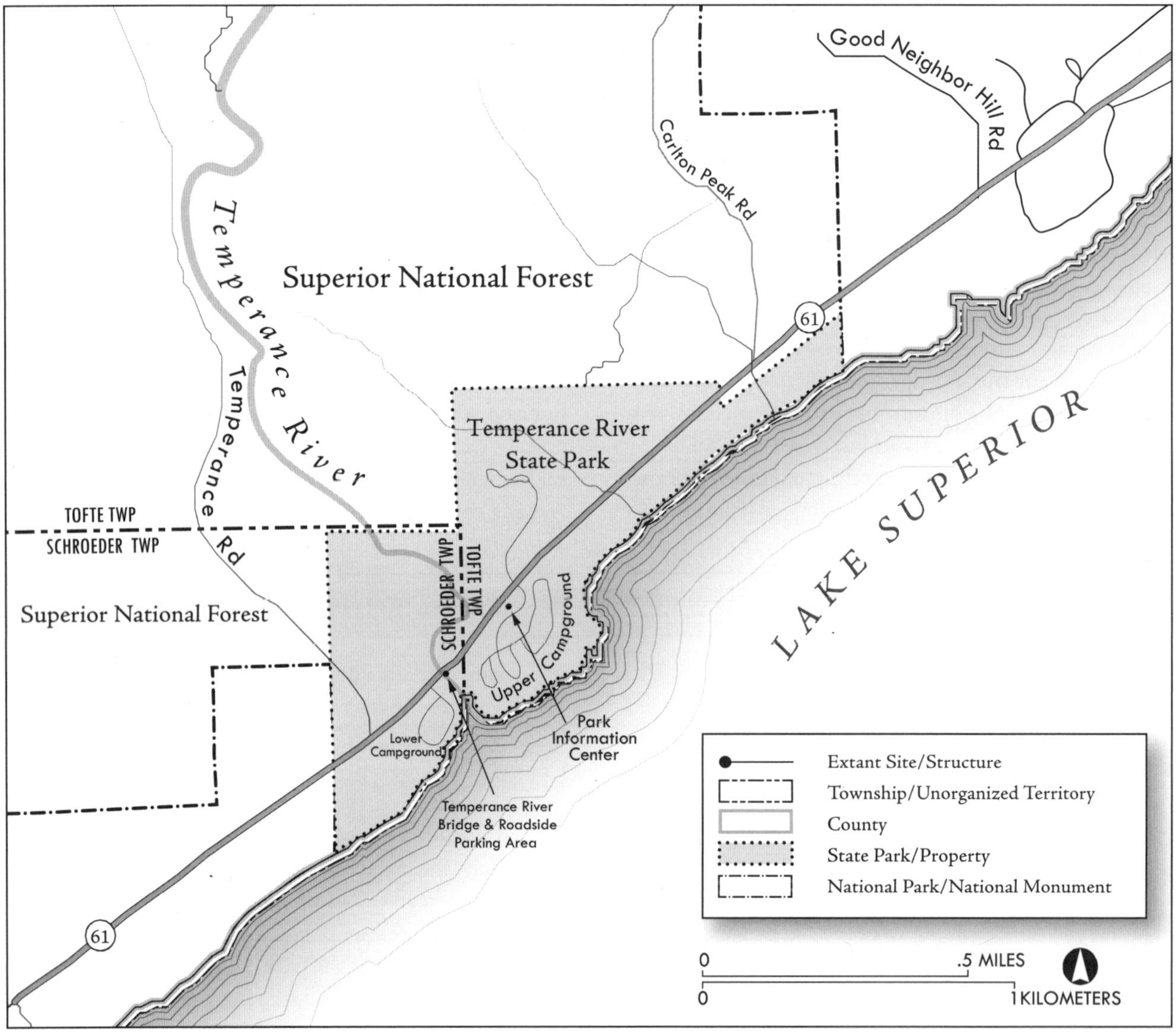

Good Neighbor Hill Rd
Carlton Peak Rd
Temperance River
Superior National Forest
61
Temperance Rd
Temperance River
State Park
LAKE SUPERIOR
TOFTE TWP
SCHROEDER TWP
SCHROEDER TWP
TOFTE TWP
Superior National Forest
Upper Campground
Lower Campground
Park Information Center
Temperance River Bridge & Roadside Parking Area
Extant Site/Structure
Township/Unorganized Territory
County
State Park/Property
National Park/National Monument
0
.5 MILES
0
1 KILOMETERS
61

The official transfer of the Temperance River property from MDH to the State Parks Division of MDC occurred in 1957. Eventually, however, concerns were expressed over the site's limited size of two hundred acres, which did not even approach the minimum five-hundred-acre standard recommended by a major 1971 study of Minnesota's state parks. Although Temperance River was officially "grandfathered" into the state park system in 1984, a later merger of the property with the nearby 2,520-acre Cross River Wayside and 2,250-acre Carlton Peak Area clearly resolved any size issues during the 1990s. The Carlton Peak summit, standing 924 feet above Lake Superior, is among Minnesota's highest points and one of only three state park sites (along with Palisade Head and Shovel Point at Tettegouche) to allow rock climbing.[51]

**The steps that CCC enrollees carved out of bedrock during the 1930s still serve as important features in the Temperance River State Park trail system.**

## Tofte Township

Tofte, the oldest of Cook County's present-day townships, was settled in 1893, primarily by Norwegian immigrants. "Carlton Peak" was proposed as the post office name in 1896, but because "Carlton" already identified a county and village in northeastern Minnesota, an alternative name, "Tofte," was chosen instead. The name, adopted officially by the U.S. Post Office Department in 1897, was derived from "Toftevaag," the diminutive Norwegian island home of several early residents.[52]

By 1900, only forty-two people, fourteen of them Norwegian immigrants, lived within the area that would become Tofte Township. When Tofte's residents sought to expand their settlement in 1902, three men departed for Toftevaag with the intention of encouraging friends and family members to return with them to settle in the North Shore community. Chris Murphy, editor of the *Cook County Herald,* observed the success of their efforts in early October, when the *America* arrived with twenty-six émigrés from the "mother country," three of whom were recent orphans. "The new arrivals are a very desirable lot of settlers," wrote Murphy, "and their coming is a very important step in the county." By 1910, the township's 131 residents included fifty-two Norwegian immigrants and twenty-six Norwegian American children.[53]

From 1899 to 1906, Tofte also embraced present-day Schroeder and Lutsen Townships. Tofte's township government came to an end in 1935, however, and was not reestablished until 1979. Its population ranged from 230 to 275 residents between 1990 and 2020, but the importance of seasonal residents is clearly evident, given that only 150 of the township's 355 housing units (42 percent) are occupied year-round. A considerable portion of Tofte's built environment reflects the high standards of design and workmanship that have been practiced by several generations of skilled builders, carpenters, and contractors. Also of importance is the Tofte Design Review Committee, which has played a major role in maintaining these standards since 1992. The

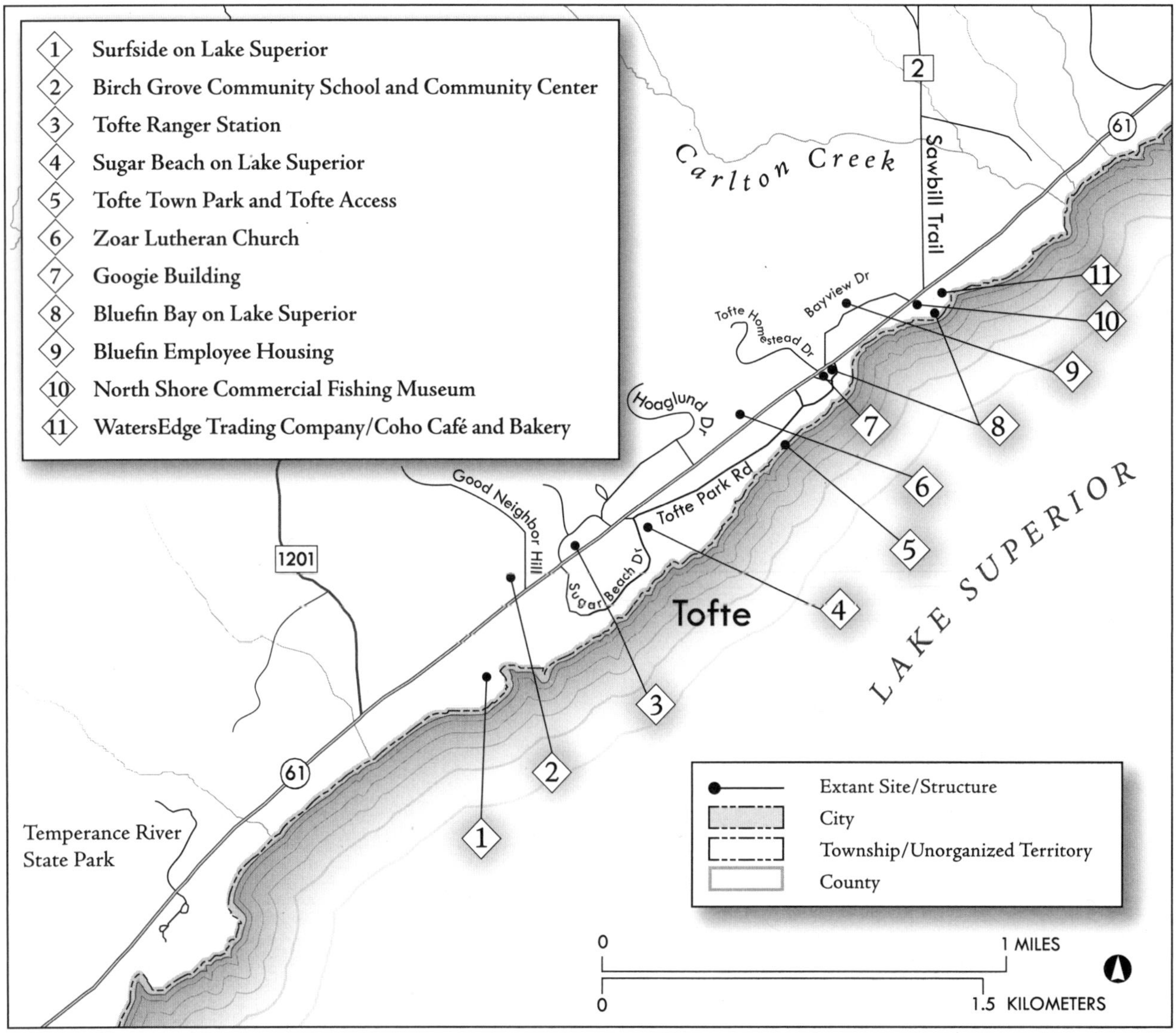

1 Surfside on Lake Superior
2 Birch Grove Community School and Community Center
3 Tofte Ranger Station
4 Sugar Beach on Lake Superior
5 Tofte Town Park and Tofte Access
6 Zoar Lutheran Church
7 Googie Building
8 Bluefin Bay on Lake Superior
9 Bluefin Employee Housing
10 North Shore Commercial Fishing Museum
11 WatersEdge Trading Company/Coho Café and Bakery
Carlton Creek
Sawbill Trail
2
61
Bayview Dr
Tofte Homestead Dr
Hoaglund Dr.
Good Neighbor Hill
Tofte Park Rd
Sugar Beach Dr
1201
Tofte
LAKE SUPERIOR
Temperance River State Park
Extant Site/Structure
City
Township/Unorganized Territory
County
0
1 MILES
0
1.5 KILOMETERS

**In early October 1902, the twenty-four immigrants who had been recruited from Toftevaag, Norway, arrived in Duluth, where they were greeted by several Tofte residents. After posing for this photograph, the entire group sailed to Tofte on the SS *America*. Courtesy of Cook County Historical Society.**

committee was formed by Dennis Rysdahl (founder of the Bluefin Bay Family of Resorts) and several other year-round and seasonal citizens who expressed alarm over the number of inquiries Tofte Township officials were receiving from franchise businesses seeking development opportunities. Concerned that such buildings might spell an "end of what was left of a small-town feel" in Tofte, the committee developed a set of design guidelines to "mimic the simplicity and authentic accretionary diversity found in old fishing villages rather than the sanitized uniformity of new developments." The guidelines seek to promote a pedestrian character throughout the community and encourage building designs that feature "traditional materials, shapes, and forms." Rather than imposing excessive restrictions on developers and builders, the committee asks them to consider "the remarkable natural beauty of the area by creating structures . . . designed to complement both their individual sites and surroundings."[54]

### Surf Side Cabins (*now* Surfside on Lake Superior)
10 Surfside Drive

The eastern side of Temperance River State Park extends into Tofte Township. A fishing camp existed just a few hundred feet from the current park boundary during the 1890s, some years before the property was acquired by Lars Godin. In 1925, Godin would sell a twenty-acre parcel with 740 feet of Lake Superior shoreline to Wisconsin resident Rudolph ("Rudy") L. Swanson, who taught in the schools of Tofte and Grand Marais from 1924 to 1927. Swanson and his wife, Cosey, "carved out" a space from the balsam and spruce forest on their lakeshore holding, put in an access road, and constructed the eleven cabins that composed their Surf Side resort. The first four units, completed in time for the 1927 tourist season, were built of split, vertical logs; a half wall of upright logs separated the combination kitchen and dining room. The couple and their two young sons departed Cook County after Swanson received a Wisconsin teaching offer for the 1927–28 school year, but the family returned to Tofte during the summers and operated the cabin complex until the United States entered World War II. Most guests, Swanson later recalled, stayed at the resort to escape the heat of the Twin Cities, to enjoy the lake views, and "to just loaf." The income provided by their cabins, which could be rented for twenty to twenty-seven dollars per week, was of great importance to the family during the summer months, when Swanson wasn't engaged in teaching.[55]

Also a photographer and storyteller, Swanson, in 1938, started taking color movies of the North Shore and Gunflint Trail, which he later presented to Wisconsin and Chicago audiences. Within a few years, the busy educator was receiving requests from several owners of midwestern industrial and commercial firms to film their factories and facilities. When Swanson's client list grew to sufficient size by 1948, he left teaching and launched a successful movie production company. By this time, Surf Side was run by new owners, who continued to tout the resort's carefully located shoreline cabins. When Roger and Betty Brustad purchased Surf Side in 1952, the couple announced their plans to modernize the resort by providing the cabins with electric refrigerators that had "deep-freeze units"; another decision that reflected the nation's overall postwar tourist environment was the addition of a four-unit motel.[56]

In 1963, Twin Citians Richard and Gloria Noren acquired the cabins and motel. Noren, a U.S. Marine Corps veteran of World War II, died in 1983, but his

**This "western-style motel" was added to Surf Side Cabins by Roger and Betty Brustad in 1952.**

widow operated the business until 2005, when she sold the property to the Tofte-based Bluefin Bay Family of Resorts. The existing buildings were replaced, in 2009, by Surfside on Lake Superior—the most recent of three developments initiated by the Bluefin Bay company. (All three resorts were purchased by new owners in July 2020.) When presenting his proposal to the Tofte Township Board in 2006–7, Bluefin developer Dennis Rysdahl, who partnered with Charles Anderson on the project, stated that the design would provide a "new look" for the area but also follow the "Scandinavian motif found in much North Shore architecture" and offer a "contemporary reinterpretation of traditional forms." Comprising five structures, each with three townhouse units that separately offer three thousand square feet of living space, Surfside is now described as a "perfect blending of coastal and contemporary architecture" that has "dramatic angles, vast expanses of glass, indescribable views," and "more balconies and patios than any other resort of Minnesota's North Shore." The townhouses are sold as one-quarter unit shares and may be rented out when not occupied by an owner.[57]

### Birch Grove Community School and Community Center
9 Good Neighbor Road

Tofte Township's Birch Grove Community School represents a story of losses and problems that small communities can encounter when a nearby resource-based facility—in this case, the Taconite Harbor dock and shipping center—is closed on sudden notice. But, at the same time, Birch Grove also reveals how the resilience and commitment of local residents and governments can protect a valuable community resource when it is under duress.

The population surge that accompanied the construction and operation of Taconite Harbor during the 1950s led to significant increases in the number of elementary-age children who resided within Cook County's three West End townships of Schroeder, Tofte, and Lutsen. Tax revenues generated by the Taconite Harbor facility provided funds for the construction of a new elementary school, Birch Grove, which opened in February 1964 with space for 230 students. Designed by the Hibbing and Duluth architectural firm of Jyring & Whiteman, Birch Grove was described by Dean Schweickhard, a former Minnesota commissioner of state education, as "not a palace, but a building that is light, safe, roomy, well-planned, and economical to maintain."[58]

Twenty years later, however, the Cook County School Board voted to close Birch Grove because of steep declines in enrollment. Despite the seemingly dire situation, the facility reopened one year later, primarily because of parental concern over subjecting young children to daily bus rides, some as long as eighty round-trip miles, between their homes and the Grand Marais school. The reopening was possible only after parents organized the Birch Grove Foundation (BGF), financed by township revenues, donations, and "just about every fund-raising trick" available to the group. Because of its ample space, the Birch Grove building also served as a community center that hosted a medical clinic, a youth hostel, special events, and one or two small businesses.[59]

Although Birch Grove remained open for the next twenty years because of BGF's efforts, the school once again faced closure in 2005 due to financial shortfalls. Just before the doors shut permanently, however, the Minnesota Department of Education gave Birch Grove a new lease on life when it was selected as one of the state's twelve public-supported charter schools. Because of its charter status, and the continued assistance provided by BGF and the three townships, Birch Grove remains open today. Tofte Township owns the building, which also serves as a community center that has tennis courts; a playground, hockey rink, and warming house; an outdoor bake oven; and, most notably, a timber-frame pavilion constructed by one Grand Marais North House Folk School class.[60]

### U.S. Forest Service, Tofte Ranger Station
7355 West Highway 61

Most North Shore CCC projects were built beyond the developed areas of towns and settlements, although an exception occurred on the forty-eight-acre Tofte Ranger Station site: here seven of the current eleven buildings were erected at the settlement's western edge in 1935–36 by members of CCC Sawbill Camp 716. (The camp, by this time, had received one of the highest ratings for work completed in the CCC's East Superior

Subdistrict.) Six structures were constructed of logs—the district office building, a ranger's garage, an oil house, a carpenter shop/storage building, and two dwelling units. The round aspen and red pine logs, with diameters ranging from seven to fourteen inches, were carefully scribed and tightly fitted together. The corner and interior supporting walls were joined together with saddle notches; the chiseled log ends extend beyond the walls. Supervising the log-construction work were three Finnish craftsmen who served as the CCC's local experienced men.[61]

The U.S. Forest Service (USFS) has done laudable work in maintaining and preserving its Tofte building ensemble. By 2015, however, several structures required attention and repair: paint was peeling off the outer walls, damaged screens needed new trim, much of the window glazing was "cracked and falling off," two porches on the ranger's dwelling were "deteriorated and rotting," and some log ends had become "punky and rotten." In 2016, a group of specialists affiliated with the Northern Bedrock Historic Preservation Corps, headquartered in Duluth, dedicated 1,160 hours of time and effort to four buildings that demanded considerable rehabilitation work. Crew members replaced the deteriorating logs, applied new caulking to log joints, refurbished windows, improved drainage systems, and removed vegetation that compromised the structures. Also assisting in restoring the "buildings to their former glory" were four volunteers from Passport in Time, an organization that engages in historical research and the preservation of public properties throughout the United States.[62] Today the building grouping continues to mark a major gateway to the 420,000-acre Tofte Ranger District, which is part of the vast SNF that stretches northward toward Canada and includes the Boundary Waters Canoe Area Wilderness (BWCAW) within its jurisdictional boundaries.

**The district office building for the Tofte Ranger Station in 1936, shortly after its completion by members of Sawbill CCC Camp 716. The tightly fitted scribed logs and saddle notch corners serve as excellent examples of the high-quality construction work accomplished by CCC workers. Courtesy of U.S. Forest Service.**

### Sugar Beach on Lake Superior
### 7316 Tofte Park Road

Following their 1905 marriage, Lars and Anna Anderson Godin, both immigrant Swedes who had arrived in Minnesota a few years earlier, settled in Tofte, where they pursued commercial fishing and established a small farm along a large expanse of Lake Superior shoreline. Their property received its name during World War I, when two thieves, who had absconded with twenty bags of sugar weighing a total of one hundred pounds, fled from the Schroeder dock. As they were being chased, the men dumped the sugar (a valuable wartime commodity) into the lake at a point proximate to Godin's cow pasture.

The original North Shore highway closely paralleled Godin's land, but a more sylvan setting emerged in 1931 when a section of the right-of-way was moved slightly inland to its current location. The resulting gain in accessible shoreline property allowed the Godins to advertise the "rugged, restful surroundings" of their new Sugar Beach holding. The first four cabins appeared in 1937 and were followed over ensuing years by eleven more units: a few were constructed of horizontal or vertical logs, others of frame and board, and some used a combination of materials. Two had exotic names, Shangri-La and Valhalla (only Shangri-La exists today). A manager was hired to run the resort when the founder's son and daughter-in-law, Ralph and Olive Godin, assumed ownership in 1952. The cabins were sold, in 1984, to individual purchasers, all of whom became members of the Sugar Beach on Lake Superior Homeowners' Association; two of the cabins are still owned by John Godin, one of the founder's grandsons. The association's fifteen cabins

**Although they have not been used for many years, three of Lars and Anna Godin's original Sugar Beach structures still overlook Lake Superior. In the foreground is the one-time fish house, constructed of poured concrete; the double-door opening is now covered by boards. To the right is the net house, also built of poured concrete. The log structure in the background, called the "wash house," served as a laundry. Courtesy of Sugar Beach on Lake Superior, https://www.toftesugarbeach.com/.**

include a few significantly upgraded units that continue to reveal their original materials and features. The majority, however, are replacements that occupy the original sites; some have been winterized, and all are available for rent when not occupied by their owners.[63]

## Tofte

The unincorporated settlement of Tofte lacks official boundaries, but the density of development increases at the intersection of Highway 61 and Johannes Lane. It was, however, the official 1925 opening of Minnesota Highway 1 that firmly placed Tofte on the North Shore tourist map. Almost immediately, local promoters were informing visitors that they would "do well to stop a while at Tofte . . . a pretty little fishing village." The community, by the 1960s, was also advertising the "Free Outdoor Theatre" at the Tofte dump, where, every evening or late afternoon during the tourist season, wild bears gathered to search for food.[64] Although the town dumps once found in Tofte and other North Shore settlements were closed and replaced by well-regulated waste disposal stations several years ago, hungry black bears still seek out dumpsters and garbage cans; fortunately, the bruins are no longer encouraged to entertain tourists.

Located within Tofte are two of the North Shore's best-known high-end resorts, which date to the 1980s and 1990s, and a small but exemplary museum where the North Shore's commercial fishing history is presented and interpreted. And, as thousands of canoeing enthusiasts know, the Sawbill Trail—one of the major BWCAW entrance roads—begins in Tofte.

### Tofte Town Park and Tofte Access
Tofte Park Road

The first motorists who entered and exited southwestern Tofte during the 1920s traveled along a section of Highway 1 that closely paralleled Lake Superior's shoreline. When the highway right-of-way was relocated farther inland in 1931, the original route was renamed Tofte Park Road—a recognition of the small park that had recently appeared on part of the forty-acre homestead John and Cecelia Tofte claimed in 1906 and that they divided among their children around 1922. The couple's twenty-year-old daughter Elizabeth (soon a teacher in the Iron Range city of Hibbing) donated her parcel for use as a public park. In 1926,

**The two bridges and former water fountain (now a wishing well) in Tofte Town Park.**

the young woman's father hired several men, who made a careful selection of red, white, and blue cobblestones they found at a lakeshore site in Schroeder Township; from there, fishing boats transported the stones to the Schroeder settlement, where they were transferred onto horse-drawn wagons and hauled to the park site. After arranging the cobblestones by color and size, the men constructed two miniature bridges and a drinking fountain (now a wishing well) fed by springwater that flowed along a tile-lined trench. Cook County commissioner Hans Engelsen would soon describe the site as the "most beautiful free camping place on Highway No. 1," while a 1926 North Shore motorist's guide termed it "a clever tourist park" that had a campground equipped with tables, stoves, and a toilet. Although the stonework eventually deteriorated because of vandalism and neglect, the features were restored during the mid-1990s by two public-spirited Tofte residents.[65] The well-maintained facility continues as a classic representation of an early, pocket-sized North Shore park.

Adjacent to the park is a sheltered access for small watercraft, built by the MDNR in 1997 and improved in 2010. Tofte Township manages the two-acre basin, which includes a protective breakwater that is eighty-five feet long. Also comprising the site are a boat ramp, a historic concrete crib dock, and a small parking lot.[66]

**Tofte's Zoar Lutheran Church, completed in 1964, is one of the North Shore's most recognizable structures because of its parabolic roof form.**

## Zoar Lutheran Church
### 7239 West Highway 61

After Tofte's Norwegian residents organized a Lutheran congregation in late 1905, the members met in homes, the schoolhouse, and the town hall until 1909, when they dedicated their new church along the Sawbill Trail. Although the church was one of many buildings destroyed by a forest fire that swept through the area in May 1910, the congregation constructed a replacement within one year. By 1948, however, after concluding that parking cars on a nearby hill during wintertime was too inconvenient, the congregation decided that the church should be moved into the settlement, where Cecelia Tofte had donated a lot adjacent to her residence.[67]

Another major decision occurred in 1961 when Zoar's members commissioned the Duluth architectural firm of Morgenstern & Stenius to design a new church, which, after removal of the existing building, would be constructed on part of the original foundation. Because of its saddle roof form, Zoar is generally considered the most unusual of several churches that emerged on the North Shore during the postwar era. Its curved roof, technically a hyperbolic paraboloid, is built of several straight, three-hinged wooden arches of different lengths, all of which are angled around a central beam. Constructed of wood, stone, and steel by Tofte contractors Kenneth and Dale Olsen, Zoar was dedicated in 1964.[68] A relatively short wooden bell tower, restored in 2020, is situated just west of the church. Because the parking lot is situated at the rear of the property, motorists approaching from the southwest have a clear view of the church and bell tower, both of which stand before a backdrop of trees and vegetation.

## Googie Building
### 7210 Highway 61

In 1965, Kenneth and Dale Olsen constructed their North Shore version of Googie architecture—a popular American design form of the 1950s and 1960s. The Googie style, which originated in California, was inspired by the streamline moderne architecture of the 1930s as well as several ideas and forms associated with the "invisible forces of speed and energy" that characterized America's automobile culture and early Space Age. The style's curvaceous roof forms, angles, bright colors, and neon lighting typically found expression in drive-ins, motels, and gas stations, although several other building types, such as the Tofte building, display less flamboyant features.[69]

Since the Olsen brothers had recently overseen the construction of Tofte's Zoar Lutheran Church, they were familiar with the structural properties of parabolic roof forms, a common feature of many Googie buildings. Nevertheless, before proceeding with the project, Kenneth Olsen's daughter Maureen,

**Local motel owners and building contractors Dale and Kenneth Olsen, who had recently built Tofte's Zoar Lutheran Church, used their knowledge of parabolic roof forms to construct this North Shore version of Googie architecture in 1965.**

a UMD mathematics major, reviewed and approved the structural calculations for the Googie's roof. When completed in 1965, the Googie initially housed the Olsons' motel office but was later used for a succession of functions, including a gift shop, a business center for the Bluefin Bay Family of Resorts, a bank, a storage building, an artist's studio and gallery space, and a day spa. Although some of the Googie's original exterior features were removed or modified during these transitions, the parabolic roof and interior spaces remain quite intact.[70]

### Engelsen Homestead and Hotel, Olsen's Motel, and Hansen's Edgewater Inn (*razed, now* Bluefin Bay on Lake Superior)
7102 West Highway 61

Norwegian immigrants Hans and Johanne Engelsen established their homestead claim along the Lake Superior shoreline in 1893. Engelsen, who would play a key role in the formative history of both Tofte and Cook Counties, departed Norway in 1882, served in the U.S. Navy, and later moved to West Duluth, where, in 1890, he married Johanne Andersen, a recent Norwegian émigré. Engelsen, over ensuing years, was joined by his brother Torger, his twin brothers-in-law John and Andrew Tofte, and a small but steady stream of other Norwegian immigrants, including the twenty-six Toftevaag immigrants who arrived in 1902. Most of the arrivals initially supported themselves by engaging in fishing, logging, trapping, and subsistence farming.[71]

The Engelsens built a more substantial residence on their property in 1898 and, one year later, donated land along Tofte's bayfront for the construction of a large, cribbed dock. Although the dock could be accessed by fishing vessels and small tugboats, the water was of insufficient depth to handle steamships like the

SS *Dixon* and SS *America*. This posed a major problem for Tofte's residents, because they were forced to row out to the anchored ships when picking up and delivering passengers and merchandise or loading fish for shipment to Duluth wholesalers. Among the more poignant stories of Tofte's early history are those that recall the "dumping" of cattle and horses over the side of a vessel and forcing "the frightened and freezing animals" to swim all the way to shore. The construction of a longer concrete dock, completed in 1915, resolved the problem. A hand truck, used to move goods, mail, and barrels of fish, was pushed along the dock's two parallel steel rails.[72]

Also located in the store, where tourist supplies could later be "bought reasonable," were the post office and, eventually, a telephone exchange. Slightly to the west was the Engelsens' sixteen-room family home, which also included the Homestead Hotel—"a friendly place, and a focal point in the town to which travelers, fishermen, and lumberjacks turned to [for] lodgings." After Johanne Engelsen died in 1915, her widowed husband continued fulfilling his obligations as Tofte's dockmaster, store owner, hotelkeeper, and postmaster. A staunch Democrat and highly motivated, principled public servant whom voters elected as their Cook County commissioner for all but two years from 1895 to 1935, Engelsen was a consistent promoter of good roads, especially the North Shore highway. And because of his wit and humor, Engelsen often spoke at public events and gatherings. For a few years prior to his passing at the age of eighty-one in 1945, Engelsen also engaged in boatbuilding—one of the pioneer settler's early passions.[73]

Engelsen, sometime before 1925, sold the Homestead and its nearby cabins to his daughter and son-in-law, Esther and Olaf Osbakken. After another Engelsen daughter and son-in-law, Cecelia and Andrew (Sjo) Olsen, acquired the Homestead in 1931, the business was renamed the Tofte Lodge. Tragically, Olsen died in a January 1931 fire that consumed the building. His sons, contractors Kenneth and Dale, reopened the cabins at the conclusion of World War II and later built a two-story motel on the former hotel site; it would eventually include the Norse Room, a popular seafood and steak house.[74]

Situated just east of the Olsens' business, and also on Engelsen's original homestead claim, was the Edgewater, a summer-season diner that opened in 1937. The proprietor was Thomas Hansen, a Norwegian fisherman who, in 1927, had emigrated to the North Shore, where, seven years later, he married Madeline Jacobsen of Beaver Bay. Their diner also included a dance floor and sufficient space for showing movies. Soon after World War II ended, the Hansens converted their diner into a year-round facility and added a general store and "Greyhound dinner stop" onto the building. Then, in 1949, the couple opened their sixteen-unit Edgewater Inn, one of Minnesota's earliest motels. Unlike the modest quarters that characterized most North Shore lodging facilities at the time, some of the Edgewater's sixteen "all-modern" motel units had two bedrooms as well as a large living room and expansive windows overlooking Lake Superior.[75]

In 1963, the Hansens replaced the original inn, store, and restaurant with a two-story, box-like structure constructed of steel and concrete. One of its attractions was the restaurant, which had a second-floor dining room and an adjacent roof garden—a place where guests could enjoy the sun during the beautiful days of summer and later view the "magnificent" moon as it was "brilliantly shining over the lake." Also provided was a convention room for meetings and small conferences.[76] Overall, the Edgewater's rental units, dining services, rooftop features, and meeting rooms would serve as a precursor for the more expansive and expensive accommodations that began appearing at a few North Shore resorts during the 1980s.

The Hansens sold the entire holding in 1971, six years before it was acquired by the Olsen brothers, Kenneth and Dale, whose acquisition consolidated much of the homestead acreage their grandparents Hans and Johanne Engelsen had secured almost seventy-five years earlier. It was, however, the purchase of the entire Edgewater property, between 1981 and 1985, by Rob Buntz and Dennis Rysdahl that marked a watershed moment in the evolution of contemporary tourist facilities in northeastern Minnesota. Their company, the Bluefin Bay Family of Resorts, would eventually develop three "new breed" luxury resorts along the North Shore.[77]

The first Buntz–Rysdahl resort project, Bluefin Bay

on Lake Superior—designed by Minneapolis architects Jafvert, Mueller & Associates—emerged in Tofte on the former Edgewater property between 1985 and 1988. The architects' proposal, designed to reflect the "shapes and orientation of traditional Norwegian and Finnish communities," utilized some of the Edgewater's original features. Most noticeable was the former dining area, which received greater "depth and animation" with the addition of balconies, sunshades, and overhangs, before it reopened as the Bluefin Restaurant. The Hansens' original no-frills, flat, boxy units, built during the 1960s, were also retained and integrated into nine new condominium units by "wrapping" two and sometimes three new "gabled levels" around the buildings. Already in 1985, Bruce Wright, the editor of *Minnesota Architecture*, a professional magazine devoted to recognizing design excellence throughout the state and Upper Midwest, offered a glowing review of the resort: Bluefin Bay, he wrote, is comparable to "a shining New England coastal village transported through time and space."[78]

The success that followed the 1994 opening of Bluefin Bay led to the construction of eighteen additional townhomes along the bay's eastern side. By 2007, Rysdahl was the sole owner of the entire Bluefin Bay enterprise, which, by then, included two other major properties, one in Schroeder (Temperance Landing, 2006), the other in Lutsen (Surfside on Lake Superior, 2008). Rysdahl's ownership continued to 2020, when the company was purchased by Joe Swanson, a Twin Cities business and financial advisor originally from Silver Bay on the North Shore and who had worked seven summer seasons at Bluefin Bay while attending high school and college. Joining Swanson in the venture was Pipasu Soni, an engineer and financial analyst from India who resided in Winnipeg, Manitoba. The

**Thomas and Madeline Hansen's Edgewater Inn in 1954, when their business included a restaurant, store, and Greyhound bus stop. The units located at the far end of the complex, built during the late 1940s, composed one of the North Shore's earliest motels.**

The development of Bluefin Bay on Lake Superior incorporated some earlier features of the Edgewater Inn into its redesign. Also noticeable at the far left is a section of the original Tofte dock; at the right is a reconstructed fish house, now used to store boating equipment.

Swanson–Soni purchase assured that the site's uninterrupted history of guest services, originally established at the Homestead Hotel by Hans and Johanne Engelsen well over a century earlier, would continue as Tofte's signature commercial enterprise.[79]

### Bluefin Employee Housing
Tofte Homestead Drive

Among the pressing problems that North Shore tourist businesses have faced for several decades is a shortage of employee housing. People who are either retiring or planning to retire are purchasing North Shore properties, commented Rysdahl during the mid-1990s, but because of their "big-city incomes," the new residents often "outprice our local people." Rysdahl and Buntz addressed this issue quickly by providing a five-bedroom dormitory-style apartment for several workers. They pursued a similar action in 2000, but at a larger scale, by purchasing land directly north of Highway 61 and Bluefin Bay. Soon, six apartment buildings, each with three townhouse units, were available for moderate rents to Bluefin's employees. In 2016, two "mini-houses" (also termed "boreal bunkhouses"), fabricated at the Riverside Boatworks in Duluth, were trucked to Tofte and erected on the site. Designed by Grand Marais architect Russell Zenk, the units' spacious interiors and vaulted roofs reflect Tofte's Design Review Guidelines, established in 2002. Also nearby are three other structures: a guest service center; a utility/laundry unit; and a common amenity building that has a pool, exercise room, café, and full-service spa. The units house some of Bluefin's seasonal employees, including several from outside the United States who hold short-term or study visas.[80]

### Tofte's Store (*razed, now* North Shore Commercial Fishing Museum)
7136 West Highway 61

One of Tofte's outstanding attractions, a museum dating to 1996 that documents the history and heritage of North Shore commercial fishing, is situated on a site once occupied by a store that Andrew Tofte Jr. established during the mid-1920s. Upon moving to Duluth during World War II, Tofte purchased and oversaw

**Tofte's North Shore Commercial Fishing Museum replicates a former twin fish house, built for Hans Engelsen and Andrew and John Tofte, that stood on a nearby site.**

a fleet of trucks that delivered bulk gasoline throughout Minnesota. Eventually, his nephews Chester and Edward Tofte ran the business, which they expanded to include groceries, tourist supplies, lunches, draft beer, oil, and gas. Longtime Cook County resident Jerry Loh owned the business from the late 1970s to 1993, when it was sold to Bluefin Bay developers Rysdahl and Buntz.[81] Though much of the property was used for the expansion and development of eighteen Bluefin Bay townhomes, the community-spirited partners also donated land for an envisioned commercial fishing museum.

Among the early advocates for such a museum was Ted Tofte, a longtime public school educator and the former store owner's brother. One year after Tofte's 1991 death, his museum dream was carried on by members of the recently formed Tofte Historical Society. Efforts to carry out the organization's mission and goals—"the collection, preservation, and dissemination of historical knowledge . . . with specific emphasis on commercial fishing and more general relationship of early lifestyles to the shore and waters of Lake Superior"—were quickly under way. Five thematic "stories" now highlight the museum's displays: factual data about Lake Superior and its challenges, including a map depicting North Shore communities and fish houses; early boatbuilding history; identification of fish species and fishing techniques; transportation on early Lake Superior ships; and documentation of individual fishermen and fishing families.[82]

The museum's ground-breaking ceremony coincided with Tofte's centenary celebration during the Fourth of July weekend of 1993. The building, designed by retired Tofte architect Willis Schellberg, replicates a former double fish house constructed decades earlier by Hans Engelsen and brothers John and Andrew Tofte. The original two-story structure, which provided space for drying and repairing nets on the upper floor, was unique to the North Shore because of its picturesque "twin" form. The two lake-facing gables were divided by a common wall—an arrangement that allowed two fishing crews to share the building while carrying out their own activities. The original appearance of the boathouse was also replicated by painting the museum "Scandinavian fish house red." Funds were provided from membership grants, dues, and donations; considerable voluntary labor, much of it highly specialized, was also devoted to the project. The museum collections now include photographs, recordings, and more than three thousand artifacts ranging in size from fishing hooks to fishing boats, along with other forms of memorabilia. Many items find use as museum exhibits or are featured in the organization's *North Shore Commercial Fishing Museum Journal*, which first appeared in 2003.[83]

A lake walk with several interpretive panels and exhibits opened between the museum and Tofte Town Park in 2011. Close to the museum entrance is the *Viking*, a commercial fishing skiff built in 1949 by Larsmont's legendary boatbuilders Charles and Reuben Hill and purchased by brothers Walter and Leonard Sve of Lake County, who used the vessel for thirty-eight years. Termed "a terrific sea boat" by the Sves, the *Viking* carried them through several severe storms, none more memorable than one sudden nor'easter that "whipped up" waves ten to twelve feet high when the men were two miles from shore.[84]

The *Viking* was later retired and put on display outside the museum but began deteriorating because of exposure to the outdoor elements. The skiff, in 2011, was moved back to Split Rock, where Walter Sve and his son Lloyd restored it. Peter Henrikson, a master wood builder affiliated with the North House Folk School in Grand Marais, was also asked to supervise the construction of a culturally appropriate shelter that would protect the *Viking* when it was returned for display outside the museum. The Folk School class that started working on the shelter in early 2013 followed an ancient Viking-era timber framing technique, *grinbygg*, which Henrikson had observed and studied in Norway. Unlike other timber-frame structures, a *grinbygg* building employs no mortices and tenons but is stabilized with braces that are pegged into the posts, plate, and tie beam. The shelter's distinctive curved birch braces and all of the other wooden materials—tamarack posts, white pine beams, and rough-sawn red pine roofing planks—came from the local area.[85]

### Lakeview Service (*now* Watersedge Trading Company *and* Coho Café and Bakery)
### 7124 West Highway 61

Ray and Florence Kinkaid Gervais, both from small towns near St. Paul, Minnesota, moved to Tofte shortly after marrying in 1931. The couple, during the decade, would open their Lakeview Service building, situated at the intersection of Highway 61 and the Sawbill Trail, which included a grocery store, tavern, gas station, and automobile maintenance garage. The Lakeview was run by a succession of other owners before developer Dennis Rysdahl purchased the property

**The Lakeview Service building during the early 1950s. The business provided Tofte residents and visitors with numerous services and goods, ranging from groceries and tobacco to gasoline and automotive parts and repairs. Courtesy of Cross River Heritage Center.**

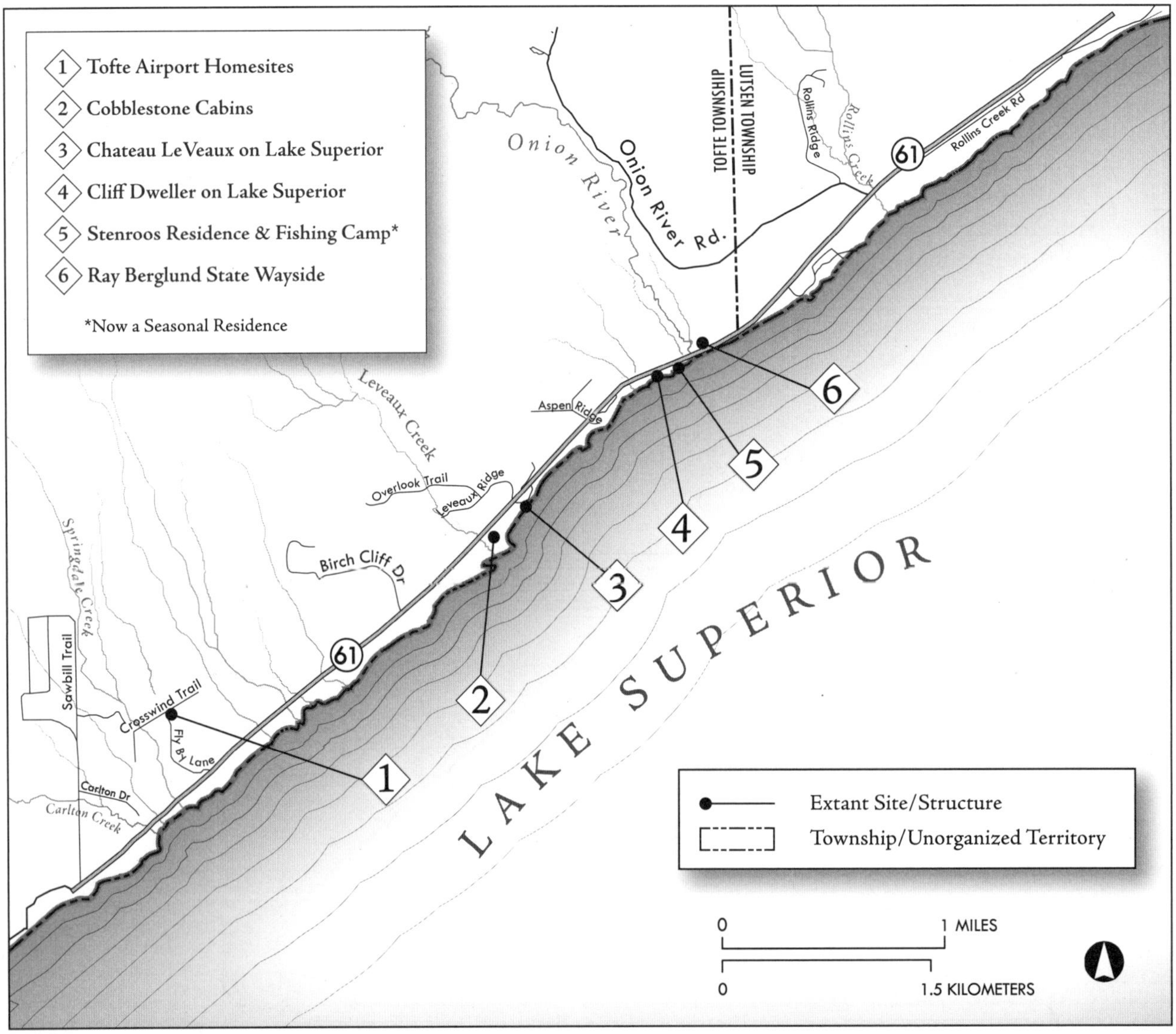

1 Tofte Airport Homesites
2 Cobblestone Cabins
3 Chateau LeVeaux on Lake Superior
4 Cliff Dweller on Lake Superior
5 Stenroos Residence & Fishing Camp*
6 Ray Berglund State Wayside
*Now a Seasonal Residence
Extant Site/Structure
Township/Unorganized Territory
0
1 MILES
0
1.5 KILOMETERS
LAKE SUPERIOR
TOFTE TOWNSHIP
LUTSEN TOWNSHIP
Onion River
Onion River Rd.
Rollins Ridge
Rollins Creek
Rollins Creek Rd
61
Aspen Ridge
Leveaux Creek
Overlook Trail
Leveaux Ridge
Birch Cliff Dr
Springdale Creek
Sawbill Trail
Crosswind Trail
Fly By Lane
Carlton Dr
Carlton Creek

in the 1980s.[86] He would subsequently modify the building, which now accommodates two businesses—the Coho Café and Bakery and the Watersedge Trading Company, a retail sales outlet that carries hiking and camping gear and outdoor clothing.

### Gervais Airstrip and Hangar (*now* Tofte Airport Homesites)

Fly By Lane, Crosswinds Trail, and Springdale Road

Tofte residents who looked skyward during the early 1940s often saw an Aeronca Super Chief, a high-winged light touring aircraft owned and piloted by Ray Gervais. In 1944, Gervais and a nine-man crew worked three weeks to clear out brush, develop an airstrip, and construct a hangar on land located a few blocks north of Highway 61. Identified as a "pilot, navigator, postwar planner, owner of the field and hangar, and pioneer in air traffic in Cook County," Gervais managed the airstrip, gave flying lessons, and even dropped illegally caught Canadian beaver pelts onto the nearby field, which were then stored in the hangar.[87]

Known as an outspoken promoter of Tofte, Gervais was an outdoor enthusiast who also photographed people and events throughout the local area. Although his property received consideration as a possible Tofte airport site in 1993, the proposal was not pursued because of the significant expenditures that were required to meet Federal Aviation Administration standards. The airstrip was abandoned in 2001 and incorporated into a 122-acre subdivision, Tofte Airport Homesites. The linear airstrip, nevertheless, still serves as an open-space buffer between the housing area's upper and lower sections. To date, only about a half dozen residences have been built on the thirty-eight lots, which are advertised as offering "some of the greatest convenience and affordability in the Lutsen–Tofte area."[88]

### Krueger/Hubbard Family Retreat (*now* Cobblestone Cabins)

6660 West Highway 61

About two and a half miles northeast of the Highway 61–Sawbill Road intersection is Cobblestone Cabins, the only remaining family-operated resort in the area. The 1925 origins of Cobblestone are tied to an extended family—members of the Krueger–Hubbard "clan"—who acquired the property some fifteen years before it was converted into a small resort. The key figures in its establishment were Minneapolis socialite Martha ("Jane") Krueger Hubbard and her husband, Charles F. Hubbard, the eldest son of Lucius F. Hubbard, Minnesota's ninth governor. Jane Hubbard, a flamboyant character in the complete sense of the term, "liked to joke, dance, and have fun"; smoked cigarettes with a long holder; and loved trout fishing, brandy, and expensive jewelry. The couple participated with several Krueger family members in purchasing the relatively large parcel of North Shore land just before a forest fire burned down its stand of old-growth trees. The optimistic Hubbards, nonetheless, oversaw the construction of their large, "showy" log residence, which was enhanced by two resplendent cobblestone fireplaces—one in the living room, the other in a bedroom.[89]

Charles Hubbard died in 1930, one year after most of the family's financial assets were lost in the worldwide stock market crash. His widow soon added a few rental cabins all covered with bark covered slash secured from a local sawmill—to the property, which she named Cobblestone Resort. In 1937, one year before her passing, the steadfast owner announced that Cobblestone was offering "24-hour service, meals at all times, running spring water in all cabins, 110 A.C. current lights, and a beautiful cobblestone beach." The resort, purchased in 1941 and subsequently owned by several other parties, was acquired, in 1975, by Jan Horak, a Twin Citian who was teaching at Tofte's Birch Grove Elementary School. Horak ran the resort by himself until 1980, when he married Kathy Jagunich, a Birch Grove music educator, originally from Eveleth on the Mesabi Range. After leaving teaching in 1987, Horak became a full-time resort operator.[90]

Although of Czech descent, Horak is a Finnish sauna enthusiast. Cobblestone's shoreline sauna, built in 1983, is regularly fired up for the owners and their renters, who, Horak asserts, definitely aren't members of the "BMW crowd." Instead, the Horaks gladly cater to the "characters and common folk" who are attracted by the sauna and free boats. Prospective patrons are also informed that they won't be disturbed by either TV or telephone and that the water provided by two wells, both 380 feet deep, is tastier than the bottled variety. Now, after a half century of resort ownership, Jan and Kathy Horak remain totally committed to the North Shore and their business. "Cobblestone is more than just cabins," Horak enthuses. "It's a way of life."[91]

**Until the Krueger family closed the North Shore Hotel in 1968, their guests could read, listen to music, and dance in the rustic lobby and office space, shown here during the 1950s. Courtesy of Cook County Historical Society.**

### North Shore Hotel (*removed, now* Chateau LeVeaux on Lake Superior)
6626 West Highway 61

Closely tied to Cobblestone was the North Shore Hotel, whose founder, Ray Krueger, was Jane Krueger Hubbard's nephew. As the director of food service at the Oak Grove Hotel in Minneapolis during the 1920s, Krueger was encouraged to open the restaurant by a wealthy St. Paul acquaintance, Frederick Dickey, owner of the No-See-Um Lodge in Lutsen. (Dickey reportedly informed Krueger that the North Shore's diners and restaurants "serve nothing but fish dinners.") Krueger bought a parcel of land next to Cobblestone in 1925 and made immediate plans for the development of a business, named the North Shore Inn. An autumn 1925 forest fire had destroyed all of the property's shoreline trees, but the conflagration didn't discourage Krueger and his two brothers from realizing their goal. Indeed, during the summers of 1926 and 1927, the men constructed their business on the "black, charred, and treeless piece of property." Soon renamed the North Shore Hotel, the two-story building had twelve rooms and two bathrooms. For the next thirty-five years, Krueger and his very hardworking wife, Lillian, served meals at all hours to as many as seventy-five patrons, some of whom were accommodated in their lodge and cabins and others who came from elsewhere on the North Shore. The hotel's guests could visit within its combination porch and sitting area, engage with the slot machines sequestered in a back room, and view a display of local rocks and minerals within a small museum. The visitors also played tennis, horseshoes, and mountain golf on the grounds and searched for agates along the shoreline. In 1960, when the couple had difficulty finding skilled cooks, they convinced the "two Joyces"—their daughters-in-law, both named Joyce Krueger—to assume the duties and thereby continue the North Shore Hotel's fine-food reputation.[92]

From 1933 to 1968, Krueger also worked as an assistant secretary for the Minnesota State Senate during the legislative session. This obligation meant that the Krueger's family life was typically divided into two segments—six months on the North Shore and six months in the Twin Cities. With the exception of a wartime interruption in 1944–45, the family operated their North Shore business for more than forty years before its 1968 closing. The lodge was subsequently taken apart, moved, and reassembled as a residence in Schroeder. Although it never again hosted tourists, it served as a home for several Vietnamese refugees during the mid-1970s. Now occupying the former North Shore Hotel site is the Chateau LeVeaux on Lake Superior, a thirty-one-unit condominium complex that opened in 1969–70.[93]

### Ray Berglund State Wayside
6355 Highway 61

This fifty-four-acre wayside has fourteen hundred feet of Lake Superior frontage and another eighteen hundred feet along the Onion River. The property was purchased in 1949 and donated to the State of Minnesota by the family and a large group of friends who wished to honor the memory of Ray R. W. Berglund—a St. Paul lumberman, conservationist, and "great lover and booster of the North Shore" who had recently died in an accident. After the land was quickly transferred to Minnesota's State Parks Division, MDH's RDD announced its ambitious plans for the wayside. Nevertheless, the improved area, when dedicated in 1959, was only one-third of an acre in size and offered little more than a blacktop parking lot and some picnic tables. Even as late as 1998, the Berglund site was still described as having "a very simple site design" and only a limited number of features.[94]

Several improvements were made to the wayside during the 2000s, thanks to funding provided by the Berglund Family Foundation and MnDOT. A redesign and rebuilding of the parking area occurred in 2009 when a section of the GGST was undergoing construction; also included among the site's improvements were its first restrooms, which appeared in 2014. Both upgrades were preceded by the construction of a stairway that leads up to the mile-long Onion River Trail, where views of Lake Superior and the river are offered.[95]

## Lutsen Township

A number of Cook County sites—including a township, a settlement, a post office, a celebrated resort, and others—are named Lutsen. In 1887, one year after filing a homestead claim at the mouth of the Poplar River, Swedish immigrants Carl Axel and Anna Peterson Nelson, accompanied by their young son Carl Jr., settled on the 156-acre site. Once the local population count reached twenty-five in 1890, Nelson's petition for a post office proved successful, although the name he requested, "Poplar," was not accepted by federal officials. Nelson then suggested "Lutzen," a German village in West Saxony where, at the midpoint of the Thirty Years' War in 1632, Swedish king Gustavus Adolphus II lost his life while leading a victorious Protestant army against Roman Catholic military forces. "Lutzen," nonetheless, was changed to the Anglicized "Lutsen" in 1895. The township was organized in 1906, disbanded in 1935, and reorganized in 1984.[96]

When the Nelsons began providing travelers with accommodations during the late 1880s, they were also establishing a foundation for the development and emergence of the North Shore as a major tourist destination. Indeed, the Nelsons are considered among the earliest resort providers in all of Minnesota. Since 1925, at least fifteen other tourist complexes, and a number of related businesses, have appeared along the eleven miles of Lutsen Township that border Lake Superior. And because of its current status as one of the Midwest's most important downhill skiing sites, Lutsen also serves as a major wintertime tourist destination.

In 1900, the area that, six years later, would be organized as Lutsen Township had a total population of sixty residents, thirty-five of whom were foreign-born, including eighteen Swedes and fourteen Canadians. The demographic composition of the township's 123 residents had shifted by the time of the 1920 census: eighty-two were born in the United States—a figure

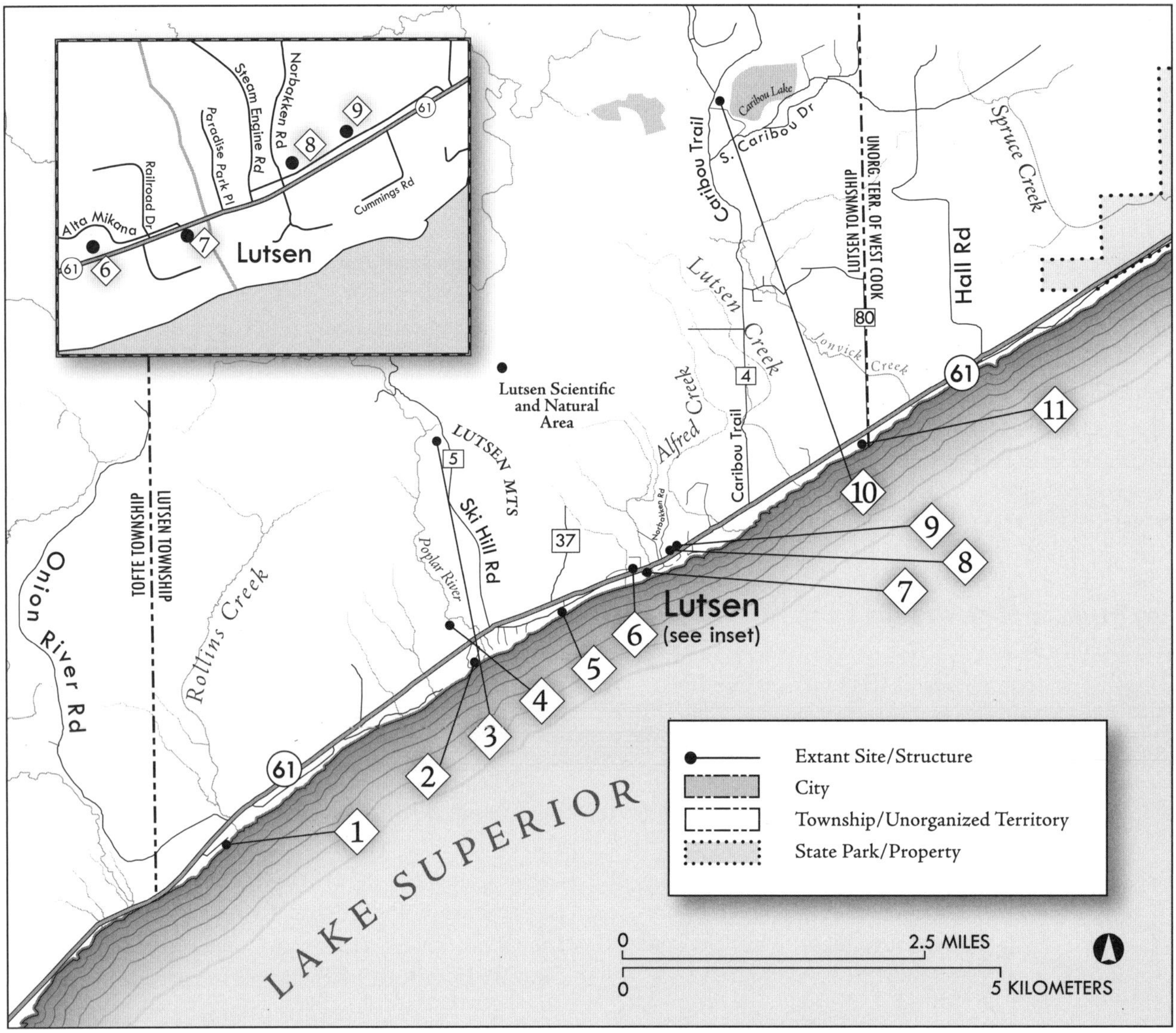


1 Lutsen Sea Villas
2 Lutsen Resort on Lake Superior
3 Lutsen Mountains Ski and Summer Resort
4 Superior National Golf Course at Lutsen
5 Ours Resort
6 Arrowhead Electric Cooperative
7 Lockport Marketplace and Deli
8 Clearview Building
9 Lutsen Evangelical Lutheran Church
10 Cathedral of the Pines
11 Grandview Park

two times greater than the forty-one foreign-born inhabitants, thirty-nine of whom were Nordics: seventeen Swedes, thirteen Norwegians, six Finland Swedes, two Danes, and one Finn. While the township's total population increased slowly throughout the immediate post–World War II decades, the numbers have expanded more noticeably after 1990, when 240 residents were counted. The figures grew to 360 people in 2000, to 415 in 2010, and to 445 in 2020. Lutsen also has much more seasonal housing than either Schroeder or Tofte Township: just 235 of its 940 housing units (25 percent) were occupied by year-round residents in 2020. The township's housing stock also reflects the socioeconomic differences that exist between two segments of its population: one group comprising the "well-to-do for which living in the area does not present a problem," the other people with low-to-moderate incomes who "are typically working two to three jobs in their attempt to meet the high cost of living in the area."[97] Similar differences, of course, characterize many areas of the North Shore.

### Sunny Dale Cabins and Spruce Point (*now* Lutsen Sea Villas)

#### 6262 West Highway 61

Located about one-half mile northeast of the Onion River is a housing complex, Lutsen Sea Villas, which stands on sites once occupied by two resorts: Sunny Dale Cabins and Spruce Point. Sunny Dale was opened during the late 1930s by John and Cecelia Loh. A Norwegian immigrant, Loh, in 1919, married Cecelia Eide, who, as a five-year-old in 1902, had arrived in Tofte with the group of twenty-four Toftevaag émigrés. The Lohs engaged in commercial fishing and small-scale farming before establishing Sunny Dale, which had cabins for one to eight people. The resort attracted several well-known guests, among them Eva Sears of Sears, Roebuck and Company and Minneapolis Symphony Orchestra violinist Charles Hollowell, who performed impromptu concerts on the porch of his cabin. Arthur and Nora Hovland acquired Sunny Dale in 1953 and operated the resort until its 1968 closing. Adjacent to Sunny Dale was Spruce Point, where Leonard and Rose Kroll Ronning opened several cabins during the early 1950s.[98]

Lutsen Sea Villas, a group of one- and two-story townhouses, replaced the two resorts in 1968–69. Considered the North Shore's first condominium property, the Sea Villas complex was developed by George Nelson Jr. (a grandson of Lutsen Resort founders Carl Sr. and Anna Nelson) in response to the growing demand for housing during both the summer and winter tourist seasons. The development now comprises eleven buildings with fifty-seven units and a 1997 guest services building that has a registration area, indoor pool, sauna, and children's play section. The Villas' townhouses, many situated on the footprints of former Sunny Dale and Spruce Point cabins, are often touted as being "as close to the lake as you can get without getting wet." The Sea Villas was planned by architects Sövik, Mathre & Madson of Northfield, Minnesota, a firm that had previously designed three North Shore Lutheran churches, including one in Lutsen.[99]

### Curtis Cabins: The Architecture of Edwin Lundie

Early Nordic immigrants who settled on Minnesota's North Shore often relied on Old World traditions when constructing their homes and buildings. These folk and vernacular structures, in turn, have inspired several generations of architects, although few receive greater attention and respect than Edwin Lundie (1886–1972), an Iowa-born, St. Paul resident of Scottish descent whose understanding of Nordic design precedents remains unsurpassed. His ability to transform these concepts into physical form is expressed in seventeen North Shore summer homes and cabins, many with ancillary buildings, which Lundie designed along an eighty-mile-long section of Highway 61. Lundie's "winsome architecture," wrote Deanna Marohn Bendix in a 1983 issue of *Minnesota Architecture*, was "expressed in Midwest dialect, with the trace of a Scandinavian accent." The local crews involved in the construction of Lundie's buildings were often supervised by master contractor and carpenter Joe Pecore.[100]

Lundie established a St. Paul architectural practice in 1919, following ten years of apprenticeship, partnership, and intense self-study. His buildings, a large majority of them residential, have proved both "timeless and imaginative," but it is on the North Shore where Lundie's "most personally expressive work" may be found.[101] Given the architect's love for the North Shore, it is only natural that one of his most telling and oft-repeated references about the local environment would appear in a Grand Marais newspaper:

> All of the elements for an indigenous architecture were present. The bold scale of the rugged coast, the background on the forest, the intriguing beauty of the building site and then the great sweep of Lake Superior provided reasons for a particular concept. Present were the materials, the lumber and timber from the surrounding forests, the stone from the hills. And present also were skills of the artisan and craftsman to be explored, encouraged, and exploited.[102]

Lundie's first Nordic-inspired North Shore building was a relatively modest Schroeder Township cabin, designed for his own family in 1941. It was constructed of cedar, pine, and stone, and Lundie personally split the shakes used on the cabin roof, carved the corner posts, and built some of the furniture. During World War II, when most private construction activities came to a halt, Lundie was able to spend summers at the cabin, which gave him more time to study and gain a better understanding of Nordic timber-frame construction.[103]

One project Lundie designed immediately after the war is an appealing and well-maintained group of four structures, commissioned by Dr. Arthur H. and Fay Watkins Curtis. A 1902 Phi Beta Kappa graduate of the University of Wisconsin–Madison, Curtis captained both the baseball and unbeaten football teams in 1901 and was the head football coach in 1903–4. Following his 1906 graduation from Chicago's Rush Medical College, Curtis spent a distinguished career, from 1910 to 1947, as a physician, educator, and administrator at Northwestern University's Medical School in Evanston, Illinois. In September 1945, just one month after World War II ended, Curtis asked Lundie to design a Lake Superior family cabin. Three more structures would follow between 1946 and 1949: a guest cabin, a garage with upper-story living quarters, and a simple timber-frame woodshed that has six posts and a gable roof with enclosed ends.[104]

The Curtis site and buildings convey an impression of Norwegian farms and cottages situated in narrow valleys or along fjords. Here, on the North Shore, the thin sliver of land is bordered by a steep bank to the north, while the southern side, formed by three hundred feet of Lake Superior shoreline, is reinforced with a stone wall. Whether one is inside or outside

**The main cabin on the Curtis compound, situated on a narrow ledge overlooking Lake Superior, displays a sensitively designed combination of native stone and wood.**

**Lundie's design for the guest cabin is comparable to its larger counterpart, but also includes some distinctive features, especially the large chimney.**

the Curtis buildings, Lake Superior's presence and awesome power are always evident. Each structure is unique and serves a specific function, but all are unified by their materials, scale, and design details.

The compound's main cabin, a timber-frame building with a rectangular plan, sits on a foundation constructed of well-crafted native stone. Especially striking are the oversized, sixteen-inch white pine corner posts, each positioned on crossed sill plates that protrude beyond the intersection in a decorative manner. The front facade has large casement windows, each with twelve lights, which face Lake Superior from the living area and provide an intimate connection with the larger exterior environment. Inside the cabin's main living area is a large, sculpted fireplace, "massed from Superior stone, variegated in color, and randomly sized."[105]

The much smaller guest cabin, dominated by a massive, stepped-stone chimney, maintains the design vocabulary of its larger counterpart. So, too, do the cabin's corner posts, although they are smaller than those of the main building. A fireplace dominates one corner of the cabin's very efficiently organized interior, provided with built-in bunk beds that flank its galley kitchen. A third structure, although termed a garage, harkens back to another historic rural Norwegian building form—a two-story *loft*, which provided farmsteads with storage space; the upper floor could also

**This building, which includes a garage at the lower level and a guest room above, is similar in appearance to the *lofts* that appeared on historic Norwegian farmsteads.**

serve as sleeping quarters for summer-season workers. In Lundie's design, this space becomes a single guest room with a bathroom in one corner; the floor is accessed by stairs leading to a lakeside gallery that extends four feet over the lower level.

## Lutsen

Lutsen, sometimes termed "two and a half hours from a town of any consequent size," is the only unincorporated North Shore settlement identified as a census-designated place (CDP) by the U.S. Census Bureau. Although a CDP has no official boundaries, it must have a name that "is recognized and used in daily communication by the residents of the community." Because Lutsen lacks a settlement center, the CDP, first specified in 2010, covers an area of almost eleven square miles, or about 10 percent of the entire township. The CDP's 2010 population of 190 grew to 265 in 2020, a figure that represents somewhat more than 40 percent of the township's year-round inhabitants.[106]

Several business and institutional buildings are located along the segment of Highway 61 that stretches between Lutsen Resort at the southwest and Lutsen Lutheran Evangelical Church to the northeast. Located along the corridor are the historic Lockport Store as well as several contemporary structures, among them the Arrowhead Electric Cooperative. About halfway between the cooperative and church is a proposed district, identified as Lutsen's potential "town center" in a series of studies undertaken from 2004 to 2007 by the Center for Changing Landscapes at the University of Minnesota. Envisioned as a combined commercial and residential district "with a small village identity," one of the primary goals for the town center—providing "a mix of housing design and cost options"—remains the report's most prescient and elusive recommendation.[107]

### Lutsen Resort on Lake Superior
### 5700 West Highway 61

Lutsen Resort has played a key role in the development and growth of tourism on the North Shore since 1888, when Swedish immigrants Carl Axel and Anna Peterson Nelson began offering food and lodging to "foot travelers, boaters, fishermen, hunters, prospectors, and homesteaders." In 1893, one year after receiving official title to the 156-acre homestead, the Nelsons' business grew appreciably when several guest rooms were opened in their new residence. Upon its completion, the *Cook County Pioneer* noted that Nelson's original "shanty" had been replaced by "a comfortable home, beautifully located, a good barn and outbuildings, and a splendid garden." At the end of the year, an obviously pleased Nelson touted the couple's success: the house "is crowded with guests upon the arrival of every boat," he exuded, "and the weary traveler is well pleased with the spacious rooms, while the meals cannot be excelled. The Lutzen House is now certainly one of the best hotels on the north shore." The Nelsons also catered to local residents, as evidenced by a group of Grand Marais young adults who sailed to the resort on the *America* in August 1902. "Mr. Nelson is noted for his hospitality," observed the *Cook County News-Herald* upon their departure, "and a good time is assured in advance." Also located in the wilderness north of Lutsen was Camp Nelson, which, from 1900 to 1925, attracted wealthy hunters who paid as much as $300 for the opportunity to bag a moose.[108]

George Jr. and his wife, Inga Toftey Nelson, were by 1922 assisting his parents in operating the family's business, which, by 1928, included the lodge and an employee dormitory called the Cottage. At capacity, the lodge accommodated as many as 225 guests in its

Lutsen Lodge as it appeared during the 1920s.

**The Birch Room in the original Lutsen Lodge displayed a unique example of Northwoods-inspired interior design. Birchbark covered much of the wall surfaces, cuttings of small birch saplings and branches were arrayed on the ceiling in geometric patterns, and the tables and plant stands may have been crafted from birchwood.**

eighty-five bedrooms, each supplied with a single and double bed. If necessary, hunters and fishermen could be asked to share a room, and even a bed, with strangers. In 1923, the senior Nelson built a hydroelectric plant along the Poplar River that provided electricity for the resort and several nearby homes; it functioned until 1941, when the REA brought power to all of Lutsen. Upon his death in early 1946, Carl Nelson was eulogized as a former resort operator, boat captain, commercial fisherman, logger, store owner, postmaster, census enumerator, Cook County commissioner, and chairman of both the local school board and Lutsen Township. Just one year earlier, the younger Nelsons had acquired the resort, a place they described as "easy to get to, but hard to leave."[109]

After a June 1948 fire destroyed the resort's twenty-room dormitory, a much more disastrous October conflagration demolished the lodge and numerous historic artifacts that the Nelsons had collected over a half century. A new lodge, constructed of virgin white pine logs that Nelson harvested from his own land, soon replaced the original building. The architect was Edwin Lundie, who already had designed a few of his acclaimed North Shore cabins. The dining room of the new lodge, although only partially finished at the time of its July 1949 opening, reportedly had "no effect on the food and [guests'] appetites, which are as good as ever." Unfortunately, the lodge, not yet completed, was also consumed by a fire, this time in December 1951. The determined couple, nonetheless, once again chose to rebuild and replicate the former structure. "It will be in the Swedish architectural style," reported Nelson, "with hand-hewn logs and carved doors on the same location near the mouth of the Poplar River." The new lodge was open for business by July 1953.[110]

Although all of Lundie's North Shore buildings represented sophisticated interpretations of rustic Nordic traditions and craftsmanship, Lutsen Lodge served as the largest and only publicly accessible example of his design skills and talents. Of special note was Lundie's ability to integrate multiple details throughout a building of such significant size. The massive entry door, built of two square forms that provided structural stability, opened into the lobby and dining room. There one immediately encountered timber posts and beams, rich wooden paneling, and a large fireplace constructed of stones rescued from the previous building. The stairway leading from the lobby to the second-floor rooms demonstrated Lundie's understanding and appreciation of intricate wood-carving and construction details: the tall newel-post was topped by a flared finial, and the spindles were carefully fastened to the handrail by wooden pins. The building's exterior also revealed the architect's touch: the lake-facing wall, sheathed with both horizontal and diagonal siding "in a rich array of directions," enhanced its timber-frame appearance, and the roof's expansive slope was "miniaturized" by a set of five identical and equally spaced dormers. The U-shaped plan, in 1959, was extended toward the northwest to accommodate a swimming pool and small conference center. Two other structures, both designed by Lundie, also appeared elsewhere on the grounds: one a roofed-over pedestrian bridge, built of timber-frame and carved posts, which crosses a nearby stream that flows into the Poplar River, the other a striking, Nordic-inspired, "obelisk-like post" with an entrance sign that appeared by the highway in July 1961.[111]

A momentous event in Lutsen Resort history occurred in 1988, when the property, after almost a century of Nelson ownership, was sold to Scott Harrison and Nancy Burns. Over the next three decades, Harrison and Burns would construct three new housing developments on nearby land—Lakeside Log Cabins, Poplar River Condos, and Cliff House Townhomes—thereby increasing the number of purchase and rental opportunities at Lutsen. Perhaps not as apparent to everyone, but certainly one of the couple's most laudable achievements, was the attention they devoted to protecting, maintaining, and preserving Lundie's iconic lodge. A telling example of their success was evident in 2012 when Minnesota's architects named Lutsen the state's "top lodge." One obviously impressed respondent even recommended that Lundie's Nordic-inspired architectural style should be adopted "as a standard vernacular . . . for sensitive development in the Northwoods."[112]

In August 2018, thirty years after their purchase, Harrison and Burns sold Lutsen to the North Shore Resort Company (formerly the Campbell Hospitality Group), owned by a Canadian son-and-mother team, Bryce and Sheila Campbell. The reported price, $8.5 million, was a North Shore record until 2020, when the Campbells secured the Superior Shores and Conference Center in Two Harbors for $15 million. Upon making the Lutsen purchase, Campell stated his intention to maintain the original appearance, features, and "historic feel" of the resort's primary attraction and showcase, namely, its "boutique lodge." While restoration of the dining area retained the hand-carved beams and columns that had been designed by Lundie, some modifications were made to the interior walls, floor, and furnishings. The revised menu included an expanded number of food options, many based on local ingredients, and some two hundred different wines that were stored in a cellar that included twelve hundred beverage bottles.[113]

Tragically, the third Lutsen Lodge also experienced an ignominious finale during a cold, early morning in February 2024, when a "ferocious and violent fire" consumed the entire structure. After hearing of the disaster, large numbers of people throughout Minnesota, the Midwest, and elsewhere immediately went on various social media sites to grieve and express their sense of loss. Among the commentators was Minnesota's U.S. senator Amy Klobuchar, a cochair of the Senate's Travel and Tourism Caucus. Minnesota has many "iconic places," she noted in her posting, "but Lutsen really stands out." Architect and "cabinologist" Dale Mulfinger, Lundie's foremost biographer, immediately observed that loss of the lodge went "far beyond those who treasure it for the personal memories made there. It's [also] a loss for those who care about architecture." Fortunately, Edwin Lundie's legacy of architectural

**The first Lutsen Lodge, destroyed by a 1948 fire, was soon replaced with a new structure designed by architect Edwin Lundie, but it also burned down in late 1951. A third lodge that replicated Lundie's former design opened in late 1953; that building, shown here in 2022, stood on the grounds until February 2024, when it, too, was reduced to ashes by another blaze.**

plans, drawings, and details had been collected, protected, and archived decades earlier. Because of their existence, resort manager Edward Vanegas made a bold prediction just hours after the disaster. "Lutsen Lodge will be rebuilt," he reported, "and new memories will be created from the newly built Lundie building."[114] Whether such a demanding, complicated, and expensive building project will ensue, of course, is impossible to predict at this time. And, as mentioned earlier in the Lake County discussion of Superior Shores, Bryce Campbell is facing legal and financial repercussions for his recent default.

### Lutsen Mountains Ski and Summer Resort
467 Ski Hill Road

The groundwork for a major Lutsen expansion occurred in early 1946, shortly after the Nelsons' son George Jr. returned from military service. While training for World War II combat duty with the U.S. Army's Tenth Mountain Division at Camp Hale in Colorado, Nelson had visions of a ski area on the Sawtooth Mountains. In July 1948, his always public relations–conscious father invited Minnesota's Republican governor Luther Youngdahl and several other dignitaries to a conference that was broadcast over the state's NBC radio stations. The program was highlighted by a major proclamation—an announcement that Minnesota's first winter resort would soon be built at Lutsen. Construction commenced almost immediately and continued even after the October 1948 fire that destroyed the family's Lutsen Lodge. A modest December celebration marked the completion of two ski runs and rope tows, a warming house, and access roads.[115]

The entire skiing area experienced numerous improvements during the 1960s: chairlifts replaced the tow bars, while snowmaking machines, a chalet, and additional ski runs appeared on the landscape. The facility received more publicity in 1976 when the Nelsons' daughter Cindy, who began downhill skiing at Lutsen as a young child, won a bronze medal at the Winter Olympic Games in Innsbruck, Austria. Twenty miles of cross-country trails and a summer alpine slide appeared between 1977 and 1979, just before Charles Skinner's 1980 purchase of the entire facility; he would soon add a gondola to the Lutsen site, a first for the Midwest. After Skinner's son Charles Jr. and son-in-law Tom Rider acquired the property (now known as the

**The major skiing facilities now evident at Lutsen began with two downhill runs and rope tows during the 1950s.**

Lutsen Mountains Corporation) in the 1990s, the two men implemented a multimillion-dollar expansion program that resulted in the development of more ski runs and lifts on four Sawtooth Mountain peaks: Moose, Eagle, Ullr, and Mystery. In 2015, an eight-passenger Deppelmayr gondola with heated seats replaced the former chairlift at Moose Mountain, regarded as one of the Midwest's most challenging alpine slopes. New and expanded skier services, dining areas, and music venues were added to the complex, as were seventy-four "ski-in/ski-out" condominiums and suites.[116]

Identified in 2009 as the "King of the Midwest Hills" by a *New York Times* correspondent, Lutsen Mountains had become, observed local author Robert McDowell three years later, one of the region's most lucrative recreational projects; it will fuel "the North Shore economy for years to come," he predicted. Nevertheless, the tremendous growth of the huge facility raised numerous environmental concerns. One immediate issue was the snowmaking process, which required an excessive drawdown of water from the Poplar River. It was not until late 2016, five years after a MDNR ruling called for an end to the withdrawal, that a pipeline connected the skiing complex to Lake Superior. Other issues concerned the recommendations presented within a long-range plan submitted for official review in 2017. The plan generated controversy because of its provisions, which, if implemented, would allow the Lutsen Mountain Corporation to extend operations onto hundreds of acres of adjacent U.S. Forest Service land. While the overall area of Lutsen Mountain's skiing terrain was projected to grow from 180 to 320 acres, the expansion and construction of existing and new facilities were expected to have even more impact: one thousand new parking spaces, five miles of permanent access road, two snowmaking reservoirs with an overall capacity of thirteen million gallons, seven chairlifts, a mountaintop chalet, a ski-patrol duty station, and more.[117]

Support for the expansion was immediately expressed by most Cook County lodging and food-service businesses as well as by downhill skiing enthusiasts from throughout the region and state. Opposition, however, began with a small number of cross-county skiers and quickly grew to include Anishinaabe tribal leaders, DarkSky Advocates, the SHTA, and several environmental organizations. In August 2023, following almost six years of review, SNF officials rejected the application, citing possible damage to local natural and ecological resources and the need to respect Native treaty rights.[118]

### Superior National Golf Course
5731 West Highway 61

A nine-hole, par-3 golf course appeared on the Lutsen Resort grounds during the late 1950s. Despite its lush greens, the short fairways proved inadequate for most golfers, who preferred to play over eighteen holes. The facility, observed Robert McDowell, represented one of the few times a fine notion of the Nelsons was poorly executed; the site now serves as a nine-hole "pitch and putt" course that affords a "no-pressure situation" for beginning golfers.[119]

In March 1987, George Nelson Jr. proposed to donate 330 acres of undeveloped land that flanked both sides of the Poplar River between Highway 61 and the Lutsen Mountains Ski Area for a championship golf course with eighteen holes. The bequest occurred one year later, following the establishment of an Economic Development Authority funded by a resort and hotel tax in Cook County's three southwestern townships. Despite numerous financial and environmental issues, including the question of how much river water could be drawn down to irrigate the greens, the first nine holes of Superior National opened in June 1991. The eighteen-hole course, its two nines named River and Canyon, were completed in 1994, as was a substantial clubhouse that replaced the existing mobile trailer. Superior National became a twenty-seven-hole course following the addition of a third nine, named Mountain.[120]

Because Superior National is publicly owned and funded, the facility remains a debated and sometimes-heated issue in Cook County. (A total of $4.8 million was expended in redesigning and rebuilding the course from 2013 to 2019.) Nonetheless, many golfers, whether skilled or duffer, are attracted by the scenic views of Lake Superior and the Sawtooth Mountains, although it is the Premier Eighteen—a combination of the River and Canyon Nines—that serves as the primary drawing card. (The Mountain Nine is now used for footgolf—a game that involves kicking a soccer ball into a cup with as few shots as possible.) Some participants, no doubt, also make their way to Lutsen because of favorable reviews that appear in publications such as *Tee Time Magazine Minnesota*, intended for the state's "affluent golfers." One *Tee Time* reporter, who identified himself, in 2018, as someone who pursues the "great game of golf" throughout the world, described Superior National as one of Minnesota's best courses—"No question. Period. Exclamation Point."[121]

### No-See-Um Lodge and Gitche Gumee Lodge (*now the* North Shore Camp)

Several tourist-oriented facilities appeared between Lutsen Lodge and the township's northeastern border during the 1920s and 1930s. One, the No-See-Um Lodge, began as an opulent fishing and hunting retreat for Frederick Dickey, a Minneapolis insurance executive and one-time chair of the Hennepin County Republican Party. Dickey's wife, Elizabeth, and daughter Marguerite often joined him at the retreat. Financial problems Marguerite Dickey experienced during the early 1930s—caused in part by the Great Depression, and especially the deaths of both parents—prompted the young woman to improve her situation by renting out the family lodge and its four cabins. In 1937, after No-See-Um was purchased by Edwin and Anna McCabe of Moorhead, Minnesota, the new owners claimed that the "beauty spot," situated among spruce and pine trees, was an "excellent place to read, roam, and relax." Although the couple's relatively brief North Shore sojourn ended with Edwin McCabe's 1942 death, they were able to build more cabins and rename their business the Gitche Gumee Lodge, which referenced poet Henry Wadsworth Longfellow's *The Song of Hiawatha*; each of the ten cabins was also identified by names derived from the epic poem. During the late 1940s and throughout the 1950s, subsequent owners advertised the resort's indoor plumbing, heated

General Electric blankets, and "wake-up to music radios." For several years, Gitche Gumee was proclaimed as the only lodge or resort located northeast of Two Harbors that had received approval and recognition by the American Automobile Association.[122]

In 1967, one year after the resort's closing, ten married couples—whose members included attorneys, professors, social workers, and National Labor Relations Board employees—formed a cooperative and purchased the property. The members, who named their acquisition the North Shore Camp, immediately devoted considerable time and effort to the repair of its recently vandalized buildings. Current shareholders carry on this tradition by engaging in two annual work weekends. Each member leases and maintains one of the camp's ten small cabins, while the original lodge serves as a communal space that has a kitchen, a dining room, bathrooms, adjacent porches, and a large hall with a substantial fireplace. The members are assessed an annual fee that covers the costs for insurance, utilities, property taxes, and supplies. Whenever a share is available for sale, the cooperative's members must review and approve the potential buyer's application. The site is private and remains open only to members and invited guests.[123]

### Earle Brown Lodge (*now* Ours Resort)
### 5530 County Road 35

Located along a section of County Road 35, which parallels Highway 61, is Ours Resort, owned since 1978 by Local 663 of the United Food and Commercial Workers (UFCW). With thirteen thousand members, most concentrated in the Twin Cities area, Local 633 is the Upper Midwest's largest UFCW union. The property was held, from 1951 to 1963, by Earle Brown (1879–1963), a well-known Minnesota personality of the late 1920s and early 1930s. Brown, in 1905, inherited his wealthy grandfather's farm in Brooklyn Center (now a suburb of Minneapolis); the property later served as the state's first commercial airstrip and as an initial training ground for Minnesota's State Highway Patrol, which Brown founded in 1929 and directed until 1932, the year he ran unsuccessfully as the Republican Party candidate for governor. The farm, donated to the University of Minnesota following Brown's 1963 death, was acquired by the City of Brooklyn Center in 1984 and converted into the Earle Brown Heritage Center. The facility, however, was renamed the Heritage Center of Brooklyn Center in 2022, after evidence of Brown's extreme racist views emerged.[124]

Because of his statewide contacts and travels, Brown was well acquainted with the North Shore and several local residents. An active outdoorsman, Brown eventually purchased some land adjacent to the Caribou River and also acquired a Lake Superior lodge in the Hovland area. In 1948, he made a quick acquisition and sale of a seven-acre property with six hundred feet of shoreline about one mile from the Lutsen Resort. Brown repurchased the holding three years later and soon oversaw the construction of a log lodge that had four bedrooms and a large fireplace. After Brown's death, the holding was sold to Walter G. and Lillian Anderson, owners of a Twin Cities printing company.[125]

The union's 1978 purchase of the Anderson property was recommended and overseen by Eugene Uttech, Local 663's astute president. Though Uttech believed that acquiring lakeshore property was a "dream" of most Minnesotans, he also realized that a vast majority of union members "would never have ownership of shoreline." Upon hearing that the Andersons were ready to sell, Uttech quickly proposed that $225,000 be allocated for the property, which included stands of mature pine and birch trees. Once Uttech received approval from Local 663's executive board and membership, the purchase was completed. Although the Andersons had initially asked for $350,000, they agreed to the lower price.[126]

Following the sale, two existing cabins were removed and replaced by new units, and three additional structures emerged on the site. The six cabins now available for rent include the former lodge, which still has many of its original furnishings. All are restricted to active, dues-paying members and to retirees who receive a pension from UFCW Local 663.[127]

### Arrowhead Electric Cooperative
### 5401 Highway 61

The Lutsen Light and Power Company, a privately owned business, began providing electric service for a limited number of businesses and homes in 1935 but quickly experienced financial problems because of high construction and maintenance costs caused by Cook County's rugged physical terrain and low settlement densities. Reorganized as the Superior North Shore

Power Company after World War II, the firm's assets were transferred to the recently formed Arrowhead Electric Cooperative in 1953. Following the immediate acquisition of a $1,110,000 low-interest loan from the REA, the cooperative was able to improve and expand its electric grid. Arrowhead, now supplied with power generated in Duluth, distributes electric and broadband service to more than four thousand customers throughout Cook County and part of Lake County. The attractive building that houses the cooperative is the result of a $2.5 million remodeling and expansion program, completed in 2008, which saved 75 percent of the original structure. The project, two years later, received Cook County's first Gold Certification from the U.S. Green Building Council's Leadership in Energy and Environmental Design Program. The design program, facilitated by Melissa Graftaas of Architecture Advantage in Duluth, was recognized for emphasizing sustainable site planning, energy efficiency, the conservation of materials, and several other factors.[128]

### Lockport Townsite and Lockport Store and Cabins (*now the* Lockport Marketplace and Deli)

5364 Highway 61

In 1911, the Cook County Board approved a plat with six blocks, which was submitted by the National Power and Paper Company for the townsite of Lockport. A hotel and some log cabins soon appeared on a few lots, and the Lutsen Tie and Post Company also built a nearby dock for its log shipments. The structures disappeared quickly, but one business become a fixture in 1928 when Jessie Young Jones opened her Lockport Store and Cabins along the highway. The young Iowa woman had recently married Charles ("Casey") Jones, a former moose-hunting guide at Carl Nelson's wilderness camp who later became a well-known local sign painter and interior decorator. (Even earlier, Jones was a professional baseball player who participated with four different major league teams from 1901 to 1908.) After the couple divorced in 1936, Jessie Jones married William Bally, a local blacksmith and well driller. By this time, her property included the store, an adjacent "cozy home-like dining room," ten rustic log cabins, and a Tydol gasoline pump. The couple moved to Florida in 1964, well after they sold their Lockport business to the first of several ensuing owners who have continued serving residents and tourists.[129] Although the cabins were removed years ago, the original store and diner, now called the Lockport Marketplace and Deli, remain a representative example of an early North Shore commercial building and business.

**The small dining room in the Lockport Store, 1940s. Several of its interior features have been maintained to the present.**

Hansen's General Store and Cabins, shown here during the late 1930s, offered groceries, gasoline, alcoholic beverages, and overnight accommodations. The current Clearview Building has occupied the site since the 1980s.

### Hansen's General Store and Cabins (*now the* Clearview Building)
5321–5325 West Highway 61

The Clearview Building, a two-story, multiunit structure, is located on much of the site once occupied by Hansen's General Store and Cabins. The original business, which eventually included a small tavern, was established in 1928 by Holst and Unni Ellingsen Hansen, both of whom emigrated separately from Norway to Minnesota before marrying in 1911. By 1937, the Hansens were boldly advertising their roadside enterprise as the "most immaculate store of the north." The couple's son and daughter-in-law, Ray and Harriet Hansen, after assuming ownership in the early 1940s, would tout the cabins' electric lights and stoves, flush toilets, and telephones as well as its common bathhouse. The Hansens also assured tourists that the information they provided about the local area was "always reliable." The store, still heated by a wood-burning stove upon its 1965 closing, would not reopen until 1981, when Jeff and Anna Latz purchased the property. During their occupancy, which extended to 2020, the couple provided space for as many as five other businesses and four affordable, second-floor apartment units. Today, the Clearview Building—including a post office, a full-service grocery store, and a few other commercial outlets—serves as Lutsen's version of a shopping center. To many residents and motorists, however, the Clearview is well known because of its Fika Coffee shop (*fika* is a Swedish term for "coffee break"), which also maintains a fitting link to the community's ethnic heritage.[130]

### Lutsen Evangelical Lutheran Church
5307 West Highway 61

A group of Lutsen Lutherans, shortly after forming a congregation in April 1938, purchased the vacant Hebron Lutheran Church in Grand Marais; the building was soon moved to Lutsen and placed on a slightly elevated triangular lot located just northeast of Hansen's General Store. In early 1956, after approving the construction of a new church, the congregation contacted architect Edward Sövik of Northfield. Sövik's firm, later in the year, completed a design for what the *Cook County News-Herald* described as a "new, modern-type church." Construction began in June 1957, shortly after the existing building was removed. Much of the initial labor was provided by ten students from St. Olaf College in Northfield, Minnesota, who were brought to Lutsen by art professor Arnold Flaten. (A decade earlier, Flaten had recruited a group of "Oles" to Hovland, also in Cook County, where they assisted in the construction of Trinity Lutheran Church.) The students, most of whom worked four weeks during summer 1957, thought they would be "wielding hammers, saws, and lumber" at the construction site. Instead, the collegians found themselves "penetrating" rock that was four feet deep. "Day after day, back to the rock, the air hammer, wrecking bars, picks spades," wrote the Reverend Otto Wedal, the congregation's pastor, in late August. "But always rock and more rock. . . . Always the concern was about rock—most to be removed from the site; some to be hauled to the project. But always rock!" After recognizing that the students needed some relief from their demanding labor, the group spent one week performing other tasks at the construction site.[131]

Isak Hansen & Sons, a Lutsen-based construction company, supervised the project, but the congregation's members also devoted considerable voluntary labor to the building effort, typically during weekends and long summer evenings. The Lutsen Lutheran Ladies Aid assured that food and coffee were always available for the volunteers and raised additional funds by offering their "famous annual smorgasbord" at Lutsen Resort. The unfinished church building opened for religious services in 1959, four years before its official July 1963 dedication.[132]

Lutsen Lutheran is smaller and less ornate than most churches the Sövik firm designed for midwestern congregations during the latter half of the twentieth century. Known for possessing a "sharp and flexible intellect," Sövik also recognized the "practical necessity" of providing suitable designs for small congregations with limited budgets, a factor that undoubtedly contributed to the choice of a single-story structure that could be built of local stone and wood by volunteer laborers. Nevertheless, Lutsen Lutheran also reveals a few subtle features that are visible in a majority of Sövik's larger, mid-century church designs, namely, a rectangular, unornamented exterior; an almost flat roof; and a slightly elevated chancel.[133] The separate, relatively short bell tower, erected some years later, is also respectful of the church and its low building profile. But the most outstanding design elements occur within the interior, namely, the cross, altar, pulpit, and baptismal font—all crafted of wood and placed in front of a south-facing glass wall that looks toward Lake Superior. Collectively, these pieces represent the

**Lutsen Lutheran, completed between 1957 and 1963, is one of four postwar North Shore churches designed by architect Edward Sövik and his firm. Photograph by Lynn Bjorkman, 2021.**

collaborative relationships Sövik established with the artists and craftspersons who designed, shaped, and built them.

### Northern Lights Resort (*now* Cathedral of the Pines)
760 Caribou Trail

Northern Lights Resort, situated about four miles north of Lutsen on the Caribou Trail from 1926 to the early 1940s, has significance as the only Cook County tourist business initiated, owned, and managed by a Black family. The family's amazing story began during the early 1900s when Hosiah ("Hosey") Posey Lyght departed Tuscaloosa, Alabama, for West Virginia. Lyght soon moved to a coal-mining community in Fayette County, Pennsylvania, where, in 1909, he married Stella Jefferson Jones, whose grandfather had been enslaved until the age of seven. In December 1913, after growing tired of "giving all his money to the company store," Lyght headed to northeastern Minnesota, where he heard that land was still available for homesteading. Lyght found work in Duluth, lived in a rooming house for a few months, and eventually traveled to Cook County, where he selected a 160-acre homestead property. Soon, Lyght would send for his wife and the couple's three sons, who arrived in Duluth in late 1914. The family then sailed on the *America* to Lutsen, arriving just before wintertime weather conditions shut down shipping traffic on Lake Superior. Alfred Nelson, the bachelor brother of Lutsen Lodge owner Charles Nelson, brought them to their property, where only a windowless trapper's shack remained on the site. The Lyght family would live with their helpful Swedish neighbor until the cabin was repaired and expanded. Upon spring's arrival, Nelson showed Lyght how to clear land and establish a subsistence farm; official title to the homestead was secured in December 1921. Twelve more children were born in Cook County; thirteen of the Lyghts' fifteen offspring survived well into adulthood.[134]

Described by one of his sons as "an ambitious type of person," Lyght built a substantial log house on the property; pursued hunting, fishing, and trapping; worked on road-construction and logging crews; drove the local school bus; ran a sawmill; and engaged in many other jobs. Because of his work ethic, Lyght raised sufficient funds for the purchase of some fifteen hundred feet of shoreline along Caribou Lake, where, during the late 1920s, the family established Northern Lights Resort, which eventually had seven cabins. Our dad "worked day and night building the cabins," stated the Lyghts' third child, Norman, who earned a master's of education degree from the University of Minnesota and was later employed by the St. Paul school system. "He had us kids peeling the bark and stacking the logs up to dry," recalled the patriarch's son; "he even taught us how to notch the corners of the cabin so they would hold up." The resort included a small store where guests could purchase candy, soda pop, and an occasional meal and also play a slot machine. And because the tourists always requested milk, the family often had one cow.[135]

Both Black and white guests were attracted to Northern Lights by word of mouth, North Shore advertising brochures, and a few Twin Cities and Chicago newspapers that occasionally noted the resort was "owned and operated by colored people." Florence Page Jaques, the celebrated nature writer who briefly visited Caribou Lake during the early 1940s, wrote that the Lyghts, "the only colored family on the North Shore . . . hold a respected place in the community"; they own a summer resort, she observed, "one of the neatest and cleanest in the whole region," and also operate a "small and picturesque sawmill." Despite the resort's success, the Lyghts were forced to close their business because of gas rationing and travel restrictions during World War II and because of the patriarch's 1944 death.[136]

During the immediate postwar years, one of the Lyght daughters, Mary, worked as a nanny for the Minneapolis family of Ruth and the Reverend Reuben Youngdahl. When she informed Youngdahl, the senior pastor at Mount Olivet Lutheran Church, about Northern Lights' availability, he decided to visit the property. Upon viewing the "genuine hand-hewn log cabin[s]," Youngdahl saw an opportunity to realize one of his longtime goals—to establish a church camp in northern Minnesota. After purchasing the property, members of Mount Olivet's congregation started converting their acquisition into a camp, called Cathedral of the Pines. The first two-week session occurred in 1949, a chapel and director's cabin were built in 1950, and the official dedication took place in 1953. Since

**Hosey and Stella Lyght pose with fourteen of their fifteen children in front of the family's hand-hewn log residence during the 1930s. Courtesy of Minnesota Historical Society.**

then, the acreage, number of buildings, and length of the camping season have expanded significantly.[137]

Several of the Lyght children remained in or returned to Cook County after World War II. Lyght Brothers Trucking, a Lutsen-based business enterprise established by some of the brothers, hauled lumber and freight throughout the United States for several years. John, the fourteenth child, became a local and even statewide celebrity following his election as Cook County's sheriff in 1972. Because of Lyght's fairness and "evenhanded concern for the well-being of constituents," he would be reelected to the position for the following twenty-two years.[138]

### Grand View Cabins and Store (*now* Grandview Park)

4944 Grandview Loop

Situated along the lakeshore side of the highway and a short distance northeast of Hansen's General Store was Grand View Cabins, later converted into a park now owned and maintained by Lutsen Township. The original acreage, acquired around 1917 by Norwegian immigrants Chris and Thea Haav Pedersen, served as a small fishing camp and farm until the 1930s, when the couple opened their cabins and an adjacent store, where fresh fish was always available. The couple's son Curtis and daughter Anne maintained ownership from 1960 to 1989. Some buildings were rented out until 1996, when the Lutsen Township Board advocated for the purchase and conversion of the land into a public park, "so people who can't afford to live on the lake don't have to drive all the way to Grand Marais." Donations paid for some of the $140,000 purchase price, but most financial support came from grants supplied by local and state agencies. Grandview Park now has a sand volleyball court, a playground, a small boat launch, picnic facilities, and, most obviously, a $50,000 "party-size pavilion" built of red pine logs in 2005–6. On the opposite side of the park (at 4821 Highway 61) is a building emblazoned with a large sign, "Isak Hansen, Home and Hardware and Custom Builder." The sign and business memorialize the name of a well-known Lutsen construction company that, for several decades, was active throughout much of Cook County. The current owner, although not related to the founder, still identifies his custom-building firm and hardware store with the Isak Hansen name.[139]

## West Cook Unorganized Territory

As Highway 61 heads northeastward from Lutsen Township toward Grand Marais, it passes through some fourteen miles of the vast West Cook Unorganized Territory. (The final four miles were once part of Rosebush Township, before its governmental functions ended during the 1930s.) Overall, West Cook's 663 square miles of land and water compose 20 percent of the county's total area. Most of its year-round residents, a total of 1,780 in 2020, live either in the vicinity of Grand Marais or along Cascade Beach Road, which parallels Highway 61 for 9.5 miles. Only 825 of West Cook's 1,955 housing units (42 percent) were occupied year-round in 2020; the majority serve as seasonal homes and cabins.[140]

The section of Minnesota Highway 1 that passed through West Cook in 1928, identified at the time as "a broad, graveled right-of-way," was, two years later, drawing criticism from local residents and public

**Chris and Thea Pedersen, who established a small farm and fishing camp at the eastern end of Lutsen around 1917, would later open their Grand View Cabins and Store. Shown here during the 1940s, the property was converted into Lutsen's Grandview Park a half century later. Courtesy of Cook County Historical Society.**

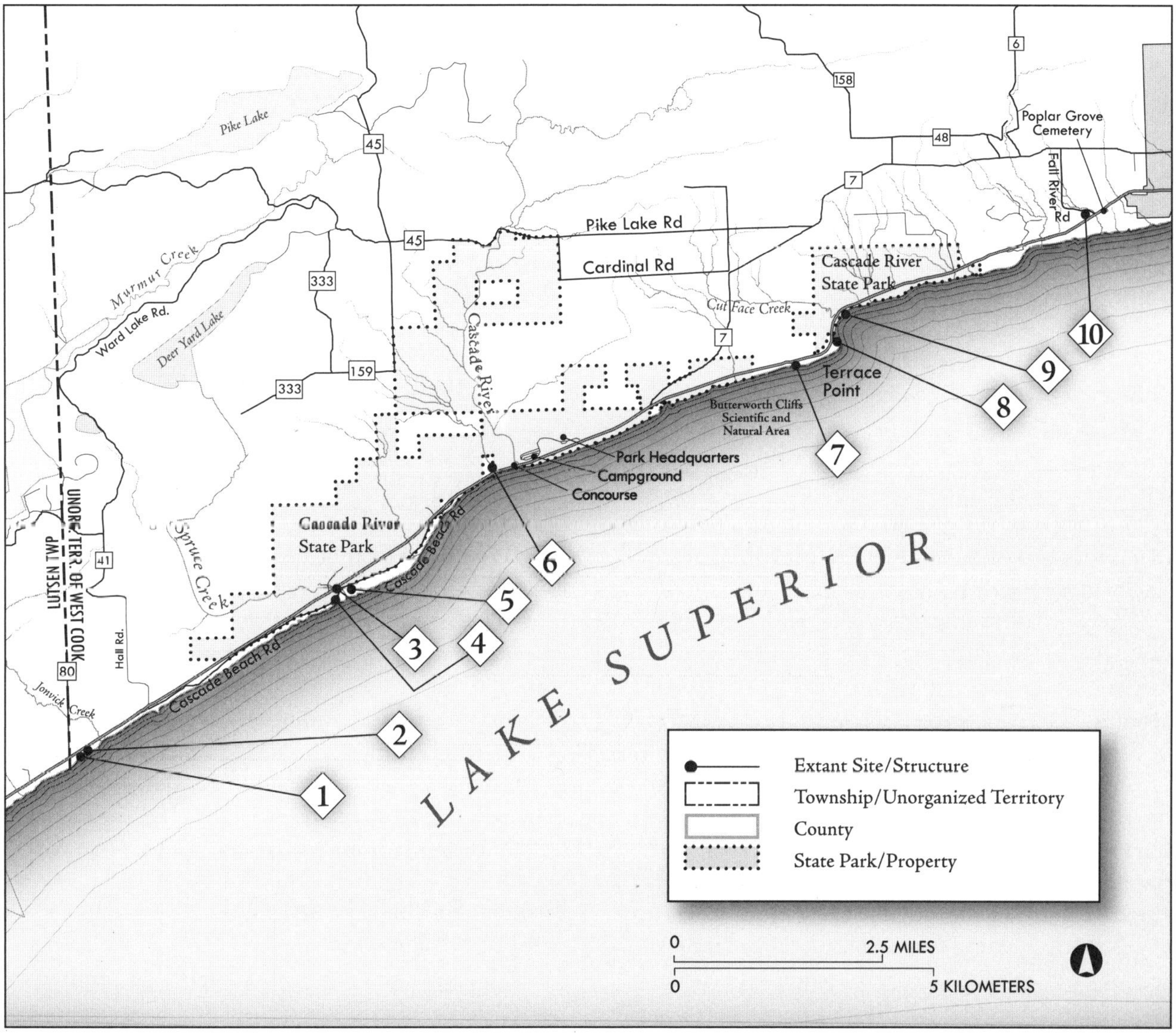


1. Solbakken Resort on Superior
2. Koeneke Shoredge Resort
3. Spruce Creek Skewed Concrete Arch Bridge
4. Spruce Creek Cabins
5. Spruce Falls Cabins
6. Cascade Lodge and Cascade Restaurant & Pub
7. Thomsonite Inn on Lake Superior
8. Terrace Point: Good Harbor Bay & S. Rex Green Overlooks
9. Cut Face Creek Rest Area
10. Timberlund's Resort

officials because of its inadequacies and dangers. When responding to these concerns in 1931, MDH officials announced that the agency would carry out three major actions: move the right-of-way somewhat closer to Lake Superior, eliminate several dangerous curves, and construct a new Cascade River bridge. The work commenced later that year when four large shovels, two powered by steam, two by gasoline, arrived at the Grand Marais dock, along with Caterpillar tractors, air compressors, drills, and some five hundred tons of coal.[141]

Most improvements, including the application of a bituminous material to the pavement's surface, were completed by August 1934, but the extensive construction work caused severe scarring and erosion along both sides of the roadway. This situation was soon addressed by MDH consultant Arthur Nichols, who completed a landscape design and management plan for the first ten miles of highway in West Cook. Nichols's plan, reported the *Duluth Herald* later that summer, was certain to introduce "new ideas in highway beautification and safety" along the entire North Shore.[142]

Rather than appearing as "a raw gash through the woods," observed the *Herald*, the roadway would "harmonize with the scenery so that the edge of the right-of-way will blend imperceptibly with the wilderness." Today the most visible examples of Nichols's recommendations are the moderate angle of the backslope on the highway's upper side and the stately conifers that have grown from seedlings planted along both sides of the corridor by CCC enrollees during the 1930s. Several narrow bands of noncontiguous public land, all part of Cascade River State Park, still flank the ten-mile-long section of Highway 61, but most motorists may not realize that Cascade Beach Road, situated between the highway and Lake Superior, provides access to more than 120 platted lots, many with private cabins and residences built on them. Although Cascade Beach Road represents one of the more densely built-up, nonurban sections of the entire North Shore, much of it is visually separated from Highway 61 by the ribbon of forested public land.[143]

### Solbakken Resort on Superior
### 4874 West Highway 61

The first of very few resorts that remain between Lutsen and Grand Marais is Solbakken (a Norwegian word for "sunny hill"), which emerged in 1936 when Russell and Lila Gunderson built some modest lakeshore cabins close to West Cook's southwestern boundary. When Don Kwakenat, a recently discharged U.S. Navy veteran from Minneapolis, purchased Solbakken in 1946, he added a combination home, office, and store to the resort.[144]

In 1983, four years after Bill and Beth Blank's acquisition of Solbakken, the couple bought a single-story log structure, Sawbill Lodge, built in 1935 by Arby and Jean Arbogust on Sawbill Lake, located twenty-six miles inland from the North Shore. Because of its carefully scribed, tightly fitted jack pine logs, all joined together by saddle notch corners, the lodge is similar to the best CCC buildings of the 1930s. The Blanks' purchase, however, was possible only because of the federal BWCAW Act of 1978—a legislative action that provided federal funds for the purchase of commercial resorts and outfitters affected by restrictions on motorized boats at wilderness entry points. Upon acquiring the lodge at an auction, the Blanks disassembled the logs and had them trucked to Solbakken. (Some logs were destroyed and required replacement when the truck crashed on one trip.) After restoring the structure over succeeding years, the lodge opened in 1994 with a lounge, a residence, an office, and a few guest rooms. Sold by the Blanks in 2006, Solbakken remains a family-owned resort with three lodge rooms, six cabins, two vacation houses, and six motel units.[145]

### Koeneke Shoredge Resort
### 4840 West Highway 61

The lodge and four cabins that compose the nearby Koeneke Shoredge Resort were built during the mid-1930s by E. O. Williams. The property was purchased in 1956 by Dr. Irene Koeneke, a longtime North Shore visitor and one of the earliest female surgeons to practice in Kansas, who also was the widow of Arthur Hertzler, a legendary "horse and buggy" doctor. Immediately after the purchase, Koeneke's sister Eloise moved from Kansas to the North Shore, where she managed the resort until her 1974 retirement at the age of eighty. Since then, three more generations of Koeneke family members, often assisted by their spouses, have operated Shoredge. Fred and Diane Koeneke assumed these responsibilities in 2015.[146]

The lobby and common room of Sawbill Lodge in 1980, three years before the entire structure was transported from Sawbill Lake to Solbakken Resort, on Lake Superior. The only changes that have been made to the room since it was moved are the addition of two windows along the south-facing (left) wall and the replacement of a wooden door with one that includes glass; some of the original chairs still remain in use.

### Spruce Creek Skewed Concrete Arch Bridge
Highway 61 and Spruce Creek

Highway 61 passes over Spruce Creek about 3.5 miles northeast of the Solbakken and Koeneke resorts. The Spruce Creek structure, although often called a culvert, is more correctly identified as a "skewed concrete arch bridge" because of its slight angular orientation to the stream. Culverts seldom garner plaudits for their design qualities, but the Spruce Creek span received recognition because of its rustic style elements, expressed in dark brownish black gabbro. Designed by Arthur Nichols and built in 1935 by members of Spruce Creek Wayside CCC Company 2702, the bridge is notable for its design features: eight stone piers; several courses of fieldstone, laid out in a random pattern on the headwalls; and a stone arch that frames both culvert openings. (Metal railings have replaced the original wooden

Other than the steel railings, which have replaced the original wooden features, the Spruce Creek Culvert still displays its 1930s rustic style details—stone piers, a random fieldstone pattern on each headwall, and a stone arch at the culvert openings.

members.) MnDOT, in 2001, deemed the culvert "significant for its association with the CCC, and as one of the few remaining roadside development facilities on State Highway 61 that date to the . . . early construction and improvement of the scenic highway." It was also included in the 2003 nomination of the Cascade River Wayside to the National Register of Historic Places.[147] The lack of a nearby parking area makes it difficult to view the span, and there is no interpretive signage at the site.

### Spruce Creek Cabins and Spruce Falls Cabins
### 4174 and 4140 West Highway 61

Between Highway 61 and Cascade Beach Road are a pair of modest tourist establishments: Spruce Creek Cabins and Spruce Falls Cabins. Spruce Creek was developed by Clarence and Edna Hemmingsen during the mid-1930s. A skilled plumber who had previously worked in Chicago, Hemmingsen built just three cabins on the property but provided an impressive water system for the site. After jackhammering through the rock, wrote one observer, Hemmingsen placed the pipes five to six feet underground, which protected them from freezing. Another owner, during the 1970s, built a few more cabins, which now serve as long-term rentals.[148]

The four units that compose Spruce Falls Cabins, located just a short distance from the Spruce Creek property, were built by local residents Mogens and Helen Jentoft during the 1930s. The property was acquired in 1969 by John Torseth and Ken Skold, partners in a Twin Cities architectural firm; two caretakers already residing on the site managed the business for several subsequent years. Skold and his wife, Janice, bought out Torseth's share in 1987 and formed a limited partnership with their four sons in 1994. The senior Skold died in 2019, but ownership is still retained by family members, who maintain the longtime rustic character of Spruce Falls. "At our cabins," they note, "you won't find TV's, phones, or an 'activities counselor.' What you will find is a place from the past. These are the cabins your parents and grandparents told you about!"[149]

### Cascade Lodge and Cascade Restaurant and Pub
### 3719 West Highway 61

In 1922, a few years before the completion of Highway 1, Edward Ogilvie selected a privately owned parcel of land, situated about two miles northeast of Spruce Creek, for an envisioned North Shore resort. Soon, a single-story log structure with two massive fireplace chimneys, along with three log cabins, appeared on the fourteen-acre property. Apparently, the resort did not open to visitors until Charles Rogers and two partners acquired the buildings and land in 1926. Cascade, however, gained its reputation as a major North Shore destination resort following Herbert and Minnie Neudahl's 1935 purchase of the holding. Their advertisements quickly touted Cascade as a "new, modern, comfortable resort, with a big, rustic log lodge and dining room," where guests were provided with opportunities to hike on former logging trails and pursue the "Kodaking" (photographing) of wild animals. A well-crafted footbridge that crosses nearby Babineau Creek was built in 1935 by members of CCC Camp 2702 who were engaged in constructing the nearby Cascade River Wayside. The small footbridge was also included in the 2003 nomination of the Cascade River Wayside to the National Register of Historic Places.[150]

The resort underwent a major change in 1939 when the Neudahls removed the original lodge and constructed a steam-heated, two-story structure with ten guest rooms and private bathrooms, a recreation room, and a large fireplace that used stones salvaged from the abandoned Spruce Creek CCC camp. A west wing, added in 1952, provided space for four more guest rooms and an owner's apartment. A separate building, completed in 1947, had a coffee and gift shop, a bar, and a dance floor that attracted the North Shore Aircooled Orchestra and other local bands; it was converted into the Cascade Lodge Dining Room during the late 1950s. In 1969, after thirty-five years of ownership, the Neudahls sold Cascade to purchasers who quickly recognized the growing local popularity of cross-country skiing and snowshoeing. Because of the groomed trails that appeared on Cascade land in 1972, the resort has received recognition as the North Shore "birthplace" of cross-country skiing. The transformation of Cascade into a year-round resort began in 1978–79, when three cabins were winterized; all of the major buildings were ready for such use by 1990.[151]

Cascade may not have the same design and historical significance as Lutsen Lodge, but it remains one of Cook County's most recognizable and prized resorts.

Cascade Lodge, shortly after the west wing, *left*, was added to the building in 1952. The antenna on that side secured television reception from stations in Duluth; the one on the right accessed Fort William–Port Arthur (now Thunder Bay), Ontario.

Undoubtedly, many North Shore aficionados can relate to an observation made by the late Larry Oakes, a Minneapolis journalist who evoked both the nostalgic and aesthetic appeal of the well-sited lodge, which overlooks Lake Superior and Highway 61. People who are wary of changes occurring in the North Shore landscape, wrote Oakes in 2002, can always "take comfort" in Cascade's "familiar old facades of half-log and split stone."[152]

### Cascade River Wayside (*now* Cascade River State Park)

#### 3481 West Highway 61

The Cascade River was already identified as an attraction by the limited number of visitors and onlookers who ventured along the trail that opened between Two Harbors and Grand Marais in late 1899. A one-way trek—undertaken in a horse-drawn sleigh, carriage, or coach—typically took two to three days. The 1917 completion of a roadway suitable for vehicles, followed by the opening of Minnesota Highway 1 in 1925, made access much easier. It was not until 1934, however, that MDH acquired 2,300 acres of land (later expanded to its current 5,050 acres) in the Cascade River area, "for utilitarian purposes, as well as to protect [it] from the encroachment of undesirable nature." Work on the site began that year when the river's mouth was moved 325 feet toward the east. A reinforced concrete spandrel bridge with a thirty-foot span crossed the river, once described by a CCC superintendent as a "torrential stream winding through a gorge of up to fifty feet deep and consisting of a series of seven falls ranging from thirty-five to five feet in height." The new structure replaced a 1916 span that itself had supplanted an 1899 wagon bridge.[153]

Arthur Nichols, also in 1934, oversaw the development of a landscape plan for the 118-acre wayside, which would include several elements: a concourse or overlook, several footbridges and viewing platforms, and numerous trails—some woven throughout the forest, others paralleling the river—all wedded by hundreds of stone and wooden steps. Sixty CCC enrollees started working on the project in late July, but because their camp, Spruce Creek 2702, was not yet completed, the young men spent three months overnighting in tents at Caribou Lake, located ten miles from the Cascade River project site. Although trucks transported the enrollees between Caribou Lake and Cascade River, Camp 2702's superintendent lamented the loss of time caused by so much travel. It was not until October—when ten barracks, a recreation hall, and a supervisor's headquarters opened next to the Cascade River outlet—that Camp 2702's enrollees gained immediate access to the worksite. (The enclave was called Spruce Creek because another camp, named Cascade River, had been established several miles to the north in 1933.) Many of the camp's two hundred workers, a majority from northern Minnesota, were replaced by 170 Missouri enrollees in late 1935; the buildings were removed in 1937–38. A small public campground, developed close to the river in 1935, remains a popular park attraction.[154]

The remarkable curved wall of the Cascade River concourse is 535 feet long and eighteen inches thick. Constructed of gabbro stones laid in a random pattern, the structure has two small lookout bays—one rectangular in form, the other curved—which are incised into the wall. Considered Minnesota's first example of a scenic overlook to integrate natural rock formations into its overall design, the late MHS historian Denis Gardner termed it a "Minnesota treasure" in 2004 as well as "one of the largest and most attractive waysides built by the Roadside Development Division of the MHD." Onlookers who gaze out from its sizable platform have views of Lake Superior, the Cascade River's mouth, and a heavily wooded inland forest.[155]

The entire Cascade River Wayside influenced subsequent rustic style landscape design projects throughout the state and also received positive reviews in Albert Good's 1938 NPS publication *Park and Recreation Structures*, which includes two images of the site. Sixty-five years later, in 2003, Rolf Anderson's National Register of Historic Places nomination highlighted several specific features that make the wayside such an exemplary model of rustic style design and construction: the "technique of using natural rock outcroppings to create a scenic overlook"; the high-quality masonry, which demonstrates "skillfully cut, selected, and laid stones"; the number of "special labor-intensive construction techniques" employed throughout the project; the "distinctive use of indigenous materials"; and the design skills of landscape architect Arthur Nichols. Quite amazingly, the wayside, even today, "still looks much as it did when finished in 1936."[156]

The first two miles of Highway 61 that proceed northeastward from the river and concourse initially pass by the park's picnic area, campground, and headquarters entrance road. A short distance farther is the Butterwort Cliffs SNA—a narrow, forty-three-acre section of Lake Superior shoreline designated and protected by the MDNR in 1990. The cool, moist microclimate of the cliffs, along with the protection offered by Ergo Bay, provides favorable conditions for the growth of rare arctic-alpine plants, among them butterwort and Hudson Bay eyebright. Because small colonies of herring gulls and peregrine falcons use the bay's cliffs as a nesting site and sanctuary, BCSNA is closed to the public for a few spring and summer months. A combination of

**The curved concourse wall at the Cascade River Wayside, shortly after its 1935 completion by members of CCC Company 2702. The wayside is considered among Minnesota's finest CCC projects.**

public and private land flanks both sides of the highway northeast of Butterwort Cliffs, but these areas are not nearly as naturalized and heavily vegetated as the ten preceding miles.[157]

### Thomsonite Beach Inn and Jewelry Shop (*now* Thomsonite Inn on Lake Superior)

2920 West Highway 61

About three and a half miles from the Cascade River is a section of Lake Superior beachfront that, since the late 1870s, has been recognized for the presence of thomsonite, a relatively rare gemstone. Among those bringing attention to thomsonite during the post–World War II era were Maurice and Tatiana ("Tania") Feigal, who moved to the Grand Marais area in 1960. Tania Feigal's personal history is unique, even on the North Shore, a place known for its many and varied immigrant stories. The daughter of Russian and German Polish parents who fled to Harbin, China, following the 1917 Russian Revolution, Tania Wolodkewicz married Maurice Feigal, a U.S. marine from Minnesota, while he was on military duty in 1946. The couple initially settled in southeastern Minnesota following their departure from China but eventually moved to Cook County, where Feigal's father had participated in hunting excursions for a half century. After acquiring five hundred feet of Lake Superior shoreline in 1960, the Feigals constructed a motel and later opened a gift shop and museum. It was, however, the addition of a jewelry workshop, with "smells reminiscent of scientific laboratories," that caught the attention of *Minneapolis Tribune* reporter Ruth Hammond in 1979. The couple's passion for thomsonite was "more than a way to make a living," noted Hammond; it motivated "their life's work." Tania Feigal spent countless hours in her workshop, where she created and crafted jewelry and other items that featured thomsonite and also offered lapidary and silversmithing classes. Museum admission was free to everyone, notably the busloads of school-age children who came to view the Feigals' gemstone collections. Tania Feigal sold the property shortly after her husband's 1995 death; it was purchased, five years later, by Scott and Lee Hansen Bergstrom—she a former Lutsen ski instructor and the granddaughter of local contractor and builder Isak Hansen. The Bergstroms operated Thomsonite Beach until 2021, when it was acquired by Joe Swanson, who, one year earlier, had purchased the Tofte-based Bluefin Bay Family of Resorts.[158]

### Terrace Point and Good Harbor Bay and S. Rex Green Overlooks

Terrace Point Road and Milepost 104

Less than one-half mile separates the Thomsonite Inn from Terrace Point, which, in 1997, was the site of a proposed luxury inn. Although the project failed to materialize, another development, Terrace Point Condominiums, did emerge a few years later. When passing by the Terrace Point entrance road, motorists experience a rather rare, if brief, North Shore moment—the opportunity to drive directly north on Highway 61 while simultaneously observing Lake Superior toward the east. Also along this section of roadway are the S. Rex Green and Good Harbor Bay Overlooks. While both are of very limited size, each provides a "big view" of Lake Superior, Seagull Rock, and, in the distance, Grand Marais. Two plaques are also perched at the overlooks' edges: one offers information about the geology of Good Harbor Bay, the other recognizes S. Rex Green, a MDH "engineer of land and right of way" who promoted and oversaw several North Shore highway improvement projects during the 1930s.

### Cut Face Creek Rest Area

2920 West Highway 61

Considerably larger than the Good Harbor Bay Overlook is the Cut Face Creek Rest Area, which appears shortly after Highway 61 makes a sharp turn to the east-northeast. The site has an interesting history because of the countless numbers of people who, since the early twentieth century, have searched for thomsonite along its shoreline. No rockhound, however, ever acquired a clearer case of "thomsonitis" than did Hans Larsen, who recognized the mineral's economic potential by 1901 and spent the remaining half century of his life searching for the gemstone. Larsen also spent many winter months polishing his accumulation of thomsonite specimens, which were later sold to tourists and collectors. The tent that sheltered the Norwegian immigrant during the months he spent at Cut Face Creek also served as Larsen's rock shop—one of the first sales outlets of this type on the North Shore. Later known as the "King of the Thomsonites," Larsen claimed that

**The attractive Cut Face Creek Rest Area offers direct access to Lake Superior and the Gitchi-Gami State Trail.**

he had gathered "enough Lake Superior stones to fill a coal car."[159]

A simple pullout for motorists existed close to the mouth of Cut Face Creek well before it was expanded, upgraded, and designated an official MnDOT rest area in 2015. Among the improvements was replacement of the former creek culvert with a passageway for the GGST, completed in 2021 and dedicated one year later, which connects Cut Face and Grand Marais. The exceptionally well-designed and constructed trail segment, 3.3 miles long, accommodates bicyclists, walkers, Rollerbladers, joggers, and people in wheelchairs. The rest area's beach also provides visitors with opportunities to search for thomsonite, even if the elusive gemstones are much more difficult to discover than in the past.[160]

### Allen's Hilltop Cabins (*now* Timberlund's Resort)
20 Fall River Road

Three miles east of Cut Face Creek is the intersection of Fall River Road and Highway 61. Located northwest of the intersection are seven units that compose Hilltop Cabins, built during the 1930s by Einar Allen on land his father and mother had acquired a quarter century earlier. Allen constructed the cabins of split vertical logs, all derived from trees that WPA workers were clearing from a new airport site located outside of Grand Marais. In 1976, Allen sold Hilltop to his nephew Robert Lund, who still operates the business as Timberlund's Resort. After the purchase, Lund added bathrooms to the cabins, updated the interiors, and covered the logs with wooden siding. The modest cabin grouping serves as an appealing reminder of an earlier era, but the most outstanding attributes are its location and setting. The site can still be described with the words that Einar Allen used decades ago when advertising Hilltop Cabins—it is a "miniature mountain retreat" that provides some of the "grandest and most gorgeous and outstanding" views of Lake Superior.[161]

The western boundary of Grand Marais occurs one-half mile east of the Fall River Road–Highway 61 intersection. Appearing a short distance before that point, on the Lake Superior side of the highway, is Poplar Grove Cemetery, established in 1916, and one of several burial grounds in the Grand Marais area.

## Grand Marais

The primary physical features of Grand Marais are its two spectacular and adjacent bays, West and East, which are separated by the "Point"—a narrow gravel bar (tombolo) that joins the mainland to a former island. To the Anishinaabe, the bays were Gichi Bitobig—

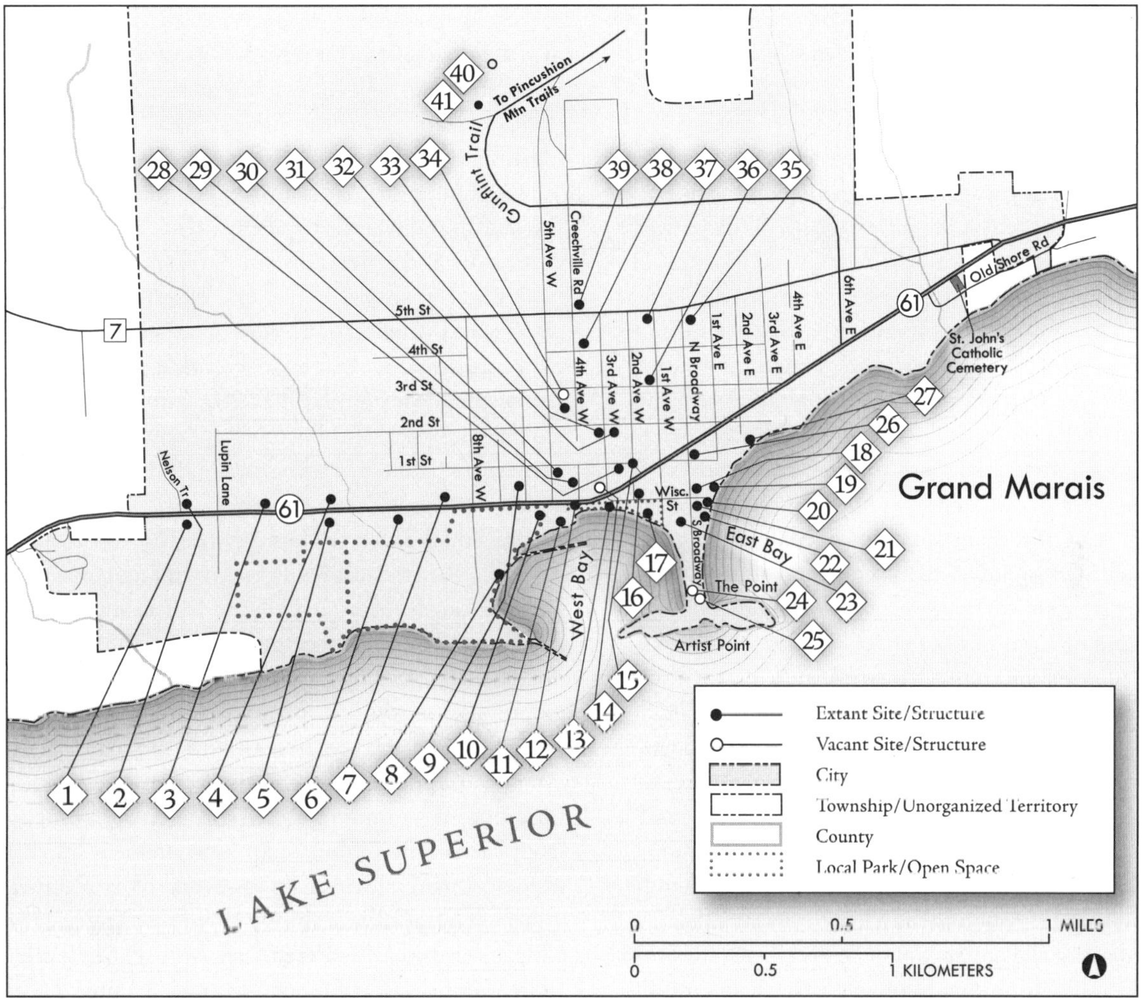


1. Grand Marais Public Works Facility
2. Benny's Collision Center
3. Up Yonder
4. Blue Moose Nursery and Gifts
5. Nelson's Traveler's Rest
6. Trailside Cabins and Motel
7. Lund's Motel and Cottages
8. Grand Marais Municipal Campground and Marina and Parkside Public Water Access
9. Birch Terrace Supper Club
10. North House Folk School
11. Jim Scott Fish House
12. Grand Marais Harbor Seawall
13. Bear Tree Park
14. Seawall Motel and Cabins
15. Gateway to the Gunflint Trail
16. Johnson's Heritage Post Art Gallery
17. Harbor Park
18. Beaver House
19. East Bay Suites
20. Drury Lane Books
21. Cook County Historical Society Museum
22. Shoreline Inn
23. Cobblestone Cove Villas and Boulder Park
24. Grand Marais Safe Harbor Boat Launch
25. U.S. Coast Guard North Superior Station
26. Bally Blacksmith Shop
27. Sisu and Löyly Nordic Sauna
28. Mökki
29. Three Sisters (Tre Søstre)
30. Russell's Cottages
31. Grand Marais Art Colony
32. First Congregational Church of the United Church of Christ
33. Cook County Courthouse
34. Historic Jail
35. St. John's Catholic Church
36. Betsy Bowen Studio
37. Bethlehem Lutheran Church
38. Lindquist Lane Motel and Cabins*
39. 4-H Club Log Building
40. Sawtooth Bluff
41. Grand Marais Water Tower

* Now private residences

the "Great Double Harbor" that provided "welcoming shelter from the surrounding, unforgiving rocky highlands" and also formed part of their "fishing, hunting, plant gathering, and maple sugaring territory." French Canadian voyageurs, who realized that the bays composed one of only a few safe harbors on the entire North Shore coastline, called them Grand Marais, a Canadian French term that is often translated as "great marsh." This interpretation, however, has been disputed by several scholars, including Grace Lee Nute, a doyen of mid-twentieth-century Minnesota historians, who argued that *marais* was an archaic French term for "a harbor or refuge, or a placid, protected cove or bay." Folklorist Timothy Cochrane, following his more recent review of numerous sources, concludes that *marais* very likely represents a "mishearing and subsequent misinterpretation" of *merée*—a Québécois French word for "a pond or calm pool of water." To the voyageurs, "Grand Marais" (actually "Grand Merée") very likely meant "grand twin bays" or "sheltered twin bays."[162]

Present-day Grand Marais traces its origins to the 1870s, although the small settlement remained relatively isolated for several decades, even after the trail for horse-drawn sleighs and stagecoaches appeared in late 1899. A road that proved suitable for motorized vehicles passed through the settlement in 1917, but as occurred along the entire North Shore, it was the 1925 completion of Minnesota Highway 1 that saw Grand Marais emerge as a destination for increasing numbers of tourists and visitors. Soon Duluth journalists were characterizing the small Cook County community as a "charming mixture of the primitive and modern." Grand Marais "still smacks of the isolation which once surrounded it," wrote a *Duluth News-Tribune* correspondent in 1928, although the North Shore highway has given the town "a new purpose, and a new hold on communication with the outside world." Since then, countless numbers of observers and commentators, among them some of Minnesota's foremost authors, have sought to capture the essence of Grand Marais's attractions. "There is more North Woods flavor to Grand Marais than to any other town on the shore," observed Grace Lee Nute in 1944. Duluth author Margaret Culkin Banning, eight years later, chose to focus on the harbor and its sheltered bays: they are, she wrote, as "comforting and comfortable as a friendly arm around a stranger." And, almost a half century later, St. Paul's well-known memoirist Patricia Hampl praised Grand Marais as "an amalgam of its gorgeous location and its small-town charms."[163]

Contemporary tourist-oriented publications that feature Grand Marais typically do not include eloquent comments and reflections similar to those expressed by the aforementioned authors. Nevertheless, given the recent inclusion of Grand Marais in many "best of" rankings, it is clear that the small city has become one of the most popular places in Minnesota and the entire Midwest: "100 Best Adventure Towns" (2009), "America's Coolest Small Town" (2015), "Best Minnesota Town for a Creative Escape" (2015), "Best Minnesota Small Town for Dining" (2016), "Best [Sixteen] Towns" (2016), "Best Midwestern Small Town" (2017), "Most Beautiful Small Town in Minnesota" (2020), "30 Small Towns You Should Visit" (2023), and so on. The descriptions point to an "energetic vibe that combines community spirit with a vibrant arts scene, great food, natural beauty, and unique history," all offered in a community that has "a little something for everyone"—ranging from "spectacular" beauty and "cozy" accommodations to an "upbeat spirit" mirrored in the colorful names given to several of its restaurants and food emporiums, among them the Angry Trout Café, Sven and Ole's Pizza, Java Moose, My Sister's Place, World's Best Donuts, Hungry Hippie Tacos, and others.[164]

## Gichi Bitobig and "Fort Misery"

Because of Timothy Cochrane's detailed investigations, we now have a greater understanding of the Anishinaabe who were present at Gichi Bitobig during the 1820s and early 1830s, when a few AFC agents spent over a decade in the area. One of the most compelling figures to emerge from Cochrane's account is Espagnol, a "principal leader of the North Shore Anishinaabeg"—a man known for his "bravery, experience, and knowledge" and for his ability to forge favorable trading relationships with AFC agents. It is quite likely, for example, that Espagnol assisted Bela Chapman, AFC's first clerk, in selecting a site for the company's Gichi Bitobig outpost in 1823.[165]

The clerks who replaced Chapman at the fur post over the next dozen years suffered from isolation, severe wintertime conditions, a lack of sufficient food, and competitive hindrances posed by the much larger Hudson Bay Company. No wonder AFC operatives termed their location "Fort Misery," "Siberia," "the Devil's own country," and other pejorative names. After abandoning the trading post in 1836, AFC maintained a fishing camp at the site for four more years. Mineral prospectors followed the fur traders and fishermen to Grand Marais in 1854, but the enclave, including its store and post office, was abandoned before 1860.[166]

## Early Days in Grand Marais

The foundation for a permanent settlement at Grand Marais occurred in 1872–73, when Hazael ("Henry") Mayhew, Ted Wakelin, and Samuel Howenstine secured considerable land along both sides of the Point. It was here that Mayhew and his brother Thomas established a trading post, hotel, post office, dock, and other structures on the eastern side of West Bay. The next significant transaction occurred in 1887–88 when the Grand Marais Real Estate and Improvement Company acquired and platted much of the land located north of the bays.[167]

Plans to make Grand Marais a major shipping center started with the dredging of its bays during the 1880s. When these activities ended in 1938, some 483,000 cubic yards of gravel and material, most shipped to Duluth for street-construction purposes, had been removed. Although deepening and expanding the bay resulted in a more accessible harbor, these actions also exposed some adjacent areas of Grand Marais to flooding during fierce storms—a process that continues to the present. (One large area, formerly known as the Pond, now a municipal parking lot located along South Broadway in downtown Grand Marais, remains a flood-prone site.) A sawmill, established in 1904, operated for several years, but it was the rafting and trucking of logs to mills, most located in Ashland and Duluth, that dominated harbor activities until 1972. Throughout this time, workers were kept busy "stacking saw logs in the winter on the gravel beaches, manhandling them to form rafts in the spring, and loading cedar railway ties and cedar poles onto skows."[168]

Horse-drawn sleighs and stagecoaches could access Grand Marias by late 1899, but once Lake Superior was free of ice, virtually all travelers arrived and departed on steamboats. Visitors found quarters in a few hotels and boardinghouses or even set up their own tents along the lakeshore. Some guests were entertained by local residents, as occurred during one week in June 1900 when three well-attended dances, all very much appreciated, took place in the Howenstine and Paine homes. "Take it all together, the past week has been quite lively," wrote a local correspondent; "we natives are naturally very quiet, and the liveliness is laid to the number of tourists that are here."[169]

The 1880 U.S. Census counted only fifty-six people in Grand Marais—forty-seven Anishinaabe and nine whites. By 1920, the total figure had grown to 425, including fifty-five Anishinaabe residents; one hundred were immigrants, seventy-two of them Nordics—thirty-six Norwegians, twenty-nine Swedes, and seven Finland Swedes. (The twenty-one Canadians were the only other foreign-born group with a relatively large representation.) Despite the small population numbers, Grand Marais's residents, by 1920, were pursuing numerous occupations, ranging from laborers, teamsters, carpenters, shoemakers, saloonkeepers, laundresses, and housekeepers to merchants, bookkeepers, stenographers, newspapermen, attorneys, bankers, teachers, and government workers. Just outside the community were several small subsistence farms, again, most established by Nordic immigrants. To the north was Maple Hill, a Swedish enclave; five miles west of the village and one mile inland from Lake Superior was Good Harbor Hill, developed by Norwegians. Because their agricultural activities were so marginal, Good Harbor's settlers soon realized that it would be "necessary to harvest the products of Lake Superior." When spring arrived, several Maple Hill families, along with their cattle and chickens, descended down the hill to Good Harbor Bay, boarded skiffs, and sailed to Grand Marais, where clusters of cabins, fish houses, and docks had been built along West Bay for use during the fishing season.[170]

Because Minnesota Highway 1 originally followed present-day County Road 7, situated five blocks to the north, it avoided the lakeshore and much of the downtown area. A noticeable change occurred after 1930, however, when local officials announced that land had been acquired "for the purpose of constructing and maintaining a state trunk highway through the Village of Grand Marais." That segment, now the most heavily trafficked section of Highway 61 in Cook County, serves motorists who are traveling to other destinations and provides local residents and tourists with access to the city's businesses, services, and attractions.

In 2020–21, a section of highway that passes through much of Grand Marais and parallels the West Bay waterfront was the focus of a "Big Dig," which began with the removal of existing road surface materials and an underlying level of contaminated soil. The ensuing reconstruction program sought to address several safety issues associated with excessive traffic speeds by introducing curb bump-outs, narrowing driving lanes and shoulders, and developing a dedicated bicycle lane. Pedestrian-oriented enhancements focused on the widening of sidewalks and pathways and the provision of enhanced lighting conditions. Roadside aesthetics were enhanced by planting trees and vegetation in the street terraces.[171]

## Grand Marais: "Low Key or High Class"?

In 1950, Margaret Culkin Banning detected something striking and even noble in the "simple daily life" of the 1,080 people who resided in Grand Marais: they exemplify, she observed, "the mesh of county and state and inter-nation, making an American pattern of order and protection and conservation and cooperation with neighbors." She also was intrigued by the residents' range of interests, which represented a "knowledge of forestry, of hunting and fishing skills, of books and paints."[172]

What might Banning, a social critic as well as a novelist, say if she were able to visit Grand Marais during recent years? Undoubtedly, the celebrated writer would make observations and comments about several of the highly accomplished and well-known people who call Grand Marais their hometown and also applaud the efforts of residents who wish to maintain the community's small-town qualities and character, while simultaneously providing them with viable incomes, affordable housing, and high-quality services. And she undoubtedly would be impressed that Grand Marais and its hinterland are still served (as they have been since 1891) by a weekly newspaper, now the *Cook County News-Herald*, and, from 1998 onward, by WTIP North Shore Community Radio (90.7 FM) in Grand Marais, which reaches the counties of Cook and Lake, the tip of Michigan's Keweenaw Peninsula, and a small section of Ontario.

Banning might have even voiced her opinions about a 1987 proposal for an upscale harbor hotel, which, after receiving a "flurry of petitions in protest" from the town's citizens, failed to gain the support of the Grand Marais City Council. The discussion, noted one observer, was driven by a key question: should Grand Marais be "low key or high class"? The issue reappeared, this time in 2005, when developers sought approval for three separate vacation condominium complexes in Grand Marais. All three were given a green light to proceed, even though several citizens criticized officials for "their lack of effort at preventing a recent proliferation of vacation condominium construction that could quickly accelerate." Only two were developed; the third was not built because of funding issues.[173]

Residents and developers may have different visions of what is best for Grand Marais's future, but the hordes of tourists and visitors who descend upon the small city must believe that the small city is "doing something right." It is highly unlikely (and fortunate) that Grand Marais will ever become a Lake Superior version of Vail, Colorado, or Nantucket, Massachusetts. Nevertheless, maintaining a viable balance between preservation and development may continue as one of the most difficult issues the city and its citizens face well into the future.

The following overview describes several places and sites, both past and present, that have shaped Grand Marais's unique "personality." To make this assessment, the city is organized into four districts: (1) the Highway 61 corridor that enters Grand Marais from the west-southwest; (2) the area that includes the downtown, the Point, and Artist's Point; (3) a section that lies between downtown and Highway 61; and (4) the large area located north of Highway 61.

## Western Highway 61 Entrance

Tourist cabins began appearing at the western entrance to Grand Marais during the mid-1920s, when Minnesota Highway 1 first approached the village. More cabins were built after a 1930 road alignment moved the highway closer to Lake Superior. Most people who operated Grand Marais's tourist businesses until the

1960s had either Swedish or Norwegian backgrounds. Today, however, only one original "Scandinavian Row" business (Lund's Motel and Cottages) is owned and managed by a descendant of the original founders; two places, however, still retain much of their original physical character and appearance. Also along the corridor are a century-old North Shore public campground, a WPA "seawall" dating to the 1930s, a distinctive sculpture that stands in a tiny park, and one of the nation's preeminent folk schools.

### Tomteboda (*razed, now the* Grand Marais Public Works Facility)

1800 West Highway 61

Swedish émigré Hildegard Forsell Beebe opened a few tourist cabins in southwestern Grand Marais during the mid-1920s, shortly after she and her husband, Elijah Beebe, and their five daughters moved from Michigan to Minnesota's Lake Superior coastline. A decade later, the woman's sister and brother-in-law, Freda and Carl Hedberg, departed Chicago for Grand Marais, where they began building fourteen Nordic log cabins on an adjacent property. The Hedbergs would name their complex Tomteboda—Swedish for "Home of the Elves." They also crafted a Little Tomteboda for display on the resort grounds and placed two carved elves at the resort's entrance. Both couples sold their businesses during the late 1940s and early 1950s, although the Hedbergs maintained a retirement home at Tomteboda for a few years. Following Carl Hedberg's 1956 death, his widow returned to Sweden, where she spent the remainder of her life.[174]

Carl and Phyliss Noyes, who purchased Tomteboda in 1952, added a motel and an eighteen-hole miniature golf course to the grounds. Many guests, and a number of Grand Marais residents, however, were attracted

**Carl and Freda Hedberg constructed a group of rental cabins at their Tomteboda resort during the 1930s and also assembled this miniature "Home of the Elves" on the grounds.**

by the Noyeses' Catalina swimming pool, which was heated, filtered, lighted, and equipped with "all of the necessary gadgets required by the state." The couple even hired an instructor to offer swimming lessons to Grand Marais–area children during the summer months. By 1972, advertisements for Tomteboda were highlighting its location—"nestled in the woods, yet within the city"—as well as the color television sets and "guest phones" available in each cabin. Tomteboda remained a North Shore fixture for almost eighty years before the City of Grand Marais purchased the property, removed its buildings and trees, and constructed a large public utilities facility on the site that opened in 2017–18.[175]

### Preine's Hilltop Lodge and Cabins and Niolina's Pensionat (*razed, now* Benny's Collision Center)
1803 West Highway 61

Fred and Mabel Smith Preine of Minneapolis opened a clothing store within Grand Marais's Arrowhead Hotel in 1931. They sold the store around 1938 and launched Preine's Hilltop Lodge and Cabins—considered one of Grand Marais's finest tourist destinations at the time. "The lodge and its cabins command attention immediately," wrote an enthusiastic *Cook County News-Herald* reviewer soon after the resort's opening, as does the circular drive "cut through the natural growth of fir and birch trees" and the rock garden that enhances the site's "natural beauties." Knotty pine covered the interior walls of the two large lodge rooms: one a tearoom that had tables of different colors, the other a lounge furnished with "cozy chairs." Mabel Preine prepared meals for patrons in a well-lighted, contemporary kitchen, which was lined with her own home-canned food. Adding a "final touch to the rustic charm of the place" were its distinctive lamps fashioned from diamond willow wood. Guests who stay at Preine's, predicted the correspondent, will definitely "spread the news of its comfort and convenience."[176]

**The knotty pine walls of the cozy tearoom at Niolina's Pensionat were covered with American and European bric-a-brac.**

Mabel Preine was active in numerous civic organizations during World War II, including service as the membership chair of Cook County's Red Cross and president of the Grand Marais Garden Club. Unfortunately, her health problems forced the couple to sell the business just prior to the 1946 tourist season opening, and one year before she died. Fred Preine served as president of the Grand Marais Commercial Club during the late 1930s and worked as Cook County's deputy auditor throughout the 1940s before his passing in 1950.[177]

Preine's Hilltop Lodge was purchased, in early 1946, by Minneapolitans Albin and Anneilia Grabowski Carlson—he the son of Swedish immigrants, she the daughter of Polish émigrés. The couple married in 1942, just weeks before Carlson departed for three years of military duty with the U.S. Navy. After his lengthy service concluded, the couple established themselves in Grand Marais and quickly sought to attract both tourists and Cook County residents to their new business. They did this by emphasizing Albin Carlson's ethnic heritage and surname: the lodge was called a *pensionat* ("guest house" in Swedish); Anneilia became the Swedish "Niolina"; a large outdoor sign enticed motorists to stop and "Enjoy Mrs. Carlson's Swedish Cooking"; and a smorgasbord, available for $1.50 a plate, was featured on the weekend menu. The Carlsons' facilities, including a twenty-unit motel built during the late 1950s, were described as modern and "comfortably equipped" during their tenure, which ended in 1965 when the couple returned to the Twin Cities. Although other owners ran the business for several years thereafter, the lodge, motel, and all but two cabins were eventually razed or moved from the property. Benny's Collision Center is now located on a portion of the original site.[178]

Elsa Johnson grew twinflowers "amongst beautiful pines" at Linnea Woods from 1947 to 1975.

### Harbor Light Supper Club (*now* Up Yonder)

1615 West Highway 61

The Nightingale Café, built and opened by Myron Hahn and Marvin Maxwell in 1930, became the Harbor Light Supper Club after its acquisition, in late 1938, by Gordon and Ann Sykes of Fort William, Ontario. The Sykeses also built several nearby rental cabins (later removed) before the property was sold in 1973. Among the ensuing owners was William J. O'Brien, a Republican politician from St. Paul who previously served two terms (1963–66) in the Minnesota House of Representatives and one term as state auditor (1969–71). The Harbor Light's sixty-five hundred square feet of interior space, which could accommodate as many as 240 people in its dining area, also offered a setting for dances, parties, and dinner theater performances.[179]

Acquired by new owners in 2017, several years after the Harbor Light had closed, the property experienced a rebirth as the WunderBar Eatery and Glampground. Unfortunately, the fledgling business closed in 2020 because of financial issues exacerbated by the Covid-19 outbreak. Renamed Up Yonder following its subsequent purchase by a group of investors, the structure currently includes a bar and restaurant and serves as a venue for live music and other large events.[180]

### Linnea Woods Motel and Cabins (*now* The Blue Moose)

1301 Highway 61 West

Henning and Elsa Andersson Johnson emigrated separately from Sweden to Chicago, where they married in 1939. When vacationing by Grand Marais with their two children in 1946, the couple purchased an undeveloped parcel of land on the northern side of Highway 61. There, one year later, the Johnsons established Linnea Woods Motel and Cabins "amongst beautiful pines." Elsa Johnson also cultivated the "beautiful flower that grows in our woods"—the *Linnaea borealis* (Sweden's national flower), commonly known as the twinflower. Henning Johnson died in 1955, but his widow operated Linnea Woods for another twenty years. Others owned the business until 1990, when Maribeth Nelson acquired the property. She and her husband, Bill Doucette, changed the name to Blue Moose Nursery and Gifts, converted the cabins into long-term rental units, transformed the motel into a gift shop, and added a nursery to the grounds. Doucette, a widower in 1995, managed The Blue Moose from spring through autumn until 2022, when he sold the business to a pair of local residents, who announced their plans to operate the business as a seasonal garden center.[181]

The first two log cabins that emerged at Traveler's Rest in 1935 have been maintained and preserved to the present.

**Nelson's Traveler's Rest**
1300 West Highway 61

Morse Rhea, a North Dakotan serving with the U.S. Coast Guard in Grand Marais, and his wife, Ethel, purchased a parcel of undeveloped land along Highway 61 in 1935. The couple, assisted by their daughter and son-in-law, established a tourist business, Traveler's Rest, which had four cabins—two built of logs, two faced with log siding. The sale of their property occurred just three years later because of Rhea's transfer to another Coast Guard station. Four additional cabins, all "nestled among the pines, quiet and restful," appeared after a mother-and-son team, Grace and William Mulligan, acquired Traveler's Rest in 1944. The addition of two more single cabins and a pair of double units (one a former CCC building) occurred during the succeeding tenure of Dale and Dale Webb Saethre, which spanned the years from 1964 to 1990.[182]

Since purchasing Traveler's Rest in 1990, Tom and Patty Eckels Nelson have retained and maintained the log and log-faced cabins, most organized around an elongated circular space that includes a playground at its center. It was the relatively unaltered features of Nelson's mom-and-pop resort that drew the attention of a MHS consultant who surveyed Grand Marais's tourist facilities during the late 1990s: Traveler's Rest, she observed, stood out as a rare example of a once-common property type in Grand Marais. Those same features are still present today, but only because of the work and dedication of the Nelsons, who "have their lives invested in Traveler's Rest."[183]

**Trailside Cabins and Motel**
1100 West Highway 61

During the late 1930s, Kenneth and Marie Cooper Healey, with the assistance of local carpenter and builder Einar Stone, constructed Trailside Cabins, a complex of eight "classic" rental cabins, seven motel units, and an adjacent combination residence and office. When Roy and Florence Byholm acquired Trailside in 1956, they added a flat-roofed "strip motel" along the highway, hoping that its location would "attract travelers and exhibit how modern the facility was." An ensuing owner, who wasn't impressed by the motel's flat roof surface, chose to construct a gable rooftop so it would better relate to Trailside's cabins.[184]

Today, the cabins maintain a distinctive presence along Highway 61. The seven initial units, each retaining its 1930s name—Tiny Tim, Big Cabin, New Cabin, Bridge, Jim, Sixteen, and Kari's Cabin—are relatively unaltered and retain evidence of their original size, materials, and construction details, including wooden-frame windows with six lights, gabled rooflines, and uniform brackets that support the offset entrance gables. Also enhancing Trailside's overall setting are the mature trees that tower over the grounds.[185]

### Lund's Motel and Cottages

#### 919 West Highway 61

Lund's Motel and Cottages has been owned for almost nine decades by just two generations of one family. The business was established by Able Lund, a son of Norwegian immigrants who had settled in the Red River Valley of far northwestern Minnesota during the late nineteenth century, and his wife, Mable Allen Lund, whose parents immigrated to Cook County from Norway and Sweden. A U.S. Navy veteran of World War I, Lund worked as a U.S. Border Patrol agent until the Prohibition Amendment of late 1933 precluded the need for his services. The couple, two years later, used Lund's military bonus to initiate the acquisition of twelve hundred feet of secluded land that bordered the highway in southwestern Grand Marais. Once their purchase was completed in late 1937, Einar Stone, who also built several cabins at Trailside and other Grand Marais sites, performed much of the construction work. The seven original units that composed the Lund cabin complex grew to eight when a combined residence/office building was completed in 1947.[186]

The Lunds' son Ron returned to Grand Marais from San Francisco in 1977 and began assisting his parents in managing their business. The decision, Lund later recalled, was made "as a labor of love, because I grew up with it and wanted to see it continue."

**Lund's Motel and Cottages is a business that has been owned and operated by just two generations of one family since 1937. Although the cabin interiors are modernized, the exteriors, here in 2016, remain remarkably intact; only outdoor decks have been added to these cabins since they were constructed during the late 1930s and early 1940s.**

Following the senior Lund's death in 1981, his son built a six-unit motel that opened in 1984; the new building, and some winterized cabins, quickly attracted skiers and snowmobilers. Lund worked with his mother during summers from 1985 to 1989 but spent each academic year at the University of Minnesota, where he completed a degree in architecture.[187]

Upon assuming sole ownership of the business in 2003, following his mother's passing, Lund realized that it would be possible to secure a "little niche" in the tourist market because of a growth in cabin popularity. Even if cabin culture remained "a little bit behind" the times, observed Lund, he surmised that mom-and-pop places still had an appeal because of their "quaintness" and privacy.[188] Lund's Motel and Cottages has continued as a traditional and attractive fixture in Grand Marais's tourist landscape—but only because of the owner's devotion and attention to its upkeep and maintenance.

### Grand Marais Tourist Park (*now the* Grand Marais Municipal Campground and Marina)
114 South Eighth Avenue West

Among Grand Marais's most popular tourist destinations, all accessed from South Eighth Avenue, are a city campground, a small marina, and a public water access. The campground, now one of the best-equipped public facilities of its type on the North Shore, was identified as a "tourist park" soon after Grand Marais officials acquired the land and adjacent shoreline access in 1924. Within a year, 22,640 visitors and almost two thousand vehicles were registered at the site. Even more tourists used the property following the implementation of a major improvement and expansion program in 1947, which included the addition of hot water, washing machines, and showers. Local officials, at that time, claimed that the park could handle "trailer houses, as well as tenters, and picnickers," and had everything required by modern outdoor campers. The facility, already by summer 1961, had attracted ten thousand "trailer people." An office opened around 1965, when the former SNF headquarters building was moved to the campground.[189]

Present-day tourists are especially attracted by the site's cobblestone beach, three hundred campsites, and well-equipped recreational facilities, all situated within walking distance of Grand Marais's downtown attractions. A small marina, protected by a J-shaped wall, extends from the campground into West Bay, while the most recent addition, the Parkside Public Water Access, was jointly sponsored and funded by the City of Grand Marais and the MDNR. The Parkside facility, following its 2022 opening, proved popular among both residents and tourists because of the outstanding views that are available from its breakwater, which is ten feet wide and two hundred feet long. Also on display at the campground is a tugboat—the *Neegee* (Anishinaabe for "friend")—built in 1936 by Jim Scott and his son Roger; it remains the only tugboat ever constructed in Cook County. Used by local fishermen until the 1960s, the workhorse tug also moved the log booms that were assembled along both West Bay and East Bay. After experiencing considerable deterioration in a Duluth drydock, the *Neegee* was donated to the Cook County Historical Society (CCHS) in 2001 and returned to Grand Marais; once there, volunteers worked three years to restore the vessel, which included rehabilitation of its broken joists, flooring, and hatch doors and reinforcement of the cabin ceiling. Standing next to the *Neegee* is a twelve-by-twenty-foot replica of an early twentieth-century fish house.[190]

### Charles and Anna Johnson Residence (*now the* Birch Terrace Supper Club)
601 West Highway 61

Completed in 1898, this log structure served as a home for C. H. and Cecelia Taylor before Swedish immigrants Charles H. and Anna Johnson purchased the property at the time of their 1907 marriage. Johnson, in 1890, had traveled from Michigan to Cook County, where he quickly became "a powerful figure in local business affairs"; Anna Johnson was known for her artistic interests and support of local cultural activities. The Johnsons also enlarged the residence, which provided more space for the numerous social and Republican Party activities they organized. The property was sold in 1946, soon after the deaths of both Johnsons, to Vern and Marge Talkovich, who converted the residence into Birch Terrace, a restaurant known for its Colonial Dining Room. A number of other owners, since 1965, have operated the business, currently known as the Birch Terrace Supper Club.[191]

The North House Folk School campus includes two large timber-frame structures (one in the background), both built in 1934 by CCC enrollees for the U.S. Forest Service. In the foreground is a *skjelter*, a folk building typically used for hay storage in remote areas of Norway, which was constructed by a small group of students enrolled in a 2017 North House class.

### Gunflint Ranger Station, Superior National Forest (*now* North House Folk School)

500 West Highway 61

When the massive SNF was established in 1909, it also included the Grand Marais–based North Shore Division (now the Gunflint Ranger District). In 1934, four SNF structures—an office/headquarters building, an oil house, and two large (thirty by fifty foot) timber-frame warehouses—were erected by CCC enrollees on a prime parcel of West Bay shoreline. Later, following the construction of a new SNF administrative building, the original headquarters building was moved to the public campground. Another transfer occurred in 1992, when all SNF functions were relocated to a new structure situated more than one mile toward the west (2020 West Highway 61).[192]

All of the former SNF properties located along West Bay, including its two large CCC buildings, were leased to the recently organized North House Folk School in 1997. Formed by volunteers and enthusiasts who began offering classes focused on "northern" skills and crafts, North House reflects the folk school (*folkehøjskoler)* concept that emerged in mid-nineteenth-century Denmark, then spread to all the Nordic countries. North House later procured more property along West Bay, including fish houses, two docks, and even a forty-two-foot sailing schooner, the *Hjørdis*. Since then, the campus has grown with the addition of wood milling and blacksmithing shops, a teaching kitchen, and a student commons. The 2018 acquisition of an adjacent business, the Dockside Fish and Seafood Market—which reopened two years later as the Fisherman's Daughter at Dockside Market (418 West Highway 61)—increased the size of the North House campus footprint by 50 percent.[193]

During a typical year, more than three thousand students enroll in as many 350 North House classes, which range from furniture craft, woodworking, food preparation, and boat- and canoe building to basketry, weaving and fiber arts, fly-fishing, northern geology and ecology, and sustainable living. The reason for its popularity is simple, says Mark Hansen, a North House founder and the first of many teachers who have followed him. "People are born to create," he observed in 2012; many who live in "a high-tech world . . . are really looking for low-tech and high-touch."[194]

### Jim Scott Fish House

South of the Highway 61 and Fifth Avenue Intersection

The Jim Scott Fish House, dating to 1907, has wooden shingle walls and an attached shed-roofed addition. Once used for cleaning and packaging fish, and for storing and repairing boats and gear, the structure

**The 1907 Jim Scott Fish House is representative of many similar structures once evident along Grand Marais's West Bay.**

was built by Jim Scott, a successful fisherman and a businessman who served as a Grand Marais bank president, helped to establish the North Shore Cooperative Fishermen's Association, and assisted in building the First Congregational Church. (Eugene Clark, Scott's bachelor business partner, also occupied a bunk in the cramped fish house attic until 1915.) Ironically, Scott's 1947 death, of natural causes, occurred on the very dock he had built forty years earlier. The well-constructed building, listed in the National Register of Historic Places in 1986, was still being used for boat and equipment storage by two of Scott's grandsons in 2018, when North House purchased the structure. The artifacts associated with the building were later donated to the CCHS, which collaborated with the Folk School and the MHS in preparing a preservation plan and interpretative program for the landmark building.[195]

### Grand Marais Harbor Seawall

#### South Side of Highway 61, between Third and Fourth Avenues West

Flanking the eastern side of Scott's fish house is the Angry Trout Café (408 West Highway 61), one of Grand Marais's best-known restaurants. From there, the highway closely parallels West Bay for a brief distance. Protecting both the shoreline and the roadway at this vulnerable point is a seawall, constructed by WPA workers in 1937. The project received approval from MDH engineers after Grand Marais officials requested replacement of the existing retaining wall, which had a history of construction problems. The new structure, its moderately curved form designed by landscape architect Arthur Nichols, was constructed along and atop an existing wall that extended for one block (four hundred feet) along the lakefront. Built of reinforced concrete and faced with black and dark red gabbro of varying sizes, the structure is anchored to the rocky bottom by steel bolts that are two and a half feet long. Approximately one hundred feet from the eastern terminus is a curved lookout bay with two explanatory plaques: one, dating to 1955, describes the harbor's geology, while the other, added around 1988, summarizes the harbor's history. A mounded barrier of rubblestone, added along the lakeshore side in 1967, provided the seawall with increased stabilization and protection. The height of the wall was reduced by several inches in 1976 when some walkway sections were repaired with poured concrete. While a subsequent assessment of the site determined that the repairs had compromised the seawall's "integrity of design, materials, workmanship, and feeling," the evaluation also concluded that the overall qualities of "location and setting" had been maintained.[196] Despite these changes, the seawall endures as a reminder of the constant interactions between land and lake in Grand Marais.

### Bear Tree Park

#### Highway 61–Wisconsin Avenue Intersection

A "serpentine curve," formed by the merger of Highway 61 and Wisconsin Avenue during the early 1930s, created a small, triangular area of shoreline space that was selected as the location for a sculpture, sponsored and implemented by the Minneapolis School of Art (MSA) in 1953. Called *The Bear Tree*, the sculpture recognized the generosity and cooperation of Grand Marais officials and citizens who supported a local art colony, organized by the MSA in 1948. The steel and concrete piece—two bear cubs on a tall, smooth, tree-like column, as they wait for their mother—was created by Minneapolis art-

*The Bear Tree,* around the time of its 1954 dedication.

ist Raymond Gormley and his students and dedicated in 1954 by former Minnesota governor Jacob A. O. Preus. A simple circular fountain, added to the base in 1965, failed to function and was soon removed.[197]

### Seawall Motel and Cabins *(razed)*

#### North of Bear Tree Park and Highway 61

Hans Olai Toftey, at the age of seventeen in 1902, departed Norway for the North Shore with his parents and siblings. In 1916, he married Clara Gilbertson, the daughter of Norwegian immigrant farmers from west-central Minnesota. The couple, during the 1930s, established Toftey's Cabins, which they operated before moving to California in 1945. A series of other owners managed the renamed Seawall Motel and Cabins until 2006, when the site was proposed for a new condominium complex, the Harbor House. A downturn in Grand Marais's real estate market led to the project's abandonment, but not before a backhoe had reduced the Seawall to rubble.[198] The lot remains vacant.

### Wigwam Theatre *(razed, now the* Gateway to the Gunflint Trail)

#### West Second Avenue, Slightly North of the Intersection with Highway 61

In October 1930, the *Cook County News-Herald* reported that the highway entering Grand Marais from the west would be moved four blocks southward to its current location. Soon, an angular slash that cut through a number of existing streets caused the removal of several structures. The newspaper's description of these actions assumed that readers possessed an intimate familiarity with Grand Marais's businesses and residences:

> The road will hit one corner of the Wigwam Theater; will go through the present Northwestern Oil Company site; pass between the Arrowhead Hotel and the Midway Service Station; barely miss the Home Trade Shoe Shop; go directly through the Hall's Battery and Electric Company's garage, will necessitate the removal of J.C. Murphy's house; will strike Mrs. Chris Holte's home and force the removal of other houses beyond.[199]

The Wigwam Theatre in Grand Marais, called the Princess at the time of its construction around 1912, served as a venue for "a lot of good times"—ranging from movies and plays to dances and other events—before it was scheduled for removal during the highway rerouting project. Following the Wigwam's 1937 demolition, a section of the vacant site was proposed as the site for a "symbolic entrance" to the Gunflint Trail—a major tourist route that begins in Grand Marais and proceeds northward into the SNF. The envisioned gateway, promoted jointly by members of the Gunflint Trail Association and the Grand Marais Commercial Club, proved successful when Mayor Homer Massie secured agreements from several units of government, including two New Deal agencies (the CCC and WPA), along with the MDH and the USFS.[200]

Although the Gunflint Trail was accessible from different roads within Grand Marais, the preferred entrance, by 1930, had coalesced around the intersection of West Second Avenue and Highway 61. The gateway, designed by MDH consultant Arthur Nichols and USFS roadside development engineer Harold E. Olson, was built in 1938–39 by several CCC enrollees,

**The Gunflint Trail entrance during the 1950s, shortly after the figures of a bear and voyageur were placed atop the two stone posts, which had been built in 1938–39.**

who may have been assisted by WPA workers. The gateway's primary features—"two pillars of natural [gabbro] stone, one on either side of the road leading up the Gunflint Trail"—also include a curved wall that extends from each pillar to a shorter post. Toward the northeast is a rectangular open space, identified by Nichols as an "open lawn" that eventually would be framed by trees and other plantings. (A formal flagpole setting proposed for the site was not developed.) Attached to the western pillar is a plaque that recognizes former governor Jacob Preus as the primary promoter of the Gunflint Trail; he would also preside at the gateway's 1941 dedication. A portion of the open lawn was used, in 1987, as the site for Grand Marais's new public library and an expansion in 2011. Although the gateway feature still remains at its original Second Avenue location, the primary Grand Marais entrance to the Gunflint Trail was relocated about one-half mile farther east in 2000.[201]

A large, painted metal sign was fixed to each gateway entrance post during the 1950s. One depicted a voyageur who was carrying a canoe that had "Gunflint Trail" emblazoned on it; below was a small sign with the words "Land of the Voyageur." Situated on the gateway's other side was a bear sitting in a motorboat, with a "Wilderness Country" sign underneath it. The motorboat was later covered by a plywood sign that depicted the bear catching a fish. By 2012, when the signs were termed in "complete disrepair," a community-based project raised sufficient funds to renovate and restore them. Gunflint Trail artists Yarrow Korf and Alicia Hein completed the project in September 2013, including restoration of the original bear in a motorboat.[202]

## Downtown and the Point

Grand Marais's small downtown district, centered at the intersection of Wisconsin Street and Broadway Avenue, lies south of the "diagonal cut" that resulted from the realignment of Highway 61 during the 1930s. Farther south and flanked by East Bay and West Bay are the Point and Artist's Point, two of Grand Marais's most scenic and popular sites. Some first- and second-generation buildings still remain in this area, although several are of more recent vintage, including two vacation condominium complexes that appeared in 2006. Also of note is one of Minnesota's few remaining Ben Franklin department stores (105 West Wisconsin Avenue); after seven decades of ownership by the Joynes family, the store was sold, in 2022, but to owners who have pledged to retain the Ben Franklin name and tradition. Since Grand Marais has fewer brick-and-mortar commercial structures than many other Minnesota towns of similar size, its mixture of predominantly frame-and-board buildings, some more than a century old, are examples of what might be termed a version of "Northwoods vernacular."

### Johnson's Trading Post (*razed, now* Johnson's Heritage Post Art Gallery)

115 West Wisconsin Street

In 1906, Charles Johnson moved his three businesses, all located in a single room within the Cook County State Bank, to a new "trading post" at the western end of Wisconsin Street. The cross-shaped log structure, with a central lobby, also housed the Grand Marais Post Office, but it was Johnson's fur trade business that made him "known far and wide among early settlers and Indians." After a 1926 fire consumed the structure, the ambitious Swedish immigrant built another trading post, this one covered with cedar shakes, which provided quarters for several small businesses and also served as a gallery where Anna Johnson's artwork was displayed and sold. The building would be operated as a gift shop following the deaths of both Johnsons in the mid-1940s.[203]

The dilapidated structure was torn down in 1989 and replaced with the Johnson Heritage Post Art Gallery, constructed of Montana lodgepole pine. (Funded by the Johnsons' son Lloyd, the building was designed by his nephew Duane Johnson.) Now managed by the CCHS, the Heritage Post includes a permanent collection of Anna Johnson's artwork, some of which is always on display, and promotes "public awareness of the cultural heritage of the arts in Cook County and the North Shore through high quality exhibits of the work of artists and artisans past and present."[204]

### Standard Oil Distribution Center (*razed, now* Harbor Park)

110 West Wisconsin Street

One of Grand Marais's remarkable land-use transitions occurred during the early 2000s when a former Standard Oil Company property, located at the corner of Wisconsin Avenue and First Street, was converted into Harbor Park. One part of the site included an automobile service station dating to the mid-1920s; nearby was a large gas and oil distribution center, completed in 1931, where ships could anchor and pump fuel into seven huge bulk tanks. The service station closed in 1998—well after the distribution center had moved to another site—when federal and state regulations required operators to remove all existing underground storage containers.[205]

In 2000, the nonprofit Trust for Public Land, a national organization engaged in protecting "iconic landscapes"—including several throughout the Lake Superior region—coordinated a distinctive private–public partnership that raised funds to purchase the "crown jewel property along the harbor." The large number of Grand Marais citizens who gathered to watch as the vacant filling station was demolished on a July day in 2000 reportedly were pleased with the new harbor and lighthouse views that were immediately opened toward the south. Completed in 2006, the highly popular harbor site is integrated with Bear Tree Park and provides space for "private reflection, passive recreation, and large-scale public events," including the annual August Fisherman's Picnic that dates to 1928.[206]

### North Shore Hotel and Cook County Cooperative Store (*now the* Beaver House)
3 East Wisconsin Street

Located at the northeastern corner of Broadway and Wisconsin is a 1925 building that has been known as the Beaver House since 1965. An earlier structure, the North Shore Hotel (later called the Broadway), constructed by Swedish immigrant Andrew Larson in 1898–99, housed members of the 1901 University of Minnesota Gophers football team who traveled to Grand Marais during late August and spent several days engaged in physical conditioning activities on the North Shore. The site, however, remained vacant for twelve years following a major 1913 fire that consumed the hotel and several nearby structures. J. C. Murphy's grocery store, built on the former hotel property in

**The Beaver House, a bait shop and destination for North Shore anglers, also attracts considerable attention from tourists and visitors, who may be either amused or bemused by its exterior.**

1925, was initially operated by his widow, then by the couple's daughter and son-in-law, who sold the business to the Cook County Cooperative Association (CCCA) in 1945; the organization disbanded and departed the building some years later.[207] The cooperative concept would be reinstituted in 1974 when the Cook County Whole Foods Co-op (now at 20 East First Street) was organized.

The vacant CCCA structure, purchased in 1964 by Bill Cronberg and Guyal Anderson, was converted into a shoe repair shop. The men soon realized, however, that the handmade fishing flies they sold in their building were more profitable than making shoe repairs. Cronberg assumed sole ownership of the Beaver House bait shop in 1976, fifteen years before it became a Broadway Avenue attraction because of the large feature, fabricated by local artist Jim Korf, which dominates the building: the head of a fiberglass walleye situated above the entrance door and the fishtail, which appears to pierce the roof. The building's exterior facades are also covered with lettering and a large mural, while the interior is crowded with fishing tackle, nets, and outboard motors.[208]

In 2016, three years after Cronberg's passing, the Beaver House was acquired by his son Tyson, who had spent considerable time in the building since 1970, when he was five years old. Because the structure required significant maintenance and repairs at this time, a number of local residents expressed concern that it might be torn down and replaced by another Grand Marais restaurant. Several volunteers immediately sought to "freshen up" the exterior murals and also "painted and patched and polished the interior." The whimsical, quirky building, one of the city's most photographed attractions, continues to maintain a connection to "old" Grand Marais.[209]

### Sterling Hotel (*now* East Bay Suites)
21 East Wisconsin Street

The business ventures associated with this site have served Grand Marais's tourists and visitors since 1910, the year George and Christina (Belle) Sterling opened the Lake Side, a hotel and restaurant. Although the Lake Side burned down in 1913, the recently widowed Belle Sterling soon had an even larger hotel, the Sterling Hotel, built on the site. She managed the Sterling until her 1945 passing, when it was sold and renamed as the East Bay Hotel. Lois Pedersen, who acquired the property with her husband in 1956, acknowledged, some twenty years later, that the East Bay had "squeaking, uneven floors" as well as "occasional new roof leaks, [and] the now and then plumbing difficulties." Nevertheless, she and a legion of satisfied patrons and local citizens believed that the much-loved building

**The original Sterling Hotel, shortly after its name was changed to the East Bay Hotel in 1945. The East Bay would remain a popular Grand Marais lodging and dining destination until its removal in 2005. The current East Bay Suites appeared on the site shortly thereafter.**

was "comfy and cozy," possessed "character, history [and a] certain dignity," and offered guests a "unique experience to stay in an old hotel." Despite numerous protestations, a subsequent purchaser chose to raze the historic structure in 2005. But rather than engaging in a typical demolition exercise, the new owners invited Grand Marais residents "to come and take a piece of their history." Some local salvagers removed the vacated hotel's mirrors, radiators, light fixtures, and even the door numbers, while others detached its three-quarter-inch maple flooring, along with doors, sinks, and floor and wall paneling (including the dining room's rosemaling)—"essentially gutting the building of anything of value to re-use and recycle into their own lives." East Bay Suites, a vacation condominium complex that opened on the site in 2006, is now owned and managed by Odyssey Resorts, a major provider of tourist services along the North Shore.[210]

**This building, one of Grand Marais's oldest residences, was successively occupied by several businesses before becoming Drury Lane Books in 2002.**

**The former Grand Marais lightkeeper's residence, dating to 1896, now serves as the Cook County Historical Society Museum.**

### Joseph Mayhew Residence (*now* Drury Lane Books)
12 East Wisconsin Street

The exact origins of this residence are not known, but it likely emerged during the 1890s and was once occupied by Joseph Mayhew, Grand Marais's first lighthouse keeper. Its side-gable entry and short cross-gable extension are undoubtedly similar to some other early houses that have subsequently disappeared from the Grand Marais landscape. The dwelling was converted into a gift store by 1952, a shoe repair shop during the late 1970s, and the Sivertson Gallery in 1982, before becoming Drury Lane Books in 2002. The bookstore was launched by the late Joan Drury, originally from the Twin Cities suburb of Richfield, who later moved to Duluth, where she organized Spinsters Ink, a feminist publishing company, and also founded Norcroft, a Lutsen women's writing retreat. Drury passed away in 2020, eighteen years after establishing the Grand Marais bookstore, which is now owned by her son and daughter, Kevin and Kelly Kager. Although it has no more than 650 square feet of retail space, the bookstore's five thousand volumes are expertly and compactly arranged throughout the building. Drury Lane attracts both regular patrons and visitors, who peruse its inventory, make purchases, and also participate in bookstore events that enhance the cultural life of Grand Marais and Cook County.[211]

### Lightkeeper's House (*now the* Cook County Historical Society Museum)
8 South Broadway Avenue

It was not until 1896, eight years after the opening of Grand Marais's lighthouse, that a residence was built for the local lightkeeper. A reporter who observed the $2,800 building undergoing construction in early August 1896 predicted that it would be Cook County's finest home and a tribute to Grand Marais. Lightkeeper Joseph Mayhew, soon a widower with three children, moved into the seven-room house in December. The two-story wooden-frame structure, basically rectangular in plan, has a concrete foundation covered with brick veneer; narrow clapboard siding envelops the lower story, while the upper level and portico are sided with sawtooth-shaped shingles.[212]

A local U.S. Coast Guard commander still occupied the residence during the 1950s, but the building, by 1963, was vacant and slated for possible consideration as a surplus property by the federal government. At this time, CCHS president Olga Soderberg launched a successful campaign that allowed the organization to acquire the residence in 1966 and convert it into a museum; the building received further recognition in 1978 when it was listed in the National Register of Historic Places. The first floor, including a 2007 addition on its eastern side, houses the CCHS's administrative offices, exhibits, and a small sales area; the upper story has additional displays. The basement provided space for archival storage until 2017–18, when serious flooding issues forced CCHS administrators to move its collections off-site and plan for the development of a safe facility.[213]

### Shoreline Inn
### 20 South Broadway Avenue

The Shoreline Inn, designed by Minneapolis architect E. J. Becchetti, emerged along East Bay between 1952 and 1954. It was the first North Shore lodging facility to display the architectural features and construction materials that became popular throughout the United States during the immediate postwar years—an L-shaped plan, flat roof, and structural steel framework; walls built of "slag aggregate blocks," all covered with brick veneer; and a large, paved parking lot, bordered by a thin band of vegetation. The Shoreline's interior, termed "luxurious" in early advertisements, was not nearly as austere as the exterior due to its furnishings—now termed examples of mid-century modern design. The "tastefully furnished lobby," observed a local newspaper reporter who toured the Shoreline upon its August 1954 opening, had blond furniture, large windows looking onto Lake Superior, a carpeted seating area, and a brick fireplace. Covering one wall was a fifteen-by-seventeen-foot mural, painted by Grand Marais Art Colony founder Birney Quick, that represented the area's natural features. Each of the Shoreline's thirty rooms, with walls all painted in "two-tone color schemes," included a television, wall-to-wall

**The 1954 opening of the Shoreline Hotel introduced mid-century modern design and furnishings to Grand Marais. The lobby had leather-like furniture (including this sectional couch), full-glass windows, and a carpet with a foliage design motif. Artist Birney Quick's mural, a representation of the area's natural characteristics, dominated one wall.**

carpeting, blond ash bedroom furniture, large picture windows, and draw drapes in contrasting colors. The owners also expressed pride in their air-conditioned Terrace Dining Room, where two walls of windows provided "unexcelled views" of East Bay.[214]

A seawall gave the hotel (soon called the Shoreline Motor Lodge, and later the Shoreline Inn) limited protection from East Bay's turbulent wave action, but even such a well-built structure could not allay the impact of a November 1960 "monster" storm that made "Broadway a lake, Wisconsin a river." Water, gravel, and a pulp log smashed into the Shoreline's dining room, causing significant flooding and damage. After another damaging storm caused serious harm just one year later, efforts were made to enforce the seawall with five-ton boulders hauled from Carlton Peak. The possibility of further extreme weather events, however, eventually led to the permanent closure of the dining room.[215] The Shoreline, especially popular among skiers during the 1950s and 1960s, remains a moderately priced option for travelers who cannot afford Grand Marais's more expensive tourist accommodations. The unadorned 1950s exterior remains relatively intact, and Birney Quick's mural still graces one of the lobby's interior walls.

### Cobblestone Cove Villas and Boulder Park
17 South Broadway Avenue

This impressive site offers close-up views of West Bay and a distant impression of the Sawtooth Mountains. Despite the prime location, little more than vacant lots and a few residences were evident at the site in 2005, when the Land and Cabins Company of Grand Marais acquired the property. The company's owners soon applied for a building permit that allowed them to build a ten-unit vacation condominium complex, Cobblestone Cove Villas, on the site. When the company's request was reviewed during a public meeting, however, several Grand Marais citizens decried the "unsightly" appearance of "vacation condos" and questioned whether they were "appropriate for the small-town character of the city." Although the Cobblestone, and East Bay Suites, applications were approved and built, no other vacation condominium projects have appeared in downtown Grand Marais since 2005. Adjacent to Cobblestone is Boulder Park, completed and dedicated in 1998: just three-quarters of an acre in size, the site is filled with coniferous trees and also marks a pathway connection between Harbor Park at the north and the Point to the south.[216]

## The Point

The gravel isthmus or tombolo known as the Point provides a spine for the double harbor the Anishinaabe called Gichi Bitobig. French Canadian voyageurs also gained familiarity with the Point when they landed and secured their canoes between its protected double bays. Although no physical evidence remains of the outpost established by AFC personnel during the 1820s, it very likely was built somewhere on the Point. A half century later, the tombolo would serve as the initial settlement site for what became Grand Marais. The spit of land, local historian Eugene Glader has confirmed, was identified as "the Point" by the early 1900s.[217]

The dredging that began along West Bay during the 1880s increased significantly throughout the 1920s and 1930s. While the removal of more than six acres of gravel from the tombolo expanded the breadth and depth of Grand Marais's harbor, these actions also destroyed much of the natural barrier that once provided the Point, Broadway Avenue, and other nearby areas with protection from flooding events. A large area of the Point was also covered, from the 1940s to the mid-1980s, by huge stacks of logs that were transported across Lake Superior to Ashland, then shipped to several Wisconsin paper mills.[218] Today the Point offers parking space for vehicles and boat trailers. At the far southern end is one of Grand Marais's outstanding early twentieth-century landmarks—a former U.S. Coast Guard station.

### Hazael and Thomas Mayhew Buildings and Consolidated Papers, Inc., Log Storage and Dock (*now the* Grand Marais Safe Harbor Boat Launch *and a vehicle parking area*)

Brothers Hazael ("Henry") and Thomas Mayhew constructed a group of buildings on the Point between 1873 and 1880. Among these structures were the Lakeview Hotel (more likely a boardinghouse, which also included the first school and courthouse) and a two-story trading post that had a store, a post office, doctor's quarters, a fur storage room, and an

**The Point, looking eastward from West Bay, about 1894. The building on the right is likely the Mayhew Hotel; to its left is the Mayhews' home, store, and post office. Farther left, at the northern entrance to the Point, is another residence. Chippewa City is visible in the distant background. Courtesy of Cook County Historical Society.**

office and bedrooms for the proprietors. Nearby were sheds, a large dock, cabins that housed several single men, and a small horse barn. The Point served as the center of Grand Marais's commercial life into the early twentieth century, but the movement of businesses toward the mainland was well under way when the Lakeview burned down in 1916 and the new North Shore highway opened between Duluth and Canada one year later.[219]

A complicated series of land transfers occurred on the Point prior to 1941, when the Filer Fiber Company of Michigan secured considerable property for its log-storage operations. Filer's holdings would be purchased successively by three other timber and lumber firms from 1952 to 1966, when the company was acquired by a Wisconsin firm, Consolidated Papers, Inc. All of the companies had modern lifting equipment, initially acquired by Filer during the late 1940s, which was used to create cordwood piles, some twenty feet high, of spruce, balsam, jack pine, birch, and aspen logs. A majority of the stacks were located along West Bay, where the sheltered inlet provided considerable protection from most weather events. East Bay was used less often because of its greater exposure to storms. The bay's vulnerability was especially evident during the storm of November 1960, an event that caused serious damage to the Shoreline Motor Lodge and other sites: "Much pulpwood . . . washed into the lake," observed the *Cook County News-Herald* in a May 1961 overview, and some logs were "pushed back into Grand Marais' streets."[220]

A number of logs were transported from the Point to Ashland in trucks, but most, for many years, were moved by tugboats. After the pulpwood was dumped into the bays, crews of men equipped with pike poles packed the logs into "booms"—large circular enclosures constructed of buoyant Sitka spruce timbers that had been chained together. (Because spruce is so soft, the chains were attached to a piece of oak that had been inserted into each log.) Once logs filled the boom, and the chains tightened, a small tugboat guided the "floating islands" into Lake Superior, where they were then organized into large rafts, the largest of which extended to a depth of ten feet into the water. Following this, a powerful tugboat, often moving little more than one mile per hour, carefully towed the "rafts of gold" to Ashland, where the logs were placed onto railcars and transported to paper mills in Wisconsin Rapids, Appleton, and Stevens Point. Consolidated Papers ended its rafting operations in 1978 but continued hauling logs, with trucks, to Wisconsin for a few more years. In 1985, soon after shutting down shipping activities, Consolidated surrendered its log-holding facilities to the City of Grand Marais; much of the Point was then converted into a large parking area for vehicles and boat trailers. The city later cooperated with the MDNR in constructing the Grand Marais Safe Harbor Boat Launch, located adjacent to the U.S. Coast Guard station. Fortunately, the Point's most outstanding features remain unchanged, namely, the exceptional views of both bays, Grand Marais, and the Sawtooth Mountains.[221]

### U.S. Coast Guard North Superior Station *(vacant)*
### 315 South Broadway

Small docks and fish houses dominated the southernmost end of the Point until the mid-twentieth century. Also making a brief appearance on the Point was a keg and box factory that A. D. Anderson opened in 1915 but that closed within a year because of financial problems. By this time, Grand Marais was serving as one of the North Shore's busiest harbors, even though no U.S. Coast Guard station was available to assist fishing boats and other vessels caught in turbulent storms. The closest Coast Guard facilities were located on Michigan's Upper Peninsula, 90 miles across Lake Superior, and in Duluth, 110 miles to the southwest.[222]

In 1920, when U.S. congressman William Carss introduced a bill requesting funds for the construction of

**Two log booms were moored along the West Bay shoreline during the late 1930s. The tugboat (probably the *Neegee*), at the upper side of the bay, moved the booms into Lake Superior, where they were joined together to create large rafts for towing to Ashland. Extending northward from the boom is First Avenue West; at the far left, surrounded by trees, is the Cook County Courthouse. The seven Standard Oil Company storage tanks situated along the shoreline were removed in 2000; Harbor Park now occupies the site.**

a U.S. Coast Guard station in Grand Marais, the Duluth Democrat (who later won two elections as a member of Minnesota's Farmer-Labor Party) spoke poignantly about the fishermen who had died when no rescue vessels were available to save them. "We have lost about fifteen men up there in the last few years," testified Congressman Carss when presenting the bill in the U.S. Congress, "just from having them caught in these storms and being swept out to sea."[223]

Carss's bill, which allocated $54,175 for a new Coast Guard station located "somewhere along the North Shore," became law in May 1920. Nevertheless, it was not until 1928 that funds were appropriated for the construction of the three Grand Marais structures, each painted white and topped by a red roof, which accommodated several Coast Guard functions: administrative offices and quarters for the crew, a square boathouse for four rescue vessels, and a combination shop and garage. The Coast Guard occupied the station in 1929 and maintained a continuous, full-time presence in Grand Marais until March 1973, when federal funding for the facility was eliminated on sudden notice. A local volunteer Coast Guard Auxiliary provided limited services for four additional years before northeastern Minnesota's DFL congressman James L. Oberstar secured a special federal appropriation that allowed the station to reopen in 1977. Nevertheless, the year-round presence of Coast Guard personnel ended in 1988, although a few reservists were assigned to the station from Memorial Day to Labor Day for the next four years. Rumors of the station's impending closure circulated during the late 1990s and early 2000s, but an official decision was not announced until 2021, when federal authorities deemed the facility "redundant." Because of this decision, the Cook County Sheriff's Office and Grand Portage Reservation Tribal Council are now responsible for monitoring some fifteen hundred square miles of Lake Superior. Although the future of the property remains uncertain, the CCHS has recommended that the longtime "closed to the public facility" become a Grand Marais maritime history center—a "compelling, magnetic attraction" that

**An aerial view of Grand Marais's U.S. Coast Guard North Superior Station, 1940s or early 1950s. In the foreground is a nineteenth-century dock and freight warehouse, built by Henry Mayhew. Businessman Charles J. Johnson later enlarged the buildings, which were used by fisherman Ed Anderson at the time of this image. Identified as one of the most photographed places in Grand Marais, the site was also popular among Grand Marais Art Colony students before the fish house burned down in March 1956. Photograph by Milford J. Humphrey. Courtesy of Cook County Historical Society.**

would contribute to "the vitality and success of other waterfront interests and the broader community."[224]

## Artist's Point

The small island at the southern end of the tombolo has been identified, at least since the 1970s, as Artist's Point, a term that reflects the postwar emergence of the Grand Marais Art Colony during the 1940s. (Because of the emphasis given to painting in the outdoors—*en plein air*—the art colony students were attracted to the island.) Countless numbers of residents and visitors, as they have since the late nineteenth century, still trek to the island, where they hike, fish, picnic, and view the Grand Marais skyline, West Bay, East Bay, Lake Superior, and the distant Sawtooth Mountains from different vantage points. Some early onlookers even spent considerable time carving the date or year of their visit (the earliest is 1892), as well as personal and hometown names, into the rocks; many of the markings remain visible today. Natural scientists, especially botanists, were drawn to the island because of its plants, many of them rare, which grew in tiny crevices and water pools. Unfortunately, the steady flow of foot traffic throughout the site has compacted and eroded the soil and eliminated much of the most delicate plant life.[225]

Another Artist's Point attraction is the breakwater, some 350 feet long, which protects the West Bay harbor. Initially constructed of log cribs in 1883–84, the structure has served as a walkway since 1926, when it was encased with concrete. The earliest lighthouse, a square, wooden structure built at the breakwater's terminus in 1885, was impacted by several storms during ensuing years. After experiencing irreparable damage in 1919, the lighthouse was replaced, one year later, by a "white, square, pyramidal skeleton steel tower" with an enclosed upper section. The tower, which still stands at the breakwater's terminus, was automated in 1937, and the keeper's position eliminated in 1946. A U.S. Coast Guard lookout tower, since removed, was built at the center of Artist's Point during the late 1920s; a fire tower also stood close to the breakwater from 1928 to 1953.[226]

## North of Downtown

The area between Grand Marais's downtown district and Highway 61 is defined by its mixture of land uses, including motels, diners, drive-ins, automotive service stations, and other commercial establishments. Also located within this district are two structures unique to Grand Marais and the entire North Shore—a former blacksmith shop and a recently established public sauna.

### Bally Blacksmith Shop (*now a* Cook County Historical Society *property*)
100 Broadway Avenue

This modest structure, constructed by Sam Bally in 1911, is a rare example of a once common building type that has all but disappeared from the American scene—a blacksmith shop. Bally, who had previously owned a blacksmith shop in Bayfield, Wisconsin, operated his Grand Marais business until 1922, when ownership was assumed by a son, Albert, who turned it over to his son William in 1946. Although the shop was no longer used at the time of its 1986 listing in the National Register of Historic Places, William Bally continued operating his business in an adjacent metal building until 2009.[227]

The most noticeable features of the unaltered, single-story, frame-and-board structure are its false front and two oversized entrance doors, "wide enough to take a team and wagon." When Bally's blacksmithing activities ended, an outburst of local support prompted the CCHS to acquire the property. In addition to the building, CCHS secured the furnishings and equipment, which ranged from the forge, the bellows, anvils, a drill press, and a wagon wheel tire bender to a wide assortment of unique, handmade tools. Volunteers cleaned and cataloged the artifacts; repaired the building; and assisted in developing a long-range plan that would interpret the local history of blacksmithing and similar industries, provide a space for public gatherings, and create facilities for exhibit preparation and storage. Blacksmithing demonstrations are now popular attractions during the tourist season.[228]

### Claus and Joakime Hansen Residence and Fishing Camp (*now* Sisu and Löyly Nordic Sauna)
110 Second Avenue East

About two blocks east of Bally's is a residence, dating to 1893, built one year after Klaus ("Claus") Hansen and Joakime Steen were married in Norway; the couple soon immigrated to Grand Marais and established

The 1911 Bally Blacksmith Shop, a rare example of a building type once found throughout the United States, is currently owned and managed by the Cook County Historical Society.

a residence and fishing camp along East Bay. The Hansens' daughter Edith and her husband, John Hill, a Finland Swede carpenter and fisherman, maintained the family's connection to the property until their passing in 1966. The Hansen–Hill residence, identified as one of Grand Marais's earliest houses upon its 1969 sale, was sold again in 1982 before its early 2021 purchase by Twin Citians Katie and Sam Usem, the owners of a family cabin in nearby Hovland. Although the Usems have no Finnish background, their acquisition was made with the intention of establishing a public sauna on the site. In a remarkably brief period of seven months, Katie Usem oversaw the transition of Hansen's former fish house into the two-unit Sisu and Löyly Nordic Sauna, which opened in October 2021. (Besides *sauna*, the name includes two other Finnish words: *sisu*, a common term often translated as "guts" or "intestinal fortitude," and *löyly*, which refers to the steam that arises when water is thrown onto the hot rocks of a sauna stove.) The project required close collaboration with Grand Marais building officials, given the need to maintain the original fish house footprint, dimensions, and appearance throughout the conversion process. Nearby are a separate sauna lounge with space for yoga classes and the Hansens' original

**Katie Usem stands by her two-unit Sisu and Löyly Nordic Sauna, converted from a fish house in 2021. The residence in the background was built by Claus and Joakime Hansen during the late 1890s.**

dwelling unit, now a residence. The entire complex, termed "spa-like but unpretentious" by the owner, offers prospects of East Bay, Artist's Point, and downtown Grand Marais from its shoreline location. Also available, since early 2023, is the Usems' mobile sauna, constructed of hand-hewn, steam-bent oak timbers;

and a floating sauna that is located eight miles from downtown Grand Marais, at Skyport Lodge on Devil Track Lake.[229]

## North of the Highway 61 Corridor

A majority of Grand Marais's housing stock is located on the northern side of Highway 61. Although Grand Marais has, over recent decades, evolved into a more cosmopolitan place, many of its residences maintain the look of a small city that is unapologetically rooted in its history and traditions. Most of the dwellings are vernacular structures that reflect the origins of a small town that was developed by hardworking citizens who relied on the natural resources of Lake Superior and the nearby region. A number are former log cabins that have been expanded by frame-and-board additions and are typically covered over with modern siding materials. Also dispersed throughout the residential area are some one-time rental cabins and motel units that have been expanded and converted into year-round dwellings. Several civic and institutional buildings are also situated throughout the district.[230]

### Mökki
210 West First Street

*Mökki*, a Finnish word for a cottage or cabin, identifies a cluster of three "tiny houses" on West First Street that are available for short-term rentals. Two were built, the other reconstructed, between 2010 and 2016 by Grand Marais resident Lonnie Dupre, an elite Arctic explorer and mountaineer. Dupre, who, in 1991, became the first person to traverse Canada's Northwest Passage from west to east (Pacific to Atlantic) with a dogsled, would later accomplish two other "human-powered firsts": circumnavigating Greenland with a kayak and sled in 2001 and reaching the North Pole, by canoe and dogsled, during summer 2006. Another of Dupre's feats, accomplished in 2015, was the first solo, January assent of North America's highest mountain peak—Denali, in Alaska. Seven years later, in January 2022, Dupre departed on another adventure, a four-month-long dogsled trek along the western coastline of Greenland. During that period, he participated in the making of a film, *Amka* (an Inuit word for "one with a friendly spirit"), which explores the bond between Inuit hunters, polar explorers, and Greenland sled dogs.[231]

Also a skilled carpenter, Dupre has taught log-building classes at Grand Marais's North House Folk School. He put these skills to use when constructing Mökki's three structures, all located on or proximate to the site of a former automobile repair garage. In 2010, Dupre began converting the garage into the Cottage, now situated within a yard that has wildflowers, ash trees, and a raised-bed garden. The Cottage was followed, in 2013, by Mökki's namesake unit, the Dovetailed Cabin, built of scribed logs that are joined together with half-dovetailed corner notches. The Birdhouse, a simple, "funky A-frame" that offers a bird's-eye view of West Bay from its loft and balcony, was undertaken in 2016. The exteriors and interiors of all three structures are trimmed with "a mix of earth-tone primary colors" that provide "hints" of the Nordic countries.[232]

### Three Sisters (Tre Søstre)
11–15 West Fourth Avenue

A relatively short distance separates the vernacular buildings that compose the Mökki group and an award-winning trio of small but architecturally distinctive structures—Aurora, Horizon, and the Skyhouse—that were designed to represent "one communal identity." Opened in 2019 by Todd and Susan Miller, the name *Tre Søstre* (Danish for "Three Sisters") honors the ethnic heritage of Miller's father and also alludes to Lake Superior's "rogue waves"—those having a height more than two times greater than nearby waves. (Three rogue waves may have been one of several factors that caused the sinking of the ore boat *Edmund Fitzgerald* in 1975.) Three Sisters is included among a number of Grand Marais vacation rental properties that the Millers own and manage.[233]

Before making Grand Marais their home in 2003, the couple, both native Minnesotans, sailed throughout the Great Lakes and the Caribbean on a sloop, the *Snow Day*. They later acquired an early twentieth-century Grand Marais fisherman's house, which included, at its core, two square cabins that had been joined together to form a single rectangular structure; each cabin was built of aspen logs, rescued from the harbor before being towed across the lake to Ashland. The Millers also purchased another property that included three badly damaged buildings. Once all four

**The Dovetailed Cabin appears in the foreground; behind it is the Birdhouse.**

structures were restored and converted into rental units, the couple built a new timber-frame structure, the "Boathouse," for their own use.[234]

Following the purchase of a nearby vacant hillside lot, the Millers proposed to build three small rental units on the site. To do so, they sought out Duluth architect David Salmela, known for the "Scandinavian influence" inherent in his projects and work and for a willingness and ability to provide "unconventional solutions to unique circumstances." Specifically, the Millers asked Salmela to create "a bold architectural statement" that would give primary attention to nearby views, while also recognizing its neighborhood setting. Salmela designed three structures, each having a remarkably small footprint (sixteen by twenty-two feet), but with cantilevers and exterior decks that expand the amount of usable space on the upper floors. The buildings' design also offers improved conditions for stormwater infiltration and provides space for the incorporation of several landscape design features, including stone walls that convey a vibrant system of patios, paths, and "softscapes." The project, already in 2019, received a design award from the Wood Products Council of the United States, while a Swedish

**The largest unit in the Three Sisters (Tre Søstre) complex is the Sky House. Photograph by Corey Gaffer. Courtesy of Salmela Architect, 2019.**

competition and exhibition, titled *The Architecture of Necessity*, honored Tre Søstre "for its closely cohesive group of three related small houses, each with its own character and a suitably simple detailing."[235]

### The Birches (*now* Russell's Cottages)
20 West Fifth Avenue

Russell's Cottages, one of Grand Marais's venerable tourist establishments, was launched as the Birches by Frederick and Edna Andert in 1931. The family's association with local tourism began even earlier, in 1921, when Andert was named principal of the nearby Maple Hill School and, one year later, superintendent of the Grand Marais School District. The couple soon purchased the Tourist Hotel on West First Avenue, which was managed by Jennie Spooner, Edna Andert's widowed mother; she would oversee the renamed Andert and Spooner Tourist Hotel until early 1932, when a fire destroyed the entire building. Despite this setback, the family soon built and established a group of rental cabins, the Birches, located close to their residence. One, a scribed log cabin, served as Jennie Spooner's home until 1946, when the entire family departed for California, where Andert had accepted a teaching position.[236]

After local residents Robert and Agnes Russell purchased Anderts' property in 1948, the new owners sold a few cabins and identified the seven remaining units as Russell's Cottages. The responsibility of managing the business was assumed by Agnes Russell following her husband's 1975 death and, in 1992, by the couple's daughter and son-in-law, Joyce and Gordon Lindquist. Even though they were retired residents of the Twin Cities, and involved in numerous philanthropic and public service activities, the Lindquists would spend the next thirty summers in Grand Marais managing the family business. Russell's Cottages, they noted, remained a place where guests could "fully enjoy the beauty of the North Shore, untethered from Wi-Fi and television. Instead of [the] Internet, we connect you with Nature, relaxation, and well-being." Until Gordon Lindquist's passing at the age of ninety-three in late 2022, and his ninety-year-old widow just a few months later, the couple belonged to a very small group of nonagenarians who have been actively involved in the management of a North Shore business. Russell's Cottages, now operated by a daughter, remains a charming reminder of an earlier era in Grand Marais history.[237]

### St. John's Catholic Church (*now the* Grand Marais Art Colony)
120 West Third Avenue

Grand Marais Catholics attended St. Francis Xavier Church in nearby Chippewa City until 1916, when local parishioners completed their own house of worship, St. John's, on West Third Avenue. A significant share of the funding for St. John's reportedly was generated by several Grand Marais women "who braved the woods country to solicit help from lumber camp employees." By 1958, however, when it became obvious that the building could no longer meet the parish's needs, the members voted to construct a larger edifice, located on Fifth Street, which opened in 1961.

The vacated Third Avenue church became the headquarters for the Grand Marais Art Colony in 1963. The colony had opened in 1947, when Duluth native Birney Quick, along with Glenn Ranney, both instructors at the MSA (renamed the Minneapolis College of Art and Design in 1970), organized summer classes in Grand Marais. Among the initial students were several World War II veterans who participated because of the educational benefits provided by the Serviceman's Readjustment Act, or GI Bill, of 1944. When MSA support was reestablished in 1952, following a two-year hiatus, Quick and several other artists offered classes for eight weeks on the second floor of the Village Hall, and the location was recognized by its new name, the Town Hall Art Colony. The MSA's affiliation ended in 1958, but Quick and fellow artist Byron Bradley soon formed an independent business, the Grand Marais Art Colony, which allowed the summer program to continue.[238]

Quick and Bradley purchased the former church building in 1963. Although Birney Quick's unexpected 1981 death challenged the colony's future, the community responded by creating a nonprofit organization, Grand Marais Arts Inc., which continues to the present. Now Minnesota's oldest art colony, the Grand Marais organization offers arts and cultural programs year-round; many occur in an adjacent 2005 building that has studios for clay, glass, and printmaking. The colony also purchased the former North Shore Pharmacy building (21 West Highway 61) in 2019, which provides exhibition, studio, and residential spaces.[239]

### United Congregational Church (*now the* First Congregational Church of the United Church of Christ)
### 300 West Second Street

The origins of Grand Marais's Congregational church may be traced to 1907 when a small group of residents began holding meetings in private homes and the village hall. Their initial house of worship, called the United Congregational Church of Grand Marais, emerged on Second Street in 1917; the name was changed to the United Protestant Church in 1941 and to the First Congregational Church of Grand Marais in 1955. A later nationwide merger with the United Church of Christ is reflected in its current name.[240]

The members of First Congregational voted, in 1968, to purchase a larger Second Street lot for their present West Second Street church, which was completed and dedicated two years later. Warren W. Kane of Austin, Minnesota, an architect whose firm would

**Architect Warren Kane's 1969 drawing for the First Congregational Church of the United Church of Christ in Grand Marais. *75th Anniversary Bulletin of the Congregation*, 1982.**

later be recognized for "helping churches accommodate growth and changes in mission," designed the building. Kane's free-form design for the relatively small structure, which shares several features with many other American churches of that era, respects the scale and character of the nearby neighborhood and includes intimate interior spaces for worship and gathering. First Congregational is also linked to the greater North Shore environment because of the local materials used in its construction. Granite rocks of different sizes were trucked thirty miles from Carlton Peak to the site, where the congregation's members cut, shaped, and mortared them together to construct the lower walls, interior columns, and fireplace. Wooden battens, milled from local timber sources, cover the second-level exterior—but unlike the thin, vertical, and uniform pieces that characterize typical board-and-batten construction, those at First Congregational display different widths and spacing, which creates a varied pattern on the surface.[241]

### Cook County Courthouse
411 West Second Street

In 1888, after Grand Marais was established as Cook County's seat of government, a modest, two-story, twenty-by-thirty-foot wooden-frame courthouse overlooked the tiny settlement from a prominent, recently acquired block of land along West Second Street. When the building was deemed "obsolete, limited in space, and far too modest an expression of the county's future" in 1910, Duluth architects Clyde Kelly and Werner Lignell were commissioned to prepare the design for a new Cook County Courthouse, which opened two years later.

Although the county's officials and residents lived in a small, isolated village, they demonstrated an awareness and acceptance of the associations that existed between government and civic architecture in much larger cities of the nation and world. The Cook County Courthouse—a formal neoclassical structure based on Greek and Roman antecedents, and including twelve entry stairs, six two-story Ionic columns, five recessed bays, and brickwork laid out in orthogonal and angular patterns—stood in marked contrast to the unpretentious buildings that characterized Grand Marais. A large annex, added to the rear of the courthouse during the mid-1990s, does not compromise the overall integrity of the original building, which was listed in the National Register of Historic Places in 1983.[242]

### Historic Jail
Northeast of the Courthouse

Also located on the courthouse grounds is the former jail, equipped with two iron cells at the time of its 1901 completion. The small structure was surrounded, for

**The neoclassical Cook County Courthouse, when completed in 1912, stood over the vernacular buildings of Grand Marais. It is shown here at the time of its one hundredth anniversary.**

a brief period of time, by a plank wall that stood eight feet high. Although Cook County's commissioners called for the condemnation and replacement of the jail in 1910, they would vote, one year later, to place a concrete slab on the roof and rebuild the outer wall, also with concrete. By 1983, however, a gaping hole in the roof was only one of several structural issues that compromised the long-abandoned and dilapidated structure. Fortunately, the jail was soon repaired and stabilized. Although not used for many decades, the building maintains a direct connection to the early history of Cook County and Grand Marais.[243]

### St. John's Catholic Church
10 Fifth Avenue West

The decision to construct a new Catholic church for St. John's congregation was made in 1958, but only after a sufficient number of parishioners pledged to support the anticipated construction costs of a building that could accommodate three hundred worshippers. The need for such a relatively large space was based on a steady growth in membership numbers as well as the increasing presence of visitors and part-time residents who attended Catholic services during the tourist season. While the congregation realized that the envisioned church was larger than what was needed by the parish, they predicted that the extra costs would be "borne in part by the tourists themselves."[244]

In 1959, St. John's parishioners began working with R. V. McCann, a former president of the Minnesota chapter of the American Institute of Architects who specialized in the design of churches and other institutional buildings. McCann's proposal was quite similar to the design of many other postwar churches, especially in its use of three-hinge arches, fabricated of "glulams" (glued laminated timbers), which create the steep roof that rests directly on the structure's sidewalls. Seven glulams towered above the construction site by November 1960, and much of the interior work was completed during the following winter months. Most material for the wooden roof decking, stone walls, and cedar-log altar and interior furnishings came from local sources. A free-standing bell tower, constructed of cedar poles and topped by a cross, was erected in August 1961. The September church dedication was overseen by Francis J. Schenk, bishop of the Duluth Diocese, with the Right Reverend Baldwin Dworschak, abbot of St. John's Abbey in Collegeville, Minnesota, serving as the primary speaker.[245]

In 1966, GMAC founder Birney Quick received a commission that led to the creation of a three-part mural, *Mystical Moments in the Life of Christ*, mounted, eight years later, on one wall of St. John's social room. Any artwork "filled with mysticism," Quick later explained, is "best expressed in a surrealistic style"—a tenet the artist followed when envisioning and creating a mural that interweaves "Biblical figures and the North Shore in a sort of 'dream world' mixed with local reality."[246] The St. John's painting is the largest of three murals—the others are at the Shoreline Inn and the Grand Marais State Bank (the latter was painted over after the building's conversion into the Gunflint Tavern)—that Quick created for the North Shore city.

### First Norwegian Evangelical Lutheran Church (*now* Betsy Bowen Studio)
301 West First Avenue

In 1899, after Mathias and Christina Johnson Johansen established a homestead on Good Harbor Hill and a fishing camp along West Bay, the couple met with several neighbors to organize the First Norwegian Evangelical Lutheran Congregation of Grand Marais. Affiliation with the Hauge Synod occurred

**The First Norwegian Evangelical Lutheran Church at 301 First Avenue West, shortly after its 1903 completion. The fence bordering the wooden sidewalk kept cattle from grazing on the church grounds. The Betsy Bowen Studio is now located in the building. Courtesy of Cook County Historical Society.**

two years later. The Norwegians then engaged in a "friendly competition" with the Swedes of Maple Hill, located north of Grand Marais, to determine which group would build the first church. The Swedes "won" the informal contest when they conducted a church service in June 1902—one year before the Norwegians replicated the event within their new building. Although the latter congregation had no more than a handful of members in 1903, the church, located at 301 First Avenue West, could seat two hundred people. The membership, nonetheless, grew so quickly that a small addition and gallery were attached to the building in 1923. The members voted, in 1938, to remove the nationality designation of the church and change its name to Bethlehem.[247]

### Bethlehem Lutheran Church

417 First Avenue

In 1953, when the existing Bethlehem Lutheran was deemed inadequate for the congregation's needs, a building committee began meeting with Arnold Flaten, a St. Olaf College art professor who previously had been involved with the development of a church in Hovland and would soon participate in similar activities at Lutsen. When Bethlehem's committee realized that the existing building could not be remodeled to meet their needs, Flaten recommended that the congregation hire his former student, the well-known architect Edward Sövik. After considering "numerous plans and counterplans" provided by Sövik and his firm, the congregation voted to purchase a large land parcel located two blocks north of their existing church. Sövik also designed a parish hall that would include an auditorium, a kitchen, a library, classrooms, and offices.[248]

The Stone Brothers Construction Company, located in nearby Colvill, started building the flat-roofed, two-story parish hall in June 1959. Most of the firm's work was completed by February 1960, when two hundred congregants processed from the existing church to the new building. After filling its auditorium, kitchen, library, and entrance hallway, the attendees listened as the Reverend Joel Anderson delivered his sermon, "The Magic of Newness." Church services would continue in the parish house until 1964, when the new sanctuary was completed.[249]

Bethlehem, the only example of a true A-frame church on the North Shore, also represents one of relatively few times that Sövik used the structural form during his lengthy and prolific career. Architectural historian Gretchen Buggeln has also observed that Sövik seldom built A-frame structures after the late 1950s, but he did employ the form on those few occasions when congregations requested it. Whether Bethlehem's congregation asked for an A-frame church is not known, but their rather modest $90,000 budget may have been a factor in the decision.[250]

The wooden members that form Bethlehem's rigid A-frame extend to the ground, where they are anchored into concrete pilings. The non-load-bearing walls, with their colored glass windows, separate the building's interior space from the outdoor environment. The expansive roof and dark-stained vertical boards that cover both of the exterior gable ends are suggestive of old churches in the small towns of northern Europe that inspired Sövik. The sanctuary's minimalist features, also characteristic of old European churches, were recognized by a local journalist who attended the January 1964 church opening: the "restrained beauty of the nave," wrote the reporter, is accomplished by the placement of "a simple cross—the only break in the vast expanse of the wall."[251]

### Lindquist Lane Motel and Cabins *(now private residences)*

Fourth Street West between Third and Fourth Avenues West

The important role that tourism plays in Grand Marais's present-day economy is apparent throughout the small city. The city's current cultural landscape also provides evidence, sometimes subtle, of previous tourist-related sites that were later adapted for other uses, often as residences. One example of this transition is a row of five former rental cabins that Emil ("Fritz") and Jennie Lindquist opened in 1948 on the other side of their Fourth Street residence.

Lindquist immigrated from Sweden to Minnesota in 1920. Seven years later, while attending Bethel Seminary in St. Paul, Lindquist married Jennie Strom, the daughter of Swedish parents residing in Mora, Minnesota. Upon receiving his theology degree in 1930, Lindquist accepted a position as the pastor of

**The A-frame supports for Grand Marais's Bethlehem Lutheran Church are fixed into concrete pilings at ground level. The sign indicates that religious services may be affected by snowmobile noise during a northeastern Minnesota winter.**

Grand Marais's First Baptist Church. Within two years, Lindquist was embarking on a career as a dedicated public official and civic volunteer, which included service as Cook County's clerk of court and deputy coroner; as Grand Marais's village clerk and trustee; and as a leader in several local organizations, including the Chamber of Commerce, and as president of the CCHS. He also was a visiting chaplain in Cook County's CCC camps during the 1930s; owned two automobile service stations; and operated a charter fishing service, based in the Grand Marais harbor, which included a pair of steel-hulled boats, the *Sea King* and *Sea Queen*. Additionally, the couple owned and operated Lindquist Lane Motel and Cabins from 1948 to the time of the patriarch's 1962 death. Lindquist's widow managed the five units for a few years before selling them; all were later converted into year-round residences.[252]

### 4-H Club Log Building
#### 317 West Fifth Street

Among the construction projects pursued by Grand Marais's WPA workers during the 1930s was this log structure, used for several decades by Cook County's 4-H clubs. The $3,510 building, located on part of the

**Grand Marais's 4-H Club log building remains an enduring tribute to the WPA workers who completed numerous projects throughout Grand Marais during the 1930s.**

Cook County Fairgrounds, was erected by ten men who labored throughout the summer of 1939. They completed the project before September, just in time for 4-H Club members to display their projects and exhibits at the annual Cook County Fair. Grand Marais's first invitational art exhibit also occurred within the building in 1944.[253]

The thirty-by-forty-foot structure, sited at a forty-five degree angle on its lot, is constructed of round spruce logs, with protruding ends, that are fastened together with saddle notches. The prominent stone chimney is part of a large interior steel-and-brick fireplace situated on the building's northwest-facing wall. Shallow dormers perched on each of the roof planes allow natural light to reach the interior. Several adjacent and deteriorating fairground buildings were removed and replaced by the Grand Marais Community Center (317 W Fifth Street) in 1992, but the 4-H building continued to accommodate some county fair activities until 2011, when the annual event was discontinued. The log structure now serves as an event space for both public and private programs and meetings.[254]

### Sawtooth Mountain Ski Slide (*razed, now* Sawtooth Bluff)

Above the Grand Marais Water Tower along the Gunflint Trail Scenic Byway

In May 1948, five volunteers began cutting small trees and saplings from Sawtooth Mountain, which overlooks Grand Marais and Lake Superior from a height of almost six hundred feet. Curious onlookers soon learned that the volunteers were clearing the path for a tow that would "eventually pull ski enthusiasts up-hill for another thrill down." Initially sponsored by the Grand Marais Chamber of Commerce, and later operated by the Sawhill Mountain Ski Club, local promoters were encouraged when Fred Haley, an enthusiastic Canadian Ski Association official, claimed that the hill "had possibilities beyond anything he had seen" in North America. The towline poles were in place by late 1949, and the first test runs on Grand Marais's Sawtooth Mountain Ski Slide occurred in early 1950. A *Cook County News-Herald* correspondent even described the experiences and sensations novice skiers might encounter when negotiating a downhill run for the first time. "You feel awkward," warned the reporter. "Your body just won't stay forward, nor will your knees bend." Experienced skiers were assured, nevertheless, that "a variety of tricky slopes" offered the challenge they might want.[255]

The ski hill's grand opening, celebrated in mid-February 1950 with a weekend "Sawtooth Sno-Fun Fest," was highlighted by downhill and slalom ski races, cross-country skiing and snowshoe competitions, hockey and broomball games, figure skating demonstrations, and the crowning of a Snow Queen. A scheduled "mutt race" was canceled when only one unharnessed dog appeared at the starting line. Despite the minimal facilities that still characterized the site, Grand Marais promoters convinced Central U.S. Ski Association (CUSSA) officials to hold the organization's February 1952 championship event at Sawtooth Mountain. Preparations for these activities would demand the efforts of some seventy-five volunteers, "including office workers and women," who assisted in clearing and improving both new and existing ski trails throughout 1951. A log chalet, its foundation constructed during an intense November rainstorm, was completed at the top of Sawtooth, but only after Minnesota governor Luther Youngdahl issued a special dispensation that allowed the club's members to harvest suitable trees from public land. Reg Gilbertson of Minneapolis designed the chalet, which Charles Boostrom, a well-known local log cabin builder, completed just before the competition was under way.[256]

To encourage local attendance at the competition, Grand Marais's ski club members organized several simultaneous "Come-see, Come-ski" activities throughout the immediate area. The overall event received high marks from a *Cook County News-Herald* reviewer, who observed that Grand Marais was "completely saturated" with skiers—most from Minnesota, Wisconsin, Michigan, and Ontario—who gave "local people their greatest skishow thus far." Most of the events were won by skiers from Ironwood, Michigan, and Duluth.[257]

The event's successful outcome obviously impressed CUSSA officials, because Grand Marais was, once again, selected for the subsequent 1953 competition. Although Sawtooth's facilities were quite well established and tested by this time, Grand Marais's ski club members could not control one vital factor—the weather. Considerable angst was expressed by local officials as Grand Marais remained snowless throughout December 1952 and January 1953. But then, just two weeks before the mid-February event, "the weatherman

**A 1937 Ford panel truck powered the Sawtooth Mountain Ski Slide's tow when it opened in early 1950. An electric motor soon replaced the vehicle. Courtesy of Cook County Historical Society.**

finally favored the snow-starved slopes of Sawtooth Mountain with a foot of feather-light snow." When additional heavy snow fell throughout much of the Midwest just before the competition, 38 of the 142 registrants canceled their Grand Marais travel plans because of adverse road conditions. Although the competition opened on Saturday morning to heavy winds and subzero weather, the situation, by afternoon, was much improved. The participants also received assurance that some of the potentially dangerous conditions recognized during the previous competition had been resolved. Most noticeable was the addition of electric safety gates, installed by Grand Marais municipal power employees, which allowed tow operators to shut down the line before skiers were "entangled in the rope." A Saturday evening banquet, held in Grand Marais's new high school gymnasium, recognized the three hundred participants, organizers, and CUSSA officials, who were entertained by Grand Marais music teacher Harold Ikola's orchestra, the "Swingsters," and by several speakers and other performers.[258]

Sawtooth remained a popular venue for several ensuing years and also provided Grand Marais students with opportunities to participate on high school ski teams that were competitive at the state level. In 1955, Don Burris, the editor of *Minnesota–Wisconsin Ski News,* even claimed that Sawtooth had the potential "to become one of the outstanding winter sports areas not only in the Midwest, but in the U.S." Nevertheless, the facility closed during the mid-1960s because of several factors, including excessive expenses, the large number of volunteers required to maintain and operate such a facility, and the competition from larger and better-equipped skiing sites in nearby Lutsen. Perhaps even more important was the problem posed by intermittent and inadequate snowfall, which made it difficult, and sometimes impossible, to maintain a satisfactory snowpack on Sawtooth's south-facing ski slope.[259]

Only a faint impression of the once-popular ski run is now evident when looking northward from Grand Marais. Currently identified as Sawtooth Bluff, the site's future is yet to be determined, although a 2017–18 Master Plan, prepared by a committee comprising members from several agencies, called for the development of a "destination regional park" on the 640-acre public holding.[260] A short distance toward the northeast and proximate to the Gunflint Trail is the heavily used Pincushion Mountain Trail System (1 Pincushion Drive), which attracts hikers, runners, and cross-country skiers.

## East Cook Unorganized Territory

Cook County's only traffic light is situated at the intersection of Highway 61 and Broadway Avenue in eastern Grand Marais. The land-use pattern that stretches northeastward from this point comprises several highway-oriented businesses and services and the tiny St. John's Catholic Cemetery. Soon thereafter, Highway 61 enters what once was Rosebush Township. During the late 1930s, Rosebush and the more distant townships of Colvill and Hovland were disbanded and included in the vast East Cook Unorganized Territory, which now extends for almost twenty-four miles between Grand Marais and the Grand Portage Indian Reservation boundary. While East Cook sprawls over 438 square miles of land and water, only 835 year-round residents lived within the territory's boundaries in 2020, which was, nevertheless, the highest number in its history. As is evident throughout the county, East Cook has many more seasonal residents than permanent inhabitants: 1,080 (72 percent) of its 1,510 dwellings were classified as part-time units in 2020. Some residents still inhabit parts of an area once identified as Chippewa City, located about one mile outside of Grand Marais. Other inhabitants are situated within or close to the small, unincorporated settlements of Croftville, Colvill, and Hovland.[261]

## Chippewa City

Chippewa City, located about one mile east of Grand Marais, emerged as an important Anishinaabe enclave during the early 1880s. At this time, dredges were deepening Grand Marais's West Bay harbor, and a large breakwater was also under construction. The employment opportunities provided by these projects attracted numerous Anishinaabe workers from the entire North Shore area to Grand Marais. Many of the men and their families moved into Chippewa City, which, years earlier, had emerged along the "Old Road" that connected the settlement to Grand Marais.

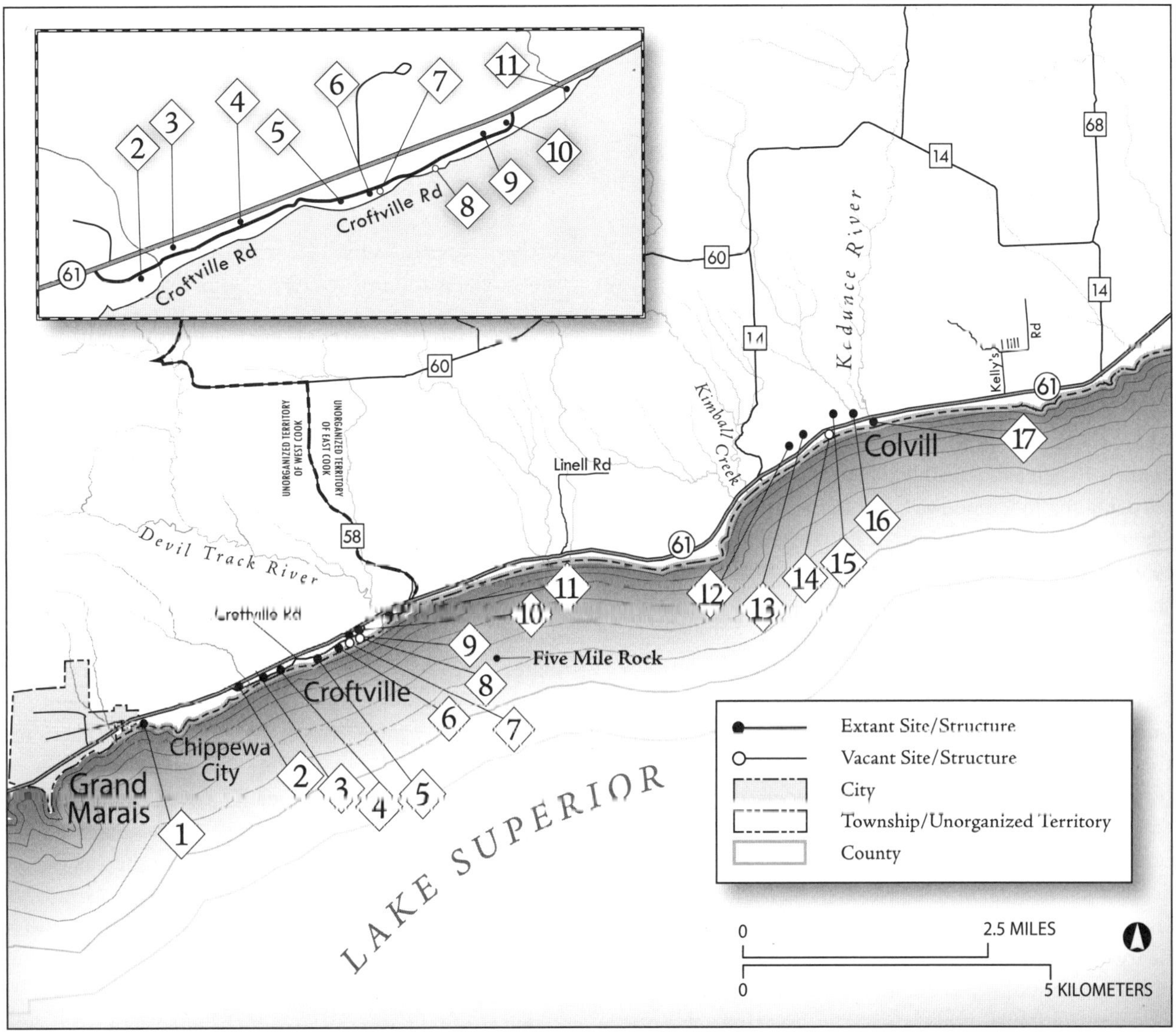


1. St. Francis Xavier Catholic Church
2. Anderson's North Shore Resort
3. Larsen's Lakeview Cabins
4. Elsie's Lakeview Cabins
5. Flower Power Gardens*
6. Croftville Road Cottages
7. Rudy's Fish
8. Rasmussen Fish House
9. J. Croft Residence
10. F. Croft Residence
11. Devil's Track Cabins*
12. Charles Wiger Vernacular Roadside Garden
13. Amyotte Residence/Kivitalo
14. Zerbach Fish House
15. Colvill Town Hall
17. Kadunce River State Wayside

*Now a residence

Chippewa City's population peaked between 1882 and 1901 when more than one hundred families lived in the settlement. Some residents inhabited small houses built of hand-hewn logs, but even more occupied "portable-style homes in the traditional Anishinaabe lodge design, which were made of birchbark, modern blankets, or hide that covered over a curved wooden framework of poles."[262]

Staci Lola Drouillard has written that Chippewa City and Grand Marais, by the early twentieth century, "developed somewhat of a convenient reliance on each other." The community's residents were dependent on Grand Marais's periodic employment opportunities, medical assistance, and contemporary conveniences, whereas the townspeople relied on Anishinaabe residents for their labor and wilderness familiarity. Also participating in Chippewa City's economy were tourists who purchased the well-crafted souvenir items produced by Anishinaabe women, perhaps none more popular than the beautiful, small containers they fashioned from porcupine quills.[263]

Among Chippewa City's notable residents was mail carrier John Beargrease. Although the carrier's wife, Louise Wishkop Beargrease, was born in Beaver Bay, she claimed Chippewa City as her original home. The couple and their five children also resided in Chippewa City at various times during the late nineteenth and early twentieth centuries. Following Beargrease's 1910 death and internment in Beaver Bay, his widow and several family members returned to Chippewa City. Louise Beargrease passed away in December 1918 during the influenza pandemic, as did George, her seventeen-year-old son, and Peter, a brother-in-law. The three share a grave in the Chippewa City cemetery.[264]

Another notable resident was Anishinaabe artist George Morrison (1919–2000), who received the name Wah Wah Tha Go Nay Ga Bo (Standing in the Northern Lights) at the time of his birth in Chippewa City. After graduating from Grand Marais's high school in 1938, Morrison departed the North Shore for art schools in Minneapolis, New York City, and France and later pursued a teaching career at several American universities. Because of his "reverence for the land and the lake," Morrison, in 1970, moved back to the North Shore, where he built a home and studio at Red Rock on the Grand Portage Indian Reservation. Morrison's subsequent production of landscape paintings and wood collages would establish his national reputation as a notable abstractionist who found fame as a "superb colorist and a landscape painter in the richest sense of the tradition." His enduring reputation, art historian W. Jackson Rushing observes, is based on an innate ability to capture the "feeling of those moments in time in those places." The late Cook County artist received further recognition in 2022 when five of his paintings were selected and printed by the U.S. Postal Service for its Forever Stamps series. The Department of American Indian Studies and Department of Art, both at the University of Minnesota, also announced the establishment of the George Morrison Center for Indigenous Arts, which supports the "creation and interpretation of Indigenous art in all its forms."[265]

Chippewa City's residents were, unfortunately, losing their property by the early twentieth century. Although the story is complicated, Drouillard has explained the process with considerable acumen in her book *Walking the Old Road*. She writes that many homes were consumed by the 1907 forest fire on the North Shore, while other losses occurred because of land condemnation actions caused by the construction of Minnesota Highway 61. Population numbers also declined after some young men left for military service during World War I and when several residents died of influenza in 1917–18. But most important was the acquisition of Chippewa City land by some of Grand Marais's white residents. A not uncommon practice was the takeover of property when the Anishinaabe could not afford county taxes imposed on their holdings during the first three decades of the twentieth century. Although a few of Chippewa City's log dwellings could still be found among the trees along the highway during the early 1940s, all disappeared years ago. Today, only a former Catholic church, now a museum that is also listed in the National Register of Historic Places, identifies the once-vibrant community.[266]

### St. Francis Xavier Catholic Church
### 1402 East Highway 61

Chippewa City's Catholic church is named for Father Francis Xavier Pierz (1785–1880), a Slovenian priest who introduced Christianity to the Grand Portage Anishinaabe. Jesuit priests from Fort William, On-

**Volunteers clear the grounds of St. Francis Xavier Catholic Church during the 1950s. The view is looking southward toward Lake Superior. The property is now owned and managed by the Cook County Historical Society.**

tario, offered services in the homes of Chippewa City residents for several years before the congregation's members built their church on a small lot donated by Antoine and Antoinette Fillison. Funds for the new building came from basket socials, where baked goods, placed in birchbark containers, were sold to eager buyers, many of them fishermen and lumberjacks. St. Francis Xavier was the first Catholic church to emerge in the Grand Marais area and one of only very few nineteenth-century American Indian mission buildings still remaining in Minnesota. Situated about one-eighth mile north of the church is the Chippewa City Cemetery, which was separated from most of the settlement following construction of Minnesota Highway 1. The cemetery has two parts: an older area with numerous unmarked graves and a newer section with several headstones.[267]

Anishinaabe carpenter Frank Wishkop built the gable-roofed church, which was ready for religious services by August 1896. The hand-hewn tamarack log walls of the twenty-five-by-thirty-foot nave represent Wishkop's familiarity with a French Canadian construction technique known as *pièce sur pièce* ("piece on piece," or literally "log on log"). To ensure that the corners would be "flush and neat," the logs are locked together with half-dovetail notches—*queue d'aronde* to French Canadians. The handcrafted pews, along with a small balcony, could seat about eighty people. Above the nave is a peaked roof that covers the square belfry and a 225-pound bell. The building's remaining sections, all constructed of frame and board, include a south-facing narthex; a north-facing, gable-roofed sacristy dating to 1903, which replaced an eight-by-fourteen-foot lean-to that once provided visiting priests with a place to sleep; and a small structure between the nave and sacristy that houses the altar. Two nearby sheds, since removed, sheltered the priest's sled dogs and stored wood for use in the church stove.[268]

Grand Marais Catholics continued worshipping at St. Francis Xavier until 1916, when they built their own church (St. John's) on West Third Avenue. St. Francis Xavier was closed in late 1936, shortly after a few families celebrated their final Christmas Mass in the church. Thereafter, as Drouillard writes, "the church would face its most difficult test: surviving the decay brought on by poverty, prejudice, and community division, three factors that ultimately led to the final decline of the village and a long period of neglect for the Chippewa church." Volunteers from St. John's congregation, along with a few Grand Marais Lions Club members, performed some restoration work on the vacated St. Francis Xavier building in 1957, one year before it was broken into and partially destroyed by unknown "vandals," who smashed all of the windows, "hammered" down the door, and damaged the stove and part of the handmade altar. Repairs were made, but it was a preservation and funding program, launched jointly in 1970 by the CCHS and St. John's congregation, that led to the completion of several projects: construction of a concrete-block foundation underneath the church, restoration of the interior, and replacement of the roof and clapboard siding with new materials. The successful outcome was recognized in 1985 with the official listing of St. Francis Xavier in the National Register of Historic Places. A major 1995 event, with artist George Morrison as principal speaker, celebrated the centenary anniversary of the church. Then, in 1998, ownership of the building was transferred to CCHS, which continues to protect, maintain, and offer tours of the building; additional financial assistance has been and is provided by donations and grants from individuals, organizations, the Grand Portage Reservation Tribal Council, and the MHS. Because of these efforts, St. Francis Xavier maintains its presence along Highway 61 as one of the North Shore's most important cultural landmarks.[269]

## Croftville

The settlement of Croftville, its southwestern entrance located almost one mile northeast of St. Francis Xavier, is defined by a relatively narrow ribbon of level land that separates much of the rocky shoreline on the south from a high ledge to the north. A few fishermen spent time at the isolated location during the 1890s and early 1900s, before the first permanent settlers made their appearance shortly after 1910. Among this group was a pair of adjacent fisheries established by two brothers and their wives—Joseph and Jennie Jensen Croft (1637 Croftville Road) and Frederick and Sally Johnson Croft (1653 Croftville Road). The brothers were sons of British immigrants Smith and Anna Croft, who had moved to rural Duluth Township during the 1870s. The two families were followed by other settlers to the Cook County settlement, among them additional members of the extensive Croft clan. By 1940, a total of eighty people inhabited Croftville: twenty-one were named Croft, and twenty-three of all twenty-eight adult males pursued fishing as their primary occupation.[270]

The initial North Shore roadway passed through Croftville before the present highway was built slightly inland in 1924–25. Nevertheless, the former section, soon renamed Croftville Road, quickly attracted tourists and motorists because of the rental cabins and fish sales stands that paralleled its right-of-way. The cabins remain very popular with current tourists, although local residents, along with numerous people from the greater Grand Marais area, still consider Croftville Road a "walking lane"—a wide pathway filled with "ever-present pedestrians ambling alone in pairs or with dogs, admiring the view, the cobble beach and ever-present waves, and the wildflowers and birds."[271] Croftville Road is appreciated not only for its pedestrian-friendly qualities but also because the corridor retains several picturesque and appealing features of the "old" North Shore cultural landscape, namely, the two original Croft residences (one still owned by a family descendant) and a number of rental cabins that reveal their mom-and-pop origins. Three vacant fish houses and a former fish sales store also represent the working life of an earlier era. A number of seasonal and year-round houses still retain their modest appearance, but several newer homes, some much larger and more opulent than their older counterparts, may portend a different future for Croftville.

### Summerville and Curley's Resort and Garage (*now* Anderson's North Shore Resort)

1390 Croftville Road

Shortly after the Highway 61–Croftville Road junction is Anderson's North Shore Resort, which occupies a site that has served motorists and tourists since the mid-1920s. The initial business, known as Summerville, was established by Norwegian immigrants Gunnar and Dina ("Gjertine") Avendahl Larson after their arrival from Two Harbors. Summerville, which included little more than a few modest rental cabins and a small Prohibition-era dance hall, closed during the mid-1930s. The property was acquired, in 1948, by Iver ("Curley") and Hannah Johnson Bentley, both the children of Minnesota immigrant parents: he the son of rural New York Mills Finns, she the daughter of Sandstone Swedes. After making numerous additions and improvements to the acquisition, named Curley's Resort, the couple advertised their "clean, modern and semi-modern housekeeping cottages" and the cabin cruiser that was available for "deep-sea trolling." Bentley, also a skilled mechanic, established a vehicle repair shop on Croftville Road, while his wife, an accomplished skeet shooter, won trophies at numerous competitions; together, the couple avidly pursued hunting and fishing opportunities throughout the North Shore area. Following the 1972 sale of their business, the Bentleys spent more than twenty years as retirees in Sandstone and Jensen Beach, Florida.[272]

Curley's was soon acquired by a purchaser who operated the business for an additional twenty years. A North Dakotan who frequented the resort during the 1970s and 1980s described it as a cluster of six half-log cabins, furnished in "very primitive garage-sale décor." Each kitchen was equipped with an old gas cook stove but had no refrigerator. The single bedroom, provided with a large, vintage steel frame bed, had large windows that looked toward the lake and allowed guests to hear the waves breaking throughout the night. The toilets and showers, located in a separate, shared bathhouse, created difficulties in managing wastewater disposal along the shoreline, while the cabins' proximity to an eroding bank that dropped about eight feet to the Lake Superior shoreline posed additional issues.[273]

The deteriorating resort buildings had been closed for a few years when Julie Anderson purchased the property in 2002. She "started from scratch" by installing a new septic system and well; rebuilding or replacing the six shoreline cabins, all now covered with board-and-batten siding; and constructing a new, two-unit cabin on the upper side of Croftville Road. Anderson was pleasantly surprised when her business "took off in leaps and bounds"—thanks in large part to previous guests who had fond memories of its four hundred feet of cobblestone beach. The owner is now assisted by her daughter and two grandchildren, who also live on the property.[274]

### Larsen's Lakeview Cabins

1423 Croftville Road

Two of Croftville's longtime, family-owned cabin businesses, both named Lakeview, are directly linked to Olai and Asta Harridsteff Larsen. The two Norwegian immigrants, like their neighbors to the west, Gunnar and Dina Larson, moved from Two Harbors to Croftville shortly after 1910. Asta Larsen, already a widow with three young children by 1921, assisted her son Lawrence in establishing a cabin business on their property in 1932. Larsen, a commercial fisherman and carpenter, married Irma Haugen in early 1942, only a few months before he would spend three years with the U.S. Army Corps of Engineers. During his military tour, Larsen participated in several World War II campaigns, including the Battle of Normandy, for which he received a Bronze Star in recognition of meritorious service. Upon returning to Croftville in

1945, Larsen once again pursued commercial fishing (his fish house and winch still remain along the Lake Superior shoreline), although the highly skilled builder was primarily employed by several local construction companies. Because of his busy work schedule, Larsen's wife and children were heavily involved in managing the cabin business. Jackie Hyovalti, one of the couple's daughters, now owns and oversees the five units that compose Larsen's Lakeview Cabins.[275]

### Elsie's Lakeview Cabins
### 1461 Croftville Road

Elsie Larsen, also assisted by her mother, Asta, established a nearby cabin rental business in 1931. The initial unit, a small house, was quickly followed by four cabins, all financed with credit secured from the nearby Hedstrom Lumber Company. In 1941, Elsie and her husband, Charles Scott, accompanied by their two children, moved to southern California, where the couple worked and resided for thirty-five years. Nevertheless, Elsie continued to embark, at the beginning of each tourist season, on a lengthy automobile excursion, typically accompanied by her mother and children, that culminated at Croftville. Once there, she engaged in the never-ending tasks linked to cabin management and maintenance.[276]

Elsie once again became a permanent Croftville resident, this time in 1980, five years after her husband's death. The indominable woman, before her passing at the age of ninety-seven in 2008, was also involved in several Grand Marais civic organizations. With almost seventy-five years of direct involvement in her Croftville enterprise, Elsie Larsen Scott undoubtedly holds the longevity record for the ownership and management of a North Shore tourist business. The cabins eventually became the responsibility of Elsie's California granddaughter Marcy Scott Waters. Despite the distance that separates Minnesota and California, Waters and her husband handle all of their reservation requests and inquiries by internet and telephone—and the Waters family continues the annual tradition of summertime trips to Croftville,

**This cottage and four nearby shoreline units have been available at Elsie's Lakeview Cabins since the early 1930s.**

where, whenever necessary, they oversee major repair and reconstruction projects, including the replacement of a cabin that burned down in 2022. The couple's diligence also honors and respects Elsie's admonishment made many years ago: "make sure you don't screw up the cabins after I'm gone."[277]

### Flower Power Gardens *(now a seasonal residence)*
### 1536 Croftville Road

During the early 1930s, Peter Hiebert of Mountain Lake, Minnesota, someone who was recognized for possessing a "life-long green thumb," began growing tomatoes, geraniums, and other plants that he predicted would be popular to buyers—even when money was scarce during the Great Depression. He and his wife, Sarah, opened their Mountain Lake greenhouse in 1935, twenty years before establishing a similar business in Sioux Falls, South Dakota. In 1960, the couple purchased one of Croftville Road's former fishing camps, which they converted into a summer home; they also developed a shoreline nursery, Flower Power Gardens. In 1992, when the senior plantsman was eighty-six years of age, his son and daughter-in-law, Gaylord and Jeanne Hiebert, acquired Flower Power. The couple closed the business in 2021 because of Covid-19-related concerns and their wish to retire from summertime work and responsibilities. The Hieberts' greenhouses and many plants still remain between Croftville Road and Lake Superior.[278]

### Carlson Cabins and Store (*now* Croftville Road Cottages)
### 1558 Croftville Road

This property was owned by several fishing families before its acquisition by Victor and Katrina Carlson, both Finland Swedes who immigrated to Duluth during the early 1900s and later settled on a Lutsen Township farm. The couple, by the late 1920s, was residing in Croftville, where Carlson engaged in commercial fishing. He died in February 1938 while fishing on Lake Superior with his youngest son, Rudy ("Red"). Many years later, Red's wife, Margaret, provided a poignant description of the impact this event had on her future husband. "Victor had a brain aneurysm and died there in the boat," she recounted. "Red had to row them back to shore—a terrible experience for a twelve-year-old boy." The family, following Victor Carlson's death, successfully maintained ownership of their Croftville property, including its three rental cabins, which his widow operated until her passing, at the age of eighty-four, in 1964. The family also established a successful fish sales business, Rudy's Fish, but only because of the inestimable assistance provided by Margaret Olson Carlson, who married Red in 1956. Born on the Grand Portage Indian Reservation, the daughter of an Anishinaabe French Canadian mother and Norwegian immigrant father, and the mother of three children, Margaret Carlson also assisted her husband with his fishing activities, including lengthy stands at the landing, where she waited to hook the boat onto its winch during bad weather. "The boxes of fish could be heavy," she recalled in a 2000 interview, "up to one hundred pounds. Lots and lots of work."[279] It was the smokehouse and store, however, that demanded most of her time and effort:

> Red caught all the herring and ciscoes we sold [after] soaking them overnight in brine and some brown sugar; we had gauges to tell us how much salt was in the brine. Fresh-caught herring were cleaned and washed before they went into the brine. Red would then stir them in the brine tubs from time to time with a big paddle, so they'd be evenly salted. They'd be in the brine eight to twelve hours. We made hooks out of heavy wire to hang the fish on. Herring and ciscoes would be hung on the hooks, and the whitefish and trout would be put out flat, on screens, in the smoker. An average batch would take three to four hours or so—we kept checking to see that they were cooking [smoked] to the right color.
>
> In the summertime, inspectors would come to test our fish and check everything and see how our store was. They'd stay with me through the smoking and they used their own thermometers to check. The whole process took hours, not just an hour or two—and there were many stages to go through. We sold to the stores, the restaurants, the hospital, and to people who came to the store. We sold a lot of fresh and smoked fish.[280]

The couple operated their smokehouse and store until health issues forced Carlson to quit fishing during

The inn and three cabins at Croftville Road Cottages, completed between 2007 and 2017, replaced a small resort and commercial fishing business that Victor and Katrina Carlson launched during the late 1920s.

the early 1970s. The former store is now used for storage, but the residence and cabins were purchased, refurbished, and expanded by a new owner who reopened the lakeside business in 1973. The buildings stood vacant in 2003, when Michael and Teresa Chemelik of Rochester, Minnesota, decided to make a "dream come true" by acquiring the property. The Chemeliks initially focused their efforts on the rehabilitation of the three all-season rental cottages, which opened in 2007. That effort was followed by a more ambitious project—the construction of an inn upon the foundation of the former residence. Completed in 2017, the building includes the Chemeliks' living quarters, an office, and five "vacation suites" with private entrances. All of their guests are provided with immediate access to 530 feet of Lake Superior shoreline.[281]

Matt and Marie Rasmussen's former fish house is one of several historic structures that remain along Croftville Road. A privy is at the left.

## Rasmussen Fish House

### Lakeshore Side of 1609 Croftville Road

Danish immigrants Matt and Marie Christiansen Rasmussen married in Wisconsin before moving to Croftville, where they built a residence and fish house in 1916. Following Rasmussen's 1944 death, the couple's son Lester continued fishing at the site until 1971, when he moved to western Washington.[282] The

The left corner of this cobblestone residence, dating to the early 1930s, sits on a former Devil's Track River bridge abutment.

long-vacant fish house, one of the largest examples of this building type in Cook County, still stands along the Lake Superior shoreline in Croftville.

### John A. and Sylvia Johnson Residence
1900 East Highway 61

Appearing a short distance beyond the Croftville Road–Highway 61 intersection is the Devil's Track River, which is typically identified as the translation of an Anishinaabe term for "the spirits (or God) walking-place-on-the-ice-river." Euro-American translations of the devil as a "supremely evil" entity, however, very likely represent an incorrect interpretation of what the Anishinaabe considered a "spirit" or a "ghost." Situated close to the Highway 61 bridge that spans the Devil's Track is a well-built residence, constructed of Lake Superior cobblestones during the early 1930s. Built for John A. and Sylvia Carlson Johnson, both children of Finnish immigrant parents, the structure included an office and store that once served the family's small resort, Devil's Track Cabins. The picturesque building, termed "a one of a kind on the North Shore," has been a single-family residence for many years.[283]

## Colvill

Appearing shortly after the Devil's Track River is a small Lake Superior geological feature, Five Mile Rock, which served as a distance marker for early mariners who were approaching or departing the Grand Marais harbor. Situated about three-quarters of a mile from the shoreline, Five Mile Rock stands close to the western boundary of what became Colvill (sometimes spelled Covill) Township following its division from Hovland Township in 1906. The separation occurred because Colvill's residents, most of whom lived close to Durfee Creek, believed they were "so remote from government at Hovland that their interests had been sadly neglected." A total of 125 people were counted in the 1920 Colvill Township census, among them 51 immigrants: 21 Norwegians, 19 Finland Swedes, 7 Swedes, and 4 others. The official existence of Colvill Township ended in 1937–38.[284]

Within the former township is an unincorporated community, also called Colvill. Both the township and the settlement were named for William J. Colvill—a Red Wing newspaper man, an attorney, and commander of the famed First Minnesota Regiment who was severely wounded at the 1863 Battle of Gettysburg. (A prominent statue within the Minnesota State Capitol building in St. Paul recognizes the former Union army colonel.) Colvill, in 1893, applied for a 167-acre homestead claim, situated between Cliff Creek and Kimball Creek. He would spend several summers improving the property until the early 1900s, when ill health, caused by wartime injuries, forced Colvill to sell the holding and move back to Red Wing, where the veteran soldier died in 1905. Residing nearby and less than one mile east of Durfee Creek was Ole E. Erickson, a Swedish immigrant and Minneapolis grocer who settled on a 145-acre homestead claim in 1896. After making required improvements to the holding, Erickson received title to his property during the early 1900s. Erickson also participated in the formation of Colvill Township and was vice president of the Grand Marais and North Shore Railroad Company, an unsuccessful venture that would have extended the rail line from Two Harbors to Fort William–Port Arthur, Ontario. Prior to Erickson's 1920 death in his Colvill cabin, the Swedish homesteader's crops and produce won several ribbons at the Minnesota State Fair.[285]

**Ole E. Erickson's descendants continue to enjoy the stunning lakeshore section of property that he homesteaded in 1896. The photograph includes members of the fourth, fifth, and sixth generations of Erickson's family; the youngest is his great-great-great-grandson. Photograph courtesy of the family, 2014.**

### Charles Wiger Vernacular Roadside Garden
2777 East Highway 61

Many first-time North Shore motorists undoubtedly are surprised, amazed, amused, perplexed, or mystified by the collection of stones, rocks, boulders, driftwood, birchbark, flowers, vegetation, used signs, hand-carved and chainsawed wildlife sculptures, a pair of frogs engaged in fishing, an almost life-size metal moose, a tin man, a Bigfoot figure, numerous mannequin heads, and much more that suddenly appear, unannounced, on the upper side of Highway 61. The display is the work of Charles ("Chuck") Wiger, an attorney and DFL state senator from the St. Paul suburb of Maplewood who was elected to the Minnesota Legislature in 1996 and served until 2024. Wiger, in 2008, purchased the acreage, including a mid-century residence, because of the site's almost endless supply of rocks and stones, most of which have fallen, and continue to descend, from a wave-cut cliff of North Shore bedrock lava that rises forty feet above the property. In 2010, some months after a previous year's storm had uprooted several large trees, Wiger converted the downed trunks into berms for an envisioned roadside attraction. His venture has involved transporting tens of thousands of rocks—in buckets, a wheelbarrow, and a four-wheeler—to the project site. The entire feature now stretches along the highway for some five hundred feet and also extends northward to the bedrock cliff.[286]

If cultural landscape scholars were asked to identify and define Wiger's endeavor, which he has described as "a message of harmony, peace, and joy," the discussion very likely would focus on some combination of the following terms: landscape, garden, vernacular, whimsical, sculptural, rock, roadside, and folk art. While "vernacular roadside garden" captures several characteristics of the feature, Wiger's own words provide an even clearer understanding of its origins. "I've always loved rocks since I was a kid," he remarked in 2015. "I love nature and trees."[287]

### Alfred and Margaret Amyotte Residence (*now* Kivitalo)

2841 East Highway 61

In 1900, Alfred (Fred) Amyotte, of French Canadian and Anishinaabe parentage, emigrated from Quebec to Cook County, where, two years later, he married Margaret Scott of Grand Marais. Amyotte built a small residence for his family, very likely during the early 1920s—just as work was under way on the section of North Shore highway that stretches between Grand Marais and Canada. Many of Amyotte's ten children, including six sons (all of whom served in World War II), were born and raised in the house, which was constructed of carefully cut bedrock lava. A later owner provided more upper-story space by modifying the original roofline and also expressed his ethnic identity by incising a Finnish word, "Kivitalo" (Stonehouse), into the front facade.[288]

### Russell Zerbach Fish House and the Breakers Motel and Cabins *(abandoned)*

2925 East Highway 61

Perched along Colvill's shoreline is a deteriorating fish house, built by Russell Zerbach during the early 1940s. Zerbach was five years old in 1905, when his German American parents moved from northern Michigan to Colvill. Zerbach "finished school" at the age of eleven and pursued fur trapping for one year before becoming a lumberjack. When barely a teenager, Zerbach decided to pursue the life of a fisherman after an older worker "convinced him that fishing was a good occupation." Zerbach was also employed as a carpenter and fishing guide and, during the 1960s, built the Breakers Motel and Cabins, which had large picture windows that offered views of Lake Superior. Married twice, the Colvill resident received significant assistance from both spouses: Thelma Nelson Zerbach, from 1935 until her passing in 1958, and Mildred Backstrom Zerbach, from 1961 until his death at the age of ninety in 2000. Zerbach's rectangular fish house still remains along the shoreline, although much of its foundation, walls, and roof have been undermined and worn away by Lake Superior's high water and storms. Much more visible on the highway's upper side are Zerbach's original home and long-vacant motel.[289]

### Moe-Del Motel (*now the* Outpost Motel)

2935 East Highway 61

Adolph and Clio ("Del") Boostrom Moe opened their Moe-Del Motel during the early summer of 1961. Described at that time as a "modernistic new court nicely located back from the highway," each of the horseshoe-shaped structure's seventeen units had picture windows that overlooked Lake Superior as well as shower baths and vented heat. Renamed the Outpost Motel following its sale to new owners some years later, the business remains a fixture within Colvill. One of relatively few lodging facilities situated between Grand Marais and Grand Portage, the Outpost remains a popular and moderately priced overnight stop for North Shore travelers and visitors.[290]

### Colvill Town Hall

2965 East Highway 61

Local residents built a town hall following the organization of Colvill Township in 1906, but the structure burned down during a March 1928 grass fire. A replacement, under construction by May, was completed in July. The single-story, hipped-roof building, which continues to overlook Lake Superior and Highway 61, is quite similar to several other town halls and one-room schoolhouses that appeared along the North Shore and throughout many areas of Minnesota and the Midwest during the early twentieth century. The hall's governmental functions ended following the 1937 dissolution of Colvill Township, but the building continued serving as a venue for community events, performances, and dances, including those that featured the popular Swedish musician and humorist Olle i Skratthult, who had a summer home in nearby Hovland. Responsibility for maintenance and insurance costs has been assumed by Cook County throughout the hall's post-township history, although the commissioners, in 2005, considered selling the building rather than authorizing $4,000 for repairs. But when numerous residents expressed their wish to keep the hall open, the commissioners quickly approved the request, admitting that the building had "its own charm" and that any privatization effort would represent a "real mistake."[291] The modest but well-maintained building still identifies both the settlement of Colvill and the former township.

### Kodonce River State Park (*now* Kadunce River State Wayside)
2986 East Highway 61

Despite its limited size, a 128-acre section of the Kadunce (also Kodonce) River watershed was added to Minnesota's state park system in 1947, but only because of the efforts undertaken by Judge Clarence R. Magney. More appropriately designated a state wayside in 1969, the property, now managed by MnDOT, serves as the entrance to a trail, less than one mile in length, that passes through the Kadunce River gorge and provides access to one large waterfall and three smaller cascades. Located at the upper end of the river is the Kadunce Spur, a link to the SHT. Also significant is the eight-mile-long expanse of Lake Superior shoreline that extends northeastward between the Kadunce Wayside and the Brule River—the most impressive gravel and sand beach on the entire North Shore.[292]

## Hovland

The name "Hovland" identifies Cook County's first township, which existed from 1894 to 1938, and also serves as the name of an existing unincorporated community. A town hall, built "with everyone contributing, everyone helping," emerged in 1893, one year before the township's official organization. Despite Hovland's small population of seventy-two residents in 1900, the township was, by this time, already termed "a vigorous, self-reliant, self-conscious community of fishermen, loggers, prospectors, [and] trappers." By 1910—three years after Colvill's residents had separated and organized their own township—Hovland's 130 citizens included 63 immigrants, among them 55 Nordic immigrants—35 Norwegians, 10 Swedes, and 10 Finland Swedes. In 1937–38, when two-thirds of Hovland's taxpayers were delinquent, and more than one-half of all land was in public ownership, the Cook County Board voted to dissolve the township, which eventually would be integrated with the East Cook Unorganized Territory. Hovland's current zip code area covers a somewhat larger area than the former township and included an estimated population of 250 permanent residents in 2020. As occurs elsewhere on the North Shore, "seasonal residents and retired snowbirds" expand the summertime numbers.[293]

### Grover Conzet WPA Camp and Brule River State Park (*now* Judge C. R. Magney State Park)
4501 East Highway 61

The Brule River, once the boundary between two former townships, Colvill and Hovland, was known as Wiskode-zibi (Half-Burned Wood River) to the Anishinaabe, the Bois Brulé (Burned Wood) to the French, and the Arrowhead River for a brief time during the early twentieth century. Different logging companies harvested timber within the river's watershed from the early 1900s to the 1930s, and major fires also caused extensive damage. The site's ensuing history is unusual because of its three-thousand-acre "transient camp" (also called a "hobo camp"), which the Minnesota Division of Forestry opened along the Brule in 1934. Named the Grover Conzet Camp in recognition of the state's first commissioner of forestry and fire prevention, the facility and its natural setting were transferred, in late 1936, to the federal government's WPA. The camp included fourteen barracks; two bathhouses; two recreation halls; three workshops; and a dining hall, bakery, garage, warehouse, and root cellar. The men constructed a trail and stairs to Devil's Kettle, the site's best-known feature; established a small park; farmed some land where they grew a portion of their own food; and fought a major forest fire north of Hovland. After building a small sawmill at the site, the camp's residents were able to salvage some lumber from the charred trees. Approximately eight hundred men passed through the facility until it was shuttered in July 1938. It then served as a summer "health camp" for 125 Anishinaabe children before being abandoned. The foundations for some camp buildings still remain on the site.[294]

The origins of what initially was called Brule River State Park date to 1957, when the Minnesota Legislature approved the purchase of a few remaining private land parcels that would complete the 940-acre holding. Officially identified as Judge C. R. Magney State Park in 1963, the name honored a man who had served as Duluth's mayor, was an associate justice of the Minnesota Supreme Court, and was highly influential in establishing eleven state parks and waysides along the North Shore. Indeed, in April 1962, while on a journey "to visit all the continents," Magney sent a letter from South Africa to the *Cook County News-Herald*,

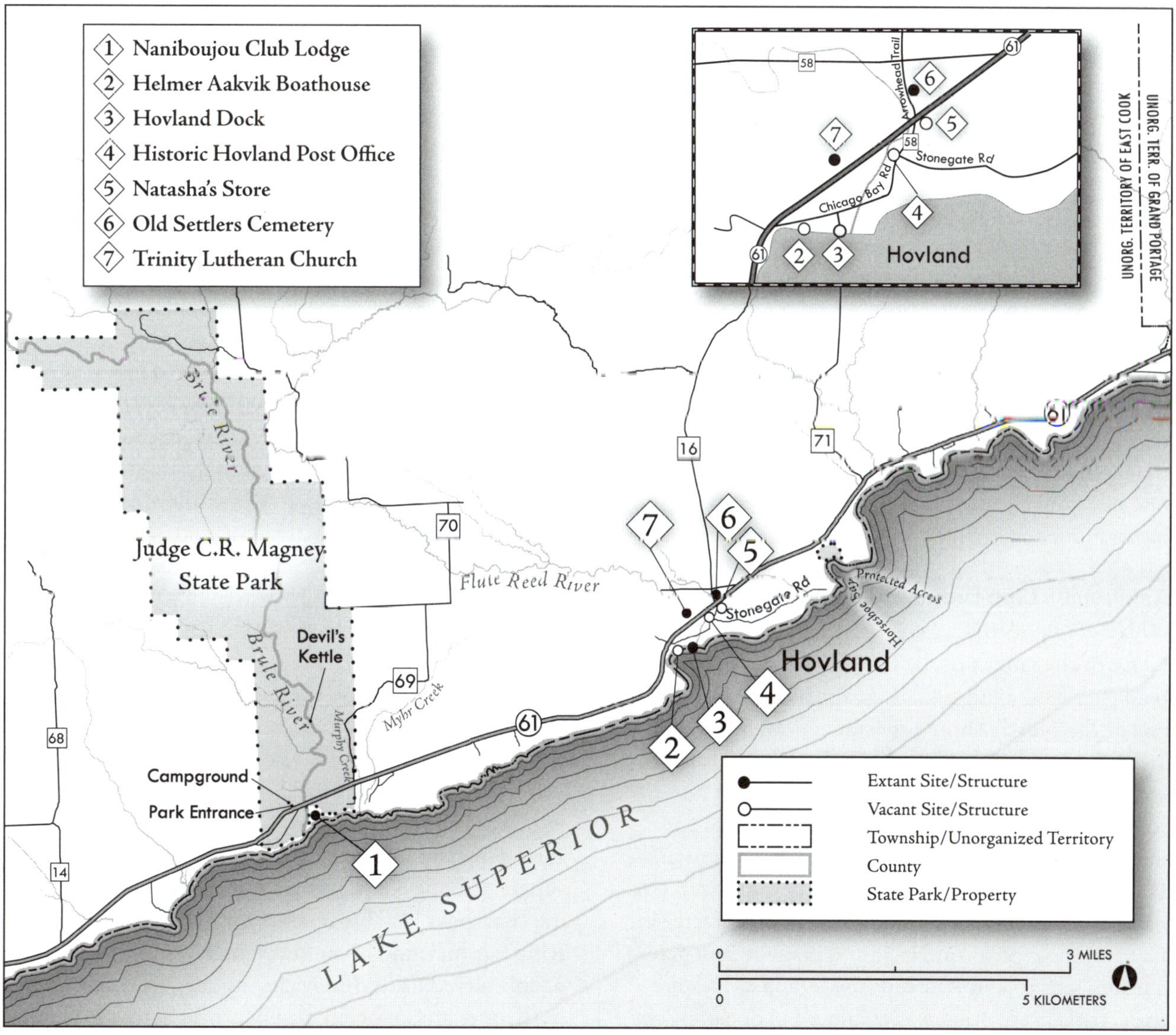

1 Naniboujou Club Lodge
2 Helmer Aakvik Boathouse
3 Hovland Dock
4 Historic Hovland Post Office
5 Natasha's Store
6 Old Settlers Cemetery
7 Trinity Lutheran Church
Arrowhead Trail
Stonegate Rd
Chicago Bay Rd
Hovland
UNORG. TERRITORY OF EAST COOK
UNORG. TERR. OF GRAND PORTAGE
Brule River
Judge C.R. Magney State Park
Devil's Kettle
Campground
Park Entrance
Murphy Creek
Mybr Creek
Flute Reed River
Protected Access
Horseshoe Bay
LAKE SUPERIOR
Extant Site/Structure
Vacant Site/Structure
Township/Unorganized Territory
County
State Park/Property
0
3 MILES
5 KILOMETERS

which the newspaper published just one month before his death in Rochester's Mayo Clinic. Magney wrote that some Minnesotans believed he had "become fanatic about the North Shore" (an assertion the jurist welcomed), because of his concern over the growing number of billboards that were appearing along Highway 61. "If such increase occurs over the next ten years," wrote Magney, "the word 'scenic' cannot be used in describing our highway. It will have become a mere ribbon of disfigured landscape."[295]

Further legislative action, in 1965, provided statutory authority for expansion of the state park to forty-five hundred acres, which was realized by the late 1980s. While C. R. Magney has, since then, experienced less development than any other North Shore state park, it does have "lots of steps"—more than 175 of them. Many lead to a pair of platforms, both perched over the Brule River, that provide overviews of Devil's Kettle—once considered a mysterious feature because some of its flowing water appeared to vanish. As determined more recently, however, the mystery is a rhyolite dome that splits the sometime raging Brule into two parts: one side flows over the falls, while the other disappears into a hole or "kettle."[296]

### Naniboujou Club Lodge and Restaurant
20 Naniboujou Trail

Close to the mouth of the Brule River, on private land that flanks Judge C. R. Magney State Park, is one of the North Shore's spectacular architectural attractions—the Naniboujou Club Lodge. Although located in the Hovland area, it has no notable Nordic features; instead, the lodge interior represents an impressionistic depiction of Cree Indian culture that Naniboujou's affluent sponsors sought to portray. (Its name, "Naniboujou," was derived from a character in Cree mythology; a similar figure, Nanabozho, plays a prominent role in Anishinaabe legends.) Despite the artistic license that was employed in depicting the Crees' cultural and spiritual life, the lodge rightfully continues to receive plaudits from many observers, some of whom have termed it a "rustic jewel," a "North Shore fantasy," and even a "kind of Versailles of the north woods," if not a "North Woods answer to the Sistine Chapel."[297]

Naniboujou's origins may be traced to May 1925, when the Brule Land and Outing Corporation, formed by a group of Duluth businessmen, unveiled an ambitious proposal for a "large summer resort and tourist hotel" that coincided with the opening of Minnesota Highway 1. Initial plans for the thirty-three hundred acres of land envisioned a new town, called Arrowhead, and a dam that would provide light and power and also create a lake on the river where bathing and other recreational pursuits could occur. None of these proposals were realized before the Naniboujou Holding Company acquired the property in 1927. The organization immediately leased the land to the Naniboujou Club, which announced its intentions to construct a lodge with 150 bedrooms and several "entertainment features." Projected for the grounds were tennis courts, a golf course, a bathhouse, an electric plant, and individual lots where each member could build a cabin that followed his own plans. Memberships in the private club, many for "friends and . . . friends of friends," were generally priced at $200, but only two votes from the board of governors' thirty-one members could veto an applicant's request. The original proposal stated that no more than 25 percent of the members could be Minnesota residents, thereby ensuring "a comfortable balance of club attendance, between those who may run up over weekends and those from a greater distance who would stay longer."[298]

Construction of the lodge was under way, but far from complete, during summer 1928, when plans were made to enroll the members' sons in a boys camp supervised by expert counselors, among them "several" tribal leaders. In June 1929, just before the grand opening, invitations were sent to Naniboujou's members, some of whom had honorary status, including baseball superstar Babe Ruth, former world heavyweight boxing champion Jack Dempsey, sportswriter and satirist Ring Lardner, and other luminaries. An estimated 550 people were served dinner during the weekend event. Perhaps it was an omen of the future, however, when the featured speaker, Minnesota governor Theodore Christianson (also a member), could not participate because of illness. Just a few months later, the stock market crash brought a sudden halt to any expansion plans. By July 1930, the membership rolls had dwindled so precipitously that Naniboujou's twenty-four rooms were opened to the general public. This effort failed

**A view of Naniboujou looking northward from the Lake Superior shoreline.**

to generate sufficient revenue, and the club experienced foreclosure in 1935. The Naniboujou would not reopen until 1939, following a sale to the Arthur Roberts Hotel Company of Rochester, Minnesota.[299]

Other owners followed in 1953 and 1963 before the Campus Church, a nondenominational Christian group located at the University of Minnesota, acquired the property in 1980. Tim and Nancy Ramey served as caretakers until 1985, when they purchased the business. Over the years, the Rameys and their seven children restored the Naniboujou and eventually offered a public dining option, which became a very popular attraction among both visitors and local residents. Unfortunately, Ramey had been paralyzed and confined to a wheelchair following a 1998 accident that occurred while he was serving as a volunteer firefighter. Nevertheless, he and his wife, along with their staff, have continued to offer a unique visitor experience at Naniboujou—"no phones, no televisions in the rooms, no Wi-Fi access, and no cell phone tower nearby"—which harkens back to the North Shore lodges of an earlier era. Since most of their children resided throughout the United States and did not wish to take over the business, the couple reluctantly put the Naniboujou up for sale in September 2016. When no satisfactory offers were forthcoming by spring 2017, the listing was removed. Although the facility was closed throughout 2020 because of Covid-19-related concerns, both the lodge and the dining area opened for a smaller number of guests in 2021—thanks to the efforts of Nancy Ramey, a few longtime employees, and one of the couple's daughters and her children, who returned to Naniboujou for the summer season. Normal restaurant and lodging activities resumed in 2022.[300]

The current view of Naniboujou offered from Highway 61 does not convey the full extent of the rambling, two-story, gambrel-roofed structure, which sits upon a level plane of grass: a much more complete impression may be gained from various lakeside vantage points. Designed by Duluth architects Holstead & Sullivan, the lodge footprint is generally horseshoe shaped, with wings that radiate diagonally from a centralized great hall. Situated at the intersection of both wings and the hall is a separate polygonal tower, topped by a hip roof. The building's exterior, completely sheathed with weathered cedar shakes, also displays the artful use of deeply tinted red trim. It is the thirty-by-eighty-foot interior dining area and public space, with a high ceiling shaped in the form of an inverted canoe and adorned with symbols and geometric forms, which continues to amaze and astound observers. The artist, Antoine J. Gouffe (1884–1976), a native of Philadelphia and a son of French immigrant parents, spent several years studying in France. Just before 1920, Gouffe and his French wife, Marie, settled in Duluth, where he pursued a career as a portrait painter, artist, and photographer. The couple continued to reside in Duluth until the early 1940s, when they moved to the Caryville, New York, headquarters of the Northeast Federation of the Theosophical Society in America.[301]

At Naniboujou, Gouffe used zigzag and other geometric forms, all painted in vivid blue, red, green, orange, and yellow colors, to create, as a *New York Times* writer claimed in 2000, "a psychedelic marriage of Art Deco and traditional Cree Indian patterns." Just below the dining area's ceiling is a row of faces that represent Gouffe's interpretation, some Cree inspired, of various nature gods. On the northern wall is a massive fireplace—constructed of rounded Lake Superior cobblestones—that stands twelve feet high and weighs an estimated two hundred tons. Carefully integrated into the fireplace chimney and just above eye level is a stone sunburst—the Cree symbol of welcome. Listed in the National Register of Historic Places in 1982, Naniboujou continues to maintain, as Adelheid Fischer has written, a North Shore "spirit of fantasy."[302]

## Chicago Bay/Hovland

Eight diminutive settlements eventually emerged in Hovland Township, four of which were located along the lakeshore—Lake Shore Road, Horseshoe Bay, Big Bay, and Chicago Bay (only the latter is featured here). Situated about four miles from the Brule River,

**Naniboujou's dining room and public space, with its massive cobblestone fireplace in the background, continues to attract and enchant observers.**

Chicago Bay was earlier identified as Sickle Bay by geologists engaged in North Shore survey work during the 1850s. The "Chicago Bay" name may have been derived from *shikag* (an Anishinaabe term for "skunk") by the Booth Packing Company some three decades later. The location served as a stop for its steamships, such as the *Hiram R. Dixon* and *T. H. Camp*, which often picked up fish that local settlers had packed into boxes and kegs. The groundwork for a permanent settlement was established during fall 1887, when Norwegian immigrants Ole Brunes and Nils Ludvig Eliasen made their way beyond Grand Marais to the Flute Reed (also Flutereed) River, which feeds into Chicago Bay. Both men had worked as cabinetmakers in Duluth, but because of poor wages, they decided to start fishing for the Booth Company. After viewing the bay and river, each man selected a 160-acre homestead property at the mouth of the Flute Reed: Eliasen's acreage was east of the stream, Brunes's on the west. Following their return to Duluth on the *T. H. Camp*, the men filed homestead applications in the city's U.S. General Land Office. During spring 1888, the two Norwegians sailed in their own fishing vessel from Duluth to Chicago Bay, where they constructed Brunes's sixteen-by-eighteen-foot log cabin, which had a sapling pole roof covered with birch and cedar bark. Soon, Anna Brunes and Nellie Eliasen, each with four children in tow, sailed to Chicago Bay; both families lived in the small cabin until Eliasen's dwelling was completed. The men secured official title to their homestead properties in January 1894.[303]

More settlers followed the Brunes and Eliasen families to Chicago Bay. By 1890, when the U.S. Census Bureau sent Bert Fesler to collect fisheries data from Isle Royale and the North Shore, the young ichthyologist reported that some twenty Norwegians resided at Chicago Bay. The residents had, already in 1889, petitioned federal authorities for a post office that would be named for Hamar, a small city bordering Norway's largest lake. Although their suggestion was rejected, approval was given to "Hovland," a name that may have been recommended by Anna Brunes because it was the home community of her Norwegian grandfather.[304]

Local promoters, as early as the 1890s, were promoting Hovland as the "Trout Capital of the World." Ole Brunes sought to capitalize on this popularity in 1893 when he expanded the family's log dwelling and added a few second-floor bedrooms for six or more people. Once the skilled carpenter made further extensions to the residence, even more anglers could be housed in Hovland's "hotel." Brunes also built a Flute Reed River tourist cabin, believed to be the first of its kind on the entire North Shore. When the Brunes family departed Hovland sometime before 1904 because of health problems, the hotel was acquired by another Norwegian couple, Lauritz ("Louis") and Nella Ellingsen, who had moved to Chicago Bay in 1897. They maintained the hotel until 1913 and operated a general store that closed in 1940, following Ellingsen's death at the age of eighty-five. The one-time hotel, now vacant and in dilapidated condition, still stands in Hovland. None of the original structures remain on Eliasen's neighboring property.[305]

Hovland, occasionally termed a "colorful boomtown" during the early twentieth century, was especially hard hit by the 1930s economic depression. A recovery began during the postwar era when increasing numbers of motorists ventured beyond the better-known tourist centers of Tofte, Lutsen, and Grand Marais to Hovland, where they found fewer people, less commercialization, and a community of residents who, though showing pride in their Nordic heritage and culture, did so in an unassuming and low-key manner. Even more recently, in 2016, a *Cook County News-Herald* reporter observed that Hovland (and Colvill) still maintained this tradition: both settlements, he commented, are "quiet places with little hustle or bustle, and that's how a lot of folks living there want to keep it."[306]

Hovland has also served as an unpretentious home for several well-known individuals, among them Swedish immigrant Hjalmar Peterson, better known as Olle i Skratthult (Olle from Laughtersville), whose humorous music and antics made him the best-known Swedish and Scandinavian vaudeville performer in the United States from the late 1910s to the early 1930s. While based in Minneapolis, Peterson acquired and expanded a Hovland cabin that served as his favorite retreat from 1922 and 1933. Also present in Hovland were architect Chilson Aldrich, the author of a popular and now-classic book, *The Real Log Cabin*, and his wife, Darragh Aldrich, a playwright, novelist, poet,

**This remarkably large hotel emerged in 1893, after Ole Brunes added on to his family's log residence. Shown here in 1910, the hotel was owned and operated at that time by Nella and Louis Ellingsen, who may be standing at the far right. An outhouse or privy, undoubtedly one of several on the property, is visible between the group of people and the hotel. Courtesy of Cook County Historical Society.**

journalist, and early Minneapolis WCCO radio announcer. After the couple purchased one-half mile of Lake Superior shoreline in the 1920s, Aldrich designed and built a one-room log cabin on their property; six more units were sold to friends. Several of the cabins would later be restored by Grand Marais wilderness guide, craftsman, and author Harry Drabik. Also of note is Swedish American author and outdoorsman Calvin Rutstrum, who lived along the Flute Reed from 1923 to 1931; Rutstrum wrote fifteen books about survival in the wild, among them a 1970 autobiography, *Challenge of the Wilderness*, that includes descriptions of his Hovland years.[307]

### Helmer Aakvik Boathouse *(razed)*
#### Aakvik Lane

Among Hovland's most revered residents were Helmer and Christine Aakvik, who established their home and a fishing camp on what was later named Aakvik Lane. The Norwegian immigrant also built a second boathouse/fish house on Chicago Bay. Aakvik already was an experienced fisherman when he emigrated in 1914, at the age of eighteen, to the southwestern Minnesota community of Clarkfield. He soon moved to an Alaskan fishing settlement but returned to Clarkfield and married Christine Haaland, the daughter of Norwegian immigrants, in 1926. Two years later, after the couple had settled in Hovland, Aakvik became a Lake Superior commercial fisherman, a pursuit that he would follow for almost six decades. But it was a momentous event in late November 1958—when Aakvik "braved near-zero temperatures on storm-whipped Lake Superior for 25 hours in a fruitless search for a fisherman who was lost tending his nets"—that made him a North Shore legend and national Carnegie Hero.[308]

Aakvik set out on the mission in an aging skiff that he had built "along the lines of a North Atlantic dory."[309] Several years later, Aakvik recalled, with vivid detail but typical Nordic understatement, the ordeal he faced in an unsuccessful attempt to rescue Carl Hammar, his young neighbor and fishing partner:

> Well anyway I got ready to go out and look for him. . . . The sea was building bigger and bigger the further I got out. . . . I'd been getting a lot of spray and everything off the top of them seas, all over the motor, it was all ice. The gas line

froze up, so I couldn't get it going. Well, I had no tools—just an axe—so I had to bare my hands to get the gas line off. Then I stuck it in my mouth and got the ice [out] you see. Well I got the motor going, and pretty soon a big sea went right over me, and the skiff was swamped—oh, I'd guess a quarter full.

All I could do was to keep into the wind. I wasn't going nowhere the sea was so big—maybe 20, 25 feet. The skiff was taking a terrible pounding. It was an old skiff anyways and it started to come apart and leak real bad. It was full to the top with water and the planks were separating, the screws pulling right out. Well, I couldn't keep going like that, or soon I'd have no skiff left, so I shut the motor off and drifted—drifted the rest of the day, all night and the next forenoon.

Well the next morning the wind had calmed some. It was still rough out there, but time to think about getting back in. . . . I had to get the motor started you see, but the rope was all ice and wouldn't fit in the groove. The whole front of the skiff where I couldn't reach the axe was ice—a foot, maybe two, thick. I had to chop my mitts off with [the] axe. I needed bare hands to unravel the starting rope, to get one strand out that would fit in that motor. Well, I got the motor going and headed back towards shore. It was real slow with [the] skiff swamped and all that ice. I couldn't chop no ice up in front. I got my legs froze in solid so I couldn't stand. I run like that about six hours. Then . . . the motor quit. No gas.

Well, I sat thinking about what to do. I still had my oars—I didn't throw them over. But my hands were too cold to grip them. . . . I looked up and there was the [Coast Guard] cutter. . . . When we got back to the town dock there must have been a hundred people there. . . . I only froze two toes where I cut the rubber boots with the axe chopping ice, and the water got in. [But as] I said before I went out: "Don't you worry, the old man will be back."[310]

In 1985, two years before Aakvik's death at the age of ninety, a Minneapolis journalist visited the fisherman in his Hovland home. "The house is broken down and weathered just like Helmer's old body," wrote the newspaperman. "The yard and interior are a collection of this and that, a graveyard of forgotten projects, notions, canned goods, and dreams." Other North Shore fishing camps certainly displayed similar characteristics, but Aakvik was ready with a wry response when he sensed that the reporter might be somewhat taken aback by such seeming disorder. "We may look kinda wild here, ya," Aakvik quipped, "but we're civilized." A few years earlier, the Hovland fisherman had asked a friend, Mark Hansen of the North House Folk School, to build a simple coffin equipped with a keel and a carved compass, so that Aakvik, upon his death, could "steer a straight course to the stars."[311] The words later inscribed on Aakvik's gravestone—"Home from the cruel sea and now in a peaceful harbor"—serve as a fitting epitaph for a fisherman who had many encounters with the vagaries and vicissitudes of Lake Superior.

**Helmer Aakvik, a few years after his Herculean but futile effort, in 1958, to rescue fellow fisherman Carl Hammar. Photograph by Barbara Richards, early 1960s. Courtesy of the photographer.**

**The remnants of Helmer Aakvik's fish house, *far right*, were still evident along the Chicago Bay shoreline in 2015. The buildings on the left are owned by other residents.**

## Hovland Dock

### 4734 Chicago Bay Road

One of Hovland's treasured landmarks is the community dock, even though the final angled piece has separated and is sagging from its adjacent crib. Before construction began in 1902, steamboats were forced to anchor a considerable distance from the shoreline, which meant that the transfer of goods and passengers—an especially dangerous procedure at night and during storms—was undertaken by rowing skiffs to and from the vessels. The dock construction project was supervised by John Eliasen, a Norwegian settler and well-known fiddler who had, already in 1899, overseen the dredging of a safe harbor for local fishermen and boats. The dock, located about five hundred feet west of the Flute Reed River mouth, was constructed of cedar logs, planks, and cribs. Eliasen and his crew started their work by building a large log crib at the shoreline, which was filled with heavy rocks; the structure was completed by erecting three more cribs, all connected by a plank deck that extended 220 feet into the bay. Over subsequent decades, huge shipments of fish, logs, horses, oats, hay, and supplies were loaded and unloaded at the dock.[312]

The Eliasen family owned the dock until 1922, when it was acquired by Hovland Township. The crib was enclosed in concrete, and its rotting deck planks were replaced by a concrete slab that rested on steel beams and a framework of corrugated metal. Cast-iron bollards were placed on the deck, and a pair of steel rails spanned the structure's length. A large cart that moved along the rails facilitated the movement of products to and from a large warehouse situated close to the shoreline. Cook County assumed ownership of the dock when Hovland Township was dissolved in 1938.[313]

A layer of concrete applied to the deck during the mid-1970s covered the steel tracks, but some of the deepest pilings began washing away around this time. In November 1999, a small group of Hovland residents called for the stabilization and preservation of the remaining dock section to protect it from further deterioration. The proposal gained little momentum, although the ARDC, in 2015, considered the dock and adjacent shoreline as a possible wayside. The dock was still noteworthy, commented an ARDC planner at the time, as one of only a few remaining examples of an early North Shore transportation system, which also represents "a significant story involving commercial fishermen, tragedy, and heroism." The wayside, nevertheless, was not developed, and the Cook County Board of Commissioners announced their decision, in 2018, to abandon any further dock preservation efforts, given that Lake Superior "will most likely claim the crumbling structure sooner than later."[314]

Close to the base of the dock is a CCHS marker that commemorates the "Old Dog Trail" used by John Beargrease and other mail carriers during the latter decades of the nineteenth century. The marker, dedicated in October 1956, with representatives from historical societies in Cook and Lake Counties and the Ontario city of Thunder Bay in attendance, originally stood just under one and a half miles southwest of the current location. The sign was moved to its current dock site location during the mid-1980s.[315]

### Hovland Post Office *(vacant)*
4811 Chicago Bay Road

Hovland's earliest post offices were located in the homes of settlers, although a small log structure, built sometime before 1914, was used for an unknown number of years. That long-abandoned building still remains along Chicago Bay Road, undoubtedly because its log walls were protected by siding for several decades. Around 2017, when the structure was on the verge of collapse, property owners Margo Otterness and David O. Olson replaced the walls with new logs. The structure still stands along Chicago Bay Road as a reminder of early twentieth-century Hovland.[316]

### Art's Place, Flutereed Store and Cabins, and Natasha's Store *(vacant)*
5038 East Highway 61

In 1937, Arthur Eliasen, a Hovland lumberjack, USFS supervisor, and builder, opened Art's Place, which offered merchandise, gasoline, and rental cottages at the Highway 61–Chicago Bay Road intersection. Eliasen's property was purchased in the mid-1940s by Werner Noreen, a Swede who had emigrated to Chicago in 1909 and later played fiddle in Olle i Skratthult's orchestra. A 1949 sale of the property also resulted in a name change, to the Flutereed Store and Cabins. Groceries, beer, gas, and oil were

**The Flutereed Store, during the 1950s, provided motorists and Hovland residents with groceries, merchandise, beer, and Shell Oil products; it also had a café and dance floor and several nearby tourist cabins.**

available for purchase; customers could order meals that were served in a small dining area; and dance music was provided on some nights. The Flutereed (also Flute Reed) was Hovland's commercial and social center until its 1980 closing.[317] Local residents and visitors now stop, shop, and gas up at the Chicago Bay Marketplace (4971 East Highway 61), which was built about one-third of a mile to the west during the 1990s.

The Flute Reed building and property were purchased by Natalia and Archie Kirk in 2003. Kirk, an injured Vietnam War veteran and Cook County home builder, met Natalia ("Natasha") Sheshina, a Russian citizen, while he was visiting St. Petersburg in 1993. The "two souls [who] found each other on opposite sides of the earth" married one year later. After their purchase, the Kirks spent several years renovating the Flute Reed building, which opened in 2011 as Natasha's—a store that featured her custom-made clothing, along with a selection of gift items, many from Russia. Following Kirk's 2016 death, his buoyant widow kept the store open intermittently before disposing of its inventory, closing the business, and putting the property up for sale during the early 2020s. Sold in 2023, the building remained vacant at the time of this writing.[318]

**The late nineteenth-century deaths of Norwegian immigrant Johan Jacobson (1837–88) and his daughter Ingeborg Anna (1887–96) are memorialized in Hovland's Old Settlers Cemetery.**

## Old Settlers Cemetery
### 18 Arrowhead Road/Trail

Hovland's earliest burial ground, established in 1894, is located northeast of the Arrowhead Road–Highway 61 intersection. Now called the Old Settlers Cemetery, the small site has about seventy-five graves and is still used for a limited number of burials. One Norwegian-language headstone commemorates Mrs. Mathilde Mickelson of Tromsø, whose birth year, 1834, is the cemetery's oldest; her immigrant journey began in Arctic Norway, likely during the 1890s, and culminated in Hovland, where she resided until her 1909 death. Predominating throughout the cemetery are two surnames—Eliasen and Jacobsen/Jacobson—each listed twelve times. Also interred in the graveyard is Werner Noreen, the Swedish musician and business owner who resided in Hovland for several years.

Buried side by side in the cemetery are a father and son, both well-known Cook County artists: John Spelman II (1880–1941) and John Spelman III (1912–69). The senior Spelman, a native of Oak Park, Illinois, studied and often exhibited his work at the Art Institute of Chicago. After developing a "keen interest in northeastern Minnesota," his artistic efforts would focus on the Lake Superior region. In 1908, Spelman bought shoreline land in the Hovland area, where, two years later, he began building a cabin and studio, named Spruce Point Lodge. Until the early North Shore roadway opened in 1917, the Spelman family, often accompanied by friends and relatives, traveled by train from Chicago to Duluth, where they boarded the SS *America* and sailed to Chicago Bay.[319]

John Spelman III, from 1939 to 1945, served as an artist-in-residence at Kentucky's Pine Mountain Settlement School, where he is still recalled and venerated for his linoleum block and wooden prints that characterized the existence and environment of people in Appalachia and illustrated the "mountain cabin in ways that convey the dignity and beauty of that vernacular style." After moving to Grand Marais in 1941, Spelman worked intermittently for the *Cook County News-Herald* and as a high school art teacher. Facing "financial realities" during the early 1950s, Spelman accepted limited-term positions in Minnesota and South Dakota high schools, where he taught both art and English. In 1960, Spelman returned to Grand Marais and once again was employed as an art teacher until his death, nine years later, at the age of fifty-seven. Today Spelman's prints, "rich in detail and historical significance," are appreciated even more so than in the past. Spelman's entire body of North Shore work, observe Scott Husby and Tracey Cullen in a recent overview of his life and career, is of "immense value, not only for its artistry but also for what he portrays of human activities that are gradually disappearing or have vanished completely."[320]

### Trinity Lutheran Church
#### 4957 East Highway 61

Less than one-half mile west of the Old Settlers Cemetery is Trinity Lutheran Church. Dedicated in 1950, Trinity is one of the North Shore's most architecturally significant postwar buildings. The congregation's origins date to 1905, when a Grand Marais pastor offered monthly sermons in the local schoolhouse. He and other early ministers often spent Sunday night in Ellingsen's Hotel before returning to Grand Marais, by foot, steamboat, stagecoach, or sleigh. The official formation of the congregation, named Zoar Lutheran, occurred in 1907.

Another group of Norwegian famers in the Flute Reed Valley (about four miles north of Chicago Bay), along with three families of Finland Swedes who resided on nearby Poplar Hill, formed a separate Trinity Lutheran congregation in 1907; this group would soon affiliate with the Hauge Synod, the "low church" wing of Norwegian Lutheranism in North America. When the Chicago Bay and Flute Reed groups merged in 1912, the Trinity name was maintained, and within two years, the congregation constructed a church along the section of roadway (now North Road) that became part of Minnesota Highway 1 during the early 1920s. The Trinity Lutheran Cemetery (4681 North Road), established in 1915 on land adjacent to the former church, remains Hovland's primary burial ground.[321]

When Highway 61 was rerouted closer to Chicago Bay in 1932–33, Trinity's members considered the possibility of moving their church from its isolated North Road location to a new site. It was not until early 1946, however, that the congregation voted to raze the 1914 building and construct a new church, named Trinity Lutheran, on two acres of land situated adjacent to Highway 61. Professor Arnold Flaten, a former Lutheran pastor who, in 1932, had founded the art program at St. Olaf College in Northfield, Minnesota, served as Trinity's first architect.[322] A skilled artist and sculptor, Flaten had little, if any, formal training in architecture; nevertheless, his proposal for Trinity demonstrated considerable design awareness, a significant understanding of site characteristics and local materials, and encyclopedic familiarity with Nordic and Lutheran traditions.

While working on the Trinity design, Flaten collaborated with his former student and 1939 St. Olaf graduate Edward Sövik, who gave special attention to its technical and structural features. Flaten, in fact, had urged his talented protégé, following Sövik's distinguished World War II service in a U.S. Marine Corps night fighter squadron in the Pacific theater, to study architecture. Their future collaboration, Flaten predicted, would "revolutionize church architecture for the Lutheran Church." The construction drawings for Trinity, some of which include Sövik's notation "Revised 10 January 1948," reveal the mind and hand of someone who already possessed considerable skills as a designer and delineator. (After earning an architecture degree from Yale University in 1949, Sövik established his firm in Northfield, Minnesota, where, within twenty years, he would be acknowledged as "the most theologically informed and articulate American church architect of his day.") Undoubtedly of greatest importance were Sövik's calculations and specifications for the seven three-hinged arches that provided Trinity with its completely open sanctuary. Such solid arches are quite unlike the prefabricated trusses that characterized most gable-roofed churches in postwar America.[323]

Also engaged in discussions with the congregation and Flaten in 1946 were two of Hovland's summer residents—St. Olaf College philosophy professor Howard Hong and his wife, Edna Hatlestad Hong—both of whom had recently returned from Europe, where they worked with the American Friends (Quakers) Service Committee in assisting refugees during the tumultuous years that followed World War II. Hong proposed the development of a Hovland "work camp," modeled on the Quakers' program, that would be staffed by St. Olaf College student volunteers. Although the Hongs soon departed for Europe, this time to serve a two-year stint with the Lutheran World Federation, the Trinity work camp emerged in June 1947, thanks to Flaten's leadership. His wife, Evelyn Solberg Flaten, and the couple's four children also joined the St. Olaf students in Hovland.[324]

After establishing their living quarters in the farmhouse and barn of Norwegian settlers Mons and Anna Hansen, the fifteen "Oles" began their ambitious project by gathering rocks from the Flute Reed River and highway right-of-way and hauling them to the construction site. They then engaged in the "slow, tedious task" of laying and mortaring the rocks to form the foundation walls, bell tower, and chimney. Anton Arnquist, a Swedish member of the congregation, lent his cow, Pokey, to the students, so they would have fresh milk and cream, and a few local fishermen provided some of their catch to ensure that everyone was fed. Ten students participated in the 1948 program, and thirteen in 1949. (Some took part during both summers.) The latter group, described by Flaten as the "artiest camp," assisted him in completing the carvings and sculptural features that appear on the altar and interior arches and above the entry doors. Congregational and community volunteers also spent countless hours

**Hovland's Trinity Lutheran Church, looking toward the north-northwest. Also visible are four of the seven three-hinged arches that support the roof. The arches become progressively larger as they approach the "elbow" located at the upper end of the wall and taper as they extend toward the roof's ridgeline.**

performing additional work and installing materials and features, such as the maple flooring, bell, and exterior doors, all salvaged from the former church. Because of limited monetary resources, indoor water and restrooms were not provided. The bulletin's cover, distributed at the July 1950 church dedication, displayed a linoleum block print of Trinity created by John Spelman III.[325]

Flaten, already in 1946, had remarked that the church would relate to the site as if it "grew out" of the landscape. The timber-frame structure, perched on stone walls, also pays homage to traditional northern European churches, some of which the Flatens had visited and observed while living and studying in Europe during the early 1930s. Extending toward the east is an exterior stone wall that has a vertical opening with a small, carefully crafted barrel vault at the top; a window-like space within the wall accommodates the original Trinity bell and Flaten's wooden carving of a Christ figure. The use of locally supplied lumber and timber sources throughout the interior conveys a sense of warmth and enclosure that is appropriate for the climate and environment of northeastern Minnesota. Flaten's carvings and artistry also display a level of refinement and elegance seldom found in rural churches.[326]

The congregation's members, in 2017–18, expanded the narthex and built a one-story gathering space at the northern end of the church. An important part of the project was accomplished by twenty members of the congregation who spent almost two weeks participating in an extended Grand Marais North House Folk School class, where they engaged in creating the carved pine trusses for the extension, which now looks "like it has always been there." A pastor's office and indoor restrooms were also part of the expansion program. And, after seventy years of going without, the church and its kitchen were finally provided with running water from a drilled well.[327]

Trinity represents the collaboration of a mature artist and a young architect, both of whom were keenly aware of Lutheran, European, and North Shore traditions and antecedents and possessed a sensitive understanding of the relationship between a building and its landscape. Additionally, Trinity has a unique history because of the thirty-three St. Olaf College students who participated in its construction during the late 1940s. But equally impressive are the congregation's members, both past and present, who, for three-quarters of a century, have maintained the landmark church and supported its ministry and programs with their gifts and donations of time, skill, and treasure.

**The Reverend Kris Rølvaag Garey served Hovland's Trinity Lutheran Church as an intern from 2006 to 2008, then as pastor until 2022. She is the granddaughter of Norwegian and American author Ole Rølvaag, who was nominated for the Nobel Prize in Literature in 1931, and the daughter of Karl F. Rolvaag, Minnesota's DFL governor from 1963 to 1967.**

### Horseshoe Bay Protected Access

#### 1.5 Miles Northeast of the Highway 61–Chicago Bay Road Intersection

Northeast of Hovland and Chicago Bay is Horseshoe Bay, which provided shelter for commercial fishermen and was occasionally used by Consolidated Papers, Inc. until its log-rafting activities ended in 1963. The MDNR, in 1992, called for the establishment of an access site on the bay, one of nine (now eleven) safe harbors the agency envisioned for the shoreline between Duluth and the Canadian border. Although the property was also being considered for sale to six leaseholders who held land surrounding the bay, the safe harbor proposal prevailed. The remote property and its scenic bay offered little more than a basic boat ramp and parking lot until 2009–10, when the site was completely renovated by the MDNR. The agency improved the access road and parking area, replaced the flimsy ramp with a large concrete structure, and constructed a new L-shaped crib dock that provides limited wave protection for boats and kayaks.[328]

## Grand Portage Indian Reservation

Five miles beyond Hovland is the Grand Portage Indian Reservation's western boundary. The ensuing eleven miles of Highway 61 pass through the least developed section of the North Shore before its oldest settlement, also named Grand Portage, appears; the highway then continues for another five miles to the Canadian border. Even today, as Anishinaabe elder Billy Blackwell wrote in 1983, "one cannot think of Grand Portage at all without noticing that it is far from other places."[329]

The entire reservation covers seventy-five square miles of territory, thirteen small islands, and eighteen miles of Lake Superior shoreline. Within its boundaries is the small, serene Grand Portage community, which includes residential, commercial, and institutional buildings. Close to the settlement is the Grand Portage National Monument, one of Minnesota's most important cultural properties. The Grand Portage National Monument recognizes and celebrates the site's importance, from 1730 to 1805, as a varied "emporium of goods and cultures" and what some have termed the "single most important fur trade location in the world."[330] Operated jointly by the Grand Portage Band and NPS, the entire Grand Portage National Monument property is accessible to the public, as are all the commercial and recreational properties that lie outside its boundaries. Nonnatives, however, must treat the Anishinaabe's residential, religious, and protected properties with respect and deference and visit those places only after receiving permission to do so. Most of the ensuing discussion is limited to sites that are open to the general public.

Grand Portage also has a "lasting relationship" with Isle Royale (Minong), which is situated thirty-five miles to the east in Lake Superior and where a human presence has been apparent for as many as forty-five hundred years. The strong ties between Isle Royale (a national park since 1940) and Grand Portage received recognition in 2019 when the Minong Traditional Cultural Property was listed in the National Register of Historic Places.[331]

The first population census for Grand Portage, conducted by an AFC trader in 1825, counted sixty-nine Anishinaabe residents. The 1920 U.S. Census listed 187 people, split almost equally between ninety-four Anishinaabe and ninety-three non-Anishinaabe inhabitants; the latter group included thirty-three immigrants—sixteen Canadians, eleven Swedes and Norwegians, and six representatives of four other groups. By 2020, when the total count reached 618, the U.S. Census Bureau listed 390 as American Indian (Anishinaabe) residents and another 71 as having mixed parentage; altogether, these 461 residents constituted three-fourths of the entire population. Grand Portage also has the highest proportion of year-round, owner-occupied housing units in Cook County: 294 of its 353 dwellings (86 percent) were inhabited throughout 2020. And, unlike many other Indian reservations in the United States, Grand Portage has relatively few nonnative properties within its boundaries.[332]

As discussed earlier, the development of Minnesota's North Shore highway was fraught with numerous problems. No section of Highway 61, however, generated greater controversy than the segment that passes through the Grand Portage Indian Reservation. Indeed, most of the current route was not completed until the early 1960s, and only after some three decades of often rancorous debate occurred in Grand Portage, Grand Marais, St. Paul, and Washington, D.C. The deliberations began in 1933, when MDH officials announced their intentions to reroute the final section of Highway 61, which, at that time, turned northward at the Reservation River and passed through Mineral Center before crossing into Canada over the Pigeon River bridge at Sextus City. The MDH proposal called for a new highway that would follow Lake Superior's shoreline from the Reservation River to the Grand Portage settlement and culminate at a new Pigeon River bridge located close to High Falls—the North Shore's highest waterfall. The proposal, MDH officials insisted, had received the "enthusiastic approval of the people of the state, the Indians, and the Canadian government."[333]

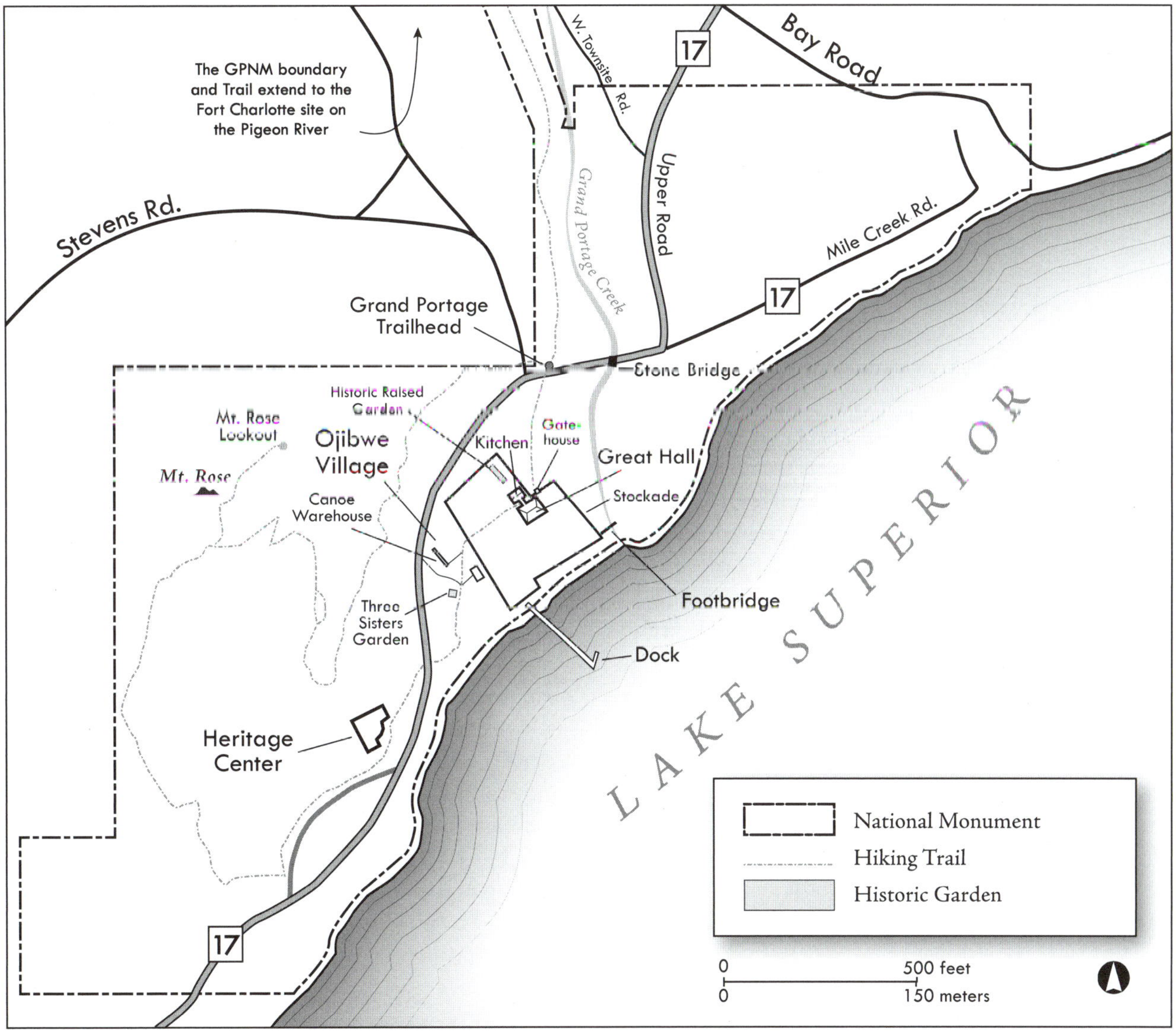

The GPNM boundary and Trail extend to the Fort Charlotte site on the Pigeon River
Stevens Rd.
W. Townsite Rd.
17
Bay Road
Upper Road
Grand Portage Creek
Mile Creek Rd.
Grand Portage Trailhead
Stone Bridge
Historic Raised Garden
Mt. Rose Lookout
Mt. Rose
Ojibwe Village
Kitchen
Gate-house
Great Hall
Stockade
Canoe Warehouse
Three Sisters Garden
Footbridge
Dock
Heritage Center
LAKE SUPERIOR
National Monument
Hiking Trail
Historic Garden
0 500 feet
0 150 meters

Nevertheless, Harold L. Ickes, U.S. secretary of the interior from 1933 to 1946, quickly vetoed the plan, basing his decision on opposition from the NPS, the Izaak Walton League, and especially the Quetico–Superior Committee, whose board members argued that the right-of-way "would violate the undisturbed wilderness area along the shore and lead to the eventual destruction of wild game and timber in the area." The State of Minnesota attempted to overturn Ickes's ruling by taking its case to the U.S. Supreme Court in 1938, but the request was turned down for jurisdictional reasons. The petition, two years later, was submitted to the U.S. Court of Appeals, which gave the state an affirmative ruling. Ickes countered this decision by urging the U.S. Department of the Interior to buy back those lands the Anishinaabe had lost. Because these properties would then revert to tribal ownership, they could not be condemned for highway-building purposes without Anishinaabe approval. Intensive legal wrangling occurred thereafter, but the disagreements were finally resolved in favor of a new road in 1943. The project, nevertheless, was postponed once again, this time to 1958, when preliminary survey work and highway construction activities were initiated. Official dedication of the completed highway, along with a new international border station and Pigeon River bridge, occurred in 1966. Fortunately, the delay provided time to reconsider and modify two of the original plan's most controversial proposals: the highway, rather than passing through the Grand Portage settlement, was rerouted north of the community, and the new Pigeon River bridge emerged about a quarter mile downriver from High Falls.[334]

The ensuing narrative begins by providing an overview of three sites—two located by the southwestern entrance to the Reservation, the other at Hollow Rock, situated several miles farther northeast. Following this, the majority of the discussion moves to the Grand Portage settlement, and its early years as an Anishinaabe enclave and fur trade outpost. Attention is then given to the period from the 1920s to the present, which includes the establishment of Grand Portage National Monument, and the development of a mutual park management plan undertaken jointly by the Grand Portage Tribe and NPS. The volume concludes with an overview of several properties and sites located between the Grand Portage settlement and international border.

### Reservation River Lodge (*now* Trovalls Lakeshore Village Subdivision, *private residences*)
Highway 61 and Trolls Trail

The original road that entered the western section of the Grand Portage Indian Reservation and a nearby bridge that passed over the Reservation River were built proximate to Lake Superior in 1917. A new bridge and short section of Highway 61, both constructed slightly inland from the shoreline in 1937, were soon followed by the opening of a nearby non-Anishinaabe business, the Reservation River Lodge. The lodge, located close to the relocated highway, included a store, a diner, a bar, and a few second-story tourist rooms; several cabins were also situated along Lake Superior. The lodge was purchased, in 1946, by Arvid and Alma Taylor Nygren of Minneapolis. The ambitious Nygrens, respectively sixty-one and fifty-seven years of age at the time, were soon advertising the attractions of their business—lodge rooms furnished with hot water and bathrooms, home-cooked meals, heated shoreline housekeeping cabins, a "full line" of guns and fishing tackle, and opportunities for both "deep-sea" and stream fishing. Nygren, a Swedish immigrant, also served as a Cook County commissioner for ten years. At the time of Nygren's passing, in 1963—one year after the sale of the business—a local newspaper reporter expressed admiration for the many improvements the lodge owner and his wife had so quickly made to their holding. Ensuing purchasers operated a campground on the site before it was acquired, in 1977, by Gary and Shirley Trovall. They sold the lodge building in the early 2000s and converted the acreage into Trovalls Lakeshore Village, a small subdivision that now includes several private residences and landholdings.[335]

### Mary and Paul La Plante Reservation River Allotment *(vacant)*

Among the Anishinaabe residents of Grand Portage who received an 1897 federal land allotment was Mary Mashkigwatig, who had married a French Canadian, Paul La Plante, in 1873. Their eighty-acre tract, located about a mile inland from the Reservation River's mouth, was the first of several sites the La Plante children and other family members acquired; by 1919, they would own more than six hundred acres of land throughout the area. To support his family, La Plante pursued a variety of jobs, including one winter spent delivering mail by dogsled over a frozen Lake Superior to Isle Royale's isolated mining enclaves. Also a carpenter, La Plante is best known for his boatbuilding skills; one of La Plante's boats, a modified Mackinaw named the *Isle*, is stored in Tofte's North Shore Commercial Fishing Museum.[336]

### John and Laura Johns Jr. Summer Residence and John and Sarah Hendricks Cabins (*now* Hollow Rock Resort)

### 7422 East Highway 61

The entrance to Hollow Rock occurs 6.5 miles northeast of the Reservation River. The name refers to an opening at the rocky base of a tiny island that has space, during periods of sufficient water, for the passage of a kayak or canoe. The craggy feature is unique to the North Shore because it was not formed by the flowing current of a river or stream. Instead, as geologist John Green explains, Hollow Rock is "a piece of old lava flow that has been separated from the mainland outcrops or bedrock by wave erosion over thousands of years." Because the lava had several fractures, Lake Superior's waves were able to "pluck out rock blocks from either side until there was a passage."[337]

Now overlooking the site is Hollow Rock Resort, currently owned by the Grand Portage Band. The initial business was established during the early 1950s on land that John F. Johns Jr. had acquired almost a half century earlier. Born in 1868, Johns was the son of Cornish parents who married Laura in 1862, shortly after both emigrated separately from England to Michigan's Copper Country. The family, in 1878, moved to Isle Royale, where the senior Johns worked at two mines, the Wendigo and Minong, before he and two of his sons developed Isle Royale's first tourist hotel in 1892; they would later establish homesteads on some of Isle Royale's small islands.[338]

The oldest son, John Johns Jr., a skilled mariner and licensed first-class Great Lakes boat pilot, married Laura Rose of Ontario in 1898. The couple resided in Duluth throughout most of their wedded life but spent summertime interludes at Hollow Rock, which they acquired during the early twentieth century. In April 1940, two years after Johns's death, a U.S. Census enumerator reported that his widow and their daughter Winnifred were engaged in fishing at Hollow Rock; also living with them was Laura Johns's nephew, John Hendricks, a fisherman who joined the U.S. Navy in September 1940. Four years later, while on military duty in England, Hendricks married Sarah Philbin of County Mayo, Ireland. Following the war's end, in 1945, the couple settled at Hollow Rock, where Hendricks once again pursued commercial fishing and operated a charter boat service.[339]

After purchasing the property outright in 1953, the Hendrickses built five tourist cabins along the shoreline and developed a campground for recreational vehicles. Many of their patrons were either waiting for or returning on boats that ferried passengers between Grand Portage and Isle Royale. Until the current North Shore highway route was completed in 1964, however, any driver who entered the Grand Portage Indian Reservation from the southwest could reach Hollow Rock only by following a circuitous fifteen-mile-long journey. Upon reaching the Reservation River, motorists turned toward the northeast and drove to Mineral Center, whereupon they headed eastward for several miles, then proceeded southward to Lake Superior and the Hendrickses' resort. Also situated at the Hollow Rock terminus were as many as five other residences and fishing camps and a "very primitive road" that culminated at Red Rock, where artist George Morrison maintained his home and studio from the mid-1970s to 1990.[340]

Although Sarah Hendricks died in a tragic 1969 automobile accident, her widowed husband continued running the resort until his passing in 1987. Hollow Rock was subsequently operated by two other owners, both of whom maintained the resort's mom-and-pop character into the early 2000s, when the twelve-acre property was acquired by the Grand Portage Band. Two new cabins appeared in 2010–11, and the existing units were rebuilt, refurbished, winterized, sheathed with log siding, and topped with metal roofs. Management of all seven Hollow Rock cabins (named Bear, Crane, Eagle, Fish, Loon, Marten, and Moose) occurs off-site at the Grand Portage Lodge and Casino.[341]

## The "Great Carrying Place": Early Anishinaabe and European Interactions at Grand Portage

About seventeen miles northeast of the Reservation River is the Pigeon River, which simultaneously serves as a boundary between Minnesota and Ontario and between the United States and Canada. Although some twenty-two miles of the river are unnavigable because of waterfalls, gorges, cascades, and rapids, Indigenous people were able to bypass the barrier thousands of years ago by following a dry preglacial valley—which served as the only natural route between the Pigeon River and Lake Superior. Called Kitchi-onigamiing by the Anishinaabe, the narrow footpath, 8.5 miles in length, provided access to the "seemingly endless waterways of interior North America."[342]

In 1729, Pierre Gaultier de Varennes, Sieur et de la Vérendrye, who oversaw France's fur trade empire in the Lake Superior region, reportedly received a map from an Indigenous guide who was very sympathetic to France. The map depicted Kitchi-onigamiing, which the French named Le Grand Portage—the "Great Carrying Place." Their fur-trade activities, established at Grand Portage a few years after La Vérendrye's 1731 exploration and reconnaissance of the site, peaked between 1740 and 1745. French Canadian voyageurs performed the essential work of transporting the furs, which were supplied by different North American Indian groups. These remarkable journeys, conducted over a challenging portage that still has some of the roughest and heavily wooded topography in present-day Minnesota, were possible only because the Anishinaabe taught the voyageurs how to build and repair their "North" canoes, made of lightweight birchbark. After reaching Grand Portage Bay, the voyageurs transferred their bounty of furs into larger and sturdier "Montreal" canoes, which could carry three tons of cargo, plus the crew. (Schooners were sometimes used for part of the journey.) Their destination was Montreal, where the major fur warehouses and distribution center were situated. Limited archaeological remnants of "post in ground" *(in pile)* structures that have been found at two sites very likely date to the period of French occupancy.[343]

The defeat suffered by France in the French and Indian War (1754–63) resulted in British domination of the fur trade. A group of investors, many of them Scottish, established an independent fur company in 1768—eleven years before the North West Company (NWC) was formed. NWC financed the construction of a fort and trading post that would become a major station or depot during the ensuing decade. The depot quickly demonstrated "all the marks of permanence: a major complex of buildings, year-round employment, [and] an Indian village." The fort had three gates, two with guardhouses, wrote George Heriot, a nineteenth-century deputy postmaster, and included storehouses and dwellings, along with a large open space or "yard," where as many as seventy canoes could be built each year. A garden provided vegetables, primarily potatoes, for the inhabitants; also on the site were some cattle, sheep, and pigs. Located at the upper end of the portage and 8.5 miles from the depot was Fort Charlotte, described as "a stockaded quadrangle, with stores and buildings within it," which included living quarters, warehouses, and a canoe yard. The journey from Fort Charlotte to Lake Superior was an arduous trek for NWC voyageurs, because each man typically carried two packs that weighed a total of 180 pounds.[344]

The American Revolution brought significant changes to Grand Portage. By 1802, many NWC structures had been moved, piece by piece, to an outpost at Fort William, Ontario. The AFC, formed by John Jacob Astor in 1808, eventually assumed control of Grand Portage, but its importance as a fur trade center soon faded; the old depot, by 1822, was deemed an "archaeological ruin." In 1834, Ramsay Crooks, Astor's one-time general manager, reorganized the company as a fishing station, which may have been located along the lakefront just above the Grand Portage Creek outlet. When these activities ended eight years later, the North Shore Anishinaabe faced a difficult economic situation.[345]

Soon after enactment of the 1854 Treaty of La Pointe, the scattered clans at Grand Portage came together to form a single Anishinaabe community or reservation. There, American authorities predicted, the Anishinaabe would break "from their past, live in one place, and become like whites." Early attempts to "civilize" the Anishinaabe envisioned them as farmers, even though Grand Portage is one of the most agriculturally intractable districts in Minnesota. Between 1859 and 1878, the area of land under cultivation expanded from just twelve acres to no more than twenty. Many years later, Anishinaabe elder Ellen Olson would describe Grand Portage as "a pile of rock . . . and trees and a lot of water, but not much else to make a living with. It's a hard place to live." The harvesting of red and white pine that began on the reservation in 1901 provided short-term employment for some men, but these activities ended within relatively few years.[346] Fishing would remain a constant presence in the local economy over a significantly longer period of time.

## Past and Present in the Cultural Landscape

A blending of past and present characterizes all North Shore cultural landscapes. Nowhere, however, does the "long tradition of overlapping historical themes and use patterns" that are imbedded within the cultural landscape resonate more meaningfully and deeply than at Grand Portage. Among its sites are three notable properties that have been identified for their lengthy history of cultural coalescence—the Grand Portage Trail, the Grand Portage settlement, and the Great Hall/Stockade that was reconstructed during the 1930s and thereafter.[347]

Anishinaabe perceptions of the "boundaries" associated with these cultural landscapes typically differ, often considerably, from the concrete and fixed conceptions of Euro-Americans. The boundaries of the Anishinaabe cultural landscape are best understood in ethnographic terms—places that "mirror the systems of meanings, ideologies, beliefs, values, and world views shared by a group of people." Some notable examples include the ridgeline that exists northeast of the old Anishinaabe village site; the southwestern face of Mount Rose (a notable promontory); Grand Portage Bay; and several features that lie outside the national monument's boundaries, including Mount Josephine, Hat Point, and the Susie Islands.[348]

## Documenting, Preserving, and Reconstructing the Past: The Minnesota Historical Society and Civilian Conservation Corps, 1922–1942

Organized efforts to preserve and manage the irreplaceable resources at Grand Portage date to the early twentieth century, when reservation residents expressed grave concerns over the encroachment of non-Indians on their land. Concurrently, a teacher at the Grand Portage Indian School observed that evidence of the early fur trade was under threat because of "erosion and development." MHS officials, who were alarmed over the loss of historic resources at Grand Portage, conducted the organization's 1922 annual meeting in Duluth (the first time outside the Twin Cities) by featuring the Great Northwest Fur Trade. During that year, a small group of artists and Anishinaabe residents were also commissioned to survey selected sites within the reservation. Among them was Twin Cities artist Dewey Albinson, described as "a Jack Londonesque romantic with a cynical view of human nature," who had recently arrived at Grand Portage in search of adventure and painting opportunities. While fulfilling his MHS duties, Albinson inspected, mapped, and photographed several locations but gave most attention to the portage trail. Although some sections were covered with fallen trees, Albinson reported that "the old heavily trodden earth was so like a cushion that a blind man could follow it."[349]

MHS officials, in 1931, organized an event that commemorated the two-hundredth anniversary of La Vérendrye's arrival at Grand Portage Bay. The organizers reported that the scene observed by attendees on a beautiful August Sunday was remarkably similar to the "little Indian village, where traders and voyageurs foregathered in the gala days of the eighteenth-century fur trade." One striking difference was evident, of course—the presence of several hundred automobiles and nearly a thousand people, among them many Canadians, who filled the grounds. After raising $2,500 in contributions for the event, the organizers used some of the proceeds to move a log cabin, built by Sam Crawford around 1895, onto the site and convert it into a museum operated by the CCHS. (The cabin would be transported once again, this time to Mineral Center during the 1960s, after historians determined that it had no direct relationship with the fur trade.) Also playing a large role in the activities was Frances Elizabeth Andrews, a Minneapolis resident and philanthropist who, during her younger years, had spent summers at the family's Isle Royale cabin. A proponent of educational and social justice issues, Andrews is best known for working alongside Ernest Oberholtzer, Sigurd Olson, and other noted environmentalists of the era to preserve what is now Minnesota's BWCAW. Andrews informed the Grand Portage attendees that she had contributed funds to reconstruct a nearby dock, which would recognize La Vérendrye's arrival at the site in 1731 and also honor her late brother, William. The new dock's cribwork was constructed of logs cut from Anishinaabe land, while the deck planks were fabricated out of twenty-five hundred feet of lumber salvaged from the recently dismantled Outlaw Bridge at Sextus City.[350]

The Great Depression of the 1930s brought considerable duress to Grand Portage. Among the governmental agencies that sought to alleviate some of the hardship was the Civilian Conservation Corps–Indian Division (CCC-ID), which organized two separate camps on the reservation: the first existed only for a few months in 1933, while the second spanned the years from 1936 to 1942. The physical improvements and construction projects undertaken by the 150 or so young men who participated in these efforts stand out as the most visible legacy of the CCC-ID at Grand Portage. Initially, however, CCC-ID officials promoted the camps because of the significant assistance they would bring to the local economy. Indeed, a 1933 agency report concluded that the impoverished conditions experienced by Grand Portage residents were "due to the present price of fish, the source of their main income, being only 1 cent a pound with a very limited demand." The first CCC-ID project occurred when a group of enrollees worked, from June to November 1933, in clearing the Grand Portage Trail; most of their labor, however, was not undertaken to improve access but primarily to reduce the danger of fires.[351]

**A group of young men from CCC-ID Camp S-62 pose after completing their first day of work at Grand Portage on 7 September 1936. Courtesy of Minnesota Historical Society.**

The Grand Portage settlement, early 1930s, a few years before the village was reestablished farther inland. In the background is Hat Point. Photograph by Ernest Oberholtzer. Courtesy of the Ernest Oberholtzer Foundation, Ranier, Minnesota.

In 1936, a second, larger group of Anishinaabe enrollees was brought together to form Grand Portage CCC-ID Camp S-62. This action was indirectly linked to the Indian Reorganization Act of 1934 (also known as the Wheeler–Howard Act), which "aimed at decreasing federal control of American Indian affairs and increasing Indian self-government and responsibility." The act permitted the state's Anishinaabe bands to create the Minnesota Chippewa Tribe: six of the state's seven reservations, including the Grand Portage Band, soon joined the organization. The Grand Portage Reservation Tribal Council (later the Reservation Business Committee), also formed at this time, handled all issues not of concern to any other reservation. Among their earliest actions was the repurchase of some private land tracts that had been lost during previous decades.[352]

Camp S-62's enrollees were housed in eleven buildings that emerged on 2.5 acres of land in 1936. The camp, at maximum, accommodated seventy-five young men; another twenty-five lived in their own homes. (Most, by far, were Grand Portage residents, but a small number came from five other Anishinaabe reservations in Minnesota.) The enrollees eagerly participated in organized sports activities and quickly demonstrated their athletic prowess: Camp S-62 won the 1936 North Shore champion trophies for both basketball and baseball; the basketball team repeated this feat in 1937 and also received the CCC-ID's Superb Sportsmanship trophy. Although the camp buildings closed in 1938 because of funding shortfalls, many enrollees were able to live at home and continue working; those young men who came from other reservations were transferred to the Nett Lake CCC-ID Camp in Koochiching County.[353]

The largest project undertaken by Camp S-62's enrollees occurred from 1936 to 1940—excavation of NWC's eighteenth-century depot and reconstruction of its Great Hall, its stockade, three watchtowers, and an entrance gate. Other CCC-ID structures were built elsewhere, including a stone bridge, a schoolhouse constructed of logs shipped from Oregon, a cobblestone ranger station, a lookout tower, and a small monument that marked the location of Fort Charlotte and the Grand Portage Trail terminus. The young men also worked on foot trails, roads, telephone lines, and picnic grounds; planted wild rice in a lake; and removed trees affected by white pine blister rust.[354]

One CCC-ID activity undertaken by Camp S-62's members, nonetheless, met with mixed reactions—a project intended to rehabilitate the former "primitive setting" of Grand Portage by "clearing out the worst of the old buildings which cluttered up the main village area adjacent to the waterfront." The former lakeside "row of whitewashed log cabins" that Dewey Albinson described in 1922 would be replaced, in 1939–40, by wooden-frame dwellings oriented to the road pattern. The new village center, including a school and community building, was constructed on a ridge that overlooked the former settlement and Lake Superior.[355]

**Sisters Christine, Louise, and Lucy Flatte display their weavings and birchbark baskets at Grand Portage in 1936. The sisters were the daughters of Mike Flatte, a hereditary leader of the Grand Portage Band. Photograph by William E. Roleff. Courtesy of Minnesota Historical Society.**

**A 1937 WPA exhibit at Grand Portage included several Anishinaabe handmade items, ranging from baskets, weavings, and snowshoes to a drum, a canoe, and a paddle.**

### North West Company Depot (*razed, now* Grand Portage National Monument)

East of Grand Portage Visitor Center and Museum

The Civilian Conservation Corps, in early 1936, authorized the expenditure of $6,200 to reconstruct a section of the former NWC depot at Grand Portage. MHS officials, however, demanded that an archaeological investigation occur at the site before any construction work could begin. Those efforts, overseen in 1936–37 by MHS archaeologist Ralph Brown and undertaken by members of his staff and CCC-ID enrollees, represented the first thorough investigation of the site and revealed the outline of the Great Hall, dating to the 1770s, along with the remnants of as many as thirteen other buildings and hundreds of artifacts. The excavations were followed, over the next two years, by reconstruction of the Great Hall and some of its associated structures. A small museum located within the Great Hall displayed handcrafted items produced by local Anishinaabe residents, many of them women who had joined the Works Progress Administration (WPA). Although the reconstructed NWC site, when completed, was regarded as one of Minnesota's primary CCC projects, the results were less than adequate, noted an archaeologist familiar with the project, primarily because the work had been performed without sufficient time or monetary resources.[356]

Once the United States entered World War II in late 1941, the Grand Portage site would be "literally abandoned and neglected" for most of the decade. The only work occurred in 1946 , when Anishinaabe workers and Boy Scouts from Duluth and Ontario cleared much of the portage trail of brush and small trees. The decade concluded with a two-day event in July 1949, held outside the Great Hall, which marked the centenary anniversary of Minnesota's designation as a U.S. territory. The celebration's pageant script included Anishinaabe, voyageur, and pioneer reenactors as well as six contemporary "princesses," among them Miss Minnesota and Miss Ontario, who arrived in "three beautiful convertible-top cars."[357]

The official 1951 designation of Grand Portage as a National Historic Site, sponsored in the U.S. Congress by Minnesota's U.S. senator Hubert H. Humphrey, brought significant national attention to the property. The August festival that celebrated this

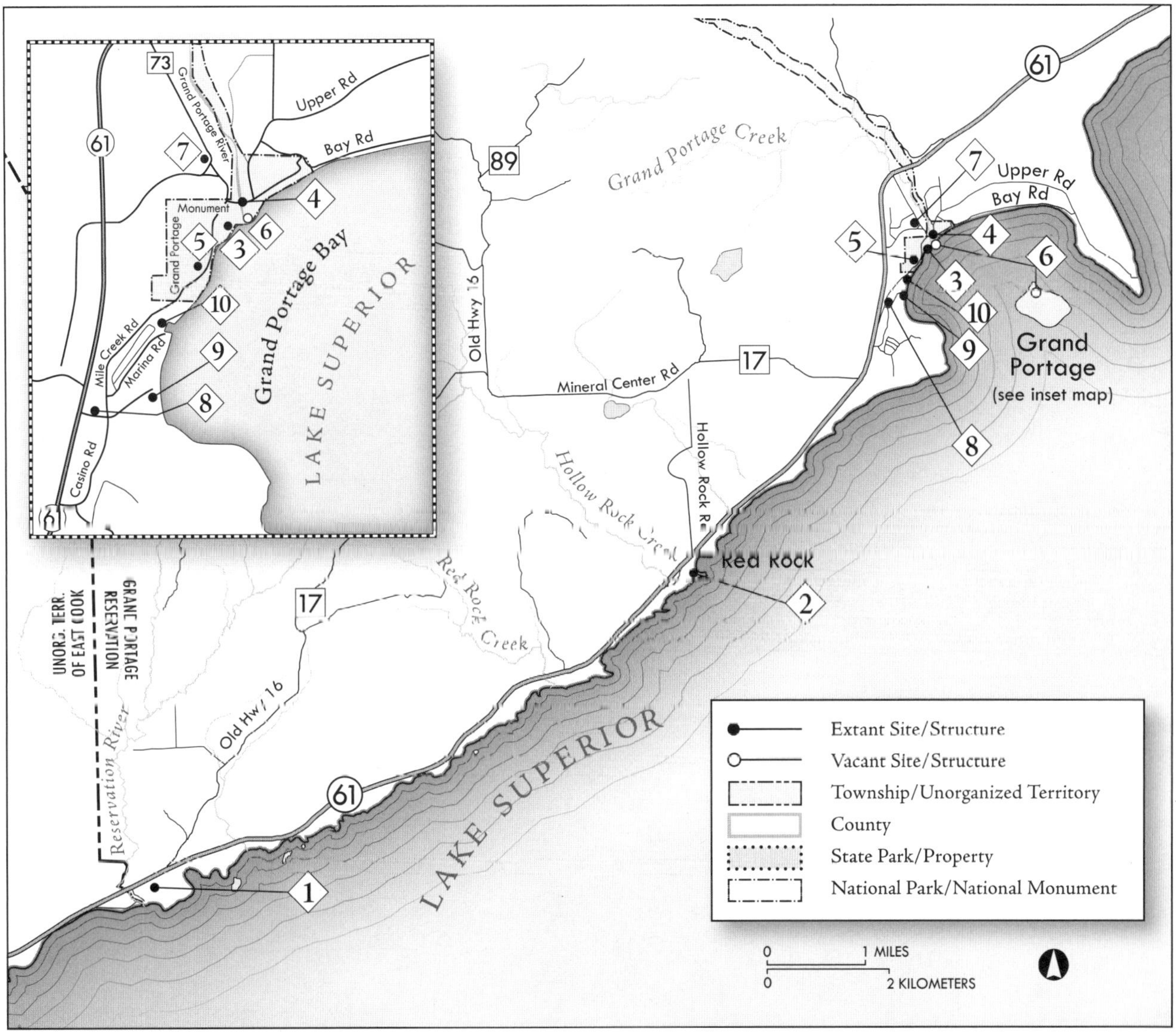


1. Reservation River Lodge*
2. Hollow Rock Resort
3. Grand Portage National Monument
4. Grand Portage Creek Stone Bridge
5. Grand Portage National Monument Heritage Center
6. Peter Gagnon Trading Post and Residences
7. Grand Portage Ambulance and Fire Station
8. Grand Portage Trading Post
9. Grand Portage Lodge and Casino
10. Hat Point Marina

*Now a private residence

The celebration of Minnesota's Territorial Centennial, held at the base of Mount Rose in July 1949, included a pageant with performances that occurred proximate to three Anishinaabe tepees.

The Grand Portage dock was rebuilt just outside the stockade in 1931. Shown here during the early 1950s, the dock has been subsequently reconstructed and repaired several times.

The August 1951 dedication of the Grand Portage National Historic Site was attended by several dignitaries and a large audience of observers. Here the attendees are gathering before they move to the viewing stand. Courtesy of Minnesota Historical Society.

action was highlighted by President Harry S. Truman's message, which conservationist Sigurd Olson read to the audience. The event concluded with the singing of "America" and "God Save the King" (Canada's national anthem at that time), accompanied by Grand Marais's high school band. Despite this recognition, a 1955–56 NPS assessment of the reconstructed site offered a stark description of its overall condition. "Sections of the palisade were falling over," reported the evaluation. "Many post butts were rotted from standing in water-filled trenches. The Great Hall weather-beaten and neglected. The exhibits were deteriorating because those . . . not enclosed in glass cases were handled indiscriminately by visitors."[358]

Grand Portage leaders, after seeing just how little funding was provided by National Historic Site designation, soon determined, albeit reluctantly, that further development would require surrendering ownership of the site to the federal government—"a rare occurrence" for any tribal organization. Additional discussions eventually led to the creation of the Grand Portage National Monument, which received U.S. congressional approval in 1960. The legislation provided funds for further archaeological work and a number of improvements that were carried out during the decade's early years.[359]

The Grand Portage National Monument legislation was considered quite uncommon at the time, given that Grand Portage Band members were granted several rights typically not offered at other NPS sites. They were able to develop and provide services and accommodations for visitors, to produce and market their products and merchandise on the Grand Portage National Monument property, and to receive preference when filling positions for construction and maintenance operations. Indeed, the Grand Portage Band for the past quarter century has been responsible for filling all such openings.[360]

A bolt of lightning completely destroyed the reconstructed Great Hall and its priceless collection of cultural artifacts in July 1969; the gatehouse, although charred, was saved. The fire, nonetheless, did provide archaeologists with opportunities to conduct more rigorous excavations on the burned-over site and to resolve several questions about inaccuracies that had occurred when the Great Hall was rebuilt in 1938–40. When the excavations revealed that a porch and kitchen originally joined the Great Hall, the "pronounced emphasis on authenticity" resulted in the reconstruction of both structures. The success of this endeavor, undertaken from 1971 to 1973, was noted by Grand Portage National Monument superintendent Richard Tousley, who lauded the Anishinaabe carpenters for their "quiet pride" in reconstructing the thirty-by-ninety-five-foot Great Hall, which employed the French *poteaux sur sole* (post-on-sill) style of building. Its hand-hewn logs, hip roof, and two fieldstone chimneys required significant expertise and perseverance, observed the superintendent. When the interior was supplied with appropriate eighteenth-century furnishings, NPS rangers were once again able to tell the "compelling stories of Grand Portage."[361]

Grand Portage National Monument now comprises 710 acres of land and water. The vast majority of visitors focus on the structures, features, and activities located along or close to Grand Portage Bay, while a smaller number follow the trails, including the historic pathway that terminates at the long-abandoned Fort Charlotte site. The Grand Portage National Monument complex, comprising entirely reconstructed structures, is immediately identifiable by its perimeter wall, which provides an impression of what the British sought when they built the stockade during the 1740s: defense and security were paramount, of course, but the wall also served as a "social barrier, animal enclosure, windbreak, and symbol of power and resolve."[362] After passing through the gatehouse and entering the enclosed space, one immediately sees the Great Hall and its large kitchen, joined by a covered walkway. A fire-watch tower stands nearby, while a Quebec-style bake oven flanks one of the kitchen's exterior walls; also evident is a fur trade–era kitchen garden, planted on two raised beds.

**Among the irreplaceable objects destroyed by the 1969 lightning strike that burned down the Great Hall was this Anishinaabe canoe.**

**The Great Hall, *right*, and its attached kitchen were reconstructed during the early 1970s.**

Just outside the stockade's western wall is a nineteen-by-fifty-two-foot warehouse with a collection of birchbark canoes. (The original foundation for this structure was found during a 1964–65 excavation.) South of the warehouse is a re-created Anishinaabe village (Anishinaabeg Odéna), with wigwams, conical lodges, and work shelters. Nearby is the Three Sisters Garden, a traditional planting style pursued by Native Americans that includes a trio of vegetables: corn, beans, and squash.[363] A voyageur encampment is also located in the vicinity.

North of the stockade is a trail that leads to Mount Rose, which ascends some 305 feet above Lake Superior. Outside the stockade's southern wall is a wooden dock that juts into Grand Portage Bay. In 1931, when Frances Andrews provided funds to replace the original structure, it was believed the remnant pilings were part of a NWC dock dating to the 1780s. Although fragments of flintlock weapons, blacksmithing and shipbuilding tools, kettles, and other items were later found at the site, the bay would have been too shallow for large supply vessels. The pilings, therefore, likely were part of small dock built later by the AFC or BIA. Although a severe storm destroyed the reconstructed dock in 1951, it was quickly repaired; major reconstruction and rebuilding efforts were also undertaken during the mid-1970s and in 2010. Now 271 feet long and 13 feet wide, with an "ell" or perpendicular extension that is 35 feet long, the dock was used, until 2006, by the *Wenonah*, one of the boats that ferries passengers to and from Isle Royale. Because of problems posed by the bay's shallow water and exposure to southeasterly winds, all commercial vessels that serve Isle Royale now use the Hat Point Marina. (The former vehicle parking lot, used by the ferry's passengers, was needed for the new Heritage Center.) Some private boaters also anchor their vessels at the stockade dock for brief periods of time.[364]

### Grand Portage Creek Stone Bridge
Mile Creek Road and Grand Portage Creek

Mile Creek Road crosses over Grand Portage Creek on a small stone-covered bridge, built between 1938 and 1940. The significance of the span was acknowledged by Minnesota's SHPO in 1996 and received national recognition in 2016 when the *Historic American Engineering Record* termed it a "representative example of the rustic aesthetic" that exemplified the best CCC and NPS design work of the late 1930s. (The name has also been adopted by the Stone Bridge Singers Drum Group, an ensemble of young men from the Grand Portage area who began performing at powwows and other events around 2007.) Built of multiplate steel arches and faced with finely cut, dressed stone, the bridge, twenty-eight feet wide and fifty feet long, displays "heavy massing, use of local materials, and a design intended to harmonize with the natural surroundings." It may, in fact, be the only remaining CCC-ID stone bridge in Minnesota. The 2016 survey also called attention to the stone arches and parapets (the retaining walls above the deck), which were showing signs of significant deterioration. The bridge was restored, two years later, with input from the Duluth-based Northern Bedrock Historic Preservation Corps, along with the recently formed Grand Portage Preservation Crew and specialists from the NPS Historic Preservation Training Center in Frederick, Maryland. Rededicated in 2018 at the annual Rendezvous Days and Pow Wow held in Grand Portage, the bridge remains "a highly significant landmark within the community, serving as not only a vital transportation link but also as a cultural symbol." And, of course, it stands as a testament to the construction skills and abilities of the young men who served with the CCC-ID many decades ago.[365]

### Grand Portage National Monument Heritage Center
170 Mile Creek Road

When the Grand Portage Band donated land to establish a national monument in 1958, it was with the understanding that a visitor center and museum would soon be built "to revitalize the reservation's struggling economy and bring jobs to Grand Portage." The visitor center and employment opportunities failed to materialize until 1999, when a "precedent setting" form of park management emerged, thanks to the collaborative efforts of Grand Portage National Monument superintendent Timothy Cochrane and the late, longtime Tribal Council chairman Norman Deschampe. By utilizing the Tribal Self-Governance Act of 1994, the two men developed a park management plan that would provide opportunities "to capitalize on mutually beneficial purposes."[366]

The agreement immediately gave the Grand Portage

**The stone bridge that crosses Grand Portage Creek, shown here shortly after its 2018 restoration, is an outstanding example of a late 1930s CCC-ID project. The historic span, following the recent completion of a road realignment and the construction of a new vehicle bridge, is now limited to pedestrians.**

Band authority to hire maintenance staff, most of them tribal members. Since then, numerous interpretative and resource management positions have been filled by the band, among them the Grand Portage Conservation Crew, which employs local youths who work on natural and cultural resource projects throughout the Grand Portage National Monument, the entire reservation, and Isle Royale National Park. But the most visible result of the collaborative effort is the Grand Portage National Monument Heritage Center that opened in 2007. The $5 million structure, situated on a hill just west of the reconstructed fur trade–era depot, is separated from the Grand Portage National Monument complex by a buffer of trees and vegetation. Supporting the Heritage Center are four large interior pillars (actually steel I-beams covered by large sections of white pine), which represent the four cardinal directions—an essential facet of traditional Anishinaabe culture. Its 16,600 square feet of interior space accommodate numerous well-designed museum exhibits that depict Anishinaabe and fur trade history with images, text, and artifacts. Also within the building are a bookstore, a small theater, and offices for Grand Portage National Monument staff members, who were previously sequestered in various Grand Marais buildings, including the former U.S. Coast Guard station. Enhancing the Heritage Center's spacious lobby is a large mural (eighteen feet long and nine to fifteen feet high), painted in "vivid hues of acrylic" by Anishinaabe Finnish artist Carl Gawboy and completed in 2007. Titled *Rendezvous Kitchi Onigamiing*, the mural depicts the annual Grand Portage rendezvous or gathering that occurred when the Anishinaabe and voyageurs came together to trade furs for goods and supplies. (The Rendezvous Days and Pow Wow are reenacted annually outside the stockade grounds during one weekend in August.) The mural also represents the "mixing and interacting" that distinguish the ongoing relationship between the Grand Portage Band and NPS.[367]

### Peter Gagnon Trading Post and Residences *(razed)*
### Grand Portage Island and Upper Side of the Mill Creek Outlet

The Grand Portage area has been home to numerous trading posts for more than two and a half centuries: the first may have been a year-round British "trading house" that opened in 1768. Among the small posts that emerged thereafter was one established by Quebec native Peter Gagnon, who immigrated to the United States in 1869 and was living on Grand Portage Island (also called Sheep Island) three years later. Gagnon purchased furs from Anishinaabe trappers and ran a fishing station, linked to the Booth Company of Duluth, that employed as many as ten men. People and goods arrived and departed on a long dock that jutted into Lake Superior. After moving to the mainland sometime during the 1920s, Gagnon, then in his seventies, built a new residence and pursued gardening, an activity that spread his fame throughout the area. Identified as the "most pretentious home in Grand Portage," Gagnon's dwelling was valued at $5,000 in the 1930 U.S. Census—the highest monetary figure for any residence in the entire area. Married twice to Grand Portage Indian Reservation women, first to Nanette Maymushkowaush, then to Lucy Spruce, Gagnon died in 1935. Today, the only remaining evidence of his mainland home and property is a chimney and three crabapple trees.[368]

### McLean's Store and Cabins (*razed, now the* Grand Portage Ambulance and Fire Station)
### 105 Store Road

Effie Falconer McLean, a former local schoolteacher, postmistress, entrepreneur, and "great friend" of the Anishinaabe, would later become one of several non-native business owners in Grand Portage. Assisted by her British Canadian husband, John McLean, the couple, in 1935, opened a store where groceries, souvenirs, and Anishinaabe handcrafts were sold. Available for rent, at two dollars a day, were several rustic cabins, all lighted with electricity provided by a generator, heated by wood-burning stoves, and supplied with outdoor privies. McLean's guests could also partake of the "heavy-duty meals" prepared by a former lumber camp cook. Many of their patrons were either going to or returning from the dock at Lucky Star Landing on Hat Point, where motorboats transported them between the mainland and Isle Royale. The McLean property was eventually razed and is now occupied by the Grand Portage Ambulance and Fire Station.[369]

### Grand Portage Trading Post
#### 77 Mill Creek Road

The Grand Portage Trading Post Association opened a cooperative store in 1968, just a few years after Highway 61 entered the settlement. The store manager observed that Grand Portage had supported an array of small trading posts since the eighteenth century, but none had regained the significance of any built during the fur trade's "golden years." It was his hope that the new cooperative store would serve as the foundation for a rebirth of similar activities at northeastern Minnesota's "ancient center of commerce." Although the cooperative was disbanded in 1982, the Reservation Business Committee maintained the outlet until 2004–5, when a substantial building with thirteen thousand square feet of interior space emerged on the site. It now has a grocery and convenience store, a fast-food cafeteria, a bakery, a gift shop, more than forty slot machines, and a post office. Outside are eight gas pumps that provide fuel for residents and visitors, many of them from Canada, and a car wash "with undoubtedly the most scenic view [of any] in the state."[370]

### Grand Portage Lodge and Casino
#### 70 Casino Drive

In 1927, a syndicate of Duluth, Minneapolis, and Chicago investors announced their proposal for the Hotel Voyageur, a white stucco building similar in style to an English manor house, which would overlook Grand Portage Bay. Also planned for the property were cottages and docks, a golf course and bathhouse, and a landing field that could be used by those "taking up the sport of aviation for summer recreation." Adding to the project's overall appeal, claimed the promoters, were the bay's historic colors and atmosphere and the area's former voyageur and fur trade trails, which would be converted into bridle paths. The ambitious proposal was never initiated, a victim of the economic depression that commenced in 1929. Another initiative, this one dating to 1947, was introduced under provisions of the Wheeler–Howard Act of 1934, which allowed tribal groups to pursue projects for their envisioned economic benefits. The plan, for a two-story, $100,000 lodge and hotel constructed of logs and stone, would prove financially successful, argued tribal officials, once the final section of Highway 61 was rerouted through the settlement.[371] This plan also failed to materialize, caused at least in part by a pause in highway construction activities until 1958 with completion in 1963.

The Anishinaabe, during the 1970s, announced their plans for a hotel based on the "ancient Ojibwe custom of hospitality." The Grand Portage Lodge and Conference Center, located below the Trading Post and overlooking Lake Superior, opened in 1975. While the Radisson Hotel Group assisted in early management operations, the band assumed total responsibility in 1980. Located east of the hotel are a marina (41 Marina Road) with thirty boat slips, dating to 1971, and a recreational vehicle park. It was, however, the 1990 opening of a nearby casino, with fifteen thousand square feet of space for "gaming action" and related activities, that brought even greater change to the reservation. Renovated in 2018, the casino now has 425 coinless slot machines; numerous tables for blackjack, three-card poker, and other card games; and space for events and small conferences. Its striking interior, featuring a three-story atrium, "honors the indigenous culture of Grand Portage," while simultaneously offering striking views of Lake Superior and the nearby environment. Not everyone, of course, resident or nonresident, appreciates the presence of a casino in such a historic and culturally rich setting. Nonetheless, the revenues it generates benefit the entire Grand Portage community, observed Grand Portage National Monument superintendent Tim Cochrane in 2009. "The band's economic rise through modest casino profits poised them for greater self-determination in their relationship with federal and state governments."[372]

### Hat Point Marina
#### 402 Upper Road

Directly east of the NWC depot is Hat Point Peninsula. This feature—along with such impressive Lake County sites as Shovel Point, Lafayette Bluff, Silver Creek Cliff, and Palisade Head—is one of the North Shore's most identifiable headlands. The peninsula shelters the eastern side of Grand Portage Bay and offers protection for Grand Portage Island. It also was the site for several early fishing camps and currently serves as a home for the Hat Point Marina, used by ferries that transport passengers between Grand Portage and Isle Royale from May to early autumn.

The proposal for a new terminal to replace the storm-damaged and outdated structure was approved in 2023; the construction project, undertaken and completed one year later, has ferry terminals, seats for two hundred passengers, and many other improvements and features.[373]

### Mount Josephine Wayside Rest Area/ Wayswaugoing Bay Overlook
Milepost 148

The five miles of Highway 61 that connect Grand Portage and the Canadian border are often termed the most scenic segment of the North Shore and even of the entire state. Located along this section of roadway is Mount Josephine, which towers more than 750 feet above Lake Superior. Well-conditioned hikers who reach its summit are able to experience a resplendent view of the scene that stretches below—notably Wayswaugoing Bay, the thirteen Susie Islands (owned and managed as natural areas by the Grand Portage Band), and, in the distant background, Isle Royale. A much more accessible site, dedicated in 1965 as the Mount Josephine Wayside Rest Area, is available to motorists who do not have either the time or the stamina to hike the trail. Construction of the wayside began in 1960, when crews started cutting through 110 feet of rock and 15 feet of overburden to create the feature—Highway 61's "highest stopping point"—situated some 450 feet above Lake Superior. By the early 2000s, however, a major upgrading of the site was necessary because of several safety and accessibility problems. The project, completed in 2012, moved the parking area away from the overlook and replaced it with a walkway and cantilevered observation deck that "magnificently frames the amazing vistas."[374]

**The largest road cut along Highway 61 occurred at Mount Josephine during the early 1960s.**

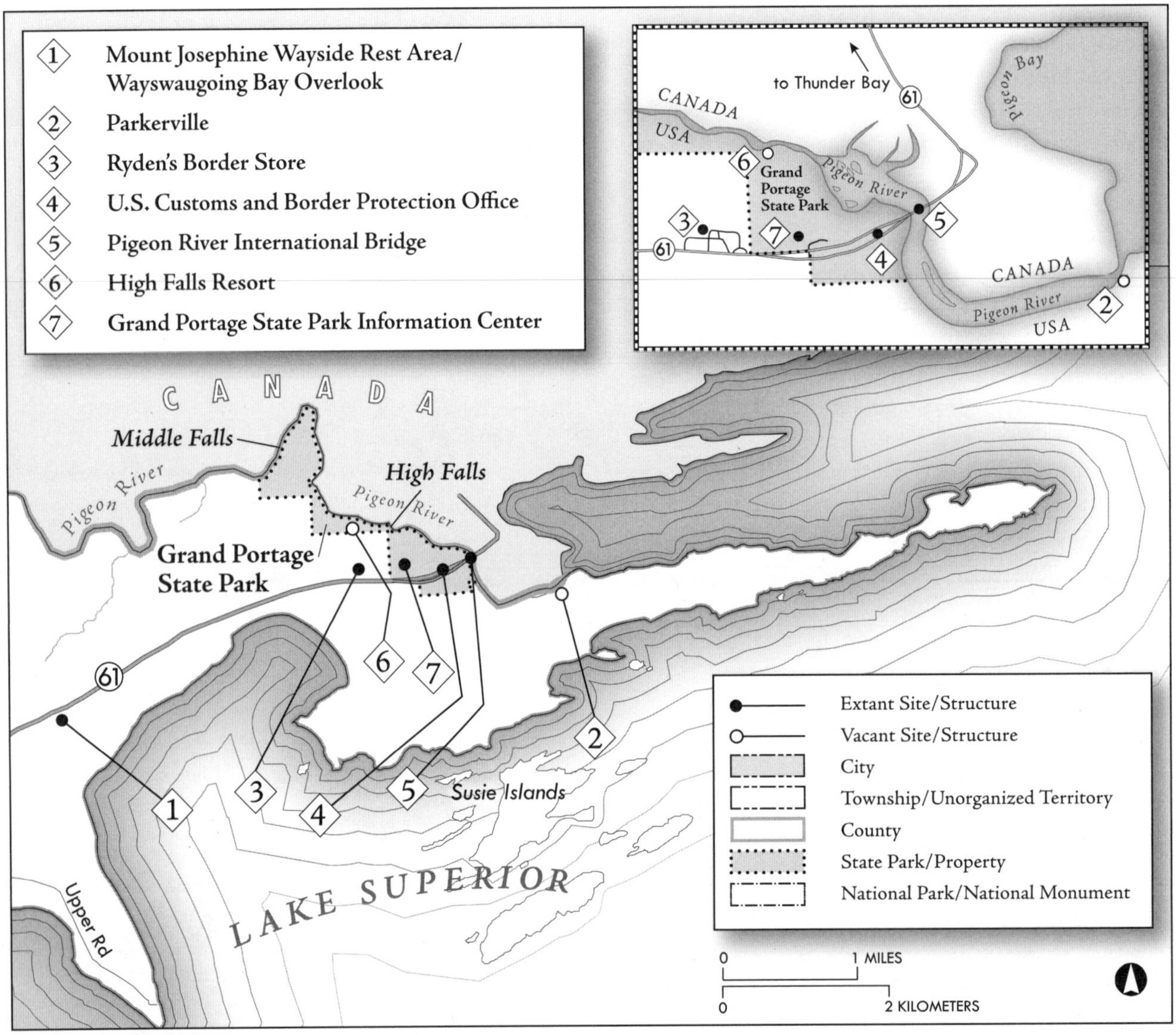

1 Mount Josephine Wayside Rest Area/ Wayswaugoing Bay Overlook
2 Parkerville
3 Ryden's Border Store
4 U.S. Customs and Border Protection Office
5 Pigeon River International Bridge
6 High Falls Resort
7 Grand Portage State Park Information Center
to Thunder Bay
CANADA
USA
Bay
Pigeon
Pigeon River
Grand Portage State Park
61
CANADA
Middle Falls
High Falls
Pigeon River
Grand Portage State Park
Susie Islands
LAKE SUPERIOR
Upper Rd
Extant Site/Structure
Vacant Site/Structure
City
Township/Unorganized Territory
County
State Park/Property
National Park/National Monument
0 1 MILES
0 2 KILOMETERS

### Mission of Immaculate Conception, Parkerville, and Alger, Smith & Company Logging Camp *(vacant)*
South of Highway 61 and the Pigeon River

The Pigeon River forms the border between Minnesota and Ontario and passes under the Highway 61 bridge before it discharges into Lake Superior. The Indigenous people who fished, trapped, hunted, and harvested wild rice throughout the Pigeon River area established trails that were used for eons. The site, from the 1830s through the 1930s, included a Catholic mission, a trading post, a post office, a logging camp, and small gardens and fields. The entire area, now undeveloped, is defined by its notable natural and cultural qualities, which are protected by one of the Grand Portage Indian Reservation's preservation zones.[375]

Father Francis Xavier Pierz, one of Minnesota's best-known nineteenth-century missionary priests, established the Mission of Immaculate Conception and a small cemetery along the river in 1838. The Slovenian prelate, who had departed Europe for Michigan in 1835, immediately set out "to change the Ojibwe lifestyle" by promoting agricultural practices that involved land clearing and the planting of gardens and fruit trees. (Soil conditions, when compared to the Grand Portage Bay area, were better along the Pigeon River.) Pierz, however, engaged in preaching and teaching for only a single year before being called back to Michigan by his superiors. Upon his return to Pigeon River for summer 1841, the prelate once again encouraged the Anishinaabe to expand their farming activities and to build a birchbark-covered chapel large enough for seventy-five people. But after Pierz departed in late autumn, the mission began falling into disrepair. Three Jesuit clerics who arrived at the enclave in 1848 expressed their dismay over the uncompleted dwellings and dilapidated chapel, "which formerly lacked only a roof, but which now falls piece by piece." After an 1849 fire destroyed their mission, the Jesuits abandoned the Pigeon River area and moved to Fort William. Also present in the area during the early 1840s was the Cleveland Company, a small, independent firm involved in the fur trade; the company established a small trading post and agricultural enclave close to the Pigeon River's mouth but was bankrupt by 1845.[376]

A mail trail that connected Duluth and Fort William during the 1850s crossed the Pigeon River in the general vicinity of the earlier mission site. It was there that Asa and Caroline Parker settled in 1867. Born in New Hampshire, and trained as a surveyor, Parker had a remarkably varied and lengthy career. He worked as a flagman on the construction of the Illinois & Michigan Canal outside of Chicago in 1838; built the first sawmill in the Michigan copper-mining town of Ontonagon in 1851; participated in the 1855 townsite survey of Superior, Wisconsin; and served as a local agent for the Canada and Liverpool Silver Mining Company until 1859, when he returned to Ontonagon.[377]

Having gained familiarity with the Pigeon River area while searching for silver in Canada, Parker acquired 160 acres of land on the Minnesota side of the border in 1865, one year after marrying Caroline Prince of Buffalo, New York. The couple, in 1867, settled along the river, where they farmed, raised livestock, fished, engaged in the fur trade, and purchased maple syrup and berries from the Anishinaabe. They also operated a farm along the river that soon was well known for producing potatoes, other vegetables, and flowers. The family, including seven children (one would later drown in Lake Superior), resided in a relatively substantial dwelling; several nearby log cabins housed their Anishinaabe workers. Parker also received an appointment as the Pigeon River postmaster in 1872, an important position, because American and Canadian mail carriers who arrived with dogsleds or horses exchanged their monthly accumulation of mail at Parkerville. After the family returned to Ontonagon in 1875, Parker again found employment as a surveyor and also served as the local postmaster and judge of probate before his 1908 death. The only significant development that occurred along this section of the Pigeon River following the Parkers' departure was the construction of a short-lived, twentieth-century logging camp.[378]

### Ryden's Border Store
9301 Ryden Road

Ed and Mabel Ryden moved to Cook County in 1947, when the couple purchased the store and several buildings at Sextus City. Although the store burned down in 1949, the Rydens rebuilt immediately but moved from Sextus City to their current location in 1963, which coincided with the new Pigeon River bridge opening. The Rydens' transfer of their inventory into the relocated building occurred so quickly that the business reopened within one week; a nearby motel and restaurant appeared later. Now owned and operated by the third generation of family members, Ryden's Store continues to offer numerous items and services: a money exchange; a "gas bar"; duty-free items, including alcohol; and a convenience store filled with merchandise that appeals to tourists—"shirts, sweatshirts, figurines, jewelry, flags and homemade beef jerky, souvenir coffee mugs (Minnesota and Canada), Canada jam, and Minnesota wild rice." Although the restaurant and motel closed several years ago, the Rydens began providing another very popular service during the early twenty-first century—a parcel pickup service that offers a low-cost alternative to the high postal rates charged for mailing items directly from the United States to Canada. After an item arrives at Ryden's, the Canadians "come down and pick up packages, get cheap gas, and cheap duty-free items." Although Covid-19 restrictions resulted in an almost total shutdown of the Minnesota–Ontario border and the parcel delivery service during late 2020 and much of 2021, standard deliveries were reestablished in 2022.[379]

### Grand Portage–Pigeon River Border Crossing, U.S. Customs and Border Protection Office, and Pigeon River International Bridge
9403 Highway 61

Less than one-half mile separates Ryden's Store from the Pigeon River Border Crossing and U.S. Customs and Border Protection Office, as well as the adjacent Pigeon River International Bridge. All appeared during the relocation and construction of Highway 61 between 1958 and 1966. The new building opened at 11:00 P.M. on 1 November 1963—at precisely the same time the Sextus City bridge crossing closed. A temporary building served the new border station until 1966, when a much more substantial two-story structure was completed. The ground level of this building included space for administrative offices and functions, while the second floor, equipped with "modern bachelor quarters," could house as many as four seasonal employees. Outside the building were two heated booths that sheltered the attendants who checked travelers' documents; nearby were a pair of "radiant heating slabs," large enough to examine trucks and automobiles, and two "tilted inspection ramps," used to scrutinize "low silhouette vehicles."[380] The facility has been modified and upgraded considerably over subsequent years to accommodate new technologies, growing traffic flows, and U.S. Department of Homeland Security regulations.

Funds to construct the nearby Pigeon River International Bridge, financed jointly by the governments of the United States and Canada, were secured in 1957. The steel-stringer bridge also opened in November 1963 and was dedicated in May 1964. The span, since then, has experienced few alterations and retains its original utilitarian features and appearance. A 2011 appraisal observed that the no-frills structure exhibits few, if any, significant design characteristics and possesses little "artistic value."[381] What the bridge does very well, however, is serve as an efficient and vital link between the United States and Canada.[382]

### Alger, Smith & Company/Pigeon Falls Lumber Company and High Falls Resort (*now the* Grand Portage State Park Visitors and Welcome Center)
9333 East Highway 61

The entrance to Grand Portage State Park occurs a short distance before the U.S. Border Station. Authorized in 1988, the park protects a section of the rugged Pigeon River gorge that has been virtually inaccessible to humans since the first Indigenous people appeared in the Lake Superior region thousands of years ago. The river, in fact, was deemed "incapable of use for the driving, handling, and floating of logs, pulpwood and timber" until 1898, when Alger, Smith & Company moved its logging headquarters from Michigan to the North Shore community of Knife River. After acquiring the timber rights, Alger–Smith dealt with the waterway's obstacles by contracting with the Pigeon River Improvement, Slide and Boom Company, which constructed a complex system of booms, dams, and sluiceways for moving the logs, without damage, to Lake Superior; once there, the logs were organized into large rafts and towed to Duluth. Another firm, the Pigeon River Lumber Company, initiated its logging operations in 1902 and purchased all of Alger–Smith's assets two years later. When the Pigeon River Lumber Company's activities concluded in 1919, the stripped

In June 1939, Jack Rhea of Port Arthur, Ontario, directs logs through one of the Pigeon River's sluiceways with his pike pole. Courtesy of Cook County Historical Society.

and scarred landscape was devoid of both aesthetic and economic value and "afflicted with unemployment, forest fires, and poor hunting."[383]

The log transportation system, nevertheless, was once again put to use during the early 1930s when a Canadian firm pursued large-scale timber-cutting activities along the Arrow River, an Ontario tributary of the Pigeon River. Although the Pigeon's sluiceways and flumes were in need of repair, recalled Branson Tripp of Thunder Bay, who worked along the river in 1940–41, they remained sufficiently sound for the transfer of pine logs to Lake Superior. But because the aging structures were on Minnesota's side of the river, American and Canadian officials engaged in a complicated series of legal arguments concerning reimbursements and toll charges. The final Pigeon River log drive occurred in 1941.[384]

A remote camp for sportfishing enthusiasts also appeared along the Pigeon during the early 1930s. Lloyd K. Johnson, the son of influential Grand Marais pioneers Charles and Anna Johnson, and an owner of considerable land on Minnesota's side of the river, expanded the camp into the High Falls Resort in 1939. Bascom Tripp, who managed the resort with his wife, Mary Randle Tripp, and her sister Dorothy Randle, built several structures by High Falls, including a lodge that had a large fireplace and chimney in the foyer; a dining room; a snack bar where ice cream cones, soda pop, chips, and candy were available; and a store that sold Wedgewood china and similar items. Several cabins were situated nearby. Until 1963, when the new Pigeon River bridge opened, High Falls Resort was much more accessible to Canadians than it was to Americans. A motorist coming from Minnesota could reach the resort only by driving to Sextus City and crossing the former Pigeon River bridge into Canada; from there it was five miles to a small park located by Middle Falls and another two miles to the river landing. After parking their vehicles, the tourists boarded a boat that ferried them back to Minnesota and the resort, located a quarter mile from High Falls.[385]

Although the remaining marketable timber of the Pigeon River and its tributaries had been harvested by the late 1930s and early 1940s, another threat soon loomed on the horizon: the proposed construction of a hydroelectric dam at High Falls. The scheme, promoted

**Veteran fishermen Einar Bloomquist and Jack Hirsch posted this advertisement in 1947, shortly before they opened their High Falls Resort.** ***Cook County News-Herald,*** **24 July 1947, 4.**

by the Pigeon River Lumber Company, drew the immediate ire of Chester S. Wilson, Minnesota's commissioner of conservation. Wilson forcefully stated, in 1946, that the dam would impair, and possibly destroy, the scenic attractiveness of what were termed some of the continent's "notable waterfalls." Apparently, the proposal never received serious consideration, but several conservation groups quickly called for the establishment of a state park that would protect the American side of both High Falls and Middle Falls—the latter a thirty-foot-high cataract located 3.5 miles northwest of its more spectacular counterpart. The envisioned state park was also seen as a complement to the small Middle Falls municipal wayside on Ontario's side of the river—later expanded into Pigeon River Provincial Park. The Minnesota sections of Middle Falls and High Falls, and almost 280 acres of land, were donated and sold by Lloyd K. Johnson to the nonprofit Minnesota Parks and Trails Council in 1988. The MDNR immediately purchased the acreage from the council for $316,000, a remarkably low price given the outstanding quality of its natural attractions. The Minnesota Legislature, one year later, approved the creation of High Falls State Park, which was soon renamed Grand Portage State Park.[386]

The property has thirteen thousand feet of Pigeon River frontage but remains one of Minnesota's smallest state parks. Despite the relatively limited acreage, establishing the park was a complicated process that began with the MDNR transferring the land to the BIA, which held it in trust for the Grand Portage Band of Chippewa, who then leased the park back to the MDNR for the sum of one dollar per year. It remains the only park in the United States comanaged by an American Indian tribe and a state government. Upon its 1994 opening, visitors immediately began walking along the level, easily accessible, one-half-mile-long trail that leads to High Falls—the tallest waterfall in Minnesota. (The waterfall at Tettegouche State Park is the highest situated entirely within the state.) Three wooden decks allow observers to gain different views of the waterfall. A more challenging trail continues for 2.5 miles from High Falls to Middle Falls. Located by both Highway 61 and the trail entrance is the Grand Portage State Park Visitors and Welcome Center, dating to 2010. Staffed by Grand Portage Band members,

**High Falls, 120 feet high, is a popular attraction at Minnesota's Grand Portage State Park. Ontario borders the eastern (right) side of the river.**

the center includes exhibits and information devoted to the cultural heritage of the Anishinaabe and also acts as a Minnesota travel information center and highway rest area.[387]

The Pigeon River serves as a boundary between two nations, as well as between an American state and Canadian province, and marks the transition from Minnesota Highway 61 to Ontario Highway 61. On the Canadian side is Ontario's Pigeon River Provincial Park, officially designated in 1957 and now twenty-two hundred acres in size, which also offers views and perspectives of the river gorge and both waterfalls. Together, the two parks protect some of the most important natural and cultural sites along the North Shore and Lake Superior. For that, all of us can be grateful.

# Acknowledgments

The following acknowledgments seek to recognize the many individuals who provided information, expertise, and support throughout the time I worked on this book about Minnesota's North Shore. I am deeply indebted to all of them and apologize if anyone is inadvertently excluded or incorrectly identified.

The late Mary Ann Norton, who first assisted me while I worked on a book about the Duluth company town of Morgan Park, was tireless in her search for information about the North Shore's southwesternmost section of Scenic Drive. Patricia Maus and Aimee Brown, respectively the former and current director of the Northeast Minnesota Research Center at the University of Minnesota Duluth, constantly responded to my requests for information in a timely manner, as did several individuals affiliated with the Duluth Public Library and St. Louis County Historical Society. Larry Sommer reviewed my description of properties situated within Duluth, while Helen Hendrickson, Merle Norgren, Alvera Pierson, John Schifsky, and Mary Ann Sironen served as primary informants for the Duluth Township section of North Shore Scenic Drive.

Mel Sando, a former director of the Lake County Historical Society (LCHS) in Two Harbors, introduced me to the organization's extensive holdings, notably the papers of the Lake Superior International Highway Association, which date to the 1920s and 1930s. Subsequent assistance was provided by several LCHS staff members. I am especially indebted to the Two Harbors Public Library, which gave me permission to reproduce a number of early twentieth-century images in its possession; all were taken by Harold Youngren, a local Swedish immigrant photographer. I also had the good fortune to employ Rebecca Norlien, a Two Harbors resident and history devotee, who tracked down considerable information, much of it obscure, about local residents and properties. Scott Roen and Art Fenstad, respectively, offered information related to the small enclaves of Castle Danger and Little Marais, whereas local historian Ed Maki and public library director Julie Billings provided background on the "taconite town" of Silver Bay. Walter Sve, a Split Rock Township resident, shared his vast knowledge of Lake Superior and the North Shore with me on several occasions, including a memorable visit during the early-morning hours of a day in October 2014, when I accompanied the eighty-seven-year-old fisherman as we ventured out in a small skiff to check his nets for lake trout.

In Grand Marais, the archives of the Cook County Historical Society (CCHS) supplied much documentation and information about the northeastern end of the North Shore.

Offering essential assistance were three former CCHS staff members: directors Katie Clark and Katie Johnson, and museum administrator Martha Marnocha. Also responding graciously to my numerous requests for information were several Grand Marais Public Library employees, most notably Jim Johnson. Another Cook County organization, the Cross River Heritage Center (CRHC)—associated with the Schroeder Area Historical Society—provided several historic photographs for inclusion in the book; all were carefully reproduced by Barbara Livdahl, a gracious volunteer docent. In addition, two CHRC-sponsored tours gave me opportunities to visit and photograph several iconic North Shore buildings designed by Edwin Lundie, one of Minnesota's premier postwar architects. Ron Lund of Grand Marais, the second-generation owner of a cabin resort that has been in his family for nine decades, answered many of my questions about the history and evolution of local tourism, while Katie Usem, the developer and owner of a Grand Marais public sauna that opened in late 2021, offered the perspectives and insights of a recent North Shore entrepreneur.

Philip J. Anderson and Timothy Cochrane, both authors of books about the North Shore, provided many useful comments and suggestions following their reviews of my initial manuscript draft. Barbara Sommer evaluated my discussion of projects undertaken by the Civilian Conservation Corps during the 1930s, and Fredric Quivik helped me to understand the structural features of several postwar churches. While most of the early twenty-first century images were taken by me, the photographs of Marlene Wisuri, Tim Counts, Barbara Richards, and Eric Keplinger further enhance the book.

I also was privileged to utilize the talents and skills provided by several of my former University of Wisconsin–Madison graduate students, all of whom have gone on to pursue successful professional careers: Dee Finnegan, a designer and cartographer, prepared the complex and detailed maps that enhance the book's usefulness and visual appearance; Lynette Neitzel-Larsen, a digital media specialist, brought new life and legibility to many faded historic images; Dean Proctor, an architect and graphic artist, prepared a sketch of one historic Duluth property; Eric MacDonald, now an associate professor of environment and design at the University of Georgia, created several early maps and sketches; and George F. Thompson, a publisher of numerous place-based books, enthusiastically supported the completion of this volume from the outset.

Lynn Bjorkman, my wife, a historic preservation planner who was previously on the staff of Keweenaw National Historical Park in Michigan's Upper Peninsula, gave me a broader understanding of the Lake Superior region and its built environment. It is only because of Lynn's insights, unwavering patience, and consistent support that this book saw the light of day.

Several staff members affiliated with the University of Minnesota Press participated in the book's development and production. Senior editor Pieter Martin was involved from the beginning, while Mike Stoffel, Rachel Moeller, and Anne Carter provided considerable assistance throughout the lengthy publication process. Copy editor Holly Monteith also provided a thorough review of the manuscript before it went to press, and Lisa Himes prepared a detailed index.

The following names recognize the many additional individuals who assisted me as I worked on this volume. Again, it must be emphasized that any errors or omissions are my responsibility and entirely unintended: Arvo Alanen, Maija Alanen, Marit Alanen, Barbara Anderson, Chel Anderson, Deborah Anderson, Emily Anderson, Jon Anderson, Julie Anderson, Lynn Anderson, Robert Anderson, Rolf Anderson, Tim G. Anderson, Sue Baker, Jill Baum, Michael Bayer, Judy Beardsley, Scott Benson, Joseph Beres, Dori Betts, Julie Billings, Angie Braud, Bayne Brown, Margaret Carlson, Dean Carpenter, Penny Carpenter, Teresa Chmelik, Charles Comnick, Pamela Cone, Tim Counts, Mae Davenport, Tony Dierckins, Livio Di Matteo, Cynthia Donner, Bill Doucette, Lonnie Dupre, Randy Ellestad, Sheryl Erickson, Lisa Flax, Emily Ford, Carl Gawboy, Mark Gilbertson, John Godin, Tara Golden, Fanny Graden, Scott Graden, Rachel Gregg, John Gustafson, Karen Gustafson, Gretchen Heath, Deserae Hendrickson, Jeanne Hiebert, Marland Hildebrandt, Jackie Hyovalti, Carrie Jennings, Lee R. Johnson, Nick Junjak, Allison Kampbell, Matti Kaups, Natasha Kirk, Diane Koeneke, Michael Koop, Carol Krynski, Joanne Kurhajec, Ron Kyllonen, Tedi Kytola, Tom Lamb, Mike Lazaretti, Arlene Lind Lehto, George Lewis, Joanne Lind, Todd Lindahl, Gordon Lindquist, Jon Luikart, Jamie MacFarlane, Duane Madison, Linda Malzak, Carolyn Marino, Frank E. Martin, Steve Martens, Lou Mattson, Karin McGinnis, Grant Merritt, Jim Miller, Tim Miller, William Miller, Kirsten Mohr, Don Motschenbacher, Jackie Mueller, Andrew Munsch, Bradley Nelson, Carol Pearson, Mary Petz, Ron Piercy, Alvera Pierson, Stevie Anna Plummer, Barbara Richards, Todd Ronning, Cindy Rowlee, Dennis Rysdahl, Chad Salmela, David Salmela, Darryl Sannes, Diane Sannes, Kirk Scheid, Fredric Schmitz, Kara Ronnerud Schock, Carolyn Schousboe, Mary Lyght Seaborg, Alvine Shatto, Julie Sievert, Maureen Singleton, Barbara Stark, David Tersteeg, Diane Tessari, Molly Thompson, Stephen Veit, Karen Waters, Daniel Watkins, Gregg Westigard, Charles Wiger, Marlys Wisch, Cathy Wurzer, Barbara Wyatt, and Tiffany Zifco.

Finally, I would be remiss if I did not mention several University of Minnesota faculty members who, years ago, provided the foundation and background that allowed me to complete this book: geographers John Borchert, Eugene "Cotton" Mather, Fred Lukerman, and Yi-Fu Tuan; American literature scholar Sarah Youngblood; landscape architect Roger Clemence; art historian Marion Nelson; architect John Meyers; and architectural historian Frederick Koeper.

# Notes

## Introduction

1 Mary Ann Grossman, "Our Hearts Know the Exact Location of 'Up North,'" TwinCities.com, 5 July 2008; Aaron Shapiro, *The Lure of the North Woods: Cultivating Tourism in the Upper Midwest* (Minneapolis: University of Minnesota Press, 2013), xii. Shapiro also notes that "Up North" is used throughout the Upper Midwest, although "it resonates most strongly in Wisconsin; far northern Michigan is well known as the Upper Peninsula, or UP—a place where "Yoopers" reside.

2 *Duluth News-Tribune*, 18 July 1918, 5; *Journal News* (Two Harbors), 18 November 1915, 1.

3 Patricia Hampl, "Small Is Beautiful," *New York Times Travel Magazine*, 5 May 1999.

4 Margaret Culkin Banning, "A Motorist's View of North Shore Drive," *Minneapolis Sunday Tribune*, Pictures, 17 July 1960.

5 *Minneapolis Sunday Tribune*, 1 October 1961, H9; "Poll: What Is the Best Minnesota Road Trip Destination?," *StarTribune*, July 2018, https://www.startribune.com/poll-what-is-the-best-minnesota-road-trip-destination/486472951.

6 Timothy Knopp and Uel Blank, *The North Shore Experience* (St. Paul: Minnesota Sea Grant Institute, 1982), 10, 35, 37, 64.

7 Laura Butterbrodt, "North Shore Housing Market Stays Hot through Winter," *Duluth News-Tribune*, 13 March 2021, A6, quoting Laura Joynes Carlson.

8 Chel Anderson and Adelheid Fischer, *North Shore: A Natural History of Minnesota's Superior Coast* (Minneapolis: University of Minnesota Press, 2015).

9 William Cronon, "Storytelling," *American Historical Review*, 118 (February 2013): 19.

10 Sarah Williams Goldhagen, *Welcome to Your World: How the Built Environment Shapes Our Lives* (New York: Harper's, 2017), xvi; Arnold R. Alanen and Robert Z. Melnick, "Why Cultural Landscape Preservation?," in *Preserving Cultural Landscapes in America*, ed. Arnold R. Alanen and Robert Z. Melnick, 3–6 (Baltimore: Johns Hopkins University Press, 2000); John A. Jakle, Keith A. Sculle, and Jefferson S. Rogers, *The Motel in America* (Baltimore: Johns Hopkins University Press, 1996), 14; Lovisa Kjerrgren, *Layers of Land: The Palimpsest Concept in Relation to Landscape Architecture* (Uppsala: Swedish University of Agricultural Sciences, 2011), https://www.academia.edu/12181616/.

11 K. E. Foote and M. Azaryahu, "Sense of Place," in *International Encyclopedia of Human Geography*, ed. Rob Kitchin and Nigel Thrift, 96–100 (Philadelphia: Elsevier, 2009), https://www.sciencedirect.com/science/article/pii/B9780080449104009986.

12 Willis H. Raff, *Pioneers in the Wilderness: Minnesota's Cook County, Grand Marais and the Gunflint in the 19th Century* (Grand Marais, Minn.: Cook County Historical Society, 1981), 291–92.

13 Raff, 291–92; *St. Paul Daily Press*, 19 June 1869, 2; Barbara Livdahl, ed., *Schroeder Area History . . . as Shared by Those Who Lived It* (Schroeder, Minn.: Schroeder Area Historical Society, 2010), 2; Robert McDowell, *A History of Lutsen: Gateway to the Wilderness* (Lutsen, Minn.: Lutsen History Press, 2012), 35.

14 Phil Ochs, cited by John Cohen and Happy Traum, "Today: Bob Dylan Released 'Highway 61 Revisited' in 1965, 48 Years Ago," *AllDylan—a Bob Dylan Blog*, August 30, 2013, https://alldylan.com/august-30-bob-dylan-released-highway-61-revisited-in-1965-2/; Michael Gray, *The Bob Dylan Encyclopedia* (London: Continuum International, 2006), 321.

15 Bob Dylan, *Chronicles, Volume 1* (New York: Simon and Schuster, 2004), 240.

16 Karin Hertel McGinnis, "Rocks, Water, Soil, and Trees,"

in *Pines, Mines, and Lakes: A Field Guide to the Architecture and Landscape of Northeastern Minnesota*, ed. Arnold R. Alanen, 1–8 (Madison: Department of Landscape Architecture, University of Wisconsin–Madison, 2000); J. G. Norwood, "Description of the Northwest Shore of Lake Superior," in *Report of a Geological Survey of Wisconsin, Iowa, and Minnesota: and Incidentally of a Portion of Nebraska Territory*, by David Dale Owen, 338–418 (Philadelphia: Lippincott, Grambo, 1852).

17 John C. Green, *Geology on Display: Geology and Scenery of Minnesota's North Shore Scenic Parks* (St. Paul: Minnesota Department of Natural Resources, 1996); Richard W. Ojakangas, *Roadside Geology of Minnesota* (Missoula, Mont.: Mountain Press, 2009). My narrative also incorporates several comments and suggestions made by Chel Anderson and Carrie Jennings following their reviews of the manuscript.

18 Ojakangas, *Roadside Geology*, 15–16; Anderson and Fischer, *North Shore*, 228–30; Green, *Geology on Display*, 8, citing Cloud.

19 Ojakangas, *Roadside Geology*, 45; Anderson and Fischer, *North Shore*, 229–31.

20 Anderson and Fischer, *North Shore*, 131–32, 230–31; comments from Carrie Jennings to the author, November 2015.

21 Nancy Langston, *Sustaining Lake Superior: An Extraordinary Lake in a Changing World* (New Haven, Conn.: Yale University Press, 2017), 1, 5; Anderson and Fischer, *North Shore*, 227–35; Jennings comments, November 2015.

22 Anderson and Fischer, *North Shore*, 227; Green, *Geology on Display*, 19.

23 Matti Kaups, "North Shore Commercial Fishing, 1849–1870," *Minnesota History* 46 (Summer 1978): 44; Anderson and Fischer, *North Shore*, 281; comments from Chel Anderson to the author, June 2019.

24 Anderson and Fischer, *North Shore*, 235–43.

25 North Shore Forest Collaborative, "Why Are the Birch Dying?," https://northshoreforest.org/what-happened-to-the-forest/; Anderson and Fischer, *North Shore*, 290–92.

26 Anderson and Fischer, *North Shore*, 113–15.

27 Anderson and Fischer, 113–15; Karly Bitsure-Meszaros, Allie McCreary, Jordan W. Smith, Erin Seekamp, Mae A. Davenport, John Nieber, Bruce Wilson, Dorothy H. Anderson, Cynthia Messer, and Mark Kanazawa, "Building Coastal Climate Readiness along the North Shore of Lake Superior," *Michigan Journal of Sustainability* 3 (Spring 2015): 211; Center for Changing Landscapes, University of Minnesota, "North Shore Climate Beliefs Report," 2018, https://www.changinglandscapes.umn.edu/sites/changinglandscapes.umn.edu/files/climate_beliefs_north_shore_fact_sheet_umn_2018_final.pdf; comments from Mae Davenport to the author, 2019.

28 Patty Loew, *Indian Nations of Wisconsin: Histories of Endurance and Renewal* (Madison: Wisconsin Historical Society Press, 2001), 2; Anderson and Fischer, *North Shore*, 253.

29 Christina Harrison, Elaine Redepenning, Christopher I. Hill, George Rapp Jr., Stanley Aschenbrenner, James K. Huber, and Susan C. Mulholland, *The Paleo-Indians of Southern St. Louis County, Minnesota: The Reservoir Lakes Complex* (Dubuque, Iowa: Kendall/Hunt, 1995), 12–16, 135–41; Carl Gawboy, "Early Peoples," in *Roots in the Past—Seeds for the Future: The Heritage and History of Clover Valley, French River, and Surrounding Communities*, ed. Clover Valley/French River Community History Committee (Duluth, Minn.: The Committee, 2000), 13–15; Anderson and Fischer, *North Shore*, 247–48; State Archaeologist, Minnesota Department of Administration, "Prehistoric Period: An Overview of Prehistoric Archaeology in Minnesota (12,000 BC–AD 1650)," https://mn.gov/admin/archaeologist/the-public/mn-archaeology/prehistoric-period/.

30 State Archaeologist, "Prehistoric Period"; Anderson and Fischer, *North Shore*, 247–48; Gawboy, "Early Peoples," 16.

31 Timothy Cochrane, *Gichi Bitobig, Grand Marais: Early Accounts of the Anishinaabeg and the North Shore Fur Trade* (Minneapolis: University of Minnesota Press, 2018), 9; Theresa M. Schenck, *The Voice of the Crane Echoes Afar: The Sociopolitical Organization of the Lake Superior Ojibwe, 1640–1855* (New York: Garland, 1997), 4, 87; Anderson and Fischer, *North Shore*, 247–48.

32 Schenk, *Voice of the Crane*, 3–4; Anderson and Fischer, *North Shore*, 250–51.

33 Anton Truer, *Ojibwe in Minnesota* (St. Paul: Minnesota Historical Society Press, 2010), 12–13, 17–28; William Lass, *Minnesota: A Bicentennial History* (New York: W. W. Norton, 1977), 49; Carolyn Gilman, *The Grand Portage Story* (St. Paul: Minnesota Historical Society Press, 1992), 30–33; comments from Timothy Cochrane to the author, 2018; Minnesota Department of Natural Resources (hereafter MDNR), "1837 Treaty," http://

www.dnr.state.mn.us/aboutdnr/laws_treaties/1837/index.html.

34 Grace Lee Nute, *The Voyageurs' Highway* (St. Paul: Minnesota Historical Society Press, 1941), 5–10, 48–58; Lass, *Minnesota*, 49–52; Norman K. Risjord, *Shining Big Sea Water: The Story of Lake Superior* (St. Paul: Minnesota Historical Society Press, 2008), 79–80.

35 William W. Folwell, *History of Minnesota*, rev. ed. (St. Paul: Minnesota Historical Society Press, 1956), 1:307; Kaups, "North Shore Commercial Fishing," 48; Glenn N. Sandvik, "Land Office Buchanan: Emporium of the North Shore," *Minnesota History* 52 (Fall 1991): 279–80, 285; James Peet Papers, 1846–71, Minnesota Historical Society Archives, St. Paul (hereafter MHS Archives).

36 Manuscript schedules for the U.S. Census, 1920.

37 Lee Bloomquist, "He's the 'Glue' of Northeastern Minnesota Tourism," *Business North*, 1 November 2019; Explore Minnesota, "Tourism and Minnesota's Economy Fact Sheet," 2019.

38 Thomas F. Waters, *The Superior North Shore: A Natural History of Lake Superior's Northern Land and Waters* (Minneapolis: University of Minnesota Press, 1987), 138–45; Sharon Moen, "Siscowet Trout: A Plague of Riches," Minnesota Sea Grant, 2002; Cochrane comments, 2018.

39 Margaret Beattie Bogue, *Fishing the Great Lakes: An Environmental History, 1783–1933* (Madison: University of Wisconsin Press, 2000), 39; Anderson and Fischer, *North Shore*, 94; Waters, *Superior North Shore*, 175.

40 Robert Barnwell Roosevelt, *Superior Fishing: The Striped Bass, Trout, and Black Bass of the Northern States* (1865; repr. Minnesota Historical Society Press, 1985); Kaups, "North Shore Commercial Fishing," 51; Anderson and Fischer, *North Shore*, 93–96.

41 Manuscript schedules for the Minnesota Census, 1895; Matti Kaups, "Norwegian Immigrants and the Development of Commercial Fisheries," in *Norwegian Influence on the Upper Midwest*, ed. Harald S. Naess (Duluth: University of Minnesota Duluth, 1976), 21, 27.

42 Kaups, "North Shore Commercial Fishing," 55, 58; Tony Dierckins and Maryann C. Norton, *Lost Duluth: Landmarks, Industries, Buildings, Homes, and the Neighborhoods in Which They Stood* (Duluth, Minn.: Zenith City Press, 2012), 122; Bogue, *Fishing the Great Lakes*, 69; Ingeborg Holte, *Ingeborg's Isle Royale* (Grand Marais, Minn.: Women's Times, 1984), 10; Grace Lee Nute, *Lake Superior* (New York: Bobbs-Merrill, 1940), 187–88.

43 Timothy Cochrane and Hawk Tolson, *A Good Boat Speaks for Itself: Isle Royale Fishermen and Their Boats* (Minneapolis: University of Minnesota Press, 2002), 72–73, 84, 91, 125, 140, 167, 230–31; Waters, *Superior North Shore*, 179.

44 Waters, *Superior North Shore*, 146–59; Cory A. Goldsworthy, Keith A. Reeves, Joshua E. Blankenheim, and Nick R. Peterson, *Fisheries Management Plan for the Minnesota Waters of Lake Superior, 2016–2025* (St. Paul: MDNR, 2017), https://files.dnr.state.mn.us/publications/fisheries/special_reports/181.pdf; MDNR, "Commercial Fishing License Information," 2023, http://www.dnr.state.mn.us/fishing/commercial/cf.html.

45 *Grand Marais Pioneer*, 3 June 1891, 2; Kaups, "Norwegian Immigrants," 27–28; Bogue, *Fishing the Great Lakes*, 67, citing Coventry.

46 John R. St. John, *A True Description of the Lake Superior Country: Its Rivers, Coast, Bays, Harbours, Islands, and Commerce* (New York: William H. Graham, 1848), 7.

47 *Duluth News-Tribune*, 18 June 1918, 5; 16 August 1923; Paul Lundgren, "Minnesota Point: Duluth's Hay Fever Haven and Summer Resort," In "Perfect Duluth Day," *Duluth News Tribune*, 23 August 2022; Larry Oakes, "Growth of Cascade Lodge Tells Story of the North Shore," *StarTribune* (Minneapolis), 14 December 2007.

48 Cochrane comments, April 2018.

49 *News from Bob's Cabins*, undated brochure available at Bob's Cabins in Larsmont; *Duluth News-Tribune*, 25 May 1952, A6, citing C. Midlam.

50 [James Agee], "The Great American Roadside," *Fortune* 10 (September 1934): 177.

51 Jakle et al., *Motel in America*, 41–51.

52 *Two Harbors News Chronicle and Times*, 11 August 1949, 1; Jakle et al., *Motel in America*, 41–51; John Margolies, *Home Away from Home: Motels in America* (Boston: Little, Brown, 1995), 30–31, 82; comments from Marlys Wisch to the author, 2021.

53 Felicia Schneiderhan, "Fractional Ownership: Buying into a Shared Getaway," *Lake Superior Magazine*, February 2015; "Fractional Ownership," Wikipedia, accessed 2023.

54 Brian Bakst, "In Minnesota Cabin Country, Rental Property Could Get New Tax Treatment," *Duluth News-Tribune*, 11 December 2019, citing Walz.

55 Iron Range Resources and Rehabilitation Board, "The Economic Impact of Leisure and Hospitality in IRRRB Service Area," March 2015.

## 1. Dogs, Horses, and Mail along the North Shore Trail

1 "United States Postal Service," Wikipedia, accessed 2023; Todd Lindahl, "Postal Perils on the North Shore," *Two Harbors Iron Port: Official Newsletter of the Lake County Historical Society*, Fall 2019, 2; Raff, *Pioneers in the Wilderness*, 293–94.

2 Lindahl, "Postal Perils on the North Shore," 2; Newton J. Bray, "The North Shore," *Two Harbors Chronicle*, 1 September 1932, 1; George H. Primmer, "Pioneer Roads Centering at Duluth," *Minnesota History* 16 (September 1935): 298; Raff, *Pioneers in the Wilderness*, 294, citing Helen Wieland Skillings; *Cook County Herald*, 24 December 1898.

3 Lindahl, "Postal Perils on the North Shore," 2; Raff, *Pioneers in the Wilderness*, 296–304; Timothy Meinch, "For the Love of Dogs," *Midwest Living* 33 (January–February 2019): 38; "John Beargrease Sled Dog Marathon," https://beargrease.com/. See also Daniel Lancaster, *John Beargrease: Legend of Minnesota's North Shore* (Duluth, Minn.: Holy Cow Press, 2008).

4 *Duluth Minnesotian*, 8 February 1872, 2; 13 July 1872, 2; 27 July 1872, 2; Hugh E. Bishop, *By Water and Rail: A History of Lake County, Minnesota* (Duluth, Minn.: Lake Superior Port Cities, 2000), 39.

5 *Duluth Minnesotian*, 15 November 1873, 3; 3 January 1874, 3.

6 *Duluth Weekly Tribune*, 17 December 1886, 1; John L. Morrison, "Two Harbors, Minnesota," in *Two Harbors in 1900* (Two Harbors); Bishop, *By Water and Rail*, 47.

7 Raff, *Pioneers in the Wilderness*, 65–66; "SS America," https://www.superiortrips.com/America_Shipwreck.htm.

8 *Cook County Herald*, 9 April 1898, 3; Raff, *Pioneers in the Wilderness*, 297.

9 *Cook County Herald*, 23 December 1899, 3; *Duluth News-Tribune*, 19 January 1900, 5; Todd Lindahl, "Transportation on the North Shore: Part 2," *Overlook: Newsletter of the Cook County Historical Society*, Summer 2001, 1, 4; Raff, *Pioneers in the Wilderness*, 311–12.

10 Nancy S. Nelson and Tony Dierckins, *Duluth's Historic Parks: Their First 160 Years* (Duluth, Minn.: Zenith City Press, 2017), 78, 121, citing Duluth Board of Park Commissioners.

11 Nelson and Dierckins, 78, 124.

12 Nelson and Dierckins, 121–22; *Duluth News-Tribune*, 26 July 1896, 12; 6 September 1896, 11; 12 April 1898, 5; David Naymark, "Memories of Yesteryears," 1955, Archives and Manuscripts, Martin Library, University of Minnesota Duluth (hereafter UMD); "Good Roads Movement," Wikipedia, accessed 2023; Joel Katz, *From Footpaths to Freeways: A Survey of Roads and Highways in Minnesota* (St. Paul: MnDOT, 2009), 13.

## 2. A Road and a Bridge to Canada, 1900–1917

1 May Stanley, "Do Something for Good Roads Slogan of Duluth Automobile Club," *Duluth News-Tribune*, Magazine, 31 May 1914, 1, 3; *Duluth News-Tribune*, 15 March 1907, 12; 17 March 1907, B8; 11 June 1919, 3; Mary Ann Lewis, "Horseless Carriage Days in Duluth," *Duluth News-Tribune*, Cosmopolitan, 26 November 1950, 12; Dorothy V. Walters, "Pioneering with the Automobile in Minnesota," *Minnesota History* 26 (March 1945): 19–20; "Filiatrault Calls for Driving Course on Minnesota Point Beach," *Zenith City Press*, 10 April 2019.

2 *Duluth News-Tribune*, 11 June 1909, 3; 18 April 1913, 8; Bishop, *By Water and Rail*, 60.

3 *Duluth News-Tribune*, 14 May 1908, 3; 11 June 1909, 3; 22 March 1910, 3; 18 April 1913, 8; Bishop, *By Water and Rail*, 60; "North Shore Scenic Railroad," http://www.northshorescenicrailroad.org/about.htm; "Ghosts of the Duluth, Missabe, and Iron Range Railroad," *Sometimes Interesting*, https://sometimes-interesting.com/2015/03/03/ghosts-of-the-duluth-missabe-and-iron-range-railroad/.

4 *Duluth News-Tribune*, 27 August 1903, 10; 14 December 1904, 6.

5 *Duluth News-Tribune*, 30 April 1908, 6; McDowell, *A History of Lutsen*, 25–26.

6 *Duluth News-Tribune*, 17 March 1907, B8; 13 April 1907, 6; 11 June 1909, 3; 7 May 1911, 6; 6 December 1912, 8; 22 March 1910, 3; *Cook County News-Herald*, 1 April 1905, 7; 9 March 1916, 1; 30 March 1916, 1; *Two Harbors Chronicle*, 9 April 1931, 1, citing Beckman.

7 Julius F. Wolff Jr., "Some Vanished Settlements of the Arrowhead Country," Minnesota History 34, no. 5 (1955): 181; Lindahl, "Transportation on the North Shore," 1, 4.

8 Leonard B. Peterson, Frieda Biggins Peterson, and Rudy V. Illgen, "Hotel Scientific Ranch on Old Hwy. No 1 Near London Crossing, 1920–1924," typewritten manuscript in the LCHS archives; *Silver Bay News*, 10 September 1958, 3; Lindahl, "Transportation on the North Shore," 1, 4.

9 Ardell Waxlax Markitans and Ansis Markitans, *Waxlax Descendants: Stories and Pictures*, 2nd ed. (privately pub-

lished, 2011), 3–4; Wolff, "Some Vanished Settlements of the Arrowhead Country," 181–82; Bishop, *By Water and Rail*, 109; Arnold R. Alanen, *Finns in Minnesota* (St. Paul: Minnesota Historical Society Press, 2012), 39; Jacob Steinberg, "The Miracle of Finland," *City Pages* (Minneapolis), 9–15 May 2018, 8–11; Anderson and Fischer, *North Shore*, 131.

10 Wolff, "Some Vanished Settlements of the Arrowhead Country," 184; *Cook County News-Herald*, 20 April 1916, 1; 27 April 1916, 1; 3 May 1916, 1.

11 Raff, *Pioneers in the Wilderness*, 267; *Duluth News-Tribune*, 12 August 1908, 3; 22 October 1911, 2; Livdahl et al., *Schroeder Area History*, 14; Minnesota Department of Transportation (hereafter MnDOT), "History of MnDOT," http://www.dot.state.mn.us/information/history.html.

12 Daniel Naymark, "Memories of Yesteryears," 1940, Vertical Files, Archives and Manuscripts, Martin Library, UMD; manuscript schedules for the U.S. Census, 1920; Arthur Wiley King, "Voyageur in a Buggy," *Duluth News-Tribune*, Cosmopolitan, 3 February 1953, 6; *Duluth News-Tribune*, 24 October 1984, A8.

13 *Duluth News-Tribune*, 2 May 1913, 10; 28 May 1913, 9; 23 July 1913, 8, citing Stephens; *Two Harbors Sentinel*, 25 September 1915, 1; MnDOT, "History of MnDOT."

14 *Duluth News-Tribune*, 6 December 1914, 4; "June 11, 1876: Birth of Edward J. Filiatrault," *Zenith City Press*, http://zenithcity.com/thisday/june-11-1876-birth-of-edward-j-filiatrault/ (inactive website).

15 *Duluth News-Tribune*, 6 December 1914, 4, citing Kirby; S. B. Kirby Sr., in Minnesota Arrowhead Association, Mathias Koll Papers, MHS Archives; *Duluth Herald*, 20 June 1934, 8, citing Kirby.

16 *Duluth News-Tribune*, 6 December 1914, 4, citing Kirby; *Duluth Herald*, 20 June 1934, 8, citing Kirby; "S.B. Kirby, Sr.," in Mathias Koll Papers.

17 *Duluth News-Tribune*, 6 December 1914, 4; 11 August 1915, 14, citing Filiatrault.

18 *Duluth News-Tribune*, 21 April 1904, 6, citing *Thunder Bay Sentinel*; 5 February 1911, C5; *Duluth Weekly Herald*, 18 October 1911, 4, citing Neal; *Cook County News-Herald*, 9 March 1916, 1.

19 *Duluth News-Tribune*, 11 August 1915, 14; 1 August 1943, Pictures, 2; *Cook County News-Herald*, 26 August 1915, 1.

20 Tony Dierckins, *Glensheen: The Official Guide to Duluth's Historic Congdon Estate* (Duluth, Minn.: Zenith City Press, 2009), 9; Nelson and Dierckins, *Duluth's Historic Parks*, 117–21; Gregory Kopischke, "Morell, Anthony Urbanski" and "Nichols, Arthur Richardson," in *Pioneers of American Landscape Design*, ed. Charles Birnbaum and Robin Karson, 253–57 (New York: McGraw-Hill, 2000); Arnold R. Alanen, *Morgan Park: Duluth, U.S. Steel, and the Forging of a Company Town* (Minneapolis: University of Minnesota Press, 2007), 72–74.

21 *Duluth Herald*, 26 May 1913, 1, 7; 27 May 1913, 13, citing Congdon; 29 May 1913, 5; *Duluth News-Tribune*, 28 May 1913, 8; 30 May 1913, 7; 12 March 1914, 14; 23 May 1914, 6; 14 November 1914, 11; 4 February 1915, 12; Nelson and Dierckins, *Duluth's Historic Parks*, 121–23; Dan Hartman, "A Legacy Forgotten—Chester Congdon and the North Shore Drive," 3 August 2016, https://glensheen.org/blog/history-blogs/a-legacy-forgotten%e2%80%8a-%e2%80%8achester-congdon-and-the-north-shore-drive/.

22 *Duluth News-Tribune*, 28 May 1913, 8; 23 May 1914, 6; 14 November 1914, 11; Nelson and Dierckins, *Duluth's Historic Parks*, 122–23.

23 *Duluth Herald*, 26 May 1913, 1, 7; *Duluth News-Tribune*, 28 May 1913, 8; 30 May 1913; Hartman, "A Legacy Forgotten."

24 *Duluth News-Tribune*, 12 March 1914, 14; 23 May 1914, 6; 14 November 1914, 11; *Duluth Herald*, 18 May 1915, 16; Nelson and Dierckins, *Duluth's Historic Parks*, 122–23; Larry Oakes, "New Look at a North Shore Legacy," *StarTribune*, 22 February 2001, B1; Hartman, "A Legacy Forgotten"; John Schifsky, "Chester Congdon and North Shore Drive," *Duluth Township Newsletter*, July 2014, 5, citing Congdon Trust Ordinance, http://www.duluthtownship.org/pdf/newsletter/2014/july2014.pdf.

25 *Cook County News-Herald*, 10 May 1916, 1; 9 August 1916, 1; 3 November 1916, 1; 20 April 1920, 1; 23 June 1955, 1; *Journal-News* (Two Harbors), 27 July 1916, 1; 24 August 1916, 1; Owlshead Transportation Museum, Maine, "1908 Sears Buggy," http://owlshead.org/collections/detail/1908-sears-motor-buggy.

26 Wirth to Ward, cited in Barbara Beving Long, "T.H. 61 in Gooseberry Falls State Park and Bridge No. 3585," prepared for the Minnesota Department of Transportation by Rivercrest Associates Inc., September 1996, *Phase III, Historical Mitigation*, https://www.dot.state.mn.us/roadsides/historic/files/iforms/CK-GMC-029.pdf; *Journal-News*, 27 July 1916, 1; 10 August 1916, 1; *Cook County News-Herald*, 9 August 1916, 1; 6 September 1916, 1; 8 November 1916, 1, citing Mullen.

27 *Cook County News-Herald*, 27 December 1916, 1; 21 February 1917, 1.

28 *Duluth News-Tribune*, 22 April 1917, B4; 8 July 1917, A3; *Duluth Herald*, 13 August 1917, 7.

29 Howard Owen, "39 Years Later Minnesota Builds Highway," *Better Roads* (March 1961), 25–26, 36–39.

30 *Cook County News-Herald*, 2 May 1917, 1; 15 August 1917, 1; *Journal News* (Two Harbors), 16 August 1917, 1; Leah Thomas, *Passport into the Past: Mineral Center, Minnesota* (video), Cook County Historical Society (hereafter CCHS), 2013; *Duluth Herald*, 2 August 1916, 3; 13 August 1917, 7; *Duluth News-Tribune*, 6 May 1917, 6B; Max M. Moore, "Outlaw Bridge: Here's the Tale of How Rotarians Bridged a Gap Back in 1917," *The Rotarian* 118 (June 1972): 48–50; Ontario Ghost Towns, "Pigeon River," 2014, http://www.ghosttownpix.com/ontario/towns/pigeonriver.html.

31 Denis Gardner, *Wood+Concrete+Stone+Steel: Minnesota's Historic Bridges* (Minneapolis: University of Minnesota Press, 2008), 9, 11, 16–17.

32 *Journal News*, 16 August 1917, 12; *Duluth Herald*, 20 August 1917, 4, citing Ferguson; *Duluth News-Tribune*, 20 August 1917, 4, citing Magney; *Cook County News-Herald*, 22 August 1917, 1; Moore, "Outlaw Bridge," 50; Ontario Ghost Towns, "Pigeon River," https://www.ghosttownpix.com/ontario/towns/pigeonriver.html.

33 *Cook County News-Herald*, 22 August 1917, 1.

## 3. A State, Federal, and International Highway, 1918–1929

1 *Duluth News-Tribune*, 18 July 1918, 5.

2 *Duluth Herald*, 1 April 1916, 17, citing Mullen; *Duluth News-Tribune*, 19 April 1919, 3, citing Simonson; *Cook County News-Herald*, 21 April 1920, 1.

3 *Cook County News-Herald*, 26 November 1919, 1; 26 May 1920, 1; 15 September 1921, 6.

4 *Duluth News-Tribune*, 24 August 1919, B5.

5 *Duluth News-Tribune*, 24 August 1919, B5.

6 *Cook County News-Herald*, 8 January 1919, 1, citing Engelsen; 3 August 1922, 1.

7 *Duluth News-Tribune*, 9 September 1919, 3; 9 March 1920, 1, 3; 4 December 1922, 3, citing Farrell; *Lake County Courier*, 12 October 1922, 1; Oakes, "New Look at a North Shore Legacy"; Nelson and Dierckins, *Duluth's Historic Parks*.

8 MnDOT, "A History of MnDOT," https://www.dot.state.mn.us/about/history.html; Paul Daniel Marriott, "Roads Designed for Pleasure: A Brief History of the Origins of Scenic Driving and Automobile Touring in the United States (Part II)," *Journal for America's Byways* 1 (October 2011): 33.

9 "The 1945 Annual Meeting of the Minnesota Historical Society," *Minnesota History* 26 (March 1945): 44; *Duluth News-Tribune*, 14 December 1921, 3; 1 January 1926, B2, citing Forbes; *Cook County News-Herald*, 20 April 1922, 4; *Lake County Courier* (Two Harbors), 19 June 1924, 5; Theodore Wirth to Harold R. Ward, 5 August 1937, cited in Long, *Phase III, Historical Mitigation*; Andrew Munsch, "U.S. Highway 61—Early Grading Projects Timeline," Deadpioneer's Historic Minnesota Highways, https://deadpioneer.com/routes/US61/us61history.htm.

10 Paul Daniel Marriott, "Roads Designed for Pleasure: A Brief History of the Origins of Scenic Driving and Automobile Touring in the United States (Part II)," *Journal of America's Byways* 1 (October 2011): 34–35; Thomas Owens to James N. Harper, 3 September 1925, in Lake Superior International Highway Association Papers, Lake County Historical Society, Two Harbors (hereafter LSIHA Papers).

11 *Duluth News-Tribune*, 14 May 1922, Auto/Sports, 1; *Lake County Chronicle*, 14 September 1922, 1; 28 September 1922, 1.

12 *Lake County Chronicle*, 14 September 1922; 28 September 1922, 1; *Duluth News-Tribune*, 21 November 1922, 4.

13 *Lake County Chronicle*, 8 March 1923, 1; 19 June 1924, 5, citing Johnson; 19 March 1925, 1; *Duluth News-Tribune*, 1 January 1926, B7, citing Forbes; *Duluth Herald*, 2 August 1923, 3; Munsch, "U.S. Highway 61—Early Grading Projects Timeline."

14 *Duluth News-Tribune*, 2 July 1922, B1; *Lake County Chronicle*, 19 June 1924, 5, citing Johnson.

15 *Duluth News-Tribune*, 1 August 1922, 4; *Duluth Herald*, 1 August 1922, 6, citing Preus; *Two Harbors Chronicle*, 17 January 1935, 1.

16 *Lake County Chronicle*, 19 June 1924, 1; *Duluth News-Tribune*, 19 June 1924, 4.

17 *Lake County Chronicle*, 18 January 1925, 1.

18 *Duluth Herald*, 11 July 1925, A1, A2, citing Johnson; *Lake County Chronicle*, 16 July 1925, 12, citing Babcock and Nolan; Clow and Nicholson Transportation Co. to Owens, 2 July 1925; Owens's press release, 8 July 1925 (both items in LSIHA Papers).

19 *Duluth News-Tribune*, 18 September 1925, B1; 26 September 1925, 1; 1 January 1926, B2; *Duluth Herald*, 25 September 1925, 20; 26 September 1925, 1; 28 September 1925, 12; Edward Congdon to Owens, 2 October

1926, LSIHA Papers; Nelson and Dierckins, *Duluth's Historic Parks*, 121–23.

20 Schifsky, "Chester Congdon and North Shore Drive," 5.

21 *Lake County Chronicle*, 26 March 1925, 1; Owens to Babcock, 2 February 1926, LSIHA Papers; Babcock to Owens, 12 March 1926, LSIHA Papers; "Minnesota State Highway 61," Wikipedia, accessed 2023; Don Dembers, "100 Years in the Making . . . Minnesota's Highway System," https://static1.squarespace.com/static/5d3e3e6c733af1000134b553/t/5d475e8073704000 01f75617/1564958338747/MN_Highway_System.pdf; Steve Riner, "Minnesota's Constitutional Routes," 2003, http://www.steve-riner.com/mnhighways/conrtes.htm; Dan Hartman, "A Legacy Forgotten—Chester Congdon and the North Shore Drive," *The Glensheen Collection*, 3 August 2016, https://medium.com/the-glensheen-collection/north-shore-drive-and-chester-a-romance-forgotten-8af7c81b131b.

22 Thomas Owens to Charles Babcock, 2 February 1926; 9 March 1926, LSIHA Papers; Charles Babcock to Thomas Owens, 12 March 1926; 17 March 1926; Rodney Paine to Thomas Owens, 5 June 1928; 18 June 1926; Thomas Owens to Edward Congdon, 22 March 1926, LSIHA Papers; *Wisconsin Sunday Times* (Superior), 6 June 1926.

23 Thomas Owens to Edward Congdon, 17 January 1927; 5 January 1928; Thomas Owens to Rodney Paine, 9 September 1927, LSIHA Papers.

24 *Lake County Chronicle*, 29 July 1926, 1; *Duluth News-Tribune*, 1 July 1928, C1.

25 *Duluth News Tribune*, 19 November 1918, 5; *Duluth Herald*, 23 December 1918, 11; *Cook County News-Herald*, 20 November 1918, 1.

26 *Cook County News-Herald*, 27 July 1922, 3; 12 June 1924, 2; *Duluth News-Tribune*, 29 March 1918, 5; 4 May 1919, 8; *Evening Telegram* (Superior), 31 May 1965; Margaret Walsh, "Tracing the Hound: The Minnesota Roots of the Greyhound Bus Company," *Minnesota History* 49 (Winter 1985): 313–14; "Greyhound Lines," Wikipedia, accessed 2023; "White Motor Company," Wikipedia, accessed 2023.

27 *Cook County News-Herald*, 29 May 1924, 2; 7 August 1924, 1; *Duluth News-Tribune*, 10 September 1919, 1; 21 April 1920, 1; *Lake County Chronicle*, 15 August 1929, 6; Walsh, "Tracing the Hound," 321; "Greyhound Lines Historical Company Timeline," https://www.zippia.com/greyhound-lines-careers-999881/history/.

28 "The Funeral of Duluth Musician Jens Flaaten, August 9, 1922," *Zenith City Press*, 9 August 1922; *Cook County News-Herald*, 21 April 1920, 1; 15 September 1921, 6; 14 July 1921, 1; *Duluth News-Tribune*, 17 July 1927, A4.

29 Manuscript schedules for the U.S. Census, 1920.

30 *Cook County News-Herald*, 26 May 1920, 1; 14 July 1921, 1, 5; 1 February 1951, 1; *Duluth News-Tribune*, 28 December 1911, 14; 1 July 1928, C5; interview with Darrel and Larry Ryden, conducted by Pat Zankman, 26 September 2002, on file with CCHS; city directories for Duluth, Virginia, and Superior, 1920–30; manuscript schedules for the U.S. Census, 1920, 1930, 1940; *Wisconsin Blue Book*, 1923, 621; 1931, 561.

31 *Cook County News-Herald*, 26 May 1920, 1; 14 July 1921, 1; 14 July 1921, 5; 1 February 1951, 1; *Duluth News-Tribune*, 28 December 1911, 14; 1 July 1928, C5; Darrel and Larry Ryden interview, 2002; "Bringing Up Father," Wikipedia, accessed 2023; Aetna Insurance Company, *Pigeon River Resort, Pigeon River, Minnesota*, fire insurance map drawn by W. W. Foster, 1949; National Park Service (hereafter NPS), Sextus City plat map, circa 1940 (both of the latter items on file with CCHS).

32 Manuscript schedules for the U.S. Census, 1920; *Cook County News-Herald*, 21 April 1920, 1; 3 August 1922, 1.

33 *Cook County News-Herald*, 23 January 1918, 1; 15 September 1921, 6; *Duluth News-Tribune*, 30 January 1918, 12; 18 July 1918, 5; 25 August 1918, 9.

34 *Duluth News-Tribune*, 18 July 1918, 5; 23 July 1920, B1; 24 July 1920, 1, 9; 28 October 1920, 1; 25 September 1921, 1; 2 July 1922, D1; Tony Dierckins and Heidi Bakk-Hansen, "Prohibition in Duluth (1916–1933)," Zenith City Archives, http://zenithcity.com/?s=prohibition+in+duluth; Gary Genosko and Scott Thompson, "Administrative Surveillance of Alcohol Consumption in Ontario, Canada: Pre-electronic Technologies of Control," *Surveillance and Society* 4, no. 1/2 (2006): 1–28; "Ontario Temperance Act," Wikipedia, accessed 2023.

35 Green, "A History of the North Shore Road"; *Cook County News-Herald*, 1 August 1929, 1; 3 July 1930, 1.

36 *Duluth News-Tribune*, 26 September 1929, 8; *Duluth Herald*, 27 September 1929, 1, 6; Charles A. Forbes, "Opening of the Pavement between Knife River and Two Harbors, September 27, 1929," manuscript on file with LCHS; Andrew Munsch, "U.S. Highway 61—Concrete Paving Project Timeline, 1921–1939," Deadpioneer's Historic Minnesota Highways, https://www.deadpioneer.com/routes/US61ref/us61earlyconcrete.htm. The listing of parade participants comes from a review of images taken by photographer Harold Youngren, filed in the Two Harbors Public Library.

## 4. The North Shore during Depression and War, 1930–1945

1 *Cook County News-Herald*, 3 July 1930, 1.

2 *Duluth News-Tribune*, 18 February 1930, 13.

3 *Two Harbors Chronicle*, 11 June 1931, 1; 17 September 1931, 1; 30 April 1934, 1, 3; Arnold R. Alanen, "Years of Change on the Iron Range," in *Minnesota in a Century of Change: The State and Its People since 1900*, ed. Clifford E. Clark (St. Paul: Minnesota Historical Society Press, 1989), 158.

4 *Cook County News-Herald*, 30 April 1931, 1; 7 May 1931, 1; *Two Harbors Chronicle*, 2 April 1931, 1, 5; 9 April 1931, 1; 18 July 1931, 1, citing Johnson.

5 *Lake County Chronicle*, 1 September 1927, 1; *Two Harbors Chronicle*, 14 February 1935, 1.

6 *Duluth News-Tribune*, 1 July 1928, C1.

7 *Cook County News-Herald*, 18 December 1930, 1; *Two Harbors Chronicle*, 16 April 1931, 1; 30 April 1931, 1; *Duluth News-Tribune*, 12 December 1930, 1; Andrew Munsch, "U.S. Highway 61—First Pavement Timeline," Deadpioneer's Historic Minnesota Highways, https://deadpioneer.com/routes/US61/us61ref/us61firstpave.htm.

8 *Two Harbors Chronicle*, 16 April 1931, 1; 30 April 1931, 1; 18 July 1931, 1; *Cook County News-Herald*, 3 December 1931, 1; *Duluth Herald*, 22 August 1934, 2; Andrew Munsch, "U.S. Highway 61," Deadpioneer's Historic Minnesota Highways, https://www.deadpioneer.com/routes/US61/index.htm.

9 *Duluth News-Tribune*, 8 July 1928, C7; 1 July 1928, C1; 27 April 1930, C1, citing Coulter; 10 August 1930, B1, citing Coulter.

10 *Lake County Chronicle*, 17 November 1927, 1; 8 November 1928, 6.

11 Munsch, "U.S. 61, Minnesota"; "U.S. Highway 61," Wikipedia, accessed 2023.

12 "Twenty-First Amendment to the United States Constitution," Wikipedia, accessed 2022.

13 William E. Leuchtenburg, *Franklin D. Roosevelt and the New Deal, 1932–1942* (New York: Harper and Row, 1963), 8, 42–61.

14 Harold W. Lathrop, "Fifty Years of State Parks in Minnesota," in *American Planning and Civic Annual, 1939*, ed. Harlean James (Washington, D.C.: American Planning and Civic Association, 1940), 198; Barbara W. Sommer, *Hard Work and a Good Deal: The Civilian Conservation Corps in Minnesota* (St. Paul: Minnesota Historical Society Press, 2008), 17; Gemini Research, *Historic Roadside Development Structures on Minnesota's Trunk Highways* (St. Paul: MnDOT, 1998), 3.14, 5.6.

15 Sommer, *Hard Work and a Good Deal*, 51, 90, 144, 147, 156–57; Gemini Research, *Historic Roadside Development*, 3.33, 5.6; Calvin W. Gower, "The CCC Indian Division: Aid for Depressed Americans, 1933–1942," *Minnesota History* 42 (Spring 1972): 11–13.

16 Sommer, *Hard Work and a Good Deal*, 26–28, 50–51, 144; Douglas Brinkley, *Rightful Heritage: Franklin D. Roosevelt and the Land of America* (New York: HarperCollins, 2016), 416.

17 Sommer, *Hard Work and a Good Deal*, 17–18; Gemini Research, *Historic Roadside Development*, 3.14, 3.32–33; Albert Good, *Park and Recreation Structures* (Washington, D.C.: U.S. Government Printing Office, 1938), 1:5.

18 Gemini Research, *Historic Roadside Development*, 3.4–6; 3.14; 3.29–31; Kopischke, "Morell" and "Nichols"; Alanen, *Morgan Park*, 72–74.

19 W. H. "Bill" Raff, *Law and Order in the Wilderness: The First 100 Years of Local Governance in Minnesota's Cook County* (Grand Marais, Minn.: CCHS, 1982), 33; Sommer, *Hard Work and a Good Deal*, 119–21, 144; Gemini Research, *Historic Roadside Development*, 5.41; *Two Harbors Chronicle*, 25 January 1934, 1; 25 March 1937, 1; 3 November 1939, 1; Tony Dierckins, *Greetings from the Arrowhead: The North Shore and Canoe Country, a Postcard Perspective of Historic Northeastern Minnesota* (Duluth, Minn.: Zenith City Press, 2011), 17.

20 *Cook County News-Herald*, 2 August 1916, 1; *Two Harbors Chronicle*, 1 October 1931, 1; 23 July 1932, 1; *Duluth Herald*, 22 August 1934, 2; 7 April 1938, 1; 28 April 1938, 1; 5 May 1938, 1; 24 August 1938, 1; 24 August 1939, 1; *Duluth News-Tribune*, 1 January 1935, 1; Munsch, "U.S. Highway 61"; Green, "History of the North Shore."

21 *Two Harbors Chronicle*, 4 March 1937, 1; 30 November 1939, 1.

22 *Two Harbors Chronicle*, 14 September 1939, 1; Howard Q. Owen, "39 Years Later Minnesota Builds Highway," *Better Roads*, March 1961, 25–26, 36–38.

23 *Two Harbors Chronicle*, 22 July 1937, 1; 11 August 1938, 1; 7 September 1939, 1; 14 September 1939, 1; *Lake County News-Chronicle*, 24 October 1940, 1.

24 *Duluth News-Tribune*, 4 May 1940, 1, 3, citing Stassen and Arrowhead Association; *Two Harbors Chronicle*, 23 May 1940, 1.

25 *Duluth News-Tribune*, 9 December 1941, 10; *Two Harbors Chronicle and Times*, 31 May 1945, 2; 5 September 1946,

8; *Cook County News-Herald,* 6 September 1945, 1; Bishop, *By Water and Rail,* 157, 159.

26 Comments from Alvera Pearson to the author, 2016; Harold W. Lathrop, "Minnesota," in *American Planning and Civic Annual, 1942,* ed. Harlean James (Washington, D.C.: American Planning and Civic Association, 1942), 156.

27 *Two Harbors Chronicle,* 16 August 1945, 1, quoting Kragseth; 30 August 1945, 1; 6 September 1945, 1; National Archives, "WWII Army Casualties: Minnesota," https://www.archives.gov/research/military/ww2/army-casualties/minnesota.html.

28 *Two Harbors Chronicle,* 16 August 1945, 1.

## 5. On the Road Again, and Again, 1946–2024

1 *Cook County News-Herald,* 6 June 1946, 1; 9 October 1947, 1; *Two Harbors Chronicle and News,* 28 August 1947, 1, citing Elmgren; 9 October 1947, 3, citing Lorntson.

2 *Cook County News-Herald,* 29 July 1948, 1; *Duluth News-Tribune,* 31 July 1948, 1; 12 December 1949, 1; 9 February 1950, 1; 10 May 1951, 1.

3 *Duluth News-Tribune,* 25 May 1952, A6, citing Midlam.

4 *Cook County News-Herald,* 4 September 1952, 1; James M. Liston, "The North Shore of Lake Superior: Duluth to Canada—the Road Hugs the Shore, Takes You into the Heart of the Country Like This," *Better Homes and Gardens* 30 (September 1952): 246.

5 *Duluth News-Tribune,* 4 December 1949, A4; *Two Harbors Chronicle and Times,* 2 August 1945, 1; 24 October 1946, 1, 3; John Lind, "Meeting Here Planned by North Shore Resorters," *Cook County News-Herald,* 30 September 1948, 1.

6 *Cook County News-Herald,* 7 July 1955, 1, 3; 8 September 1955, 1; *Duluth News-Tribune,* 25 July 1957, 1–2.

7 *Duluth News-Tribune,* 21 June 1955, 9; *Cook County News-Herald,* 16 June 1955, 1; 10 November 1955, 1, citing Benson; 26 January 1961, 1, 2, citing St. Paul Garden Club and Rod Krueger.

8 *Duluth News-Tribune,* 16 February 1950, 13; *Cook County News-Herald,* 19 February 1952, 1.

9 *Cook County News-Herald,* 21 May 1953, 6; 3 May 1956, 2.

10 Brady Slater, "Talk to Shed Light on Duluth's History as a Cold War Defense Hub," *Duluth News-Tribune,* 12 May 2014; "North American P-51 Mustang," Wikipedia, accessed 2023; "343d Wing," Wikipedia, accessed 2023; "31st Air Division," Wikipedia, accessed 2023; Clover Valley/French River Community History Committee, *Roots in the Past,* 186–88.

11 *Cook County News-Herald,* 1 February 1951, 1; 8 September 1955, 1; Ryden interview.

12 *Cook County News-Herald,* 12 March 1959, 1; Rhonda Silence, "60 Years of History at Ryden's Border Store," *Cook County Star* (Grand Marais), 8 October 2007, 1; Ryden interview.

13 Martha Marnocha, "Joanne Hart: A View from the Border," *Overlook: Newsletter of the Cook County Historical Society,* Winter 2019, 1, 4; *Cook County News-Herald,* 26 May 2018; Ryden interview.

14 Mineral Center photograph, 1940s, on file with CCHS; Cochrane comments, 2018.

15 *Cook County News-Herald,* 26 November 1957, 1.

16 Jack Kerr, "Motorcade Heads for Circle Tour," *Duluth News-Tribune,* 16 September 1960, 1–2; "New Highway's Scenery 'Best in the World,'" *Duluth News-Tribune,* 16 September 1960, citing Lloyd K. Johnson, 1, 11; "Lake Superior Admirals' End Pioneering Trip," *Duluth News-Tribune,* 19 September 1960, 1–2; "Great Lakes Circle Tour," http://greatlakescircletour.org/; Jeff Klassen, "Introducing Wawa Goose, the Third," *Bay Today,* 19 June 2017, https://www.baytoday.ca/local-news/introducing-wawa-goose-the-third-646891; Livio Di Matteo, "Cross-Border Travel at Pigeon River," *Northern Economist,* 23 October 2011.

17 *Duluth News-Tribune,* 32 December 1955, 2; 17 July 1959, 18; John A. Weeks III, "Minnesota Named Highways," https://www.johnweeks.com/highway/mnnamedhighways/index.html.

18 Hillary Olsen, "Ober's Legacy," *Ernest Oberholtzer: Unsung Hero of the BWCAW* (blog), 15 November 2011, http://oberholtzerbwca.blogspot.com/. Oberholtzer's letter may be found in the Ernest C. Oberholtzer Foundation Archives, Mallard Island, Ranier, Minn. A highly modified version of the letter was published in the *Minneapolis Star,* 14 September 1958, E3.

19 Di Matteo, "Cross-Border Travel at Pigeon River"; IBI Group, "Northern Ontario Passenger Vehicle Travel Profile," 2013, ES2–3; Bob Berg, "Wayside Stop at Ryden's, a 70-Year-Old Pullover on Your Way to (and from) Canada," *Lake Superior Magazine,* 22 December 2017; comments from Beverly Soloway to the author, 2018.

20 *Duluth News-Tribune,* 25 July 1957, 1, 2; Doris Kreitlow, "Locals Testify about Unsafe Highway 61," *Cook County News-Herald,* 2 October 1989, 1, 9.

21 *New York Times,* 4 January 1990, A16.

22 *New York Times*, 4 January 1990, A16; CNN Consulting Engineers, "Underground Transportation Facilities," http://www.cnaengineers.com/underground-transportation-facilities.htm; FWHA Excellence in Highway Design, "Category 2: The Rural Highways Merit Award," https://www.fhwa.dot.gov/eihd/2002/cat2pic3.cfm.

23 Jan Horak, interviewed by Anna Klobuchar, 5 November 2002, copy on file with CCHS.

24 Brady Slater, "MnDOT Brings 'Mumble Strips' to North Shore," *Duluth News-Tribune*, 17 August 2019, A6; Center for Changing Landscapes, University of Minnesota, "Existing Road Section on the North Shore: Appendix," in *North Shore Scenic Drive: All-American Road*, 179–83 (Minneapolis: University of Minnesota, 2003).

25 "Minnesota State Highway 61," Wikipedia, accessed 2024. The Scenic Byway Program considers Duluth's Canal Park as the point of origin for North Shore Scenic Drive.

26 "National Scenic Byway," Wikipedia, accessed 2024; Federal Highway Administration, "National Scenic Byways & All American Roads," https://fhwaapps.fhwa.dot.gov/bywaysp; North Shore Scenic Drive Council, "North Shore Scenic Drive Corridor Management Plan," 2000, updated 2015 and 2019, http://www.dot.state.mn.us/scenicbyways/pdf/corridor-mgmt-plans/n-shore-cmp.pdf; Arrowhead Regional Development Commission, "North Shore Scenic Drive Wayside Rest Improvement Plan-Phase II—2015 Update," http://www.arrowheadplanning.org/nssd/2015.Update.WRIP.pdf; MDNR, "Minnesota Scientific and Natural Areas," http://www.dnr.state.mn.us/snas/index.html; MnDOT, "Safety Rest Areas and Waysides: Rest Areas along Hwy 61," http://www.dot.state.mn.us/restareas/hwy61amenities.html; Parks and Trails Council of Minnesota, "Grand Portage State Park," https://www.parksandtrails.org/portfolio/grand-portage-state-park/.

27 U. W. Hella, "Minnesota," in *American Planning and Civic Annual, 1953*, ed. Harlean James (Washington, D.C.: American Planning and Civic Association, 1954), 136; Roy W. Meyer, *Everyone's Country Estate: A History of Minnesota's State Parks* (St. Paul: Minnesota Historical Society Press, 1991), 38–40, 155–58, 166–67, 176–77, 297–99.

28 Meyer, *Everyone's Country Estate*, 138–40, 155–58, 178–80, 208–10, 248–49, 273–78, 279–81; MDNR, "State Parks," https://www.dnr.state.mn.us/faq/mnfacts/state_parks.html.

29 "North Shore Scenic Railroad," Wikipedia, accessed 2023; "North Shore Scenic Railroad, 2011–2023," https://duluthtrains.com/about.

30 Superior Hiking Trail Association, *Superior Hiking Trail Guidebook*, 9th ed. (Two Harbors, Minn.: The Association, 2022), 2–5, 198; "Superior Hiking Trail," Wikipedia, accessed 2024.

31 Gitchi-Gami Trail Association, "Gitchi-Gami State Trail: 2016 Plan Update and Scoping Project," https://www.ggta.org/; MDNR, "Gitchi-Gami Trail Rider," Summer 2023.

32 MDNR, "Lake Superior State Water Trail," https://www.dnr.state.mn.us/watertrails/lakesuperior/index.html.

## Part II

1 "Transect," Wikipedia, accessed 2023; Transect Geography," Wikipedia, accessed 2023; Andrès Duany and Emily Talen, "Transect Planning," *Journal of the American Planning Association* 68, no. 3 (2002): 245.

2 Grady Clay, *Real Places: An Unconventional Guide to America's Generic Landscape* (Chicago: University of Chicago Press, 1994), xi.

## St. Louis County

1 Nelson and Dierckins, *Duluth's Historic Parks*, 121–22, citing Duluth Board of Park Commissioners, 121; Paul Clifford Larson, "Duluth: Where Style Went Wild," *Architecture Minnesota*, September/October 1983, 44.

2 Twin Ports Genealogical Society, "Scandia Cemetery Burial Database," on file in the North Shore Room, Duluth Public Library; *Duluth News-Tribune*, 10 April 2020, A3; *Duluth Monitor*, 12 March 2023.

3 Larry Millett, *Minnesota's Own: Preserving Our Grand Homes* (St. Paul: Minnesota Historical Society Press, 2014), 287; Michael Koop, "National Register of Historic Places Registration Form for Glensheen, the Chester and Clara Congdon Estate," 1991, State Historic Preservation Office, Minnesota Department of Administration (hereafter SHPO-MDA); Dierckens and Norton, *Duluth's Grand Old Architecture*, 163–65; "Chester Adgate Congdon," Wikipedia, accessed 2023.

4 Koop, "Registration Form for Glensheen"; Millet, *Minnesota's Own*, 288–89; Dierckins, *Glensheen*, 11, 31–105.

5 Koop, "Registration Form for Glensheen"; Dierckins, *Glensheen*, 117, 128–35.

6 Dierckins, *Glensheen*, 9, 109; "Country Place Era," Wikipedia, accessed 2024; Candace Renalls, "Return to Glory," *Duluth News-Tribune*, 17 June 2006, A3; Cultural Landscape Foundation, "Country Place Era Garden," https://tclf.org/category/designed-landscape-types/garden-and-estate/country-place-era-garden.

7 Dierckins, *Glensheen*, 109, 118–19; Renalls, "Return to Glory," A1, A3; Emily Ford, "Hello, from an Unlikely Head Gardener," *Glensheen* (blog), 2 October 2017, https://glensheen.org/blog/garden-blogs/hello-from-an-unlikely-head-gardener/.

8 Renalls, "Return to Glory," A3, citing Mike Lowe.

9 Koop, "Registration Form for Glensheen"; Dierckins, *Glensheen*, 120–27, 136–37, 144–46.

10 Suzanne Congdon LeRoy, *Nightingale: A Memoir of Murder, Madness, and the Messenger of Spring* (Minneapolis, Minn.: Kirai Press, 2013); "Glensheen Murders," Wikipedia, accessed 2024; "Glensheen Historic Estate," Wikipedia, accessed 2024.

11 *Duluth News-Tribune*, 4 April 2018, 2; Brady Slader, "Northland Wish List: Glensheen Gives Backdrop for Bonding Tour," *Duluth News-Tribune*, 24 September 2021, 1; University of Minnesota Foundation, "Glensheen Mansion," 2017, http://legacy.umn.edu/stories/glensheen-mansion; Dan Hartman, "What Is Going On?," *Glensheen* (blog), 28 December 2015, https://glensheen.org/blog/restoration-blogs/what-is-going-on/; Hartman, "Shoreline and Boathouse Damage," *Glensheen* (blog), 30 October 2017, https://glensheen.org/blog/restoration-blogs/shoreline-and-boathouse-damage/; Lucie B. Amundson, "From Stodgy to Story," American Alliance of Museums, 25 April 2018, https://www.aam-us.org/2018/04/25/from-stodgy-to-story-glensheens-historic-transformation/.

12 Millett, *Minnesota's Own*, 281.

13 *Duluth Herald*, 8 December 1930, 22; Lawrence Sommer, *The Mansions of Duluth* (Duluth, Minn.: St. Louis County Historical Society, c. 1985); Dierckins and Norton, *Duluth's Grand Old Architecture*, 182; Duluth Preservation Alliance, "2013 Preservation Awards," https://duluthpreservation.org/event-category/preservation-centennial-awards/; Carrie Hatler, "The Dudley Mansion in Duluth," *Forgotten Minnesota*, 9 August 2017, https://www.forgottenminnesota.com/2017/08/09/2017-08-the-dudley-mansion-in-duluth/.

14 Manuscript schedules for the U.S. Census, 1900, 1910, 1920, 1930; Dierckins and Norton, *Lost Duluth*, 159; "The Shores," https://www.assistedliving.com/minnesota/duluth/the-shores/; comments from Maryanne Norton to the author, 2018.

15 Manuscript schedules for the U.S. Census, 1870, 1880, 1900, 1910, 1920, 1930, and for the Minnesota Census, 1905; Duluth city directories; James Allen Scott, *Duluth's Legacy: Architecture* (Duluth, Minn.: Department of Research and Planning, City of Duluth, 1974), 1:137; Dierckens and Norton, *Duluth's Grand Old Architecture*, 130; Duluth Preservation Alliance, "Third Annual House Tour," 1983, and "29th Annual Historic House Tour, Sept. 15, 2013"; comments from Michael Bayern to the author, 2015, 2019.

16 Manuscript schedules for the U.S. Census, 1930, 1940; Nelson and Dierckins, *Duluth's Historic Parks*, 224; David Gebhard and Tom Martinson, *A Guide to the Architecture of Minnesota* (Minneapolis: University of Minnesota Press, 1977), 198–99; *Duluth Visitor* 6 (15 May–1 June 1951), 20, Duluth city directories.

17 Gebhard and Martinson, *A Guide to the Architecture of Minnesota*, 198–99; Scott, *Duluth's Legacy*, 139.

18 Manuscript schedules for the U.S. Census, 1900, 1910, 1920, 1930, 1940; Wendy Grethen, "Historic Reflections: Lakeside–Lester Park Self-Guided Walking Tour," *Grey Green* (blog), 2006, http://www.greygreen.org/lakeside; "Lakeshore Manor Assisted Living," http://lakesidemanormn.com/.

19 *Duluth News-Tribune*, 11 January 1920, 3; 18 January 1920, E1; Nelson and Dierckins, *Duluth's Public Parks*, 224.

20 *Lake Superior News*, 12 March 1887, 4–5, citing the Association; 17 December 1887, 7; Dierckins and Norton, *Duluth's Grand Old Architecture*, 33.

21 *Lake Superior News*, 20 August 1886, 7; 17 December 1887, 7; Dierckins and Norton, *Duluth's Grand Old Architecture*, 33.

22 *Lake Superior News*, 17 December 1887, 7; *Duluth News-Tribune*, 29 October 1917, 7, citing Wires; Liza Nagel, "National Register of Historic Places Inventory—Nomination Form for the Limnological Station," 1978, SHPO-MDA.

23 *Duluth News-Tribune*, 12 December 1946, 1; Dierckins and Norton, *Duluth's Grand Old Architecture*, 33; Cathy

Wurzer, *Tales of the Road: Highway 61* (St. Paul: Minnesota Historical Society Press, 2008), 52–53.

24 Nagel, "Nomination Form for the Limnological Station"; Duluth Preservation Alliance, "2013 Preservation Awards"; UMD News Center, "Where Lake Superior Research Was Hatched," 8 October 2019, https://news.d.umn.edu/news-center/articles/limnology-building-preserved.

25 Manuscript schedules for the U.S. Census, 1900, 1910, 1920, 1930; Dierckins and Norton, *Duluth's Grand Old Architecture,* 33; Norton comments, 2018.

26 Manuscript schedules for the U.S. Census, 1910, 1920, 1930, 1940; *Duluth News-Tribune,* 6 September 1993, B6.

27 Tourist brochure, 1953; Duluth Preservation Alliance, "Third Annual House Tour"; *Duluth News-Tribune,* 6 September 1993, B6; Duluth city directories; Norton comments, 2018.

28 Duluth Preservation Alliance, "Third Annual House Tour"; Nelson and Dierckins, *Duluth's Historic Parks,* 229.

29 *Duluth News-Tribune,* 1 January 1926, B2; Mead & Hunt, "Minnesota Department of Transportation (Mn/DOT) Historic Bridge Management Plan—Bridge Number: 5772" (Minneapolis, Minn.: Mead & Hunt, 2006); Denis Gardner, *Wood+Concrete+Stone+Steel: Minnesota's Historic Bridges* (Minneapolis: University of Minnesota Press, 2008), 126; Nelson and Dierckins, *Duluth's Historic Parks,* 123–27.

30 Susan Granger, Scott Kelly, and Sue Grossman, "National Register of Historic Places Nomination Form for the Lester River Bridge (Bridge 5772)," 2002, SHPO-MDA; Preservation Alliance of Minnesota, "2006 Minnesota Preservation Awards," http://archive.mnpreservation.org/programs/minnesota-preservation-awards/2006-minnesota-preservation-awards/; ICRI, "Award of Merit: Transportation Category," 2011, https://www.icri.org/awards/icri-project-awards-2011/, Lester River Bridge.

31 *Duluth News-Tribune,* 1 January 1935, 1; George W. Kelley, "The Northshore Has Its Face Uplifted: CCC Boys Help Beautify a Famous Lake Driveway," *Duluth News-Tribune,* Current Events/Feature Stories, 24 May 1936, 1, citing Paine.

32 Nelson and Dierckins, *Duluth's Historic Parks,* 124–26; *Duluth News-Tribune,* 7 May 1922, Auto, 1, citing Snively; 6 August 1922, C8.

33 Nelson and Dierckins, *Duluth's Historic Parks,* 125–26; *Duluth News-Tribune,* 4 June 1922, 3; 20 July 1931, B1; 13 March 1938, A1; 17 August 1941, Pictures, 5; 28 August 1949, B5.

34 *Duluth News-Tribune,* 28 August 1949, B5, citing Hogue; George Lewis, "History Corner—Brighton Beach Tourist Camp," *Look at Lakeside,* October 2012, 3.

35 Gilman D. Feith, "History of the U.S. Environmental Research Laboratory at Duluth, MN, from Its Inception through 1987," typescript, Environmental Research Laboratory–Duluth, 1988; *Milwaukee Journal,* 17 August 1967, 9, citing Udall; Nelson and Dierckins, *Duluth's Historic Parks,* 126; USEPA, Duluth, Minn., Laboratory, "About the Great Lakes Toxicology and Ecology Division: What We Do," 2023, https://www.epa.gov/aboutepa/about-great-lakes-toxicology-and-ecology-division.

36 *Duluth News-Tribune,* 7 July 1921, 3; Nelson and Dierckins, *Duluth's Historic Parks,* 124–26.

37 Nelson and Dierckins, *Duluth's Historic Parks,* 125; Kathryn Mayo and William Mayo, *61 Gems of Highway 61* (Cambridge, Minn.: Adventure Publications, 2009), 18–19; comments from George Lewis to the author, 2013.

38 Mayo and Mayo, *61 Gems of Highway 61,* 18–19; Ron Morton, *A Road Guide: The North Shore of Lake Superior on Highway 61* (Duluth, Minn.: Rockflower Press, 2001), Kindle ed.; Peter Passi, "Makeover for Bruised Brighton Beach?," *Duluth News-Tribune,* 12 November 2018, A1, A4; *Duluth News-Tribune,* 22 March 2019, A2; 3 July 2021, A3; 28 May 2023, A2; comments from Barbara Stark to the author, October 2018.

39 Manuscript schedules for the U.S. Census, 1930, 1940; Duluth city directories; Lake Superior North Shore Association, travel brochure, 1953; Duluth Guide Co., *Duluth Souvenir Guide: Gateway Shores* (Duluth, Minn.: The Guide Company, 1958), 13; comments from Duane Madison to the author, 2015–16; comments from Mark Gilbertson to the author, 2016.

40 Manuscript schedules for the U.S. Census, 1940; tourist brochure, 1953; Duluth city directories; postcard caption for "Turk's Clearview Court," late 1950s.

41 Maryanne Norton, "Ask the Historian: Lost Golf Courses of the Twin Ports," *Zenith City Online,* 30 May 2013, http://zenithcity.com/archive/parks-landmarks/lost-golf-courses-of-the-twin-ports/.

42 Ronald K. Huch, "'Typhoid' Truelsen, Water, and Politics in Duluth, 1896–1900," *Minnesota History* 47 (Spring 1981): 191–93; Dierckens and Norton, *Duluth's Grand Old Architecture,* 33.

43 "National Register of Historic Places Inventory—

Nomination Form for the Lakewood Pumping Station," 1994, SHPO-MDA (the Pumping Station has not been listed in the National Register); Shawn Perich, *The North Shore: A Four-Season Guide to Minnesota's Favorite Destination* (Minneapolis: University of Minnesota Press, 1992), 10; Dierckens and Norton, *Duluth's Grand Old Architecture*, 33.

44 *Duluth Herald*, 26 April 1943, 1–2; 21 July 1943, 12; 27 August 1946, 13; 27 August 1946, 13; 2 November 1954; "Northern Shores Townhomes, LLC," 2016, https://www.bizapedia.com/mn/northern-shores-townhomes-llc.html.

45 Duluth city directories; manuscript schedules for the U.S. Census, 1910, 1920, 1930, 1940; tourist brochure, 1953; comments from Julie Sievert to the author, 2015.

46 Comments from Julie Sievert to the author, 2015; Briells Bredsten, "New Owners, Same Charm at Inn on Gitche Gumee," *Duluth News Tribune*, 27 November 2023.

47 *Duluth News-Tribune*, 30 May 1915, 14; 8 August 1915, B16; 19 September 1915, A9.

48 Manuscript schedules for the U.S. Census, 1940; comments from Helen Silander Hendrickson to the author, 2014; Madison comments, 2014–16.

49 Duluth city directories; Lake Breeze Motel Resort, http://www.lakebreeze.com/.

50 "Plat for Bristol Beach Subdivision," Register of Deeds, Duluth Courthouse, 1922.

51 Duluth city directories, 1943, 1951, 1956, 1960; manuscript schedules for the U.S. Census, 1940; *Duluth News-Tribune*, 24 February 1962, 1; comments from Cynthia Donner to the author, 2015, 2021; Duluth City building permits, 2023.

52 Manuscript schedules for the U.S. Census, 1910, 1920, 1930, 1940; tourist brochures, 1940, 1942, circa early 1940s, 1946, 1948, 1950, 1953; *Duluth Visitor*, 15–31 July 1965, 26; Duluth city directories; Wurzer, *Highway 61*, 18–19; Gardenwood, http://gardenwoodresort.com/about; comments from Pam Cone to the author, 2018.

53 Wurzer, *Highway 61*, 18–19; telephone directory, Duluth region, December 1962; *North Shore Regional Telephone Directory*, April 1979; tourist brochure, 1972; Gardenwood Resort & Motel, https://www.gardenwoodresort.com/; Hendrickson comments, 2016; Cone comments, 2018; Motschenbacher comments, 2023.

54 Kathryn Strand Koutsky and Linda Koutsky, *Minnesota Eats Out: An Illustrated History* (St. Paul: Minnesota Historical Society Press, 2003), 19; Clover Valley/French River Community History Committee, *Roots in the Past*, 71; tourist brochures, 1944, 1945, 1950, 1953; *Duluth News-Tribune*, 25 May 1952, A6; 7 June 1953, 18. Claude Midlam married Evelyn Cowden in 1961 after he and his first wife divorced.

55 Tourist brochure, 1953; *Duluth News-Tribune*, 30 September 2000, A1, A5; Larry Oaks, "New Look at a North Shore Legacy," *StarTribune*, 22 February 2002, B1, B4, citing Evera; *StarTribune*, 10 June 2009, B1; "Sheldon Aubut's Duluth History: McQuade Road Fish Fry, Store and Campground," http://www.cityhistory.us/duluth/stories/mcquade.htm; Hendrickson comments, 2016; comments from Alvera Sternberg Shatto to the author, 2016; comments from John Schifsky to the author, 2019, 2020, 2023.

56 MDNR, "McQuade Access," http://www.dnr.state.mn.us/water_access/harbors/mcquade.html.

57 Manuscript schedules for the U.S. Census, 1930.

58 Paul Lawson, "Withered Promise: Century Leaves Clifton Less Than Metropolis," *Duluth News-Tribune*, 30 October 1955, A45; Schifsky comments, 2018, 2019.

59 Schifsky comments, 2019; comments from Mary Ann Sironen to the author, 2023; comments from Angie Braud to the author, 2023.

60 "Plat for Clifton, Lake Superior County, Minnesota Territory," 1856, on file in the St. Louis County Register of Deeds Office, Duluth, Minn.; Walter Van Brunt, ed., *Duluth and St. Louis County: Their Story and People* (Chicago: American Historical Society, 1921), 387–88; Minnesota Legislative Reference Library, "Legislators Past and Present," http://www.leg.state.mn.us/legdb/fulldetail.aspx7ID+12004; John Fritzen, *Historic Sites and Place Names of Minnesota's North Shore* (Duluth, Minn.: St. Louis County Historical Society, 1974), 4; Clover Valley/French River Community History Committee, *Roots in the Past*, 27–28; Sandvik, "Land Office Buchanan," 180–81.

61 Charles S. Bryant, *History of the Upper Mississippi Valley* (St. Paul: Minnesota Historical Society Press, 1881); *Duluth Weekly Tribune*, 6 April 1886, 4; *Duluth News-Tribune*, 20 April 1902, 8; 16 November 1953; *Duluth Herald*, 22 February 1915, 14; "Sharon Croft Johnson Shares Her Memories," *The Landmarks*, June 1973, 3 (*The Landmarks*, a monthly newsletter for the townships of Lakewood, Alden, Normanna, and Duluth, was published from September 1968 through June 1979 and from June 1985 through July 1989); Gerald Egger, "The Smith Croft Family of Fishermen," *North Shore Commercial Fishing Museum Journal* 22 (Fall 2014).

62 *Duluth News-Tribune,* 22 October 1897, 5; Clover Valley/French River Community History Committee, *Roots in the Past,* 36, 49; Fritzen, *Historic Sites and Place Names,* 4; Todd Lindahl, "The Clifton Depot," *Duluth Township Newsletter,* March 2005, 3, http://www.duluthtownship.org/pdf/newsletter/march2005.pdf.

63 Walter Eldot, "North Shore Tells Tales of Hoffman," *Duluth News-Tribune,* Cosmopolitan, 4 March 1956, 3.

64 Manuscript schedules for the U.S. Census, 1910, 1920, 1930, 1940; Minneapolis–St. Paul and Duluth city directories; Walter Eldot, "'Baron' Prefers the North Shore," *Duluth News-Tribune,* Cosmopolitan, 1 August 1954, 4; *Duluth News-Tribune,* 10 January 1964; 4 January 1969, 9; comments from Merle Norgren to the author, 2016.

65 Manuscript schedules for the U.S. Census, 1920, 1930, 1940; Duluth city directories; Norgren comments, 2016; *Duluth News-Tribune,* 4 January 1969, 9.

66 Tourist brochure, 1953; business cards for the Beachway Motel & Cabins (Minn.) and the Beach Resort Motel & Cabins (Wisc.), 2013; Norgren comments, 2014.

67 "Beachway Motel and Cabins," Yahoo! Travel, 2009; "Beachway Motel and Cabins," Yelp, 2014.

68 Hildebrandt comments, 2013; *StarTribune,* 17 May 2016.

69 Manuscript schedules for the U.S. Census, 1910, 1920, 1930, 1940; Duluth city directories; tourist brochure, 1949; *Duluth News-Tribune,* 11 March 1964, 13; 24 March 1997, A7; Shatto comments, 2016.

70 Manuscript schedules for the U.S. Census, 1930; Shatto comments, 2014, 2016.

71 *Duluth Visitor,* 16–31 July 1960, 12; John Lundy, "New Business Model at Lakeview Castle Site," *Duluth News-Tribune,* 11 August 2010, A1; Shatto comments, 2016; Cory Fechner, "RIP Lakeview Castle," *Perfect Duluth Day* (blog), 30 December 2009, https://www.perfectduluthday.com/2009/12/30/rip-lakeview-castle-duluth/.

72 *Duluth News-Tribune,* 31 December 2009, B1; Lundy, "New Business Model"; Candace Renalls, "New Name, New Look for 'The Castle,'" *Duluth News-Tribune,* 6 December 2010, B1, B3; Shatto comments, 2016; Red Swan Catering and Event Center, http://greatlakesdrive.com/GLD/property/the-clearwater-event-center/.

73 Hess, Roise & Co., "Bridge No. 003797 [Talmadge River]," Minnesota Historic Bridge Inventory, 1996, SHPO-MDA; Andrew Munsch, "Historic U.S. 61: Talmadge River Bridge," Deadpioneer's Historic Minnesota Highways, https://www.deadpioneer.com/routes/US61/historicus61se/talmadgeriver/talmadgeriver.html.

74 Tourist brochures, 1937, 1949, 1953; Hendrickson comments, 2014; Sironen comments, 2016; Norgren comments, 2016.

75 Fritzen, *Historic Sites and Place Names,* 5; Norwood, "Description of the Northwest Shore of Lake Superior," 349, 356; Wolff, "Some Vanished Settlements of the Arrowhead Country," 177; Sandvik, "Land Office Buchanan," 280.

76 Fritzen, *Historic Sites and Place Names,* 5–6; Wolff, "Some Vanished Settlements of the Arrowhead Country," 177; Vernon A. Palms, "A Brief History of the French River District," in Clover Valley/French River Community History Committee, *Roots in the Past,* 105, 31–35; manuscript schedules for the U.S. Census, 1920, 1930; Nute, *Lake Superior,* 202.

77 Manuscript schedules for the U.S. Census, 1910, 1920, 1930, 1940, 1950; tourist brochure, 1950; Hendrickson comments, 2015.

78 Manuscript schedules for the U.S. Census, 1930, 1940; Duluth city directories; "'Country Stores' in Duluth Township," *The Landmarks,* May 1974, 3–4, https://www.duluthtownship.org/arts-and-heritage-group/landmarks-archive/; Hendrickson comments, 2015.

79 Alanen, *Finns in Minnesota,* 86–88; French River Lutheran Church Congregation, "Dedication Service: 50th Anniversary, 1924–74."

80 French River Lutheran Church Congregation, "Dedication Service: French River Lutheran Church, October 6th, 1957"; French River Lutheran Church Congregation, "Dedication Service: 50th Anniversary"; comments from Tiffany Lefner-Zifco to the author, 2021; Alanen, *Finns in Minnesota,* 88.

81 MnDOT, "Clifton–French River Historical Marker: Historic Roadside Development Structures on Minnesota Trunk Highways, 1998," SHPO-MDA; Gemini Research, *Historic Roadside Development,* 5.20, 5.21.

82 Manuscript schedules for the U.S. Census, 1920, 1930, 1940; *Two Harbors Chronicle-Times,* 10 July 1958, 1.

83 Chilton D. Aldrich, *The Real Log Cabin* (New York: Macmillan, 1928), xi; "Chilson Darragh Aldrich, Architect, 1876–1948—an Appreciation," *Northwest Architect* 15 (July–August 1951): 40–41.

84 Page and Hill, *Cabins of Real Logs* (Minneapolis, Minn.: Page and Hill, 1936).

85 Page and Hill, citing Mary Snyder.

86 Manuscript schedules for the U.S. Census, 1940; *Two Harbors Chronicle-Times,* 10 July 1958, 1; comments from Mike Lazaretti and Tim Counts to the author, 2014,

2016; information posted by Snyder family members on Ancestry.com.

87 Lazaretti and Counts comments, 2016; Duluth Preservation Alliance, "2016 Preservation Awards Event," https://duluthpreservation.org/events/2016-preservation-awards-event/. The historic preservation specialists and builders were Leone Graf and Matt Favet.

88 Hess, Roise & Co., "Bridge No. 003797 [French River]," Minnesota Historic Bridge Inventory, 1996, SHPO-MDA; Andrew Munsch, "Historic U.S. 61: French River Bridge," Deadpioneer's Historic Minnesota Highways, https://www.deadpioneer.com/routes/US61/historicus61se/frenchriver/frenchriver.html; *Duluth News-Tribune*, 22 March 2019, A2; comments from Rachel Gregg to the author, 2019; AFLA, "French River Wayside," https://aflandarc.com/work/french-river/.

89 *Duluth News-Tribune*, 30 March 1913, 7; 29 July 1914, 14; *General Laws of the State of Minnesota, Thirty-Eighth Session of the Legislature* (St. Paul, Minn.: Earle S. Goodrich, State Printer, 1913), 703; HDR Engineering, *French River Cold Water Hatchery Rehabilitation Analysis* (St. Paul: MDNR, 2013), II-2, IV-1.

90 Cory A. Goldsworthy, Keith A. Reeves, Joshua E. Blankenheim, and Nick R. Peterson, *Fisheries Management Plan for the Minnesota Waters of Lake Superior, 2016–2025*, 3rd ed. (St. Paul: MDNR, 2017); Minnesota Steelheader, "Lake Superior Kamloops Rainbow Trout," https://minnesotasteelheader.com/our-fish/kamloops/; HDR Engineering, *French River Cold Water Hatchery*, II-2, IV-1; Dennis Andersen, "On the North Shore, Wild-Strain Steelhead Stocking Revives after Covid Pause," *StarTribune*, 25 February 2022; comments from Deserae Hendrickson to the author, 2019; comments from Fredric J. Schmitz to the author, 2020.

91 Goldsworthy et al., *Fisheries Management Plan*, 86–92; HDR Engineering, *French River Cold Water Hatchery*, II-2, IV-1; Sam Cook, "French River Hatchery Repairs Could Cost $7.6 Million," *Duluth News-Tribune*, 27 October 2013, C8–C9.

92 Manuscript schedules for the U.S. Census, 1920, 1930, 1940; comments from Jackie Mueller to the author, 2014, 2016.

93 Earl Finberg, "'Swissota': A North Shore Log Lodge Patterned on Swiss Models," *Duluth News-Tribune*, Cosmopolitan, 6 October 1946, 20; Mueller comments, 2016. I am indebted to the late Ron Kyllonen, who provided access to the Swissota in 2015.

94 Mueller comments, 2016.

95 Tourist brochures, 1957; Duluth Guide Co., *Duluth Souvenir Guide*, 13; *Duluth Visitor*, 15–31 August 1960, 25; *Duluth News-Tribune*, 20 May 2012, D4; Mueller comments, 2016.

96 Manuscript schedules for the U.S. Census, 1910, 1920; comments from Lou Mattson to the author, 2019; interview with Hjalmer L. Mattson, conducted by Barbara W. Sommer, 7 November 1977, Archives and Manuscripts, Martin Library, UMD, http://reflections.mndigital.org/cdm/ref/collection/nemhc/id/4901.

97 Manuscript schedules for the U.S. Census, 1900, 1910, 1920, 1930, 1940; Mattson comments, 2019, citing Hjalmer Mattson; Clover Valley/French River Community History Committee, *Roots in the Past*, 37.

98 Tourist brochures, 1950, 1953; *Duluth News-Tribune*, 17 February 1946, 4; Robert Gerber, "North Shore Ice Bars Trout Harvest," *Duluth News-Tribune*, 16 April 1950, 1, 6; Jim Blubaugh, "One Man's Junk Is Another's . . . ," *Duluth News-Tribune*, 10 April 1977, B1, B7; Mattson interview; Hendrickson comments, 2015; Mattson comments, 2019; Schifsky comments, 2020.

99 Blubaugh, "One Man's Junk," B1, B7; Mattson comments, 2019.

100 Mattson comments, 2019.

101 Manuscript schedules for the U.S. Census, 1910, 1920; Richard Hudelson, "The Scandinavian Local of the Duluth Socialist Party: 1910–1924," *Swedish-American Historical Quarterly* 44 (October 1993): 181–90; *Duluth Herald*, 3 March 1937, 8; 13 June 1977, C5; *Duluth News-Tribune*, 9 March 1941, 14; comments from Tara Bates Golden to the author, February 2016; "'Country Stores' in Duluth Township."

102 Manuscript schedules for the U.S. Census, 1940; tourist brochures, 1953; Duluth Guide Co., *Duluth Souvenir Guide*, 13; Wonderland Resort Facebook page, https://www.facebook.com/wonderlandresortke/.

103 Golden comments, 2016; Wonderland Resort Facebook page; "Wonderland Resort," Wikibin, accessed 2023; *Duluth News-Tribune*, 27 September 2015, D5.

104 *Duluth Visitor*, 15 August–1 September 1949, 21; Wurzer, *Highway 61*, 49–51; "Paul Gilmore," Wikipedia, accessed 2003; Shatto comments, 2014, 2016; "Quonset: Metal Living for a Modern Age," http://www.quonsethuts.org/huts/.

105 *Duluth Visitor*, 1–15 July 1949, 21; 15 August–1 September 1949, 21; 1–15 September 1949, 17; 15 September–1 October 1949, 17.

106 *Duluth Visitor*, 15–31 July 1955, 4; 1–15 September 1955,

4; 1–15 July 1956, 21; 15–31 July 1957, 7; Wurzer, *Highway 61*, 49–51.

107 Manuscript schedules for the U.S. Census, 1930, 1940, 1950; Duluth Guide Co., *Duluth Souvenir Guide*, 14; tourist brochure, 1953; *Duluth Visitor*, 15–31 July 1965, 26; Madison comments, 2016.

108 Rick Nelson, "Duluth's New Scenic Café Is a 20-Year Success Story," *StarTribune*, 30 December 2019; Jana Hollingsworth, "Dining Out: New Scenic Café Still Inspires," *Duluth News-Tribune*, 8 July 2015, C1.

109 Scott Graden, with Arlene Anderson, *New Scenic Café: The Cookbook* (Duluth, Minn.: New Scenic Café, 2014), 28–29; Duluth Guide Co., *Duluth Souvenir Guide*, 14; Brady Slater, "Making Magic on the North Shore: New Scenic Celebrates 20 Years," *Duluth News-Tribune*, 21 March 2019, A1; Madison comments, 2014–16; comments from Carolyn Marino to the author, 2016.

110 Arlene Anderson, "A Conversation with Scott," in Graden, *New Scenic Café*, 31–34; Graden, *New Scenic Café*, 28–29; Slater, "Making Magic on the North Shore."

111 Anderson, "A Conversation with Scott," 31–34; Shawn Perich, "New Scenic Café Celebrates 20 Years," *Northern Wilds Magazine*, April 2019, https://northernwilds.com/new-scenic-cafe-celebrates-20-years/; comments from Scott Graden to the author, 2019.

112 James Norton, *Lake Superior Flavors: A Field Guide to Food and Drink along the Circle Tour* (Minneapolis: University of Minnesota Press, 2014), 58; Nelson, "Duluth's New Scenic Café"; Graden, *New Scenic Café*; Scott Graden, *New Scenic Café: The Second Cookbook* (privately published, 2023).

113 "Obituary of Glen C. Nelson: Artist, Mentor and Author," Jane Street Clayworks, 2011, http://janestreetclayworks.com/2011/03/06/obituary-of-glenn-nelson-artist-mentor-and-author/ (inactive website); Hendrickson comments, 2014–15; comments from Alvera Pierson to the author, 2016.

114 "Glenn Nelsons Leaving the Area," *The Landmarks*, September 1975, 3. I am indebted to Marlene Wisuri for the written notes and floor plan sketches of Ironstone that she provided in September 2014.

115 "Glenn Nelsons Leaving the Area"; "Obituary of Glen C. Nelson."

116 Pierson comments, 2016; Hendrickson comments, 2014–19; Rich Sill, "Back Roads, Back Porches," *The Landmarks*, May 1988, 4.

117 Manuscript schedules for the U.S. Census, 1940; tourist brochure, 1945; *Duluth Visitor*, 1–15 August 1946, 18; 1–15 August 1953, 25; Sill, "Back Roads, Back Porches"; Pierson comments, 2016; Hendrickson comments, 2015–19.

118 Tourist brochure, 1953; James Norton, "Sean Lewis of Nokomis in Duluth, MN," *Heavy Table*, 15 September 2009, http://heavytable.com/sean-lewis-of-nokomis-in-duluth-mn/; Rick Nelson, "Bummer: Duluth's Nokomis Is Calling It Quits," *StarTribune*, 3 October 2012.

119 Manuscript schedules for the U.S. Census, 1900, 1920, 1920, 1930; "U.S. Headstone Applications for Military Veterans, Alphonse M. Anderson, 1953," Ancestry.com; Pierson comments, 2016; Lynne Compton, "Gertrude Osbakken," *The Landmarks*, February 1988, 1, 2.

120 Manuscript schedules for the U.S. Census, 1910, 1920, 1930, 1940; Pierson comments, 2016.

121 Manuscript schedules for the U.S. Census, 1930, 1940; tourist brochures, 1946, 1949, 1950; Duluth Guide Co., *Duluth Souvenir Guide*, 14; Pierson comments, 2016.

122 Manuscript schedules for the U.S. Census, 1920, 1930, 1940; Sironen comments, 2014–16.

123 Manuscript schedules for the U.S. Census, 1920, 1930, 1940, 1950; Clover Valley/French River Community History Committee, *Roots in the Past*, 41; Evelyn Lukkonen and Alvera Pierson, "Blue Bird Landing," *The Landmarks*, December 1971, 4; Mary Ann Sironen Lukkonen, "Blue Bird Landing," 31 August 2000 (unpublished typewritten account provided to the author); Sironen comments, 2014–16, 2023–24.

124 Lukkonen and Pierson, "Blue Bird Landing"; Sironen, "Blue Bird Landing"; Sironen comments, 2014.

125 Sironen, "Blue Bird Landing"; Sironen comments, 2014, 2023; *Duluth News-Tribune*, 23 December 2018, D5.

126 Lukkonen and Pierson, "Blue Bird Landing"; Sironen, "Blue Bird Landing"; Sironen comments, 2016, 2023.

127 Fritzen, *Historic Sites and Place Names*, 6; Todd Lindahl, "The Start of Palmers," *Duluth Township Newsletter*, January 2008, 2.

128 Manuscript schedules for the U.S. Census, 1900, 1910, 1920, 1930, 1940; *Duluth News-Tribune*, 20 February 1956, 1.

129 Comments from Jon Luikart to the author, 2016; Hendrickson comments, 2016; Pierson comments, 2016.

130 Tourist brochures, 1948, 1949, 1961; Hendrickson comments, 2016; Pierson comments, 2016; Luikart comments, 2016.

131 Luikart comments, 2016; Pierson comments, 2016; Hendrickson comments, 2016; Molly Hoeg, "Lodge Logic," *Lake Superior Magazine*, August/September 2016, 46–52.

132 Fritzen, *Historic Sites and Place Names*, 6; *Duluth Weekly*

*Herald*, 26 November 1913, 10; Pierson comments, 2016; comments from Carolyn Marino to the author, 2016.

133 Tom Willkowske, "Lighthouse's Breaded Herring Recalls the Shorecrest," *Duluth News-Tribune*, 23 August 2007, G6; Schifsky comments, 2020; Eric Faust, "Lighthouse on Homestead in Duluth, MN," *Heavy Table*, 17 November 2009, http://heavytable.com/lighthouse-on-homestead-in-duluth-mn/.

134 Candace Renalls, "Former Lighthouse on Homestead Building Gets New Life as Vacation Rental," *Duluth News-Tribune*, 23 November 2015, C1; "North Shore Lighthouse Suites," http://www.northshorelighthousesuites.com/north-shore-lighthouse-suites.html.

135 Clover Valley Forum, 26 January 2007; Two Harbors Forum, 22 September 2010; Deborah Morse-Kahn, *Lake Superior's Historic North Shore: A Guided Tour* (St. Paul: Minnesota Historical Society Press, 2008), 60; "American Missionary Fellowship," Wikipedia, accessed 2023.

136 Minneapolis–St. Paul and Duluth city directories; Eldot, "'Baron' Prefers the North Shore," 4; tourist brochure, 1953; *Duluth Visitor*, 1–15 July 1960, 12–13; 1–15 July 1964, 27; 2–15 July 1965, 26; Marino comments, 2016.

137 *Duluth Visitor*, 15–31 July 1954, 12; 1–15 July 1957, 18; 1–15 July 1960, 12–13; 1–15 July 1964, 27; 2–15 July 1965, 26; *Duluth News-Tribune*, 10 January 1964; Marino comments, 2016; Norgren comments, 2016.

138 Manuscript schedules for the U.S. Census, 1940; Morse-Kahn, *Lake Superior's Historic North Shore*, 60; Tom's Historic Logging Camp and Old Northwest Co. Trading Post, http://www.tomsloggingcamp.com/.

139 *Duluth Visitor*, 1–15 June 1966, 24; tourist brochure, 1972; Tom's Historic Logging Camp; Marino comments, 2016; "Minnesota's Scenic 61," *MidwestWeekends*, 19 October 2015, citing Weckman, http://www.midwestweekends.com/plan_a_trip/touring/scenic_byways/north_shore_scenic_highway.html (inactive website).

140 *Duluth News-Tribune*, 13 May 1913.

141 Kelley, "Northshore Has Its Face Lifted," 1; B. C. Rogers, "Camp Improvement," *Lakeshore Camp News*, 21 May 1936, 2; Rogers, "Congratulations," *Lakeshore Camp News*, 21 June 1936, 2; John Pawlek, "Photograph Album of CCC Co. 1751, Project SP-18." *Lakeshore Camp News* and the photograph album are on file at the Iron Range Research Center, Chisholm, Minn.

142 Sommer, *Hard Work and a Good Deal*, 147; *Lakeshore Camp News*, 21 May 1936, 3–4; Kelley, "North Shore Has Its Face Lifted," 1.

143 Sommer, *Hard Work and a Good Deal*, 147; *Two Harbors Chronicle*, 4 November 1937, 1; Stacy Mitchell, "Union in the North Woods: The Timber Strike of 1937," *Minnesota History* 56 (Spring 1999): 272; Schifsky comments, 2019–20.

144 LHB Inc., "St. Louis County Public Works Stoney Point Wayside: Report on Existing Conditions and Rehabilitation Recommendations for the Stony [*sic*] Point Wayside," Duluth, Minn., 14 April 2006, SHPO-MDA.

145 LHB Inc.

146 Manuscript schedules for the U.S. Census, 1940; *Duluth News-Tribune*, 4 October 1989, B7; Pearson comments, 2016; Hendrickson comments, 2016; Sironen comments, 2023.

147 Pearson comments, 2016.

148 Manuscript schedules for the U.S. Census, 1920, 1930, 1940; Hendrickson comments 2016; Richards comments, 2016.

149 Brian Stablinger, "Stoney Point: USA, Northeast, the Great Lakes," WannaSurf (undated; inactive website); Dan Kraker, "Lake Superior Surfers Brave Frigid Weather for Giant Freshwater Waves," MPR News, 6 January 2022, https://www.mprnews.org/story/2022/01/06/lake-superior-surfers-brave-frigid-weather-for-giant-freshwater-waves.

150 Manuscript schedules for the U.S. Census, 1920, 1930, 1940; information from Ancestry.com.

151 Comments from Daniel Watkins to the author, 2016.

152 Information from Ancestry.com; Dodges Log Lodges, http://www.dodgeslog.com/; Watkins comments, 2016.

153 *Duluth Visitor*, 15–31 August 1946, 7; August 1947, 17; 1–15 July 1951, 17; 15–31 July 1962, 7; *Duluth News-Tribune*, 9 May 1997, B9; comments from Christine Schousboe to the author, 2016; comments from Allison Kampbell to the author, 2016.

154 Comments from Bayne Brown to the author, 2015; Richards comments, 2016.

155 Brown comments, 2015; Richards comments, 2019.

156 Glenn N. Sandvik, "Land Office Buchanan: Emporium of the North Shore," *Minnesota History* 52 (Fall 1991): 281, 288.

157 Sandvik, "Land Office Buchanan," 281, 285–87.

158 Sandvik, 281, 285–87.

159 Sandvik, 283–88.

160 NPS and State of Minnesota Department of Highways, "Lakeshore Wayside Historical Monument, S.P.6926-01 (TH61)," 26 September 1936, 4 March 1937, on file with MnDOT. I am indebted to Andrew Munsch, who provided a copy of this document.

161 Mayo and Mayo, *61 Gems of Highway 61*, 22; NPS and State of Minnesota Department of Highways, "Lakeshore Wayside Historical Monument."

## Lake County

1 "Unorganized Territory," Wikipedia, accessed 2023.
2 U.S. Census of Population, 1890–2020.
3 U.S. Census of Population, 2020.
4 Warren Upham, *Minnesota Place Names: A Geographical Encyclopedia* (1920; repr., St. Paul: Minnesota Historical Society Press, 2001), 311; *Journal-News*, 18 January 1917; Fritzen, *Historic Sites and Place Names*, 7; Bishop, *By Water and Rail*, 95; Knife River Heritage and Cultural Center interpretive panel; Morton, *A Road Guide*.
5 Bishop, *By Water and Rail*, 96–98; John A. Monger, "Knife River's Growing Importance," *Duluth News-Tribune*, 6 June 1915, 15; *Memoirs of Knife River* (privately published, c. 1985), 4; "Charles Anderson (c.1841–1926), Genealogy," Wikipedia, accessed 2023.
6 Franklin A. King, "Logging Railroads of Northern Minnesota," *Railway and Locomotive Historical Society Bulletin* 93 (October 1955): 94, 108–110; *Duluth News-Tribune*, 17 November 1901.
7 Bishop, *By Water and Rail*, 82–85, 96–98; Fritzen, *Historic Sites and Place Names*, 8; *Memoirs of Knife River*, 7–8; Monger, "Knife River's Growing Importance," 11.
8 Manuscript schedules for the U.S. Census, 1900, 1910, 1920, 1930; Monger, "Knife River's Growing Importance," 11; *Memoirs of Knife River*, 9; Bishop, *By Water and Rail*, 98.
9 Manuscript schedules for the U.S. Census, 1900, 1910, 1930; Monger, "Knife River's Growing Importance," 11; "Knife River, Minnesota," Wikipedia, accessed 2023.
10 Manuscript schedules for the U.S. Census, 1910.
11 Manuscript schedules for the U.S. Census, 1920, 1930; *Journal-News*, 19 January 1917, 12; *Duluth News-Tribune*, 27 April 1930, C1; Bishop, *By Water and Rail*, 91; "Knife River, Minnesota"; "Lake No. 2, Minnesota," Wikipedia, accessed 2022.
12 Adelle Whitefoot, "Knife River Celebration of Julebyen Recognized by Norwegian News Outlet," *Duluth News-Tribune*, 4 December 2015, A8; "Julebyen 2022," Julebyen Christmas Village, December 3–4, 2022.
13 Andrew Slade, *Hiking the North Shore*, 2nd ed. (Duluth, Minn.: There and Back Books, 2018), 41–43; Eve and Gary Wallinga, *Waterfalls of Minnesota's North Shore and More*, 2nd ed. (Grand Marais, Minn.: North Shore Books, 2015), 46–49; Sarah P. Rubenstein, *Minnesota History along the Highways: A Guide to Historic Markers and Sites* (St. Paul: Minnesota Historical Society Press, 2003), 208–9.
14 Krech Ojard, "North Shore Scenic Railroad Bridge 19A," https://www.krechojard.com/project/railroad-bridge-19a/.
15 Ojard; Mike Creger, "Old North Shore Bridge Comes Down," *Duluth News-Tribune*, 15 November 2009, C1.
16 Manuscript schedules for the Minnesota Census, 1905, and U.S. Census, 1910, 1920, 1930, 1940; tourist brochure, 1937; *Two Harbors News-Chronicle*, 11 August 1949; *Duluth News-Tribune*, 23 October 1959, 24; 4 October 1974; Madison comments, 2015; comments from Joanne Erickson Lind to the author, 2016; comments from Randy Ellestad to the author, 2017.
17 Manuscript schedules for the U.S. Census, 1900, 1910, 1920, 1930; *Memoirs of Knife River*, 23.
18 *Lake County News-Chronicle*, 23 October 1940; tourist brochure, 1937; *Duluth Visitor*, 15 September–1 October 1947, 6; *Memoirs of Knife River*, 23.
19 Manuscript schedules for the U.S. Census, 1940; *Duluth Visitor*, 1–15 July 1957, 19; 1–15 July 1958, 26; 2 July 1965, 27; *Duluth News-Tribune*, 4 September 2007.
20 *Duluth Visitor*, 1–15 July 1957, 19; 1–15 July 1958, 26; 2 July 1965, 27; Eric Faust, "Russ Kendall's Smoke House in Knife River, MN: In Their Own Words," *Heavy Table*, 17 December 2009, http://heavytable.com/russ-kendalls-smoke-house-in-knife-river-mn/; "Bizarre Foods with Andrew Zimmern—Minnesota," Travel Channel, 19 April 2010, http://livedash.ark.com/transcript/bizarre_foods_with_andrew_zimmern- (inactive website).
21 Andrew Krueger, "Fire Severely Damages Russ Kendall's Smokehouse on North Shore," *Duluth News-Tribune*, 13 May 2014, A1; Brady Slater, "Less Than Six Weeks after a Devastating Fire, and with Community Help, Russ Kendall's Smokehouse Is Ready for Business—and So Are the Customers," *Duluth News-Tribune*, 21 June 2014, A1; Faust, "Russ Kendall's Smoke House"; Michelle Miller, "Russ Kendall's Smokehouse: A Century of Tradition," *Northern Wilds*, 21 February 2023, https://northernwilds.com/russ-kendalls-smokehouse-a-century-of-tradition/.
22 Manuscript schedules for the U.S. Census, 1880, 1900, 1910, 1920, 1930, 1940; "Memoirs of Knife River," 57, 59; tourist brochure, 1949.
23 U.S. Patents, "Trolling Plane: Lloyd E. Coolidge and Francis I. Coolidge, Knife River, Minn., Application September 5, 1940, Serial No. US355420A, Patented March 25, 1941"; Madison comments, 2016; Norgren comments, 2016; *Knife River Heritage and Cultural Center Newsletter*, January 2021, citing Ellestad.

24 Jane Brissett, "Invasion of the Rich," *Duluth News-Tribune*, 7 August 2005, A6.

25 *Two Harbors Chronicle*, 29 June 1939, 1; 5 October 1939, 1; Einar Karlstrand, "Knife River Residents Build a Basin," *Duluth News-Tribune*, Cosmopolitan, 3 October 1948, 3.

26 Ford Eastman, "Harbors of Refuge," *Duluth News-Tribune*, Cosmopolitan, 24 October 1948, 14; *Duluth News-Tribune*, 3 April 1960, 1; Karlstrand, "Knife River Residents Build a Basin"; MDNR, "Knife River Marina and Access," https://www.dnr.state.mn.us/water_access/harbors/knife_river.html.

27 Tourist brochure, 1972; *Duluth Herald*, 31 July 1974; *Duluth News-Tribune*, 31 July 1974; *Chronicle & Times* (Two Harbors), 8 August 1974; MDNR, "Knife River Marina and Access"; Paul von Goertz, "Future of Knife River Marina Is Anyone's Guess," *Historic Knife River Heritage & Cultural Center Newsletter* (October 2023), 1–4.

28 Manuscript schedules for the U.S. Census, 1930, 1940, 1950; tourist brochure, 1972; Ellestad comments, 2017; *Duluth News-Tribune*, 11 January 1972, 17; 2 May 1990, D2.

29 Knife River Campground: RV & Tent Sites, http://www.kniferivercampground.com/.

30 Jamey Malcomb, "Knife River Looks to Restore Train Depot," *Lake County News-Chronicle*, 29 January 2018, 1; Terri Cadeau, "Knife River Depot Project Chugs Along," *Lake County News-Chronicle*, 29 March 2019, A1; "Volunteers Make Progress on Knife River Depot Restoration," *Lake County News-Chronicle*, 13 September 2019, A1, citing Ronning.

31 *Duluth News-Tribune*, 17 June 1939, 3; Samantha Erkkila, "Historical Society Donates Fishing Tug to Knife River," *Duluth News-Tribune*, 22 December 2016, A7, citing Randy Ellestad; Terru Cadeau, "Passion Projects Unite Community," *Duluth News-Tribune*, 2 September 2023, A1; *Knife River Heritage & Cultural Center Newsletter* (March 2024), 1.

32 Gerhard Folgero, "Across the North Atlantic in an Open Boat," diary translation, http://leiferiksonvikingship.com/portfolio-items/folgeros-story/.

33 Cadeau, "Passion Projects Unite Community"; "*Leif Erickson* (Ship)," Wikipedia, accessed 2023; Peter Passi, "Replica Viking Ship Heads to New Port," *Duluth News-Tribune*, 3 August 2022, 1; Editorial Board, "Norse Funeral Avoided in Knife River," *Duluth News-Tribune*, 5 August 2022, 4.

34 "Knife River Ladies Aid," manuscript in possession of Knife River Lutheran Church; "Knife River Lutheran Church History," https://www.kniferiverlutheran.church/history.

35 "Knife River Ladies Aid"; "Knife River Lutheran Church History"; comments from Marv Hold to the author, 2016; comments from the Rev. Susan Berge to the author, 2021.

36 Manuscript schedules for the U.S. Census, 1910, 1920, 1930, 1940; tourist brochures, 1948, 1949; Hold comments, 2016; Berge comments, 2021.

37 Alanen, *Pines, Mines, and Lakes*, 3–47, 3–48; *Lake County News-Chronicle*, 9 June 2000, 1–2; Chuck Frederick, "Community Post," *Duluth News-Tribune*, 15 June 2000, B1–B2; Candace Renalls, "Lighthouse Restaurant Opens at New Location in Knife River," *Duluth News-Tribune*, 11 September 2011, C1; "Owners Say Lighthouse at Emily's in Knife River Is Closing for Good," *Duluth News-Tribune*, 18 October 2015, C1; Brady Slater, "New Life Ahead for Knife River Landmark—Emily's Eatery Looks toward July Opening," *Duluth News-Tribune*, 20 June 2017, A3; David Witt (Louie the Loon), "The Lighthouse at Emily's in Knife River, MN," *Heavy Table*, 5 September 2013, https://heavytable.com/the-lighthouse-at-emilys-in-knife-river-mn/.

38 Manuscript schedules for the U.S. Census, 1900, 1910, 1920, 1930, 1940; *Duluth News-Tribune*, 2 July 1971, 17; Madison comments, 2016; Lind comments, 2016.

39 Manuscript schedules for the U.S. Census, 1910, 1920, 1930, 1940; Harvey Hadland, "Fishing Vessels of the Great Lakes," http://www.harveyhadland.com/rostern.htm; Brett Laidlaw, "Smoke 'Em If You Got 'Em," *Trout Caviar: Foraging the North* (blog), 13 March 2008, http://troutcaviar.blogspot.com/2008/03/smoke-em-if-you-got-em-i-was-vegetarian.html.

40 "Great! Lakes Candy Kitchen: Our Story," https://www.greatlakescandy.com/about-us.html#/.

41 Tourist brochure, 1945; "About Us: Island View Resort," https://islandviewresortmn.com/about-us; comments from Sheryl Ericksen to the author, 2014.

42 "Island View Resort History"; Ericksen comments, 2014.

43 "Island View Resort History"; Ericksen comments, 2019.

44 Manuscript schedules for the U.S. Census, 1900, 1910, 1920, 1930; Oliver Isaacson and Irene Hill Norgard, *Larsmont Yesterday* (privately printed, 1980); Carl Silfversten, "What Is a Finland Swede?," *Chisholm Tribune-Herald*, 23 June 1932.

45 Isaacson and Norgard, *Larsmont Yesterday*; Alanen, *Finns in Minnesota*, 83–84; Roberta Sve, "The Hill Boatworks,

Part I," *North Shore Commercial Fishing Journal*, Summer 2010, 1–3.

46 Manuscript schedules for the U.S. Census, 1900, 1910, 1920, 1930, 1940; Isaacson and Norgard, "The Earliest Days," summer 2011; Timothy Cochrane and Hawk Tolson, *A Good Boat Speaks for Itself: Isle Royale Fishermen and Their Boats* (Minneapolis: University of Minnesota Press, 2002), 40–41.

47 *Duluth News-Tribune*, 16 June 1997, A7; Sve, "Hill Boatworks, Part I," 2; Cochrane and Tolson, *A Good Boat Speaks for Itself*, 142, 147–48, 230; Alvera Pierson, "Reuben Hill: 'The Boat Builder,'" *The Landmarks*, June 1979, 11.

48 Chuck Fredrick, "Boat Builder Was True Craftsman," *Duluth News-Tribune*, 17 June 1997, B1, citing Sve; Cochrane and Tolson, *A Good Boat Speaks for Itself*, 175–76; Roberta Sve, "The Hill Boatworks, Part II," *North Shore Commercial Fishing Museum Journal* 18 (Fall 2010): 2.

49 Manuscript schedules for the U.S. Census, 1900, 1910, 1920, 1930; Oliver Isaacson and Irene Hill Norgard, "Larsmont Yesterday—a History," *The Larsmont Line*, Spring 2013, http://www.larsmont.org/1304lccnwsltr.pdf.

50 Manuscript schedules for U.S. Census, 1920, 1930, 1940; tourist brochure, 1950; "Stonegate on Superior," https://www.stonegateonsuperior.com/.

51 Tourist brochures, 1942, 1950; *Duluth News-Tribune*, 16 August 1976, B4; 7 November 1996, 6.

52 Schneiderhan, "Fractional Ownership"; Teri Cadeau, "North Shore Resorts Sold," *Two Harbors News-Chronicle*, 31 May 2019, A1, A3; Interval International, "Larsmont Cottages on Lake Superior," https://www.intervalworld.com/web/cs?a=1503&resortCode=LRM.

53 Manuscript schedules for the U.S. Census, 1900, 1910, 1920, 1930, 1940; *Duluth Herald*, 4 June 1919, 3; *Duluth News-Tribune*, 21 February 1962, C5; 17 April 2010, B5; comments from William Miller to the author, 2016.

54 Tourist brochures, 1937, 1947, 1948; *Duluth News-Tribune*, 21 February 1962, C5; 24 July 2004, B6; Janna Goerdt, "Home on the Lake," 2 July 2006, C1–C2; 17 April 2010, B5; *Lake County News-Chronicle*, 23 July 2004, A4; 26 April 2019, B3; comments from William Miller and Tim Miller to the author, 2016.

55 Manuscript schedules for the U.S. Census, 1900, 1910, 1920, 1930, 1940; tourist brochure, 1948; Isaacson and Norgard, "Larsmont Yesterday—a History"; *Duluth News-Tribune*, 28 February 1997, B9; 21 August 2008, B4; comments from Judy Sjoblom Beardsley to the author, 2016; comments from Marlys Wisch to the author, 2016.

56 Beardsley comments, 2016; *Duluth News-Tribune*, 25 September 1951, 7; 23 July 1980, A12; Kier Zimmerman, "Breezy Point Cabins Set for Four-Season Operation Near Two Harbors," *Duluth News-Tribune*, 13 June 2016, C1.

57 Jamey Malcomb, "County Board Approves Plan for Breezy Point," *Lake County News-Chronicle*, 30 October 2015, A3; Micki Sievwright, "Lake Effect: Odyssey Resorts Preserves the All-American Allure of Breezy Point," *Artful Living Magazine*, Spring 2016, 216–17; Zimmerman, "Breezy Point Cabins Set for Four-Season Operation"; Breezy Point Cabins on Lake Superior, "1930s Heritage with a Modern Twist."

58 Manuscript schedules for the U.S. Census, 1920, 1930, 1940; Isaacson and Norgard, "Larsmont Yesterday—a History"; *Duluth News-Tribune*, 28 February 1997, B9; 21 August 2008, B4; Beardsley comments, 2016; Wisch comments, 2016.

59 LaReesa Sandretsky, "Mother–Daughter Team Takes Over Mocha Moose," *Lake County News-Chronicle*, 21 February 2013, A3; Teri Cadeau, "Mocha Moose for Sale—to Right Owner," *Lake County News-Chronicle*, 10 January 2020, B3; Beardsley comments, 2020; comments from Micki Agar to the author, 2020; Mocha Moose Facebook page, https://www.facebook.com/mochamoosemnFacebook.

60 Manuscript schedules for the U.S. Census, 1910, 1920, 1930; Beardsley comments, 2020.

61 Beardsley comments, 2020.

62 David Anderson, "National Register of Historic Places Nomination Form for the Larsmont School," 1992, SHPO-MDA; Alanen, *Finns in Minnesota*, 88; Wisch comments, 2016.

63 Anderson, "Nomination Form for the Larsmont School."

64 Anderson; Philip Hommes, "A Day of Fun in Larsmont," *Lake County News-Chronicle*, 29 July 2016, A3; Wisch comments, 2016.

65 Manuscript schedules for the U.S. Census, 1910, 1920, 1930, 1940; *Two Harbors News-Chronicle*, 24 September 1970, 1; "A Tribute to Oliver Isaacson (1906–1970)," *The Landmarks*, March 1971, 3; Isaacson and Norgard, "Larsmont Yesterday—a History"; obituary for Richard Sjoblom, http://www.millerfuneralfridley.com/obituary/Richard-Eric-Sjoblom/Minneapolis-MN/1531013.

66 Comments from Bradley Nelson to the author, 2000 and 2015; Jerri Holan, *Norwegian Wood: A Tradition of Building* (New York: Rizzoli, 1990), 90, 177.

67 Nelson comments, 2000 and 2015.

68 Manuscript schedules for the U.S. Census, 1910, 1920, 1930, 1940; tourist brochures, 1937, 1942; Bill Guse, "News [from] Bob's Cabins on Lake Superior's North Shore," newsletter available at the resort.

69 *Duluth News-Tribune,* 21 March 1969, 17; 16 October 1978, A5; Guse, "News [from] Bob's Cabins."

70 Guse, "News [from] Bob's Cabins"; "History of Bob's Cabins," https://www.bobscabinsonlakesuperior.com/history.

71 Penmarallter Campsite, http://www.penmarallter campsite.com/.

72 *Two Harbors News-Chronicle,* 5 July 1979, 4; Wisch comments, 2021.

73 Mike Creger, "For MnDot, It Was Personal," *Lake County News-Chronicle,* 30 April 2010; "Honking Tree Case Remains a Mystery 10 Years Later," *Perfect Duluth Day,* 30 April 2019, https://www.perfectduluthday.com/2019/04/30/honking-tree-case-remains-a-mystery-10-years-later/

74 Jane Brissett, "Sonju, Two Harbors Ford to Merge," *Duluth News-Tribune,* 1 March 2008, D7; Sonju Two Harbors, https://about.me/sonjutwoharbors#1; Bishop, *By Water and Rail,* 173–75; Grandma's Marathon, https://grandmasmarathon.com/; Glen Andrews, "Top 48th Grandma's Marathon Results: Barno, Mazuronak Take the Win," *World-Track,* 22 June 2024, https://www.amazon.com/s?k=grandmas+marathon&adgrpid.

75 Manuscript schedules for the U.S. Census, 1920, 1930, 1940; *Duluth News-Tribune,* 6 June 1948, 8.

76 Earthwood Inn, Bar, and Grill, https://thearthwood.com/.

77 Matt Suoja, "Piece by Piece, Pierre Makes Final Voyage," *Duluth News-Tribune,* 12 February 2011, A1, A5; Lisa Kaczke, "High Winds Damage Two Harbors Landmark Pierre the Voyageur," *Duluth News-Tribune,* 8 March 2017, A1, A4.

78 Teri Cadeau, "Stolen, Painted and Ransomed: Stories behind Some of Northland's Many Unique Statues," *Duluth News-Tribune,* 5 August 2023, 1A, 8A; Spirit Animal Mysteries, http://spiritanimalmysteries.com/.

79 Todd E. Lindahl, *The Rise and Fall of Whiskey Row, and the Building of the Duluth & Iron Range Railroad* (Two Harbors, Minn.: Lake County Historical Society, 2013), 50; comments from Lakeview Cemetery Association employees to the author, 2019; comments from Becky Norlien to the author, 2019.

80 Bishop, *By Water and Rail,* 20–22, 69; Todd Lindahl, "Welcome to Burlington Bay," *Two Harbors Iron Port: Official Newsletter of the Lake County Historical Society,* July 2016, 1.

81 Timothy Andrew Tumberg, "Digging Up Whiskey Row: An Archaeological and Historical Investigation of Industrial Capitalism on the North Shore of Lake Superior," PhD diss., University of Arizona, 2010, 52–53; Bishop, *By Water and Rail,* 24; Lindahl, "Welcome to Burlington Bay," 2.

82 Tumberg, "Digging Up Whiskey Row," 42–43; Two Harbors Centennial Commission and Lake County Historical Society, *Two Harbors One Hundred Years: A Pictorial History of Two Harbors, Minnesota, and Surrounding Communities* (Two Harbors, Minn.: The Commission and Society, 1984), 40; David A. Walker, *The Iron Frontier: The Discovery and Early Development of Minnesota's Three Ranges* (St. Paul: Minnesota Historical Society Press, 1979), 40.

83 *Duluth Daily Tribune,* 12 June 1883, 4; 20 June 1883, 4; 21 July 1883, 4; 24 July 1884, 4; John L. Morrison, "Two Harbors, Minnesota," in *Two Harbors, Minn., in 1900* (Two Harbors, 1900); Thomas H. Trelford, compiler, *Two Harbors in 1910* (Two Harbors, 1910), citing Nelson; George A. Rock, "How a Dedicated Few Built a Church Despite 'Whiskey Row,'" *Two Harbors Chronicle and News,* 26 June 1956, 6 (reprint of 1912 report); Lindahl, *Rise and Fall of Whiskey Row,* 62; Bishop, *By Water and Rail,* 28–32; Tumberg, "Digging Up Whiskey Row," 62–64, 74, 76.

84 Hal Bridges, *Iron Millionaire, Life of Charlemagne Tower* (Philadelphia: University of Pennsylvania Press, 1952), 196; Tumberg, "Digging Up Whiskey Row," 62–63, 141–42.

85 Tumberg, "Digging Up Whiskey Row," 43; Bishop, *By Water and Rail,* 45–47.

86 Walker, *Iron Frontier,* 61; Two Harbors Centennial Commission and Lake County Historical Society, *Two Harbors One Hundred Years,* 18–19; Bishop, *By Water and Rail,* 47.

87 Minnesota State Census, 1895, 1905; U.S. Census of Population, 1890–2020.

88 Manuscript schedules for the U.S. Census, 1910, 1920; Bishop, *By Water and Rail,* 55–57.

89 Minnesota Legislative Reference Library, "Minnesota Legislators Past and Present: Strand, Ernest G.," http://www.leg.state.mn.us/legdb/fulldetail.aspx?ID=14979; K. Marianne Wargelin Brown, "Three 'Founding Mothers' of Finnish America," in *Women Who Dared: The History of Finnish American Women,* ed. Carl Ross and K. Marianne Wargelin Brown, 136–42 (St. Paul: Immigration History Research Center, University of Minnesota, 1986); Bruce M. White, compiler, *Minnesota Votes:*

*Election Returns for Presidents, Senators, Congressmen, and Governors, 1957–1977* (St. Paul: Minnesota Historical Society Press, 1977), 17–30; "United States Presidential Elections in Minnesota, 1980–2024," Wikipedia, accessed 2025.

90 "Duluth, Missabe and Iron Range Railway," Wikipedia, accessed 2023; Canadian National (DW&P and WC), http://www.twinportsrail.com/.

91 Bishop, *By Water and Rail*, 164, 167, 176–78; History of Mining in Minnesota, "Iron Ore Shipping," http://www.miningartifacts.org/Iron-Ore-Shipping.html; "Two Harbors, Minnesota," http://city-data.com/.

92 Chuck Frederick, "Two Harbors' Development Plans Praised in Study," *Duluth News-Tribune*, 7 October 1999, B1, B3.

93 Diane L. Pike, Britta Andress, Jordan Boy Gallagos, Jordan Marth, and Jaz Vallin, *Quality of Place: Two Harbors, MN—Learning to Be a City* (Minneapolis, Minn.: Department of Sociology, Augsburg University, 2018), 8; Creger, "Honking Tree Case."

94 Mel Sando, "Boarding Houses, 1900," *Two Harbors Iron Port: Official Newsletter of the Lake County Historical Society*, 2 January 2015, 1; William A. McGonagle, "Reminiscences of Agate Bay," *Lake County Chronicle*, 3 July 1924; Bishop, *By Water and Rail*, 45–47; Two Harbors Centennial Commission and Lake County Historical Society, *Two Harbors One Hundred Years*, 63; Charlene Roise, *Between Mines to Mills: An Historical/Architectural Survey and Evaluation of Agate Bay and Its Environs* (Washington, D.C.: U.S. Army Corps of Engineers, 2002); Liz Holum, "National Register of Historic Places Inventory—Nomination Form for the Duluth and Iron Range Railway Ore Dock No 6"; in *Minnesota Statewide Historic Sites Survey*, 1984, SHPO-MDA. Although declared eligible for National Register designation in 1986, the dock was not listed because of objections from the DM&IR.

95 Roise, *Between Mines to Mills*; DM&IR, *Two Harbors Storage and Shiploading Facility* (Duluth, Minn.: DM&IR, c. 1982); Holum, "Nomination Form for the Duluth and Iron Range Railway Ore Dock No. 6."

96 Roise, *Between Mines to Mills*; Alanen, *Pines, Mines, and Lakes*, 3.73.

97 Karen Lee Kreps, "National Register of Historic Places Inventory—Nomination Form for the Samuel Ely Shipwreck," 1992, SHPO-MDA; James R. Marshall, *Shipwrecks of Lake Superior*, 2nd ed. (Duluth, Minn.: Lake Superior Port Cities, 2005), 19–20; Roise, *Between Mines to Mills*.

98 Kreps, "Nomination Form for the Samuel Ely Shipwreck"; Marshall, *Shipwrecks of Lake Superior*, 19; "*Samuel Ely* (Shipwreck)," Wikipedia, accessed 2023.

99 *Duluth News-Tribune*, 22 June 1950, 1; Roise, *Between Mines to Mills*.

100 Hackett, "National Register of Historic Places Inventory—Nomination Form for the Tugboat Edna G," 2007, SHPO-MDA; Mel Sando, "Happy Birthday Edna G," *Two Harbors Iron Port: Official Newsletter of the Lake County Historical Society*, July 2016, 1–4; Teri Cadeau, "Tug-of-War," *Lake County News-Chronicle*, 9 August 2019, A1, A8; Pam Louwagie, "Minnesota Town of Two Harbors Struggles with Saving Beloved Tug," *StarTribune*, 30 September 2019; Friends of the Edna G, "Preserving, Restoring, Educating," https://friendsofednag.org/; Thomas V. Koehler, "Preserving the Tugboat Edna G, Two Harbors," *Lake Superior News*, 4 April 2018; Thomas Koehler comments to the author, 2024.

101 Cadeau, "Tug-of-War"; Pam Louwagie, "Minnesota Town of Two Harbors Struggles with Saving Beloved Tug," *StarTribune*, 30 September 2019; Friends of the Edna G, "Preserving, Restoring, Educating"; Koehler, "Preserving the Tugboat Edna G"; Koehler comments to the author.

102 *Two Harbors Iron News*, 10 May 1907, 1; Two Harbors Centennial Commission and Lake County Historical Society, *Two Harbors One Hundred Years*, 18; Bishop, *By Water and Rail*, 23, 28; Roise, *Between Mines to Mills*; City of Two Harbors, *City of Two Harbors Comprehensive Plan, August 2015* (Duluth, Minn.: Arrowhead Regional Development Commission, Regional Planning Division, 2015), 53.

103 Bishop, *By Water and Rail*, 51–52, 188.

104 MDNR, "Two Harbors Protected Access," https://www.dnr.state.mn.us/water_access/harbors/two_harbors.html.

105 Charles K. Hyde, *The Northern Lights: Lighthouses of the Upper Great Lakes* (Lansing, Mich.: TwoPeninsula Press, 1986).

106 Hyde; Lake County Historical Society, "Museums," https://lakecountyhistoricalsociety.org/museums/.

107 Teri Cadeau, "Two Harbors Light Station Goes Dark," *Lake County News-Chronicle*, 29 November 2019, A3; Cadeau, "Two Harbors Shines," *Duluth News-Tribune*, 9 June 2021, A1, A10; Lake County Historical Society, "Two Harbors Light Station," https://lakecountyhistoricalsociety.org/lighthouse/.

108 Monica Isley, "Council Commits Funds to Marina Land Purchase," *Lake County News-Chronicle*, 3 January 2003, 1; Forrest Johnson, "Lighthouse Point, Railroad Lands,

Sold in Two Harbors," *Lake County News-Chronicle*, 10 January 2003, 1; Chris Hamilton, "Plans Change for Lakeshore Land," *Duluth News-Tribune*, 12 August 2003, B1, B2; Janna Goerdt, "Two Harbors, Developer Reach Agreement on Lighthouse Point," *Duluth News-Tribune*, 28 October 2006, A1, A4; LaReesa Sandretsky, "Lighthouse Point Finally in City of Two Harbors' Hands," *Duluth News-Tribune*, 6 July 2013, B1; Dan Kraker, "Two Harbors Council Nixes Proposed Townhomes," MPR News, 29 March 2023, https://www.mprnews.org/story/2023/03/29/two-harbors-council-nixes-proposed-townhomes; comments from Todd Ronning to the author, 2019; Norlien comments, 2019, 2013.

109 *Duluth Evening Herald*, 2 March 1907, 5; *Two Harbors Journal*, 26 September 1907, 2; Susan Roth and Charles Nelson, "National Register of Historic Places Inventory—Nomination Form: Duluth and Iron Range Railroad Company Depot," 1982, SHPO-MDA.

110 Roth and Nelson, "Nomination Form: Duluth and Iron Range Railroad Company Depot."

111 *Duluth Evening Herald*, 2 March 1907, 5; *Two Harbors Chronicle and Times*, 17 May 1962, 1; North Shore Scenic Railroad, https://duluthtrains.com/.

112 Lake County Historical Society, "DM&IR Locomotive #3, Ore Car #251 and Caboose #22," http://www.lakecountyhistoricalsociety.org/museums/view/3-spot-and-caboose.

113 Lake County Historical Society, "DM&IR Yellowstone Mallet #229 Locomotive," http://www.lakecountyhistoricalsociety.org/museums/view/mallet-steam-engine.

114 Author's observation.

115 Cascade Vacation Rentals, "Falu Hus," 2001, https://www.cascadevacationrentals.com/.

116 Manuscript for the U.S. Census, 1910, 1940; *Lake County Chronicle*, 27 August 1920, 1; comments from Fanny Graden to the author, 2000.

117 *Duluth News-Tribune*, 17 October 1909, A6; Two Harbors Centennial Commission and Lake County Historical Society, *Two Harbors One Hundred Years*, 206; Bishop, *By Water and Rail*, 46; Mel Sando, "Then and Now in the Historic Waterfront District," *Two Harbors Iron Port: Official Newsletter of the Lake County Historical Society*, April 2014, 1.

118 Castle Danger Brewery, "Story," https://www.castledangerbrewery.com/story/; Jeremy Malcomb, "Castle Danger Brewery Plans Expansion," *Duluth News-Tribune*, 26 February 2017, D1; Malcomb, "Castle Danger Brewery Celebrates Six Years," *Duluth News-Tribune*, 12 August 2017, D1.

119 Two Harbors Centennial Commission and Lake County Historical Society, *Two Harbors One Hundred Years*, 178–79; Holum, "Property Inventory Forms: Two Harbors."

120 Holum, "Property Inventory Forms: Two Harbors"; Norlien comments, 2019.

121 McGonagle, "Reminiscences of Agate Bay," 6; Two Harbors Centennial Commission and Lake County Historical Society, *Two Harbors One Hundred Years*, 126; Holum, "Property Inventory Forms: Two Harbors"; Roise, *Between Mines to Mills*.

122 Holum, "Property Inventory Forms: Two Harbors"; Roise, *Between Mines to Mills*.

123 Manuscript schedules for the U.S. Census, 1900, 1910, 1920, 1930, 1940, and for the Minnesota Census, 1895, 1905; *Two Harbors Chronicle*, 30 July 1931, 1; Bishop, *By Water and Rail*, 158; Two Harbors Centennial Commission and Lake County Historical Society, *Two Harbors One Hundred Years*, 40.

124 Holum, "Property Inventory Forms: Two Harbors."

125 Trelford, *Two Harbors in 1910*, 32; Two Harbors Centennial Commission and Lake County Historical Society, *Two Harbors One Hundred Years*, 163–64; Roise, *Between Mines to Mills*; Mel Sando, "The Budd Hospital," *Two Harbors Iron Port: Official Newsletter of the Lake County Historical Society*, July 2015, 1, citing Budd; Mel Sando, "East Two Harbors," *Two Harbors Iron Port: Official Newsletter of the Lake County Historical Society*, January 2016, 3.

126 Two Harbors Centennial Commission and Lake County Historical Society, *Two Harbors One Hundred Years*, 163–65; Roise, *Between Mines to Mills*; Sando, "East Two Harbors," 3; "Lake View Memorial Hospital Incorporated in Two Harbors, Minnesota," http://www.nonprofitfacts.com/MN/Lake-View-Memorial-Hospital-Incorporated.html; Budd House Board and Lodge LLC, https://www.mnhelp.info/Providers/Budd_House_Board_and_Lodge_LLC/Housing_Stabilization_Services_HSS/1.

127 Manuscript schedules for the U.S. Census, 1920, 1930, 1940; Holum, "Property Inventory Forms: Two Harbors"; Roise, *Between Mines to Mills*; Graden comments, 2000; comments from Lill (Maija) Magnusson to the author, 2000.

128 Manuscript schedules for the U.S. Census, 1900, 1910, 1920, 1930, 1940, and for the Minnesota Census, 1905; Polk city directory, 1922; Two Harbors Centennial

Commission and Lake County Historical Society, *Two Harbors One Hundred Years*, 115, 117.

129 Katherine Cole Stevenson and H. Ward Jandl, *Houses by Mail: A Guide to Houses from Sears, Roebuck and Company* (New York: John Wiley, 1986), 116.

130 *Lake County Chronicle*, 24 June 1929; Fanny Graden comments, 2000; Magnusson comments, 2000.

131 *Lake County Chronicle*, 1 September 1927, 1; 22 August 1929, 1.

132 *Two Harbors Socialist*, 22 May 1915, 6; *Lake County Chronicle*, 16 July 1925, 8; 2 June 1927, 2; Two Harbors Centennial Commission and Lake County Historical Society, *Two Harbors One Hundred Years*, 22.

133 "The Original Mission" and "The New Mission," interpretive signs in Lakeview Park.

134 Holum, "Property Inventory Forms: Two Harbors," in *Minnesota Statewide Historic Sites Survey*.

135 Bishop, *By Water and Rail*, 60–64; Charlene K. Roiss, "National Register of Historic Places Registration Form—Dwan, John, Office Building," 1992, SHPO-MDA; Lake County Historical Society, "3M Birthplace Museum," https://www.lakecountyhistoricalsociety.org/museums/view/3m-museum.

136 Bishop, *By Water and Rail*, 60–64; Roiss, "Registration Form—Dwan, John, Office Building."

137 Roiss, "Registration Form—Dwan, John, Office Building"; Lake County Historical Society, "3M Museum."

138 Holum, "Property Inventory Forms: Two Harbors."

139 Manuscript schedules for the U.S. Census, 1880, 1900, 1910, 1920, 1930, and for the Minnesota Census, 1885, 1895, 1905; Albert Headley, "The Evolution of the Ore Car," paper read at the meeting of the Duluth & Iron Range Supervisor's Club, November 1925, and Headley, "Autobiography of Albert Headley," both items on file in Archives and Special Collections, Martin Library, UMD; Bishop, *By Water and Rail*, 64.

140 Manuscript schedules for the U.S. Census, 1860, 1870, 1880, 1900, 1910, 1920, 1930, 1940; Bishop, *By Water and Rail*, 158; Rev. Thomas E. Hughes, David Edwards, Hugh G. Edwards, and Thomas Hughes, eds., *The History of the Welsh in Minnesota, Foreston and Lime Springs, IA: Gathered by the Old Settlers* (1895), http://kimkat.org/amryw/1_glasbridd/minnesota_13_bywgraffiadau_04lewis-pugh_08683.htm.

141 Trelford, *Two Harbors in 1910*, 35; Holum, "Property Inventory Forms: Two Harbors."

142 Manuscript schedules for the U.S. Census, 1880, 1900, 1910, 1920.

143 *Little Sketches of Big Folks in Minnesota 1907: An Alphabetical List of Representative Men of Minnesota, with Biographical Sketches* (St. Paul, Minn.: R. L. Polk, 1907); *Proceedings of the Minnesota State Bar Association: Minnesota Law Review* 7, Suppl. (1922): 149; Trelford, *Two Harbors in 1910*, 39.

144 Holum, "Property Inventory Forms: Two Harbors."

145 Manuscript schedules for the U.S. Census, 1900, 1910, 1920, 1930; *Two Harbors Chronicle*, 21 April 1932, 1.

146 Sando, "East Two Harbors," 2.

147 Trelford, *Two Harbors in 1910*, 43; Two Harbors Centennial Commission and Lake County Historical Society, *Two Harbors One Hundred Years*, 124; *Lake County Chronicle*, 8 November 1924, 1; *Two Harbors Chronicle*, 11 June 1931, 5.

148 Two Harbors Centennial Commission and Lake County Historical Society, *Two Harbors One Hundred Years*, 124; Bishop, *By Water and Rail*, 55; Candace Renalls, "Vintage Building Materials Company Expands," *Duluth News-Tribune*, 27 May 2013, B1, B4; North Shore Architectural Antiques, http://www.north-shore-architectural-antiques.com/.

149 Susan Roth and Charles Nelson, "National Register of Historic Places Inventory—Nomination Form: Lake County Courthouse and Sheriff's Residence," 1982, SHPO-MDA.

150 Roth and Nelson; Gebhard and Martinson, *A Guide to the Architecture of Minnesota*, 209.

151 *Bay Area Historical Society Newsletter* 34 (Spring 2018); "Lake County Courthouse," *Lovin' Lake County*, https://lovinlakecounty.com/business-directory/lake-county-courthouse/.

152 Rock, "How a Dedicated Few Built a Church," 6; Two Harbors Centennial Commission and Lake County Historical Society, *Two Harbors One Hundred Years*, 179–80; "National Register of Historic Places Inventory—Nomination Form: First Presbyterian Church," 1984, SHPO-MDA. The nomination failed to receive approval in 1986.

153 Rock, "How a Dedicated Few Built a Church," 6; Two Harbors Centennial Commission and Lake County Historical Society, *Two Harbors One Hundred Years*, 179–80; "Nomination Form: First Presbyterian Church," 1984.

154 *Lake County Chronicle*, 8 September 1921, 1; *Two Harbors Chronicle*, 20 April 1931, 1; *Duluth Herald*, 31 August 1934, 24; Pratt, "Phase I: Architectural History Investigation," 56–57; Friends of the Band Shell Park, https://friendsofthebandshellpark.com/; *North Shore Journal*, 24 May 2024.

155 Two Harbors Centennial Commission and Lake County Historical Society, *Two Harbors One Hundred Years*, 177, 194; Holum, "Property Inventory Forms: Two Harbors."

156 Manuscript schedules for the U.S. Census, 1900, 1910, 1920, 1930; *Journal-News*, 27 October 1910, 1, 15; *Commercial West*, 16 October 1912, 10; *Duluth Evening Herald*, 1 April 1910, 11; *Lake County Chronicle*, 15 November 1928, 1; Holum, "Property Inventory Forms: Two Harbors."

157 Two Harbors Centennial Commission and Lake County Historical Society, *Two Harbors One Hundred Years*, 178–81; Holum, "Property Inventory Forms: Two Harbors"; comments from Rev. Kirk Scheid to the author, 2019.

158 Manuscript schedules for the U.S. Census, 1870, 1880, 1900, 1920, 1930; *Two Harbors Chronicle*, 8 December 1938, 1; Two Harbors Centennial Commission and Lake County Historical Society, *Two Harbors One Hundred Years*, 33.

159 Holum, "Property Inventory Forms: Two Harbors."

160 Holum.

161 Manuscript schedules for the U.S. Census, 1900, 1910, 1920, 1930, 1940; *Lake County News-Chronicle*, 29 July 1987, 1; Holum, "Property Inventory Forms: Two Harbors."

162 Manuscript schedules for the U.S. Census, 1900, 1910, 1920, and for the Minnesota Census, 1895; *Lake County Chronicle*, 11 October 1928, 1; 4 March 1929, 1; 28 November 1929, 1; 24 March 1932, 1, citing Haugen; Holum, "Property Inventory Forms: Two Harbors."

163 Manuscript schedules for the U.S. Census, 1900, 1910, 1920, 1930, 1940; *Journal-News*, 20 January 1920, 1; *Two Harbors Chronicle and News*, 13 May 1948, 1; Two Harbors Centennial Commission and Lake County Historical Society, *Two Harbors One Hundred Years*, 191; Lisa Menor, "The Falk House," *The Leader* (Duluth), March 2000; Holum, "Property Inventory Forms: Two Harbors"; comments from Jon and Deborah Anderson to the author, 2000.

164 Menor, "Falk House"; Holum, "Property Inventory Forms: Two Harbors."

165 Menor, "Falk House"; Jon and Deborah Anderson comments, 2000; Norlien comments, 2019.

166 Manuscript schedules for the U.S. Census, 1850, 1860, 1870, 1880, 1900, 1910, 1920, 1930, 1940, 1950, and from the Minnesota Census, 1895; *Little Sketches of Big Folks*, 57; *Two Harbors Chronicle*, 24 March 1932, 1; Bishop, *By Water and Rail*, 60; Minnesota Death Index, 1908–2002; Holum, "Property Inventory Forms: Two Harbors."

167 Manuscript schedules for the U.S. Census, 1880, 1900, 1910, 1920, 1930, 1940; *Two Harbors Chronicle and News*, 19 September 1946, 1; Two Harbors Centennial Commission and Lake County Historical Society, *Two Harbors One Hundred Years*, 133; "Harbor Point," Affordable Housing Online, http://affordablehousingonline.com/housing-search/Minnesota/Two-Harbors/Harbor-Point/25076/.

168 *Two Harbors Chronicle*, 12 May 1932, 1; *Two Harbors Chronicle and News*, 19 September 1946, 1; Two Harbors Centennial Commission and Lake County Historical Society, *Two Harbors One Hundred Years*, 133; "Harbor Point."

169 Two Harbors Centennial Commission and Lake County Historical Society, *Two Harbors One Hundred Years*, 18, 127, 128; Bishop, *By Water and Rail*, 42; Lindahl, *Rise and Fall of Whiskey Row*, 57–59; Mel Sando, "Boarding Houses 1900," *Two Harbors Iron Port: Official Newsletter of the Lake County Historical Society*, January [illegible].

170 Two Harbors Centennial Commission and Lake County Historical Society, *Two Harbors One Hundred Years*, 173–75.

171 Gretchen Buggeln, *The Suburban Church: Modernism and Community in Postwar America* (Minneapolis: University of Minnesota Press, 2015), 10–11; Two Harbors Centennial Commission and Lake County Historical Society, *Two Harbors One Hundred Years*, 175.

172 Trelford, *Two Harbors in 1910*, 15; Liz Holum, "National Register of Historic Places Inventory—Nomination Form: Two Harbors Carnegie Library," 1984, SHPO-MDA.

173 Holum, "Nomination Form: Two Harbors Carnegie Library."

174 *Lake County News-Chronicle*, 26 September 1984, 1; Holum, "Nomination Form: Two Harbors Carnegie Library."

175 *Duluth News-Tribune*, 11 June 1939, A14; *Two Harbors Chronicle*, 8 February 1940, 1, 8; Two Harbors Centennial Commission and Lake County Historical Society, *Two Harbors One Hundred Years*, 104; Wurzer, *Tales of the Road*, 43–45; Ron Brochu, "Voters Approve Referendum," *Duluth News-Tribune*, 14 March 2002, C1–C2; Janna Goerdt, "Board Decides to Demolish Old School," *Duluth News-Tribune*, 25 February 2007, C1, C7.

176 Manuscript schedules for the U.S. Census, 1900, 1910, 1920, 1930, 1940, and for the Minnesota Census, 1905;

Trelford, *Two Harbors in 1910,* 31; comments from Robert Anderson to the author, 2000.

177 Robert Anderson comments, 2000; Malinda Lavine, "Midcentury Main Attraction: Two Harbors Retro Airbnb Is a Big Hit," *Duluth News-Tribune,* 18 February 2023, C1.

178 Manuscript schedules for the U.S. Census, 1900, 1910, 1920, 1930, 1940, and for the Minnesota Census, 1905; Two Harbors Centennial Commission and Lake County Historical Society, *Two Harbors One Hundred Years,* 121, 131–32; Bishop, *By Water and Rail,* 56; postcard of Oscar's Norshore, late 1950s to early 1960s.

179 *Lake County Chronicle,* 16 July 1925, 8; 30 July 1925, 6; Burlington Bay Campground, http://twoharborsmn.gov/city_departments/burlington_bay_campground/.

180 Two Harbors Centennial Commission and Lake County Historical Society, *Two Harbors One Hundred Years,* 31; Bishop, *By Water and Rail,* 177; Mayo and Mayo, *61 Gems of Highway 61,* 36; "R.J. Houle Visitor Information Center," http://www.waymarking.com/waymarks/WMC1G2_TIC_RJ_Houle_Visitor_Information_Center, 2024; *Duluth News-Tribune,* 29 July 2008.

181 *Lake County Chronicle,* 26 September 1929, 1; Two Harbors Centennial Commission and Lake County Historical Society, *Two Harbors One Hundred Years,* 113, 157–58; Bishop, *By Water and Rail,* 177; Lakeview National, http://www.lakeviewnationalgolfcourse.com; Two Harbors Curling Club, "History," http://twoharborscurling.com/history.

182 U.S. Census of Population, 1990, 2000, 2010, 2020; Town of Silver Creek, *Silver Creek Comprehensive Plan* (Duluth, Minn.: Arrowhead Regional Development Commission, 2007), 2, 5; Silver Creek Township, https://minnesota.hometownlocator.com/mn/lake/silver-creek.cfm.

183 Tourist brochure, 1937; Two Harbors Centennial Commission and Lake County Historical Society, *Two Harbors One Hundred Years,* 144–45; Bishop, *By Water and Rail,* 172, 177; *Two Harbors Chronicle and Herald,* 11 December 1947, 1.

184 Teri Cadeau, "Superior Shores Resorts Sold for $15 Million," *Lake County News-Chronicle,* 10 January 2020, A1, A3; Superior Shores Resort and Conference Center, https://superiorshores.com/superior-shores-sells/.

185 Cadeau, "Superior Shores Resorts Sold for $15 Million"; Superior Shores Resort and Conference Center, https://superiorshores.com/superior-shores-sells/.

186 *StarTribune,* 21 July 2024.

187 Tourist brochures, 1949, 1972.

188 Upham, *Minnesota Place Names,* 314; "Lake County Past, October 1999," *Lake County News-Chronicle,* 21 October 2016; Bishop, *By Water and Rail,* 28; Meyer, *Everyone's Country Estate,* 248–49; MDNR, "Flood Bay State Wayside," https://www.dnr.state.mn.us/state_parks/waysides/index.html.

189 Manuscript schedules for the U.S. Census, 1930, 1940; Hugh E. Bishop, "I Am Betty," *Lake Superior Magazine,* October–November 2001, 31–33, citing Lessard; Liz Sawyer, "North Shore Founder of Betty's Pies Dies at 90," *StarTribune,* 25 March 2015.

190 Bishop, "I Am Betty," 31–33; Sawyer, "North Shore Founder."

191 Bishop, "I Am Betty," 33; Sawyer, "North Shore Founder"; Chuck Frederick, "Survival of the Sweetest," *Duluth News-Tribune,* 12 March 2000, D1, D8; Lynne Olson, "Betty's Pies Are World Famous," *Duluth News-Tribune,* Outlook, March 15, 2001, F8; *Duluth News-Tribune,* 25 April 2002, D1.

192 Upham, *Minnesota Place Names,* 314; *Two Harbors Chronicle,* 8 June 1939, 1; Jeffrey Hess, "National Register of Historic Places Inventory—Nomination Form for Bridge 3589," 1998, SHPO-MDA; Gardner, *Wood+Concrete+Stone+Steel,* 128.

193 Hess, "Nomination Form for Bridge 3589."

194 MnDOT, "Historic Bridges Rehabilitation Projects," 2019, http://www.dot.state.mn.us/historicbridges/rehabilitation.html; MnDOT, "Silver Creek and Stewart River Bridges," 2020, http://www.dot.state.mn.us/d1/projects/hwy61-bridges/index.html; comments from Tom Lamb (MnDOT) to the author, 2021.

195 Silver Creek Gifts and Gallery, "History of Our Building"; Silver Creek Company, https://www.silvercreekcomn.com/ (inactive website); "Silver Creek Co. Announces Closure Plan," *Business North,* 9 September 2022.

196 MnDOT, "Historic Bridges Rehabilitation Project"; Lamb comments, 2021.

197 Manuscript schedules for the U.S. Census, 1920, 1930, 1940; G. M. Schwartz, *A Guidebook to Minnesota Trunk Highway No. 1,* Minnesota Geological Survey Bulletin 20 (Minneapolis: University of Minnesota, 1925), 71; *Lake County Chronicle,* 21 January 1926, 1; tourist brochures, 1938, 1942, 1945.

198 *Lake County Chronicle and Times,* 6 December 1951, 4; postcard caption for Bill Nauha's Silver Cliff Motel, 1950s; tourist brochure, 1953; comments from Gretchen Heath to the author, 2017–19.

199 Brissett, "Invasion of the Rich," A6; Sheryl Jensen, "Em-

bracing Lake Superior from Silver Cliff Homes," *Woman Today*, August–September 2007, 72–76; Silver Cliff Homes, http://silvercliffhomes.com/.

200 *Lake County Chronicle*, 8 March 1923, 1; 19 August 1923, 1; 19 March 1925, 1; 7 May 1925, 1.

201 *Duluth Herald*, 2 August 1923, 3; *Lake County Chronicle*, 19 August 1923, 1; Schwartz, *A Guidebook to Minnesota Trunk Highway No. 1*, 71; *Northern Trails*, May 1926, 39.

202 *Lake County Chronicle*, 24 June 1926, 1.

203 *Duluth News-Tribune*, 19 November 1929, 1; 12 December 1930, 20; *Lake County Chronicle*, 21 November 1929, 1; 23 January 1930, 1, 8; 18 September 1930, 1; *Cook County News-Chronicle*, May 1930, 1; 22 May 1930, 1; *Two Harbors Chronicle*, 7 May 1931, 1; 21 April 1932, 1.

204 *Two Harbors Chronicle*, 21 April 1932, 1; *Duluth News-Tribune*, 2 April 1938, 1; *Cook County News-Herald*, 21 March 1957, 1.

205 CNA Consulting Engineers, "Underground Transportation Facilities," http://www.cnaengineers.com/underground-transportation-facilities.htm.

206 Manuscript schedules for the U.S. Census, 1930, 1940; Halcyon Harbor Cabins, *Romancing the Shore . . . Halcyon Harbor*, 1990s brochure.

207 Halcyon Harbor Cabins, *Romancing the Shore*; June Kallestad, "Out on the Cliff," *Lake County News Chronicle*, 14 May 2010, 18; Heath comments, 2016.

208 Joseph R. Kingman, *History of Encampment Forest Association: November 1921 to November 1945* (privately printed, 1945), 7–12, 22–23; Schwartz, *A Guidebook to Minnesota Trunk Highway No. 1*, 71; Andrew Munsch, "Historic U.S. 61: Old Road at the Encampment River," Deadpioneer's Historic Minnesota Highways, https://www.deadpioneer.com/routes/US61/historicus61se/encampmentriver/encampmentriver.html; Alyssa Ford, "Encampment Is Minnesota's Most Elite Northwoods Enclave," *Artful Living*, May 13, 2013, https://artfulliving.com/encampment-is-minnesotas-most-elite-northwoods-enclave/.

209 Kingman, *History of Encampment*, 11–12, 22–23; Campie Anderson and Ebba Anderson, *North Shore Reminiscences* (Minneapolis, Minn.: Encampment Forest Association, 1956), 8–9, 22–25; Liz Holum, "Notes on the EFA Main Lodge" and "Notes on the EFA River Cabin," 1984, SHPO-MDA; Ford, "Encampment Is Minnesota's Most Elite Northwoods Enclave."

210 Ford, "Encampment Is Minnesota's Most Elite Northwoods Enclave"; Walker Art Center, "Encampment," *Minnesota by Design*, 2015, http://www.walkerart.org/minnesotabydesign/.

211 "SS *Lafayette*," Wikipedia, accessed 2024; James Lovrien, "What Was Lake Superior's Strongest Gale?," *Duluth News-Tribune*, 11 November 2011, A2; "Lafayette," Great Lakes Vessel History, http://www.greatlakesvesselhistory.com/histories-by-name/l/lafayette.

212 CNA Consulting Engineers, "Underground Transportation Facilities"; Perich, *North Shore*, 35–36; Heath comments, 2017.

213 Fritzen, *Historic Sites and Place Names*, 12; Mrs. John (Agnes) Stone, "Castle Danger to Honor Its Pioneers," *Two Harbors Chronicle*, 22 April 1931, 1, 4; *Duluth News-Tribune*, Cosmopolitan, 14 October 1951, 6; comments from Scott Roen to the author, 2016, 2019.

214 Our Savior's Lutheran Church in Castle Danger, Minnesota, "History," https://sites.google.com/site/oursavioursincastledanger/home/our-saviour-s-history (inactive website); Bishop, *By Water and Rail*, 53; George W. Kelley, "Uncle Sam Breeds Potatoes in the North," *Duluth News-Tribune*, 6 September 1936, C8; Stone, "Castle Danger to Honor Its Pioneers," 1; *Lake County News-Herald*, 23 July 2009, 16.

215 Our Savior's Lutheran Church in Castle Danger, Minnesota, "History"; *Lake County News-Herald*, 23 July 2009, 16.

216 Comments from Beth Sullivan to the author, 2014; Roen comments, 2018, 2019; Bishop, *By Water and Rail*, 178; Stone, "Castle Danger to Honor Its Pioneers," 4, citing Edisen; Blesener Dahlberg Architects to R. Kauzlaric, MnDOT, 22 August 1995, and Fryberger, Buchanan, Smith & Frederick to D. Gimmestad, 20 September 1995, both items on file with SHPO-MDA; Rustic Inn Café and Gifts, "Our History," http://rusticinn.cafe/our-history/ (inactive website).

217 Norton and Dilley, *Lake Superior Flavors*, 59; Rustic Inn Café, "Our Story," http://rusticinn.cafe/our-story/; Anne Weaver, "Rustic Inn Café: Minnesota's Pie and More Place," Real Food Traveler, http://www.realfoodtraveler.com/2017/06/rustic-inn-cafe-minnesotas-pie-and-more-place/ (inactive website).

218 Gooseberry Park Cottages and Motel; comments from Kirsten Mohr to the author, 2019; comments from Nick Junjak to the author, 2023.

219 Manuscript schedules for the U.S. Census, 1910, 1920, 1930, 1940; "Split Rock Memories: Lake County's Gay Golden 60's, 1866 to 1966," one-page typescript provided by Scott Roen; Roen comments, 2019.

220 "Campers Home on North Shore of Lake Superior; Castle Danger, Minnesota," early 1930s advertisement provided by Scott Roen; tourist brochures, 1938, 1939, 1944, 1945, 1948.

221 "Star Harbor Resort Cabin Field Notes," 6 October 1990, SHPO-MDA; Heath comments, 2022; Roen comments, 2019; Grand Superior Lodge, https://odysseyresorts.com/grand-superior/.

222 Camper's Home Lodge Menu, circa 1930s, provided by Scott Roen; Ren Holland, *The Early Resorts of Minnesota: Tourism in the Land of 10,000 Lakes* (Edina, Minn.: Beaver's Pond Press, 2013), 417–18; tourist brochures, 1938, 1939, 1944, 1945, 1948.

223 Northwoods Pioneer Gallery and Gifts, "Our History," http://www.pioneercrafts.com/our-history.html.

224 Manuscript schedules for the U.S. Census, 1910, 1920, 1930, 1940; tourist brochure, 1933; Castle Haven Cabins, "Welcome to Castle Haven Cabins," http://www.castlehaven.net/.

225 Tourist brochure, 1953; comments from Jamie Lind MacFarlane to the author, 2015, 2019; Castle Haven Cabins, "Welcome to Castle Haven Cabins."

226 Castle Haven Cabins, "Welcome to Castle Haven Cabins."

227 MDNR, "State Parks."

228 Grace Lee Nute, "Gooseberry Falls State Park: Its History and Natural History," part 1, *Conservation Volunteer* 10 (May–June 1947): 27–30; Upham, *Minnesota Place Names*, 314; Meyer, *Everyone's Country Estate*, 111–12; Fritzen, *Historic Sites and Place Names*, 12; Todd Lindahl, "The Estate of Thomas Nestor Railroad, and the Logging of the Gooseberry River Watershed" (privately printed, 2004), 5; Marie Savage, "Gooseberry Falls State Park," MNopedia, https://www.mnopedia.org/place/gooseberry-falls-state-park.

229 Manuscript schedules for the U.S. Census, 1910, 1920, 1930, 1940; tourist brochures, 1937, 1942; Meyer, *Everyone's Country Estate*, 111; *Duluth News-Tribune*, 12 November 1945, 4.

230 *Duluth Herald*, 3 July 1934, 16; Rolf Anderson, "National Register of Historic Places Nomination—Registration Form for Gooseberry Falls State Park CCC/Rustic Style Historic Resources, Gooseberry Falls State Park," 1989, SHPO-MDA; Sommer, *Hard Work and a Good Deal*, 144.

231 *Duluth News-Tribune*, 4 September 1938, Cosmopolitan, 1; Anderson, "National Register Nomination for Gooseberry Falls State Park"; Sommer, *Hard Work and a Good Deal*, 104.

232 Ron Morton and Steve Morse, *Gooseberry Falls to Grand Portage: A Walking Guide to the Hiking Trails in Minnesota's North Shore State Parks* (Knife River, Minn.: Rockflower Press, 2007), 17–18; Anderson, "National Register Nomination for Gooseberry Falls State Park"; MnDOT Historic Roadside Development Structures Inventory, "Gooseberry Falls Concourse," http://www.dot.state.mn.us/roadsides/historic/files/iforms/LA-SVC-046.pdf.

233 SMSQ Architects and Gemini Research, *Mn/DOT Historic Roadside Property and Safety Rest Area: Gooseberry Falls Concourse—Preservation and Restoration Report* (Northfield, Minn.: SMSQ, 1991–93), A4.3.

234 *Civilian Conservation Corps Stonework* (blog), http://cccstonework.blogspot.com/; Minnesota Historical Society, "Gooseberry Falls State Park: Descriptions of Selected Resources."

235 Eric Kudalis, "Northern Respite," *Architecture Minnesota*, January/February 1998, 20–25, quotation on 24; Thomas Fisher, *Salmela Architect* (Minneapolis: University of Minnesota Press, 2005), 75; MDNR and MnDOT, "Fact Sheet: Gooseberry Falls State Park Visitor Center and Highway Rest Area," 1996.

236 Roy Evans, "Madonna of the Ice," *Missabe Iron Ranger*, July 1954, 51; Duluth Guide Co., *Duluth Souvenir Guide*, 17; comments from Walter Sve to the author, 2015, 2019; Heath comments, 2023.

237 Manuscript schedules for the U.S. Census, 1930, 1940, 1942, 1948; tourist brochures, 1940, 1949, 1953, 1960; *Duluth News-Tribune*, 13 December 1998, B15; Steve Pihjala, "Iona Lind's Environmental Legacy," *The Sugarloaf Interpreter* 4 (Fall 1996): 3; comments from Arlene Lind Lehto to the author, 2017.

238 Pihjala, "Iona Lind's Environmental Legacy," 3.

239 Arlene Lehto, "Save Lake Superior Association Oral History Project, 2006," interview by Nancy Nelson, Save Lake Superior Association Records, Archives and Manuscripts, Martin Library, UMD; Parks and Trails Council of Minnesota, "Alden Lind," 30 March 2001, https://www.parksandtrails.org/news/alden-lind/; Lehto comments, 2017; Elmer L. Anderson, *A Man's Reach* (Minneapolis: University of Minnesota Press), 371–72.

240 Pihjala, "Iona Lind's Environmental Legacy," 3; Save Lake Superior Association meeting minutes for 1969–70; *Sugarloaf Interpreter* 4 (Summer 1994), 1; SICA meeting minutes for 13 July 1994, 14 July 1994, 16 July 1994, February 1995, 18 May 1996, 4 October 1997 (all items on file with Archives and Special Collections, Martin Library, UMD); MDNR, "Iona's Beach Scientific and

Natural Area," http://www.dnr.state.mn.us/snas/detail.html?id=sna01000; Lehto comments, 2017.

241 Interview with Ragnvald and Ragnhild Sve, conducted by Barbara Sommer, 15 July 1977, transcript on file in Archives and Special Collections, Martin Library, UMD; Bishop, *By Water and Rail*, 69–73; Ken Vogel, "Four Generations of Fishermen on Lake Superior," *Lake County News-Chronicle*, 26 September 2014, 1; Sve comments, 2015, 2019; Roberta Sve, "Steve and Eric Sve: Heirs to a Tradition," *North Shore Commercial Fishing Museum Journal* 25 (Winter 2017): 1.

242 Ragnvald and Ragnhild Sve interview.

243 Sve comments, 2015, 2019.

244 Author's observations and Sve comments, 2015, 2019; Bishop, *By Water and Rail*, 73; Vogel, "Four Generations of Fishermen"; Sve, "Steve and Eric Sve," 2–3.

245 Sve comments, 2015, 2019.

246 Heath comments, 2023.

247 U.S. Census of Population, 1860–2020.

248 MDNR, "State Parks."

249 Stephen B. Daniel, *Shipwrecks along Lake Superior's North Shore: A Diver's Guide* (St. Paul: Minnesota Historical Society Press, 2008), 89–92; Fritzen, *Historic Sites and Place Names*, 13; Wurzer, *Tales of the Road*, 37; "Splitrock," Wikipedia, accessed 2024.

250 *Duluth News-Tribune*, 21 October 2011; "Split Rock River Trailhead Concept Plan," 3 March 2008, http://www.arrowheadplanning.org/documents/NSSD/FINAL%20BOOKLET%20acknowledgements.pdf.

251 Dierckins, *Greetings from the Arrowhead*, 34–35; Brian J. Faltinson, "National Historic Landmark Nomination: Split Rock Light Station," NPS–National Historic Landmarks Program, Washington, D.C., 2011; Les Radzak, "Split Rock Lighthouse," MNopedia, https://www.mnopedia.org/structure/split-rock-lighthouse; "Split Rock Lighthouse," Wikipedia, accessed 2023; Morton and Morse, *Gooseberry Falls to Grand Portage*, 63.

252 Hugh E. Bishop, "Time's Sentinel: The History of Split Rock Lighthouse," *Lake Superior Magazine*, 1 August 2001, https://www.lakesuperior.com/the-lake/maritime/history-of-split-rock-lighthouse/; Andrew Munsch, "Historic U.S. 61: Split Rock Lighthouse Overlook," Deadpioneer's Historic Minnesota Highways, https://www.deadpioneer.com/routes/US61/historicus61se/splitrockoverlook/splitrockoverlook.html; Wurzer, *Tales of the Road*, 38–39; tourist brochure, 1972; postcard captions for Split Rock Trading Post and Lookout Tower, 1950s and 1960s.

253 Munsch, "Historic U.S. 61: Split Rock Lighthouse Overlook."

254 Stephan A. Hall, *Split Rock: Epoch of a Lighthouse* (St. Paul: Minnesota Historical Society Press, 1978), quotation on 4; Faltinson, "Nomination: Split Rock Light Station."

255 Radzak, "Split Rock Lighthouse"; Faltinson, "Nomination: Split Rock Light Station."

256 Radzak, "Split Rock Lighthouse"; Faltinson, "Nomination: Split Rock Light Station," quotation.

257 Andrew Krueger, "New Campground Under Construction at Split Rock Lighthouse State Park," Minnesota Public Radio News, 8 March 2021; Jimmy Lovrien, "North Shore Goes Hardcore: Mountain Bike Trails Open between Split Rock, Beaver Bay," *Duluth News-Tribune*, 2 October 2021, D1, D2.

258 Briana J. Agrana and Kevin J. Foster, "National Register of Historic Places Registration Form for the Madeira," 1993, SHPO-MDA; Marshall, *Shipwrecks of Lake Superior*, 17, 19; Daniel, *Shipwrecks along Lake Superior's North Shore*, 99–103.

259 Manuscript schedules for the U.S. Census, 1900, 1910, 1920, 1930; *Duluth News-Tribune*, 17 March 1976, [illegible]; 24 February 1976, A5.

260 *Two Harbors Chronicle*, 24 August 1939, 1.

261 Fritzen, *Historic Sites and Place Names*, 15; Upham, *Minnesota Place Names*, 309; Jessie C. Davis, *Beaver Bay: Original North Shore Village* (1968; repr. Duluth, Minn.: Bay Area Historical Society, 2004), 13–16, citing Robert McClean, 16.

262 Davis, *Beaver Bay*, 21–22; Peets diary entry.

263 Manuscript schedules for the U.S. Census, 1860; Davis, *Beaver Bay*, 31, 37, 45, 47, 59; Bishop, *By Water and Rail*, 17–19; John Beargrease Sled Dog Marathon, http://www.beargrease.com/.

264 Manuscript schedules for the U.S. Census, 1900, 1910, 1920; Davis, *Beaver Bay*, 100; Bishop, *By Water and Rail*, 7–19; Maggie King, "What Happened to the Dispute over an Old Fish House in Beaver Bay?," *North Shore Commercial Fishing Museum Journal* 26 (Summer 2017): 1.

265 Reginald Buck, "Lady Fisherman: Lydia Jacobsen, at Fifty-Eight, Shows Up the Men at Beaver Bay When It Comes to Netting Herring," *Duluth News-Tribune*, Cosmopolitan, 19 December 1943, 2, citing Jacobsen; Duluth city directory, 1957; Bishop, *By Water and Rail*, 10; "Christian Albert Jacobsen," California Death Index; "Mrs. Lydia Jacobsen," Minnesota Death Index.

266 *Minnesota State Gazetteer and Business Directory for 1922–1923* (St. Paul, Minn.: Polk, 1922), 1336; Ed Maki,

*Treaties to Taconite: The Settling of Beaver Bay/Silver Bay* (privately printed, 1990s), 17.

267 U.S. Census of Population, 1960, 1970, 1980, 1990, 2000, 2010; U.S. Census Bureau, "Explore Census Data," https://data.census.gov/cedsci/.

268 *North Shore Commercial Fishing Museum Journal* 12 (Summer 2004): 1–3.

269 Hans Eisenbeis, "Nothing Doing," *The Rake*, July 2005, 42–43 (*The Rake* was published in the Twin Cities from 2002 to 2008); Cove Point Lodge, https://www.covepointlodge.com/.

270 North Shore Camping Company, https://www.northshorecampingco.com/.

271 Chuck Frederick, "Beaver Bay Cabin Becomes Information Center," *Duluth News-Tribune*, 8 September 2001, B1; Ed Maki, "What Is Happening with the Beaver Bay Apartments?" *Bay Area Historical Society Newsletter* 33 (2017): 1–5; Maki, *Treaties to Taconite*, 34.

272 Teri Cadeau, "Sale Pending of Beaver Bay Historic Building," *Lake County News-Chronicle*, 9 August 2019, 1, 7; Cadeau, "Beaver Bay Historical Property Sale Tabled," *Lake County News-Chronicle*, 16 August 2019, 3; *Bay Area Historical Society Newsletter* 37 (Summer 2021): 2–4.

273 Maki, "What Is Happening with the Beaver Bay Apartments?"; comments from Tedi Kytola to the author, 2022.

274 Manuscript schedules for the U.S. Census, 1930, 1940; *Northern Trails: The North's Premier Tourist Publication*, May 1926, 41; tourist brochure, 1942; Bishop, *By Water and Rail*, 13, 15, 17; Davis, *Beaver Bay*, 104; *Duluth News-Tribune*, 28 March 1959, 8; 17 February 1999; Pat Reed, *Looking Back*, undated Bay Area Historical Society pamphlet; comments from Linda Malzak to the author, 2017; comments from Tim G. Anderson to the author, 2018; comments from Ed Maki to the author, 2019.

275 *Bay Area Historical Society Newsletter* 33 (Fall 2017): 3–4.

276 *Bay Area Historical Society Newsletter* 33 (Fall 2017): 2–3.

277 Manuscript schedules for the U.S. Census, 1930, 1940; tourist brochures, 1937, 1949, 1953; Davis, *Beaver Bay*, 61; *Duluth News-Tribune and Herald*, 23 February 1986, D8; *Duluth News-Tribune*, 4 November 1988, D2.

278 Tourist brochure, 1972; Davis, *Beaver Bay*, 61; B. Berrens, "Couple Keeps Historic Touch at Beaver Bay's Camp 61," *Lake County News-Chronicle*, 26 August 2011; comments from Carol Krynski to the author, 2016.

279 *Lake County Chronicle*, 20 June 1996, 1; Keith and Teresa Bartell, "Brief History of the Beaver Bay Agate Shop," information panel on display in the Agate Shop museum.

280 Davis, *Beaver Bay*, 38, 63; Liz Holum, "MHPIF, Beaver Bay School," 1984, SHPO-MDA; Elizabeth Lovold Garrison, "Beaver Bay School," *Bay Area Historical Society Newsletter* 31 (October 2015); *Bay Area Shopper* (Silver Bay), April 1998; Maki comments, 2019.

281 Davis, *Beaver Bay*, 38, 63; Holum, "MHPIF, Beaver Bay School"; Garrison, "Beaver Bay School"; *Bay Area Shopper*, April 1998; Maki comments, 2019.

282 Davis, *Beaver Bay*, 25, 57–58, 64, 105.

283 Mrs. George F. Case, *Beaver Bay Club* (privately published, 1945); Maki, *Treaties to Taconite*, 17; Davis, *Beaver Bay*, 105; Holum, "MHPIF, Beaver Bay Club."

284 Steve Kuchera, "North Nonprofit Aims to Evict Century-Old Fish House," *Duluth News-Tribune*, 30 July 2013; "Beaver Bay Club Seeks Resolution of Dispute over Old Fish House," *Duluth News-Tribune*, 1 August 2013; "The Lorntson Story Began with Martin and Hannah . . . and Led to 'Stump-Rancher-Turned-Fisherman Conrad,'" *North Shore Commercial Fishing Museum Journal* 12 (Summer 2004); "What Happened to the Dispute over an Old Fish House in Beaver Bay?," *North Shore Commercial Fishing Museum Journal* 26 (Summer 2017); Ed Maki Jr., notice to Bay Area Historical Society members, September 2023.

285 Davis, *Beaver Bay*, 55–57; Andrew Munsch, "Historic U.S. 61: Beaver River Bridges," Deadpioneer's Historic Minnesota Highways, http://www.deadpioneer.com/routes/US61/us61images/us61postcards.htm; Jamey Malcomb, "New Trail Section, Connects Silver Bay, Beaver Bay," *Lake County News-Chronicle*, 1 June 2018, B1.

286 Agnes Thorngren, undated interview provided to the author by Ed Maki.

287 Manuscript schedules for the U.S. Census, 1900, 1910, 1930, 1940, and for the Minnesota Census, 1905; Minnesota Arrowhead Country, "List of Resorts and Hotels," late 1920s; tourist brochures, late 1940s and early 1950s; *Duluth Herald*, 7 February 1942, 10; *Duluth News-Tribune*, 23 August 1950, 2; Holland, *Early Resorts of Minnesota*, 409, 414; Maki comments, 2010.

288 Manuscript schedules for the U.S. Census, 1910, 1930, 1940, and for the Minnesota Census, 1905; Michael Koop, "National Register of Historic Places Registration Form for the Edward and Lisa Mattson House and Fish House," 1990, SHPO-MDA; Maki comments, 2010.

289 Manuscript schedules for the U.S. Census, 1900, 1910, 1930, 1940; Koop, "Edward and Lisa Mattson House and Fish House."

290 Koop, "Edward and Lisa Mattson House and Fish House."

291 Koop; Morse-Kahn, *Lake Superior's Historic North Shore,* 100.

292 *Cook County News-Herald,* 13 October 1955, 1, citing W. M. Kelley.

293 Manuscript schedules for the U.S. Census, 1920, 1930, 1940; *Two Harbors Chronicle and Times,* 8 April 1954, 1; Maki, *Treaties to Taconite,* 23; Robert V. Bartlett, *The Reserve Mining Controversy: Science, Technology, and Environmental Quality* (Bloomington: Indiana University Press, 1980), 22; John Henrickson, "Silver Bay, Minnesota: Sunrise for a Phoenix," *Lake Superior Magazine,* October–November 1989, 25–26; Bishop, *By Water and Rail,* 141–42.

294 Bishop, *By Water and Rail,* 143–46; Bartlett, *Reserve Mining Controversy,* 20–23; Frank D. Schaumburg, *Judgment Reserved: A Landmark Environmental Case* (Reston, Va.: Reston, 1976), 45–58; *Duluth News-Tribune,* 9 October 1946, 1, citing R. C. Allen; 6 June 1947, 1, 5; 18 June 1947, 1, 7; 10 July 1947, 1, 4; 12 July 1947, 1, 8, citing Fischer and Weinberg; 26 November 1947, 1; 17 December 1947, 1, 4, citing Control Commission.

295 Lloyd V. Gustafson, "Beaver Bay Sees Bright Horizon," *Duluth News-Tribune,* Cosmopolitan, 23 February 1947, 10–11; Siinto Wessman, "Beaver Bay Feels Growing Pains," *Duluth News-Tribune,* 24 February 1952, A6; Emil Schneider, "Nameless North Shore 'Ghost Town' Becoming a Wilderness Metropolis," *Duluth News-Tribune,* Cosmopolitan, 26 October 1952, 8–9; *Duluth News-Tribune,* 26 July 1952, 2, citing Schmid; *Cook County News-Herald,* 3 April 1953, 1; *Skillings' Mining Review,* 30 October 1954; Bishop, *By Water and Rail,* 143, 148.

296 E. W. Davis, *Pioneering with Taconite* (St. Paul: Minnesota Historical Society Press, 1964), 178–81; Bishop, *By Water and Rail,* 141–45; City of Silver Bay, Minnesota, http://www.silverbay.com/.

297 Jane Brody, "Iron Ore Company vs. the Changing Times," *New York Times,* 8 August 1973, 58; Bartlett, *Reserve Mining Controversy,* 118–60; Grant J. Merritt, *Iron and Water: My Life Protecting Minnesota's Environment* (Minneapolis: University of Minnesota Press, 2018), 31–40, 59–60.

298 Jeffrey T. Manuel, *Taconite Dreams: The Struggle to Sustain Mining on Minnesota's Iron Range, 1915–2000* (Minneapolis: University of Minnesota Press, 2015), 100–117, quotation on 114; Merritt, *Iron and Water,* 72–77; Bartlett, *Reserve Mining Controversy,* 205–9.

299 Al Miller, "Bankruptcy Petition Filed for Reserve," *Duluth News-Tribune and Herald,* 8 August 1986, A1; Peter Passi, "Northshore Mining Co. Celebrates Reopening of Furnace No. 5," *Duluth News-Tribune,* 14 June 2008; John Myers, "Cliffs Will Reopen Northshore Mining in May," *Duluth News-Tribune,* 14 May 2016; Dee DePass, "Cliffs Natural Resources Will Restart Two Taconite Lines at Its Minnesota Plant," *StarTribune,* 25 October 2013; Jimmy Lovrien, "In Silver Bay, New Pellet Points towards Cliffs' Future," *Duluth News-Tribune,* 7 August 2019, A1, A7; Dan Kraker, "Cleveland-Cliffs Extends Closure of Northshore Mining Until Next Year," *Duluth News-Tribune,* 23 July 2022, A11; 23 February, 2023, 3.

300 Jean Jones, "Students Build Models for Model Town," *Minneapolis Tribune,* 20 November 1949, L12; *Duluth News-Tribune,* 3 August 1953, A7; City of Silver Bay, Minnesota, http://www.silverbay.com/.

301 *Engineering News-Record* 23 (October 1952): 34; *Duluth News-Tribune,* 26 July 1952, 2, citing Edward Schmid; *Cook County News-Herald,* 13 October 1955, 1, citing Kelley; *Duluth News-Tribune,* Outlook Edition, 9 January 1955, 6.

302 Arnold R. Alanen, "Postwar Planning and Conservation in America, with Special Reference to Remote Mining and Industrial Communities in Minnesota and Michigan," in *Cultural Heritage in the Sustainability of Remote Communities,* ed. Christine Garnaut and Robert Freestone (Melbourne, Australia: University of New South Wales, 2007), 61–63.

303 Emil Schneider, "Taconite Projects to Boom Prosperity of Area," *Duluth News-Tribune,* 1 January 1953, 1; *Duluth News-Tribune,* 26 July 1953, A4; *Duluth News-Tribune,* "Iron for Tomorrow," 9 August 1953, 6; "Reserve Mining Company's Taconite Development," *Minnesota Engineer,* April 1955, 15; Kurt Kaiser, ed., *Company Town: An Oral History about Life in Silver Bay, Minnesota, 1950s–1980s* (Silver Bay, Minn.: William M. Kelley High School, 2012), 21, quoting Ruth Koepke.

304 *Duluth News-Tribune,* 25 August 1953, 1; Isadore Cohen, "'Company Towns': Silver Bay, Babbitt Revise Meaning of Ugly Term," *Duluth News-Tribune,* 5 September 1954, 8; David Setnicker, "The Beginning of the End of Mining Company Towns: Biwabik's Modern Home Manufacturing Corporation," *Hometown Focus* (Virginia, Minn.), 26 May 2017, 23–26.

305 Kaiser, *Company Town,* 21–24, 33; Maki comments, 2021; Alanen, *Morgan Park,* 255–59, 278.

306 Schneider, "Nameless North Shore 'Ghost Town,'" 8; *Duluth News-Tribune,* 12 September 1956, 10; Donald Torbert, *A Century of Minnesota Architecture*

(Minneapolis, Minn.: Minneapolis Society of Fine Arts, 1958); *Minneapolis Tribune*, 20 May 1956; Evan Jones, "Company Town a la Mode," *Steelways* 12 (December 1956): 1.

307 U.S. Census of Population, 1960–2010; U.S. Census of Housing, 1960; Pat Prince, "Silver Bay Wants to Be More Than Summer Heaven," *Minneapolis Star and Tribune*, 17 May 1987, B1, B7.

308 Kaiser, *Company Town*, 29, citing Ruth Koepke.

309 *Two Harbors Chronicle and Times*, 17 December 1953, 1, 4; *Duluth Herald*, 22 April 1955, 26; Debra Kellner, "Historic Study of Silver Bay's School System," 2008, 3, SHPO-MDA.

310 *Duluth News-Tribune*, 4 May 1955, 3; Ed Goodpaster, "Our New Taconite Towns," *Minneapolis Tribune, Picture Magazine*, 19 June 1955.

311 Chuck Frederick, "Safe Harbor Could Be Boon for Silver Bay," *Duluth News-Tribune*, 18 March 1993, A1, A10; Chuck Frederick, "Silver Bay to Christen Marina, Safe Harbor," *Duluth News-Tribune*, 20 May 1999, A1, A6; Margaret Bogue and Virginia A. Palmer, *Around the Shores of Lake Superior: A Guide to Historic Sites* (Madison: University of Wisconsin Sea Grant Program, 1979), 28–29; MDNR, "Silver Bay Marina, Protected Access," https://www.dnr.state.mn.us/water_access/harbors/silver_bay.html.

312 Frederick, "Silver Bay to Christen Marina"; Denis Gardner, "Sinking of the Hesper," *Minnesota History* 58 (Winter–Spring 2003–4): 58; MDNR, "Silver Bay Marina, Protected Access."

313 Ken Vogel, "North Shore Adventure Park Breaks Ground," *Lake County News-Chronicle*, 9 June 2017, 1; *Lake County News-Chronicle*, 31 May 2019, 1; North Shore Adventure Park, https://northshoreadventurepark.com/.

314 Wallace W. Morgan, "Symbolic 'Mr. Taconite' Unveiled at Silver Bay," *Duluth News-Tribune*, 25 February 1962; inscription on "Rocky Taconite" statue.

315 Teri Cadeau, "A 'Rocky' History: Builder Tells Story behind Silver Bay Landmark," *Lake County News-Chronicle*, 26 October 2018; Maki comments, 2019.

316 *Two Harbors Chronicle and Times*, 17 December 1953, 1, 4; *Duluth News-Tribune*, 8 March 1956, 13; Kellner, "Historic Study of Silver Bay's School System," 12–13.

317 John Krebs, "Nursing Facility Near Completion," *Duluth News-Tribune*, 20 December 1990, A7, citing F. Janklow; Minnesota Department of Veterans Affairs, "Veterans Homes: Silver Bay," https://mn.gov/mdva/homes/silver-bay/.

318 *Duluth News-Tribune*, 16 March 1954, 1; 17 October 1956; Walter Eldot, "Silver Bay Incorporates: Village Council Starts from Scratch," *Duluth News-Tribune*, 6 January 1957, 21; comments from Julie Billings to the author, 2020.

319 Kaiser, *Company Town*, 45–47, 52, citing Lucy Malmo, 45.

320 Kaiser, 45–47; *Duluth News-Tribune*, 9 January 1955, 1; *Mesabi Daily News* (Virginia, Minn.), 31 January 1955; *Silver Bay News*, 18 June 1957, 1; 1 July 1958, 1; Maki, *Treaties to Taconite*, 31.

321 *Two Harbors Chronicle and Times*, 4 June 1953, 1; 17 December 1953, 1; 13 October 1955, 1; Wayne C. Johnson, "The Formation and Development of Sychar Lutheran Church," in *Sychar Remembers: Sixty Years* (Silver Bay, Minn.: Sychar Lutheran Church, 2013), 33–37; Sychar Lutheran Church, *2013 Church Directory* (Silver Bay, Minn.: Sychar Lutheran Church, 2013), 2, 6; Buggeln, *Suburban Church*, 30, 85–88, 273–74; Albert Christ Janner and Mary Mix Foley, *Modern Church Architecture: A Guide to the Form and Spirit of 20th Century Religious Buildings* (New York: McGraw-Hill, 1968), 138.

322 *Cook County News-Tribune*, 25 February 1965, 1; Sychar Lutheran Church, *2013 Church Directory*, 3, 7; Buggeln, *Suburban Church*, 85–88, quotation on 86.

323 Sychar Lutheran Church, *2013 Church Directory*, 5, 9; comments from Kristina Pirsig to the author, 2017.

324 Hayden L. Straight, *Together: The Story of Church Cooperation in Minnesota* (Minneapolis, Minn.: T. S. Denison, 1971), 218–23; *Duluth News-Tribune*, 19 November 1954, 3; 22 July 1956, A15; *New York Times*, 23 September 1956, 44; Alanen, *Morgan Park*, 170–72.

325 *Duluth News-Tribune*, 22 July 1956, 15, citing Hankins; Richard Kieckhefer, *Theology in Stone: Church Architecture from Byzantium to Berkeley* (New York: Oxford University Press, 2004); comments from Lynn Anderson to the author, 2018.

326 *Duluth News-Tribune*, 22 July 1956, 15; United Protestant Church of Silver Bay, "Church History," http://unitedprotestant.org/.

327 "Reserve Mining Company's Taconite Development," *Minnesota Engineer*, April 1955; George Starkovich, cited in Kaiser, *Company Town*, 60; O. E. Domain, cited in Kellner, "Historic Study of Silver Bay's School System," 5.

328 *Silver Bay News*, 31 March 1959, 1; Janna Goerdt, "Life's Purpose Finds New Use for Old School," *Duluth News-Tribune*, 17 September 2006, C1–C2; Kellner, "Historic Study of Silver Bay's School System," 9–11.

329 St. Mary's Catholic Church, "Litany of the Blessed Virgin Mary" and "History," https://stmarysilverbay.org/news; comments from Cindy Rowlee to the author, 2018, 2020.

330 Harold Hollis, "Taconite Finds Place in Church," *Duluth Herald*, 27 February 1957.

331 Ken Vogel, "North Shore's 'Black Beach' to Open to Public by Memorial Day," *Lake County News-Chronicle*, 16 May 2015; Parks and Recreation, City of Silver Bay, Minnesota, http://www.silverbay.com/?page_id=26; Bob Berg, "Exploring a Different Kind of Beach, Silver Bay Now Welcomes Beachcombers to Once-Private Shore," *Lake Superior Magazine*, 15 October 2018, https://www.lakesuperior.com/travel/minnesota/402travelmn/.

332 Anderson and Fischer, *North Shore*, 230; *Duluth News-Tribune*, 7 March 1936, 9, citing G. Archibald.

333 MDNR, "Tettegouche State Park," http://www.dnr.state.mn.us/state_parks/tettegouche/index.html; Mountain Project, "Tettegouche SP (North Shore) Climbing," https://www.mountainproject.com/area/105812783/tettegouche-sp-north-shore

334 MDNR, "State Parks."

335 MDNR; MDNR, "Tettegouche State Park."

336 Manuscript schedules for the U.S. Census, 1900, 1910; John E. Hunt, "Fishing Clubs along the Baptism River," *Minnesota History* 59 (Summer 2005): 229–31, 234.

337 Hunt, "Fishing Clubs along the Baptism River," citing Cooley, 232.

338 Gustave Axelson, "Backwoods Manor," *Minnesota Conservation Volunteer*, July–August 2011, 24–29, citing Ostman, 29; Meyer, *Everyone's Country Estate*, 273–78; MDNR, "Tettegouche State Park."

339 Michael Koop, "National Register of Historic Places Registration Form for the Tettegouche Camp Historic District," 1999, SHPO-MDA; MDNR, "Tettegouche State Park."

340 Hunt, "Fishing Clubs along the Baptism River," 235; MnDOT, "Historic Bridges; Bridge 3549, Baptism River," http://www.dot.state.mn.us/historicbridges/; Andrew Munsch, "Historic U.S. 61: Old Baptism River Bridge and Highway," Deadpioneer's Historic Minnesota Highways, https://deadpioneer.com/routes/US61/historicus61se/baptismriver/baptismriver.html; "Iona's Singing Beach," *Northern Wilds*, June 2022, 15.

341 Konnie LeMay, "Adieu, Sea Stack: A Last Look at a Natural Icon," *Lake Superior Magazine*, February–March 2020, 15–17; Anderson and Fischer, *North Shore*, 284; Emily Bright, "Storm Topples Often-Photographed Sea Stack at Tettegouche State Park," MPR News, 1 December 2019, https://www.mprnews.org/story/2019/12/01/storm-topples-oftenphotographed-sea-stack-at-tettegouche-state-park.

342 Bishop, *By Water and Rail*, 59–64; Wurzer, *Tales of the Road*, 31–32.

343 Manuscript schedules for the U.S. Census, 1930, 1940; tourist brochure, 1949; Bishop, *By Water and Rail*, 64; "Illgen City," Wikipedia, accessed 2024.

344 Leonard Peterson, Frieda Peterson, and Rudy Illgen, "Illgen City," circa 1990, typescript prepared for Lake County Historical Society; *Silver Bay News*, 10 June 1958, 3; Marjorie Ingle, *Mayan Revival Style: Art Deco Mayan Fantasy* (Salt Lake City, Utah: Peregrine Smith Books, 1984), 1; Ella Andra-Warner, "The North Shore's Mayan-Inspired Resort," *Northern Wilds*, 28 March 2017.

345 "Chichen Itze," Wikipedia, accessed 2022; "Ancient Maya Architecture," Wikipedia, accessed 2022.

346 *Lake County Chronicle*, 11 October 1928, 10; tourist brochures, 1942, 1949; *Silver Bay News*, 10 June 1958, 3; Wurzer, *Tales of the Road*, 28–30.

347 *Two Harbors Chronicle*, 14 June 1934, 3; 21 June 1945, 7, citing the Illgens; *Silver Bay News*, 10 June 1958, 3; tourist brochure, 1949; Duluth Guide Co., *Duluth Souvenir Guide*, 15; Wurzer, *Tales of the Road*, 29–30; Andrew Munsch, "Historic U.S. 61: Old Alignment at Illgen City," Deadpioneer's Historic Minnesota Highways, https://www.deadpioneer.com/routes/US61/historicus61se/illgencity/illgencity.html.

348 Manuscript schedules for the Minnesota Census, 1905; Finland Schools Reunion Committee, *Keeping Our Heritage: Finland, Minnesota, 1895–1976* (Finland, Minn.: The Committee), 29–30.

349 Postcard caption for Kennedy's Landing Campground, 1980s; Andrew Munsch, "Historic U.S. 61: Old Highway 61 between Illgen City and Little Marais," Deadpioneer's Historic Minnesota Highways, https://deadpioneer.com/routes/US61/historicus61se/illgennorth/illgennorth.html.

350 Fritzen, *Historic Sites and Place Names*, 17; Upham, *Minnesota Place Names*, 311; Nute, *Lake Superior*, 302; Bishop, *By Water and Rail*, 109–13; "Little Marais, Minnesota," Wikipedia, accessed 2023.

351 Frank Antilla, *Left Home at 16: A Memoir of Strength, Courage and Faith* (privately published, 2010), 2–3, 17, 74–75, 195–210; North Shore Visitor, "A Fish out of Water," https://northshorevisitor.com/business/a-fish-out-of-water/.

352 Tourist brochures, 1949, 1950; "Leonard and Evelyn Rudstrom," Florida Death Index, 1877–1998; *Duluth*

*News-Tribune,* 13 February 1972, 34; *Bay Area Historical Society Newsletter* 34 (Spring 2018): 1–4; Wurzer, *Tales of the Road,* 26–28.

353 *Duluth News-Tribune,* 13 February 1972, 34; Wurzer, *Tales of the Road,* 26–28; comments from Dean and Patty Carpenter to the author, 2017, 2024.

354 *Duluth Herald,* 9 December 1933, 11; Art Fenstad, *The Lake Is Your Life: The Fenstads at Little Marais* (privately printed, 2021), 20–21, 63–65.

355 Manuscript schedules for the U.S. Census, 1930; travel brochures, circa 1949, 1972; *Duluth News-Tribune,* 8 April 1990, C2; Carpenter comments, 2017, 2024.

356 *Duluth Herald,* 9 December 1933, 12; comments from Art Fenstad to the author, 2022, 2024.

357 Manuscript schedules for the U.S. Census, 1900, 1910, 1930, 1940; "Minnesota, Homestead and Cash Entry Patents, Pre-1908," http://search.ancestry.com/.

358 Bishop, *By Water and Rail,* 109 11; "A History of Eastern Lake County," 15–16; "Fenstads: Little Marais, Minnesota," biographical account at the North Shore Commercial Fishing Museum, Tofte.

359 *Northern Trails: The North's Premier Tourist Publication,* May 1926; tourist brochure, 1937; *Duluth News-Tribune,* 12 December 2000, B5; Beth Gauper, "Seeking the Old North Shore: On Minnesota's Beloved Vacation Spot, Change Is Coming Fast," *Midwest Weekends* (undated); Fenstad's Resort, https://fenstadsresort.com/.

360 Meyer, *Everyone's Country Estate,* 178–81; Chris Clayton, "Winter Camp at George Crosby Manitou State Park," *Minnesota Conservation Volunteer* 86 (January–February 2023): 21; MDNR, "George H. Crosby Manitou State Park," https://www.dnr.state.mn.us/state_parks/park.html.

361 *Cook County News-Herald,* 23 June 1955, 1; "Manitou River Bridge: Lake County, Minnesota," BridgeHunter, http://bridgehunter.com/mn/lake/9002/ (inactive website).

362 Manuscript schedules for the U.S. Census, 1930, 1940; Workers of the Writers' Program of the Work Projects Administration in the State of Minnesota, *The Minnesota Arrowhead Country* (Chicago: Albert Whitman, 1941), 164–65; tourist brochures, 1937, 1972; *Duluth News-Tribune,* 23 December 1955, 1, 3.

363 Meyer, *Everyone's Country Estate,* 166–67; MDNR, "State Waysides in Minnesota," http://www.dnr.state.mn.us/state_parks/waysides/index.html.

## Cook County

1 Adolph A. Toftey, "Cook County," in *Who's Who in Minnesota in 1941,* ed. C. N. Corwell and Esther Stutheit (St. Paul: Minnesota Editorial Association, 1941); Cook County GIS, *Plat Book and Land Atlas: Cook County, Minnesota* (Grand Marais, Minn.: Cook County Courthouse, 2013), 3.

2 U.S. Census of Population, 1890–2020; manuscript schedules for the U.S. Census, 1920.

3 Cochrane, *Gichi Bitobig,* quotation on 139; Gene Rebeck, "The 'Cook County Shuffle': Making It Work in Minnesota's North East Corridor," *MinnPost,* 11 February 2016; Rae Poynter, "Exclusive: Moving to Cook County. Part 1: Why Cook County?," *Boreal Community Media,* 15 November 2021; Bob Thompson, "New Construction in Cook County, Minnesota," *Cook County News-Herald,* 21 January 2022, A1, B5.

4 "U.S. Presidential Elections in Minnesota," Wikipedia, accessed 2024.

5 U.S. Census of Population, 1890–2020; "Cook County, Minnesota," Wikipedia, accessed 2024; "Grand Portage Reservation," Wikipedia, accessed 2023.

6 Raff, *Law and Order in the Wilderness,* 13–16, 20–25, 35–42; Raff, *Pioneers in the Wilderness,* 182.

7 Minutes of the Regular Meeting of the Board of Cook County Commissioners, 9 September 1942, https://www.leg.mn.gov/archive/sos/film/pdf.9117.pdf (this account also includes minutes from 1935 and 1939).

8 Raff, *Law and Order in the Wilderness,* 13–16, 20–25, 35–42.

9 Manuscript schedules for the U.S. Census, 1900, 1910, 1920, 1930, 1940; U.S. Census of Population, 1950–2020; Raff, *Law and Order in the Wilderness,* 61; Livdahl et al., *Schroeder Area History,* 55; "Township of Schroeder, MN," *Minnesota Gazetteer,* https://minnesota.hometownlocator.com/counties/subdivisions/data,n,township%20of%20schroeder,id,2703158999,cfips,031.cfm#google_vignette.

10 Livdahl et al., *Schroeder Area History,* 24–25; Barbara Livdahl and Cross River Heritage Center, *Lost Resorts,* exhibit at the Cross River Heritage Center, 2015–16; "Amboy and George Spencer Shipwreck Sites," Wikipedia, accessed 2023.

11 Manuscript schedules for the U.S. Census, 1900, 1910, 1920; Bureau of Land Management, "General Land Office Records for John Gunderson," 1899; Livdahl and Cross River Heritage Center, *Lost Resorts;* Ford Eastman,

"From Logs to Magazines: Paper Begins Long Trip on North Shore," *Duluth News-Tribune*, 16 September 1951, C2; *Cook County News-Herald*, 21 June 1962, 1; Linda Lamb, "Timber . . . !," *Schroeder Area Historical Society Newsletter* 21 (May 2012): 1; interpretive panels for Sugarloaf Harbor at the former Taconite Harbor Townsite.

12 Elmer L. Andersen, *A Man's Reach* (Minneapolis: University of Minnesota Press, 2000), 365–66; Sugarloaf: The North Shore Stewardship Association, "History [and] Brief History Timeline, 2018," https://sugarloafnorthshore.org/about-sugarloaf/our-story/.

13 Andersen, *A Man's Reach*, 366–67; Sugarloaf, "History"; comments from Emily Andersen to the author, 2020.

14 MDNR, "Sugarloaf Point SNA," https://www.dnr.state.mn.us/snas/description; Sugarloaf, "History"; comments from Molly Thompson to the author, 2023.

15 Upham, *Minnesota Place Names*, 144, 146; tourist brochure, 1937; *Cook County News-Herald*, 28 February 1953, 1; 24 September 1953, 1; *Duluth News-Tribune*, 6 November 1953, 1; Livdahl et al., *Schroeder Area History*, 39–40; Livdahl and Cross River Heritage Center, *Lost Resorts*.

16 *Cook County News-Herald*, 3 June 1954, 1; Erie Mining Company History Project Team, *Taconite: New Life for Minnesota's Iron Range—the History of Erie Mining Company* (Brookfield, Mo.: Donning, 2019), 68.

17 *Cook County News-Herald*, 3 June 1954, 1; Cross River Heritage Center, *Boom Town to Ghost Town: Taconite Harbor*, exhibit, 2016; Wurzer, *Tales of the Road*, 25–26.

18 Cross River Heritage Center, *Boom Town to Ghost Town*; "Plat of Taconite Harbor Subdivision," on file with CCHS.

19 Cross River Heritage Center, *Boom Town to Ghost Town*; Pat Prince, "Taconite Harbor to Be Dismantled, Ending an Era," *Minneapolis Star and Tribune*, 14 March 1986, A1, A6; Laurie Hertzel, "Taconite Harbor Residents Win Reprieve," *News-Tribune and Herald* (Duluth), 22 May 1986, A1, A10; Janet Pinkston, "Taconite Harbor Gets a Glimpse of the End," *News-Tribune and Herald*, 5 November 1987, A1, A7; Mark Stodghill, "Houses Cost Less in Taconite Harbor; You Haul 'Em Away," *Duluth News-Tribune*, 6 December 1989, A2; Wurzer, *Tales of the Road*, 26–38.

20 Rhonda Silence, "Community Gets Update from MN Power," WTIP North Shore Community Radio, 14 December 2019, https://wtip.org/community-gets-taconite-harbor-update-mn-power.

21 Livdahl et al., *Schroeder Area History*, 41, 44; Cross River Heritage Center, *Boom Town to Ghost Town*.

22 Livdahl et al., *Schroeder Area History*, 40–42, 61; "Broom Falls on Car 000: Last Erie/LTV Steel Load," https://www.trainorders.com/discussion/read.php?11,4122007.

23 Brady Slater, "Coal-Fired Operations to End at Taconite Harbor Energy Center; Plant Will Be Idled in 2016," *Duluth News-Tribune*, 9 July 2015; Livdahl et al., *Schroeder Area History*, 39–44; "Cliffs Erie Railroad," Wikipedia, accessed 2024; Silence, "Community Gets Update from MN Power."

24 MDNR, "Taconite Harbor: Small Craft Harbor," in *Lake Superior Boating Guide: A Guide to Boating on the Minnesota Side of Lake Superior* (St. Paul: MDNR, 2004), 48; MDNR, "Taconite Harbor: Small Craft Harbor," https://www.dnr.state.mn.us/water_access/harbors/taconite.html.

25 Livdahl et al., *Schroeder Area History*, 5.

26 Manuscript schedules for the U.S. Census, 1900, 1910, 1920, 1930, 1940; U.S. General Land Office, Bureau of Land Management Records for Henry J. Redmyer, 1889; Livdahl et al., *Schroeder Area History*, 5; Raff, *Pioneers in the Wilderness*, 83–88; Amy M. Lucas, "Stickney Inn and Store: National Register of Historic Places Evaluation of Significance," prepared for the Schroeder Area Historical Society, 2015, 18–19; Sverre Arestad, "Reindeer in Alaska," *Pacific Northwest Quarterly* 42 (July 1951): 211, citing Jackson.

27 *Cook County News-Herald*, 11 October 1916, 1; Mary T. Bell, *Cutting across Time: Logging, Rafting and Milling the Forests of Lake Superior* (Schroeder, Minn.: Schroeder Area Historical Society, 1999), 9; Raff, *Pioneers in the Wilderness*, 88; Lucas, "Stickney Inn and Store," 19; Livdahl et al., *Schroeder Area History*, 7–8; death certificates for Henrik, Emilie, and Hedrick Redmyer, in "Washington Deaths, 1883–1960."

28 Raff, *Pioneers in the Wilderness*, 89; Bell, *Cutting across Time*, ix, 6–7; Livdahl et al., *Schroeder Area History*, 7–10, 22, 36; Lucas, "Stickney Inn and Store," 19.

29 Livdahl et al., *Schroeder Area History*, 10, 20; Livdahl and Cross River Heritage Center, *Lost Resorts*; Lucas, "Stickney Inn and Store," 26, 41–42.

30 Lucas, "Stickney Inn and Store," 20–21, 42.

31 *Cook County News-Herald*, 6 June 1929, Lucas, "Stickney Inn and Store, 20–24, 42; Livdahl et al., *Schroeder Area History*, 30–31; Florence Page Jaques, *Snowshoe Country* (Minneapolis: University of Minnesota Press, 1944), 39.

32 Livdahl et al., *Schroeder Area History*, 31–35; Wurzer, *Tales of the Road*, 23–24.

33 Laurie Hertzel, "Resort Is Sweetly Stuck in the Past,"

*StarTribune*, 12 June 2011, https://www.startribune.com/resort-is-sweetly-stuck-in-the-past/123613904/; Livdahl et al., *Schroeder Area History*, 30–36; Lucas, "Stickney Inn and Store," 26–29, 46.

34 Hertzel, "Resort Is Sweetly Stuck in the Past"; Livdahl et al., *Schroeder Area History*, 27; Lamb's Resort on Lake Superior, https://lambsresort.com/.

35 Jeffrey A. Hess, "National Register of Historic Places Inventory—Nomination Form for the Schroeder Lumber Company Building," 1986, SHPO-MDA.

36 Livdahl et al., *Schroeder Area History*, 22; MnDOT, "Historic Roadside Properties on Minnesota Highways Inventory Forms: Cross River Rest Area," 1998, http://www.dot.state.mn.us/roadsides/historic/inv-form.html.

37 Willoughby M. Babcock, "Highways and History," *Minnesota History* 13 (December 1932): 381–82; Gemini Research, *Historic Roadside Development Structures*, 3.7, 4.13, 5.21–22.

38 MnDOT, "Historic Roadside Properties on Minnesota Highways."

39 Livdahl et al., *Schroeder Area History*, 7, 9, 10, 20–22, 36; Gemini Research, *Historic Roadside Development Structures*, 3.7, 5.4, 5.20–21, 5.45; Roger Blakely, *Tourist and Hiking Guide for Minnesota's North Shore* (Moorhead, Minn.: New Rivers Press, 1981), 18; MnDOT, "Historic Roadside Properties on Minnesota Highways," https://www.dot.state.mn.us/roadsides/historic/index.html.

40 MDNR, Office of Planning, "Cross River State Wayside and Temperance River State Park Management Plan," circa 1981, 77, https://www.lrl.mn.gov/docs/pre2003/other/821249.pdf; Meyer, *Everyone's Country Estate*, 208–9; comments from Gregg Westigard to the author, 2020.

41 Livdahl and Cross River Heritage Center, *Lost Resorts*; Raff, *Pioneers in the Wilderness*, 77–78; *Duluth News-Tribune*, 12 September 1932, 1; *Two Harbors Chronicle*, 22 September 1932, 2.

42 Arthur Gunderson, "Frontier Bishop," *Duluth News-Tribune*, 13 April 1941, Cosmopolitan, 13; Lesley DuTemple, "Our Snowshoe Saint," *Lake Superior Magazine*, 30 July 2018, https://www.lakesuperior.com/travel/michigan/402snowshoe-saint-the-long-trek-to-sainthood-for-father-frederi/; "Frederick Baraga," Wikipedia, accessed 2023.

43 Manuscript schedules for the U.S. Census, 1920, 1930, 1940; Minneapolis city directories, 1914, 1918; tourist brochures, late 1920s, 1930, 1942, 1944, 1946; "Joseph Elmer Pecore," U.S. World War II Navy Muster Rolls, 1938–1949; "Hazel C. Pecore" and "Joseph E. Pecore," Find a Grave Index, 1861–1912.

44 Minneapolis city directories, 1935, 1937; manuscript schedules for the U.S. Census, 1940; *Cook County News-Herald*, 14 June 1945, 1; Livdahl et al., *Schroeder Area History*, 24–25; comments from Barbara Livdahl to the author, 2017.

45 Nancye Belding, "Schroeder Supports Temperance Landing," *Cook County News-Herald*, 23 September 2005, A1, A10; Temperance Landing on Lake Superior, http://www.resortsandlodges.com/lodging/usa/minnesota/north-shore/temperance-landing-on-lake-superior.html.

46 Manuscript schedules for the U.S. Census, 1920, 1930, 1940; tourist brochures, 1937, 1946; *North Shore Commercial Fishing Journal* 10 (Spring 2002): 1–2; Livdahl et al., *Schroeder Area History*, 25; Livdahl and Cross River Historical Center, *Lost Resorts*.

47 *Cook County News-Herald*, 21 June 1962, 1; 19 April 1994; tourist brochure, 1946; Livdahl and Cross River Historical Center, *Lost Resorts*.

48 Upham, *Minnesota Place Names*, 143, citing Norton and Clark; MDNR, "Temperance River State Park," https://www.dnr.state.mn.us/state_parks/park.html?id=spk00268#information.

49 MnDOT Historic Roadside Development Structures Inventory, "Temperance River Roadside Parking Area," 1998, https://www.dot.state.mn.us/roadsides/historic/files/iforms/CK-UOG-046.pdf; Meyer, *Everyone's Country Estate*, 318, N87; Sommer, *Hard Work and a Good Deal*, 25, 157, citing Tofte Township Clerk records, 51–52.

50 MnDOT, "Temperance River Roadside Parking Area"; Sommer, *Hard Work and a Good Deal*, 155; *Two Harbors Chronicle*, 28 April 1938, 4.

51 Meyer, *Everyone's Country Estate*, 140, 287; MDNR, "Temperance River State Park."

52 Chris Tormondsen, *Tofte: A Collection of Facts and Tales of the North Shore Area of Lake Superior* (Tofte, Minn.: Tofte Brothers, 1968), 4; Raff, *Pioneers in the Wilderness*, 107–8.

53 Manuscript schedules for the U.S. Census, 1900, 1910; Tormondsen, *Tofte*, 4–5; Raff, *Pioneers in the Wilderness*, 107–8; *Cook County Herald*, 11 October 1902, 6, citing Murphy; 9 October 1952, 1.

54 U.S. Census of Population, 1900–2020; Raff, *Law and Order in the Wilderness*, "Tofte (in Cook County, MN) Populated Place Profile," *Minnesota Gazeteer*, https://minnesota.hometownlocator.com/mn/cook/tofte.cfm;

Adelheid Fischer, "On the Shores of Gitchigummi," *Architecture Minnesota*, March/April 1994, 53, citing Risdahl; Cook County Board of Commissioners, "Tofte Design Review District Ordinance," 1992, https://www.toftemn.com/wp-content/uploads/2020/08/Tofte-Design-Review-Ordinance.pdf.

55 Manuscript schedules for the U.S. Census, 1910, 1920, 1930 1940; Raff, *Pioneers in the Wilderness*, 108; tourist brochures, 1937, 1947; *Cook County News-Herald*, 11 September 1952, 1; 2 February 1956, 1; interview with Rudolph Swanson, conducted by Merlin Humphrey, 30 March 1981, CCHS; obituary notice for Rudolph Swanson, April 1984, CCHS.

56 Tourist brochures, 1947, 1950; *Cook County News-Herald*, 11 September 1952, 1; 2 February 1956, 1; Swanson obituary and interview.

57 Josh Jipson, "Surfside Development Supported by Tofte," *Cook County Star* (Grand Marais), 15 May 2006, B2; Bluefin Bay Family of Resorts, "Surfside on Lake Superior," http://www.bluefinbay.com/surfside/.

58 *Cook County News-Herald*, 13 February 1964, 1; 27 August 1964, 1, citing Schweickhard.

59 *Duluth News-Tribune*, 27 August 2002.

60 *Cook County News-Herald*, 23 September 2005, A10; *Duluth News-Tribune*, 20 October 2012.

61 Edith Dunn, "National Register of Historic Places Register Form, Tofte Ranger Station—Cook County, MN," 1998, MDA-MHS (the station has not yet been listed in the National Register); Lee Johnson, "Superior National Forest–Northern Bedrock Historic Preservation Corps Partnership Project: Tofte Ranger Station Rehabilitation, August 23–30, 2016; September 6–13, 2016," on file with the U.S. Forest Service, Tofte Ranger District; Sommer, *Hard Work and a Good Deal*, 155.

62 Johnson, "Superior National Forest–Northern Bedrock"; Northern Bedrock Historic Preservation Corps, "2016 Field Season: Tofte Report," https://www.northernbedrockcorps.org/wp-content/uploads/NBHPC2016-Field-Season-Report-1.pdf; Passport in Time, "Tofte Ranger Station Historic Rehabilitation Project—SuperiorNF-MN," http://www.passportintime.com/tofte-rs-2016.html.

63 Tourist brochures, 1948, 1961; Sugar Beach on Lake Superior, https://www.toftesugarbeach.com/; Scott Godin, oral history recording, 6 November 2002, CCHS; comments from John Godin to the author, 2020; Andrew Munsch, "Historic U.S. 61: Private Driveway at Tofte," Deadpioneer's Historic Minnesota Highways, https://www.deadpioneer.com/routes/US61/historicus61se/toftedriveway/toftedriveway.html.

64 *Northern Trails: Premier Tourist Publication of the North*, Midsummer ed., 1926, 51; Fritzen, *Historic Sites and Place Names*, 20; tourist brochure, 1965.

65 *Northern Trails*, Midsummer ed., 1926; Mary Alice Hanson, "Tofte Park History," descriptive panel on the park grounds.

66 MDNR, "Tofte Access," https://www.dnr.state.mn.us/water_access/harbors/tofte.html.

67 Mrs. John [Cecelia] Tofte, "Brief History of Zion Lutheran Church, Tofte," *Cook County News-Herald*, 22 October 1962, 2; *Duluth News-Tribune*, 12 May 1910, 1, 7.

68 *Cook County News-Herald*, 6 June 1963, 1; 22 October 1964, 1.

69 "Googie Architecture," Wikipedia, accessed 2024; Alan Hess, *Googie Redux: Ultramodern Roadside Architecture* (San Francisco: Chronicle Books, 2004), 29; Larry Millett, *Minnesota Modern: Architecture and Life at Midcentury* (Minneapolis: University of Minnesota Press, 2015), 123.

70 Comments from Maureen Olsen Singleton to the author, 2015; comments from Ron Piercy to the author, 2022, 2023.

71 Bureau of Land Management, "General Land Office Records for Hans Engelsen," 1899; Tormondsen, *Tofte*, 4; Raff, *Pioneers in the Wilderness*, 107–8.

72 Raff, *Pioneers in the Wilderness*, 107–9, 113.

73 *Cook County News-Herald*, 1 March 1945, 1; Raff, *Pioneers in the Wilderness*, 43, 107, 110, 134, 181, 304–5, 322.

74 *Northern Trails*, Midsummer ed., 1926, 51; tourist brochure, 1937; *Cook County News-Herald*, 23 January 1941, 1; 2 February 1956, 1; 12 June 1977, 3.

75 Manuscript schedules for the U.S. Census, 1930, 1940; *Cook County News-Herald*, 14 November 1963, 1; May 1966; "Thomas Hansen Oral History," interviewed by Willis Raff, 12 March 1981, CCHS; Tom Hansen, "Tom Hansen Recalls Early Settlers in Tofte-Schroeder," *Schroeder Area Historical Society Newsletter* 16 (May 2010): 3; postcard caption for the Edgewater Inn, early 1950s.

76 *Cook County News-Herald*, 14 November 1963, 1; "Thomas Hansen Oral History"; Ted Tofte, Rob Buntz, and Tommy Hansen, "One Hundred Years of Hospitality," *The Fishwrapper* (Bluefin Bay, Tofte) 10 (Summer 1993): 1.

77 Tofte et al., "One Hundred Years of Hospitality," 1.

78 Tourist brochures, 1942, 1946, 1949; *Cook County News-Herald*, 23 May 1963, 3; Link, "Bluefin Bay," 64; John

Myers, "$4.3 Million Project Adds 18 Townhomes at Bluefin Bay," *Duluth News-Tribune,* 12 June 1993, A1, A6; Livdahl and Cross River Historical Center, *Lost Resorts;* interview with Dennis Rysdahl, conducted by Anna Klobuchar, 5 November 2002, on file with CCHS; Bruce N. Wright, "New England in the North: An Old North Shore Resort Takes on a Fresh Look," *Architecture Minnesota,* July/August 1985, 24.

79 *Cook County News-Herald,* 10 July 2020, 1.

80 Comments from Dennis Rysdahl to the author, 2022; Peter Paasi, "'Boreal Bunkhouse' to Fill North Shore Niche," *Duluth News-Tribune,* 26 June 2016, A1, A8, citing Rysdahl.

81 Ted Tofte, *Wonderland of the Herring Choker: Tales from the Early Days of Commercial Fishing on the North Shore of Lake Superior* (Charleston, W.V.: Blackwater Press, 1982), 18; Ted Tofte, "The Double Red Fish House," *Tofte Historical Society Newsletter* 1 (Summer 1993): 1, 3; *Cook County News-Herald,* 6 December 2019; Mary Alice Hanson, "It's Time to Celebrate," *North Shore Commercial Fishing Journal* 21 (Summer 2013): 1–3; Rysdahl comments, 2022; North Shore Commercial Fishing Museum, https://www.commercialfishingmuseum.org/.

82 Hanson, "It's Time to Celebrate"; North Shore Commercial Fishing Museum, http://www.commercialfishingmuseum.org/.

83 Tofte, *Wonderland of the Herring Choker,* 18; Tofte, "Double Red Fish House"; *Cook County News-Herald,* 6 December 2019; Hanson, "It's Time to Celebrate"; Rysdahl comments, 2022; North Shore Commercial Fishing Museum, http://www.commercialfishingmuseum.org/.

84 Virginia Reiner, "New Lakewalk Exhibit Opens in Tofte Park," *North Shore Commercial Fishing Journal* 19 (Winter 2011): 1–2; Reiner, "Celebrating 20 Years of Making History," *North Shore Commercial Fishing Journal* 21 (Fall 2013): 1–2, citing W. Sve.

85 Rhonda Silence, "Folk School and Fishing Museum Work Together on Historic Shelter," *Cook County News-Herald,* 6 April 2013; Reiner, "Celebrating 20 Years," 2; Peter Henrikson, "Grindbygg Boat House—North Shore Commercial Fishing Museum," http://peterhenrikson.com/project/grindbygg-boat-house-north-shore-commercial-fishing-museum.

86 Manuscript schedules for the U.S. Census, 1930, 1940; Ray Gervais, obituary, May 2002, on file with CCHS.

87 "Aeronca Super Chief Family," Wikipedia, accessed 2024; *Cook County News-Herald,* 5 October 1944, 1; Livdahl comments, 2020.

88 *Cook County News-Herald,* 5 October 1944, 1; Gervais obituary; Livdahl comments, 2020; comments from Martha Marnocha to the author, 2020.

89 *North Shore Commercial Fishing Museum Journal* 12 (Spring 2004): 1–3.

90 Tourist brochures, 1937, 1946, 1949; *Cook County News-Herald,* 25 April 1946, 1; *Minneapolis Tribune,* 7 February 1930, 18; interview with Jan Horak by Anna Klobuchar, 5 November 2002, on file with CCHS; Cobblestone Cabins, http://www.cobblestonecabins.biz/.

91 Horak interview; Cobblestone Cabins, http://www.cobblestonecabins.biz/.

92 Tourist brochures, 1928–29, 1937, 1939–40; *Cook County News-Herald,* 9 May 1968; *North Shore Commercial Fishing Museum Journal* 12 (Spring 2004); Livdahl and Cross River Historical Center, *Lost Resorts;* Livdahl comments, 2020.

93 *Cook County News-Herald,* 9 May 1968; 13 September 1968; *North Shore Commercial Fishing Museum Journal* 12 (Spring 2004); Livdahl and Cross River Historical Center, *Lost Resorts.*

94 *Cook County News-Herald,* 22 October 1959, 1; Meyer, *Everyone's Country Estate,* 173–74; MnDOT Historic Roadside Development Structures Inventory, "Berglund, Ray, Roadside Parking Area," 1998, http://www.dot.state.mn.us/roadsides/historic/files/iforms/CK-TFT-001.pdf.

95 *Cook County News-Herald,* 9 November 2013; 2 August 2014; 9 August 2014.

96 Raff, *Pioneers in the Wilderness,* 80–82; McDowell, *A History of Lutsen,* 4–8, 24, 40; "Battle of Lützen (1632)," Wikipedia, accessed 2024.

97 Manuscript schedules for the U.S. Census, 1900, 1920; U.S. Census of Population, 1930–2020; *Cook County News-Chronicle,* 14 November 2015; Township of Lutsen, Minn., demographic data and boundary map, https://minnesota.hometownlocator.com/counties/subdivisions/data,n,township%20of%20lutsen,id,2703138550,cfips,031.cfm; "Best Places: Lutsen, Minnesota," http://www.bestplaces.net/housing/city/minnesota/lutsen.

98 Manuscript schedules for the U.S. Census, 1910, 1920, 1930, 1940; *Cook County News-Herald,* 1 March 1951, 1; 16 June 1960, 1; tourist brochures, 1945, late 1940s, 1953; Livdahl and Cross River Historical Center, *Lost Resorts.*

99 McDowell, *A History of Lutsen,* 127; Lutsen Resort of Lake Superior, "Sea Villas," https://www.lutsenresort.com/lodging/sea-villas/; comments from SMSQ Architects to the author, 2018.

100 Deanna Marohn Bendix, "Ed Lundie," *Architecture Minnesota,* July/August 1983, 46.

101 Eileen Michaels, "Edwin Lundie, 1886–1972," in *The Architecture of Edwin Lundie,* by Dale Mulfinger (St. Paul: Minnesota Historical Society Press, 1995), 10.

102 *Cook County News-Herald,* 10 February 1959.

103 Michaels, "Edwin Lundie," 17.

104 Peter J. O'Toole, *Edwin H. Lundie: Five Decades—a Journey of Art and Architecture* (St. Paul, Minn.: Artist Book Press, 2016), 153.

105 Mulfinger, *Architecture of Edwin Lundie.*

106 "Census-Designated Place," Wikipedia, accessed 2023; Township of Lutsen; Lutsen CDP; Joshua Lindstrom, quoted in "Build-Outs of Summer: Fika Coffee of Lutsen, Minnesota," *Sprudge* (blog), 14 September 2016, http://coffeegeekio.blogspot.com/.

107 Center for Changing Landscapes, University of Minnesota, "Crafting a Northwoods Town: Lutsen Town Center Design and Gitchi Gami Trail Alignment Analysis," 2004–7.

108 Bureau of Land Management, General Land Office, Homestead Record 1351 for Charley Nelson, 1892; *Cook County News-Herald,* 9 August 1902; McDowell, *A History of Lutsen,* 17–18, 27, citing 1893 *Cook County Pioneer,* 28, 42.

109 *Cook County News-Herald,* 15 January 1946, 1; tourist brochure, 1948; McDowell, *A History of Lutsen,* 72–74, 84, 94.

110 *Cook County News-Herald,* 10 June 1948, 1; 21 October 1948, 1; 28 July 1949, 1; 30 December 1949, 11; 9 February 1950, 1; 6 December 1951, 1; 21 February 1952, 1; *Duluth News-Tribune,* 2 February 1952, 2; McDowell, *A History of Lutsen,* 100–103, 109–11.

111 Mulfinger, *Architecture of Edwin Lundie,* 108; McDowell, *A History of Lutsen,* 112, 120–21; Camille LeFevre, "Historic Hotels," *Architecture Minnesota,* January–February 2009, 11; *Cook County News-Herald,* 20 July 1961, 1.

112 McDowell, *A History of Lutsen,* 144–55; James Cramer, "Northwoods Resorts Architects Love," *Architecture Minnesota,* July/August 2012, 42–45; Lutsen Resort on Lake Superior, "Our History," https://www.lutsenresort.com/our-history/.

113 Michael Creger, "Familiar Places, Fresh Faces . . . New Owners at Favorite Spaces," *Lake Superior Magazine,* 21 March 2019; Katie Krantz, "Lutsen Resort Restores Restaurant, Adds New Cuisine to Menu," *Cook County News-Herald,* 7 June 2019; Cadeau, "Superior Shores Resorts Sold for $15 Million"; Paul Walsh, "Judge Takes Away Operation of Superior Shores Resort from Owner of Fire-Ravaged Ludsen Lodge," *StarTribune,* 30 July 2024.

114 Brielle Bredsten, "Historic Lutsen Lodge Destroyed in Fire," *Duluth News-Tribune Podcast Minute,* 7 February 2024, https://www.duluthnewstribune.com/news/local/historic-lutsen-lodge-destroyed-in-fire, citing Klobuchar; Jim Buchta, "Lutsen Lodge Was a 'Phenomenal Legacy' of a Top Minnesota Architect," *StarTribune,* 7 February 2024; Dan Kraker and Andrew Krueger, "Historic North Shore Lodge Destroyed in Overnight Fire, Owner Plans to Rebuild," MPR News, 6 February 2024, citing Vanegas, https://www.mprnews.org/story/2024/02/06/historic-lusten-resort-north-shore-lodge-destroyed-in-overnight-fire-lutsen-resort.

115 *Cook County News-Herald,* 29 July 1948, 1; 21 October 1948, 1; 29 December 1949, 1; 9 February 1950, 1; McDowell, *A History of Lutsen,* 89, 100–108.

116 McDowell, *A History of Lutsen,* 115, 123, 127–34; Lutsen Mountains, "Our History," https://www.lutsen.com/about/history/.

117 Stephen Regenold, "Lutsen Mountains: King of the Midwest Hills," *New York Times,* 26 March 2009; Rhonda Silence, "Water District Project Nears Completion," *Cook County News-Herald,* 2 July 2016; Brian Larson, "Lutsen Ski Hill EIS for Expansion on Superior National Forest," *Cook County News-Herald,* 1 May 2020; McDowell, *A History of Lutsen,* 89, 100–108.

118 Jimmy Lovrien, "Forest Service Rejects Lutsen Expansion," *Duluth News-Tribune,* 27 August 2023, 1A, 5A.

119 McDowell, *A History of Lutsen,* 119; Lutsen Resort on Lake Superior, http://www.lutsenresort.com/.

120 McDowell, *A History of Lutsen,* 144–55; E. Nolan, "Superior National at Lutsen—the North Shore of Minnesota," *Tee Times Magazine Minnesota,* 24 May 2018.

121 Nolan, "Superior National at Lutsen"; Superior National Golf Course, https://superiornational.com/.

122 Manuscript schedules for the U.S. Census, 1920, 1930, 1940; *Cook County News-Herald,* 13 May 1937, 1; tourist brochures, 1937, 1949; "Gitche Gummee Lodge on the North Shore of Lake Superior," circa 1950s, advertisement provided by Dianne Tessari; *North Shore Commercial Fishing Museum Journal* 12 (Spring 2004): 2; comments from Dianne Tessari to the author, 2016, 2017.

123 Tessari comments, 2017.

124 Jackie Crosby, "Merger Creates Largest UFCW Local in Five-State Area," *StarTribune,* 27 September 2018; comments from Diane and Darryl Sannes to the author,

2020; Heritage Center Conference & Event Center, http://heritagecenter.mn/; Tim Harlow, "Brooklyn Center's Earle Brown Heritage Center Has a New Name," *Star-Tribune*, 21 June 2022.

125 Eugene J. Utecht, *Labor Pains: The Birth and Growth of UFCW Local 653* (privately published, c. 2000), 109–10; Sannes comments, 2020; "Earle Brown," Wikipedia, 2024.

126 Utecht, *Labor Pains*, 107, 109–10.

127 Sannes comments, 2020; UFCW Local 663, "Ours Resort," https://www.ufcw663.org/member-benefits/ours-resort.

128 "Electrifying the Gunflint," circa 1958, CCHS; Jack Porter, "A History of Lutsen Light and Power Company," 2004, CCHS; *Cook County News-Herald*, 25 June 1953; "Arrowhead Electric," *Architecture Advantage*, 2012, https://architectureadvantage.com/project/arrowhead-electric-2/; Rhonda Silence, "Arrowhead's Green Building Gets Gold," *Cook County News-Herald*, 12 June 2010.

129 Manuscript schedules for the U.S. Census, 1920, 1930, 1940; tourist brochures, 1937, 1949; *Cook County News-Herald*, 10 April 1947; 15 November 1972; "Cook County Historical Sites," CCHS; obituary notice for Jessie Bally, December 1972, CCHS.

130 Manuscript schedules for the U.S. Census, 1920, 1930, 1940; tourist brochures, 1937, 1947, 1949; *Cook County News-Herald*, 11 November 1965; 14 August 1981, 1; Harriet Hansen Hams obituary notice, November 2014, CCHS; Eric Weicht, "Jeff and Anna Latz: Building a North Shore Legacy," *North Shore Wilds*, 29 October 1967, 2.

131 *Cook County News-Herald*, 10 November 1955, 1; 1 February 1956, 1; Otto Wedal, "They Helped Build the Church," *Cook County News-Herald*, 29 August 1957, 5; *North Shore Commercial Fishing Museum Journal* 14 (Spring 2006): 4.

132 *Cook County News-Herald*, 10 November 1955, 1; 2 February 1956, 1; 13 September 1956, 1; 2 April 1959, 1; 11 July 1963, 1; McDowell, *A History of Lutsen*, 116–17.

133 Buggeln, *Suburban Church*, 34–35, 130, 133.

134 Bureau of Land Management, General Land Office Records for Hosey Lyght, 1921; interview with John Lyght, conducted by Margaret Robertson, 13 March 1992, on file with MHS Archives; Samuel Meshbesher, "Lyght, John (1927–2010)," MNopedia, https://www.mnopedia.org/person/lyght-john-1927-2010; Rick Adkisson, "Hosiah Lyght," Homestead National Park, NPS, 22 November 2021, https://www.nps.gov/people/hosiah-p-lyght.htm.

135 John Lyght and Margaret Robertson interviews; Meshbesher, "Lyght"; Todd Beamon, "Without People There Is No History: 2 Families Have Special Stake in This Region," *Duluth News-Tribune*, 7 March 1962, D1, D5, quoting Norman Lyght; John Lyght, interviewed by Barbara Puch, 1996, summary provided in "Northern Lights Resort," *Overlook: Newsletter of the Cook County Historical Society*, Spring 2004, 1, 4.

136 Tourist brochure, 1937; John Lyght interview; Meshbesher, "Lyght"; Florence Page Jaques, *Snowshoe Country* (Minneapolis: University of Minnesota Press, 1944), 48.

137 John Lyght interview; Meshbesher, "Lyght"; comments from Mary Lyght Seaborg and Barbara Livdahl to the author, 2020; *Cook County News-Herald*, 4 August 1953; 2 July 1962; Arthur Wiley King, "Cathedral of the Pines," *Duluth News-Tribune*, Cosmopolitan, 30 August 1953, 9–10.

138 Meshbesher, "Lyght."

139 Manuscript schedules for the U.S. Census, 1920, 1930, 1940; Livdahl and Cross River Historical Center, *Lost Resorts*; *Cook County News-Herald*, 3 December 1953, 1; 30 June 1960, 1; 20 November 1990, 8; 28 April 1997, 1; Grand View file, CCHS; North Shore Explorer, "10 Beautiful Picnic Areas on the North Shore," http://northshoreexplorermn.com.north-shore-picnic-areas (inactive website).

140 Unorganized territory of West Cook, Minnesota, demographic data and boundary map, 2020.

141 *Duluth News-Tribune*, 8 July 1928, C7; *Cook County News-Herald*, 18 December 1930, 1; *Two Harbors Chronicle*, 1 October 1931, 1; Rolf Anderson, "National Register of Historic Places Nomination Form for the Cascade River Wayside," 2003, SHPO-MDA.

142 *Duluth Herald*, 23 August 1934, 2.

143 *Two Harbors Chronicle*, 17 May 1934, 1; 12 July 1934, 1; *Duluth Herald*, 15 May 1934, 1; 23 August 1934, 2; Meyer, *Everyone's County Estate*, 139; Anderson, "Nomination Form for the Cascade River Wayside," citing Gemini Research; Cook County GIS, *Plat Book and Land Atlas*, 19–21, 31–33.

144 Comments from Scott Benson to the author, 2015, 2017; manuscript schedules for the U.S. Census, 1930; John Lind, "North Shore Briefs," *Two Harbors Chronicle and Times*, 12 December 1946, 7; *Cook County News-Herald*, 31 October 1983, 8; Livdahl and Cross River Historical Center, *Lost Resorts*; Solbakken Resort on Superior, http://solbakkenresort.com/.

145 Manuscript schedules for the U.S. Census, 1930; Lind, "North Shore Briefs"; *Cook County News-Herald*, 31 Oc-

tober 1983, 8; Livdahl and Cross River Historical Center, *Lost Resorts*; Mary Alice Hanson, *Sawbill History and Tales* (Tofte, Minn.: Sawbill Press, 2005), 62–65; Solbakken Resort on Superior, http://solbakkenresort.com/; Benson comments, 2015, 2017.

146 *Cook County News-Herald*, 2 August 1979; "Arthur Emanual Hertzler," *Kansapedia*; Livdahl and Cross River Historical Center, *Lost Resorts*; comments from Diane Koeneke to the author, 2020.

147 MDNR, Division of Parks and Recreation, *Cascade River State Park Management Plan* (St. Paul: MDNR, February 2003), 1; MnDOT, "Comments on SMSQ Architects Preservation and Restoration Report of December 2001," http://www.dot.state.mn.us/roadsides/historic/files/sample-spruce-creek.pdf; Anderson, "Nomination Form for the Cascade River Wayside."

148 Manuscript schedules for the U.S. Census, 1930, 1940; Charles Pearson, *The Cascade Beach Road*, vol. 1 (2000), typescript in the Grand Marais Public Library.

149 Pearson, *Cascade Beach Road*; Spruce Falls Cabins, https://www.sprucefallscabins.com/.

150 Eugene A. Glader, *Cascade Lodge: The History of a North Shore Landmark* (Duluth, Minn.: Cascade Lodge, 2010), 15–19, 21–29, 59, 68–69, 136–38; Anderson, "Nomination Form for the Cascade River Wayside."

151 Glader, *Cascade Lodge*, 61, 75, 76, 82, 96, 109, 159; *Cook County News-Herald* (Explore Winter ed.), 29 December 2006, 8.

152 Glader, *Cascade Lodge*, 75–77, 82–85, 96–97; tourist brochure, 1953; Larry Oakes, "Haven by the Lake," *StarTribune*, 22 December 2001, B1, B2; Cascade Lodge, Your Historic Basecamp on the North Shore, http://cascadelodgemn.com/.

153 Glader, *Cascade Lodge*, 1–3; MnDOT Historic Roadside Development Structures Inventory, "Cascade River Overlook," 1998, citing RDD officials and U. W. Hella, 1935, http://www.dot.state.mn.us/roadsides/historic/files/forms/CK-UDG-044.pdf. Hella would later serve as director of the State Parks Division of the Minnesota Department of Conservation.

154 MnDOT Historic Roadside Development Structures Inventory, "Cascade River Overlook," 1998, citing RDD officials; Sommer, *Hard Work and a Good Deal*, 156.

155 Anderson, "Nomination Form for the Cascade River Wayside"; Denis P. Gardner, *Minnesota Treasures: Stories behind the State's Historic Places* (St. Paul: Minnesota Historical Society Press, 2004), 67–68.

156 Anderson, "Nomination Form for the Cascade River Wayside"; Good, *Park and Recreation Structures*, 163, 165; Gardner, *Minnesota Treasures*, 265.

157 Anderson, "Nomination Form for the Cascade River Wayside"; MDNR, "Butterworth Cliffs SNA," https://www.dnr.state.mn.us/snas/detail.html?id=sna20245.

158 Max Feigal obituary notice, 1962, CCHS; *Cook County News-Herald*, 23 October 1995, 2B; 14 June 2002, 6A; manuscript schedules for the U.S. Census, 1950; Ruth Hammond, "Couples' Life Revolves around 'the Gem of 10,000 Faces,'" *Minneapolis Tribune*, 30 June 1979; Jim Cordes, *The Treasures of Minnesota's North Shore and Gunflint Trail: A Lake Superior Journey* (privately published, 2008), 109; Mark Leatherman, "Radiant Minnesota Thomsonite: The World's Most Colorful Opaque Gemstone," *Rock and Gem*, 15 February 2019; Thomsonite Beach Inn and Suites, https://thomsonite.com/.

159 Cordes, *Treasures of Minnesota's North Shore*, 107; undated *Duluth News-Tribune* article, circa 1949, CCHS.

160 Arrowhead Regional Development Commission, *Cook County Comprehensive Trails Plan* (Duluth, Minn.: Arrowhead Regional Development Commission, 2018), 9.

161 Manuscript schedules for the U.S. Census, 1900, 1910, 1920, 1930, 1940; tourist brochures, 1946, 1953; interview with Ronald and Mable Lund, conducted by Pat Zankman, 7 January 2002, on file with CCHS; comments from Ron Lund to the author, 2016, 2017.

162 Cochrane, *Gichi Bitobig*, 41–44, 136; Nute, *Lake Superior*, 302.

163 *Duluth News-Tribune*, 7 July 1928; Margaret Culkin Banning, "My Favorite Town—Grand Marais," *Ford Times* 42 (April 1950): 3–4; Hampl, "Small Is Beautiful."

164 "Best Adventure Towns: Grand Marais, Minnesota," *National Geographic Adventure*, October 2009, http://adventure.nationalgeographic.com/weekend-getaways/minnesota/grand-marais-travel; Robert Firpo-Cappiello, "Meet America's Coolest Small Town 2015!," *Budget Travel*, 5 March 2015, https://www.budgettravel.com/article/meet-americas-coolest-small-town-2015_52445; "Best Small Town for a Creative Escape—Grand Marais—2015 Best of Minnesota," *StarTribune*, 14 May 2015, http://www.startribune.com/best-small-town-for-a-creative-escape-grand-marais/303435121/; "Best Small Town for Dining: Grand Marais," *StarTribune*, 21 April 2016, http://www.startribune.com/best-small-town-for-dining-grand-marais/375763601/; "Best Towns 2016," *Outside*, 25 April 2016, https://www.outsideonline.com/2056761/best-towns-2016; "Best Midwestern Small Town: Grand Marais, Minn.," *USA Today*, 28 April 2017,

http://www.10best.com/awards/travel/best-midwestern-small-town/; "The 20 Best Small Towns to Visit in 2017," Smithsonian, http://www.smithsonianmag.com/travel/20-best-small-towns-visit-2017-180962925/; Karen Zamora, "Grand Marais Wins 'Best Midwestern Small Town' Award," *StarTribune*, 29 April 2017, citing Linda Jurek, http://www.startribune.com/grand-marais-wins-best-midwestern-small-town-award/420790383/; Brie Dyas, Kara Ladd, and Hadley Mendelsohn, "Most Beautiful Small Towns in Every State," *House Beautiful*, 10 January 2020, https://www.housebeautiful.com/lifestyle/g4458/the-most-beautiful-small-towns-in-america/; Betsy Rathburn, "Named the Most Beautiful Small Town in Minnesota, Take a Closer Look at Grand Marais," Only in Your State, https://www.onlyinyourstate.com/minnesota/grand-marais-mn/; "10 Most Beautiful Towns in Minnesota," *Attractions of America*, https://www.attractionsofamerica.com/travel/most-beautiful-small-towns-minnesota.php; "30 Small Towns Recognized by Country Living Magazine," *Country Living*, February March 2023, https://www.magzter.com/stories/home/Country-Living/.

165 Cochrane, *Gichi Bitobig*, 95–106, 135.

166 Cochrane, 9, 83, 88, 125–32; Nute, *Lake Superior*, 302; Raff, *Pioneers in the Wilderness*, 4–7, 58–60.

167 Raff, *Pioneers in the Wilderness*, 13–19, 58; Eugene Glader, *Downtown Grand Marais*, 2nd ed. (Grand Marais, Minn.: Downtown Grand Marais, 2016), 1:2–5.

168 Raff, *Pioneers in the Wilderness*, 63 (quotation), 118, 252, 355–56; Glader, *Downtown Grand Marais*, 1:13–15; CCHS and Harbor Friends, "Harbor History Tour," YouTube video, 2016, https://www.youtube.com/watch?v=TKSauhEcCQ8.

169 Raff, *Pioneers in the Wilderness*, 60–61; *Cook County Herald*, 21 June 1900, 5.

170 Manuscript schedules for the U.S. Census, 1920; Staci Lola Drouillard, *Walking the Old Road: A People's History of Chippewa City and the Grand Marais Anishinaabe* (Minneapolis: University of Minnesota Press, 2019), 88; Raff, *Pioneers in the Wilderness*, 63, 68–70, 116–18 (quotation), 252, 355–56.

171 *Cook County News-Herald*, 2 October 1930, 1; MnDOT, "Highway 61 Reconstruction Project in Cook County, 2020–21," https://www.dot.state.mn.us/d1/projects/hwy-61-grand-marais/index.html.

172 *Duluth News-Tribune*, 8 July 1928, C7; Culkin Banning, "My Favorite Town," 4, 6; U.S. Census of Population, 1950–2010; Grand Marais, Minn., profile, https://minnesota.hometownlocator.com/mn/cook/grand-marais.cfm.

173 Pat Prince, "Grand Marais Faces Development Dilemma," *StarTribune*, 16 August 1987, B1; Joan Farnam, "And Then There Were Three," *Cook County News-Herald*, 30 September 2005, A9; Bill Nell, "Three's Not a Charm for Third Condo Builder," *Cook County News-Herald*, 25 October 2005, A1; Lund comments, 2021.

174 Manuscript schedules for the U.S. Census, 1930, 1940; *Cook County News-Chronicle*, 10 August 1956; tourist brochures, 1946, 1949.

175 *Cook County News-Chronicle*, 29 July 1961; 20 June 1963; 4 July 1968; 17 June 1965; January 1969; November 1972; tourist brochures, 1957, 1959, 1964–65, 1972.

176 Manuscript schedules for the U.S. Census, 1920, 1930, 1940; *Cook County News-Herald*, 9 June 1938, 1; 16 June 1938, 4; Glader, *Downtown Grand Marais*, 2:120.

177 *Cook County News-Herald*, 9 June 1938, 1; 29 May 1947, 1; 20 July 1950, 1.

178 Manuscript schedules for the U.S. Census, 1930, 1940; tourist brochures, 1949, 1953, 1959; *Minneapolis Tribune*, 31 May 1977, C5; *StarTribune*, 4 April 1999, B8.

179 *Cook County News-Herald*, 24 November 1938; 25 June 2007; 8 September 2012; 27 February 2016 ("Historical Reflections"); obituary notices for Ann and Gordon Sykes, 1990, 1996, and William J. O'Brien, 2007, CCHS; "William O. Brien (Minnesota Politician)," Wikipedia, accessed 2023.

180 *Cook County News-Herald*, 24 November 1938; 25 June 2007; 8 September 2012; 27 February 2016 ("Historical Reflections"); obituary notices for Ann and Gordon Sykes, 1990, 1996, and William J. O'Brien, 2007 CCHS; "William O. Brien (Minnesota Politician)," Wikipedia, accessed 2023; Eric Weicht, "Change Is Coming to Cook County," *Northern Wilds*, 30 November 2022.

181 Manuscript schedules for the U.S. Census, 1930; *Cook County News-Herald*, 26 May 1955; 24 September 1975; Glader, *Downtown Grand Marais*, 2:217–18; comments from Bill Doucette to the author, 2019; Eric Weicht, "The Blue Moose Changes Hands," *Northern Wilds Magazine*, 28 December 2022.

182 Tourist brochure, 1959; Barbara Henning, "Minnesota History/Architecture Survey Form for Traveler's Rest," 1997, SHPO-MDA; *Cook County News-Chronicle*, 26 November 1996, B1, B6; Glader, *Downtown Grand Marais*, 2:217.

183 *Cook County News-Herald*, 25 November 1965, B1, B6; Glader, *Downtown Grand Marais*, 2:217.

184 "History of Trailside," one-page typescript written by Trailside's owner, late 1990, CCHS; Barbara J. Henning, "Minnesota History/Architecture Survey Form for Trailside Cabins and Motel," 1997, SHPO-MDA.

185 Henning, "Trailside Cabins and Motel"; "History of Trailside"; Trailside Cabins and Motel, http://www.stayattrailside.com/.

186 Manuscript schedules for the U.S. Census, 1900, 1910, 1920, 1930, 1940; tourist brochure, 1959; Ron and Mabel Lund interview, 2002; Lund comments, 2016, 2017, 2021.

187 Ron and Mabel Lund interview, 2002; Lund comments, 2016, 2017, 2021.

188 Tourist brochure, 1959; Ron and Mabel Lund interview, 2002; Lund comments, 2016, 2017.

189 Glader, *Downtown Grand Marais,* 1:191–93; *Cook County News-Herald,* 30 September 1946, 2; 6 June 1947, 1; 21 September 1961, 1.

190 Gardner, *Minnesota's Treasures,* 124–25; Terry Pepper, "Grand Marais Light," *Seeing the Light: Lighthouses of the Western Great Lakes* (blog), September 2012, http://www.terrypepper.com/Lights/superior/gdmarais-mn/index.htm; CCHS, *Our Vision for the Future: Historical Sites Evaluation and Long-Range Plan* (Duluth, Minn.: CCI IS, October 2013), 34–36; CCHS, "Fish House and Tug the Neegee," http://www.cookcountyhistory.org/fishhouse; Grand Marais Campground and Marina, http://www.grandmaraisrecreationarea.com/campground/; Kitty Mayo, "Grand Marais Waterfront Expands Options," *Business North* (Duluth), 7 September 2022; comments from Dave Tersteeg to the author, 2024.

191 *Cook County News-Herald,* 15 March 1945, 1; Raff, *Pioneers in the Wilderness,* 80–81, 350, 367–74; tourist brochures 1953, 1972; M. J. Humphrey, Ade Toftey, Marion Killmer, and Steven J. Wright, *Pioneer Faces and Places, 1850–1930* (Grand Marais, Minn.: CCHS, 1979), 22–23; comments by Doug and Becky Gilchrist in the Grand Marais Old House Study, CCHS.

192 Glader, *Downtown Grand Marais,* 1:186–91; comments from Lee R. Johnson to the author, June 2017.

193 "North House Folk School: Grand Marais, MN, est. 1997," https://indd.adobe.com/view/8482f3dc-84a6-48de-9ddb-f0e122283243; North House Folk School, "About Us, 2018 Annual Report," https://northhouse.org/about-us/about-north-house; *Cook County News-Herald,* 24 March 2018; 20 March 2020; comments from Joseph Beres to the author, 2021.

194 "North House Folk School"; Dan Kraker, "Low-Tech Handcraft Has Never Been More Popular at North House Folk School," MPR News, 23 March 2012, citing Hanson, ttps://www.mprnews.org/story/2012/03/23/woodworking-low-tech-craft (inactive website).

195 Manuscript schedules for the U.S. Census, 1900, 1910, 1920, 1930, 1940; Glader, *Downtown Grand Marais,* 1:192; Jeffrey A Hess, "National Register of Historic Places Inventory—Nomination Form for the Jim Scott Fishhouse," 1986, SHPO-MDA; Gardner, *Minnesota Treasures,* 123–26; Marnocha comments, 2020.

196 *Cook County News-Herald,* 23 July 1936, 1; 18 February 1937, 1; Gemini Research, "MnDOT Historic Roadside Development Structures Inventory: Grand Marais Historic Sea Wall," 11 October 1997, http://www.dot.state.mn.us/roadsides/historic/files/iforms/CK-GMC-029.pdf.

197 *Cook County News-Herald,* 2 April 1953, 1; 1 July 1954, 1; 22 July 1954, 1; 11 November 1965, 1; Glader, *Downtown Grand Marais,* 1:116–18; Coleen J. Sheehy, "Making a Place for Art: 50 Years at the Grand Marais Art Colony," *Minnesota History* 55 (Summer 1997): 261; Gemini Research, "Grand Marais Historic Sea Wall"; Lund comments, 2016.

198 Reba Gilchrist, interviewed by Pat Zankman, 11 September 2002, transcript on file with CCHS; Farnam, "And Then There Were Three"; Nell, "Three's Not a Charm"; Lund comments, 2016.

199 *Cook County News-Herald,* 2 October 1930, 1.

200 *Cook County News-Herald,* 18 February 1937, 1; 7 October 1937, 1; Glader, *Downtown Grand Marais,* 2:116–19.

201 Glader, *Downtown Grand Marais,* 2:119; Minnesota Department of Highways, "Tentative Study for Proposed Forest Entrance Plan: Gateway to Gunflint Trail," October 1938, CCHS; Andrew J. Schmidt, "Minnesota Architecture—History Inventory Form for the Gunflint Trail, Grand Marais Segment," 1990, SHPO-MDA.

202 *Cook County News-Herald,* 25 May 2013; 12 September 2013.

203 *Cook County News-Herald,* 25 March 1945, 1; Glader, *Downtown Grand Marais,* 1:125–29; Historic Cook County, "Johnson Heritage Post Art Gallery," https://www.cookcountyhistory.org/the-history-of-the-jhp-art-gallery.

204 Historic Cook County, "Johnson Heritage Post Art Gallery."

205 Glader, *Downtown Grand Marais,* 1:105–14.

206 *Cook County News-Herald*, 7 August 2000, B4; Trust for Public Land, "Grand Marais Harbor Park," https://www.tpl.org/our-work/grand-marais-harbor-park; *The Trust for Public Land Northwoods Initiative*, http://cloud.tpl.org/pubs/local-mi-northwoods-brochure-2.p.

207 Glader, *Downtown Grand Marais*, 1:56–59, 1:69–71, 2:70–71; *Cook County News-Herald*, 31 August 1901, 3.

208 Glader, *Downtown Grand Marais*, 1:70–71; Sam Cook, "Flicks, Fun at Beaver House," *Duluth News-Tribune*, 23 May 2010, C6.

209 Glader, *Downtown Grand Marais*, 1:71; Cook, "Flicks, Fun at Beaver House"; CCHS, "Broadway and Wisconsin—the Beaver House Corner," *Overlook: Newsletter of the Cook County Historical Society*, Fall 2015, 1, 4; Jon Tevlin, "Grand Marais Saves Beaver House and a Bit of Our History," *StarTribune*, 4 May 2016.

210 Manuscript schedules for the U.S. Census, 1910, 1920, 1930, 1940; Glader, *Downtown Grand Marais*, 1:60–68, quoting Lois Pedersen, 1:67–68; Joan Farnam, "Taking the East Bay Home Piece by Piece," *Cook County News-Herald*, 17 June 2005, A1, A3.

211 Glader, *Downtown Grand Marais*, 1:150–51; Jay Gabler, "Picture Book Cute: Grand Marais' Drury Lane Books More Than Just a Pretty Space," *Duluth News-Tribune*, 29 April 2023, A1, A9; Drury Lane Books, http://drurylanebooks.com/.

212 Charles W. Nelson, "National Register of Historic Places Inventory—Nomination Form for the Grand Marais Lightkeeper's House," 1978, SHPO-MDA.

213 *Cook County Herald*, 8 August 1896, 2; *Cook County News-Herald*, 11 August 1966, 1; Nelson, "Nomination Form for the Grand Marais Lightkeeper's House"; CCHS, *Our Vision for the Future*, 29.

214 *Cook County News-Herald*, 25 September 1952, 1; 5 August 1954, 1; postcard caption for the Shoreview Hotel, late 1950s; Glader, *Downtown Grand Marais*, 1:99–101; Jakle et al., *Motel in America*, 47.

215 *Cook County News-Herald*, 1 December 1960, 1; 23 November 1961, 1.

216 *Cook County News-Herald*, 29 July 2005, A9; Pat Clochetto, "Will Grand Marais Become a City of Condos?," *Cook County Star* (Grand Marais), 20 October 2005, 1; Farnham, "And Then There Were Three"; Nell, "Three's Not a Charm," A1, A3.

217 Cochrane, *Gichi Bitobig*, 42–46; Glader, *Downtown Grand Marais*, 1:165; Ruth E. Allard, *Stories from Superior's Northern Shore: Historic Cook County, Minnesota* (Grand Marais, Minn.: CCHS, 2018), n.p.

218 Cochrane, *Gichi Bitobig*, 46; Allard, *Stories from Superior's Northern Shore*.

219 Raff, *Pioneers in the Wilderness*, 58; Glader, *Downtown Grand Marais*, 1:53–55; Allard, *Stories from Superior's Northern Shore*.

220 Glader, *Downtown Grand Marais*, 1:167–69; *Cook County News-Herald*, 12 March 1953, 1; 25 May 1961, 6.

221 Glader, *Downtown Grand Marais*, 1:167–69; Arthur Wiley King, "Rafts of 'Gold' Towed in Lake," *Duluth News-Tribune*, Feature, 23 August 1954, 1; Ford Eastman, "Log Islands Afloat," *Duluth News-Tribune*, Cosmopolitan Section, 17 July 1949, 5; MDNR, "Grand Marais Access," in *Lake Superior Boating Guide*, 52.

222 CCHS, "The Fight for Protection on Lake Superior," *Overlook: Newsletter of the Cook County Historical Society*, Spring 2019, 1, 6–7; Glader, *Downtown Grand Marais*, 1:167–69.

223 CCHS, "Fight for Protection on Lake Superior," citing the W. L. Carrs Papers, MHS Archives; "William Leighton Carss," Wikipedia, accessed 2024.

224 *Cook County News-Herald*, 29 March 1956, 1; 2 June 1977, 1; Kalliee Hawkins, "Past to Present: North Superior Coast Guard Station," *Northern Wilds*, March 2023; CCHS, "2018 Facilities Plan," 26, https://static1.squarespace.com/static/59eb668c2278e7603e197248/t/5c80551753450aee0ff4a49d/1551914271178/cchs+site+plan+2018.pdf.

225 Raff, *Pioneers in the Wilderness*, 36–38, 61–63; Anderson and Fischer, *North Shore*, 230, 285, 335; Glader, *Downtown Grand Marais*, 1:165.

226 Harry F. Drabik, *The Story of Coast Guard Point, at Grand Marais, MN* (Grand Marais, Minn.: CCHS, 2005), 15–18; Glader, *Downtown Grand Marais*, 1:172–74; "Grand Marais Lighthouse," Lighthouse Friends, http://lighthousefriends.com/light.asp?ID=652; Pepper, "Grand Marais Light."

227 Jeffrey A. Hess, "National Register of Historic Places Inventory—Nomination Form for the Bally Blacksmith Shop," 2023, SHPO-MDA; CCHS, *Our Vision for the Future*, 20–23.

228 CCHS, *Our Vision for the Future*, 20–23.

229 Manuscript schedules for the U.S. Census, 1900, 1910, 1920, 1930, 1940; *Cook County News-Herald*, 6 July 1967, 4; Rhonda Silence, "A Nordic Sauna Experience Coming to Grand Marais," WTIP North Shore Community Radio, 29 August 2021; comments from Katie Usem to the author, 2021, 2023, 2024; Kalli Hawkins, "Sisu and Löyly Expand Business to Offer Mobile Sauna Service,"

WTIP North Shore Community Radio, 29 April 2023, https://wtip.org/sisu-and-loyly-expand-business-to-offer-mobile-sauna-service/; "Sisu and Löyly A Lakeside Nordic Sauna Experience," Sisu and Löyly.com.

230 I am indebted to Todd Miller for his comments about the structural features of many older homes in Grand Marais.

231 "Lonnie Dupre," Wikipedia, accessed 2023; Lonnie Dupre, *Greenland Expedition: Where Ice Is Born* (Minnetonka, Minn.: NorthWord Press, 2000); comments from Lonnie Dupre to the author, 2021; Pascale Marceau, "AMKA," *Pascale Marceau* (blog), 3 September 2023, https://www.pascalemarceau.com/post/amka-film.

232 Dupre comments, 2021; website postings for Mökki; comments from Stevie Anna Plummer to the author, 2020; Brian Larsen, "After 20 Years, Lonnie Dupre Will Return to Greenland," *Cook County News-Herald*, 9 April 2022, B1.

233 "Tre Søstre Housing/Salmela Architect," *Architecture Daily*, 2 July 2019, https://www.archdaily.com/920108/tre-sostre-housing-salmela-architect/; "The Three Sisters," *Wilderness North*, 10 December 2015.

234 "Tre Søstre, Salmela Architect"; comments from Todd Miller to the author, 2021.

235 "U.S. Building of the Week, Tre Søstre, Salmela Architect," 16 September 2019, https://www.world-architects.com/en/architecture-news/reviews/tre-sostre; Wood Products Council, "Top of the Crop: Here Are the 2020 U.S. Wood Works Wood Design Awards Winners," *Architect's Newspaper*, 5 February 2020; Virserum Art Museum, Sweden, "Nødvändightens Arkitektur: Architecture of Necessity," 2019.

236 Manuscript schedules for the U.S. Census, 1920, 1930, 1940; *Cook County News-Herald*, 7 January 1932; 26 July 1946, 1; obituary notice for Frederick Andert, October 1962, CCHS; comments from Gordon Lindquist to the author, 2021.

237 Manuscript schedules for the U.S. Census, 1930, 1940; Lindquist comments, 2021; Russell's Cottages, https://www.russellscottages.org/; *Cook County News-Herald*, 9 December 2022, 4; 11 March 2023, 4.

238 *Cook County News-Herald*, 10 April 1947, 1; *Duluth News-Tribune*, Cosmopolitan, 15 June 1947, 6; Humphrey et al., *Pioneer Faces and Places*, 34; Glader, *Downtown Grand Marais*, 1:165; Kathryn R. Goetz, "Grand Marais Is Home to Minnesota's Longest-Lived Art Colony," *MinnPost*, 26 March 2013; Grand Marais Art Colony, https://grandmaraisartcolony.org/.

239 Goetz, "Grand Marais Is Home to Minnesota's Longest-Lived Art Colony"; Grand Marais Art Colony, https://grandmaraisartcolony.org/.

240 *Cook County News-Herald*, 18 April 1957; 8 July 1982, 1; Gail Huschle, "First Congregational Church Celebrates a Milestone," *Overlook: Newsletter of the Cook County Historical Society*, Spring 2017, 1, 4.

241 *Cook County News-Herald*, 18 April 1957; 8 July 1982, 1; *Austin Daily Herald*, 11 January 2019.

242 Raff, *Law and Order in the Wilderness*, 26; Raff, *Pioneers in the Wilderness*, 21–22, 76; "Cook County Courthouse (Minnesota)," Wikipedia, accessed 2023; Dennis A. Gimmestad, "National Register of Historic Places Inventory—Nomination Form for the Cook County Courthouse," 1983, SHPO-MDA.

243 Raff, *Law and Order in the Wilderness*, 26; Raff, *Pioneers in the Wilderness*, 76; Gimmestad, "Nomination Form for the Cook County Courthouse."

244 *Cook County News-Herald*, 10 July 1958, 1; 17 November 1960, 1.

245 R. V. McCann Papers, Northwest Architectural Archives, Elmer L. Andersen Library, University of Minnesota; *Cook County News-Herald*, 4 September 1960, 1; 17 November 1960, 1; 16 February 1961, 1; 22 June 1961, 1; 29 June 1961, 1; 6 July 1961, 1; 10 August 1961, 2; 7 September 1961, 1.

246 Birney Quick, comments about the St. John's Mural, on file at CCHS.

247 Raff, *Pioneers in the Wilderness*, 68–70, 284–88; typewritten history of Bethlehem Lutheran Church, on file in the church office.

248 *Cook County News-Herald*, 3 February 1955, 1; 2 February 1956, 1; 30 January 1959, 1.

249 *Cook County News-Herald*, 28 May 1959, 1; 18 February 1960; 5 March 1960, 1.

250 Buggeln, *Suburban Church*, 100, 102 (quotations); *Cook County News-Herald*, 2 May 1963, 1.

251 Buggeln, *Suburban Church*, 33, 101; *Cook County News-Herald*, 23 January 1964, 1; comments from Fredric Quivik to the author, 2021.

252 *Cook County News-Herald*, 7 February 1962; obituary notice for Jennie Lindquist, 1990, CCHS Archives; Lindquist comments, 2021.

253 *Cook County News-Herald*, 22 June 1939, 1; 31 August 1939, 1.

254 *Cook County News-Herald*, 22 June 1939, 1; 31 August 1939, 1; comments from Dori Betts and Cook County Extension Service to the author, 2017.

255 *Cook County News-Herald*, 20 May 1948, 1; 29 December 1949, 11; 5 January 1950, 1; 2 February 1950, 6; 9 February 1950, 1.

256 *Cook County News-Herald*, 16 February 1950, 1; 29 November 1951, 8; 21 February 1952, 1; Arthur Wiley King, "Sawtooth Ski Chalet," *Duluth News-Tribune*, Cosmopolitan, 16 December 1951, 8.

257 *Cook County News-Herald*, 21 February 1952, 1.

258 *Cook County News-Herald*, 5 February 1953, 1; 26 February 1953, 1.

259 *Cook County News-Herald*, 5 February 1952, 1; 17 February 1955, 1, quoting Don Burris.

260 Sawtooth Bluff Regional Park Planning Committee, *Sawtooth Bluff Regional Park Master Plan* (Duluth, Minn.: Arrowhead Regional Development Commission, 2018), https://www.ci.grand-marais.mn.us/index.asp?SEC=BA65C375-F022-4780-83AB-23D1DD5A61B4.

261 Minnesota Gazetteer Home Town Locator, "Unorganized Territory of East Cook Data and Demographics," 2020.

262 Drouillard, *Walking the Old Road*, 10, 89, 105.

263 Drouillard, 172; Allard, *Stories from Superior's Northern Shore*, n.p.

264 Drouillard, *Walking the Old Road*, 284–85; Raff, *Pioneers in the Wilderness*, 311.

265 Drouillard, *Walking the Old Road*, 130, 273, citing Morrison; Allard, *Stories from Superior's Northern Shore*; "George Morrison (Artist)," Wikipedia, accessed 2024; "George Morrison (American Artist, 1919–2000)," http://www.artnet.com/artists/george-morrison.

266 Drouillard, *Walking the Old Road*, 241, 243, 247–53, 257–58.

267 Jeffrey A. Hess, "National Register of Historic Places Inventory—Nomination Form for St. Francis Xavier Church," 1986, SHPO-MDA; Drouillard, *Walking the Old Road*, 14–16, 195–203.

268 *Cook County Herald*, 10 May 1896; Hess, "Nomination Form for St. Francis Xavier Church"; Drouillard, *Walking the Old Road*, 16–17; Peter Ennals and Deryck W. Holdsworth, *Homeplace: The Making of the Canadian Dwelling over Three Centuries* (Toronto: University of Toronto Press, 1998), 60–61.

269 *Cook County News-Herald*, 19 June 1957, 1; 26 June 1957, 1; 3 July 1958, 1; 30 March 1998, 1; Drouillard, *Walking the Old Road*, 22–23, 272–73; Raff, *Pioneers in the Wilderness*, 52; CCHS, "The History of the St. Francis Xavier Church," https://www.cookcountyhistory.org/the-history-of-the-chippewa-city-church.

270 Raff, *Pioneers in the Wilderness*, 118; manuscript schedules for the U.S. Census, 1910, 1920, 1930, 1940.

271 Morse-Kahn, *Lake Superior's Historic North Shore*, 161.

272 Manuscript schedules for the U.S. Census, 1910, 1920, 1930, 1940; Minnesota Death Index for Gunnar Larson (1935) and Hannah Larson (1939); tourist brochure, 1959; obituary notice for Hannah Bentley, 2004, CCHS; comments from Julie Anderson to the author, 2021.

273 Comments from Steve Martens to the author, 2021.

274 Bob Berg, "Spotlighting Mom-and-Pop Resorts: Anderson's," *Lake Superior Magazine*, 7 August 2011, https://www.lakesuperior.com/travel/minnesota/333mompop1/; Anderson's North Shore Resort, https://andersonscabins.com/; Julie Anderson comments, 2021.

275 *Cook County News-Herald*, 24 October 1996; *Mesabi Tribune* (Virginia, Minn.), 25 February 2014; Larsen's Lakeview Cabins, http://www.elsiescabins.com/; comments from Jackie Hyovalti to the author, 2019, 2022.

276 Manuscript schedules for the U.S. Census, 1920, 1930, 1940; *Cook County News-Herald*, 8 January 1976; 12 June 2008; comments from Karen Waters to the author, 2020.

277 *Cook County News-Herald*, 12 June 2008; Elsie's Lakeview Cabins, http://www.elsiescabins.com/; Waters comments, 2020.

278 *Argus-Leader* (Sioux Falls, S.D.), 26 August 1996, 25; 13 October 1999, 12; comments from Jeanne Hiebert to the author, 2022.

279 "Margaret Carlson," in *Tough Men, Tough Boats: Look over Your Shoulder*, ed. F. Keith Hunt (Grand Marais, Minn.: CCHS, 2018), 85; comments from Margaret Carlson to the author, 2019.

280 Carlson comments, 2019; "Margaret Carlson," 85–89 (the sentences in the quotation have been rearranged for purposes of clarity).

281 Sue Groenmeyer, "Croftville Cottages Felt Like a Return to Earlier Days," *Cook County News-Herald*, 20 March 2007, A9; Jane Howard, "Croftville Road Cottages Expanding to Include an Inn," *Cook County News-Herald*, 21 January 2012, A1, A9; Teresa Chemelik, "Croftville Road Cottages History," https://www.croftvilleroadcottages.com/.

282 Manuscript schedules for the U.S. Census, 1920, 1930, 1940, 1950; *Cook County News-Herald*, 16 May 1944; *Tacoma News Tribune*, 12 August 1999.

283 Manuscript schedules for the U.S. Census, 1920; Upham, *Minnesota Geographic Names*, 144; Mayo and Mayo, *61 Gems of Highway 61*, 108–9.

284 Manuscript schedules for the U.S. Census, 1910, 1920, 1930; Raff, *Pioneers in the Wilderness*, 115–16.

285 Philip J. Anderson, "A Scandinavian Enclave on Lake Superior's North Shore: Settlement and Community Building among Norwegians, Swedes, and Swede Finns in Hovland, Minnesota, 1888–1932," in *Norwegians and Swedes in the United States: Friends and Neighbors*, ed. Philip J. Anderson and Dag Blanck (St. Paul: Minnesota Historical Society Press, 2012), 236, 240, 242–43, 253–54; Frederick L. Johnson, "Colvill, William (1830–1905)," MNopedia, https://www.mnopedia.org/person/colvill-william-1830-1905; Raff, *Law and Order in the Wilderness*, 15–16; U.S. Bureau of Land Management, General Land Office Records for William Colvill and Ole E. Erickson.

286 Minnesota Legislative Reference Library, "Wiger, Sr., Charles W. 'Chuck,'" https://www.lrl.mn.gov/legdb/fulldetail?id=10713; Dick Hagen, "Meet a Rock-Collecting Minnesota State Senator," *The Land* (Mankato, Minn.), 5 November 2015; Jon Tevlin, "State Senator's Garden Project Is One Thing He Can Control," *Star Tribune*, 12 September 2015; Mekissa Dressely, "Amazing Sculpture Yard, Covill, MN," *North Shore Explorer*, 21 October 2022; comments from Charles Wiger to the author, 2015, 2021. Chel Anderson identified the geological origins of the lava cliff on Wiger's property.

287 Tevlin, "State Senator's Garden Project"; Wiger comments, 2021. I am indebted to Barbara Wyatt, NPS (retired), for discussing the different landscape terms with me in 2021.

288 Manuscript schedules for the U.S. Census, 1910, 1920, 1930, 1940; "Bill Anyotte," in *Grand Portage Chippewa: Stories and Experiences of Portage Band Members* (Grand Portage, Minn.: Grand Portage Tribal Council/Sugarloaf Interpretive Center Association, 2000), 25–30.

289 Manuscript schedules for the U.S. Census, 1910, 1920, 1930, 1940; biographical information for Russell Zerbach in the North Shore fishermen's file, North Shore Commercial Fishing Museum, Tofte, Minn.; tourist brochure, circa 1965.

290 *Cook County News-Herald*, 14 June 1951, 4; caption for Moe-Del Motel postcard, 1950s. Comments about the Outpost's popularity came from online postings.

291 All of the following are from the *Cook County News-Herald*: 31 May 1928; 19 July 1928; Bill Hall, "Fate of Colvill Town Hall in Limbo Awaiting Public Input," 29 July 2005; "County Votes to Repair Town Hall," 26 August 2005.

292 *Duluth News-Tribune*, Cosmopolitan, 1 June 1947, 17; Meyer, *Everyone's Country Estate*, 166; Anderson and Fischer, *North Shore*, 233–35.

293 Manuscript schedules for the U.S. Census, 1900, 1910; Raff, *Law and Order in the Wilderness*, 14, citing Carrie Brunes; Raff, *Pioneers in the Wilderness*, 39–40; Best Places, "Hovland (Zip 55606), Minnesota," http://bestplaces.net/zip; Anderson, "A Scandinavian Enclave," 244.

294 "Judge C. R. Magney State Park," Wikipedia, accessed 2024.

295 Meyer, *Everyone's Country Estate*, 181–82; "Judge Magney," *Cook County News-Herald*, 12 April 1962, 2, 4; "Judge Magney Concerned about North Shore," *Cook County News-Herald*, 19 April 1962, 2; "Judge C. R. Magney State Park," Wikipedia, accessed 2024.

296 Meyer, *Everyone's Country Estate*, 181–82; Eve Wallinga and Gary Wallinga, *Waterfalls of Minnesota's North Shore and More*, 2nd ed. (Grand Marais, Minn.: North Shore Press, 2015), 149–51; Andrew Slade, *Hiking the North Shore*, 2nd ed. (Duluth, Minn.: There and Back Books, 2015), 154–56; MDNR, "Judge C. R. Magney State Park," https://files.dnr.state.mn.us/maps/state_parks/spk00193.pdf.

297 "Naniboujou Club Lodge," Wikipedia, accessed 2023; Adelheid Fischer, "Indian Lore," *Architecture Minnesota*, March/April 1992, 42–43; Douglas Martin, "Rustic Retreat on Gitche Gumee," *New York Times*, Travel, 15 August 2000, 10, 12.

298 *Lake County Chronicle*, 28 May 1925, 1; *Cook County News-Herald*, 24 November 1927, 1; *Duluth News-Tribune*, 18 January 1928, 5; Stewart Taylor Co., "The Naniboujou Club in the Tip of the Famous Arrowhead Country" (twenty-page prospectus issued to prospective members in 1927—reprinted in 2014 and made available for sale at the Naniboujou Lodge); "About: History of Naniboujou Lodge and Restaurant," https://www.naniboujpi.com/about.

299 *Duluth News-Tribune*, 1 July 1928, C7; 27 July 1930, A2; 7 February 1953, 6; *Lake County Chronicle*, 27 June 1929, 1; *Cook County News-Herald*, 11 July 1929, 4; Gardner, *Minnesota Treasures*, 267–69.

300 "Welcome to Naniboujou!," a five-page printed and illustrated document, dating to approximately 2014, that was available for purchase; interview with Tim and Nancy Ramey, conducted by Pat Zankman, 6 May 2002, on file with CCHS; Bailey Wolding, "Naniboujou Lodge Is Up for Sale," *Northern Wilds*, 4 December 2016; Matt

McKinney, "For Sale: North Shore's Stunning Naniboujou Lodge," *StarTribune*, 4 September 2016, B5.

301 Manuscript schedules for the U.S. Census, 1900, 1910, 1920, 1930, 1940; Gouffet family tree, posted on Ancestry.com.

302 Martin, "Rustic Retreat on Gitche Gumee"; Charles W. Nelson and Mark E. Haidet, "National Register of Historic Places Inventory—Nomination Form for the Naniboujou Club Lodge," 1982, SHPO-MDA; Gardner, *Minnesota Treasures*, 267–69; "Naniboujou," Wikipedia, accessed 2023; Fischer, "Indian Lore," 42–44.

303 Manuscript schedules for the U.S. Census, 1900; *Cook County News-Herald*, 28 June 1925, 1 (the article is based on an interview with Ole Brunes); August Brunes, "My Memories," CCHS; Raff, *Pioneers in the Wilderness*, 93–95, 97, 103 (quotation); U.S. Bureau of Land Management, General Land Office Records for Ole Brunes (1904) and Nels Ludwig Eliasen (1904).

304 Bert Fesler, "The North Shore in 1890," Fesler Papers, Northeastern Minnesota Historical Center (also cited in Raff, *Pioneers in the Wilderness*, 95); Brunes, "My Memories"; *Cook County News-Herald*, 24 January 1929, 1.

305 *Cook County News-Herald*, 8 August 1940, 1; Raff, *Pioneers in the Wilderness*, 96–97; Philip J. Anderson comments, 2017, 2021.

306 Unorganized territory of East Cook data and demographics; Brian Larson, "How Should History of Hovland and Colvill Be Preserved?," *Cook County News-Herald*, 26 March 2016; Raff, *Pioneers in the Wilderness*, 93, 97, 103.

307 Unorganized territory of East Cook data and demographics; Larson, "How Should History of Hovland and Colvill be Preserved?"; Raff, *Pioneers in the Wilderness*, 93, 97, 103; Anderson, "A Scandinavian Enclave," 249–50, 256–57; "Hjalmar Peterson," Wikipedia, accessed 2023; Aldrich, *Real Log Cabin*; Hugh E. Bishop, "Restoring Rustic Dreams," *Lake Superior Magazine*, June–July 2001, 35–39; Calvin Rutstrum, *Challenge of the Wilderness* (Minneapolis, Minn.: T. S. Denison, 1970).

308 Manuscript schedules for the U.S. Census, 1920, 1930, 1940; Carnegie Hero Fund Commission, "Helmer M. Aakvik, Grand Marais, Minnesota," 1958, https://mychfc.org/hero.aspx?hero=44566; *Oakland* (Calif.) *Tribune*, 31 October 1959, B25.

309 Marlin Bree, "The Old Man and the Inland Sea," *The Ensign: Magazine of the United States Power Squadrons*, January–February 2007, 20.

310 "Helmer Aakvik's Daring Rescue Attempt: Story Told by Helmer Aakvik," *North Shore Commercial Fishing Journal* 3 (Fall 1995).

311 Bob Ehlert, "Faces of the North Shore," *Minneapolis Star and Tribune, Sunday Magazine*, 28 July 1985, 14; Bree, "Old Man and the Inland Sea," 24.

312 Raff, *Pioneers in the Wilderness*, 94–95; "National Register of Historic Places Inventory—Nomination Form for the Chicago Bay Dock," 1981, SHPO-MDA (the dock was determined not eligible for National Register listing).

313 "Nomination Form for the Chicago Bay Dock"; CCHS, "Hovland's Commercial Dock at Chicago Bay," *Overlook: Newsletter of the Cook County Historical Society*, Winter 2015, 1, 6.

314 "Nomination Form for the Chicago Bay Dock"; CCHS, "Hovland's Commercial Dock at Chicago Bay," 1, 6; Rhonda Silence, "Comments Wanted on Possible Hovland Dock Shoreline Improvements," *Cook County News-Herald*, 24 October 2015, citing Andy Hubley (ARDC); Brian Larson, "County Will Not Pursue Hovland Dock Project at This Time," *Cook County News-Herald*, 13 January 2018.

315 *Cook County News-Herald*, 14 October 1965, 1; Philip J. Anderson comments, 2021.

316 Comments from Margo Otterness to the author, 2018; Philip J. Anderson comments, 2021.

317 Manuscript schedules for the U.S. Census, 1900, 1910; Toftey, "Cook County"; military draft card for Arthur Eliasen, 1942, posted on Ancestry.com; tourist brochures, circa 1946, 1949.

318 Rhonda Silence, "Natasha's Flute Reed Store Now Open," *Cook County News-Herald*, 6 August 2011; "Archie George Kirk, Jr.," *Cook County News-Herald*, 29 October 2016; comments from Natalia Kirk to the author, 2021, 2023.

319 Scott Husby and Tracey Cullen, *John A. Spelman III* (Duluth: Historic Minnesota, 2021), 8–9.

320 "John A. Spelman III," https://pinemountainsettlement.net/?page_id=2496; *Cook County News-Herald*, 30 October 1969; Husby and Cullen, *John A. Spelman III*, 7–12, 19, quotation.

321 David Holmes, *Salt of the Earth: A History of Hovland, Minnesota, and Its People* (St. Cloud, Minn.: North Star Press, 2010), 94–95; Trinity Lutheran Church, *The Centennial Anniversary Celebration of Trinity Lutheran Church: Hovland, Minnesota, 1909–2009* (Hovland, Minn.: Trinity Lutheran Church, 2009).

322 Trinity Lutheran Church, *Centennial Anniversary Celebration*.

323 Buggeln, *Suburban Church*, xix, 30–31. The blueprints are

stored in the church archives. I am indebted to Fredric Quivik, who provided me with a detailed explanation of Trinity's structural features in 2021.

324 *Cook County News-Herald*, 12 June 1947, 1; Victor Christ-Janer, *Arnold Flaten, Sculptor* (Minneapolis, Minn.: Augsburg, 1974), 10; Trinity Lutheran Church, *Centennial Anniversary Celebration*.

325 Holmes, *Salt of the Earth*, 98; *Cook County News-Herald*, 12 June 1947, 1; 21 August 1947, 1; 20 July 1950, 1; Trinity Lutheran Church, *Centennial Anniversary Celebration*; Kathryn Gorman, "When Happy Young Crew Built Church," *St. Paul Sunday Pioneer Press*, Feature, 2 September 1950.

326 *Cook County News-Herald*, 12 June 1946, 1, citing Flaten; Christ-Janner, *Flaten, Sculptor*, 10; Gorman, "When Happy Young Crew Built Church."

327 Philip J. Anderson comments, 2017; Quivik comments, 2021.

328 *Cook County News-Herald*, 20 June 1963; 23 March 1992; 1 August 2009, 31 July 2010; MDNR, "Horseshoe Bay Protected Access," *Lake Superior Boating Guide*, 51.

329 Billy Blackwell, Norman Deschampe Jr., Liza Thibeault, Tom Olson, and Gilbert Caribou, *A History of Kitchi Onigaming: Grand Portage and Its People* (Cass Lake, Minn.: Minnesota Chippewa Tribe, 1983), 3.

330 Gilman, *Grand Portage Story*, 5; Lass, *Minnesota*, 49.

331 Timothy Cochrane, *Minong—the Good Place: Ojibwe and Isle Royale* (East Lansing: Michigan State University Press, 2009), 9–19; "Minong Traditional Cultural Property," Wikipedia, accessed 2024.

332 "Grand Portage (Gichi Onigamiing)," MNopedia, https://www.mnopedia.org/place/grand-portage-gichi-onigamiing; manuscript schedules for the U.S. Census, 1920; City Population, "Grand Portage: Unorganized Territory in Minnesota," 2024, http://www.citypopulation.de/en/usa/minnesota/admin/cook/2703125071__grand_portage/.

333 Howard Owen, "39 Years Later Minnesota Builds Highway," *Better Roads*, March 1961, 25–26, 36–39; Gilman, *Grand Portage Story*, 126–27.

334 Owen, "39 Years Later"; Gilman, *Grand Portage Story*, 126–27; *Cook County News-Herald*, 31 October 1963, 1; 7 November 1963 1; 28 May 1964, 1; 11 August 1966, 1.

335 Tourist brochures, 1947, 1950; *Cook County News-Herald*, 18 July 1963; 3 August 1972; 25 March 2021; "Reservation River Bridge," BridgeHunter, https://bridgehunter.com/mn/cook/5307; Philip J. Anderson comments, 2021.

336 Manuscript schedules for the U.S. Census, 1900, 1910, 1920, 1930; "U.S. Indian Allotment Records for Minnesota, 1888–1919," from Ancestry.com; "Statement of Paul LaPlante Made at Grand Portage, April 20, 1931," MHS Archives; Cochrane, *It Takes a Good Boat*, 84–88.

337 Rhonda Silence, "Hollow Rock Is a North Shore Natural Treasure," WTIP North Shore Community Radio, citing John Green, 2 May 2016, https://www.wtip.org/hollow-rock-north-shore-natural-treasure; tourist brochure 1949; *Cook County News-Herald*, 18 February 1963; 3 August 1972.

338 Manuscript schedules for the U.S. Census, 1870, 1880, 1900, 1910, 1920, 1930, 1940; comments from Mary Hendricks Petz to the author, 2021; Tim Cochrane, "Isle Royale Leisure," in *Borealis: An Isle Royale Potpourri* (Houghton, Mich.: Isle Royale Natural History Association, 1992), 87.

339 Manuscript schedules for the U.S. Census, 1940; *Cook County News-Herald*, 4 September 1969; Petz comments, 2021.

340 Manuscript schedules for the U.S. Census, 1940; "Johns Family Tree," posted on Ancestry.com; Petz comments, 2021.

341 Petz comments, 2021; Ada Igoe, "Rock Solid Idea: What Hollow Rock Teaches about Metal Roofs," *Lake Superior Magazine*, October–November 2011, 33–36; Grand Portage Lodge and Casino, https://www.grandportage.com/.

342 George M. Schwartz, "The Topography and Geology of the Grand Portage," *Minnesota History* 9 (March 1928): 30; Janna Knittel, *Moccasins and Red Sashes* (Fort Washington, Pa.: Eastern National, 2000), 4; NPS, "History & Culture: Grand Portage National Monument, Minnesota," 2024, https://www.nps.gov/grpo/learn/historyculture/index.htm.

343 Gilman, *Grand Portage Story*, 32–40, 74, 92; Nute, *Lake Superior*, 34–35; Douglas A. Birk, *A Study of Nineteenth Century Travel Routes between Grand Portage, Minnesota, and Fort William, Ontario* (Grand Portage, Minn.: Grand Portage National Monument, NPS, 1998), 4; NPS, "History & Culture,"; NPS, "Minnesota: Grand Portage National Monument," 2017, https://www.nps.gov/articles/grandport.htm; Douglas A. Birk, "National Register of Historic Places Inventory—Nomination Form for Grand Portage National Monument," 1976–77, 8-1, 8-4, 8-5, SHPO-MDA, https://npshistory.com/publications/grpo/nr-grand-portage-nm.pdf; Stephen Veit comments to the author, 2024.

344 Erwin N. Thompson, *Grand Portage: A History of the Site,*

*People, and Fur Trade* (Washington, D.C.: Division of History, U.S. Department of the Interior, 1969), citing Herriot; Knittel, *Moccasins and Red Sashes,* 22; Gilman *Grand Portage Story,* 19; Birk, "Nomination Form for Grand Portage National Monument," 7-12, 8-5; Veit comments, 2024.

345 Nute, *Lake Superior,* 34–35; Gilman, *Grand Portage Story,* 104–6; Birk, "Nomination Form for Grand Portage National Monument," 7-20, 89; Cochrane, *Minong,* 117; NPS, "History and Culture"; NPS, *Cultural Landscape at Grand Portage National Monument; Stockade, Portage, Grand Portage Village* (Omaha, Neb.: Midwest Regional Office, National Park Service, 2002), NPS, NPS Park Cultural Landscapes Program, 2016, https://npsparkclp.tumblr.com/post/142865457032/heritage-in-motion-preservation-and-reconstruction.

346 Gilman, *Grand Portage Story,* 109; Cochrane, *Minong,* 112, 138, citing Olson, 149–50.

347 NPS, "Grand Portage National Monument: Cultural Landscapes Inventory," 2001, 1; NPS, *Cultural Landscape at Grand Portage National Monument.*

348 NPS, "Grand Portage National Monument: Cultural Landscapes Inventory," 2; Donald Hardesty, "Ethnographic Landscapes: Transforming Nature into Culture," in Alanen and Melnick, *Preserving Cultural Landscapes in America,* 169.

349 Ron Cockrell, *Grand Portage National Monument, Minnesota: An Administrative History* (Omaha, Neb.: Midwest Regional Office, NPS, 1982, revised 1983), 10, https://npshistory.com/publications/grpo/adhi/index.htm; https://www.loc.gov/pictures/item/mn0626/; Birk, "Nomination Form for Grand Portage National Monument," 8.12; Gilman, *Grand Portage Story,* 122, 127–28; Dewey Albinson, "A Grand Portage Story and Some Tales from the North Country," typescript, 19–22, MHS Archives.

350 Pam Neil and Mike Plummer-Stern, "A Monumental Task: Grand Portage National Monument Celebrates 50 Years," in *The Grand Portage Guide* (Grand Portage, Minn.: Grand Portage National Monument, 2008), 9, https://npshistory.com/publications/grpo/newsletter/2008.pdf; Cockrell, *Grand Portage National Monument,* 13; Birk, "Nomination Form for Grand Portage National Monument," 7, 18; MHS, "Historical Exploring in the 'Arrowhead Country': The State Historical Convention of 1931," *Minnesota History* 12 (September 1931): 281–96, quotation on 288; Marjorie Savage and Mya Coursey, "Andrews, Frances (1884–1961)," MNopedia, https://www.mnopedia.org/person/andrews-frances-1884-1961.

351 National Park Service, "The Historic Stone Bridge at Grand Portage National Monument," https://www.nps.gov/articles/000/the-historic-stone-bridge-at-grand-portage-national-monument.htm; Justine Christianson, "Stone Bridge, CSAH 17 Spanning Grand Portage Creek, Grand Portage, Cook County, MN," https://www.loc.gov/pictures/item/mn0626/; Neil and Plummer-Stern, "A Monumental Task," 9–10, citing the CCC-ID; Gilman, *Grand Portage Story,* 125–26; Sommer, *Hard Work and a Good Deal,* 144, 150.

352 Neil and Plummer-Stern, "A Monumental Task," 10; Gilman, *Grand Portage Story,* 126; "Indian Reorganization Act: United States [1934]," Wikipedia, accessed 2024.

353 Christianson, "Stone Bridge (Bridge 7614)," 6–10; Sommer, *Hard Work and a Good Deal,* 144.

354 Christianson, "Stone Bridge (Bridge 7614)," 7–8; Sommer, *Hard Work and a Good Deal,* 117, 121.

355 Gilman, *Grand Portage Story,* citing Albinson, 126.

356 Gilman, *Grand Portage Story,* 128–29; Neil and Plummer-Stern, "A Monumental Task," 10; Christianson, "Stone Bridge (Bridge 7614)," 7; Sommer, *Hard Work and a Good Deal,* 121; Cockrell, *Grand Portage National Monument,* 16, citing Alan Woolworth.

357 Cockrell, *Grand Portage National Monument,* 16, quoting Alan Woolworth; *Cook County News-Herald,* 31 July 1949, 1.

358 Cockrell, *Grand Portage National Monument,* 16, quoting Alan Woolworth.

359 *Cook County News-Herald,* 14 June 1951, 1; 16 August 1951, 1; Gilman, *Grand Portage Story,* 130–31; Neil and Plummer-Stern, "A Monumental Task," 12; National Park Service, "Grand Portage Administrative History, Part I (continued)—the MHS and the National Park Service," 2005

360 Gilman, *Grand Portage Story,* 126, 130–31; Sommer, *Hard Work and a Good Deal,* 121.

361 Thomas P. Busch, "National Register of Historic Places Inventory—Nomination Form for Grand Portage National Monument," 7–21, SHPO-MDA; Neil and Plummer-Stern, "A Monumental Task," 14–16, citing Tousley.

362 Neil and Plummer-Stern, "A Monumental Task."

363 NPS, "Historic Gardens at Grand Portage," 2022, https://www.nps.gov/articles/000/historic-gardens-at-grand-portage.htm; NPS, "Canoe Warehouse," 2015,

https://www.nps.gov/grpo/learn/photosmultimedia/canoe-warehouse.htm; Birk, "Nomination Form for Grand Portage National Monument," 7-21, 7-22.

364 Birk, "Nomination Form for Grand Portage National Monument," 7-32; NPS, "Superintendent's Compendium," https://www.nps.gov/grpo/learn/management/superintendent-s-compendium.htm; Cochrane comments, 2021, 2022.

365 Christianson, "Stone Bridge (Bridge 7614)," 9–11; comments from Jill Baum (NBCC) to the author, 2021; *Cook County News-Herald*, 2 August 2018; NPS, "Stewardship at Grand Portage National Monument," 2020, https://www.nps.gov/articles/grand-portage-national-monument-ojibwe-management.htm; Anderson comments, 2025.

366 Neil and Plummer-Steen, "A Monumental Task," 17; Gilman, *Grand Portage Story*, 129–36; Cochrane, *Minong*, 163.

367 Neil and Plummer-Steen, "A Monumental Task," 17–18; NPS, "Stewardship at Grand Portage National Monument"; Sarah Doty, "A Grand Painting for Grand Portage," *Duluth News-Tribune*, 26 July 2007, B1, B4.

368 Gilman, *Grand Portage Story*, 115–16, 122; James Hull, "Trade at Grand Portage," *Cook County News-Herald*, 20 June 1935, 1, 4; Birk, "Nomination Form for Grand Portage National Monument," 7.27; Cochrane comments, 2022.

369 Gilman, *Grand Portage Story*, 125; Tofte, *Who's Who in Minnesota*, 1941; *Cook County News-Herald*, 16 August 1951, 1; 12 July 1962; Cochrane comments, 2021.

370 Hull, "Trade at Grand Portage"; Cook County News Herald, 2 September 1982; 12 November 2004; 11 March 2005; 14 August 2010.

371 *Lake County Chronicle*, 1 September 1927, 8; *Duluth News-Tribune*, 23 January 1928, 2; Lloyd V. Gustafson, "Chippewas Gear for Economic Freedom," *Duluth News-Tribune*, Cosmopolitan, 2 March 1947, 3.

372 Gilman, *Grand Portage Story*, 130; Cochrane, *Minong*, 162–63; *Cook County News-Herald*, 14 July 2018.

373 Anderson and Fischer, *North Shore*, 227; Brian Larsen, "Grand Portage Begins Work to Redevelop Hat Point Marina and Ferry Terminal," *Cook County News-Herald*, 13 November 2020; Brian Larson, "Portage Hat Point Ferry Terminal to Undergo Major Rebuild," *Cook County News-Herald*, 24 November 2023.

374 James Hull, "The New Road at Grand Portage," *Cook County News-Herald*, 11 August 1960, 7; Rhonda Silence, "Mount Josephine Wayside Rest Improvements Celebrated," *Cook County News-Herald*, 26 May 2010; Nature Conservancy, "Top 10 Best Views in Minnesota, 2020," 24 June 2020, https://www.nature.org/en-us/about-us/where-we-work/united-states/minnesota/stories-in-minnesota/best-views-minnesota/.

375 Cochrane comments, 2022.

376 Gilman, *Grand Portage Story*, 106–8, quoting Jesuit accounts, 108; Birk, "Nomination Form for Grand Portage National Monument," 8-9, 8-10; Birk, *Travel Routes*, 16–17.

377 *Memorial Record of the Northern Peninsula of Michigan* (Chicago: Lewis, 1895), 459–60; Cochrane comments, 2022.

378 Manuscript schedules for the U.S. Census, 1870, 1880, 1900, and for the Minnesota State Census, 1875; U.S. General Land Office record for Asa A. Parker, 1865; appointments of U.S. postmasters: Asa A. Parker, 1872; Gilman, *Grand Portage Story*, 112; *Memorial Record of the Northern Peninsula of Michigan*, 459–60.

379 Bob Berg, "Wayside Stop at Ryden's, a 70-Year-Old Pull-over on Your Way to (and from) Canada," *Lake Superior Magazine*, December 2017, citing Mike Boomer, https://www.lakesuperior.com/travel/minnesota/395tavelmn/.

380 *Cook County News-Herald*, 7 November 1963, 1; 25 November 1965, 1.

381 *Cook County News-Herald*, 26 December 1957, 1; MnDOT, "Historic Bridges—Bridge 5923," https://www.dot.state.mn.us/historicbridges/5923.html.

382 Livio Di Matteo, "Cross-Border Travel at Pigeon River," *Northern Economist*, 23 October 2011; IBI Group, "Northern Ontario Passenger Vehicle Travel Profile," 2013, ES-2, ES-3; comments and unpublished data from Livio Di Matteo to the author, 2015, 2018.

383 "Pigeon River Improvement, Slide & Boom Co. v. Charles W. Cox. Ltd," *American Journal of International Law* 29 (January 1935): 150; *Cook County News-Herald*, 25 July 1946, 1; Gilman, *Grand Portage Story*, 112; *Duluth News-Tribune*, 18 June 1939, A8; "Grand Portage State Park," Wikipedia, accessed 2024.

384 "Pigeon River Improvement, Slide & Boom Co. v. Charles W. Cox. Ltd," 150; *Duluth News-Tribune*, 18 June 1939, A8; Debbie Tornblom, "Pigeon River's High Falls Resort," *Green Mantle* (Thunder Bay, Ont.), 3 July 1996, 1, citing Tripp.

385 *Cook County News-Herald*, 24 July 1947, 4; "Grand Portage State Park," Wikipedia, accessed 2024; Ed and Mabel Ryden interview, OH-0127-1980 CCHS, 1980.

386 Chester S. Wilson, "The Fate of High Falls on the Pigeon River: Scenic Beauty or Water Power?," *Minnesota Conservation Volunteer* 9 (July–August 1946): 1–2; "Pigeon River Improvement, Slide & Boom Co. v. Charles W. Cox. Ltd," 150; *Duluth News-Tribune*, 18 June 1939, A8; Meyer, *Everyone's Country Estate*, 279–81.

387 "Grand Portage State Park," Wikipedia, accessed 2024; Meyer, *Everyone's Country Estate*, 279–81.

# Index

**Arnold R. Alanen** is professor emeritus in the Department of Planning and Landscape Architecture at the University of Wisconsin–Madison. He is author of *Morgan Park: Duluth, U.S. Steel, and the Forging of a Company Town* (Minnesota, 2007) and *Finns in Minnesota*, coauthor of *Main Street Ready-Made: The New Deal Community of Greendale, Wisconsin*, and coeditor of *Preserving Cultural Landscapes in America*.